CHANTS DEMOCRATIC

CHANTS DEMOCRATIC

New York City and the Rise of the
American Working Class, 1788-1850

Twentieth-Anniversary Edition

SEAN WILENTZ

OXFORD
UNIVERSITY PRESS
2004

OXFORD

UNIVERSITY PRESS

Oxford   New York
Auckland   Bangkok   Buenos Aires   Cape Town   Chennai
Dar es Salaam   Delhi   Hong Kong   Istanbul   Karachi   Kolkata
Kuala Lumpur   Madrid   Melbourne   Mexico City   Mumbai   Nairobi
São Paulo   Shanghai   Taipei   Tokyo   Toronto

First published by Oxford University Press, Inc., 1984
First issued as an Oxford University Press paperback, 1986
Oxford University Press Twentieth-Anniversary Edition issued 2004
Published by Oxford University Press, Inc.
198 Madison Avenue, New York, New York 10016
www.oup.com

Oxford is a registered trademark of Oxford University Press

Library of Congress Cataloging-in-Publication Data
Wilentz, Sean.
Chants democratic: New York City and the rise of the American working class, 1788–1850 /
Sean Wilentz—20th anniversary ed.

p. cm.
Includes bibliographical references and index.

ISBN 978-0-19-517449-6

1. Working class—New York (State)—New York—History.
2. New York (N.Y.)—History.
I. Title.
HD8085.N53W54   2004   305.5'62'0974710903—dc22   2004054794

Printed in the United States of America
on acid-free paper

To Eli Wilentz
Jeanne Campbell Wilentz
Christine Stansell

Preface

This is an extended historical essay on capitalism and democracy in the United States. Between the American Revolution and the completion of emancipation in 1865, this country experienced a series of profound social changes, among them the emergence of a working class. In New York City—then consisting only of what we know today as lower Manhattan— these changes occurred with unusual force and rapidity: more than a decade before the Civil War, the working-class presence was established in the American metropolis. Like the rise of the city itself, the rise of an American working class in New York raised fundamental questions about the character of the democratic Republic—questions that would be asked again, across the nation, over the rest of the nineteenth century.

Now and then, Lionel Trilling once wrote, it is possible to observe the moral life in process of revising itself. Such moral revisions were basic to the history of the city in the age of Jefferson and Jackson, as New Yorkers came to redefine the meaning of America in the light of new exigencies of life and labor. What follows is a social interpretation of these revisions and what they tell us about the American past.

My interest in these matters dates back to my undergraduate years, when I was fortunate enough to be a history major at Columbia College. After all this time, it is a pleasure to thank David Rothman, James Shenton, and Lee Benson for their early instruction and abiding encouragement. I am also pleased to thank the history dons of Balliol College, Oxford—especially Richard Cobb (now of Worcester), Maurice Keen, and Colin Lucas—for their patience and their enthusiasm.

My deepest intellectual debt is to David Brion Davis. From the start,

Professor Davis thought that this project was worth doing, and he supported it generously with a combination of tough criticism and fresh suggestions. More than anyone, it was he who convinced me that a history of
labor must also in large measure be a history of the life of the mind. To
glance at these pages is to see the influence of his own efforts at coming to
terms with the age of revolution.

My other teachers at Yale also helped me enormously with advice and
counsel. I am particularly grateful to C. Vann Woodward, Paul Johnson,
Peter Gay, and John Merriman for extended hours of conversation about
the possibilities—and the limits—of this undertaking.

At Princeton, I have been lucky to be able to profit from an extraordi-
narily stimulating assembly of historians. Special thanks to David Abraham, Natalie Zemon Davis, Stanley Katz, Arno Mayer, John Murrin,
Daniel Rodgers, Carl Schorske, and Lawrence Stone for their camaraderie
and their comments on an earlier draft. Thanks, also, to my skeptical
graduate students, who sent me back to the manuscript even after I
thought it was done.

The Mrs. Giles M. Whiting Foundation, the Yale Center for the Study
of American Art and Material Culture, the Council on West European
Studies, and the Princeton University Committee on Research in the Humanities and Social Sciences contributed important financial assistance to
help me complete my research and writing. The librarians and their staffs
at Columbia, Yale, and Princeton have been unfailingly helpful over the
years. For making their place of work mine as well, I owe a special debt to
the librarians and staff of the New-York Historical Society and to Idilio
Pena Garcia and his staff at the Municipal Archives and Record Center.

Florence Thomas typed several versions of the manuscript, including my
dissertation, with accuracy and abundant good cheer, keeping my spirits
up during the rough patches. Andrew Bechman, Dina Copelman, Elizabeth
Farrar, Steven Jaffee, Darcy Lebau, and Louis Masur gave some invaluable
aid during the final stages of research and proofreading.

Several friends and colleagues read and commented on some portion of
the manuscript. I am especially grateful to Alan Dawley, Eric Foner, Eugene Genovese, Herbert Gutman, Paul Johnson, Bruce Laurie, Michael
Merrill, and David Montgomery for their help. Earlier versions of various
chapters were scrutinized, to my great benefit, by the Columbia University
Seminar on the History of the Working Class, Professor Gutman's seminar at the City University Graduate Center, the New York Institute for
the Humanities, and a workshop at the University of Pennsylvania. My
fellow researchers Elizabeth Blackmar, Peter Buckley, and Paul Gilje
shared in the inevitable trench humor and guided me to several important
sources. My conversations with Fred Siegel and Paul Berman made me

think about the larger political and literary issues at stake; they helped prompt me to draw my title and my epigraphs from Walt Whitman, *Leaves of Grass* (Boston, 1860). Walter Hugins graciously sent me his raw data on the Working Men, without which this study would have been far poorer.

For several years, Alfred Young has been an irreplaceable friend of this book and its author. His suggestions on revisions forced me to go for broke, even when I was timid; with his unmatched knowledge of the early history of American labor, he alerted me to ideas and sources I would otherwise have overlooked.

Otto Sonntag copy-edited the typescript with consummate mastery and precision. Leona Capeless and the staff at Oxford University Press pretended to be unconcerned when I telephoned or arrived at the office with news of yet another delay. So did my editor, Sheldon Meyer. To all, my deep appreciation for shepherding me through with unflagging optimism and the highest of editorial standards.

Along with James Wilentz, the people whose names are on the dedication page are those to whom I owe the most. Their intellectual contributions, apart from everything else, have been incalculable. My parents' sensitivity to the past and their dislike of cant have helped keep me honest; their fortitude, in hard times and good, has been an inspiration. I first met Christine Stansell on a winter's day at the Historical Society. Since then she has shared her notes, her brains, her freethinking passion to get things right. The rest still takes my breath away.

Princeton, N.J.   S.W.
December 1983.

Note to the Paperback Edition

Some typographical and other minor errors from the cloth edition have been corrected. I am grateful to Stanley Engerman, Paul Gilje, and Herbert Gutman for their help. A special note is due Herb Gutman, who, particularly over the last few months, was an extraordinary friend and mentor. His recent death leaves me, along with so many other social historians, without a beloved intellectual champion.

Some excellent studies, either unknown to me or still in progress when *Chants Democratic* went to press, should be consulted by anyone interested in the issues I discuss. These include Richard B. Stott's splendid dissertation, "The Worker in the Metropolis: New York, 1820–1860" (Ph.D.,

Cornell University, 1983); Peter Buckley's long-awaited thesis (soon to be published by Oxford), "To the Opera House: Culture and Society in New York City, 1820–1860" (Ph.D., State University of New York at Stony Brook, 1984); John Ashworth's fine revisionist study, *"Agrarians" and "Aristocrats": Party Political Ideology in the United States, 1837–1846* (London, 1983); Gary Kornblith, "From Artisans to Businessmen: Master Mechanics in New England, 1789–1850" (Ph.D., Princeton University, 1983); and Celia Morris Eckhardt, *Fanny Wright: A Rebel in America* (Cambridge, Mass., 1984). My book would have been far better if I'd had these works on hand; their contributions make it far clearer where we should now be headed in the continuing reinterpretation of nineteenth-century society, culture, and politics.

Princeton, N.J.   S. W.
August 1985.

Preface to the
Twentieth-Anniversary Edition

It is a great honor to write this new preface to an old book.

Late in 1977, I was living in New York, working on my dissertation for Yale University, and getting nowhere fast. I knew my subject, knew the kind of book I wanted to write, and had located abundant sources, but the themes were not cohering. Two serendipitous finds changed that: a manuscript autobiography by one John Petheram, a New York immigrant who worked for a drug maker in the early 1830s, and the account of the 1825 Erie Canal celebration compiled by Cadwallader Colden. Suddenly, I thought I saw something new, and I started reading and rereading all my sources in that light.

A year later, with two draft chapters done, I talked my way into an enviable university teaching job. The condition for accepting the job was that I finish the dissertation quickly. I wrote and wrote, and hit the deadline. Then I jumped on another treadmill to get the dissertation revised and published in time to come up for tenure. Thanks to more friends and loved ones than I had any right to expect, that got done, too, amid the multiple demands and distractions of being a young professor.

Looking back, if I'd had more time, this book would be much better than it is. But I might also still be writing it. In some ways, I still am.

The book grew in part from my encounter with the radicalism of the 1960s. Three important new trends in American history writing arose during those years. The first two—reinterpreting the history of slavery and race relations and reinterpreting the history of women—have had a deep and enduring effect on the way that historians and the public think about our past. The third, sometimes referred to as the new labor history, has had less obvious influence, for reasons that have never fully been explained. *Chants Democratic* belonged to that third trend, although it also aimed at something larger.

Like the work on slavery and women, the new studies of American labor challenged the consensus view of American history that had flourished since the late 1940s. According to the consensus writers, many of whom had started out on the radical political Left, American politics had never been wracked by any fundamental intellectual or ideological divisions. Liberal and capitalist at its birth, the country supposedly remained united by liberal values and by the crass, hustling, money-making drives that liberalism at once softened and encouraged. Anything else was either inauthentic or marginal. American democracy, as Richard Hofstadter, the most iconoclastic of the consensus historians, remarked, was more an exercise in cupidity than fraternity.

By the late 1960s, as Hofstadter conceded, the consensus view lost its intellectual force. Too much in American history, above all the Civil War, could not be accommodated to the consensus framework. Too much in the American present could not be accommodated either — the bitter divisions over civil rights, America's military involvement in Vietnam, and the rise of anti-liberal countercultures on both the Right and the Left. A number of books and articles by a younger generation of labor historians, including Herbert Gutman, David Montgomery, Alfred Young, and Melvyn Dubofsky, unearthed a history of class conflict that conformed neither to the consensus formulas nor to the interpretations offered by earlier Progressive- and New Deal–era writers, Marxist and liberal. Still-younger historians, grouped around their own journals such as *Studies on the Left, Radical America,* and, later, the *Radical History Review,* rediscovered American labor history and tried to view it from the democratic perspective of the early New Left and the civil rights movement.

Here was history with a mission, to rediscover the experiences and voices of those ordinary Americans, then habitually dismissed as inarticulate, who had built the country and had had to fight to gain their share of the nation's promise. For the new labor historians, the key work was, ironically and tellingly, not about America at all — it was E. P. Thompson's *The Making of the English Working Class,* originally published in 1963. Thompson, a heterodox socialist historian, offered a way of thinking about class as a social and cultural as well as an economic relation — a living, breathing relation that involved real people in difficult and at times bewildering circumstances, trying to make sense of huge forces that were beyond their control. I get the impression that today's young American historians do not read Thompson's book much, but twenty-five years ago, in the circles I frequented, it was a well-thumbed talisman, along with the writings of Gutman, Montgomery, Young, and Dubofsky. We knew that American history was very different from British history, but we still wanted to try to do for American working people and their past something of what Thompson had done for the English.

Thompson's influence on *Chants Democratic* is obvious. But there were other strong influences. Despite the inadequacies of consensus interpretations, Richard Hofstadter's writings still impressed me, especially with their emphasis on ambiguity, irony, and complexity. Hofstadter's mordant approach seemed an antidote to a history that could easily become a simplified and sentimental chronicle of winners and losers, good people and bad people. A revulsion against the sentimentalism in an earlier round of radical history writing from the 1930s had been vital to the rise of the consensus writers twenty years later. I wanted to try to retain that anti-sentimental sensibility without losing an empathy for ordinary Americans. That would mean sorting out the many aspects of working-class life, drawing distinctions among different trends and impulses, and taking adequate account of the sadder, uglier, and more brutal sides of my subjects. It would also mean trying to understand employers, anti-labor writers, and hidebound conservatives in their own great variety, and as they understood themselves.

I had other interests as well. A native New Yorker, I had long been fascinated by the city's history. New York had not, however, figured as large as other places in the writing of American social history. There was a presumption that New York was too large, too complex—and, perhaps, too Jewish—to reveal much about the American experience. Better to find a small place like Trempealeau County, Wisconsin, or Newburyport, Massachusetts, and exploit the easily handled census material and other primary sources. Or, if a city had to be studied, better it was Boston—close to Harvard, the home of the principal urban historians of the previous two generations, Arthur M. Schlesinger Sr. and Oscar Handlin. Primary sources on New York had been neglected, both by local officials (whom, one suspected, had every reason to keep historical records hidden) and by a patriciate that lacked the powerful historical sensibility of its counterparts in Boston, Philadelphia, or even Chicago. There had been some exceptional studies of New York, especially a wonderful book by Moses Rischin, *The Promised City*, about the Lower East Side—and, while I was writing, another would appear on the same neighborhood, Irving Howe's, *World of Our Fathers*. But New York's history generally lagged behind.

Apart from my personal loyalties, I had never understood the case against New York as atypical. London was atypical of Britain, and Paris was atypical of France, yet this had never stopped scholars from writing their histories. Handlin and his students had overcome the bias against

cities in American culture, but an anti-metropolitan bias lingered. I hoped
to break through it, making the argument that to the extent New York was
atypical, it was all the more important. If the history of the United States
could not be understood solely from the vantage point of New York, neither could that history be understood with New York excluded. It was a
perception that, fortunately, others shared. When I finally arrived in the
New York archives and libraries to begin my research, I found several
historians, old and young, writing dissertations and books about the city.
In coffee shops and seminar rooms around Manhattan and, occasionally,
Queens and Brooklyn, we made sense of our material together.

My interest in politics was as large as my interest in New York, above
all the politics of the Jacksonian era. Amid the explosion in social and
cultural history that accompanied the search for the inarticulate, interest
in political history had declined. Mine had not. Many in my cohort viewed
past politics with a certain wariness, as a place where so-called elites—
later slighted as "dead white men"—drowned out or compromised ordinary voices. I was more inclined to see politics as an arena where con-
testing forces had to come to terms with every variety of discontent—and
where, if only indirectly, even the most marginal Americans could have
great influence. This was especially true for what had become my favorite
period in American history, from the end of the War of 1812 to the coming
of the Civil War. An early reading of Arthur M. Schlesinger Jr.'s *The Age
of Jackson*—a book largely written off by the academic avant garde at the
time—had swept me up in the intrigues and battles of the formative period
of American political democracy. With his interest in the less celebrated
as well as in Jackson and his rivals, Schlesinger had introduced me to the
likes of the radical freethinker Fanny Wright and the workingman politician Ely Moore. He gave me a model for writing history as seen from
below as well as from above. His book's obvious shortcomings, especially
its utter neglect of Indian removal, had allowed its critics to dismiss it—
but to me its virtues vastly outweighed its defects, especially on the subject
of labor politics.

Finally, I wanted to write about ideas as well as about society, culture,
and politics. More, I thought, than many of his admirers allowed, E. P.
Thompson's book has been carried along by its examination of intellectuals, including workers and middle-class reformers, and their ideas. They
ranged from the famous, such as the utopian manufacturer Robert Owen,
to such obscure writers as John Gray and Thomas Hodgskin; their scope
included theology and literature along with political economy. Thompson
had not simply given back to the English working class its dignity and its
culture; he had given it back its gift of intellection. Schlesinger's *Age of
Jackson* had, in a different way, done something similar for the Jacksonian-

era radicals. And if Hofstadter tended to be dismissive of popular thought, he offered still another way to understand the internal divisions, paradoxes, and unanticipated consequences in American intellectual history.

As it happened, the history of early American political ideas was going through a transformation in the 1960s and 1970s, wholly outside, it seemed, the field of social history. At Yale, David Brion Davis, who to my great good fortune directed my dissertation work, was re-creating a genealogy of antislavery thought that upset the tidy categories of liberal consensus and continuity. Elsewhere, other historians, preeminently Bernard Bailyn, Gordon Wood, and J. G. A. Pocock, rediscovered a cluster of political ideas above and beyond the early liberalism of John Locke, and which they argued formed the intellectual foundations of the American Revolution. That cluster of ideas, called, broadly, "civic humanism" or "republicanism," displaced Locke's *Second Treatise on Government* as the intellectual progenitor of American politics—and, it seemed at the time, drove the final nail into the coffin of the liberal consensus interpretation of American history. Between Davis's works and those of the "republican" writers, it seemed to me that the way had been cleared to reassess the labor radicals of the Jacksonian era, and their adversaries, in wholly new ways.

Thus armed with these influences—disparate and in many ways incompatible with each other, except in my own mind—I plunged into the archives. The first thing that became obvious was that the economic history of New York differed greatly from that of other major industrializing cities like Lowell or Lynn, Massachusetts—and also from earlier accounts that had stressed New York's mercantile and financial activities above all. The early chapters of a new book by the young British historian Gareth Stedman Jones, *Outcast London*, clarified matters by showing how the great cities had passed through their own version of the Industrial Revolution, but following a pattern very different from the factory towns that dominated the history books.

Convinced that New York had exemplified what I called, in shorthand, metropolitan industrialization, I then floundered about trying to make new sense of the political and intellectual history of New York's workers. The Petheram manuscript and the Colden volume gave me the breakthrough I needed. Petheram's recollections remarked memorably on how rearrangements of work in the early-nineteenth-century city had created new lines of authority deeply at variance with American egalitarian values. Colden's illustrated descriptions of artisan emblems and public rituals made clear how, despite the enormous differences between Britain and the early United States, early American artisans had retrieved old ideals of "the Trade" and mingled them with the democratic ideals of the new republic. Together, these sources helped me formulate the outlines of what I called,

again in shorthand, "artisan republicanism." After six years of more research and overly hasty writing, that idea remained at the core of my
dissertation and then of this book.

Since then, some critics have been generous with *Chants Democratic*
and others have been very critical of it. When it was first published, the
kinder reviewers (including, to my great satisfaction, Herbert Gutman)
understood the book's disputing of the consensus school and its efforts to
blend social, intellectual and political history. Others took the book to task
less for what it said than for what it failed to say about one issue or
another—racial antagonisms, the remaking of the city's working class after
1850, and the effects of nativism on local politics. Some detected a hidden
political agenda, about explaining the failure and the possibilities of radical
politics in the present as well as the past. I had actually worked hard to
avoid this pitfall, lest the book lose its sense of the pastness of the past.
Although history and the here-and-now are in constant dialogue, the idea
of constructing a "usable" past out of the preoccupations of the present
has always struck me as an invitation to distorting history.

Despite the spirited criticisms directed at *Chants Democratic*, I remain
persuaded of the book's basic validity. With hindsight, I might have said
more than I did about the racism that afflicted many of New York's workers, about the unskilled laborers of the era, about how slavery helped
shaped the city's early working class, about the wharfside world as well as
about New York's sweatshops and working-class theaters. I wish the book
had more salt air in it, and more of the ropes, hawsers, and adzes of the
city's shipbuilders and other maritime tradesmen. I also wish that I had
carried it forward to 1860 and developed even more fully the vast impact
that the immigration of the late 1840s and early 1850s had upon New York
working-class life. None of these changes, however, would have affected
the essential argument, only enriched it. And, I am pleased to say, a number of books published since 1984 have done precisely that, not least Edwin
G. Burrows and Mike Wallace's remarkable and distinguished study,
Gotham: A History of New York City to 1898, which appeared in 1999.

My continuing work on the period has exposed other shortcomings that
I consider more severe. *Chants Democratic* is the work of a young historian, still feeling his way and finding his voice. There are passages that I
wish I could rephrase, either because they are overwritten or because they
are so solemnly academic. Although I was always interested in politics, I
was less patient than I have become with the choices made by those figures, including dissenters such as the Loco Focos, who tried to exercise
power as well as to gain it. Were I writing the book based on what I have
learned during the past twenty years and hope to continue writing about
in future, I would have emphasized the democratic elements of early

American democratic republicanism more than I did. I also would have seen the Jacksonian political mainstream as less unified and more filled with hopeful possibilities, some of which, even on the slavery issue, came to fruition.

These shifts reflect, no doubt, my continuing involvement in contemporary politics as well as my continuing research on political history. For various reasons, I have been able to witness the machinations of political leaders at the center as well as the periphery of American power, during a time of intense polarization not unlike the era discussed in this book. The experience has not always been pretty, least of all amid the acrid atmosphere in Washington, D.C., during the impeachment autumn and winter of 1998 and 1999. These travails have left me with a far clearer understanding of the contingencies, treachery, and enduring idealism of democratic politics. Even more, they have reinforced my certainty that, without a detached and well-informed historical understanding of the early republic, current and future generations of Americans will easily lose their way in trying to sustain and enlarge the best of our political inheritance.

Luckily, *Chants Democratic* has survived despite its flaws. I have resisted the idea of revising it, not because it doesn't need revision but because the result would not be *Chants Democratic*. As history is argument without end, I am delighted that the original has been granted a new life. Let the arguments continue.

Princeton, N.J.   S. W.
January 10, 2004

Contents

Plates 2–21 appear between pages 216–217.
Maps 1 and 2 appear at the end of the Appendix.

Abbreviations

AHR	*American Historical Review*
AQ	*American Quarterly*
BAAD	Board of Assistant Aldermen, Documents
CCFP	City Clerk Filed Papers
GSMT	General Society of Mechanics and Tradesmen
HDC	Historical Documents Collections, Queens College, City University of New York
JAH	*Journal of American History*
JEH	*Journal of Economic History*
JIH	*Journal of Interdisciplinary History*
JNH	*Journal of Negro History*
JSN	*Journal of Social History*
LH	*Labor History*
MARC	Municipal Archives and Record Center, New York
MCC	*Minutes of the Common Council, 1785–1831*
MVHR	*Mississippi Valley Historical Review*
NYH	*New York History*
N-YHS	New-York Historical Society
N-YHSQ	*New-York Historical Society Quarterly*
NYPL	New York Public Library
P & P	*Past & Present*
PMHB	*Pennsylvania Magazine of History and Biography*
PSQ	*Political Science Quarterly*
SAJ	Senate Assembly Journal, New York
WMQ	*William and Mary Quarterly*

CHANTS DEMOCRATIC

1. Stollenwerck's Panorama, 1815.

Introduction
Stollenwerck's Panorama,
1815

You may read in many languages, yet read nothing about it,
You may read the President's Message, and read nothing about it
   there,
Nothing in the reports from the State department or Treasury department, or in the daily papers or the weekly papers,
Or in the census returns, assessors' returns, prices current, or any
   accounts of stock.

Chants Democratic, III, 17

In 1815, Peter Stollenwerck, a New York watchmaker, put on display in
his shop a panorama of a manufacturing and commercial city by the sea,
a fantasy of a city like his own Manhattan (Plate 1). It was something
of a cultural event. Although panoramas (or dioramas) of historical
scenes had been a familiar New York entertainment for years, Stollenwerck's was the first in America in which the figures actually moved and
in which the artist tried to represent the ordinary clamor of a contemporary expanding city. In such urban busyness, another artisan, Walt Whitman, would later find the poetry of the self and the democratic mass.
Stollenwerck, a craftsman working during the twilight of the American
Enlightenment, was more literal; like the first photographers (whom the
dioramists anticipated), he was interested in exactness, in reproducing
city life as perfectly as possible, omitting only the most intimate of scenes.
Here, lured to the back of Stollenwerck's shop, patrons could see themselves as they could not in the window reflections at street level, as part of
a comprehensible order, of a rational (if not necessarily divine) design,
coming and going in harmonious balance, all part of the pleasing spectacle.[1]

1. *Longworth's American Almanac for 1816* (New York, 1816). On panoramas in
England and the United States, see Richard Altick, *The Shows of London* (Cambridge,

3

Obviously, Stollenwerck had commercial motives when he built his model; if the departing customers paused to inspect the master's watches and clocks, so much the better. But Stollenwerck was also a dedicated craftsman proud of his artistry and his trade, a pride that showed in his decision to make the city's artisans the featured performers in his panorama. Instead of the usual diorama fare—Washington crossing the Delaware, Vesuvius in flames—Stollenwerck gave his public skilled men, at work in the different mechanical arts. We are left only a glimpse of one of these vignettes, a small group erecting an elaborate building; elsewhere, shoemakers worked their awls, tailors flashed their needles, shipbuilders raised Lilliputian masts. Throughout, Stollenwerck depicted material progress achieved within an artisan system of masters, journeymen, and apprentice craftsmen—all dressed in work clothes, all at their labor, enlarging their city and its goods, carving civilization out of what was still semiwilderness, imposing their own rational design on nature's fruits. If Stollenwerck celebrated anything in his model, he celebrated these men—his fellows—and their work. He may have understood only dimly that even as he cranked up his ingenious contraption, the system of labor and the way of life he had so carefully copied and idealized were disintegrating.

The decline of Stollenwerck's universe, and of the frame of mind that inspired his panorama, was part of a series of epochal historical transformations, what Karl Polanyi collectively called the great transformation and others describe as the emergence of modern bourgeois society and the working class.[2] For more than a millennium, urban crafts had been organized along roughly similar lines, successively adapted to different modes of production—geared to limited markets, based on the skilled use of hand tools, passed through generations of masters and apprentices. The artisan system persisted in early commercial capitalist Britain and Europe, instituted and formalized in the great urban guilds, and containing what Marx cogently described as an all-important duality in the social relations of the workshop:

> The master does indeed own the conditions of production—tools, materials, etc. (although the tools may be owned by the journeyman too)—and he owns the product. To that extent he is a *capitalist*. But it is not as capitalist that he is *master*. He is an artisan in the first instance and is supposed to be a master of his craft. Within the process of production he appears as an artisan, like his journeymen, and it is he who initiates his apprentices into the mysteries of the craft. He has precisely the same relationship to his apprentices as a professor to his

---

Mass., 1978), 128–210. Altick, on the basis of extensive research, concluded that the first moving diorama mounted in the United States dated from 1828; that date may now be pushed forward by more than a decade.

2. Polanyi, *The Great Transformation* (Boston, 1957).

students. Hence his approach to his apprentices is not that of a capitalist but of a *master* of his craft.[3]

In the most advanced parts of Britain and Europe, the interposition of merchant capital and continued expansion of capitalist markets rendered this duality a contradiction: gradually, from the sixteenth century through the early nineteenth, merchant capitalists and master craftsmen restructured the social relations of production, transformed wage labor into a market commodity, and established the basis for new sets of class relations and conflicts. In America, colonial rule, slavery (and other forms of unfree labor), the weakness of mercantilist guilds, and an abundance of land created a different economic matrix; nevertheless, a similar process occurred at an accelerated rate beginning in the late eighteenth century in the New England countryside and the established northern seaboard cities. Along with the destruction of plantation slavery, this disruption of the American artisan system of labor ranks as one of the outstanding triumphs of nineteenth-century American capitalism, part of the reordering of formal social relations to fit the bourgeois ideal of labor, market, and man.[4]

3. Karl Marx, *Capital*, trans. Ben Fowkes (London, 1976), I, 1029.

4. This paragraph draws upon a wide-ranging body of research by historians and economists, much of which is summarized in Stephen Marglin, "What Do Bosses Do? The Origin and Function of Hierarchy in Capitalist Production," *Review of Radical Political Economics* 6 (1974): 33–60. On craftsmen in antiquity, see Alison Burford, *Craftsmen in Greek and Roman Society* (Ithaca, 1972). On English and European craftsmen and early industrial capitalism, see Maurice Agulhon, *Une Ville ouvrière au temps du socialisme utopique: Toulon de 1815 à 1851* (Paris and The Hague, 1970); Theodore S. Hamerow, *Restoration, Revolution, Reaction: Economics and Politics in Germany, 1815–1871* (Princeton, 1958); Christopher H. Johnson, *Utopian Communism in France: Cabet and the Icarians, 1839–1851* (Ithaca, 1974); Bernard H. Moss, *The Origins of the French Labor Movement: The Socialism of Skilled Workers* (Berkeley and Los Angeles, 1976); Iorwerth Prothero, *Artisans and Politics in Early Nineteenth-Century London: John Gast and His Times* (Folkestone, 1979); Joan Wallach Scott, *The Glassworkers of Carmaux: French Craftsmen and Political Action in a Nineteenth-Century City* (Cambridge, Mass., 1974); William H. Sewell, Jr., *Work and Revolution in France: The Language of Labor from the Old Regime to 1848* (Cambridge, 1980); E. P. Thompson, *The Making of the English Working Class* (New York, 1964). Recent work on the crafts in the United States has concentrated on local studies. On the eighteenth century, see Charles Olton, *Artisans for Independence: Philadelphia Mechanics and the American Revolution* (Syracuse, 1975); Eric Foner, *Tom Paine and Revolutionary America* (New York, 1976); Gary B. Nash, *The Urban Crucible: Social Change, Political Consciousness, and the Origins of the American Revolution* (Cambridge, Mass., 1979). On the nineteenth century, the work of Alan Dawley, Paul G. Faler, Bruce G. Laurie, Howard B. Rock, and Anthony F. C. Wallace has been of exceptional importance; for a review of these and related works, see Sean Wilentz, "Artisan Origins of the American Working Class," *International Labor and Working Class History* 18 (1981): 1–22. Still of enormous influence are two essays by David Montgomery, "The Working Classes of the Pre-Industrial American City, 1780–1830," *LH* 9 (1968): 3–22; and "The Shuttle and the Cross: Weavers and Artisans in the

Stollenwerck's fate was tied both to the decline of the artisan system and to the rise of new kinds of urban life. Every era has, of course, had its great cities, which have displayed social and economic assumptions, conflicts, and accommodations of the age in a concentrated form. In the early and mid-nineteenth century, the new towns and cities of Lancashire, the Lyonnais, and New England quickly captured the imagination of both the champions and critics of early industrial capitalism, as sites where the ambitions and exploitation of capitalist enterprise seemed most evident, congealed in the very architecture of the mills, the mansions, and the rows of workers' housing. Of no less interest—and, arguably, of greater importance—were the established capitalist metropolitan centers. Some had long been important as political capitals or commercial cities, but as the fruits of merchant capital accumulated and as the structure of national and international economic life altered, these cities experienced rapid change along unfamiliar lines. The metropolises became the headquarters of new agencies of national and international finance, communications, and commerce; usually, they became important manufacturing cities as well. With the arrival of poor migrants and venturesome entrepreneurs, they contained the greatest extremes of new forms of conspicuous luxury and squalid poverty—and every gradation of splendor and misery in between. It was in these metropolises that the idealism and anxiety of what came to be called "modern life" were most keenly felt and expressed. The most influential early labor movements took root in such centers earlier and more tenaciously than elsewhere. By 1850, London and Paris had become the model metropolises of the Old World, the capitals, to borrow Walter Benjamin's phrase, of the nineteenth century. So, by 1850, Stollenwerck's New York, although no longer a political capital, had become the metropolis of America.[5]

To link these two developments—to write the history of class relations and the rise of the working class in the emerging American metropolis—is a vital task if we are to comprehend the social history of the United States. Historians have long understood the need for this. More than

Kensington Riots of 1844," *JSH* 5 (1972): 411–46; and Herbert G. Gutman, *Work, Culture, and Society in Industrializing America* (New York, 1976), esp. 3–78.

5. On the culture of nineteenth-century metropolitan life, see Walter Benjamin, "Paris—The Capital of the Nineteenth Century," in *Charles Baudelaire: A Lyric Poet in the Era of High Capitalism* (London, 1973), 155–76; and Richard Sennett, *The Fall of Public Man* (New York, 1978). Unfortunately, no early-nineteenth-century metropolis, including New York, has received the kind of polyvalent appraisal accorded Vienna in Carl E. Schorske, *Fin-de-Siècle Vienna: Politics and Culture* (New York, 1980). Recent social and urban historians have been especially slow to examine the metropolis in comparative terms, as a distinct social formation. For one approach, though, see Lynn H. Lees, "Metropolitan Types," in *The Victorian City: Images and Realities* ed. H. J. Dyos and Michael Wolff (London, 1973), I, 413–28.

sixty years ago, William V. Trimble singled out Jacksonian New York as a key site for historical investigation, America's foremost center for the initiation and spread of political opinion, a rapidly growing city "where massing of population, a new capitalistic domination of industry, and the emergence of a proletariat were raising imperative questions."[6] Ever since, some of the foremost American historians—including Dixon Ryan Fox, Arthur Schlesinger, Jr., Richard Hofstadter, and Lee Benson—have based their conclusions on early national and Jacksonian America largely or wholly on their studies of class and politics in New York. None, however, have offered entirely satisfactory accounts and interpretations of New York's "great transformation"; thus, the most influential interpretations of the era's significance have been either flawed or limited in important ways.

Progressives like Trimble, Fox, and (in a later, New Deal variation) Schlesinger, Jr., thought that the heart of the matter lay in party politics—that the early industrial revolution and the advent of the Jacksonian Democrats marked the political rise of "proletarian," liberal forces, centered in New York and Massachusetts, which aimed to curb the excesses of conservative "capitalists." The Progressives' contributions—in some of the first sustained efforts to write a social history of American politics—were immense. Unfortunately, although the Progressives understood that social coalitions and conflicts were fundamental to political battles, they utilized a concept of class that now seems rudimentary. In place of an examination of changing social relations and the process of class formation—the *emergence* of new social classes in the early nineteenth century—they substituted a series of flat, fixed social categories (proletarians, capitalists), lacking in historical specificity and explanatory power. The Progressives' insistence that political parties, in New York and elsewhere, directly embodied class interests—that the Whigs were the party of business, the Democrats the party of farmers and labor, or simply "the people"—led them in turn to ignore the plain truth that in New York and in the rest of the country, both major parties were led by established and emerging elites and their professional allies, usually lawyers. By then looking at employers and workers primarily through the distorting lens of party politics, the Progressives further narrowed their understanding of popular social consciousness, virtually equating it with the ideas espoused by either the Whigs or the Democrats; simultaneously, they took the politicians' most fiery "class" rhetoric at face value, as a full and accurate expression of the *politicians'* social views and allegiances. The work of the most important labor historians of the Progressive Era and afterward did not speak directly to that of the political historians

6. William V. Trimble, "Diverging Tendencies in the New York Democracy in the Period of the Loco Focos," *AHR* 24 (1919): 398.

(although there were unmistakable affinities); their elucidation of "practical," wage-conscious American unionism did, however, help forestall more expansive treatments of class relations and of working-class beliefs and behavior.[7]

Counter-Progressives like Hofstadter and Benson demolished what had become Progressive orthodoxy by taking another look at the liberal ideology and social composition of the Democrats and Whigs—and by finding that the two parties' similarities overwhelmed their differences. In refuting the Progressives, however, American historians from the late 1940s through the early 1970s retained some of their elders' assumptions, above all their fixation on party politics and their willingness to understand class as an abstract institution. By equating class with wealth and occupation, and by taking either voting behavior or the actual social philosophy of party politicians (and of a few supposedly "radical" splinter parties) as leading indicators of popular consciousness, the counter-Progressives discovered a past in which political conflict turned on deep ethnic, religious, and "status" divisions but in which class and class consciousness were either nonexistent or submerged by an American entrepreneurial consensus.[8]

While they cleared the way for a more realistic appraisal of party politics and political culture, the counter-Progressives left a great deal to be explained about Jacksonian New York and Jacksonian America. The obvious and growing inequalities of wealth and power in the early-nineteenth-century metropolis seemed to demand closer attention than most counter-Progressives were willing to pay. It was still possible, of course, to argue that these inequalities did not shake the fundamental American consensus or that the politicians handled them in ways that did not upset their own political power. Nevertheless, the sheer mass of the evidence placed enormous strains on the notion that ethnicity or consensus negated class differences.[9] Moreover, the counter-Progressives offered no way for understanding the abundant evidence of labor radicalism and of class formation and recurrent conflict in early-nineteenth-century New York. How could the counter-Progressives with their "ethnocultural models" ex-

7. See Dixon Ryan Fox, *The Decline of Aristocracy in the Politics of New York, 1801–1840* (New York, 1919); Arthur M. Schlesinger, Jr., *The Age of Jackson* (Boston, 1945); John R. Commons et al., *History of Labour in the United States* (New York, 1916), I; Selig Perlman, *A Theory of the Labor Movement* (New York, 1928).

8. Richard Hofstadter, "William Leggett, Spokesman of Jacksonian Democracy," *PSQ* 58 (1943): 581–94; idem, *The American Political Tradition* (New York, 1948), 56–85; Lee Benson, *The Concept of Jacksonian Democracy: New York as a Test Case* (Princeton, 1961). For fuller remarks and a brief overview, see Sean Wilentz, "On Class and Politics in Jacksonian America," in *The Promise of American History: Progress and Prospects*, ed. Stanley I. Kutler and Stanley N. Katz (Baltimore, 1982), 45–63.

9. See Edward Pessen, *Riches, Class, and Power before the Civil War* (Lexington, Mass., 1973).

plain the rise and brief political success of the Working Men of 1829 and their leader Thomas Skidmore—a man who called for a civil revolution and the equalization of property relations? How could they make sense of the class-conscious, inter-ethnic New York labor movement of the mid-1830s, the strike waves and labor uprisings of 1836 and 1850, or the working-class unrest discussed by Robert Ernst in his important study of the city's immigrants?[10] The most sustained counter-Progressive attempt to do so, by Walter E. Hugins, preserved the consensus formula, but only by adapting the work of the early labor historians to describe artisan radicals as entrepreneurial reformers and the labor movement as an expression of narrow, "practical" trade unionism.[11] Yet ever since, apart from Edward Pessen's examination of the ideas of some of New York's "uncommon" Jacksonian labor leaders, no plausible alternative to the counter-Progressives' arguments has appeared.[12]

Recent work on the history of early industrial workers and nineteenth-century democratic movements helps us take the first steps toward just such a reinterpretation, in ways that allow us to incorporate the important insights of previous work.[13] Slicing across the unfortunate compartments

10. Ernst, *Immigrant Life in New York City, 1825–1863* (New York, 1949), 99–121.

11. Hugins, *Jacksonian Democracy and the Working Class: A Study of the New York Workingmen's Movement, 1829–1837* (Stanford, 1960).

12. Pessen, *Most Uncommon Jacksonians: Radical Leaders of the Early Labor Movement* (Albany, 1967). Douglas M. Miller, *Jacksonian Aristocracy: Class and Democracy in New York, 1830–1860* (New York, 1967), contradicts the counter-Progressives but offers little in the way of an analysis of class formation and consciousness beyond what was presented earlier by the Progressives and the Commons school. Counter-Progressive formulations have been more successfully challenged in studies of other states and regions. See above all, Donald B. Cole, *Jacksonian Democracy in New Hampshire, 1800–1851* (Cambridge, Mass., 1970); James Roger Sharp, *The Jacksonians versus the Banks: Politics in the States after the Panic of 1837* (New York, 1970); Harry L. Watson, *Jacksonian Politics and Community Conflict: The Emergence of the Second Party System in Cumberland County, North Carolina* (Baton Rouge, 1981).

13. Among the most important of these works on the history of the United States are Alan Dawley, *Class and Community: The Industrial Revolution in Lynn* (Cambridge, Mass., 1976); Paul G. Faler, *Mechanics and Manufacturers in the Early Industrial Revolution* (Albany, 1981); Leon Fink, *Workingmen's Democracy: The Knights of Labor and American Politics* (Urbana, 1983); Lawrence Goodwyn, *Democratic Promise: The Populist Moment in America* (New York, 1976); Gutman, *Work, Culture, and Society*; Bruce G. Laurie, *Working People of Philadelphia, 1800–1850* (Philadelphia, 1980); David Montgomery, *Beyond Equality: Labor and the Radical Republicans, 1862–1872* (New York, 1967). On the eighteenth century, see Foner, *Tom Paine*; on the twentieth, see James R. Green, *Grass Roots Socialism: Radical Movements in the Southwest, 1895–1943* (Baton Rouge, 1978). In other ways, the revitalization of historical materialism undertaken by Eugene D. Genovese (in recent years, in collaboration with Elizabeth Fox-Genovese) has had a continuing influence on my thinking about capitalism, ideology, and property relations. See, above all, their articles collected in *Fruits of Merchant Capital: Slavery and Bourgeois Property in the Rise and Expansion of Capitalism* (New York, 1983).

of academic fashion—the "new" social history, the "new" urban history, "anthropological" history—these studies have begun to change the ways in which American historians understand social development and consciousness. In place of a static, instrumentalist economic determinism, they have treated class as a dynamic social relation, a form of social domination, determined largely by changing relations of production but shaped by cultural and political factors (including ethnicity and religion) without any apparent logic of economic interest. They take for granted the inescapable fact that class relations order power and social relationships; they have examined the numerous conflicts and accommodations that give rise to and accompany these relations as a complex series of social encounters, fusing culture and politics as well as economics. In short, they insist that the history of class relations cannot be deduced by some "economic" or sociological calculus and imposed on the past; nor can it be ignored if it does not appear just as the historian thinks it should, either in or out of politics. It must be examined as part of a human achievement in which men and women struggle to comprehend the social relations into which they were born (or entered involuntarily) and in which, by the collective exercise of power, they sustain or challenge those relations, in every phase of social life. From this perspective, the history of class relations in the emerging metropolis quickly begins to look very different from those offered or implied in earlier writings. The wish to enlarge and, in part, to correct that perspective, and to rewrite the history of the formation of the metropolitan working class, with all its larger implications about the history of capitalism and democracy in the United States, was my major reason for undertaking this study.

The final product approaches the problem through a series of interconnected middle-range themes. The first will come as no surprise: the central role of the crafts. Craft workers—sometimes treated by labor historians as a working-class elite, the aristocracy of urban labor—were in fact at the heart of New York's emerging working class from the 1790s until midcentury, embracing a wide range of people, from well-paid skilled journeymen to outworkers getting by on starvation wages. Clerks and unskilled laborers represented a numerous but decided minority of male metropolitan workers before the Civil War; except for domestic servants, a very special group, the vast majority of female wage earners as well were craft workers.[14] Al-

14. In all, clerks and unskilled laborers (including common laborers, porters, stevedores, cartmen) made up about 40 percent of the male wage-labor force in 1855. For figures on men and women, see Ernst, *Immigrant Life*, 214-17. The treatment of certain groups of craft workers as a privileged sector has been most marked—and disputed—in the recent British literature on the labor "aristocracy"; see R. Q. Gray, *The Labour Aristocracy in Victorian Edinburgh* (Oxford, 1976); John Foster, *Class Struggle and the Industrial Revolution: Early Industrial Capitalism in Three English Towns*

though male laborers and dockhands did organize on their own behalf, it was the craft workers (including the women) who, in concert with radical small producers, elaborated the first articulate forms of plebeian radicalism, and who dominated the most powerful labor organizations of the era. Other groups have to be considered, but it is to the craft workers and their employers that we must look in order to understand the most dramatic changes in class relations in early-nineteenth-century New York.

Interpreting the history of the crafts leads directly to what might be called the problem of the middle class. In large measure, the best recent work on class and class formation in the North has approached the history of a single class in isolation; we now know a great deal about how workers, petty proprietors, and merchant capitalists forged what Paul Johnson has called the "moral imperative" around which they formed class identities, but very little about how these classes-in-formation affected each other.[15] In particular, historians of the working class have been too willing either to portray middle-class employers as Dickensian parodies of the parvenu or to ignore them altogether; likewise, they have made little progress in analyzing the importance of petty proprietors, especially those shopkeepers and small master artisans who helped direct various radical and labor reform movements.[16] No study of New York's workers, particu-

---

(London, 1974); Geoffrey Crossick, *An Artisan Elite in Victorian Society: Kentish London, 1840–1880* (London, 1978). The supposedly privileged position of all craft workers—based usually on an idealized conception of craft workers as opposed to factory workers and common laborers—is commonly taken for granted in the United States. One recent text book, by a respected group of economic historians, goes so far as to transform the journeymen wage earners of the general trades' unions of the 1830s into "small businessmen" who "used their membership largely to assist price fixing in their business transactions." See Lance E. Davis et al., *American Economic Growth: An Economist's History of the United States* (New York, 1972), 228.

15. Paul E. Johnson, *A Shopkeeper's Millennium: Society and Revivals in Rochester, New York, 1815–1837* (New York, 1978), 8. See also Mary P. Ryan, *Cradle of the Middle Class: The Family in Oneida County, New York, 1790–1865* (New York, 1981), on middle-class imperatives and family life.

16. The failure to treat petty proprietors has been particularly troublesome, given, as Arno Mayer has observed, that the United States in the first half of the nineteenth century "may well have been the closest thing there has ever been to a country of small producers and property owners." I sympathize with Mayer's argument—that America has long been a lower-middle-class nation that lives by spurious middle-class myths and visions—but my emphasis here is rather different. Whatever their character (and they were, I think, considerably more complex and multifarious than Mayer had the opportunity to discuss), the culture and myths of the urban American lower-middle class took shape only as part of a process of class formation and conflict before the Civil War. In this respect, shopkeepers and, even more, small master artisans in New York had a central, if at times somewhat ambiguous, influence on the making of the working class, and vice versa. As we shall see, through 1850, at least some of these small producers saw their primary social and political allegiances resting with wage earners, and against financiers and capitalist employers. See Arno J. Mayer, "The Lower Middle Class as Historical Problem," *Journal of Modern History* 47 (1975): 422.

larly not one that tries to analyze working-class beliefs as well as behavior, can leave these people out; moreover, even if New York had its own, homegrown Bounderbys and Veneerings, the middle class merits respectful study. If, as Bryan Palmer has astutely observed, the history of class and class formation is the history of the "process of confrontation" between classes, then the terms of confrontation were set by the ideals, aspirations, rationalizations, and activities of New York's employers and independent small producers as well as by the city's workers.[17] To make sense of the emerging middle class in this context is to begin to comprehend the dialectics of power and social change.

The economic history of early industrialization in New York also demands more thorough evaluation. Recently, English and Continental historians have challenged the familiar "leading sector" synthesis on the industrial revolution, in order to stress the combined and uneven character of nineteenth-century capitalist growth. Gone is the nearly exclusive concern with mechanization, with the rise of the factory system, and with the prehistory of twentieth-century forms of mass production. Instead, attention has shifted to the larger process of capitalist transformation—a process that fostered a *variety* of possible forms of industrial organization, that hastened the intensification of human labor and the proliferation of sweating as well as the introduction of labor-saving machinery, and that affected some sectors of production more than others.[18] American urban and labor historians have been slower to reconsider the conventional wisdom; most pertinent here, the history of manufacturing in early-nineteenth-century New York continues to be presented as part of a seemingly inevitable national shift toward a factory system.[19] In fact, that history was far more

17. Bryan D. Palmer, A *Culture in Conflict: Skilled Workers and Industrial Capitalism in Hamilton, Ontario, 1860–1914* (Montreal, 1979), xvi.

18. The conventional wisdom appears in Marxist, non-Marxist, and anti-Marxist writings alike. The locus classicus is Marx, *Capital*, I, chaps. 13–16, but see also W. W. Rostow, *The Stages of Economic Growth: A Non-Communist Manifesto* (Cambridge, 1960), and David S. Landes, *The Unbound Prometheus: Technological Change and Development in Western Europe from 1750 to the Present* (Cambridge, 1969). The most sustained and intelligent critique on the English case is Raphael Samuel, "The Workshop of the World: Steam Power and Hand Technology in Mid-Victorian Britain," *History Workshop*, no. 3 (1977): 6–72.

19. Most of the "new" labor history has concentrated on various "leading sectors" and single-industry towns, despite the early warnings of George Rogers Taylor, in *The Transportation Revolution, 1815–1860* (New York, 1951), that these were not the sole, or even the most significant, sites of early industrial change. Susan E. Hirsch, *The Roots of the American Working Class: The Industrialization of Crafts in Newark, 1800–1860* (Philadelphia, 1978), offers a more complex account of antebellum manufacturing, but remains committed to showing that industrialization and the rise of the factory system are best handled as identical terms. More illuminating is Bruce Laurie's discussion of uneven development in Philadelphia, in *Working People of Philadelphia*, chap. 1. On New York, see virtually every book that has even touched on the city's

complex and interesting, an example of the early stages of what I have chosen to call metropolitan industrialization. Any attempt to reinterpret the ideology and social conflicts of the era would be hopeless without a detailed examination of metropolitan industrialization, from its first stirrings in the 1780s through the 1840s.

Ideology—the emerging systems of belief of employers and workers— and how to recover it present the most intractable problems of all. In 1909, John H. Morrison, the historian of New York's shipyards, reported that the history of labor relations in New York's early-nineteenth-century trades had never fully been written, on account of the scarcity of material.[20] Morrison exaggerated the dearth; nevertheless, the historian of New York labor is left few of the diaries, family papers, account books, and narratives that have enriched recent social histories of the South, of New England, and of the West. To interpret social consciousness as broadly as possible, I have turned to what I could find of other kinds of evidence, located in court records, ceremonial speeches, contemporary prints and drawings, and accounts of parades and festivals. These sources, especially the speeches, carry their own perils, as the counter-Progressives pointed out. Many take the form of rhetorical exhortations, directed at workers or employers (and sometimes both) to win their confidence and support, usually for a political cause. As such, they are, in William Empson's term, "myths," intended by their authors to flatten out a multitude of prejudices, hopes, and motives for the sake of easy assimilation and graphic power.[21] If interpreted too literally, they can disguise as much as they reveal about social perceptions and relations. But there is also meaning in these sources, as historians discover from time to time; such "myths," after all, draw on popular beliefs and assumptions; once formulated, they help order people's understanding of the world and tell us something about social relations. Nowhere was this truer than in early-nineteenth-century America, where political rhetoric and spectacle were subjects of passionate popular interest and debate.[22] That the "myths" were manipu-

---

manufacturing economy before 1860, including Edward K. Spann's encyclopedic *The New Metropolis: New York City, 1840–1857* (New York, 1981).

20. Morrison, *A History of New York Ship Yards* (New York, 1909), 64.

21. Empson, *Some Versions of Pastoral* (London, 1935), 35.

22. Such, of course, was the leading article of faith for what used to be known as the "symbolist" American-studies movement, in its discussions of Jacksonian politics and industrialization. See, for example, Henry Nash Smith, *Virgin Land: The American West as Symbol and Myth* (Cambridge, Mass., 1950); John William Ward, *Andrew Jackson: Symbol for an Age* (New York, 1955); Marvin Meyers, *The Jacksonian Persuasion: Politics and Belief* (Stanford 1957); Leo Marx, *The Machine in the Garden: Technology and the Pastoral Ideal in America* (New York, 1964). More recent work in this vein includes John Kasson, *Civilizing the Machine: Technology and Republican Values in the United States, 1776–1900* (New York, 1977). Each of these works, with

lated for a variety of ends and came to mean different things to different people only confirms that they held substantive and evocative meanings for the audiences to whom they were directed. Taken at this level, a historical reading of these materials—an examination of how the "myths" changed and were invested with different meanings by different groups—can help bring us closer to some understanding of how old forms of social solidarity and consciousness decayed and new ones arose.

Such a study of ideology and class demands coming to terms with political culture and with shifting definitions of republicanism. In almost every conceivable public context—and some private ones as well—the subjects of this book turned to the language of the Republic to explain their views, attack their enemies, and support their friends. As recovered by J. G. A. Pocock, this discourse rested largely on four interlocking concepts: first, that the ultimate goal of any political society should be the preservation of the public good, or *commonwealth*; second, that in order to maintain the commonwealth, the citizens of a republic had to be able and willing to exercise *virtue*, to subordinate private ends to the legislation of the public good when they conflicted; third, that in order to be virtuous, citizens had to be *independent* of the political will of other men, lest they lose sight of the common good; fourth, that in order to guard against the encroachments of would-be tyrants, citizens had to be active in politics, to exercise their *citizenship*. To these concepts, eighteenth-century Americans, above all "middling" merchants and artisans, added *equality*, the liberal idea that all citizens should be entitled to their natural civil and political rights under a representative, democratic system of laws.[23]

The history of class formation in New York is comprehensible only if it is understood in this broad ideological context: faced with profound changes in the social relations of production, ordinary New Yorkers began to reinterpret their shared ideals of commonwealth, virtue, independence, citizenship, and equality, and struggled over the very meaning of the terms. In so doing, they also revealed the social meanings of republicanism

---

all of its merits, is hampered by its insufficient attention to social relations, power, and class. The significance of cultural myths and symbols has, however, been presented in a revised form, in a number of new studies of working-class culture. The most systematic of these is Sewell, *Work and Revolution in France*. Critical influences here—on the present study as on others—have been Thompson, *Making of the English Working Class*; Maurice Agulhon, *La République au village* (Paris, 1970); idem, *Une Ville ouvrière*; idem, *Marianne au combat: L'Imagerie et la symbolique républicaines de 1789 à 1880* (Paris, 1977).

23. J. G. A. Pocock, "Virtue and Commerce in the Eighteenth Century," *JIH* 3 (1972): 119–34; idem, *The Machiavellian Moment: Florentine Political Thought and the Atlantic Republican Tradition* (Princeton, 1975). On equality, see Gordon S. Wood, *The Creation of the American Republic, 1776–1787* (Chapel Hill, 1969), esp. 72–73; and Foner, *Tom Paine*, 123–24, 225–26.

for urban producers—and how they changed. Formal republican thought was a political ideology, a world view that distinguished sharply between society and government and held that social disorder stemmed from political corruption. Nevertheless, it bore close associations to social relations outside of politics, associations that were severely tested as Americans came to consider their own way of life as peculiarly conducive to a proper republican order. In the decades just after the Revolution, New York's artisans (like their counterparts in other cities) elaborated their own democratic variant of American republican ideology, bound to their expectations about workshop production.[24] By 1850, with the erosion of the artisan system, that shared vision had virtually collapsed and been replaced by new and opposing conceptions of republican politics and the social relations that would best sustain them. This process of social reformation and ideological transformation was neither simple nor linear; to trace its sometimes baffling course from the most direct of class confrontations through nativism and immigration, political intrigue, gang warfare, and numerous reform movements, is the greatest challenge for the historian of early-nineteenth-century urban labor. Nevertheless, the process happened, and can be shown to have happened, in the republican metropolis.

What to call the new forms of social consciousness that appeared has long been subject to debate. Early on, I abandoned the familiar, essentialist concept of class consciousness, still dominant in the Marxist and Weberian traditions, that would define the term as an all-embracing (usually revolutionary) critique of capitalist wage-labor relations, held by the mass of proletarians and expressed in all consequential matters of public and private concern, above all in politics. The problem, as I see it, is not with such abstractions per se; they have their uses for social historians, who must sift through a multitude of historical particulars and untidy events. It is, rather, that historians who have stuck to this particular concept have usually allowed it to tyrannize them, so that they try to see how closely the past approximated the ideal—thereby using a concept to account for why something that presumably *should* have happened did not, before coming to terms with what *did* happen. Very quickly, the historian discovers that the ideal "conscious class" has never existed in the United States as, supposedly, it has in England and on the Continent; characteristically, this leads to attempts to explain why the past let down the ideal, why there has been no class consciousness (or, as Werner Som-

24. I argued this point, in a preliminary fashion, in "Artisan Republican Festivals and the Rise of Class Conflict in New York City, 1788–1837," in *Working-Class America: Essays in Labor, Community, and American Society*, ed. Michael Frisch and Daniel Walkowitz (Urbana, 1983), 37–77. I have corrected and refined the materials and interpretations presented in that essay.

bart put it, no socialism) in the United States.[25] It is the wrong question, one that is based on a woefully stylized impression of class consciousness abroad, one that short-circuits our attempts to understand the class perceptions that did exist in this country, one that pulls history through the looking glass into a make-believe world of "false consciousness" and "liberal consensus." Instead of writing about this aspect of the history of American class relations, we have usually written it off from the start.

Rejection of the old ideal has not, however, led me to abandon the concept of class consciousness altogether or to collapse it into a broader category like "plebeian," or "populist." Recent historians and sociologists have argued that such categories help us to understand numerous nineteenth-century British popular movements, including some that scholars habitually classify as working-class protest. Some of the movements examined here may also be understood in such terms. But the label "populist" fails to account for those movements that did comprehend social conflict as being, at least in part, a result of capitalist labor relations. Nor does the term "class loyalty"—commonly used to describe a recognition of class differences that falls short of class consciousness—adequately cover the purposeful critiques of capitalist wage labor elaborated in Jacksonian New York.[26] Rather, between 1829—the annus mirabilis of New York artisan radicalism—and 1850, both a process and a strain of consciousness emerged in numerous ways from the swirl of popular politics, in which people came

25. Sombart, *Warum gibt es in den Vereinigten Staaten keinen Sozialismus?* (Tübingen, 1906). The tenacity of the Sombartian fallacy is evident in several of the essays in John H. M. Laslett and S. M. Lipset, eds., *Failure of a Dream? Essays in the History of American Socialism* (Garden City, N.Y., 1974). Christopher Lasch has made a similar point, in a different but related context, observing, "The understanding of American radicalism and its history has suffered from a recurrent tendency either to force it into European categories or to make its very resistance to this procedure the basis of a general condemnation of the American Left." See Lasch's preface, along with Olaf Hansen's introduction, to Randolph Bourne, *The Radical Will: Randolph Bourne, Selected Writings, 1911–1918*, ed. Olaf Hansen (New York, 1977).

26. On the "populism" of English workers' movements, see Craig Calhoun, *The Question of Class Struggle: Social Foundations of Popular Radicalism during the Industrial Revolution* (Chicago, 1982). Gareth Stedman Jones has argued more persuasively that several movements of the 1830s and 1840s—above all Chartism—are better understood as extensions of eighteenth-century radicalism than as the bearers of a new working-class critique of capitalist wage relations or as a pre-Marxian socialism. In part, the same holds true in the United States; nonetheless, I would argue that various strains of class consciousness, deeply attached to republican values but distinguishable from "classical" artisan republicanism, and linked to critiques of workshop dependency and exploitation, also emerged in the 1830s and 1840s. See Gareth Stedman Jones, "The Language of Chartism," in *The Chartist Experience: Studies in Working-Class Radicalism and Culture, 1830–1860*, ed. James Epstein and Dorothy Thompson (London, 1982), 3–58. The concept of "class loyalty" (*Klassengefühl*) was first developed clearly by Samuel Gompers; for a brief discussion, see Dawley, *Class and Community*, 239–40.

at various points to interpret social disorder and the decline of the Republic at least partly in terms of class divisions between capitalist employers and employees. More specifically, workers and radicals elaborated a notion of labor as a form of personal property, in direct opposition to capitalist conceptions of wage labor as a market commodity. For much of the period, this consciousness of class appeared within a broader defense of the "producing classes," an amalgam of "honorable" anticapitalist small masters and wage earners; in moments of particularly acute crisis, however, as in the mid-1830s and in 1850, critiques of wage relations came to the fore, usually (but not exclusively) in trade-union movements.

It is in these terms, rejecting the more familiar definition of class consciousness as the only one, recognizing the possible coexistence of several tendencies and outlooks, sometimes in a single movement or in the minds of individual participants, that I think we can better understand the social and ideological tensions at work in early-nineteenth-century New York. We encounter a continuing working out of emerging class conflicts, in which different groups, including employers, drew upon and transformed an established "plebeian" artisan republicanism to make sense of their experience and to act upon it. This process did not turn into a fixed battle at any one point; class consciousness and labor radicalism (in various and changing forms) emerged and abated, depending on a myriad of circumstances. Overall, however, we can detect a pattern, indicating that New Yorkers—especially in brief periods of what André-Jean Tudesq has aptly called "social fear"[27]—returned to class issues and to class identities and allegiances to defend their interests, and those of the democratic Republic itself, as they saw them. It is in this pattern of human relationships over time—and not the creation of abstract social categories or "groups"—that I find it possible to locate and describe the process of class formation as a central development in early-nineteenth-century New York.

In principle, such a study could encompass every realm of social life for all New Yorkers before the Civil War: if new forms of class relations and social consciousness arose, as I believe they did, they should show up in redefinitions of gender, sexuality, and family, in the conduct of politics, in childhood, in housing patterns, in the meanest transactions of everyday life. No such total history is attempted here. In some cases, the decision to eliminate material or pass over entire questions was eased by the spate of excellent recent works on New York, which promise finally to put the history of the metropolis in a full and proper perspective.[28] More impor-

27. André-Jean Tudesq, *Les Grands Notables en France* (1840–1849): *Étude historique d'une psychologie sociale* (Paris, 1964), II, 1236.
28. See, e.g., Elizabeth Strother Blackmar, "Housing and Property Relations in New York City, 1780–1850" (Ph.D. diss., Harvard University, 1980); Amy Bridges, *A City*

tant, by sticking mainly to familiar subjects—especially the trade unionists, labor radicals, and their opponents—I hope to place what have long been recognized as central problems in a new light. For three generations, historians have told and retold the history of class relations and labor movements in early-nineteenth-century New York. This book will have served its purpose if it can help to tell that history again in a more convincing way.

Above all, while I treat one, highly unusual city, I hope to contribute to the continuing attempts to reconceptualize the history of the American working class. By this, I do not mean to suggest that a single entity came into being in the antebellum years never to change or to be changed, ever bound by a unity of sentiment across the shifting barriers of trade, region, race, sex, or ethnicity, autonomous and eternally resentful of all other classes. This Working Class never existed, least of all before the Civil War. But a new order of human relations did emerge, primarily (but not exclusively) in the North and West, defined chiefly (though again not exclusively) by the subordination of wage labor to capital.[29] What is more, men and women came in the same period to understand that this was happening, and they began to think and act, in E. P. Thompson's phrase, in new "class ways," unlike those of the mid–eighteenth century.[30] Worldwide capitalist development continued to alter the locus and texture of these relations; all of the fundamental tensions, issues, and dilemmas of class remained. In this sense, it is proper to treat the so-called

in the Republic: The Origins of Machine Politics in New York City (forthcoming); Carol Groneman [Pernicone], "The 'Bloody Ould Sixth': A Social Analysis of a New York Working-Class Community in the Mid-Nineteenth Century" (Ph.D. diss., University of Rochester, 1974); Paul E. Gilje, "Mobocracy: Popular Disturbances in Post-Revolutionary New York City, 1780–1829" (Ph.D. diss., Brown University, 1980); John B. Jentz, "Artisans, Evangelicals, and the City: A Social History of Abolition and Labor Reform in Jacksonian New York" (Ph.D. diss., City University of New York, 1977); Elaine Weber Pascu, "From the Philanthropic Tradition to the Common School Ideal: Schooling in New York City, 1815–1832" (Ph.D. diss., Northern Illinois University, 1980); Howard B. Rock, Artisans of the New Republic: The Tradesmen of New York City in the Age of Jefferson (New York, 1979); Spann, The New Metropolis; Christine Stansell, City of Women: The Female Laboring Poor in New York, 1785–1860 (New York, forthcoming); Paul O. Weinbaum, Mobs and Demagogues: The New York Response to Collective Violence in the Early Nineteenth Century (Ann Arbor, 1979).

29. In somewhat broader terms (based on the best available data), the United States changed, between the late eighteenth century and 1870, from a nation of independent producers, slaves, and slaveholders to one in which most gainfully employed persons worked for wages. Emancipation in the South after 1865 was an important but secondary factor in this statistical shift. See Jackson Turner Main, The Social Structure of Revolutionary America (Princeton, 1965), 271–76; and Montgomery, Beyond Equality, 25–31.

30. Thompson, "Eighteenth-Century English Society: Class Struggle without Class?" Social History 3 (1972): 147.

early national and Jacksonian eras as a period of class formation in the United States. People and events in New York City were a vital part of that process; by examining them, from the 1780s to the final establishment of the New York working-class presence in 1850, this book aims not to study a "typical" case, a microcosm, but to supply an important part of the historical puzzle and to suggest ways in which class formation might be approached in other areas of the country.

A final word on organization. In the main, the argument is structured as a chronological, analytical narrative—a useful form in which to describe the process of class formation *as* a process. Part I, on the artisan republic, is, however, more synoptic, a setting of the stage. It should be clear that the period 1788–1825 was not a static or harmonious one—far from it. Nonetheless, it is a period that is best seen as prelude to what was to come. For that reason, I have deliberately been as panoramic as possible in the opening section, in order to touch on the several themes that united New York's workers and employers as well as on those that divided them, on those themes of harmony and of suspicion that would come into play as the early crises of the artisan republic deepened into new forms of social understanding and conflict. We begin, then, with a city in celebration.

I

The Artisan Republic,
1788-1825

Neither a servant nor a master am I,
I take no sooner a large price than a small price—I will have my own,
    whoever enjoys me,
I will be even with you, and you shall be even with me.
                                  Chants Democratic, III, 7.

1

"By Hammer and Hand":
Artisans in the Mercantile City

In February 1815, a sloop arrived in New York harbor with first news of the signing of the Treaty of Ghent. Almost immediately, a spontaneous festival erupted, and for over a week, New Yorkers rejoiced at the expected return of commerce after four years of diplomatic wrangling and nearly three years of war. None were more jubilant than the city's artisans. At closing time, masters, journeymen, and apprentices filled their shops with their finest wares and snake-danced tipsy through the streets, their paths lit by shimmering transparencies, of eagles and dollars spilling from a cornucopia, of brawny arms lifting mallets, above the legends "Peace, The Mechanic's Friend" and "By Hammer And Hand All Arts Do Stand." At dawn, they wobbled back to the shops, only to begin another round of patriotic toasting. An exultant artisan rhymester named Werckmeister caught the mood well with a pun: "*Work* is over, Peace is *master* / Friendship ties her knot now faster."[1]

These were the trades in their favorite array, the citizen-craftsmen, distinguished by their insignias and their leather aprons and united by a fierce pride in their skills and products—a self-proclaimed social estate embracing those the journalists called "the plain, honest men" of the mercantile city.[2] All craftsmen, employers and employees alike, had reason to cheer; clear sailing for the merchants and sea captains augured ample work and good wages for even the lowliest local mechanic. No one

1. *Evening Post* [New York], February 27, 28, March 1, 1815; *Columbian* [New York] February 27, 1815; R. S. Guernsey, *New York and Vicinity during the War of 1812* (New York, 1895), II, 483–94.

2. For typical references, see *American Citizen* [New York], March 11, April 13, 1801.

seemed perturbed by the gaps between the festive craft imagery and the actual conditions in the workshops and artisan neighborhoods. No one mentioned the strikes that had hit the shops before the war and that threatened to resume with the revival of business. For at least this one auspicious moment, the artisans' devotion to country, craft, and commercial prosperity submerged memory and premonition.

So New York's craftsmen greeted the peace that would bring the collapse of the artisan republic. What, then, were the changing social conditions and relations in the city's trades? And why, on those nights of jubilee, had the economic and moral universe of craft and workshop already begun to fall apart?

The Crafts in Flux

Jefferson's embargo and the War of 1812 marked a calamitous interlude in New York's rise to supremacy among America's mercantile cities.[3] In 1788, Manhattan was one of several important ports of call along the Atlantic sugar routes, a city of sufficient size and prestige to be selected as the new nation's capital but not yet even remotely a commercial metropolis. Ruins left from the great fires of 1776 and 1778 remained untouched, charred reminders of the British occupation during the Revolution; the merchant Samuel Breck, on his return from France in the late 1780s, found it "a neglected place, built chiefly of wood, and in a state of prostration and decay."[4] Ten years later, the national government had relocated to the pestiferous Potomac, safe from urban crowds, while New York emerged as the busiest of the seaboard trading cities; over the next quarter of a century, the pleasant, provincial port became a commercial emporium and a financial market of international prominence. New York's merchants, already blessed with one of the world's finest harbors and with excellent waterways to the hinterland, seized control of coastal commerce and established Manhattan as the chief entrepôt for shipping to and from Britain. The early introduction of an auction system for imports and of regular transatlantic packet-ship service widened access to British capital and increased the city's advantages over its chief rivals, Philadelphia and

3. The material in the following paragraph is drawn mainly from Sidney I. Pomerantz, *New York, An American City, 1783–1803: A Study in Urban Life* (New York, 1938), 147–225; Robert Greenhalgh Albion, *The Rise of New York Port, 1815–1860* (New York, 1939), 1–15; Myron H. Luke, *The Port of New York, 1800–1810* (New York, 1953); Douglass C. North, *The Economic Growth of the United States, 1790–1860* (New York, 1966), 32, 42, 51, 62–63; Bayrd Still, *Mirror for Gotham: New York as Seen by Contemporaries from Dutch Days to the Present* (New York, 1956), 54–81.

4. Breck, *Recollections of Samuel Breck* (Philadelphia, 1877), 89–90; T. E. V. Smith, *The City of New York in the Year of Washington's Inauguration, 1789* (New York, 1889), 5–6.

Baltimore. The early-nineteenth-century transport revolution—hastened by the completion of the Erie Canal in 1825—tightened New York's grip on commerce from the Atlantic to the most distant American markets. New and improved banking and credit institutions, insurance companies, brokerage houses, and a stock market kept lower Manhattan at the center of what one writer has described as the era's "business revolution."[5] New York became a mandatory stop for foreign tourists, who marveled at its bustling streets, its merchants' brick town houses, and its forests of masts. The more astute among them noted what the city's growth meant to those inside the counting houses: henceforth, one wrote in 1823, "[n]ot a tree will be felled which does not necessarily operate to increase the trade and riches of New York."[6]

With prosperity came a mounting population, fed by rural migrants from the city's hinterland, vagabonds, and small waves of immigrants from Britain and Ireland. In the first rush of expansion, between 1790 and 1800, the number of residents counted in the census increased by more than 80 percent; by 1805, New York was the nation's largest city. Twenty years later, despite the embargo, the war, and several outbreaks of yellow fever, the recorded population had nearly tripled again, to over 160,000. The city's physical growth was almost as impressive. Although incapable of ending chronic housing shortages, new construction to the north and the subdivision of existing structures surpassed the expectations of the most enterprising New Yorkers. In 1803, when municipal officials drafted plans for a new, marble city hall, to be built on the city's outskirts, they authorized the use of red sandstone for the rear north wall, "inasmuch as it was not likely to attract much notice." By 1825, the limits of most concentrated settlement, running from river to river, reached to Fourteenth Street—almost two miles north of the hall (Map 1).[7]

This rapid development deepened existing contrasts between rich and poor. Between 1790 and 1825, New York's total wealth per capita rose by approximately 60 percent, but the distribution of wealth became increasingly unequal, accentuating disparities already evident before the Revolu-

5. Thomas C. Cochran, "The Business Revolution," AHR 79 (1974): 1444–66. See also idem, Frontiers of Change: Early Industrialism in America (New York, 1981), 17–37.

6. John M. Duncan, Travels through Part of the United States and Canada in 1818 and 1819 (New York, 1823), II, 25.

7. Ira P. Rosenwaike, The Population History of New York City (Syracuse, 1972), 15–28; Pomerantz, New York, 201–9; John W. Francis, Old New York: or, Reminiscences of the Last Sixty Years (New York, 1858), 15. On housing shortages, see James Ford, Slums and Housing with Special Reference to New York City (Cambridge, Mass., 1936), I, 87–90; Betsy Blackmar, "Re-walking the 'Walking City': Housing and Property Relations in New York City, 1780–1840," Radical History Review 21 (1979): 131–48.

tion; by the late 1820s, a mere 4 percent of the population owned half of the city's noncorporate wealth.[8] At the pinnacle of local society stood a cosmopolitan mercantile elite of old Knickerbockers, of transplanted New Englanders, and of the odd self-made parvenu like the immigrant John Jacob Astor. Aggressive in their pursuit of regional, southern, and western markets, innovative in their use of credit, sometimes opulent in their private displays of fortune (a style exemplified by Astor, whose very name, Herman Melville would later write, "rings like unto bullion"), New York's merchants and financiers formed the most conspicuous and energetic American aristocracy of urban capitalist wealth. Clustered in their residential enclaves along Broadway and the southern portions of the city, they dined in each other's homes and married into each other's families; they also directed the city's network of charitable and cultural associations and dominated city government.[9]

At the other extreme were the laboring poor—migrants and immigrants, sailors, free blacks, day laborers, widows, orphans, and transients. No one was sure how many New Yorkers found themselves in these straits, but their numbers were obviously large and growing. In the mid-1790s, approximately six hundred paupers were lodged in the city's almshouse; by 1817, the number of inmates had almost tripled, while more than fifteen thousand persons, about one-seventh of the city's population, required some sort of public or private charity relief.[10] The more fortunate of the city's manual laborers found jobs along the waterfront; the most fortunate of all managed to obtain licenses as cartmen, draymen, and hackney-coach drivers—mean, rough work but also regular, independent, and profitable work.[11] Thousands of others lived with more marginal prospects. By 1825, pockets of the city's central and outer wards had become dilapidated

8. Edmund P. Willis, "Social Origins of Political Leadership in New York City from the Revolution to 1815" (Ph.D. diss., University of California at Berkeley, 1967), 103–32; Rock, Artisans of the New Republic, 238; Pessen, Riches, Class, and Power, 33. On poverty and inequality in New York before 1776, see Nash, Urban Crucible, 125–27, 239–40, 254–56, 331–32.

9. Albion, Rise of New York Port, 235–59; Willis, "Social Origins," 156–74, 220–21; M. J. Heale, "From City Fathers to Social Critics: Humanitarianism and Government in New York, 1790–1860," JAH 63 (1976): 21–41; Pessen, Riches, Class, and Power, 9–73, 169–248; Frederick Cople Jaher, The Urban Establishment: Upper Strata in Boston, New York, Charleston, Chicago, and Los Angeles (Urbana, 1982), 187–96, 208–22, 231–50; Herman Melville, "Bartleby the Scrivener," in Great Short Works of Herman Melville, ed. Warner Berthoff (New York, 1969), 40.

10. Raymond Mohl, Poverty in New York, 1783–1825 (New York, 1970), 14–34, 87–90.

11. Isaac Lyon, Recollections of an Old Cartman (Newark, 1872), 3–5; Pomerantz, New York, 211–12; Rock, Artisans of the New Republic, 205–34; Graham Hodges, "The Cartmen of New York City, 1667–1801" (Ph.D. diss., New York University 1982).

slums where even the most determined missionaries to Christ's poor walked with fear. Along Bancker Street in the Fourth Ward, poor blacks crammed into tumbledown houses, where overcrowding and poor sanitation led to periodic outbreaks of disease and fever. To the east, Corlears Hook, the sailors' resort, became a lower-class haven, a mixture of small shops, barrooms, boarding houses, and minuscule flats. Only a few blocks from the new City Hall, the Five Points district, built hastily on a landfill over the old Collect Pond, began to decay into a vaporous neighborhood of clapboard homes abandoned by their original artisan owners. Most gentlemen and visitors shunned these areas, but they could not deny the absence of what the Englishman John Lambert called a "pure republican equality." Nor could they avoid the poorest of the poor, who could be seen all over town, living as best they could from the scraps of the mercantile economy, as ragpickers, hucksters, street sweepers, wood-chip collectors (a job for children), seamstresses, and prostitutes.[12]

Between these social extremes (but overlapping them at either end) were the master craftsmen and their journeymen employees, the largest group of working people in New York.[13] Well before the turn of the cen-

12. Ward Stafford, *New Missionary Field: A Report to the Female Missionary Society for the Poor of the City of New-York and Its Vicinity* (New York, 1817), 12–15; *Evening Post*, January 23, 1805; *New-York Spectator*, July 13, 1816; *Report of the Committee of the Medical Society of the City and County of New York* (New York, 1821); MCC, XI, 440–41; Groneman, " 'Bloody Ould Sixth,' " 20–33; John Lambert, *Travels through Canada and the United States* (London, 1814), 102–3; CCFP, Police Committee, January 31, 1825; Mary Christine Stansell, "Women of the Laboring Poor in New York City, 1820–1860" (Ph.D. diss., Yale University, 1979), 17–56 passim.

13. Here I am defining artisans as all those engaged in the direct production of commodities, masters as well as journeymen, but not apprentices. The precise proportion of artisans in the early-nineteenth-century work force in New York City is not clear. Carl F. Kaestle, using the 1796 city directory, finds that 52.6 percent of the city's workers were artisans. See Kaestle, *The Evolution of an Urban School System: New York City, 1750–1850* (Cambridge, Mass., 1973), 31–32. Rock computes figures from the jury book of 1819 and estimates that between 50 and 60 percent of the city's workers could be classified as "mechanics"; Rock's figures, however, include cartmen and draymen as mechanics; his sources and Kaestle's tend to underestimate the numbers of laborers in the city and take no account of domestic servants. A random sample of names from the 1815 city directory revealed that 36.2 percent of those listed were artisans. Because the directory underenumerated younger workers and journeymen as well as day laborers, I would estimate that approximately two-fifths to one-half of the male work force worked in the trades, either as masters or as journeymen—a slightly larger proportion than prevailed in eighteenth-century New York. See Rock, *Artisans of the New Republic*, 14–16. On the work force in eighteenth-century New York, see Jacob Price, "Economic Function and the Growth of American Port Towns," *Perspectives in American History*, no. 8 (1974): 131–37, 184–85. Price's figures show a dramatic decline in the relative size of New York's "industrial" sector, from 1746 to 1795. His figures and the others cited here are very different, largely because Price places individuals in various artisan trades, including carpenters, in his "service" sector. By reclassifying Price's figures, to place his subsectors II. C and D in the industrial sector, we find that about 40 percent of the male labor force worked in the trades in 1795.

tury, New York's artisans had won considerable acclaim for producing goods that compared favorably with the finest English workmanship; like their counterparts in England, they also remained a decidedly secondary power in the commercial capitalist city.[14] In 1815, only a slender portion of the city's wealthiest men had any direct connection with the trades (Table 1), a situation that would persist into the 1820s and beyond.[15] Although their skills differentiated them from the laborers and the poor, the majority of the artisans—masters and journeymen combined—held little or no taxable property (Table 2). The craft economy included a diverse collection of occupations, from light consumer crafts like tailoring and shoemaking to heavier local industries like sugar refining. Virtually all relied directly or indirectly on the success of the port.[16]

Compared with the city's merchant capitalists these artisans seemed to some New Yorkers like remnants of another era, tied to an ancient craft world of production and marketing. Through the 1820s, the majority of artisan firms were tiny: the journeyman bookbinder John Bradford's whimsical description of a typical bindery in 1815, with its three or four candlesticks and as many workers, may be taken as a rough norm for the major New York trades.[17] Most of the artisans' advertisements and the jobs they enumerated in their price lists stated that their work was largely oriented to specific orders, based on informal direct credit sales. Apprenticeship remained a standard arrangement in 1820, when employers estimated that between six and eight thousand apprentice boys served local producers. Journeymen in every craft outside the building trades were paid by the piece, according, at least in principle, to a set book or list of "just" prices—evidence that artisan wage labor was not yet fully regarded as a market commodity, as labor-power subject to the impersonal laws of supply and demand. Although most municipal regulation of production and

14. Carl Bridenbaugh, *The Colonial Craftsman* (Chicago, 1950), 65–124 passim.
15. Pessen, *Riches, Class, and Power*, 47–48.
16. On the range of crafts, see Rock, *Artisans of the New Republic*, 12–13. On other manufacturing pursuits before 1825, see Albion, *Rise of New York Port*, 165–93; Pomerantz, *New York*, 158–59, 194–99. See also, for a similar situation, Sam Bass Warner, *The Private City: Philadelphia in Three Periods of Its Growth* (Philadelphia, 1968), 65–67. For a theoretical overview of the economic structure of a mercantile city, see Max Weber, *Economy and Society*, ed. Guenther Roth and Claus Wittich (Berkeley, 1978), II, 1215–17.
17. John Bradford, *The Poetic Vagaries of a Knight of the Folding Stick of Paste Castle* (Gotham [New York], 1815), 9–10. The ratio of masters to journeymen in the 1816 sample (1 : 3.0), although not definitive, suggests most craft firms were small; in some of the smaller trades, as Rock notes, the numbers of journeymen and masters were roughly equal. See Rock, *Artisans of the New Republic*, 266–68. On the simplicity of manufacturing firms in general in this period, see Alfred D. Chandler, Jr., *The Visible Hand: The Managerial Revolution in American Business* (Cambridge, Mass., 1977), 17–19, 50–52.

distribution was abandoned before 1788, the assize on bread remained in force until 1821; government administration of butchering and the public markets would last well beyond the 1820s. Master craftsmen at least claimed that they expected to earn no more than a "competence," an independent estate of simple comforts. The declared axioms of artisan business, outlined in a snippet of verse dedicated to the stonemasons in 1805 and published in the city directory, were as appropriate to a seventeenth-century village as to an emerging nineteenth-century metropolis:

> —I pay my debts
> I steal from no man; would not cut a throat
> To gain admission to a great man's purse
> Or a whore's bed; I'd not betray my friend
> To get his place of fortune; I scorn to flatter
> A blown up fool above me or crush
> The wretch beneath me

Barter persisted along with petty-commodity exchange in some corners of the trades; in 1812, it was still possible for a small master builder to tote up the occasional account in terms of turkeys or gold watches paid rather than in terms of cash tendered.[18]

Several factors conspired to make the growth of any more substantial industrial base seem most unlikely. Bereft of any easily harnessed water-power, Manhattan Island offered few advantages to would-be textile or cloth magnates of the kind who financed the early industrialization of New England and of the Delaware Valley. Mounting real-estate costs set off by the rapid development of mercantile facilities and the shortage of residential space further discouraged the building of mills or large central shops in the city proper. In all branches of production, even the most eager would-be craft entrepreneurs faced enormous obstacles in securing investment capital for any venture outside of shipping, transport speculation, marine insurance, or land investment: in most New York banks, the *Evening Post* observed in 1804, "the application of the laborious mechanic is treated with contempt and rejected with disdain." As late as 1827, the

18. Rita Suswein Gottesman, *The Arts and Crafts in New York, 1800–1804* (New York, 1965), 241–65, 374–79, and passim; "To the Journeymen Carpenters and Masons" (1805), N-YHS Broadside; "To the Master Printers" (1809), N-YHS Broadside; New York Society of Journeymen Cabinetmakers, *New-York Book of Prices for Manufacturing Cabinet and Chair Work* (New York, 1817); Thomas Earle and Charles Congdon, *Annals of the General Society of Mechanics and Tradesmen in the City of New York, 1785–1880* (New York, 1882), 281; Thomas R. Mercein, *An Address Delivered on the Opening of the Apprentices' Library* (New York, 1820), 21; *Longworth's American Almanack for 1805* (New York, 1805), 138–39; Ledger Book, Unidentified contractor and builder, New York City, 1812–19, December 26, 1812, January 2, 1813, December 11, 1814, NYPL MSS.

merchant John Dix could only conclude that, despite its myriad crafts, New York would forever remain "purely a trading city."[19]

Yet while Dix's observations had some merit, and while the artisan system of labor remained sturdy in large sectors of the craft economy, important changes were unfolding in the early national workshops. A few entrepreneurs in some of the heavier craft industries—leather tanning, shipbuilding, sugar refining—greatly enlarged their operations in New York, aided by the expansion of local merchant capital and by the growth of the local market. Others—above all in the consumer finishing, construction, and printing trades—moved even more decisively into the world of nineteenth-century capitalist production and exchange. As early as the 1750s, consumer finishing masters and builders had begun to free themselves from old mercantile clientage networks and to cultivate their own markets; the decline of slavery and indentured servitude in the third quarter of the eighteenth century fostered new markets in free wage labor. By the 1790s, a few consumer-trade masters had geared most of their output to supply either local retailers, regional markets, or the southern coasting trade. After 1800, improved transport links to the North and West made large-scale production of light consumer goods even more feasible and profitable. The city's burgeoning population provided the labor pool and enlarged demand to encourage the growth of new and highly competitive local markets in house construction, shoemaking, and tailoring. Merchant demand for printed materials and newspapers lured printers from around the country to New York. By the 1820s, even the money market, although still largely the preserve of mercantile speculators, had begun slowly to open to entrepreneurs in those crafts most stimulated by the acceleration of commerce. Obscured though they were by the more dazzling expansion of the port, these developments prepared the way for a new system of enterprise in the city's largest and most important handicrafts. By 1825, that system had already begun to replace established artisan practices with new forms of wage labor and distribution.[20]

The city's first small crop of manufactories suggested something of the

<hr/>

19. Charles H. Haswell, *Reminiscences of an Octogenarian of the City of New York* (New York, 1897), 109–30; *Evening Post*, March 3, 1804; John A. Dix, *Sketch of the Resources of the City of New-York* (New York, 1827), 85.

20. Nash, *Urban Crucible*, 258–63; 320–21; Allan R. Pred, "Manufacturing in the Mercantile City, 1800–1840," *Annals of the Society of American Geographers* 56 (1966): 307–25; David T. Gilchrist, ed., *The Growth of the Seaboard Cities, 1790–1825* (Charlottesville, 1967), 95–99; Montgomery, "Working Classes." For a splendid concise account of similar developments in Philadelphia, see Sharon V. Salinger, "Artisans, Journeymen, and the Transformation of Labor in Late Eighteenth-Century Philadelphia," *WMQ* 40 (1983): 62–84. On slavery in the crafts in eighteenth-century New York, see Edgar J. McManus, *A History of Negro Slavery in New York* (Syracuse, 1966), 47.

changing scale and relations of craft production. In 1820, a fragmentary census of some of the city's largest firms located twelve, predominantly in the building and consumer finishing crafts, that hired more than twenty-five persons, and thirty-five that hired ten or more—hardly a major industrial agglomeration by later standards, but impressive enough for an American city of the time. A handful of these were prototypes for later factories, but most were manufactories in the literal sense—oversized workshops that gathered between five and ten skilled workers with a few boys and women to produce, by hand, large lots of light consumer goods. In line with the limits to industrial growth in New York, few produced anything but the usual urban-craft items (a lone cotton-textile firm appeared in the census); only one in three used any kind of machinery more complicated than simple lathes and the traditional handicraft tools; almost all were unincorporated firms, run by a single master or a simple copartnership. For all their modesty, however, operations like Isaac Minard's shoe manufactory (a major supplier to the southern trade), or M. and W. Benton's boot-and-shoe works (tied to local and regional markets), signaled a shift toward the greater concentration of divided craft labor and the increased use of semiskilled workers—the first step in what is commonly described as the classic process of industrialization.[21]

More telling, and more indicative of future developments in New York, were the innovations in the smaller shops. Between (roughly) 1790 and 1825, a small group of New York merchant tailors, led in time by the peripatetic immigrant James Chesterman, began adding inexpensive, prepared British goods to their supplies. By 1820, what had once been a marginal trade in locally prepared unfitted "slop" sailors' clothing began to challenge the importers and expand into the production of cheap, ready-to-wear goods and slave clothing for the southern market. Master tailors, chafing at the competition, subcontracted a larger share of their work either to newly arrived outwork journeymen or to poor women, who worked at home at rates 25 to 50 percent of those paid to men. Shoemakers—alarmed at the flood of shoes from Lynn, Massachusetts, and other New England towns into New York—skimped on the quality of their leathers (using what one journeyman derided as "bad stuff"), crowded their workrooms with apprentice labor, hired outwork journeymen, found women and girls to work as binders, and prepared cargoes of cheap shoes for the South. Cabinetmakers, although slower to resort to subcontract-

---

21. Census of Manufacturing Establishments, New York County, 1820, National Archives, MSS, microfilm, Ward 1, nos. 5, 13. A total of twelve New York manufacturing firms received incorporations from the state legislature between 1790 and 1819; only one of these, a steam-engine manufactory, turned up in the 1820 census. See Aaron Clark, *List of All Incorporations in the State of New York* (Albany, 1819), 42–53.

ing than others, divided their work into its simplest procedures and re-adjusted piece rates to circumvent the regular price-book standards. Printers, caught in a spiral of underbidding for merchant orders, began to rely on the cheap labor of young men and boys scorned by regular journeymen as "half-ways." Real-estate speculators turned to entrepreneurial contractors (mocked by experienced journeymen as "master builders in name only") to hire and oversee construction crews of skilled and semiskilled men.[22]

This rearrangement of the structure of small-shop production to tap Manhattan's swelling labor pool, even more than the appearance of the manufactories, marked the beginnings of a peculiarly metropolitan form of industrialization. It was to be no simple or sudden revolution. Trades tied primarily to local neighborhood markets, above all baking and butchering, changed little. The luxury trades, and crafts like ship carpentry and coopering that could not readily be subdivided, preserved the artisanal regime. In the consumer finishing crafts, a sizable sector remained to cater to the custom trade or to local clientele, in shops that retained the traditional craft conventions. Even the most severe changes in the New York trades were far less dramatic than those afoot in the early industrial towns of New England and Pennsylvania. Nevertheless, there was cause for both exhilaration and concern especially among those artisans who worked in consumer finishing, building, and printing—between one-quarter and one-third of all the city's masters, and between one-half and three-quarters of the journeymen.[23]

Some of the problems arose directly from the acceleration of trade and affected traditional artisans as well as the most innovative entrepreneurs. Luxury-trade masters, tanners, and heavy-metal tradesmen, along with local producers of light consumer goods, watched the tariff schedules closely as New York became a major transatlantic shipping center; agitation for upward revision of duties, begun in the 1780s, continued through the early 1820s. Credit, a troublesome feature of artisan business in the eighteenth

22. Tailoring: Albion, *Rise of New York Port*, 63–64; *Evening Post*, April 20, July 13, 1819; Egal Feldman, *Fit for Men: A Study of New York's Clothing Trade* (Washington, D.C., 1960), 1–2; Haswell, *Reminiscences*, 76–77; Stansell, "Women of the Laboring Poor, 57–64; *Longworth's Almanack*, 1805, 124, 160–62; shoemaking: *The Independent Mechanic* [New York], January 25, 1812; *Columbian* [New York], December 9, 1813; John R. Commons et al., *Documentary History of American Industrial Society* (Cleveland, 1910), III, 300; cabinetmaking: Robert Walker to Charles Watts, November 25, 1809, May 11, 1810, December 11, 12, 1815, March 4, 1816, Watts-Jones Papers, N-YHS; Charles Montgomery, *American Furniture: The Federal Period* (New York, 1966), 11–26; printing: George A. Stevens, *New York Typographical Union No. 6: Study of a Modern Trade Union and Its Predecessors* (Albany, 1913), 65–69; Rollo G. Silver, *The American Printer, 1787–1825* (Charlottesville, 1967), 29–62; building: Robert Christie, *Empire in Wood: A History of the Carpenters' Union* (Ithaca, 1967), 5–12; *American Citizen*, May 23, 1810; *Evening Post*, June 19, 1810.

23. These figures are drawn from Rock, *Artisans of the New Republic*, 246. For more on the persistence of small-shop production, see below, Chapter 3.

century, became a pressing one, as the city's economy became increasingly sensitive to international terms of trade and as entrepreneurial masters attempted to reorganize their businesses and expand their regional markets.[24]

But it was labor—the changing relations of production, the very meaning of wage payment—that loomed as the most vexing problem of all in the fastest-changing trades. The transformation of the apprenticeship system dramatized the decline of the old artisan labor relations. By the mid-1820s, several craft veterans and concerned master craftsmen had complained that while apprenticeship remained almost universal, the daily life of an apprenticed boy in the city's major trades rarely matched the arrangements outlined in the signed indentures. Master tailors and shoemakers reportedly taught their apprentices only the simpler of the journeymen's tasks and used the boys as helpers. The printers were even more notorious for luring half-trained apprentices from their nominal masters and substituting them for journeymen. Throughout the trades, employers converted their customary obligations for room, board, and education to cash payments to the boy's parents, turning the system into a glorified form of juvenile wage labor for children from the city's poorest families. By 1820, an articulate apprentice could remark in public, without fear of reprimand or contradiction, that "a paternal care and circumspect watchfulness of our moral and intellectual education are seldom compatible with an apprenticed condition."[25]

Related to the mutation of apprenticeship, but of even greater significance, were the changing relations between masters and journeymen in those trades in which the employers tried to keep pace in the new competitive markets. The division of labor was only the most visible sign of these alterations; beyond the dilution of skill, the masters—even some in "honorable" trades[26]—had begun to abandon their workshop role to foremen and contractors. Others evaded or ignored the old "just" price-book

24. Albion, *Rise of New York Port*, 12–13; *Independent Mechanic*, September 9, 1812; George Rogers Taylor, *The Transportation Revolution, 1815–1860* (New York, 1951), 239–40, 360–63; Rock, *Artisans of the New Republic*, 165, 177–86; Glenn Porter and Harold Livesay, *Merchants and Manufacturers: Studies in the Changing Structure of Nineteenth-Century Marketing* (Baltimore, 1971), 72–77; Chandler, *Visible Hand*, 20–22, 29.

25. Mercein, *Address*, 21. On the decline of the apprenticeship system, see GSMT, "To the Citizens of New York" (1820), N-YHS Broadside Collection; GSMT, "Report of the Education Committee," GSMT MSS, Education; *New York Observer*, November 4, 1826; Stevens, *Typographical Union*, 65–70. See also Richard B. Morris, *Government and Labor in Early America* (New York, 1946), 363–87; Ian M. G. Quimby, "Apprenticeship in Colonial Philadelphia" (M.A. thesis, University of Delaware, 1963), on the latter stages of colonial urban apprenticeship and on the early signs of decline.

26. On the employment of a foreman and the removal of the master from production in an "honorable" shop, see Account Book, Solomon Townsend [anchor manufacturer], 1795–97, N-YHS MSS. Townsend's enterprise is thoroughly studied in Alan S. Marber, "The New York Iron Merchant and Manufacturer: A Study in Eighteenth-Century Entrepreneurship" (Ph.D. diss., New York University, 1974).

arrangements and, where possible, hired the least-expensive hands available—including, if need be, the women and children of the laboring poor. Under the circumstances, neither master nor journeyman appeared in the process of production as an artisan; the wage, based on the market and not on custom or "justice," became the only bond between them.

Reflecting on what all this meant, the coachmaker Abraham Quick observed in 1820 that the crafts were becoming the captives of a new breed of craft entrepreneurs, as often as not men "without any regards for their reputation or respect for their Creditors," who would arrange to produce goods as cheaply as they could and to sell them "at any price which offers to convert them to cash." Quick was a respected master in a trade virtually synonymous with custom work, and thus had less reason to fear the future than did local tailors, shoemakers, and cabinetmakers; still, he saw capitalist labor, cost cutting, and the creation of new markets for cut-rate goods as "very pernicious in their effects on any Mechanical Business and the Greatest Bane to honest Industry":

> Economy has like everything Else when Carried to Extreem become an Evil to the Labouring part of Society—that is the very persons who pretend to be most Strenuous & Patriotic in Supporting our Manufactories are the most opposed in Compensating the Mechanic with a fair and honest price above his Expense to Enable him to live in Encouraging, good & faithful work, all of which proves very Discouraging to those wishing to do their Employer Justice or has any regard for his reputation as a Mechanic.[27]

These, of course, were the partial judgments of an artisan raised to older, increasingly fragile conceptions of the market, labor, industry, and justice. They glossed over the less attractive features of eighteenth-century artisanal production—the use, for a time, of slave labor and indentured servants, the web of deference and clientage that governed the workshop as well as the craft economy, the marginal prospects of the mass of independent producers. Not every craft employer would have agreed with Quick, least of all the enterprising men who abetted the system Quick so despised. But we should not take Quick's remarks as mere posturing. At the very least, they indicate that the capitalist innovations in the trades only just begun in 1788 were well underway by 1820, enough to perturb even a coachmaker. Even more, they remind us that some mechanics experienced these transformations not as an entrepreneurial opportunity but as a disaster.

Like Quick, other New York craftsmen tried to make sense of what was changing in the first decades of the century, with varying degrees of op-

27. Report of Abraham Quick, 1820 Manufacturing Census, New York County, Ward 1, no. 30. See also *Independent Mechanic*, September 7, 1811.

timism and dread. From their different experiences and expectations came early indications that in some crafts new divisions of class were shattering the supposed brotherhood of "honest Industry."

Entrepreneurs

In principle, as their informal title indicated, New York's master craftsmen stood at the head of their trades, as men whose skills and attention to business had won an independent estate, a mastery of their respective crafts. Viewed en bloc, they appear to have prospered with the expansion of the port. In a sample drawn from the 1816 New York jury list, more than half of the masters owned their own house or shop (Table 3). The median total taxable wealth of those assessed was a respectable (if unspectacular) $3,200.[28] Roughly one-third of the masters—and in some crafts, many more than that—lived among the merchants in the exclusive neighborhoods south of Chambers Street (Table 4). They formed a remarkably settled group, considering what is known of the geographic mobility of early-nineteenth-century American urban dwellers: roughly half remained in the city from one decade to the next, and about one in six stayed at the same address.[29] On closer inspection, however, important differences crop up among the masters. In some of the largest crafts, between one-third and two-thirds of them owned less than $500 in taxable wealth (Table 5). A handful of those in the sample—4.8 percent of the total—held 39.1 percent of all the assessed real and personal wealth among

28. Edmund P. Willis estimates ("Social Origins," 119–25) that the median assessed wealth of New Yorkers in 1815 was about $5,000.

29. Rough persistence rates were computed from a trade directory of craftsmen included with the regular street listings in the city directory for 1805. I checked the names from the trade directory list in the street directory; the following were the persistence rates (in percentages) of those located in 1805 who were still in the city directory in 1815:

Trade	In 1815 directory	At same address in 1815
Cabinetmakers (N=57)	50.9	14.0
Carpenters (N=274)	50.0	16.8
Coopers (N=77)	50.6	29.9
Metal workers (N=44)	40.9	31.8
Shoemakers (N=214)	68.2	9.8
TOTAL (N=666)	55.4	16.8

Although very little is known about urban geographical mobility in Jeffersonian America, these figures stand in marked contrast to those gathered for craft workers and entire urban populations in the 1830s. See Peter R. Knights, *The Plain People of Boston, 1830–1860: A Study in City Growth* (New York, 1971), 48–77; Johnson, *Shopkeeper's Millennium*, 37, 170; William Neill Black, "The Union Society of Journeymen House Carpenters: A Test in Residential Mobility in New York City, 1830–1840" (M.A. thesis, Columbia University, 1975).

them. As a group, the masters may have been the leaders of their trades, but by 1815 they were dominated by an emerging elite of craft entrepreneurs, very roughly one-fifth of all the city's masters.

The craft entrepreneurs were by no means the most affluent of New Yorkers—even the wealthiest masters commanded far less capital than their merchant counterparts—but they did set a tone of solid comfort at variance with descriptions of the plain city mechanics. Although the vast majority were trained artisans, their alertness to cultivating and expanding markets and credit enabled them to run operations with as many as three workshops and dozens of journeymen employees. Their furniture was of mahogany instead of the more common pine; fineries like gilt-edged mirrors, silver cutlery, and chinaware adorned their homes. Most probably kept at least one servant; before the completion of emancipation in New York in 1827, a very few owned slaves. While none invested in real estate and other speculations on a level with John Jacob Astor and his associates, some branched out of their workshops to make additional investments in land, banking, and insurance.[30]

Duncan Phyfe, the cabinetmaker, epitomized the successful master in the custom and consumer export trades, with a career that read like an artisan version of Astor's mercantile rise from rags to riches. Phyfe first set up shop in New York in 1792, a penniless young Scotsman with consummate skills but few contacts; except for a chance encounter with Astor's daughter, who touted his work among her friends, he would have been forced to close. By 1815, his labors and those of his journeymen had earned him three shops and extensive real-estate holdings in Manhattan and Brooklyn. All along the eastern seaboard, the distinctive Phyfe Regency styles could be found in the homes of local notables, testimony to the master's fame and his acumen for exploring the coastal market in fine goods and extending credit to his distant customers. At their busiest, Phyfe's shops would eventually employ up to one hundred journeymen at

30. For an idea of the furnishings in a master's home, see Probate Inventories, New York County, HDC, B-160, W-153. Unfortunately, the available jury books for this period do not disclose whether a household included a servant. On the employment of servants in urban areas in this period, see David Katzman, *Seven Days a Week: Women and Domestic Service in Industrializing America* (New York, 1978), 104–5; Stansell, "Women of the Laboring Poor," 138, 143–44. Of the masters in the 1816 sample, two owned slaves—the ladies' shoemaker Reuben Bunn (one male and two females) and the shoemaker Jeremiah Alley (one female). On artisan landholding, see Tax Assessment Lists, New York County, Eighth Ward, 1815, MARC; no fewer than twenty-five craftsmen owned unimproved lots in the ward. On artisan speculation in land and other investments, see Stephen Allen, "The Memoirs of Stephen Allen (1767–1852)," ed. John C. Travis, typescript, N-YHS, 45–46; Ledger Book, Unidentified builder and carpenter, March 22, 1817, NYPL MSS; Indenture, Patrick and Margaret McKay with Jacob Halsey and Charles Watts, November 20, 1810, and May 1, 1817, Inventory of Estate in Charleston, both in Watts-Jones Papers, N-YHS.

a time. While the master was known for his quiet Calvinist discipline and simple demeanor—a dedicated craftsman proud of his ancestry and his art, to judge from a portrait painted about 1820 (Plate 2), the quintessential retiring Scot according to his contemporaries—Phyfe's elaborate warehouse, workshop, and showrooms confirmed his wealth and tastes as those of a merchant prince (Plate 3).[31]

Other successful masters included pioneers in the "ready made" trade, and men more directly tied to the port and the maritime crafts. A handful of merchant tailors had accumulated considerable wealth by 1815, as had a few other consumer-trade entrepreneurs (Table 6). Leather tanning, an ancient craft, became a source of enormous profit to the firms located in Frankfort and Jacob streets, a district then popularly known as "the Swamp." Gideon Lee—like Phyfe a self-educated, self-made former apprentice—was the most clever of the "Swamp clique," especially when it came to shifting from cash to credit sales and sending his agents to the Argentine to enter the world market in skins: in 1817, Lee established the nation's first joint-stock tanning enterprise; three years later, his New York Tannery Company, with an estimated capital of $60,000, carried on its trade in two manufactories and ten retail outlets; Lee himself was on his way to becoming a major figure in local banking and political circles. The city's leading shipbuilders—Henry Eckford, Christian Bergh, and the brothers Adam and Noah Brown, all talented businessmen and veterans of the craft—weathered the embargo and the wartime lulls in trade to make Manhattan the most important shipbuilding center in the country. Near the dry docks, Stephen Allen, the sailmaker, cleared by his own estimate $100,000 between 1802 and 1825, largely because of his early success in bypassing the city's ship chandlers to purchase his materials directly from the wholesalers. By the time Allen retired, at age fifty-eight, his financial interests and his reputation had won him a career in politics and seats on the boards of two banks and two insurance companies.[32]

As they consolidated their businesses, these masters and others like them continued to honor the ideal of craft fellowship and collectively helped to set the conditions and destiny of their trades. As in the colonial period, they tended to live and work near their fellow tradesmen: shoe-

---

31. Ellen Vincent McClelland, *Duncan Phyfe and the English Regency* (New York, 1929), 91–138; Walter A. Dyer, *Early American Craftsmen* (New York, 1915), 43–69; Thomas H. Ormsbee, *Early American Furniture Makers: A Social and Biographical Study* (New York, 1930), 63–81.

32. Frank Norcross, *A History of New York Swamp* (New York, 1901), 1–8, 51–60; Shepherd Knapp to Gideon Lee, March 3, 24, 25, 1823, Gideon Lee Papers, N-YHS; "Sketch of the Life and Character of the Late Gideon Lee," *Hunt's Merchants' Magazine* 8 (1843); 57–64; Albion, *Rise of New York Port*, 288–92; *New York Herald*, December 31, 1852; Allen, "Memoirs," 46, 111–14.

makers settled along William Street and Maiden Lane, cabinetmakers along Beekman Street, Broad Street, and Greenwich Street, and so on. In some crafts, the masters organized friendly societies (occasionally open to journeymen), "to Promote mutual fellowship, Confidence, good Understanding, and Mechanic Knowledge," to provide funds to support families of the sick or indigent and assist in burial expenses, and to resolve disputes among the members. Employers' committees discussed guidelines for credit to customers and drew up lists of piece rates to enforce what in one case was called "wage control." Ad hoc groups petitioned the municipality on various matters, from the unfair competition of out-of-state interlopers to alleged combinations to raise the price of raw materials. In more informal surroundings, the masters sprinkled their tavern talk with negotiations for loans, inquiries about new partnerships, and news of talented journeymen available for hire.[33]

The meetings of the General Society of Mechanics and Tradesmen extended these bonds across trade lines; they also, in time, testified to the transformations that were overtaking the craft economy. Founded in 1785 as a revival of the Mechanics' Committee of the 1770s, the General Society was originally intended to be a semipolitical umbrella organization for all of the city's independent mechanics, to help oversee the trades and secure favorable legislation from local and national government. Suspicions that the group would prove a foyer of political intrigue led the state legislature to frame its charter to permit only philanthropic projects, but within these formal limits, the group captured the ideal of mutuality and craft pride essential to artisan fraternities since the Middle Ages. Society men, one member observed, grew "accustomed to meet each other as brothers and to reciprocate sentiments of attachments"; a typical gathering at the society's Mechanic Hall brought intense conversations, in which masters "contrasted their systems of labor," before returning to the shops, "improved from the intercourse." In a city where merchants and bankers were the most powerful social and political leaders, the activities of the society testified that the artisans, too, were a resourceful and purposeful group, "a body of men who do much in sustaining the prosperity of this Metropolis," the master baker Thomas Mercein proclaimed in 1821, forming "one of the firmest pillars of our social Edifice." While the society's emblem and motto (Plate 4) reminded the city that no art could stand

33. Jury Books, 1816, Wards 1–3, 5, 8; Morris, *Government and Labor*, 150, 202–4; *The Constitution of the Associated Body of House Carpenters of the City of New-York* (1767; reprint, New York, 1792), 3; *Daily Advertiser* [New York], November 18, 1800; Charlotte Morgan, *The Origin and History of the New York Employing Printers' Organization* (New York, 1930), 3–24; New-York Friendly Association of Master Bookbinders, "List of Prices" (1822), N-YHS Broadsides; MCC, XII, 709, February 17, 1823; Norcross, *Swamp*, 10–42.

without the aid of artisan labor, the members pointed to their Mechanics' School and Apprentices' Library (both founded in 1820) as proof of their benevolent intents. With these institutions, Mercein contended, the city's young mechanics would "look back with delight on the bright season of their youthful days," when the foundation of their prosperity was laid. So the masters displayed their affection in other mutual-aid schemes, above all in their loans to worthy members and their financial support of deceased members' widows.[34]

Despite the restrictions in its charter, the society also maintained an active interest in local political and business affairs. In the mid-1790s, the membership informally joined with other craft societies in the emerging Jeffersonian coalition while they encouraged campaigns to secure higher tariffs. After 1800, the society, emboldened by the Jeffersonian victory, more openly defended the trades from foreign competition; more important, as it became increasingly dominated by the city's craft entrepreneurs, the society shifted its attention from protection to the business revolution and to breaking the mercantile monopoly on credit. Its early efforts culminated in the founding of the society's own Mechanics' Bank, in 1810. From the start, the bank attracted a brisk business discounting small notes and opening credit lines to enterprising masters; unfortunately, the masters' collective expertise at high-level finance was less sure than their command of their trades, and the bank was soon plagued by mismanagement of its investments. Within two years, the directors were driven to declare temporary insolvency; by the time the bank recovered, the society had sold off most of its shares. Nevertheless, the Mechanics' survived, with several leading masters as shareholders, to become one of the largest banks in the city. Although it never proved to be the panacea for the artisans' credit problem envisioned by its creators, it provided the first important entry for craft entrepreneurs into the money market and helped to ensure, as the society pointed out in 1829, that the city's "credible mechanics" had access to their share of financial accommodations. If nothing else, it announced the masters' alertness to the changing commercial realities of the day.[35]

34. Earle and Congdon, Annals, 7-36; Alfred F. Young, The Democratic Republicans of New York: The Origins, 1763-1797 (Chapel Hill, 1967), 62, 100, 157, 201, 250; M. M. Noah, An Address Delivered before the General Society of Mechanics and Tradesmen (New York, 1822), 7; Thomas R. Mercein, Remarks on Laying the Cornerstone of the Mechanic Institution (New York, 1821), 24; Mercein, Address, 13.

35. On the tariff, see GSMT Minute Book, September 3, 1788, November 3, 1788, April 1, 1789, January 28, 1799, March 14, 1800. On the Mechanics' Bank, see GSMT Minute Book, May 2, August 1, 10, September 5, 11, December 13, 1810, January 2, February 6, 1811, January 6, 14, 29, 1823; Charles Watts, Jr., to Charles Watts, February 21, 1811, Watts-Jones Papers, N-YHS; SAJ, 1828, pp. 757-58; Memorial of the General Society of Mechanics and Tradesmen Praying for a Renewal of the Charter of

As the society struggled to alter and improve the crafts' position, it also discovered a mission that would preoccupy the city's masters for decades to come—reshaping the mechanics' morality and work habits, to fit the new demands of the more competitive workshops and to compensate for the erosion of apprenticeship. Shortly before the War of 1812, a wide range of New York mechanics began publicly to condemn the casual customs still common in the city's shops. One article in an artisan weekly warned that "loungers who do not work to full capacity" threatened the well-being of all; others attacked the ubiquitous workshop drinking, gambling, and other wasteful entertainments with equal vehemence. In the early 1820s, the General Society—itself given to considerable toasting and drinking in the early years of the century—suddenly came to endorse its own version of the well-regulated life, blending professions of piety and maxims on thrift, sobriety, and commercial adaptation. The Mechanics' School and the Apprentices' Library became the focal points for the new campaign. The school, although limited for the most part to children of deceased members and to those whose parents could afford the annual tuition of twenty dollars, offered some assurance that future artisans would keep clear of vice. In 1825, when the apprentices turned out for a parade to celebrate the opening of the Erie Canal, the staff summarized the library's intents and its holdings by unfurling a banner emblazoned with a picture of two books, *The Life of Franklin* and the Bible. The library, more than an attempt to shore up the apprenticeship-education system, was also deemed a bulwark against moral waywardness and lassitude. "Cherish, I beseech you, a deep-rooted abhorrence of the alluring but fatal paths of vice and dissipation," Mercein told the city's apprentices on the library's opening day. "Industry, ardour, sobriety, and perseverance in your different pursuits will lead to a successful competition in the world. . . ."[36]

Other efforts supplemented the General Society's new departures. In 1822, John Griscom, the prominent Quaker professor of chemistry and promoter of urban reform, assembled some leading merchants, philanthropists, and General Society members and founded the New York Mechanical and Scientific Institution. To enhance the mechanical arts and stimu-

the Mechanics' Bank (New York, 1829); Earle and Congdon, Annals, 49–52. See also Rock, Artisans of the New Republic, 166–69; Margaret G. Myers, The New York Money Market, vol. 1, The Origins and Development (New York, 1931), 111, 114, 119, 159, 163. The bank merged in 1865 to form the Mechanics' and Metals Bank and was ultimately absorbed into the Chase Bank group. The earliest surviving records date from 1854 and are held by the Chase Manhattan Bank Archives, Record Group no. 3, Merged Banks, Chase National Bank, no. 28/4/1.

36. Independent Mechanic [New York], August 10, 17, 31, 1811; GSMT Minute Book, January 1, February 3, June 2, 1813, March 17, 1819, November 1, 1820, March 6, 1821; Cadwallader D. Colden, Memoir Completed at the Request of a Committee of the Common Council (New York, 1825), 237–38; Mercein, Address, 12–13.

late native genius, the MSI sponsored an assortment of lecture programs on science and invention; to encourage the requisite competitive spirit, it undertook an annual fair of artisan products from New York and around the country, awarding cash prizes to the cleverest, best-wrought displays. A few masters' newspapers tried to reach an even wider audience. The New York *Mechanics' Gazette*, started in 1822 by Thomas Mercein and his brother William (like Thomas, an activist in the General Society), promised to improve "the usefulness and respectability of mechanics in general." In fact, it was more of a compendium of exhortations to industriousness and clean living. Biographical sketches of successful masters trumpeted that the way to wealth was still open to all artisans of talent and sober habits. Advertisements bid prudent craft businessmen to protect their investments by taking out insurance. Special reports discussed the benefits of savings banks and loan institutions, some of them administered by other master craftsmen. The *Gazette* did offer copious news about scientific improvements: beneath this democratic, Americanized *encyclopédisme* rested the deeper message to adapt, to expand, and otherwise to improve the commercial and productive capacities of the workshops.[37]

Labor questions and disputes over wages—an increasingly troublesome set of problems after 1800—set the limits of entrepreneurial benevolence, but not of the masters' professed dedication to "the Trade." On occasion, employers negotiated freely with their men—for a time, the master cabinet-makers went so far as to select a delegation to sit jointly with the organized journeymen on a permanent grievance committee—but for the most part, the city's organized masters remained adamant about their ultimate control of wage rates, to the point of firing and blacklisting journeymen who challenged them, and bringing the most refractory men to court. Even then, they construed their role as that of paternal overseers, the artisans who knew best about conditions in the shops and whose authority had been won with years of work and experience. The cabinetmakers, in refusing their men's wage demands in 1802, took pains to point out that they did so for the benefit of all, to ensure that all employers could receive an adequate profit while the journeymen received an "equitable rate." The master printers, speaking "in the spirit of conciliation and harmony," refused similar demands from their journeymen in 1809 because

37. *Charter, Constitution, and Bye-Laws of the New York Mechanical and Scientific Institution* (New York, 1822), 3–15 and passim; Pascu, "Philanthropic Tradition," 415–19; *Mechanics' Gazette* [New York], June 8, 1822, April 26, May 3, 7, 14, 17, 21, 24, 28, 31, June 1, 1823. See also *American Mechanics' Magazine* [New York], 1 (1824). Stephen Allen served as the first president of the MSI and Gideon Lee as vice-president; other officers included Henry Eckford (second vice-president), John Slidell (third vice-president), and Thomas Mercein (secretary), all of them leading members of the General Society.

the masters' proposed rates were necessary (or so they claimed) to keep their businesses going, a maximum "beyond which it would be highly injurious, if not ruinous, *to the interests of the trade* to venture."[38]

The men behind these projects and pronouncements were neither cynical capitalists nor guileless mechanics. They distinguished themselves in their public lives as craftsmen, a word that stirred their deepest pride—independent men who, like Duncan Phyfe, were eager to be portrayed as skilled workers, men who were, as Stephen Allen remarked about his fellow sailmakers, "on friendly terms with each other," proud of "the respect attached to their business." They claimed with all apparent sincerity to have the interests of all mechanics at heart—especially those of the apprentices whom they expected one day to take their places at the head of the crafts. Yet at the same time, even as they continued to gather beneath the sign of the hammer and hand, the city's leading masters began to project a broadened vision of capitalist growth—one that proclaimed the maxims of Poor Richard but forecast an order of economic change unimaginable to Franklin, that deemed commercial and financial innovation and capitalist improvement prerequisites for the future progress of the trades, and that stressed, in unprecedented ways, the importance of self-discipline, business sense, and the pursuit of Mercein's "successful competition in the world."[39] Later years would see a heightening of the tensions between the "communal" and the commercial features of the masters' engagements, as craft employers turned to more elaborate social and economic theories and to new methods of labor control and moral reform. Already by the 1820s, however, they had begun to anticipate the shared anxieties and idealism of a manufacturing bourgeoisie. They had begun to live in a world quite different from that of the city's small master craftsmen and journeymen wage earners.

Small Masters

The majority of master craftsmen held little or no property and knew little or nothing of keeping up with the coasting trade or winning a banker's heart: their habits and capacities tied them to the old ways. Joined perhaps by a partner, they and their families performed most of the work in the shops themselves, hired at most one or two journeymen, and served a

38. *Constitution and Rules of Order of the New York Society of Cabinetmakers* (New York, 1810), 3–4; *American Citizen* [New York], December 31, 1802; George Barnett, "The Printers: A Study in Trade Unionism," *American Economic Association Quarterly* 10 (1909): 363 (italics mine).

39. Allen, "Memoirs," 51–52. On Franklin's political economy, see Drew R. McCoy, "Benjamin Franklin's Vision of a Republican Political Economy for America," *WMQ* 35 (1978): 605–28.

local custom clientele. They lived and worked in the roughshod central and outer wards among the journeymen, day laborers, and recent immigrants. The Fifth Ward, a maze of modest, densely packed dwellings, was home to many: of the master craftsmen identified there in the 1816 sample, fewer than half (43.4 percent) owned any form of assessed property. They were mainly family men, for whom a benefit society or generous friends could be critical assets; while some were youths in their twenties, the majority in the sample (60.7 percent) were older men with dependents, masters who, because of adversity, the inherent limitations of their trades, or disinterest toward capitalist enterprise, did not fully share in the early national New York boom.[40]

The small masters' petty trade brought its share of opportunity, to win a competence if not a fortune. Of those identified from the 1816 jury list, more than half were still in business in 1825; most had at least as much property as they had held nine years earlier. In those crafts relatively untouched by the rearrangements of the shops, especially butchering and baking, small masters continued to dominate their trades in the 1820s and could usually count on maintaining at least a modest competence; in no craft were small masters thoroughly eliminated. A few small masters were destined to become members in good standing in the General Society.[41] Those who managed to accumulate small amounts of property also acquired at least a few luxury goods. The estate of the shoemaker Garrett Sickles was indicative of the small master's comforts: in 1822, Sickles left his heirs, among other things, one house clock, two pairs of brass andirons, chinaware, silverware, and three gilt-edged picture frames holding his most treasured documents, a reproduction of the Declaration of Independence, a picture of the Declaration's signers, and his certificate of membership in the Tammany Society.[42]

But these were hardly the annals of spectacular entrepreneurial success or intentions; they hid both the difficulties that all small masters had to endure and the customary forms of small-shop business. Even in the food-provisioning trades, with their guaranteed markets, a combination of bad weather, interruptions in transport, and any of the other problems connected with livestock or grain supply could bring acute distress, to producer

---

40. Jury Books, Wards 3, 5, 8, 1816, microfilm, N-YHS.

41. The names of all masters in the 1816 sample with $1,000 total property or less (N=91) were checked in the city directory for 1825; 52.7 percent were found in the directory and the tax list. Small masters in the sample who later joined the society included the shoemaker John Earle and the cabinetmakers Samuel Carter and John Tallman. See Congdon and Earle, *Annals*, 358–415. For more on small tradesmen and the persistence of the artisan system, see below, Chapter 3. On successful butchers, see Thomas F. De Voe, *The Market Book* (New York, 1862), passim; Rock, *Artisans of the New Republic*, 205–6.

42. Probate Inventory, S-134, HDC.

and public alike. The emotional and financial perils of fragile simple partnerships sometimes led to grim circumstances: in one celebrated case, the small master baker George Hart was ruined by an embezzler partner, only to descend into a life of journeywork, street selling, and drunken misery that closed in 1812 at the end of a noose. For small masters who lived on the margins of independence, any common misfortune—disease, fire, a slump in trade—meant disaster, and a tightening of customary networks of neighborhood support. The narrative of the shoemaker Samuel Avery was not an uncommon one. Avery kept a steady, if humble business in Catherine Street until 1822, when illness struck his home. Forced into debt, he borrowed from friends, withheld rent for his house and shop and payments to his leather suppliers, and began taking credit from local storekeepers. In 1824, still owing one hundred dollars to his intractable physicians, Avery declared insolvency, his only possessions being his tools, some kitchen utensils, one pine table, and his family's clothing.[43]

Apart from business difficulties, the small masters found themselves pitted against a battery of economic and legal regulations, some old, some new, many a source of intense resentment. Certain measures, like the tariff, met with approval, especially in the consumer trades. Others, above all internal taxes, they deemed regressive encroachments on their liberties. The shoemakers, hatters, and curriers complained mightily about having to pay wartime duties on leather, which they denounced as unequal and odious, "foreign to the habits of free independent citizens." Periodic attempts by the Common Council to regulate street traffic and to rid the streets of pigs—used by poorer New Yorkers for meat as well as for rubbish clearance—raised similar complaints. Certain civil obligations, from compulsory jury duty to service in the militia, were especially obnoxious to small masters, who could ill afford to take time off from work and could not pay for stand-ins; likewise, with the growth of speculative credit, they objected to the prevailing system of arrest for debt because it was so contrary to customary notions of borrowing and reciprocity, and left so little leeway to men of small means to clear their accounts. "If a man seeks credit," one bewildered small master wrote, "he does not pledge his *personal* liberty for payment. . . ."[44]

43. De Voe, *Market Book*, 234, 457; *Trial for Murder. Court of Oyer and Terminer . . . 1811. The People vs. George Hart, Murder* (n.p., n.d. [ca. 1812]); Insolvency Assignment no. 1824/4, HDC. See also Insolvency Assignments nos. 1815/41, 1816/ 232, 1817/6, 1817/16, 1817/430, 1819/31, 1819/97, 1819/171, 1819/260.

44. *Evening Post*, April 8, 21, September 4, 1815; Howard B. Rock, "A Delicate Balance: The Mechanics and the City in the Age of Jefferson," *N-YHSQ* 63 (1979): 83–114; *Independent Mechanic*, April 6, 1811. One Byronic artisan—imprisoned for debt after illness kept him from his work—summed up the problem:

Say, will this noisome air, and clay-cold floor
His feeble frame to health and strength restore?

At its worst, the small master's lot brought extreme poverty and unremitting labor producing cheap work for the city's exporters or slopshops in a grim urban equivalent of the outwork domestic system. In 1812, the Reverend Ezra Stiles Ely, then the chaplain of the New York Alms House, discovered one such situation on his daily rounds. He was searching for the son of an invalid inmate when he was directed to one of the city's cellar dwellings, where he found the boy living with a cobbler and his family who supported themselves by selling vegetables and making coarse shoes. The cobbler, Ely learned, had generously sheltered the youngster for a week but could not keep him any longer "because he was too small to sit on the bench of the profession." Even when his entire family worked, this frugal master could not feed the additional small mouth without extra income. "He cannot earn anything yet," he repeated sorrowfully to Ely, as the Reverend took his leave, boy in tow.[45]

Such scenes would in time touch the souls and fire the imaginations of a generation of sentimental reformers; by the 1820s, they were the small masters' nightmares. They loomed ever larger as the commercialization of production began to leave the small masters in the fastest-changing trades with the starkest choices, that of braving the hazards of the new market, struggling on in the time-honored manner, or quitting the craft. As petty producers, the small masters confronted an unfamiliar ambiguity. On one level, the expansion of commerce and the withering away of some old restraints on production might expand petty trade; on another, most small masters had lacked either the resources or the inclination to transform their enterprises, change their own way of life, and compete successfully against those with easier access to capital. Small masters like the builder who would still work for barter followed economic imperatives alien to capitalist exchange. Men like the cellar-dwelling cobbler were unable to save money by cutting wages and could stay in business only by exploiting themselves and their families to the limits of their endurance; another, writing in 1811 under the pseudonym "Misery," claimed, "If you be a mechanic, you must promise everyone that applies to you, although it be five times as much as you can accomplish."[46] An alternative among building

---

Could he his liberty and health regain
To pay thy debt he every nerve would strain

See *Independent Mechanic*, August 1, 1812. Historians have only begun to analyze the significance of arrest for debt, but see Edwin T. Randall, "Imprisonment for Debt in America: Fact and Fiction," *MVHR* 39 (1952): 89–102. On the decay of municipal regulation, see Jon C. Teaford, *The Municipal Revolution in America* (Chicago, 1975).

45. Rev. Ezra Stiles Ely, *Visits of Mercy: Being the Journal of the Stated Preacher to the Hospital and Alms House in the City of New York, 1811* (New York, 1812), 162–63.

46. See *Independent Mechanic*, May 11, 18, August 31, October 12, 1811, September 12, 1812.

tradesmen was to gamble on getting contract work from speculators and hiring the cheapest labor; even then, assuming they raised the requisite credit, they ran the enormous risk that a sudden bankruptcy or decline in trade would halt their operations, leaving them responsible for all materials purchased. Masters in the finishing trades might try to become slopshop contractors, but they, too, had to gamble on the whims of the market and the merchants while scurrying to undercut their competitors. Neither was a life of independence; neither was the life of a craftsman.

Such choices and the threat that craft capitalists and interlopers would destroy the small masters' petty trade led to occasional rumblings of discontent, long before Abraham Quick set down his observations in 1820. The attempt by John B. Church, a brother-in-law of Alexander Hamilton, to set up the joint-stock New York Bread Company in 1801 raised a brief but spectacular ad hoc protest led by a committee of tradesmen; for several weeks, as the company attempted to begin its operation, small masters filled the local press with protests (some quite radical in tone) pleading for a patriotic boycott of the "monied capitalists," bidding "mechanics to be united; to be ONE" in their opposition to the company, "or a degrading vassalage will reduce the greater part of them to the vile ambition and avarice of *monopolists*." None charged arson when a suspicious fire burned the company's main building to the ground several months later, but neither was there any conspicuous display of grief at the firm's demise. So, in less organized ways, small masters complained about invading capitalists and the dangers of the new market.[47]

Other small masters joined the ranks of the pious and temperate, finding in personal discipline and improvement the best means to gain self-respect and to adjust to new conditions. Joseph Harmer, a small master printer, caught their mood well in the columns of his artisan weekly, the *Independent Mechanic*, where he regularly published moral fables and scenes drawn from life on the evils of the taverns, those "nurseries of vice and receptacles of the abandoned." The tone here was very different from that of the *Mechanics' Gazette* or the General Society; Harmer and the small producers who wrote for his newspaper had little to say about commercial improvement, capital accumulation, and competition except to denounce overwork and the anxious pursuit of wealth as licentious and cruel. Industriousness was fine, one correspondent opined, "but the man that endangers his constitution by too much labour squanders away a treasure." Such men were more like the original Poor Richard than the entrepreneurs who cited Franklin as a matter of course—small masters who genuinely expected relatively little in the way of riches but who wanted to make sure that they got their independent due. For them, it

47. Rock, *Artisans of the New Republic*, 189–95.

became more necessary than ever, as Harmer pointed out, to "improve the mind and strengthen the heart" by practicing the Christian virtues, working steadily, and keeping clear of the city's numerous temptations to dissipation.[48]

It was not that hardship and (for some) poverty were anything new to the city's small masters; we may read accounts from the bust periods of the eighteenth century of similar disappointments.[49] It was not that the small masters had turned their backs on material wealth or the market. Nor was duress inevitable, even for small masters in the most rapidly changing trades. It was the context of the small masters' difficulties and opportunities that was changing, at least in the city's largest crafts. The widening sphere of the cheap and nasty trade, of the multiple degradations that went with "slop" and contract work, made a mockery of even the meanest small masters' expectations; even more, the new inequalities and the dissonances in the small masters' experiences in trades led by successful entrepreneurs foretold greater divisions to come. There remained enough common ground between more prominent craft capitalists and small masters for them to join together in demands for higher tariffs and lower taxes, as they managed to do regularly from 1789 to 1825.[50] A fortunate few in the largest trades successfully negotiated the new rules of business. But neither a high tariff wall nor commercial innovation would offer much protection to most small shoemakers, tailors, and others forced to compete against New York's new breed of masters and the merchant capitalists of New England. The existence of an artisan bank, with all its promises of help to the creditable, did not enable Samuel Avery and scores of others to avoid financial ruin. The society's school and library were irrelevant to families living in cellars, who had neither time nor money for edification. Duncan Phyfe and Stephen Allen could easily retain their optimism regarding the future and their pride in the mechanical arts; a different kind of pride was reserved for a small master cobbler who had to sweat his family. Prior to 1825, small masters afflicted by these differences responded either with indictments of monopoly and untoward speculative accumulation or with a rededication to hard work, thrift, and self-reliance. After 1825, when the transformation of the trades accelerated beyond the

48. *Independent Mechanic,* April 6, 1811, September 12, 1812.

49. Nash, *Urban Crucible,* 250–53. The refrain was repeated in the post-Revolutionary period. In 1788, the Society for the Relief of Poor Debtors noted that, for many poor craftsmen, "incessant application to labor will not enable them to subsist themselves and their families. . . ." Three years later, the *Daily Advertiser* charged that "many of our skilled tradesmen, cartmen, day labourers, and others dwell upon the borders of poverty and live hand to mouth," *Daily Advertiser* [New York], January 30, January 13, 1791, cited in Mohl, *Poverty in New York,* 29.

50. Rock, *Artisans of the New Republic,* 172–77.

entrepreneurs' wildest hopes, many more small masters would reach a moment of reckoning.

Journeymen

New York's early national journeymen, like their employers, were a mixed lot, but considered as a group they formed by 1815 a distinct and growing propertyless stratum in the trades (Table 3). Virtually all were white, and most had been born either in this country or in Protestant Britain; Irish Catholics and blacks, as yet a small fraction of the city's population, were consigned largely to manual labor and casual work in and around the port.[51] Nearly all journeymen lived in rented rooms (Table 3). Few knew the familial coziness supposedly typical of the preindustrial workshop household: only about one in ten boarded with his master; masters and journeymen tended to live in different neighborhoods (Table 4). While most appear to have earned enough to support a family of five— cited by the journeymen as a minimal accepted standard—their circumstances were often spartan.[52] Advancement to independence, although not impossible, was far from assured.

51. On immigrants, see James Owre, "The Effect of Immigration on New York City, 1800–1819" (M.A. thesis, Queens College, City University of New York, 1971). Unfortunately, we can only guess at the ethnic composition of the artisan work force in this period, since available census materials do not specify place of birth. Of those artisans gathered in the 1816 sample, however, only 7.0 percent were aliens; of these, all but ten bore Anglo-Saxon names; only eleven held any assessed property. Groneman, "'Bloody Ould Sixth,'" chap. 2, finds that while aliens made up 24.3 percent of the ward's population in 1819, they accounted for 27.0 percent of its artisans; half of the aliens were day laborers. On the basis of these figures, it is reasonable to argue that (a) the percentage of aliens in the trades was roughly the same as their proportion in the population as a whole—6.3 percent in 1806 and 9.8 percent in 1819; (b) British immigrant workers were overrepresented among the aliens in the trades; (c) most alien artisans were journeymen; (d) most immigrants—including most Irish—probably took day-laboring jobs.

The picture is much clearer regarding blacks. Although blacks composed 8.8 percent of the city's free population in 1816, only thirteen—under 2.0 percent of the total—turned up in the 1816 sample. None owned any property. There were signs of a tiny but healthy black artisan community in Jeffersonian New York: among the founding members of the New York African Society for Mutual Relief were six bootmakers; the society's first president was a house carpenter and its secretary a mechanic. Blacks also secured a strong foothold in several service and petty-retailing occupations, including barbering, catering, and laundering. Overall, however, blacks remained consigned to lowlier jobs, and played at best a marginal role in the trades. See Leo H. Hirsch, Jr., "The Negro and New York, 1783 to 1865," JNH 16 (1931): 382–473; Rhoda Freeman, "The Free Negro in New York City during the Pre-Civil War Era" (Ph.D. diss., Columbia University, 1966), 269–80, 291–94; Roi Ottley and William J. Weatherby, eds., The Negro in New York: An Informal Social History (New York, 1967), 61.

52. On journeymen's wage demands and minimum standards, see American Citizen,

A significant number of the journeymen—roughly one in four—were single men in their twenties with flat purses and high hopes, the proverbial craft novices in search of training, a quick savings, and with luck a career to match that of Phyfe or Allen. The young printer Thurlow Weed met several when he drifted to New York from Albany in 1816. Like Weed, they encountered a life of chance, their prospects hanging on a lucky break, a good recommendation from another master, or an ability to make ends meet until they landed jobs. Given their inexperience, they could expect to lose several positions, as businesses failed or trade slackened; Weed, who had better credentials than most from his boss upstate, worked for four different masters during his first ten months in the city. Masters used numerous cost-cutting schemes—from substitution of "half-ways" to outright failure to pay wages—to keep these young men at bay; Weed recalled one who warned him that he would never get anywhere in the trade unless he was willing to persist in dunning his master for back wages. No doubt many—particularly those lured to New York from the hinterland—left the city shortly after they had begun their search for work.[53]

Other journeymen shuttled between being small masters and wage earners, and occasionally rose to prominence. Consider the career of Elisha Blossom, a versatile cabinetmaker who set up shop in New York in 1811. Over the next seven years, Blossom worked, in turn, as a journeyman cabinetmaker, a bookseller's clerk, and a shipwright, before settling down in 1818 as a master shipwright and a member of the General Society. In this case and others, the border between independence and journeyman's status was extremely blurry; a handful of journeymen in the 1816 sample, having scrupulously saved their wages, married well, or received funds from their parents, owned as much property as did some masters in their trades (Table 5).[54]

But by 1815, most journeymen were neither part-time masters nor hopeful youths. About half were aged thirty or more, while about one in five was over forty (Table 7). The vast majority were married men, of whom about half supported households with four or more dependents. Despite their years of experience, these older journeymen were not, as a rule, much

---

April 10, 1809; *Evening Post*, May 31, 1819. It remains to be determined how much the proportion of journeymen to masters changed over the late eighteenth and early nineteenth centuries; no sources yet located from before 1816 provide an adequate breakdown of masters and journeymen.

53. Harriet A. Weed, ed., *Autobiography of Thurlow Weed* (Boston, 1883), 52–66. Of the journeymen in the jury-book sample from 1816, 25.1 percent were single men without dependents; of these, the great majority (80.0 percent) were under thirty.

54. Journal of Elisha Blossom, 1811–15, N-YHS MSS; Minute Book, New York Society of Journeymen Shipwrights and Caulkers, January 22, March 12, April 9, 1818, NYPL MSS; GSMT Minute Book, February 4, 1818.

more affluent than their younger peers; few were close to winning their competence, although a larger proportion of them held some property (Tables 5 and 8). In all, approximately two out of three artisans over thirty years of age were journeymen; so were two out of three artisans over forty. Some may have been former masters who, like the unfortunate baker George Hart, had migrated to New York to work as journeymen before setting up on their own again; some may have been, like Hart in his later years, former masters plagued by drink. Weed later observed, with some surprise, that most of his fellow printers seemed destined to remain "journeymen through life," and he blamed their fate on drunkenness and impecunity. But individual exigencies alone cannot fully explain the proportions of older journeymen; by 1815, what Weed observed was due not to individual shortcomings alone, but to the structural limitations that accompanied the expansion of the wage-labor supply and the subdivision of the trades.[55]

What little evidence remains of prices and artisan wage rates sketches the limits of opportunity. Two reports on journeymen's budgets, one from the carpenters in 1809, the other from the masons in 1819, estimated the basic expenses for a family of five as between $6.50 and $7.00 per week. According to available wage lists, journeymen could expect to earn, on the average, between $6.00 and $10.00 per week, although some, including the masons and the most highly skilled tailors, took home as much as $12.00.[56] Obviously, as long as work was available, younger journeymen with a job could easily support themselves, and the older men could provide for their families. But few journeymen, however enterprising and diligent, could expect year-round, full employment in New York, given the severe seasonal fluctuations in demand and the interruptions of winter and bad weather. During the usual seasonal slowdowns and unforeseen interruptions in trade, the journeymen had a difficult time meeting even basic costs: the tailors, for example, estimated in 1819 that they could count on working only six months a year, making their true annual average income only $6.00 per week, a bit below the minimal family wage. Journeymen in other trades, with shorter slack periods, fared better, averaging about $7.50 per week; those in the less skilled branches of shoemaking and tailoring probably averaged closer to $5.00 per week. During periods of prolonged distress and inflation, the journeymen's real earnings were even lower, most likely dipping close to those of common laborers.[57] Expenses for any

55. Weed, *Autobiography*, 58. In the journeymen sample, 74.9 percent headed households with a female dependent; of these, 49.5 percent had four or more dependents.

56. *American Citizen*, April 10, 1809; *Evening Post*, May 31, 1819; *Evening Post*, July 13, 1819; Rock, *Artisans of the New Republic*, 249–53.

57. *Evening Post*, July 13, 1819; Commons, *Documentary History*, III, 121. No systematic record has been found of the wage rates for unskilled laborers in New York in

individual mishaps—illness, injury, fire—could put a journeyman and his dependents on the charity relief rolls; purchase of any small extravagance might court long-term hardship unless some extra income came into the house. In the consumer finishing trades, a master's decision to put out even the lowliest piece of work had immediate and obvious repercussions for the journeyman and his family.

To supplement their earnings, the journeymen turned to other resources. Unfortunately, the information on women's work in New York prior to 1820 is very meager, and no evidence has been found to determine how many journeymen's wives and daughters worked for wages. What does remain, in the jury lists and city directories, suggests an established pattern much like that discovered in early modern Europe, in which a small but significant sector of the needle trades was open to independent women and girl apprentices. Otherwise, paid work for journeymen's wives and daughters—apart from those girls who left home to enter domestic service—was limited mainly to keeping boarders (although the jury books are unclear on this too), laundering, and the tiny returns of outwork seamstressing and binding. Given this dearth of women's wage work and given the powerful assumption, expressed several times in the *Independent Mechanic*, that the honorable artisan expected to be the family breadwinner, the family economy among married journeymen was almost certainly restricted largely to the outwork journeymen's households, in which women helped their husbands and fathers with their work.[58] A far more

---

this period. Donald T. Adams's studies of Philadelphia clearly suggest that unskilled men earned considerably less than journeymen—roughly 60 percent of a skilled man's wages. Adams also argues, however, that skilled wages fluctuated more than unskilled—particularly during times of commercial distress. It seems reasonable to suppose that the same held true in New York. See Donald T. Adams, "Wage Rates in the Early National Period: 1780–1830," *JEH* 28 (1968): 404–26.

58. On women's employments in Jeffersonian New York, see *Longworth's Almanack for 1805*, 124–25, 128, 136–38, 154, 157–61, 163–64. Other primary sources are silent on wage-earning women in artisan households. Groneman located 382 women enumerated as household heads in the Sixth Ward in 1819. Of these, only 78 (20.4 percent) were listed with occupations other than "lady," and of these, half ran stores or boardinghouses. Moreover, Groneman's figures show that the great majority of wage-earning women were widows, as were the majority of independent women in the ward. The dearth of paid occupations among these independent women suggests that while there was a female labor market in the Jeffersonian trades, it was still a very restricted one. Unfortunately, the sources also reveal practically nothing about domestic service, but it seems reasonable to suspect that some New York artisans' daughters worked in service before marriage. In sum, the picture looks quite similar to those drawn for early modern European cities in Natalie Zemon Davis, "Women in the Crafts in Sixteenth-Century Lyon," *Feminist Studies* 8 (1982): 46–80; and Joan Scott and Louise Tilly, *Women, Work, and Family* (New York, 1978), 47–51. On the artisans' sense of sexual norms, "breadwinning," and gender, see *Independent Mechanic*, June 15, July 21, September 14, November 23, 1811, March 21, 1812; *American Citizen*, May 23, 1810. On the scarcity of female employment, see also Stansell, "Women of the Laboring Poor," 59–60.

common course, for young journeymen and married men alike, was to tramp. A young journeyman like Thurlow Weed thought nothing of walking from Albany to New York City and to Auburn, New York, in search of steady work; master bootmakers from as far away as Rochester considered their finest workmen to be the older journeymen on call from Manhattan. A formal tramping system, complete with trade tickets and labor exchanges, aided the journeymen carpenters, who also established a house of call for tramps from other cities in 1800. The printers traveled within the even more elaborate network, an American equivalent of the European grand tour, that stretched from New England to Pennsylvania.[59]

While they were in the city, the journeymen lived in the central and outer wards; even here, they, unlike the masters, were anything but settled. The social and economic ecology of the mercantile city helped shape their residential patterns: journeymen in the maritime trades naturally tried to live as close as possible to the waterfront, while building tradesmen roomed near the construction sites in the northern wards.[60] More often, the increasingly competitive housing market drove them to find whatever space they could in the early flats and rooming houses that lined the more crowded and rundown parts of the city and the outer wards. Journeymen changed their addresses constantly, either to avoid payment on their short-term leases or to search for cheaper lodgings. The First of May, the traditional terminal date for spring-quarter leases and all annual leases, saw the streets of the central and outer wards clogged with nomadic journeymen and day laborers, possessions on their backs, looking for new places to live, a raucous (and costly) transit, as the *Independent Mechanic* recounted: "Wives scold, dogs bark, and children cry, / Pots break, chairs crack, pans ring, and jarring notes of harshest discord rise on every side." To make do, the men sought help where they could, from friends, relations, and other craft workers. Families unable to afford rent on a house shared buildings with other journeymen, sometimes crowding three or four families in a dwelling originally designed to house one or two. A common resort for the single men was the craft boardinghouse, where for as little as three dollars per week, they could get meals, a place to bed down, and word of mouth about available jobs in the city.[61]

59. Weed, *Autobiography*, 28–32, 50–51; Jesse W. Hatch, "The Old-Time Shoemaker and Shoemaking," *Rochester Historical Society Publications* 5 (1926): 82–83; *Mercantile Advertiser*, April 25, 1810; Stevens, *Typographical Union*, 72–73. On the English system, see Eric Hobsbawm, "The Tramping Artisan," in *Labouring Men: Studies in the History of Labour* (London, 1968), 34–63.

60. Jury Book, 1816, Wards 5, 8. The building tradesmen's patterns, in particular, are reflected in Table 4.

61. *Independent Mechanic*, April 13, 1811, May 9, 1812; Weed, *Autobiography*, 55; A. [pseud.], "Letters from New York," *New Monthly Magazine and Literary Journal* [London], 2 (1830): 450.

From the boardinghouses and flats, it was a short walk to the tavern and the world of lower-class leisure—a world that increasingly set some journeymen apart from their masters. Walnut Street, near Corlears Hook, was a center of these pleasures, its grogshops, ballrooms, and bawdy houses enticing young mechanics, sailors, and drifters; elsewhere, cellars and saloon back rooms became impromptu gambling halls. As in the eighteenth century, cockfighting and bull baiting were favorite pastimes for journeymen with fresh wages: for several years, Samuel Winship, a small master butcher, kept a bison in the cellar beneath his market room for use in the latter. Disorderly houses, where prostitutes were permitted to ply their trade, dotted the city's poorer districts and catered to apprentices and journeymen, sometimes to the surprise and consternation of the master craftsmen: it took one master baker, Jacob Ackerman, several weeks to discover that his twelve-year-old apprentice, while supposedly vending cakes and pies in the street, was actually using the proceeds to "have connection" with a young girl. Sundry slightly more reputable recreations— nude bathing, riding the "flying horses" carousels, attending the shows of traveling musicians, daredevils, and acrobats—enlivened the journeymen's existence the year round; holidays, especially the Fourth of July, were occasions for boxing matches, horse races, and determined overeating.[62]

We may presume that this workingman's culture was a hybrid of eighteenth-century urban customs and those brought from the countryside by the continuing migration from the hinterland and abroad. At all events, it was a culture that was very much alive in the 1820s, even as the city's entrepreneurs and small masters began making a virtue of abstemious necessity. Its centerpiece was alcohol: at all times, in and out of the shops, New York's journeymen could be expected to drink. By the 1820s, workingmen's saloons and grocery-grog shops had achieved a separate identity within New York's renowned barroom culture, one that marked the limits of a semiautonomous, unpretentious, masculine milieu, free from the responsibilities of home and workshop. Some of these drinking places served as informal labor exchanges, where employers from outside of the state set up temporary hiring halls; more directly, the publicans and liquor-vending grocers offered the journeymen credit and the quick cash loan, as well as a warm spot in which to relax, talk, and drink. At work, meanwhile, prodigious amounts of alcohol appeared at the very benches of the

62. *Independent Mechanic*, May 4, 18, 1812; *Columbian*, October 3, 1820; De Voe, *Market Book*, I, 389; People v. Patrick Daly and Rachel Green, Court of General Sessions, August 11, 1811, MARC; MCC, IX, 27, February 24, IX, 393, December 15, 1817, XIII, 300–303, October 13, 1823; CCFP, Police Committee, July 7, 1822, August 1, 1825; Gabriel Furman, "How New York City Used to Celebrate Independence Day," *N-YHSQ* 21 (1937): 93–96.

trades as a sort of secular sacrament, to seal the journeymen's social bonds within the customary artisan regime. Thurlow Weed remembered that journeymen in one printer's shop put down their tools each morning at eleven so that they could "jeff" for beer; often, Weed recalled, they would punctuate the day with several more intoxicating breaks. Old drinking customs and rituals like "footing"—the payment of whiskey to the shop by every newly hired journeyman on his first day of work—flourished, emblems of the trade and a means by which journeymen could enforce an informal control over the pace of their labor.[63]

Not every master minded these stoppages. The more traditional employers actually encouraged the breaks as part of their paternal respect for the proper order of "the Trade"; while some paid their men partly in drink, most, if later temperance tracts are an indication, probably remained heavy drinkers themselves through the mid-1820s.[64] But this recognition of the journeymen's drinking rights was clearly breaking down, as the wage earners' alcoholic pastimes became matters of grave concern to the more enterprising employers. In the early 1820s, the mayor's desk was crossed by a steady stream of complaints from master craftsmen angry at the various abuses of local grocers and publicans, including violations of Sabbath drinking laws and the harboring of runaway apprentices. Inside the shops, a few masters, inspired perhaps by the General Society and other groups, tried to convince the men of the folly of the traditional Blue Monday. For the more recalcitrant journeymen, these attempts at reformation only made drinking a badge of self-esteem and manliness, setting them apart from their more upright masters. One printer's hex, hurled at an employer accused of mistreating his men, suggested the prickliness of the problem: "May you be bother'd all your life / With workmen—brandy lovers. . . ."[65]

63. Montgomery, "Working Classes," 10; Weed, *Autobiography*, 58. For evidence on tavern keepers' loans, see Insolvency Assignments nos. 1816/14, 20, 119, 282; 1817/6, HDC. On drinking in early-nineteenth-century America, see W. J. Rorabaugh, *The Alcoholic Republic: An American Tradition* (New York, 1979), 15, 131–32, and passim; on New York, see W. Harrison Bayles, *Old Taverns of New York* (New York, 1915). I am grateful to Elizabeth Craven of Princeton University for discussions on drinking in New York; her dissertation, on the culture of New York taverns from the Revolution to the Civil War, will, upon completion, recast these matters in wholly new ways.

64. Account Book, Unidentified carpenter and mason, June 25, 1814, NYPL MSS; New-York City Temperance Society, *First Annual Report* (New York, 1830), index, pp. 18–20.

65. Complaints against Taverns—April 1822, Stephen Allen Papers, N-YHS; CCFP, Police Committee, January 12, 1818; New York City Common Council, *Report of the Committee on the Means to Carry Into Effect the Provisions of the Act for Suppressing Immorality* (New York, 1812), 4–5 and passim; *Independent Mechanic*, June 29, 1811. For a typical rowdy night's roundup of carousing artisans, see People v. Peter McIntyre, People v. John J. Moore, and People v. Rufus Ogden, all April 6, 1816, Court of General Sessions, MARC.

Drinking, however, was but one side of the journeymen's world; as Weed's remarks and the printer's hex made clear, not every craft worker was exclusively a brandy lover. Some enjoyed more uplifting efforts at self-education, and they shared their preference with their like-minded colleagues. In the shops, discussions of the principles of a particular trade easily turned to more general subjects. John Frazee, the stonecutter and sculptor, recalled these conversations from his apprentice days with fondness, as informal but earnest symposia that would have amused Archimedes and Newton but that "first inspired me to think philosophically." The more curious of the city's literate journeymen also read. Their chosen fare was not always refined: the typefounder David Bruce remembered that an especially popular genre about 1820 was the cheap chapbook, sold under such titles as "the 'Complete Letter Writer,' 'Dreambooks,' and malefactor's 'Dying Confessions,'" quick diversions, mostly, along with the occasional book "principally of sea-songs, ancient ballads, and 'Dibdins' melodies." But just as often, Bruce recalled, the skilled workmen came to prefer more edifying material. Popular miscellanies like James Oram's and Alexander Ming's *Weekly Museum* offered them short reports on practical science and world affairs and the work of such journeymen poets as the printer Samuel Woodworth. Shakespeare, to say nothing of more accessible dramatists, was favored in some journeymen's circles; Stephen Allen described one journeyman he encountered during his apprentice days as "the best scholar in the loft," who would entertain his fellows and disarm his foes with long recitations from memory of scenes from *Hamlet* and *Romeo and Juliet*. Frazee, having completed his apprenticeship, quickly graduated from workshop talk, first to *Charlotte Temple* and *Robinson Crusoe* and then to Cellini's autobiography. Other journeymen read the classics for a nominal fee in the city's libraries and reading rooms and kept up with current events in the taverns, which regularly stocked several local newspapers.[66]

The diverse social life of the workshops, houses of call, taverns, boardinghouses and reading rooms in turn bred a variety of formal and informal journeymen's associations. Little is known of these ad hoc drinking fraternities, "box" clubs, and reading groups, but we can be sure that the rudest of them were the gangs of younger journeymen and apprentices that roamed the streets after work and on Sundays. Taking their names either from their neighborhoods—for example, the Broadway Boys—or their trades—for example, the butchers' gang known as the Hide-Binders or High Binders—the gangs were an insular lot, who found a rough collective prestige in mimicking the styles of the city's affluent dandies and

66. John Frazee, "Autobiography. John Frazee, First American Sculptor," Transcript at N-YHS, no pagination; David Bruce, "Autobiography of David Bruce, or, Then and Now," N-YHS MSS, 6, 9; Allen, "Memoirs," 26; Weed, *Autobiography*, 59.

"bloods," attending theatricals, ogling young women, and picking fights with other gangs or with immigrant day laborers. David Bruce, who "traveled" with the Old Slippers, a gang of bookbinders and printers, recalled when he and a friend had been grabbed by two of their bitterest rivals, watermen from the White Hallers gang, and covered with molasses and sand. Court records include accounts of bands of young mechanics who sallied into crowds of dockworkers and passersby, with no other apparent purpose than to start a brawl. A primitive justice governed their set-tos— Bruce thought it a mean thing for his assailants to pick on him and his friend "as they were at least five years our senior"—but otherwise the gangs betrayed little concern for any matters more monumental than protecting their street honor or proving their courage.[67]

Very different issues concerned the journeymen's benevolent societies and unions that arose independent of the masters' mutual-aid societies. These were not the first such associations in New York; at least some journeymen organized before the Revolution. The earlier efforts were rare, however, and notable mostly for their circumspection: in the first New York journeymen's "strike" in 1768—one of only three strikes on record before 1788—twenty tailors set up their own shop and complained about insufficient wages but carefully avoided any mention that they had refused to work for their masters. In 1785, a strike of journeymen shoemakers, also over wages, provoked their masters to retaliate with an employers' combination, indicating a sharpening of conflicts within the trade. Only in 1794, when several printers formed the Franklin Typographical Society, did any New York journeymen attempt to establish a permanent body of their own. Over the next thirty years, journeymen cabinetmakers, chairmakers, ship carpenters and caulkers, cordwainers, coopers, house carpenters, tailors, hatters, and masons followed suit.[68]

The journeymen's societies were as much fraternal associations as trade unions: all mirrored, to some degree, the masters' dedication to mutual aid and to the harmony of "the Trade." In some societies, business revolved almost entirely around the planning of patriotic celebrations and the collection of sick funds. At times, the journeymen stressed the unity of workshop interests and glossed over the differences between themselves and the masters, even when disputes arose: in 1809, the printers' society, while successfully negotiating a new price book, declared that "between

67. Bruce, "Autobiography," 19–20; CCFP, Police Committee, August 25, 1817; People v. William Anderson et al., December 3, 1815, People v. Benjamin Smith et al., July 1, 1818, Court of General Sessions, MARC; *Independent Mechanic*, August 24, 1812; Norcross, *Swamp*, 5–6. See also Gilje, "Mobocracy," 159–66.

68. On the earliest associations, see Morris, *Government and Labor*, 193–207, and Nash, *Urban Crucible*, 324. On the period 1800–1820, see Rock, *Artisans of the New Republic*, 264–94.

employers and employees there are mutual interests dependent; mutual duties to be performed."[69] Nonetheless, simply by setting up on their own, the journeymen admitted that they and their masters diverged in *some* ways, that the community of "the Trade" did not fully satisfy their needs. Steadily, between 1800 and 1825, the changing structure of the crafts fostered a more militant bearing, particularly in the consumer finishing crafts. In 1804, the organized journeyman tailors asserted that they had joined forces to prevent their masters from forcing impositions on them, something that happened "frequently in every mechanical branch." A year later, the shoemakers prefaced their constitution with a call to "guard against the artifices or intrigues that may be used by our employers to reduce our wages lower than what we deem an adequate reward for our labour." Between 1795 and 1825, more than two dozen strikes took place, a low figure by the standards of the 1830s but an unmistakable sign of an awakening militancy. In other protests, journeymen turned to boycotts and newspaper appeals; striking cabinetmakers and shoemakers established their own cooperative shops; during their strike of 1810, a group of journeymen house carpenters led a crowd of several hundred boys and workers in breaking the windows of the offices of two unfriendly newspapers and of the General Society's Mechanic Hall.[70]

Like their counterparts in London and Paris, these society men were hardly the most exploited, worst-paid wage earners in New York, but they may be considered among the chief immediate victims of the new workshop order. Year by year, they saw their livelihoods and positions undermined, by those they attacked as the "few who are generally concerned in the *slop* shoes line," the "unmanly and ungenerous . . . Merchant Tailors," masters of "indifferent workmanship" whose "only object is to accumulate money." Their protests aimed to stop this deterioration, to protect themselves and all they associated with the workshop. Naturally, in a time of repeated inflation, wages were a primary issue, and most of the strikes concerned demands for a "just" rate of pay; simultaneously, however, the societies also tried to regulate shop conditions. Implicit in their insistence on a regular book of prices was their attempt to restrain masters from subcontracting, subdividing the work, or hiring "scab" journeymen who defied the society's authority. The most celebrated New York labor confrontation of the era, the cordwainers' general strike of 1808, only incidentally concerned wages, and focused on those masters who hired nonsociety men and "illegal" apprentices. The journeymen printers, threat-

69. George Daitsman, "Labor and the Welfare State in Early New York," LH 4 (1963): 248–56; Stevens, *Typographical Union*, 4–18, 52.

70. *Evening Post*, November 24, 1804; Commons, *Documentary History*, III, 364–65; *American Citizen*, May 3, 23, 1810.

ened by the use of juvenile labor, were vociferous on this point as well; so were the ship carpenters and caulkers, wary that the master shipwrights might find some way to increase the number of semiskilled helpers and degrade standards in the trade.[71]

The more they struck, the more the journeymen learned about the nature of the issues at stake: what had in the eighteenth century appeared as the isolated grievances of a few unfortunate journeymen in a few shops now appeared as problems of more widespread concern, intrinsic to the restructured workshops, setting masters and men unavoidably at odds. The first general strikes of single trades—by the cordwainers in 1808 and 1811 and the masons in 1819—sharpened the boundaries of conflict as the boundaries of class; so, in its way, did the carpenters' attack on Mechanic Hall. The societies' rhetoric further betrayed how much the supposed harmony of the crafts had deteriorated. The tone of civility typical of the earliest protests vanished, as journeymen addressed the offending masters with all printable terms of opprobrium, from "haughty" aristocrats to "merciless tyrants." A few more audacious souls ventured to claim that the masters had no right at all to control wages; in 1819, an English immigrant journeyman tailor insisted that the societies alone should set piece rates, since "the Journeyman is better able to decide upon the merit of his labor than the employer is for him." More often, the journeymen simply demanded their rights to bargain, either collectively or with each master individually, in order to offset what now appeared as ineluctable conflicts. The printers exemplified the shift in attitude shortly after a strike in 1817—a mere eight years after their declaration of "mutual interests"— when they banned employers (including former society members) from their meetings and announced that "the interests of the journeymen are separate and in some respects opposite those of the employers. . . ." The attempts by the various masters' associations to repress the journeymen, through the courts and with blacklists, only strengthened the men's resolve.[72]

The societies also reinforced the members' sense of themselves as sober, self-reliant, respectable men, capable of running their own affairs. To administer sickness and burial funds and to wage strikes required a discipline and aptitude for formal organization absent in the dramshops and boardinghouses. Society constitutions forbade "frequent intoxication,"

71. Commons, *Documentary History*, III, 300; *Columbian*, December 9, 1813; *Evening Post*, April 30, July 13, 1819; Stevens, *Typographical Union*, 65–70; Constitution of the New York Society of Journeymen Shipwrights and Caulkers, NYPL MSS; People v. James Melvin, November 9, 1811, Court of General Sessions, MARC.

72. *American Citizen*, December 31, 1802; *Evening Post*, July 13, 1819; Stevens, *Typographical Union*, 76.

"gross immorality," and "neglect of business." Rules governing union meetings paid meticulous attention to decorous procedures, to the extent of covering such arcane infractions as cursing at a dismissed brother who had been reinstated in the society. Members found guilty of negligent workmanship were fined.[73] In the ever expanding numbers of society committees—on prices, on tramping, on apprentices—the men acquired a taste for independent action and learned the necessary organizing skills. This new discipline came not from the pleading or coercion of their masters, but from the journeymen's own collective efforts; it also altered, at least in the journeymen's minds, the balance of power in the trade. Where once the masters alone had regulated the workshop, the journeymen now asserted their own rights to some form of control, inspired by a new sense of their own unity and mutuality. "Man of himself is nothing," ran the maxim of one society constitution, "but when he becomes united to his fellow mortals he becomes *useful*."[74] Such was the raw material of class consciousness.

The journeymen's opposition, with its glimmers of a language of class, was limited in comparison with the struggles of the unions of the 1830s. At its peak, the best-organized society in the city, the cordwainers', included fewer than 200 members, about half of all the journeymen cordwainers in New York. At no point did the societies come close to forming an organization embracing different trades. Although at least one society, the cordwainers', organized outworkers in order to prevent strikebreaking, nothing was said directly about unskilled or semiskilled workers in or out of the trades—except to complain about them, as in 1819, when the journeymen tailors struck those masters who hired "inferior" women "slop" workers. Even the most militant societies, meanwhile, declined rapidly over the period from the postwar readjustment through the panic of 1819, either to disappear altogether or to accept incorporation from the state legislature on terms that denied them any powers to regulate work or wages. Yet the societies' example was not lost on the trades; nor could their decline halt the ongoing collisions between masters and men. At least five independent journeymen's benevolent associations survived into the mid-1820s. Quiet efforts to organize journeymen hatters and tailors led to further conspiracy trials in 1823 and 1824. A flurry of strikes during the postpanic inflation of 1824 and 1825 momentarily revived the semblance of a union movement. By the time the Erie Canal beckoned to still

---

73. Commons, *Documentary History*, III, 364–68; Constitution, New York Society of Journeymen Shipwrights and Caulkers, Article XIII, NYPL MSS; Stevens, *Typographical Union*, 46–47, 70.

74. Commons, *Documentary History*, III, 300–301; Bradford, *Poetical Vagaries*, 13.

greater changes in the shops, journeymen in the city's largest trades had more than a quarter of a century of fitful experience at organizing on their own. More profound divisions and conflicts were on the horizon.[75]

A Restive Peace

New York's artisans had many things to celebrate in 1815, but not, it would seem, the harmony and unity of the crafts. If, literally speaking, the arts still stood by hammer and hand, the artisan system was clearly in decay. Masters, small masters, and journeymen could not expect to share equally in the cornucopia of dollars. Peace, the mechanic's friend, brought ample opportunity for some but uncertain prospects for many more.

And yet, with all of these divisions, it would be mistaken to view the peace celebrations only as a high-spirited patriotic masquerade. The social changes separating masters and journeymen in the largest trades were still in their infancy. Strikes, although fast becoming a fact of workshop life, remained something of a novelty. Large sectors of the craft economy preserved the artisan system. More important, the artisans, even in the most troubled trades, still shared a sense of distinctiveness from the mercantile elite and the laboring poor, one that breathed life into an artisan idiom of mutuality and softened the new conflicts. The 1815 celebrations hinted at this idiom; beyond these hints lay a powerful set of associations, centered on the meaning of the Revolution and the craftsmen's conception of their proper place in a republican polity and society. As much as the tools of the trades, this ideology defined the artisan republic. As it shaped the artisans' perceptions of the past and present, so it prepared them for an even more unsettling future.

75. Commons, *Documentary History*, III, 370; *Evening Post*, July 13, 1819; Stevens, *Typographical Union*, 78–81; Minutes, Society of Shipwrights and Caulkers, February 20, 1818; Colden, *Memoir*, 213, 215, 225, 227, 228–29; United Societies of Journeymen Tailors "List of Prices" (1825), N-YHS Broadsides; *Evening Post*, April 24, May 18, 24, 1824, May 22, 1825; Jacob Wheeler, *Reports of Criminal Cases* (New York, 1854), I, 154; People v. William Smith and others, August 12, 1824, Court of General Sessions, MARC; Commons, *History of Labour*, I, 153–57.

2
Artisan Republicanism

In the early nineteenth century, to be an American citizen was by definition to be a republican, the inheritor of a revolutionary legacy in a world ruled by aristocrats and kings. What it meant to be an American republican, though, was by no means self-evident. As early as 1788, James Madison observed that political writers had used so many definitions of the term that "no satisfactory one would ever be found" by recourse to texts alone; more democratic-minded New Yorkers agreed.[1] With the social and political transformations of the next half-century, the versions of American republicanism multiplied, as men of different backgrounds and conflicting social views—eastern bankers and western yeomen, slaveholders and abolitionists, evangelicals and infidels—came to judge themselves and each other by their adduced adherence to republican principles. A singular political language bound Americans together, an extraordinary manifestation of apparent unity when set against the continental and British experience of the age of revolution. Beneath this superficial consensus, Americans fought passionately over the fundamentals of their own Revolution, in a nation gripped by profound (if fitful) changes in economic and social life.[2]

1. *The Federalist,* ed. Jacob E. Cooke (Middletown, Conn., 1961), 250; "Address to the Republican Citizens of the United States, May 28, 1794," reprinted in Philip Foner, ed., *The Democratic-Republican Societies, 1790–1800: A Documentary Sourcebook of Constitutions, Declarations, Addresses, Resolutions, and Toasts* (Westport, Conn., 1976), 173. The Democratic-Republicans, taking note of Madison's remarks, guessed incorrectly that they had been written by Alexander Hamilton.
2. For a synopsis of the recent literature on this point, see Robert Shalhope, "Republicanism in Early America," *WMQ* 38 (1982): 334–56.

New York's artisans, masters and journeymen, had their own sense of what it was to be a republican, as the English writer James Boardman discovered during a visit in the late 1820s. Like some of his more celebrated countrymen, Boardman was fascinated by America and its commercial capital, but he refused to restrict himself to the urbane literary drawing rooms that misled many visitors into describing New York as a genteel haven from the barbarism of the backwoods. Boardman was after the lowly shopkeepers, the poor mechanics who he hoped would enlighten him about ordinary Americans. One afternoon, he interviewed a local jeweler, who summarized the artisans' political beliefs with an anecdote. It seemed that earlier that day the jeweler had sold an ornate brooch, "executed in garnets and of French workmanship," to a fortunate young mechanic. The youth, it turned out, could not distinguish an emblem of royalty from other designs, and when a friend later told him that his new prize was in fact the Bourbon device, he blanched. "His republican feelings would not permit him to wear the badge of tyranny for a moment," Boardman later recalled, "and with breathless haste he hurried back to the jeweller for something more congenial to democratic feelings."[3]

Some months later, an immigrant workman named John Petheram learned that the artisans' "republican feelings" were sufficiently strong to help dictate the organization of the workshop. Petheram, the articulate son of a family of textile workers, fled to New York to seek his fortune in 1830, as rick burning and loom smashing spread across the English countryside. Trying his hand in several shops and stores, the young man was amazed at the apparent backwardness of the city's employers. He later remembered one, the drug maker John Morrison, as typical. "I tried to make the old fool Morrison believe," Petheram related, "that by dividing the labour, which was not done there as it [is] in England, more work could be done." The benighted man, it seemed, "had never read Adam Smith," nor had he considered "the volume of experience which is open to every man but which ignorance, bigotry, or prejudice prevents so many from ever looking into." "This, sir, is a free country," the offended Morrison shot back. "We want no one person over another which would be the case if you divided the labour." Morrison, it turned out, was not alone in his "prejudice." "They were all alike," Petheram lamented of the small master employers, "I have heard this over again, with the addition of 'Tories may be very well in England but we want none here.' "[4]

Reading these stories today brings a jolt: here is an America that confounds our expectations, one that does not entirely square with the impressions of the most thoughtful traveler of the age, Alexis de Tocqueville.

3. James Boardman, *America and the Americans* (London, 1833), 328.
4. John Petheram, "Sketches of My Life," MS, N-YHS, 52–53.

As Boardman found out, conformity to the egalitarian ideal, far from a pretext for money grubbing, still had visceral political meanings for ordinary mechanics; Petheram, apart from suffering the irony of having to tell his bosses how to be better capitalists, discovered that acquisitive individualism, the pursuit of profit, was not necessarily the summum bonum of the American republican character, at least when it came to division of labor in the workshops. Both men, in their search for America, stumbled upon what remained of a distinctive system of meanings, one that associated the emblems, language, and politics of the Republic with the labor system, the social traditions, the very products of the crafts.

First evident in the pre-Revolutionary crisis, this artisan republicanism hardened in the 1790s, as the craftsmen came to terms with what the Revolution meant to them; through the late 1820s, it helped mold them as a social group and offered some real basis of solidarity between masters, small masters, and journeymen. At the same time, however, the craftsmen re-examined the meanings of both craftsmanship and republicanism, in view of the ongoing changes in the social relations of the trades. As late as 1825, artisans of all ranks could still join together, much as in 1815, in mass proclamations of artisan republican unity; simultaneously, a complex process was underway, in which masters and journeymen in the dividing crafts began to invent opposing interpretations of the artisan republican legacy. From this ideological counterpoint, between continuity and change, consensus and conflict, came evidence of both the lingering power of old patterns of thought and the emerging shape of class consciousness. Its origins lay in politics and in the artisans' fight against political subordination in the mercantile city.

Redeeming the Revolution

For the leading citizens of eighteenth- and early-nineteenth-century New York, society was meant to be a network of lower-class loyalty and elite influence. Social distinctions derived from a combination of occupation, wealth, religion, ethnicity, and family ties; the artisans, even the wealthiest among them, were generally held at arm's length by the mercantile elite, scorned as "meer mechanicks," men of the lower or middling sort. When applied to New York's shifting array of competing family interests, this social code helped foster a fractious political system of patrician control and popular participation. Independent artisans did have an important place in electoral affairs as early as the seventeenth century, both as candidates and as voters; far more than their counterparts in Boston and Philadelphia, New York's contending gentry and merchants actively (if with detectable condescension) sought the craftsmen's support. Participation in politics did not, however, guarantee the artisans power or unity. Caught as they were in webs of patronage, restricted by the scrutiny of viva voce polling and divided to a degree by the competing religious claims of Anglicans and Presbyterians, the artisans remained politically fragmented and beholden to their social superiors until the eve of the Revolution.[5] The popular movements of the 1760s and 1770s widened some cracks in this establishment and permanently altered the way in which mechanics and other urban plebes took part in New York City politics. But as the elitist political persuasion revived after the Revolution and persisted after 1800, the artisans once again had to find their political voice and fight for a share of local power. Over the next two decades, in alliance with nonartisan politicians, they consolidated their position as a vital political interest and affirmed, in the reflection of the Revolution, an egalitarian political tradition all their own.

To understand fully the passions and traditions behind these developments, we must retrace our steps back to the streets and committee rooms of the 1760s and 1770s. Historians have long puzzled over the social significance of the Revolution for the urban mechanics; most recent work agrees that a democratic artisan-based popular movement evolved in New York from the Stamp Act crisis to the coming of the Revolution (culminating between 1774 and 1776), one allied with and for a time led by West Indies–trade merchants and shippers but one with its own awakening political consciousness.[6] The movement arose only gradually and on several fronts. Mobbing and ritualized street demonstrations, the chief forms of collective protest for urban plebes in the Old World, were quite familiar to late-eighteenth-century New Yorkers, accepted as normal (if, to some, undesirable) manifestations of lower-class displeasure and high spirits. As in Hanoverian London, the causes of these disturbances ranged from the mundane to the seemingly bizarre, from competition for work and suspected price fixing to alleged grave robbing by cadaver-hungry medical students from Columbia College. So, too, the New York crowds generally stuck to the Anglo-American norms of highly symbolic actions (burning of effigies, wearing of costumes) interspersed with limited and

5. Nicholas Varga, "Election Procedures and Practices in Colonial New York," *NYH* 41 (1960): 249–77; Patricia U. Bonomi, *A Factious People: Politics and Society in Colonial New York* (New York, 1971), 178–223; Nash, *Urban Crucible*, 144–48, 362–74.

6. Bonomi, *Factious People*, 254–55; Roger Champagne, "Liberty Boys and Mechanics in New York City, 1764–1774," *LH* 8 (1967): 115–35; Staughton Lynd, "The Mechanics in New York City Politics, 1774–1785," *LH* 5 (1964): 225–46; Edward Countryman, *A People in Revolution: The American Revolution and Political Society in New York, 1760–1790* (Baltimore, 1981), 124–25, 162–65. Cf. Pauline Maier, *The Old Revolutionaries: Political Lives in the Age of Samuel Adams* (New York, 1980), 78–81.

discriminate violence to property.[7] During the Stamp Act crisis, the mobs also assumed a distinctly political and oppositional character, as crowds of Liberty Boys, led by small merchants and privateersmen, sacked the home of one British officer, forced the resignation of the local stamp distributor, burned effigies, destroyed the governor's coach, and posted placards, signed "Vox Populi," that threatened any printer who used stamped paper. Political crowds reappeared to defend the liberty pole against royal soldiers in 1766, to cheer a jailed leader of the Sons of Liberty in 1769, to engage the garrison in bloody street fights in 1770, to dump a small consignment of tea into the harbor in 1774, and to seize the local armory after news arrived of the Lexington battle. In June 1776, crowds stripped professed Tories of their clothes, rode them through the streets on rails, and threw them in jail. Political ideals and more everyday social resentments mingled in these outbursts: anger at impressment and at moonlighting troops, for example, was indistinguishable from broader issues of American liberty in the confrontations of 1766 and 1770. By taking to the streets, however, and by exerting their will—sometimes beyond the intentions of their leaders—the crowds also challenged the course and prerogatives of New York's loyalists and more conservative Whigs, in ways far more threatening to established political standards than those of earlier crowds—or so it seemed to their opponents, one of whom wrote in 1774 of the need to halt the activities of "*Cobblers and Tailors* so long as they take upon their everlasting and immeasurable shoulders the power of directing the loyal and sensible inhabitants of this city."[8]

While the mobs established a ritualized, boisterous artisan political presence, regularly organized groups created a new framework for popular patriot politics and in time elaborated a coherent set of democratic political ideals. The first semiformal associations arose alongside the mobs, as radical mechanics helped lead the anti-British agitation by adapting established campaign techniques. Open-air meetings and door-to-door canvassing, coordinated by the Sons of Liberty, galvanized opposition to the Quartering Acts and support for nonimportation. Similar activities followed the imposition of the Intolerable Acts. The formation of an independent Mechanics' Committee to replace the Sons of Liberty in 1774

7. J. T. Headley, *The Great Riots of New York, 1712–1873* (New York, 1873), 56–65; Jules C. Ladenheim, "The Doctor's Mob," *Journal of the History of Medicine* 5 (1950): 23–53; Gilje, "Mobocracy," 1–49.

8. Quoted in Nash, *Urban Crucible*, 369. See Lee R. Boyer, "Lobster Backs, Liberty Boys, and Laborers in the Streets: New York's Golden Hill and Nassau Street Riots," *N.YHSQ* 57 (1973): 281–308; Countryman, *People in Revolution*, 36–47, 55–77; as well as Carl Lotus Becker, *The History of Political Parties in the Province of New York, 1760–1776* (1909; reprint, Madison, Wis., 1960), chaps. 2–3.

revealed a maturing artisan self-confidence in political affairs, as well as a deep distrust for the city's more moderate Whigs. It also insured the survival of what Alfred Young has described as the city's militantly anti-British, increasingly democratic brand of popular Whiggery. Plenary sessions met in the committee's new Mechanic Hall, sometimes as often as once a week, to debate the intensifying crisis and coordinate radical actions. In 1776, as war became inevitable and Loyalists temporarily fled the city, the committee exercised a growing measure of power, issuing a string of declarations on American independence and demands for political reforms, including universal manhood suffrage. For one heady spring and summer, the city fell under the sway of an extraordinary popular political debate, heavily influenced by Paine's electrifying *Common Sense* (published the preceding January). The groundswell at once coalesced anti-British opinion and opened discussion about what an independent America would look like. Gouverneur Morris, that shrewd conservative, had seen what was coming two years earlier: the "mob" had, indeed, begun to think and reason.[9]

A new political world took shape in these efforts; although the British military occupation in 1776 halted popular politics in New York, the artisans resumed political action as soon as the redcoats departed. Mobbing and street demonstrations reappeared as instruments of the popular will, when reactions to the French Revolution, the panic of 1792, the announcement of the Jay Treaty in 1794, and several more minor disputes prompted the usual parades and destruction. The spectacular William Keteltas affair of 1796 repeated the pattern, with all the bravura of the London Wilkesite disturbances and the Sons of Liberty campaigns of thirty years earlier. The fracas began when two Irish ferryboat men were convicted and sentenced—one to a public whipping—for having cursed a local alderman and refused to depart from their schedule to carry him across the East River. Keteltas, a young, struggling Democratic–Republican lawyer, took up the ferrymen's case, calling the court's decision an abomination and the state legislature's failure to intercede "the most flagrant abuse of rights . . . since the Revolution." Keteltas's persistence earned him a jail sentence as well, for contempt of the authority of the assembly— but not before Keteltas and his Republican friends had mobilized the political nation out-of-doors, to accompany the lawyer to his final showdown with the legislators. The passions were genuine, but the proceedings could have been prepared as a script, as Keteltas (the assembly chamber

9. Young, *Democratic Republicans*, 11; Morris, *Government and Labor*, 188–92; Peter Force, comp., *American Archives* (Washington, D.C., 1837–53), 4th ser., I, 312. Lynd, "Mechanics in New York City Politics," remains the best detailed account of artisan political activity between 1774 and 1776, but see also Countryman, *People in Revolution*, 124–26.

hushed, its galleries packed to overflowing) delivered his final defiant refusal to recant, only to be lifted on a chair and carried through the streets to the jailhouse while thousands chanted, "The Spirit of '76." Two months later, when Keteltas was released, he was met by another crowd that once again carried him in parade, this time on a phaeton bedecked with American and French flags, a phrygian cap, and the inscription "What, you rascal, insult your superiors."[10]

All of this would have been familiar to anyone who had lived through the 1770s. The difference, betrayed in the almost comic tone of some of the press reports on the Keteltas affair, was that the dramaturgy of the crowd was of decidedly secondary importance in the 1790s, displaced by the more regular forms of participation begun by the artisan committees. In 1783, the mechanics' votes elected a popular Whig ticket to the assembly; in 1784 and 1785, a new committee of mechanics nominated its own slates; committee petitions pressed the legislature and the Congress for protective tariffs, payment of state debts, free public education, and restrictions on the political rights of former loyalists. Over the next two years, the mechanics' links with politicians soon to be identified with the city's Federalists also strengthened, as concerns over the tariff—and approval of a national Constitution strong enough to enact one—led them directly to Alexander Hamilton and the city's conservative nationalists. The conservatives, for their part, courted the trades, with hopes of gaining a popular base to break the radical ascendancy in state politics. When George Washington was inaugurated president in 1789, no group in the country was more fervently pro-Federalist than the New York artisans.[11]

The Federalist liaison, convenient for a time, was far too rife with contradictions to last long. From the start, the conservatives' political assumptions flew in the face of the legacy of democratic action left to the artisans after the Revolution. Although Hamilton learned to suppress his elitism and politic among the mechanics, he never quite abandoned his faith that the artisans regarded the elite as their natural superiors—that "Mechanics and Manufacturers will always be inclined with a few exceptions to give their voices to merchants in preference to persons of their own professions and trades." Any chances for a more permanent Federalist-artisan alliance eroded in the early 1790s, amid numerous local controversies—above all over the chartering of the mercantile bank and the legislature's failure to charter the Mechanics' Committee—all exacerbated by the Washington

10. *New-York Journal*, March 8, 11, 1796; Young, *Democratic Republicans*, 476–95. For additional references to the Keteltas affair and other crowd activities, see Gilje, "Mobocracy," 50–84.

11. *New York Packet*, April 4, 7, 14, 21, 27, 1785; Lynd, "Mechanics in New York City Politics," 232–41; Young, *Democratic Republicans*, 100–102; Countryman, *People in Revolution*, 252–79.

administration's Anglophilic foreign policy and backtracking on the tariff. By 1794, some of the city's most politically active artisans had grown so disgruntled that they allied with like-minded men from outside the trades to form the Democratic Society of New York.[12]

"[B]utchers, tinkers, broken hucksters, and trans-Atlantic traitors"— thus the temporary exile William Cobbett (still the Cobbett of "Peter Porcupine," not yet the Radical Cobbett of the *Political Register*) on the Democratic-Republicans. The New York society came, in time, to turn such descriptions to its advantage; some members even took a measure of pride in the titles attributed to them. All such descriptions misled: the Democratic Society was far from wholly plebeian; in the American context, it bore only fleeting resemblance to the French Jacobin clubs, and still less to the sansculotte sections of revolutionary Paris or the "Jacobin" artisan corresponding societies of London and the English provincial cities. Its officers were merchants and professionals of wealth like the redoubtable rentier Henry Rutgers; only in the ranks of the secondary leadership did craftsmen begin to show up in any numbers, along with young lawyers and teachers. The membership was small, probably numbering no more than two hundred. Although fiercely antiaristocratic, its circulars and protests displayed none of the root-and-branch democracy, none of the belief in "Members Unlimited" and universal suffrage that propelled the British and French artisan societies. Its public stance cannot be understood as "radical," let alone "revolutionary"; in the truest test of its faith, during the Whiskey Rebellion, the society condemned government repression and the excise tax system but also stoutly disapproved of the rebels' armed resistance to "the execution of constitutional law." In its structure, temperament, and intent, the Democratic Society was more an embryonic political party–cum–vigilance committee than a revolutionary club or a mass movement. Although decidedly more egalitarian and outspoken than the mainstream of the emerging Republican opposition, it was destined to remain within the boundaries of what one historian has called New York's post-Revolutionary "partisan culture."[13]

12. *The Federalist*, 219; Young, *Democratic Republicans*, 201–7, 211–30, 354–65, 373–75.

13. William Cobbett, *A Little Plain English Addressed to the People of the United States* (Philadelphia, 1795), 70; "Address to the Republican Citizens," *New-York Journal*, May 28, 1794; *General Advertiser* [Philadelphia], January 26, 1797, in Foner, *Democratic-Republican Societies*, 195; Countryman, *People in Revolution*, 193–94. Cobbett's remarks were directed against the Democratic-Republican "mother society" in Philadelphia, but the implication was obviously broader. The most useful account of the New York society appears in Alfred F. Young, "The Mechanics and the Jeffersonians: New York, 1789–1801," *LH* 5 (1964): 247–76, but see also Eugene P. Link, *Democratic-Republican Societies, 1790–1800* (New York, 1942). On the English and French artisan societies, see Thompson, *Making of the English Working Class*, 17–25, 102–85; Albert

To stop there, however, would be to miss the importance of all that prompted Cobbett's denunciation and the society men's ripostes—and hence of the Democratic Society itself. While led by the familiar radical elite—the well-to-do libertarian dissenters, young lawyers, and shopkeepers who frequented the coffee houses and taverns off Liberty Street and Wall Street—the society also stretched into the artisan wards. How far is not clear. We know that the society held its meetings after dark because, it claimed, "[w]orkingmen must meet in the evening"; Alfred Young reckons that the vast majority of the rank and file were men of the "middling" and "lower" sort. Certainly the society reached the downtown printing shops and the tanneries and workshops in and around "the Swamp." More important, it built its primary alliances with the Mechanics' Committee (finally incorporated in 1792 as the General Society), the individual craft groups, and the militia—the updated versions of what had been the hard center of the popular democratic movement of the mid-1770s.[14]

Furthermore, it is important to recall the political context of the mid-1790s—the *tone* of politics as conservatives dropped their conciliatory rhetoric for an undisguised contempt for democracy, the French Revolution, and (in some cases) the lower classes in general. Cobbett's rantings and the ham-fisted elitism surrounding the Keteltas affair were only examples of a pattern of antidemocratic alarmism in the eastern cities, a pattern less virulent in New York than in New England or Pennsylvania but just as ominously unctious in temperament. Charges that opposition to the administration was promoting demagogic factionalism soon passed into the pseudonymous slurs of one "Acquiline Nimble Chops, Democrat," who saw fit, in one of his milder passages, to dismiss the dissenting mechanics as "the greasy caps," the mindless multitude. A New York cartoonist's lampoons of the Democratic-Republicans made sure to include a tailor along with a pirate as part of the ignorant democratical crowd (Plate 5). Federalists were not being complimentary when they claimed that the Democratic Society had managed to attract "the lowest order of mechanics, laborers, and draymen." "Rabble," "a monster," "an incoherent mass of people"—all this (and there was more) might have been excused as the hyperbolic paranoia of procrustean conservatives, had it not been delivered by the very men, and the friends of those men, who now governed in the name of the Republic, men who denounced republican France and supported the Jay Treaty and who took heart at the admonition that one high-minded Federalist directed to the upstart mechanics:

Soboul, *Les Sans-culottes Parisiens en l'an II* (Paris, 1958); Gwyn A. Williams, *Artisans and Sans-Culottes* (New York, 1969), 58–80 and passim.

14. Young, *Democratic Republicans*, 395, 398–405.

> No tinker bold with brazen pate
> Should set himself to patch the state
> No cobbler leave, at Faction's call
> His *last*, and thereby lose his *all*.

It all at least sounded like 1774.[15]

Against these outbursts and against Washington's excoriation of all "self-created societies," the Democratic Society raised the banner of Paine's *Rights of Man*, a defense of the French republican regicides and an egalitarian interpretation of the American Revolution, based on "sentiments of Democracy, founded upon the Equal Rights of Mankind." In strictly institutional terms, its efforts were most important in helping bring individual, and sometimes lowly, craftsmen and craft groups (including a portion of the fraternal, artisan-dominated Tammany Society) into what was becoming a disciplined local political opposition in Manhattan. In ideological terms, it captured the democratic thrust lost amid the Constitution debates and the consolidation of power by New York's conservative nationalists, in effect making democracy a sine qua non of republicanism. "Painite" describes the society's politics best, with its hatred of all deferential forms, its distrust of the past and mere tradition, and its admiration for the man himself (who, ironically enough, spent most of 1794 languishing in a Jacobin prison, a victim of Robespierrist virtue):

> To conclude—Here's success to honest TOM PAINE:
> May he live to enjoy what he does well explain.
> The just Rights of Man we never forget
> For they'll save Britain's friends from the BOTTOMLESS PITT.

In time, such pronouncements, delivered at a Democratic-artisan Fourth of July festival in 1795, acquired something of a social coloration as well, as the society and its allies moved beyond defense of their right to associate, to ponder issues like the Hamiltonian finance program. Without coming close to questioning private property or raising the rights of the dependent poor, Democratic-Republicans did turn the classical republican fears of centralized financial power into suggestions that those who accumulated property without following a productive trade (that is, bankers, merchants, speculators) were politically suspect—suggestions that had arisen at the time of the nonimportation struggles, but never with such

15. Acquiline Nimble Chops, *Democracy: An Epic Poem* (New York, 1794); William Woolsey to Oliver Wolcott, Jr., March 6, 1794, cited in Link, *Democratic-Republican Societies*, 94; Young, *Democratic Republicans*, 454; Regina Ann Morantz, "'Democracy' and 'Republic' in American Ideology, 1787–1840" (Ph.D. diss., Columbia University, 1971), 147–52. See also Marshall Smelser, "The Jacobin Phrenzy: Federalism and the Menace of Liberty, Equality, and Fraternity," *Review of Politics* 13 (1951): 457–82; Gary B. Nash, "The American Clergy and the French Revolution," *WMQ* 22 (1965): 397–98.

clarity and force. "Less respect to the consuming speculator, who wallows in luxury, than to the productive mechanic, who struggles with indigence," ran one toast of the New York Juvenile Republican Society in 1795.[16] Such ideas, far from those of potential social revolutionaries, would be most effective in bringing the artisans into a developing party system. They also established in New York at the dawn of the industrial revolution the rough equation, elaborated for the British context in the second part of *The Rights of Man*, between political virtue and what would later be called the producing classes. For decades to come, such references to the spirit of '76 and the nobility of the productive mechanics would be the warp and woof of artisan political rhetoric.

It was, then, as a way-station, between revolution and egalitarian party politics, that the Democratic Society made its mark; although the group began to fade in 1797, the artisans it helped galvanize were already well on the way to forming more enduring coalitions to beat back the threat of "aristocratic" supremacy. By 1800, a clear mechanics' interest had developed, in league with Republican politicians, fed by protariff sentiments in the trades, and fully integrated as a pressure group in the city's politics. (Mobbing, of course, continued in early-nineteenth-century New York, with, if anything, greater frequency than before, but through the mid-1820s, New York crowds arose more from ethnic and racial conflicts and the punch-ups of the gangs than from political controversy. In politics, the artisans and others concentrated on party campaigns—with a street theater of their own—and on battles for local power.) Although they never challenged the mercantile elite's hold on most elective offices, craftsmen and former craftsmen, working mainly but not solely with the Jeffersonians, won a significant share of nominations between 1800 and 1815, especially to the state assembly and municipal posts. The selection of the sailmaker Stephen Allen as mayor in 1821 and the continued presence of craftsmen on party tickets until 1825 confirmed their political presence through the Era of Good Feelings. Throughout, the city's most prominent mechanics, particularly those in the General Society, used their good offices and political clout to win concessions, on restricting state prison labor, rejecting municipal workshop plans, widening the suffrage, and furthering endless more private concerns.[17]

16. *New-York Journal*, May 31, 1794, July 8, 1795; *American Daily Advertiser* [Philadelphia], July 10, 1795, reprinted in Foner, *Democratic-Republican Societies*, 233. On Paine, see Foner, *Tom Paine*, 75–106, 253–56.

17. Allen, "Memoirs," 88–106; Rock, *Artisans of the New Republic*, 101–22. A scan of the *Evening Post*, 1815–25, reveals that while lawyers and attorneys represented the largest proportion of all nominees to state-senate and assembly posts, all Republican factions nominated at least some artisans every year—though almost all of the craft candidates seem to have been successful masters. Among the more successful artisan

Plying the machinery of the early party system, the mechanics' interest assumed a political style that later generations of New Yorkers would come to associate with the New York Democracy. Unbending elitists like the young Washington Irving looked on aghast while "old cartmen, cobblers, and tailors" clambered onto the hustings, as if a set of demotic lunatics had been turned loose to arouse "that awful despot, the people." In fact, they were witnessing the emergence of a new social type, the enterprising artisan party politician. Stephen Allen was the exemplar; indeed, his political career, like his rise in business, read like a parable of the transitions from the 1770s to the Jeffersonian era. As a boy, Allen had thrilled to the activities of the popular pre-Revolutionary movement and pored over the popular Whig and radical republican texts, above all *The Crisis*: reading Paine aloud to his uncle, he later recalled, inspired "a feeling of reverence" and drew the youngster into "the enthusiasm of the people of this city in favor of liberty." This informal political education—reinforced by the frustrations of living in a patriot household during the British occupation of the city—set Allen's democratic views, and in the 1790s he joined the Democratic-Republican opposition. Soon thereafter, Allen's rising stature in the trades, capped by his election to the presidency of the General Society in 1802, attracted Jeffersonian politicians to him. In 1812, he was elected to the Common Council, where he remained for nearly a decade to devote special attention to reordering the city's finances and minor democratic reforms. His success and undisputed popularity among the mechanic voters won him three terms as mayor from 1821 to 1824.[18]

---

politicians nominated more than once were the whip maker Peter Sharpe and the stoneware manufacturer Clarkson Crolius. In 1825, voters could choose between the following tickets of People's Party (Clintonian) and Regular (Van Burenite) Republicans:

People's Nomination	*Regular Nomination*
Senate	Senate
Henry Wyckoff*	Joshua Smith, boatman
Assembly	Assembly
Samuel Cowdrey, attorney	Stephen Allen, sailmaker
Charles Drake, physician	Philip Brasher, lawyer
Timothy Hedges, attorney	Francis Cooper*
Thomas Hertell, attorney	Maltby Gelston, notary
Elisha W. King, attorney	James Hall**
Abraham Le Foy*	Isaac Minard, boots and shoes
Richard E. Mount, bellows	Shivers Parker, brush
manufacturer	manufacturer
David Seaman, smith	Jonathan E. Robinson, merchant
Dudley Selden*	Alpheus Sherman, attorney
Ira B. Wheeler, hotelkeeper	William A. Thompson*

* no occupation listed; ** name too common to identify

See *Evening Post*, November 12, 1825; *Longworth's Directory*, 1825.

18. George D. Luetscher, *Early Political Machinery in the United States* (Phila-

Another side of artisan politics appeared in the person of the Tammany brave, Matthew Livingston Davis. Davis, a printer, was like Allen an officer in the General Society and, at least initially, a genuinely dedicated Democratic-Republican partisan. In the 1790s, Davis and his partner, the journalist-poet Philip Freneau, led the counterattack in defense of the "self-created" societies; in 1800, having joined the Tammany Society, he actively supported Thomas Jefferson. Casting his lot with the friends of Aaron Burr, Davis became, over the next quarter of a century, one of the most accomplished wire-pullers and political agents in the city, pioneering the art of painting his opponents (whatever their creed) as aristocrats, while he appropriated the rhetoric of the humble artisan. In 1803, he tried to lead the mechanics' interest into a Burrite schism, playing upon artisan dissatisfaction with Mayor Edward Livingston over the mayor's proposal for a municipal workshop for criminals and the poor; Davis's speeches rang with charges that Livingston's humanitarianism disguised aristocratic plans to build a state monopoly with convict labor and "reduce the mechanics of this city to the degraded state of those of England." Five years later, unperturbed by the failure of his scheme, Davis outlined a precocious vision of organized party politics, in which party regularity and loyalty—staying "in unison with the wishes and expectations of the party" —would be the main standard of political virtue. Davis's personal power fluctuated through the 1820s, but his achievements helped pave the way for a kind of thoroughly professional democratic party politics that would come into its own during the ascendancy of Martin Van Buren.[19]

These artisan Jeffersonians were effective. The tallies for the state-assembly elections, in which virtually all masters and probably most journeymen were eligible to vote, leave little question that the mechanics' interest and the artisan vote usually remained loyal to the Jeffersonians. This did not, of course, imply absolute political unanimity in the trades. Even as the crises of the 1790s shook artisan allegiances, some craftsmen—above all those not in need of tariff protection, poorer mechanics caught in clientage networks, some more substantial masters, and the relatively few ex-Loyalist artisans—remained in the Federalist fold. After 1800, the Federalists could count on winning at least one-third of the vote in the central and outer wards, and they never failed to field tickets on which at

delphia, 1903); [Washington Irving], *Salmagundi*, no. 11 (New York, 1807), 207–18 (quotation on 211); Allen, "Memoirs," 8–9, 49–51, 60–88.

19. *American Citizen*, April 14, 1803; Matthew L. Davis to William P. Van Ness, August 1808, June 3, 1811, Davis Papers, N-YHS; Jerome Mushkat, *Tammany: The Evolution of a Political Machine, 1789–1865* (Syracuse, 1971), 22–25, 35–36; Rock, *Artisans of the New Republic*, 66–68. On Livingston, the General Society, and the workshop scheme, see GSMT Minute Book, January 4, 1803; Mohl, *Poverty in New York*, 228–37.

least one of four candidates was from the crafts. Some of the city's most renowned master artisans, including Duncan Phyfe and the tanner Jacob Lorrilard, were active Federalists. Other artisans, disgusted at the rise of the new parties, condemned Republican and Federalist alike, as fixers who would make "abject slaves" of independent republicans. Joseph Harmer, for one, emphasized that the title of his newspaper, *The Independent Mechanic*, should be taken literally with respect to party politics, those "filthy sloughs of party declamation, those seas of error which have neither bottom nor shore." By Matthew Davis's estimate, upward of one-half of the eligible "lower-class" voters (including mechanics and laborers) failed to vote in any given election, a normal figure by today's standards, but a mark of some apathy and early "anti-party" feeling among the trades. Nonetheless, apart from the years of the embargo, when Federalist candidates made inroads into the normally Republican districts, the Jeffersonians consistently carried the central and outer wards, with totals significantly higher than those they received from the city as a whole. For most of the active artisans, masters and journeymen, politics meant supporting the mechanics' interest and voting the Jeffersonian ticket.[20]

The political and ideological ramifications of these developments were profound. As in the debates of the 1790s, the early Jeffersonian campaigns, whether led by apparently sincere men like Stephen Allen or by more opportunistic pols like Davis, connected the fate of American equality to the political well-being of the middling producers—and of the Jeffersonians. Their messages were less "democratic" than those of the Democratic Society and its allies; the society, for example, had, in good Painite fashion, included several abolitionists in its ranks, while both the General Society and the Sailmakers' Society called for the end of slavery; the Jeffersonians, partners in an increasingly Negrophobic national political coalition, left the city's small black vote to the Federalists. Paine himself, his outspoken deism a political liability after his return to New York in 1803, was forsaken by the Republican politicians; he died nearly forgotten, in 1809.[21] Within the limits of partisan politics, however, the Jeffersonians did their best to turn contests for the most minor of city posts into reprises of the 1790s—and, they implied, of the Revolution itself. Until 1807, the rhetoric changed little, as New York's slow-learning Federalists made no pretense about their belief that the Revolution had been fought for limited political goals, or about their Burkian fears that "Jacobin" Jeffersonians would excite "irreconcilable enmity between the rich and the

20. Rock, *Artisans of the New Republic*, 30–36, 86–90; Willis, "Social Origins," 152, 164–67, 239; *Independent Mechanic*, April 6, 1811.

21. Young, *Democratic Republicans*, 529–32; Link, *Democratic-Republican Societies*, 153–54; GSMT Minute Book, July 1, 1795; Foner, *Tom Paine*, 256–63.

poor" by stirring the swinish multitude. The Republicans—no Jacobins—gleefully attacked such notions as the musings of "Federal lords," the well-born nabobs and aristocrats whose goal was to "rob the mechanics and laborers of their independence of mind," and (as the Republican "Mechanic" told the trades in 1805) to "wantonly and basely take away your rights."[22] After 1807, when the embargo and the war finally handed New York City's Federalists some popular issues, they altered their tone, and reached for popular support with their own "club," the Washington Benevolent Society—but they could do no better than to appropriate the artisan as hero and condemn their foes as "pampered sons of luxury" out of touch with the suffering workingmen. Even then, the Federalists retained some of their Anglophilic anti-Jacobinism of the 1790s, so much so that they reprinted pieces like Robert Southey's well-known philippic "The Friend of Humanity" in their party newspaper. The Republicans, for their part, denounced the Federalists as secret allies of the British war effort, fomenters of American disunity and therefore enemies of popular rights and independence. The links between the crafts and the vindication of political equality remained about the same as when they had first been forged during the Revolution. They lasted through the "one-party" politics of the 1820s.[23]

The importance of this discourse, apart from its evocation of 1776 and the 1790s, was its social imagery: just as the largest of the city's trades were beginning to divide along new lines, the artisans remained, in politics, the "noble mechanics," graced with an assumed unity of purpose and interest against aristocratic foes that belied all evidence of strife in the shops. In fact, the mechanics' interest, the purported political voice of all tradesmen, was decidedly controlled by the city's leading masters. Nothing assured an artisan's success in politics more than election as an officer of the General Society. All but three of the twenty-eight society presidents who served between 1785 and 1815 were eventually nominated for either the Common Council or the assembly, and of those nominated nineteen were elected.[24] None of the nominees for the Common Council or assembly was

22. *Evening Post*, November 16, 1801; *American Citizen*, April 13, 1801; Rock, *Artisans of the New Republic*, 45–76.
23. *Washington Republican* [New York], July 29 and August 5, 1809. The Southey piece, first published in the *Anti-Jacobin* in 1797, attacked Jacobinical MPs who would rouse the lowly with the ideals of Tom Paine; as Southey saw it, the People (represented as a poor, honest knife grinder) preferred their poverty and wanted to be left in peace. On the background to the poem and on James Gillray's hand in publicizing it in a satirical print, see Draper Hill, ed., *The Satirical Etchings of James Gillray* (New York, 1976), 114–15. On Federalist ideology, see also Linda K. Kerber, *Federalists in Dissent: Imagery and Ideology in Jeffersonian America* (Ithaca, 1970); and Rock, *Artisans of the New Republic*, 77–100.
24. Willis, "Social Origins," 239.

a journeyman at the time of his nomination. While the issues raised by mechanic politicians—convict labor, the tariff, Livingston's workshop scheme—touched the lives of lesser artisans and journeymen, they were of utmost direct import to independent artisans. The journeymen's protests provoked very different responses. The organized cordwainers tried for conspiracy in 1809 received virtually no political support, apart from that of their two Republican lawyers. Strikes, when reported in the party press, were treated gingerly, usually with a simple statement of the facts. One of the few exceptions, a commentary on the carpenters' turnout in 1810 by the English Jacobin emigré and Republican editor James Cheetham—himself a former journeyman hatter—denounced the strikers for raising "unreasonable" demands and threatening commerce.[25] In a rare instance when one of the parties addressed the journeymen, it was a Federalist apologist, "Brutus," who attacked certain Republican tanners and master shoemakers for alleged meanness to their employees; "Brutus" 's sincerity, though, was suspect from the beginning, suspicions borne out when he dropped all references to the journeymen after the autumn election.[26] By otherwise sidestepping emerging class divisions within the trades, the mechanics' interest and its allies at once revealed the limits of their concerns and insulated politics from possibly fractious disputes; attacks on alleged "aristocrats" tapped an older set of anti-aristocratic, anti-elitist social resentments to provide all artisans with a common ground.

Thus, the Revolutionary legacy left artisan political life with a potentially powerful set of contradictions between the rhetoric of collective equality and the actual conditions in the trades, between the street cries of party democracy and the realities of who, in fact, held political power. In time, the underlying social divisions in the crafts and the political alienation shared by some artisans would replace the mechanics' interest and the Republican alliance with very different kinds of commitments and coalitions—but only after the Republican coalition itself collapsed in the late 1820s, the victim of its own internecine strife. In the aftermath of the 1790s, and for a quarter of a century thereafter, New York's masters and journeymen retained and responded to the ideals of the late eighteenth century, for the protection and expansion of their collective political rights against the static, deferential harmony of unquestioned elite supremacy—or, more loosely, for "equality" against "aristocracy." Even as they came to blows in the workshops and the courts, they were as one in politics—the "sinews and muscles of our country," as one Jeffersonian put it—ever prepared to redeem *their* Revolution against any who would trample on

---

25. *American Citizen*, May 3, 23, 31, June 1, 1810. On Cheetham, see Richard J. Twomey, "Jacobins and Jeffersonians: Anglo-American Radicalism in the United States" (Ph.D. diss., Northern Illinois University, 1974).

26. *Commercial Advertiser*, April 20, 1801.

their political liberties, against any who would inject "corruption . . . through the veins of the body politic."[27]

Republican Religion

While politics offered the artisans some unifying continuities with the Revolution, the city's religious life reinforced their egalitarianism and widened their cultural distance from the mercantile elite. Colonial New York had been the most Anglican of American cities; through the early 1790s the Episcopalians (especially) and the Presbyterians, along with the remnants of the Old Dutch Reform establishment, were the city's reigning denominations. Apart from those dissenting Presbyterians who had been caught up in the millennial fervor of the Great Awakening or been pushed to the borders of Unitarianism, New Yorkers worshiped their fathers' faiths, with a dogma and sense of social exclusiveness—symbolized by the church pew rents—that enhanced the prestige of the city's leading families. Trinity Church, that former bastion of elite Anglican respectability, was formally disestablished in 1784 but retained the immense tracts of land that made it the wealthiest institution in Manhattan. So the smaller churches continued to give New York high society much of its prestige. Timothy Dwight, during his famous visit, noted with satisfaction that the city was an eminently religious one, where "few, even of the licentious, think it proper to behave disrespectfully toward persons or things to which a religious character is attached."[28]

No one body of doctrine prevailed among New York's artisans during these years. A minority belonged to the more respectable Episcopalian and Presbyterian congregations; a disproportionate number of artisan Democratic-Republicans seem to have adhered to Presbyterianism, with its strong connections to American Whiggery and the patriot cause. The remainder included infidels, Methodists, Baptists, and an unchurched majority. Religion certainly played a part in the collective life of the trades: the craft societies' annual Fourth of July exercises, for example, invariably ended in a church, usually Presbyterian or Dutch Reform, and often included a sermon from a local clergyman.[29] Even in church, however, the

27. John T. Irving, *An Oration Delivered on the Fourth of July 1809, before the Tammany Society, or Columbian Order, Tailors', Coopers', Hatters', Hibernian Provident, Masons, Shipwrights', House Carpenters', and Columbian Societies* (New York, 1809), 10–11, 19.
28. Timothy Dwight, *Travels in New York and New England*, ed. Barbara M. Solomon (Cambridge, Mass., 1969), III, 331. On Trinity Church, see William Berrian, *A Historical Sketch of Trinity Church, New York* (New York, 1847); Jaher, *Urban Establishment*, 167–69, 229–31. See also Lambert, *Travels*, 72–73.
29. See Young, *Democratic Republicans*, 570; Shepherd Knapp, *A History of the Brick Presbyterian Church* (New York, 1909), 184–202.

artisans warned of the evils of ecclesiastical authority and of the lurking dangers of a resurgent, corrupt, European-style clericalism. In their diversity, they shared common ideals about the place of religion in a secular republic.

The deist movement of the late 1790s contributed, if only in a minor way, to the stock of artisan religious views. To the shock of Federalist leaders and orthodox clerics, Elihu Palmer, a blind itinerant preacher, managed to turn his newspaper, the *Temple of Reason*, into the leading exponent of early national American freethought. Lambasting Christianity as an instrument of despotism, Palmer (in time, with the help of Thomas Paine) blended humanist ethics and the natural religion of Paine's *Age of Reason* in a celebration of science and republican equality: "Poverty and riches, misery and happiness, are generally the results and consequences of good or bad governments—of wise or unwise laws—of the influence of virtue, or the prevalence of vice; and all the *natural* offsprings of human actions, not the *partial* operations of an all-just and all-wise Being."[30] Drawn both from the French and from the rich body of English Dissenting skepticism, Palmer's American deism attracted a mixture of home-grown merchant philosophes, liberal professionals, and artisans (with their own backgrounds in workshop science and democratic politics). Their numbers were hardly overwhelming. Even in the libertarian milieu of the Democratic Society (of which Palmer was a member) at best a handful of activists joined the deists. The milder Unitarianism of Joseph Priestley (welcomed by the Democratic-Republicans upon his arrival in New York as an exile in 1795) was better suited to New York's unorthodox democrats; when the Republican Patriotic Junior Association toasted Thomas Paine in 1797, it celebrated *The Rights of Man* but condemned *The Age of Reason*.[31] The deists' real impact reached beyond their followers to reinforce more widespread and nebulous anticlerical suspicions. Thus the Democratic Society, in a circular letter issued in 1794, noted that "SU-PERSTITION in a religious creed, and DESPOTISM in civil institutions, bear

---

30. *Temple of Reason* [New York], December 6, 1800. The standard work on deism in the 1790s remains G. Adolph Koch, *Republican Religion: The American Revolution and the Cult of Reason* (New York, 1933), 51–74, 130–68. On Palmer, Roderick S. French, "Elihu Palmer, Radical Deist, Radical Republican: A Reconsideration of American Freethought," *Studies in Eighteenth-Century Culture*, no. 8 (1979): 87–108, develops themes presented here; see also Herbert M. Morais, *Deism in Eighteenth-Century America* (New York, 1934); Foner, *Tom Paine*, 258–59.

31. "Address of the Democratic Society of New-York to Joseph Priestley," in Foner, *Democratic-Republican Societies*, 182; *Argus* [New York], February 7, 1797, quoted in Young, *Democratic Republicans*, 404. For a more bitter view of Paine—complete with the familiar apocrypha about his deathbed pangs of conscience—see the remarks of the ironmonger-turned-seed merchant Grant Thorburn, *Fifty Years' Reminiscences of New York* (New York, 1845), 74–82. See also Francis, *Old New York*, 134–43.

a relation to each other similar to that which exists between the children of common parents." For a time, it was enough to convince even level-headed Episcopalian conservatives like the Reverend Clement Clarke Moore that the de-Christianizing Jacobin uprising had begun, led by the Democratic-Republican followers of "those imps who have inspired all the wickedness with which the world has of late been infested."[32]

Nothing of the kind was in the offing: organized deism declined rapidly between 1804 and 1810, caught between the Second Great Awakening and Republican confidence that the re-election of the freethinker Jefferson had vindicated the separation of church and state. But its traces—and the traces of a rowdier popular impiety joined to democratic politics—lingered. A few small Universalist sects like the Society of United Christian Friends struggled and survived, kindling among the craftsmen ideas on universal salvation not entirely unlike those of Paine and Palmer. Cruder activities brought legal consequences for a few men hauled before the Court of General Sessions to answer charges that they had scandalized Christianity. Anti-Federalist politics sometimes mixed with irreverence, as they had in the 1790s: in 1821, the printer Jared Bell was arrested for allegedly entering a store, "cursing and swearing and using profane language saying 'God Almighty was a *dam fool*' for creating such men as composed the Hartford Convention and that if it was in his power he would send them and the whole British nation to Hell together. . . ." More forthrightly blasphemous was the reported crime of one John Danforth—a shout in the street that "Jesus Christ is a bastard, his mother a whore, and God a damned old whore master." Even angrier spirits attacked clerics with chamber pots, menaced would-be missionaries, and destroyed church property.[33]

The passions of revivalist religion, quite unlike the intensely cerebral

32. "Circular. Democratic Society, New York to the Democratic Society of Philadelphia" (1794), N-YHS Broadsides; [Clement Clarke Moore], *Observations upon Certain Passages in Mr. Jefferson's Notes on Virginia* (New York, 1804), 29. Among those most prominent in Painite deist circles were the lawyer Henry Fay and the printer Alexander Ming, both of whom we will encounter again. See Gilbert Vale, *The Life of Thomas Paine* (New York, 1841), 159.

33. Koch, *Religion*, 108–13, 168–84; Russell E. Miller, *The Larger Hope: The First Century of the Universalist Church in America, 1770–1870* (Boston, 1978), 161–62, 681–83; Francis, *Old New York*, 143–44; Weed, *Autobiography*, 61; People v. Jared Bell, May 4, 1821; People v. John Danforth, July 6, 1825, Court of General Sessions Records, MARC; Stafford, *New Missionary Field*, 15; Gilje, "Mobocracy," 114–26. On Universalism, see also Minutes and Membership Roll, Society of United Christian Friends, N-YHS MSS. The society's records show that while the membership never exceeded 100, the group grew steadily from 1800 to 1810, stagnated through 1815, then grew again until the mid-1820s.

The sort of blasphemy of which Danforth was accused had long been familiar among English lower and middling classes; its history in colonial America has yet to be written. See Christopher Hill, "Plebeian Irreligion in 17th Century England," in *Studien über die Revolution*, ed. Manfred Kossock (Berlin, 1969), 46–61.

democracy of the deists or the impiety of the rowdies, also distanced its adherents from orthodox devotions. Compared with other eastern cities, particularly Boston, New York had shown little interest in the great religious upheavals of the eighteenth century, but the Second Great Awakening brought a sharp rise in church membership between 1800 and 1825. Encouraged by itinerant veterans of the British and rural American circuits, a series of increasingly intense waves of revivals hit Manhattan after 1805, on a scale that surprised even seasoned clergymen. The Methodists, a persecuted sect in colonial New York, made the greatest progress. Due largely to the efforts of Methodist missionaries in the city's central and outer wards, what had been a handful of congregations in 1800 became, in twenty-five years, one of the three leading centers of Methodist worship in the United States.[34]

Methodism, like the other evangelizing faiths, carried with it a gamut of impulses to New York—all tied to the tensions between submissiveness and egalitarianism that lay at Methodism's core. None of the Methodist congregations, not even the most "popular," preached a faith comparable to the deists' and liberal Presbyterians'; as Sydney Ahlstrom reminds us, early-nineteenth-century Methodism derived neither from an optimistic view of human nature nor from American democracy, "but from John Wesley—a different source indeed."[35] More orthodox, authoritarian Wesleyans like the Reverend Nathan Bangs deplored the "extravagant excitements," the "clapping of hands, screaming, and even jumping" reported in congregations that kept to the looser ways common in eighteenth-century popular churches. Eventually, Methodist leaders, headed by Bangs and allied with the city's New School Presbyterians, would be more closely identified with efforts to enforce an industrious morality of self-discipline. But this took time to achieve: in post-Revolutionary and early national New York, Methodism was pre-eminently a religion of and for the middling and the poor, its Arminian doctrines on grace slicing through the social exclusivity of conventional Episcopalians and orthodox Calvinists. Preachers from humble backgrounds themselves—Bangs was the son of a Connecticut blacksmith—pointed out that in their churches, seats were free and open to all. Here, even journeymen and lowly day laborers could know the Redeemer, He who, in Bangs's words, "hath died for all men, and thereby opened the door of mercy for all to return and find peace and

34. Samuel Seaman, *Annals of New York Methodism* (New York, 1892), 158–214; Carroll Smith Rosenberg, *Religion and the Rise of the American City: The New York City Mission Movement, 1812–1870* (Ithaca, 1970), 45–51; Richard Carwardine, "The Second Great Awakening in the Urban Centers: An Examination of Methodism and the 'New Measures,'" *JAH* 58 (1971): 327–40. On early Presbyterian revivals, see J. D. Alexander, *The Presbytery of New York* (New York, 1887), 81–83.

35. Ahlstrom, *A Religious History of the American People* (New Haven, 1972), 438.

pardon." It was a message that families of the middle and outer wards had never heard; the overwhelming majority of those who heeded it were small shopkeepers, artisans, and laborers.[36]

The more democratic aspects of evangelical religion permeated all sorts of popular devotions. Thurlow Weed noticed the difference when he visited the Methodist congregation of the immensely popular John Summerfield after having spent his first Sundays in New York at more staid Presbyterian and Episcopalian churches. What struck Weed most was the near charismatic rapport between the preacher and his audience:

> He was followed from church to church by great numbers, charming and chastening all ears and all hearts. If any went to scoff, they inevitably "remained to pray." . . . [H]e was himself a simple, unostentatious, "meek and lowly" believer and follower of that Saviour to whom, in person and character, he bore such striking resemblance.[37]

More idiosyncratic—and still more democratic in faith and style—were the sectarian preachers, the "religious enthusiasts of every belief" who David Bruce recalled could be seen along New York's thoroughfares at almost any time of day. These included some well-known locals and visitors— Lorenzo Dow, the Methodist apostle of love who used New York as a rest stop during his eastern travels; Domanic Van Velsor, the so-called stove-fence preacher; and Amos Broad, the much-persecuted upholsterer and evangelist of Rose Street—but none attracted more attention than Johnny Edwards, the Welsh immigrant and midding master scalemaker of the Ninth Ward. Edwards (it appears to have been his real name) arrived in New York in 1801 and swiftly passed through a series of religious affiliations, from Anglican to Methodist and Baptist and Quaker, before he founded his own Church of Christ, in Greene Street in about 1808. As much showman as evangelist, Edwards would drive his scale-beam wagon

36. Seaman, *Annals*, 182–83; Abel Stevens, *Life and Times of Nathan Bangs, D.D.* (New York, 1863), 183; Nathan Bangs, *The Substance of a Sermon Preached on Opening the Methodist Church in John-Street* (New York, 1818), 31–32. In order to get a rough indication of the Methodists' social base, names of Methodist class leaders from the entire city in 1812 were taken from Seaman, *Annals*, appendix P, and checked in the 1812 city directory and tax list. The occupations of those identified in the directory ($N = 64$) broke down as follows:

Merchants and professionals	9.4
Shopkeepers and retail	10.9
Master craftsmen	14.1
Small masters and journeymen	48.4
Laborers and unskilled	17.2
TOTAL	100.0

37. Weed, *Autobiography*, 61–62. On Summerfield, see Richard Carwardine, *Transatlantic Revivalism: Popular Evangelicalism in Britain and America, 1790–1865* (Westport, Conn., 1978), 42.

to the most crowded parts of the city to regale the sinful passersby. His thoroughgoing vision of earthly corruption (according to Bruce, he would always balance his beams in his cellar because he insisted that "there is no virtue on the surface of the earth"), his devotion to the poor, and his defiance of the rich all marked him as a "mechanick preacher," in a tradition that stretched back to the English radicals of the Commonwealth. In 1810, when Edwards joined with one Dorothy Ripley to attempt a revival, he took to appearing in Wall Street, where he shouted through a three-foot-long tin trumpet for the moneylenders to repent. Undaunted by the failure of his prediction that the world would end on June 10, 1810, he remained active; more than a dozen years later, he scoffed at efforts by city fathers to subsidize missionary efforts by more reputable clergymen: "I firmly believe it would be far more acceptable to God and all good and wise men," he wrote in one petition to the Common Council, "had you laid out 300 dollars in fat geese and turkeys and given them to the poor who have seen better days and they would prefer it any time to 300 dollars worth of wind." Other lay preachers expounded more directly political beliefs. One, a gardener named David Whitehead, delivered a mock Fourth of July sermon at Potters' Field in 1826, calling down wrath upon New York's "pretty set" who dressed in rich attire and lived in luxury and abundance. "They have established robbery by law and a law for the protection of robbers," Whitehead exclaimed; all they cared for was wrestling property from workingmen and propping up their privileges with "threats of sedition and blasphemy" borrowed from "King John the First"—John Adams.[38]

Politics and religion also commingled in the artisan neighborhoods as matters for intense debate and discovery. They dominated the discussions of one group of artisans who met regularly in "Saturday night sessions" at the shop of Cox the Cooper, near Corlears Hook, about 1820. Celebrations of republican heroes and attacks on supposed Tory villains dominated the conversations; military relics from the Revolution and the War of 1812 were occasionally passed around for appropriate veneration. Several participants also had "brimstone on their shoulders," and endless ar-

38. Bruce, "Autobiography," 8, 15–16; Francis, *Old New York*, 146–50; Charles C. Sellers, *Lorenzo Dow: Bearer of the Word* (New York, 1928); People v. Samuel E. Thompson, November 5, 1812, Court of General Sessions Records, MARC; Alvin Harlow, *Old Bowery Days* (New York, 1931), 175; *Account of the Trial of John Edwards of the City of New York* (New York, 1822); CCFP, Charity Committee, January 26, 1824; David Whitehead, *An Oration Delivered at Potters' Field on the Fourth of July 1826—By the First Adopted, by the Thirteen Mothers of the Union Whose Seal Is Union and Secretary Is Truth* (New York, n.d. [1826]). Christopher Hill has brilliantly elucidated the English background of the more heretical preachers; see *The World Turned Upside Down: Radical Ideas in the English Revolution* (New York, 1972), 28–30, 79–80, 231–46.

guments pitted a few Calvinists and Presbyterians against an array of Methodists, Close Communion Baptists, Universalists, and a man who arrived one evening to declare that he had "renounced the iron-clad mysteries of the [Presbyterian] Westminster Oath." The most heterodox views received a hearing, if not always a friendly one: at least one of Cox's friends reported he had been swayed by the sea-captain disciple of a Universalist minister "who had invented a new religion that left Hell out altogether." "Soon as I get time," the curious blacksmith Joe Holden wrote to his mother, "I intend to study the matter for myself and see what there is in it. Like as not his doctrine may not be so bad after all."[39]

Yet in the end, while impiety and popular enthusiasm exerted their influences, most artisans held to a profound and shameless indifference toward any kind of organized devotion. The extent of apathy became clear just after the War of 1812, when groups of younger, affluent Presbyterians, mindful of the evangelicals' success, tried to bridge the social gap by sponsoring interdenominational missions, Sunday schools, and Bible groups in the central and outer wards. On ordinary Sundays, the tract missionary Ward Stafford found in 1817, fewer than one in four New Yorkers—and far fewer in the poorer areas of the city—attended church. Emblems with a magical (and, to Stafford, pagan) significance—horseshoes and other talismans—were more in evidence in lower-class homes than were Bibles. "We have found the people deplorably ignorant as it respects the subject of religion," Stafford lamented.[40]

It would be foolish to try to impose unity upon such diverse currents of artisan piety, irreligion, and apathy; most of the time, these tendencies were at war. Even so, the most contradictory forms of artisan devotion had some things in common. Among those of some faith, Christian and non-Christian, doctrines of spiritual equality and objections to unquestioned deference recurred in various contexts, implying a cultural independence and mistrust of the city's gentlemen and their clerics. The deists and Universalists were explicit on this: "It is a point of policy in the hierarchy," Palmer held, "to cherish [a] submissive temperament, and cultivate in the soul of man the divine virtue of humility." More pious declarations stressed that possession of earthly riches and power did not signify grace—indeed, to some, the accumulation of great personal wealth raised suspicions of sinfulness. The Methodists' appeal to the lower classes, despite the Wesleyan hierarchy, was quite direct here, as were the professions of spiritual equality published in the Independent Mechanic. The poem "Saturday Night," by "Journeyman Mechanic," was typical in its emphasis on the "blessed peace" that came with the Sabbath:

39. Ralph Christopher Hawkins, Corlears Hook in 1820 (New York, 1904), 19-39.
40. Stafford, New Missionary Field, 7, 11.

Of rich and poor the difference what?—
In working or in working not
Why then on Sunday we're as great
As those who own some vast estate.

From such statements, with all of their implied resignation to *earthly* inequality, it was a short distance to more forthright denunciations of the
anxious pursuit of money and of all those who would imitate the ways of
the mercantile elite, described by one mechanic as "the absurd and vicious
positions of a gay, thoughtless, and licentious people," trappèd in "a personal hell." And from here, it was a direct path to Johnny Edwards on
Wall Street and David Whitehead at Potters' Field.[41]

More straightforward was the artisans' overriding resentment at what
craft spokesmen of all faiths described into the 1820s as unrepublican religious authority. Only in Old World aristocracies, they charged, would
"presumptuous men" of "insolent morality" use God as an adjunct to political power and social prestige. Only enemies of the Republic would hold
superstitious beliefs that elevated the clergy and some classes of men over
others and that chained men's minds to a prescribed faith. As Thomas
King, a Universalist shoemaker, told an Independence Day assembly of
craftsmen in 1821, such "ecclesiastical despotism" had proven "the most
cruel—the most unrelenting kind of despotism that ever tormented man."
Fortunately, religious reformation and republican revolution had shaped
an America where such power was supposed to be illegitimate; all the
same, in the wake of continuing clerical denunciations of the French Revolution and the "Jacobinical" Jefferson, the artisans and the politicians
who sought their votes urged vigilance. The Republican George Eacker
was direct in 1801 when he accused the Federalists of assuming a "garb of
hypocritical sanctity," and warned the tradesmen to beware the combination of monied influence and ecclesiastical influence, "in the hands of faction . . . instruments more dreadful than the dart wielded by Death!" A
generation later, speakers reminded the artisans that the Republic had
been founded "on the broad basis of *rational* liberty," without any religious cast. For Thomas King, as for his fellow Universalists, such sentiments led to a celebration of rationalism and "the Sun of Science"; for the
Methodists, it suggested pursuit of the millennium free from state interference; for most craftsmen, it meant that they should be left alone.[42]

41. *Temple of Reason*, December 20, 1800; *Independent Mechanic*, June 15, November 23, 1811. Cf. Thompson, *Making of the English Working Class*, 26–54.
42. Thomas F. King, *An Oration Delivered on the 4th of July 1821 before the
Tammany, Hibernian, Stone Cutters', Tailors,' and Cordwainers' Societies in the Mul-
berry Street Church* (New York, 1821), 5–7; George I. Eacker, *An Oration Delivered
at the Bequest of the Officers of the Brigade of the City and County of New-York and
of the County of Richmond and the Mechanic, Tammany, and Coopers' Societies on
the Fourth of July, 1801* (New York, 1801), 14.

Only very late in the early national period did more portentous signs of religious strife begin to appear in artisan discourse. The most striking, anti-Catholicism, had always been implicit in artisan rhetoric and republican politics and religion. No "idolatrous invocation to saints" marred the artisans' public gatherings, Eacker told the crafts in 1801; on the contrary, their celebrations expressed only "abhorrence against such unblushing wickedness." In the streets, the maraudings of the gangs sometimes turned into full-fledged riots, pitting natives and Irish Protestants against Irish Catholics; there is evidence that a New York version of the Orange order gathered some underground support in the trades just after the War of 1812. But the Scarlet Whore of Babylon never quite turned up in artisan speeches in the early years of the century, and was unlikely to, given the relatively small numbers of Catholics in the city and their even smaller proportion in the crafts. If anything, Irish resistance to British and landlord rule prompted sympathy for the "persecuted catholick" and "poor peasant," whose talents, and intrepidity, Samuel Berrian pointed out in 1815, had won a "scanty and uncertain harvest." By the 1820s, however, antipapist expressions became more open, as Irish Catholics—carriers of what one printer's ode called "papal gloom"—figured more prominently in New York social and political life. In 1824, an Orange celebration of July 12, Battle of the Boyne Day, brought furious sectarian violence in and around the taverns of the Irish weavers' community in Greenwich Village. Nothing distinguished the men of Corlears Hook more, one chronicler of the 1820s noted, than their "intense, ardent, and deep-seated" detestation of Catholicism. It would re-emerge, in more organized forms, in the 1830s and 1840s.[43]

The continuing ferment of the Awakening and the changing relations in the workshops further altered the place of Protestantism in New York artisan life after about 1815. The tightening of Methodist discipline effected by Bangs had the dual effect of marginalizing some of the more enthusiastic preachers and congregations and binding evangelical religion ever closer to the creed of morality and self-repression. Simultaneously, the city's largely Presbyterian and missionary tract societies began to relax their more rigid Calvinist doctrines on conversion and grace. With their

43. Eacker, *Oration*, 6–7; Gilje, "Mobocracy," 91–105; Samuel Berrian, *An Oration Delivered before the Tammany, Hibernian Provident, Columbian, and Shipwrights Societies* (New York, 1815), 22–26; *Independent Mechanic*, May 11, July 6, August 3 and 10, and September 4, 1811, March 28, 1812; George Asbridge, *Oration Delivered before the New-York Typographical Society* (New York, 1811), 27; Hawkins, *Corlears Hook*, 14–15. On Orangism, see People v. Jonathan Burke Murphy, December 23, 1818, Court of General Sessions, MARC; on the 1824 riot, see An Unbiased Irishman, *Orangism Exposed* (New York, 1824); Rowland T. Berthoff, *British Immigrants in Industrial America, 1790–1950* (Cambridge, Mass., 1953), 189–90.

increased emphasis on actually winning poorer men to Christ, the tract societies and Sunday-school reformers stepped up their work, to make New York, by 1825, a leading center of what was soon to become an effective national evangelical united front. Their success at winning master craftsmen to the cause was evident in the Apprentices' Library banner in the Erie Canal march; a broader evangelical insurgence lay behind the master stereotyper Adoniram Chandler's plea to his colleagues in 1816 to "suppress vice as well as encourage virtue," and behind the exhortation of a Presbyterian minister, delivered to the city's artisan-dominated fire companies nine years later, to take "a Bible in one hand and a sword in the other" in a popular crusade against deism, Socinianism, and other infidelities.[44]

After 1825, artisan anti-Catholicism and the evolving strains of evangelical Protestantism would culminate in organized nativism and in abrasive clashes between infidels and believers, churched and unchurched. The point to stress, however, is that these later developments, with all of their divisiveness, should not be abstracted from their historical context. Although ethnic tensions were constant, only in the 1830s, when migration to New York from the most heavily Catholic peasant areas of Ireland accelerated, would antipapism become a potential political tool for organizing artisans and craft workers; only in the middle and late 1840s, when the famine wave hit New York and entered a far more fractured, industrializing craft economy, would economic nativism become a vital force in the crafts. Similarly, evangelicalism began to affect the shops directly only when the new workshop regime—and the social boundaries of class—that had begun to emerge in the Jeffersonian period matured. Until then, the artisans' disparate religious views provided a rough analogue to their democratic politics, opposed to all men of "insolent morality" who would ratify their presumed social superiority with the Word of God.

And so we return to democracy and egalitarianism, to the artisans' resistance to political and social deference, as a source of unanimity in the trades. Beyond this reverence of equality lay the deeper ideological connections, noted by Boardman and Petheram, that the artisans made between their ideals of the Republic and their ideals of craft. More than egalitarianism alone, it was the ways in which the craftsmen associated politics and craft production that distinguished them as artisan republicans in a city just entering the world of the nineteenth-century workshop and market. To understand what these connections were, we must look

44. Charles Foster, *An Errand of Mercy: The Evangelical United Front, 1790–1837* (Chapel Hill, 1960), 121–77; Adoniram Chandler, *An Oration Delivered before the New York Typographical Society, July 4, 1816* (New York, 1816), 9; Hooper Cumming, *An Oration Commemorative of American Independence Delivered in the Bowery Church, July 5, 1824* (New York, 1824), 19–22. See also Noah, *Address*, 10. On the fire companies, see below, Chapter 7.

again, in more detail, at all of the artisans' regalia—for it was precisely in order to make the connections explicit that the trades maintained an extraordinary series of public ceremonies.[45]

"Articels Emblemattical of Our Trade"

On July 23, 1788, between five and six thousand craftsmen—virtually every artisan in New York City—turned out for a grand procession to support ratification of the Constitution. It was a well-organized political event (a similar parade had been held in Philadelphia two weeks earlier), "pleasing for every Federalist to see," one journalist observed—the first major street demonstration in the city since the Revolution and the emotional highpoint of the Federalist-artisan alliance. It also turned into a celebration of craft, as masters, journeymen, and apprentices marched together, each trade under its own banner, to affirm the artisans' contributions to the city and the benefits to be won with a protective tariff. The display of the blacksmiths, sailors, and ship joiners was typical, headed by a scaled-down model of a frigate (named, appropriately, *Alexander Hamilton*) and featuring a banner that proclaimed: "This federal ship will our commerce revive / And merchants and shipwrights and joiners shall thrive."[46]

Nearly forty years later, and a decade after the celebration of the Treaty of Ghent, the craftsmen joined the procession to celebrate the opening of the Erie Canal. A great deal had changed—among other things, the hero on this day was Gov. DeWitt Clinton, the nephew of Hamilton's archrival in New York, George Clinton—but the crafts' regalia had not. Marching by trade (although a few journeymen's groups marched apart from their masters), the artisans once again honored their arts with ancient symbols and greeted the latest advance for American commerce as a boon to the commonwealth. Once more, nearly all employers and employees turned out, to carry banners (including some that had been used in 1788), to perform craft pageants in mock workshops, and otherwise to praise their arts. The printers' song extolled the typical themes:

> The Art, which enables her sons to aspire
> Beyond all wonders in story
> For an unshackled press is the pillar of fire
> Which lights them to freedom and glory.

45. In turning here to an analysis of parades and rituals, I have been most influenced by the writings of several European historians, above all Agulhon, *Marianne au combat*, and Alain Faure, *Paris carême-prenant: Du carnaval à Paris au XIXe siècle*, 1800–1914 (Paris, 1978). More directly related to the American scene is Alfred F. Young, "Pope's Day, Tarring and Feathering, and Cornet Joyce, Jr." (Unpublished Paper, courtesy of Professor Young). See also Thompson, *Making of the English Working Class*, 424–29.

46. *New York Packet*, June 27, July 22, August 4, 1788; *Independent Journal*, July 23, 1788. On similar festivities in Philadelphia, see Foner, *Tom Paine*, 206–9.

As before, the artisans seized the opportunity to celebrate themselves.[47]
So the trades trooped their colors continually in the early national years.
In 1794, a grand parade of different crafts (now under Republican, not
Federalist, leadership) marched with fife and drum to the Battery and
then, by boat, to Governor's Island, to help reinforce the city's fortifications and demonstrate their displeasure at the Jay Treaty. Similar processions, complete with trade banners, traveled to Brooklyn in the summer of
1814 to work on the Brooklyn fortifications. Independence Day, initiated
by craft groups and the Tammany Society in 1794, assembled masters,
journeymen, and Republican politicians through the 1820s. On a less gran-
diose scale, the trades held exercises with the militia companies each November 25, to honor with "profuse and patriotic jollification" the day in
1783 when the British army evacuated Manhattan. Through the first decade of the nineteenth century, the General Society was almost as preoccupied with ceremony and with public displays of its crest as with its
benevolent and financial projects. Journeymen's groups like the Society of
Shipwrights and Caulkers spent most of the membership's dues on such
items as "a skooner to be carried in procession," "musick at celebration of
the Grand Canal," certificates, badges, ceremonial caulking mallet, and
other "articels emblemattical of our Trade." Special events—laying the
cornerstone of the Mechanics' Institution, dedicating the Apprentices' Library—brought colorful exercises prepared by the General Society.[48]

What are we to make of these demonstrations? Certainly they were
something new on the American scene: although the scrappy evidence left
by eighteenth-century mutual-aid societies suggests that American artisans
had at least some familiarity with older British trade iconography, nothing
that has so far been uncovered shows that the craftsmen in New York or
any other seaboard city held any craft processions or ceremonies prior to
the Revolution. Nor were the early national parades antiquarian curiosi-
ties, staged to honor a distant past: the largest processions, after all, celebrated the artisans' support for economic expansion. Progress, innovation,

47. Colden, Memoir, 213–36, 250–55, 261–62; William L. Stone, Narrative of the
Festivities Observed in Honor of the Completion of the Grand Erie Canal (New York,
1825), 319–28.

48. New York Journal, July 4, 5, 1794; New York Weekly Chronicle, July 9, 1795;
GSMT Minute Book, January 6, 1789, June 7, 1797, March 7, June 6, 1798, January
1, 1800, June 17, 1801, December 4, 1804, July 4, 1807, March 8, 1808, January 9,
1821, January 19, 1823; Thomas Hamilton, Men and Manners in America (London,
1833), I, 59; Minute Book, Society of Shipwrights and Caulkers, NYPL MSS, May
29, June 5, 8, 19, 30, September 14, October 12, 1815, January 22, 1816, February
12, 1818; Bank Book, Union Society of Shipwrights and Caulkers, NYPL MSS, December 8, 1825, May 1, 1826; Edwin P. Kilroe, St. Tammany and the Origin of the
Society of Tammany, or Columbian Order in the City of New York (New York, 1913),
177–83.

and prosperity—these were the artisans' themes, not static traditionalism or corporate deference.[49] With all of their innovations, however, festivities also linked the artisans to long-standing craft ideals, to emblems and images that had grown from the matrix of British guild regulations and that evoked what one historian has called "the shadowy image of a benevolent corporate state."[50] In England many of the outward displays of craft pride—the Lord Mayors' Shows, the banners, the craft pageants, the patron saints—had long since faded or disappeared by the early nineteenth century, victims of the dislocations of capitalist development—but they had not died out completely. In New York, with the winning of independence and the creation of a benevolent republic, the old emblems still seemed appropriate enough to serve as proper representations of the crafts. A full-scale retrieval of British craft ritual ensued. In 1785, when the Mechanics' Committee designed its seal, it borrowed the arm-and-hammer sign used by several London trades as early as the fifteenth century and appropriated the artful slogan of the London blacksmiths. The Constitution procession included several features of an old Lord Mayor's Show: separate trades performed workshop pageants and carried banners that, apart from their political allusions, would have been familiar to any Elizabethan Londoner. The tailors' banner, like those in English parades, depicted Adam and Eve and bore the legend "And They Did Sew Fig Leaves Together." The cordwainers' flag included a view of the good ship *Crispin* arriving in New York harbor. The ship model carried by the joiners and shipwrights may have done Hamilton's heart good; it was also a reprise of a motif dear to seventeenth-century London shipbuilders.[51]

The symbolism survived over the next four decades, to reappear in even grander form in the Erie Canal parade. The journeymen tailors returned to a pastoral image in 1825, with their banner of a "Native" receiving a cloak, above the motto "Naked Was I and Ye Clothed Me." The coopers

49. See Alfred F. Young, "English Plebeian Culture and Eighteenth-Century Political Movements" (Paper delivered to the International Conference on the Origins of Anglo-American Radicalism, New York, October 1980), pt. 3. On survivals of craft culture, see Morris, *Government and Labor*, 135–56, 198–99; Stephen Barto and Paul O. Weinbaum, "Stone Marks in America and Their Origin, 1790–1860" (North Atlantic Region Curatorial Paper, National Parks Service, 1980), 1–4.

50. Thompson, *Making of the English Working Class*, 432.

51. William Hone, *Ancient Mysteries Described* (London, 1823), 255; idem, *The Every-Day Book* (London, 1825–26), I, 1387, 1397–402, 1439–54, II, 470–71, 627–29, 669–76; John Brand, *Observations on Popular Antiquities* (London, 1823), I, 356–67, 408–10; Frederick W. Fairholt, *Lord Mayors' Pageants* (London, 1843–44); Robert W. Malcolmson, *Popular Recreations in English Society, 1700–1850* (Cambridge, 1973), 51–52; John Bromley and Heather Child, *The Armorial Bearings of the Guilds of London* (London, 1960), 15, 22, 79, 86, 262; *New York Packet*, July 8, 11, 22, 1788; *Independent Journal*, July 23, 1788.

carried the same banner they had used in 1788 and erected a platform on which two men and a boy—the conventional trio of master, journeyman, and apprentice—built a large cask. The printers, as before, worked presses and turned out celebratory odes to the day. The master, journeymen, and apprentice combmakers featured a miniature workshop, in which seven men and boys "of the trade," using the latest in simple hand-powered machines, finished 600 combs. Seven other trades performed similar pageants in motion. The hatters carried a picture of their adopted patron with the words "St. Clement—Hats Invented in Paris in 1404." The Bakers' Benefit Society frankly copied its banner from the one presented by Edward II to the London Company of Bakers in 1307. Other insignias, guild heralds and incorporation dates appeared beside more predictable republican images, like the chairmakers' American eagle (Plate 6).[52]

Between innovation and retrieval lay a set of connections between craft and politics spelled out in the banners, speeches, and street dramas. At one level, the ceremonies announced the artisans' determination to be part of the body politic—no longer "meer mechanicks," no longer part of the vague lower and middling sort of the revolutionary mobs, but proud craftsmen, appearing for all to see on important civic occasions, marching in orderly formation up and down lower Broadway with the regalia and tools of their crafts. Apart from their skills, this pride appeared lodged in the social solidarities evoked by the ideal craft communities of "the Trade." Marching together, the employers and employees in each craft formed a symbolic body of their own. To be sure, the independent masters took their rightful place at the head of the artisan order, a position emphasized in 1825 when highly respected masters from the different trades led their respective delegations; nonetheless, each trade stressed its collective harmony, cooperation, and self-respect. Even the most arcane icons contributed to the corporate trade ideal. The biblical allusions in the banners, for example, were no demonstrations of a secret baroque piety; rather, as in the earlier English artisan festivals, they offered each trade a collective identity, sometimes underscored in the banners' mottoes like the coopers' "Love As Brethren" and the cordwainers' "United We Stand."[53]

Just as important were the marchers' contentions that their work was essential to the well-being of all, an integral component in the commonwealth of trade, agriculture, and industry. The tailors' banner, pointed out not only that their labors were as old as Eden or that they were unknown only to "Natives" but also that all God's children need tailors. At times, the artisans advanced what appear to have been residual "precapitalist" ideals about their relationships to their clients as well as about the relations of production: utility—the use value of the handicrafts, and not the

52. Colden, Memoir, 213–38; Stone, Narrative, 372–74.
53. Colden, Memoir, 217, 235.

luxury or special advantages of the artisans' goods—was their central claim for their products, voiced in the name of the trade as a whole rather than as a kind of boastful advertising ploy. As if to summarize their direct services to the city, some delegations to the 1825 march, most notably the printers and combmakers, handed out samples of their work to the throngs of spectators. Several trade emblems, like the chairmakers' picture of a chair with the motto "Rest For the Weary," emphasized both pride in craftsmanship and a collective sense of public service. In all cases, a sense of worthiness prevailed, tied to an idealization of the artisan system of production and distribution quite unlike the entrepreneurial regime that had begun to emerge in the city's workshops. To drive the point home, craftsmen and Jeffersonian politicians at various celebrations noted that they had gathered to celebrate what the masters called "the common bond and mutual sympathy," the "ties and attachments . . . interwoven with the strongest feelings of the heart," that supposedly governed the artisan community.[54]

Linked to the commemorations of "the Trade" was the craftsmen's treatment of politics. Guild heraldry established the antiquity of the crafts but not the craftsmen's attitude toward monarchy; in place of the old holidays and saints' feasts observed in England, the artisans substituted suitably republican red-letter days. Independence Day and Evacuation Day were the most important annual celebrations; even in their occasional ceremonies, the trades tried to assemble on July 4 or November 25, when they would "swear eternal allegiance to the principles of Republicanism." In the processions of 1788 and 1825, patriotic banners billowed beside craft banners; on the Fourth, either an artisan or a Jeffersonian politician delivered an address on the blessings of republican government; through the 1820s, speeches rang with denunciations of Old World luxury and pomp and repeated the contention of an early spokesman that "the feelings expressed by a freeman on an occasion like this are unknown to the subjects of Kings." The craftsmen's grandest efforts celebrated a benevolent republican state—one that would enact tariffs and finance canal building—but also celebrated their own sovereignty over that state. The regalia had royal pedigrees; the artisans themselves were attached to "republican simplicity," "the genius of America" and "just notions of Liberty, founded upon the RIGHTS OF MAN."[55]

These exhortations did not merely displace British loyalties with more

54. Ibid., 215, 220; Mercein, *Address*, 11–12; Noah, *Oration*, 7–8.

55. Eacker, *Oration*, 5; Noah, *Oration*, 12; P[eter] H. Wendover, *National Deliverance: An Oration Delivered in the New Dutch Church in the City of New York on the Fourth of July*, 1806 (New York, 1806), 11; Dr. George Cuming, *An Oration Delivered at the Presbyterian Church on East Rutgers Street before the Tammany, Tailors', Hatters', Hibernian Provident, Masons', Shipwrights', Carpenters', and Columbian Societies* (New York, 1810), 8–9.

patriotic, democratic sentiments; rather, they indicated how thoroughly the tradesmen understood the framework of republican political thought and how they associated the Republic with their conception of "the Trade." Most striking were the ways in which the speakers invoked the key concepts of eighteenth-century American republicanism—independence, virtue, equality, citizenship, and commonwealth (or community)—and explained their meaning for the crafts. Independence signified, in the first place, independence from Britain and the freedom of New Yorkers to ply their arts without foreign interference. "However great our natural advantage," the Reverend Samuel Miller claimed at one of the first artisan festivals, "they would have been in vain had the shackles of British power continued to bind and restrain us." Prior to the Revolution, the editor and General Society member M. M. Noah argued a quarter of a century later, "we saw and felt our dependent state," as "the native ingenuity of our Mechanics was checked"; only after the "legitimate owners of the soil" had reclaimed the city could mechanical genius flourish. Even more, independence connoted *personal* independence, or what John Irving called "independent equality"—the ability of each citizen to think and act free of the restraints of others and of the corrupt privilege so evident abroad. "Suffer no one to DICTATE imperiously what line of conduct you are to pursue," the sailmaker George Warner told the crafts in 1797, "but at the same time let no one be sacrificed on the altar of public opinion for a cordial and liberal expression of his sentiments." Later spokesmen picked up the argument and charted a course of personal independence through the preservation of "the rights of man," and resistance to all attempts to turn American mechanics into "vassals and slaves."[56]

As they spoke of independence, the artisans also shied away from endorsing the pursuit of self-interest for its own sake: each citizen, spokesmen explained, had to be able to place the community's good before his own, exercising what they called, in classical republican style, virtue. Warner made it plain that those who sought personal gain alone, particularly in politics, were "distinct from the general interests of the community," unvirtuous men who would lead America, like the civilizations of old, "on an inalterable course towards despotism, where the dividing line between the rich and poor will be distinctly drawn and the *latter* will be found in a state of dependence on the former." "[L]et virtue be the foundation of distinction," George Eacker concurred a few years later. A proper republic, John Irving declared in 1809, sustained a polity where "those are ex-

56. Samuel Miller, A Sermon Delivered in the New Presbyterian Church, New-York, July the Fourth, 1795, . . . at the Bequest of and before the Mechanic, Tammany, and Democratic Societies, and the Military Officers (New York, 1795), 13; Noah, Oration, 13; Irving, Oration, 20; George James Warner, Means for the Preservation of Liberty (New York, 1797), 14.

alted whose . . . superior virtue entitles them to confidence." Love for America's "splendid monument of political wisdom," Samuel Romaine remarked three years later, required recalling "that virtue is its basis."[57]

These were ideas that came from the Painite tradition and broader currents of republican thought; accordingly, for the artisans, equality and citizenship did not imply a leveled society of absolute economic and social democracy. Not until the late 1820s did propertyless small masters and journeymen express any basic objection to what Mercein called society's "artificial distinctions" of wealth, or the inevitability that these would persist. Nor did the artisans, masters or journeymen, show any interest in promoting the fortunes of the poor, those dependent persons who could easily become the tools of tyrants, men Irving described as "that uniformed class . . . who, like dull weeds, sleep secure at the bottom of the stream." Equality instead connoted political equality, the right of all independent, virtuous citizens—including the artisans—to exercise their will without interference from a nobility of privilege, wealth, or title; citizenship, by extension, stood for men's obligations to exercise their natural political rights. It was in this sense, balancing libertarian ideas of political equality with social duties, that Warner berated those men of honest industry who "considered themselves of TOO LITTLE CONSEQUENCE to the body politic" as unintentional traitors; so, too, it was to equality and citizenship that Irving referred when he extolled the republican polity as one where leaders are "revered as legislators, obeyed as magistrates, but considered as equals."[58]

These familiar republican concepts, on their own, linked the artisans with well-established patterns of American political thought and expression. What made their observations singular were the ways in which they blended American republicanism with the ideals of "the Trade." Even as they marched with other civic associations and celebrated the commonwealth, the artisans diverged from older assumptions that the trades were merely one of many important groups, a deferential estate within a larger social corporation. While they extolled commerce, they expressed misgivings about capital; without denying that prosperity demanded a proper balance between merchants, farmers, and mechanics, the artisans made quite clear that they considered the small shop as the very embodiment of republican values. Contrary to what some New Yorkers believed, Warner told the mechanics' societies, "the possession of riches is not necessarily accompanied by superior understanding or goodness of heart"; indeed, he

57. Warner, *Means*, 13; Eacker, *Oration*, 19; Irving, *Oration*, 20; Samuel B. Romaine, *An Oration Delivered before the Tammany Society, Tailors', Hibernian Provident, Shipwrights', Columbian, Manhattan, and Cordwainers' Societies in the City of New-York on the Fourth Day of July 1812* (New York, 1812), 8.

58. Mercein, *Address*, 18; Irving, *Oration*, 11; Warner, *Means*, 13.

remarked, "the experience of ages confirms that a state of mediocrity is more favorable to them both." Independence would be lost if men of great wealth ruled the Republic since, as the educator and Republican politician Samuel Mitchill (not a poor man himself) indicated, "it is soon discovered that *money is power*, that power gives the possessor of it *importance*, and that *importance begets respect*." Men of relatively little means like the craftsmen were less likely to be seduced by "the studied refinements of luxury" or "the splendid follies of wealth," the mason John Rodman hinted in 1813; the domestic arts were, he thought, "more congenial with the nature of our government and conducive to the general happiness" than any other calling. In sum, an urban variation of the Jeffersonian social theme of the virtuous husbandman emerged, one that fused craft pride and resentment of deference and fear of dependence into a republican celebration of the trades. John Irving offered the image of the artisans as "the very axis of society," in whose hands "must the palladium of our liberty rest." Others stated flatly that the craftsmen's skilled labors facilitated republican politics and exposed aristocratic threats. The printers were especially eager to point out, as George Asbridge told his fellows in 1811, that their trade was "one of the most deadly engines of destruction that can possibly be arrayed against the encroachments of despotic power." Samuel Woodworth's odes to his trade made similar claims, with suggestions that Faust, the printer of legend, was the world's first republican.[59]

The metaphorical association between the Republic and "the Trade" fortified the artisans' egalitarian republicanism. Like the Republic, the crafts themselves reputedly respected individual abilities but also stressed virtuous mutuality and cooperation. Each competent master appeared, in his workshop relations, as the quintessence of independence, free to exercise his virtue uncorrupted; the dependence of journeymen and apprentices—in principle a temporary condition—was tempered by their possession of a skill and graced with the affection and respect of their masters, in what Noah described as a web of "reciprocal" obligation. The workshop, a site of collaborative labor, ideally turned out both handicrafts useful to the public and new independent craftsmen to replenish the ranks of the trades. The masters supposedly lived not solely by the labor of others but also, as in the mock workshops, by their skills and by the sweat of their brows; they along with the skilled employees were precisely the kinds of unselfish, productive men whom the Republic needed, for they neither

59. Warner, *Means*, 13–14; Samuel Mitchill, *Address to the Citizens of New York* (New York, 1800), 21; John Rodman, *An Oration Delivered before the Tammany Society, or Columbian Order, Tailors', Hibernian Provident, Columbian, Cordwainers', and George Clinton Societies* (New York, 1813), 9; Irving, *Oration*, 10–11. Asbridge, *Oration*, 11, 25–26; Chandler, *Oration*, 14–15.

exploited others nor were, in the words of one General Society speaker, "slavishly devoted" to anyone else. Moreover, the artisans' association between craft and politics was a dialectical one: just as the bonds of the craft supported and complemented the Republic, so republicanism, as the artisans interpreted it, enhanced the economic as well as the political position of the crafts. It did not surprise the New Yorkers that British and European craftsmen were "in subjection at the point of a bayonet." Only in republican America, they claimed, where workingmen were citizens, could the artisans hope to protect themselves from the whims of would-be aristocrats; only in a land where virtue and cooperation were prized would the arts be fostered and the connections between masters and employers endure. So corrupt were the Old World monarchies, Eacker noted, that "even with their masters, manly dignity degenerates into haughtiness and sullen pride." It was, by contrast, "in consequence of our Republican form of government," Samuel Berrian intoned in 1815, that "our whole experience has been a series of brilliant improvements and expanding prosperity."[60]

Here, all the strands of artisan political egalitarianism, craft pride, and social commonwealth pulled together. Like other social groups, the artisans sustained a classical republican political language long after what Gordon Wood has described as the death of "classical politics" in America.[61] With that language, the artisans blended the cooperative ethos of "the Trade" with the democratic, libertarian sentiments characteristic of Paine, the artisan committees of the Revolution, and the Democratic Society—all to the point where each was indistinguishable from the other. Adaptation of those long-established ideals did not signal a mass yearning for a static past; repeatedly, the artisans railed against their former economic and political dependence and looked with optimism to a prosperous future. Their vision was egalitarian and suffused with the ethic of the small producer—but not "liberal" or "petit-bourgeois," as the twentieth century understands the terms. It was a vision of a democratic society that balanced individual rights with communal responsibilities—of independent, competent citizens and men who would soon win their competence, whose industry in the pursuit of happiness, as in politics, was undertaken not for personal gain alone but for the public good.

Obviously, the longer the artisans repeated these idealizations, the more they diverged from actual conditions in the shops. At times, the artisans appeared to take account of these disparities by altering their rituals and speeches accordingly, attaching new meanings to the old language. On at least three occasions (and probably more often), individual journeymen's

60. Noah, *Oration*, 17; Eacker, *Oration*, 5-6; Berrian, *Oration*, 27-28.
61. Wood, *Creation of the American Republic*, 606-18.

societies held their own Fourth of July ceremonies independent of their masters, to toast themselves, as the shoemakers did in 1813, as "a useful and intelligent class in society." In the Erie Canal march, five journeymen's groups assembled under their own banners. For their part, the master craftsmen, from about 1815 on, began adding exhortations to entrepreneurship to their glorification of rights and virtue, transforming the very definitions of the familiar terms. "Equality," for M. M. Noah in his 1822 address to the mechanics, also stood for equality of opportunity for men to rise in the world by dint of their own ambitions, talents, and merits. "In large cities," Thomas Mercein told the celebration to honor the Apprentice Library in 1820, "employment and intercourse with the rest of the community are extensive and multifarious, and contracts and responsibilities are constantly entered into"; thus, each artisan had to learn the ways of the countinghouse, to avoid dissipation and follow "the paths of industry and virtue, morality and religion" in order to enlarge his "capacity and knowledge to understand rights and detect errors" in his contractual dealings. Even with these adjustments, however, the festivities preserved at least a semblance of their original purport. Journeymen, even those who celebrated on their own, usually stuck to honoring the Republic, their arts, and the trades. In the Erie Canal parade, at least two of the journeymen's societies saw fit to march side by side with their masters, in joint contingents of "the Trade"; the vast majority of journeymen, including the shoemakers and hatters, performed in the time-honored fashion. The masters still spoke of their obligations to the crafts, still performed in the pageants of 1825, still retained the forms of the republican trades.[62]

In the 1830s, even such ceremonial camaraderie could not be reconstructed; celebrations and symbols reappeared, but to define the rifts of class between masters and journeymen, not to celebrate the harmony of craft. As E. P. Thompson has remarked about similar changes in English craft ritual, this passage from the corporate identity of "the Trade" to the duality of employers' groups and journeymen's unions "takes us into the central experience of the Industrial Revolution."[63] For the moment, however, it is essential to note the power and persistence of craft themes of mutuality and cooperation in early national New York. Despite all that was dissolving the customary social connections, the artisans' egalitarianism remained inseparable from their small producers' ethic. At the dawn of the nineteenth century, with the American Revolution still a fresh memory—to be rehearsed and refought in elections—and with New York's variant of the industrial revolution barely underway, this set of associa-

62. *National Advocate*, March 8, 1813, quoted in Rock, *Artisans of the New Republic*, 141; Colden, *Memoir*; Noah, *Address*, 8; Mercein, *Address*, 17.
63. Thompson, *Making of the English Working Class*, 426.

tions produced the most clearcut definitions of artisan pride and social identity. They remained strong enough to unify the republican trades through the early 1820s, if only for a few days a year.

Republicanism and Conflict

What, then, became of artisan republicanism during those episodes when the harmony celebrated in the mock workshops dissolved into strikes and protests? Evidence about the ideological dimension of these events is scanty, amounting to little more than a few brief newspaper dispatches, some letters, and some courtroom speeches and testimony, only a fraction of it by the artisans themselves. What remains reveals craftsmen struggling to match their artisan republican idealism with their recognition that the trades were changing and, in some cases, had begun to disintegrate. Neither republicanism nor its artisan variant could on its own fully explain or solve the issues raised; even so, artisan republicanism, though tested and at times revised, was not obliterated. This struggle to fit old ideals to new conflicts was most clearly displayed at the trial of the journeymen cordwainers in 1809.

The trial followed one of the many attempts by journeymen in the consumer finishing trades to regulate the composition of the work force. In 1808, members of the Journeymen's Cordwainers' Society, the best-organized in the city, accused the partners James Corwin and Charles Aimes of hiring an elderly nonsociety journeyman and an illegal apprentice, contrary to society regulations. Corwin and Aimes begrudgingly fired the objectionable journeyman but refused to release the boy, and their men walked out. When, soon afterward, other masters agreed to take on Corwin and Aimes's orders, the society called a general strike of the trade and demanded both an end to the masters' collusion and an increase in piece rates. Some twenty master shoemakers, including the city's largest shoe employers, then swore out a complaint against two dozen union leaders, charging them with raising a conspiracy to interfere with trade and deprive the journeyman fired by Corwin and Aimes of his livelihood. By requesting a conspiracy prosecution, the masters hoped to sustain a judgment brought in a similar case in Philadelphia in 1806; at the least, the masters might break the union; at most, they might obtain a de facto legal ban on trade unionism. For their defense, the journeymen managed to acquire the services of the exiled Irish Jacobin and Jeffersonian William Sampson; the prosecution was handled by another Irish Jeffersonian with equally impressive Jacobin credentials, Thomas Addis Emmet, Robert Emmet's brother. Although the prosecution would resort to arguments about the applicability of the common law that were then popular in

Federalist circles, there is no evidence that the trial was a surrogate battle between antilabor Federalists and prolabor Jeffersonians, as historians once supposed; Sampson and his assistants were the only Jeffersonians to come to the journeymen's aid. New social problems, far more perplexing than the ins and outs of party philosophy and politics, prompted the legal debate.[64]

Emmet opened up an attack on the journeymen for violations of both political and economic equality. How, he asked, could the unionists' attempts to coerce their masters and their impositions on the nonsociety journeymen and the shoeless customers be deemed "the mere exercise of individual rights?" More directly, how could the right to strike be considered "sound political economy"? Individual rights, Emmet insisted, were secured by allowing "every man, according to his own will, follow his own pursuits"; by making a combination for their own private benefit, the journeymen had perpetrated the most tyrannical violations of private right. Sampson, lacking any coherent theory of trade unionism but well-schooled in the ambiguities of political economy, tried to demolish the prosecution with the arguments of "the profound and perspicacious Adam Smith." As the defense interpreted him, Smith had proven that master tradesmen were in permanent conspiracy against their workmen, "so much so," Sampson observed, "that it passes unobservable as the natural course of things, which challenges no attention." It was this prior "sordid combination" to oppress the journeymen that led the unionists to organize; their right to do so was questioned, in Sampson's view, only by those smitten by the "superstitious idolatry" of the common law.[65]

Such arguments could not have demonstrated more forcefully that conceptions of labor as a commodity, free and unrestricted in the market, had badly eroded older artisan notions of workshop justice and mutuality, at least among the master shoemakers. The trial's significance, however, rests less in the differences between master and journeyman than in how both sides tried to adapt egalitarian republican politics to a still unfamiliar confrontation: above all, it is the *plasticity* of ideals about individual rights

64. Commons, *Documentary History*, III, 252–385. See also Richard B. Morris, "Criminal Conspiracy and Early Labor Combinations," *PSQ* 52 (1937): 52–57; Marjorie Turner, *The Early American Labor Conspiracy Cases, Their Place in Labor Law: A Reinterpretation* (San Diego, 1967), 172–75 and passim; Ian M. G. Quimby, "The Cordwainers' Protest: A Crisis in American Labor Relations," *Winterthur Portfolio* 3 (1967): 83–101.

65. Commons, *Documentary History*, III, 261–63, 270–78, 328–29. Sampson's use of Smith should not at all be taken as an endorsement of the notion that labor is a commodity; rather, it was much more in keeping with the "benevolist," small-producer ethos that recent scholars have suggested lay at the heart of Smith's enterprise. See Donald Winch, *Adam Smith's Politics: An Essay in Historiographic Revision* (Cambridge, 1978).

that stands out. Compared with the adversaries of the 1830s, the parties of 1809 appear oddly awkward, unsure of where their arguments might lead; it was as if they were improvising for the first time, in the closeness of a New York courtroom, the accusations and appeals that would arouse thousands in the future. Even more, artisan republican standards of commonwealth and independence remained at the heart of the matter. As Emmet explained it, the selfish journeymen had violated not only the masters' market rights but their own duty to the commonwealth, that "tacit compact which all classes reciprocally enter into, that when they have partitioned and distributed among the different occupations . . . they will pursue those occupations so as to contribute to the general happiness." Having been seduced by private interest, they had declared war on public policy and tried to constrain the independence of others, exerting what one prosecution lawyer labelled an "aristocratic and tyrannical control." The journeymen's defense in turn admonished the employers for their hypocrisy and their own unrepublican tyranny. Paradoxically, by his own use of Smith, Sampson tried to undercut the idea that the masters were simply individuals pursuing their rights; as much as ever, he proclaimed, they had collective interests—interests invisible to a casual observer. The problem, Sampson insisted, was that the "rapacity of the masters" had led them to switch their allegiances from the trade to themselves, to violate accepted workshop practices and deny their obligations, in Sampson's phrase, to "do justice by" their apprentices. Even worse, the masters, with the aid of the prosecution, tried to reinforce their position by smuggling aristocratic, unequal laws to America. "[I]s this not repugnant to the rights of man?" Sampson queried. "If it be, is it not repugnant to our constitution? If it be repugnant to our constitution, is it law?"[66]

The trial ended in something of a draw. A guilty verdict was almost assured once the court had rejected defense motions to quash the indictment on the common-law question. In passing sentence, however, Mayor Jacob Radcliff equivocated, claiming that the journeymen's equal rights included "the right to meet and regulate their concerns and to ask for wages, and to work or refuse," but not to deprive their fellow citizens of their rights. He then imposed the light fine of one dollar plus court costs. It was hardly a judgment immediately to squelch journeymen's unions; within six months, the journeymen carpenters had commenced a long and bitter strike for higher wages; in 1811, the cordwainers' society—led by the very men indicted earlier—won a raise in pay with another general strike.[67]

As the tensions in the crafts remained, the artisans in the city's fastest-changing trades continued to adjust their outlooks and their language.

66. Ibid., 279–80, 300, 329.
67. Ibid., 382–85; *American Citizen*, May 3, 1810; People v. James Melvin (1811).

The masters, on several occasions, condemned the selfishness and unreasonableness of journeymen's demands and mixed a liberal interpretation of their market rights with professions of their supposed benevolence and superior knowledge of the conditions in the trades—those ideas proclaimed, in different contexts, by the General Society and the *Mechanics' Gazette.* By 1825, they were on the verge of making Smithian ideas irrevocably their own. Haltingly, meanwhile, the organized journeymen tried to construct a consistent justification for their actions. The union printers' declaration of 1817 on the inevitably opposing interests of masters and journeymen suggested a temporary hardening of distinctions; by the early 1820s, some journeymen had begun to examine the deeper social and economic matrix of their plight. Throughout, however, artisan republicanism provided the journeymen a kind of moral ledger with which to judge their masters and defend themselves. Their new understanding of artisan republicanism surfaced with peculiar force during the carpenters' strike of 1810. The masters, joined by the city's architects and surveyors, adamantly refused to concede their privileges in the face of the "increasing evils and distressing tendency" of the journeymen's militancy; least of all would they grant a standard rate of wages, by which they could no longer decide what to pay journeymen "according to their several abilities and industry." The journeymen replied that they had struck because their "haughty, overbearing" masters—including some "master builders in name only"— had misinterpreted their own interests and those of all carpenters by hiring men below accepted wage rates and by depressing the earnings of all, so that the journeymen could not expect to become masters. Even those employers whose abilities as workmen still held respect had forfeited all allegiance, by riding about in their carriages, building themselves brick homes, and assuming a demeanor that "better fits them to give laws to slaves" than to be master mechanics. The masters had denied both their fellow tradesmen and the Republic and had become paragons of acquisitive corruption; the journeymen struck as free men for republican justice. "Among the inalienable rights of man are life, liberty, and the pursuit of happiness," the journeymen declared:

> By the social contract every class in society ought to be entitled to benefit in proportion to its qualifications. . . . Among the duties which society owes individuals is to grant them just compensation not only for current expenses of livelihood, but to the formation of a fund for the support of that time when nature requires a cessation of work.

After 1825, such thoughts on class, natural rights, just wages, and the proper expectations of "journeymen through life" would help lead organized wage earners to draw even more audacious conclusions—conclusions which stressed individual liberty and moral benevolence but which also took a step beyond the perspicacious Adam Smith.[68]

Artisan Republicanism and the Limits of Bourgeois Individualism

It has long been a fashion among historians of disparate viewpoints to describe American northern society as "bourgeois"—"middle-class," "profit-oriented," and "modern" are other common terms—virtually from the seventeenth century on. Apart, perhaps, from the would-be demesnes of the Hudson Valley landlords and patroons, no real vestiges of feudalism ever developed in this country. With its abundance of land, its great need for initiative, and a population that had fled the authoritarian monarchies of the Old World (so the argument goes), America escaped the social tensions and political economy of Europe. Capitalism arrived with the first shiploads of white men: within the fluctuating limits imposed by London, the yeoman farmers, city merchants, and industrious artisans of the colonies eagerly competed in local and, in some cases, regional markets, exemplars of a competitive and democratic individualism, neither aristocratic landlords nor downtrodden cottiers. Richard Hofstadter, who caught the emptiness as well as the opportunities of this culture, most cogently stated as a "profound truth" that in order to understand early America, one had to envisage a "middle-class world." Early-nineteenth-century economic growth required no great ideological or social changes, but only those "revolutions" in transportation and communication necessary to unleash a pre-existing capitalist spirit, what Hezekiah Niles of *Niles' Review* called, in 1815, "the almost universal ambition to get forward."[69]

In some respects, the artisans of early national New York conformed to these descriptions. Producing for a widening and increasingly competitive market, they could be clever entrepreneurs. The masters, or at least the leading craft entrepreneurs, had proven alive to (if not always adept at) capitalist business practices. Any doubts about the artisans' acquisitiveness would be overturned by the oratory of the General Society or the sign of the cornucopia of dollars that illuminated the peace celebrations of 1815. If any visitors questioned their abilities as businessmen, they had only to drop by Duncan Phyfe's workshop or to observe masters arranging for export of their goods to other cities. If any suspected that the

68. *American Citizen*, May 3, 23, 31, 1810.

69. Richard Hofstadter, *America at 1750: A Social Portrait* (New York, 1971), 131; Niles, quoted in Benson, *Concept of Jacksonian Democracy*, 12. For an intelligent preliminary overview of this literature and its critics, see Edwin G. Burrows, "The Transition Question in Early American History: A Checklist of Recent Books, Articles, and Dissertations," *Radical History Review*, no. 18 (1978): 173–90.

masters and journeymen lacked appreciation of the benefits of commercial expansion, they had only to view the parade in celebration of the Erie Canal.

The "middling" republican politics of the mechanics—with their distrust of the power and culture of New York's nabobs and their lack of sympathy for the dependent poor—also call to mind what C. B. Macpherson has described as the more radical variants of bourgeois possessive individualism. The artisans' praise of their crafts, their resentment of the unskilled, and their attacks on merchant aristocrats and overbearing clergymen, all tempered by a respect for private property, exemplified a belief that independent men of relatively small means were both entitled to full citizenship and best equipped to exercise it. Their democratic assaults on political and religious deference, their professed respect for individual initiative, and their efforts in support of the economic interests of the trades all made them appear champions of those Franklinesque virtues that have long been interpreted as the germ of bourgeois propriety.[70]

Yet the mechanics, with their artisan republicanism, also stood for much more. With a rhetoric rich in the republican language of corruption, equality, and independence, they remained committed to a benevolent hierarchy of skill and the cooperative workshop. Artisan independence conjured up, not a vision of ceaseless, self-interested industry, but a moral order in which all craftsmen would eventually become self-governing, independent, competent masters—an order to match the stonemasons' ditty that they would "steal from no man." Men's energies would be devoted, not to personal ambition or profit alone, but to the commonwealth; in the workshop, mutual obligation and respect—"the strongest ties of the heart"—would prevail; in more public spheres, the craftsmen would insist on their equal rights and exercise their citizenship with a view to preserving the rule of virtue as well as to protecting their collective interests against an eminently corruptible mercantile and financial elite. This fusion of independent liberties and personal sovereignty with social and corporate responsibilities—very akin to what others have called "collective individualism," the core of early American political thought—remained in uneasy and increasingly contradictory relation to the bourgeois tendencies of artisan thinking and to the inescapable fact that with the expansion of the craft economy and the transformation of labor relations, some crafts-

70. C. B. Macpherson, *The Political Theory of Possessive Individualism: Hobbes, to Locke* (Oxford, 1962), 137–60 and passim. See also, however, Winch, *Adam Smith's Politics*, 70–102 and passim. Winch's stress on the libertarian and "affective" features of Smith's political economy helps make sense of American "liberal" thought in this era as well.

men would never escape dependence on their masters and on the wage.[71] Certainly, by 1825, much of what vitiated artisan republicanism had at some point been re-examined, interpreted by some masters as a justification for their own economic well-being and their innovations in the shops, and by the organized journeymen as a defense of their societies and strikes. Yet even then, the trades had to travel some social and ideological distance and to endure more momentous changes in the crafts before they would be governed by the kind of individualism that Tocqueville observed in the 1830s. And as the journeymen shoemakers' and other early strikes portended, this transit would be resisted.

71. Yehoshua Arieli, *Individualism and Nationalism in American Ideology* (Cambridge, Mass., 1964), 178–80, 183–210.

II
The Bastard Workshop,
1825-1850

The usual routine, the work-shop, factory, yard, office, store, desk,
. . . .
The anvil, tongs, hammer, the axe and wedge, the square, mitre, jointer, smoothing-plane,
. . . .
Ship-carpentering, dock-building, fish-curing, ferrying, stone-breaking, flagging on side-walks by flaggers,
. . . .
In them the heft of the heaviest—in them far more than you estimated, and far less also,
. . . .
In them themes, hints, provokers—if not, the whole earth has no themes, hints, provokers, and never had.

Chants Democratic, III, 29

3

Metropolitan Industrialization

Between 1825 and 1850, New York became the most productive manufacturing city in the United States—the metropolitan center of a manufacturing complex that reached as far south as Delaware and that by the late 1840s was probably the fastest-growing large industrial area in the world.[1] These extraordinary developments utterly changed the city's crafts, but in ways very different from those evoked by the usual images of early industrial growth. Huge firms absorbed thousands of craft workers—but did not eradicate the city's small producers. New, highly sophisticated steam-powered machines thundered in the factory districts—but most of New York's largest manufacturers intensified the division of labor already underway rather than invest in labor-saving machinery. Although a few, rapidly growing trades dominated the city's manufacturing economy, hundreds more remained, leaving New York with a manufacturing sector of almost baffling diversity. Then, as now, Americans looked elsewhere to interpret the coming industrial era. Nevertheless, at midcentury the most productive manufacturing center in the nation was neither a mechanized contrivance like Lowell nor a single-trade boomtown like Lynn, but a metropolitan labyrinth of factories and tiny artisan establishments, central workrooms and outworkers' cellars, luxury firms and sweatwork strapping shops.[2]

The physical oddities of the early industrial metropolis should not de-

1. Cochran, *Frontiers of Change*, 112.
2. The most comprehensive study to date of New York manufacturing in this period is August Baer Gold, "A History of Manufacturing in New York City, 1825–1840" (M.A. thesis, Columbia University, 1932). See also Ernst, *Immigrant Life*, 73–83, 87, 90–94.

ceive us: a revolution, and not just an expansion of production, took place in New York's workshops—a revolution that *Hunt's Merchants' Magazine* described in 1849 as very much "in keeping with the spirit of the age."[3] It was a revolution already begun in 1825; although it would continue into the Gilded Age and beyond, by 1850 it had transformed the very meaning of labor and independence in the city's largest trades. It was a revolution that is difficult to describe. We may begin at its source, the ever dominant port.

Metropolitan Manufacturing and the Bastardization of Craft

"Overturn, overturn, overturn! is the maxim of New York," Philip Hone wrote in his diary in 1845. "The very bones of our ancestors are not permitted to lie quiet a quarter of a century and one generation of men seem studious to remove all relics of those who precede them." It is a cry that is still heard in Manhattan—a sudden, early recognition of what two very different German social critics would three years later describe as the constant destructions and reconstructions of a mature bourgeois society, where all that is solid melts into air.[4] Such thoughts did not come to New Yorkers twenty years earlier, when Hone and his colleagues had only begun their careers; the pathos of Hone's entry lies in his inability to comprehend how his own achievements had helped prepare the way for a new, more aggressive order. Something had happened in twenty years to change the very ethos of the city. That something was tied to commerce, but it touched every aspect of New York life.

The economic and political history of New York's commercial growth after 1825 has been described in detail in several studies and need not detain us, but a few points must be stressed. First, the rising dominance of antebellum New York over American trade and finance is still staggering to contemplate. The trade statistics only hint at this growth; so thorough was Manhattan's consolidation of commercial capital and transport routes (first the canals, then the railroads) that one observer was led to suggest, "The great city of New York wields more of the destinies of this great nation than five times the population of any other portion of the country." As New York dominated the nation's commerce, so its mercantile bourgeoisie of merchants, financiers, and lawyers dominated the metropolis, setting the standards of taste and refinement and holding the

---

3. *Hunt's Merchants' Magazine* 20 (1849): 116.
4. Nevins, *Diary of Philip Hone*, 729–30; Karl Marx and Friedrich Engels, "Manifesto of the Communist Party (1848)," in Max Eastman, ed., *Capital, the Communist Manifesto, and Other Writings by Karl Marx* (New York, 1932), 324. See also Marshall Berman, *All That Is Solid Melts into Air: The Experience of Modernity* (New York, 1982), 87–129 and passim.

critical positions of power in both major political parties.[5] Second, with this rapid acceleration of New York trade and with the stunning prosperity of the city as a whole came a further deepening of economic inequality and a general deterioration of living conditions in the poorer and middling neighborhoods, especially in the central Fourth and Sixth wards and along the East Side (Map 2). The statistics on wealth in the 1820s and 1840s mark the steady redistribution to the top, a phenomenon common to all expanding commercial capitals; the grimmer toll of overcrowding, disease, filth, and mortality in New York's poorer and working-class districts reveals the human cost, in a city that ranked second to none as a disaster of laissez-faire urban development.[6] Finally and above all, there was the sheer crush of numbers, as rural migrants and poor immigrants flooded into the port. Between 1825 and 1850, New York's population grew over threefold, making its rate of growth since 1800—750 percent—one of the highest in the world, twice as high as Liverpool's, three times higher than Manchester's, higher than that of all the jerry-built catastrophes of Dickensian lore. Until about 1830, the increase was fed primarily by newcomers from New England and the city's immediate hinterland, by British Protestants, and by a small but growing stream of Irish Catholics and Germans. The tide shifted in the 1830s and shifted again even more sharply in the 1840s with the arrival of tens of thousands of Germans and famine-plagued rural Irish. In just over twenty years, from

5. Albion, *Rise of New York Port*, passim; Taylor, *Transportation Revolution*, 6–9, 178–80, 397–98; Philip Foner, *Business and Slavery: The New York Merchants and the Irrepressible Conflict* (Chapel Hill, 1941), 1–14; Spann, *New Metropolis*, 1–22, 205–41, 281–312; Willis A. Gorman in *Congressional Globe*, 31st Cong., 2d sess., 1851, p. 417, quoted in Spann, *New Metropolis*, 17; Pessen, *Riches, Class, and Power*, 281–301; Brian J. Danforth, "The Influence of Socioeconomic Factors upon Political Behavior: A Quantitative Look at New York City Merchants, 1828–1844" (Ph.D. diss., New York University, 1974), 98–103, 191–92, and passim; Jaher, *Urban Establishment*, 173–250 passim.

6. Pessen, *Riches, Class, and Power*, 33–35; Spann, *New Metropolis*, 67–91; Kaestle, *Evolution of an Urban School System*, 189; Charles E. Rosenberg, *The Cholera Years: The United States in 1832, 1849, and 1866* (Chicago, 1962), 20–29, 57. Alarm about the city's rising mortality rate began in 1835, when the city inspector reported that the number of deaths the preceding year was more than 50 percent higher than it had been in 1833. Average mortality rates for ages 0–4 in New York rose from 85.5 per thousand in 1840–44 to 165.8 in 1850–54; by the mid-1850s, city officials estimated that half of the children born in New York would not live to the age of six. See John A. Duffy, *A History of Public Health in New York City, 1625–1886* (New York, 1968), 578–79. These figures were roughly similar to those gathered in the fastest-growing industrial towns in England in the 1840s; see Thompson, *Making of the English Working Class*, 324–31. The classic contemporary account of New York poverty and overcrowding is John Griscom, *The Sanitary Condition of the Laboring Population of New York* (New York, 1845). On the 1830s, see *Annual Report of Deaths in the City and County of New York for the Year 1834* (New York, 1835), 15–16; on housing, overcrowding, and real-estate development, see Ford, *Slums and Housing*, I, 92–121; Blackmar, "Housing and Property Relations," chaps. 3 and 4.

the early 1830s to the mid-1850s, New York changed from a major seaport where the vast majority of citizens were native born to a metropolis where more than half of the population had been born abroad and where more than four-fifths of the immigrants had come from either Ireland or Germany.[7]

This demographic explosion, coupled with the expansion of the port, set the terms for the emergence of New York's working class (Table 9). The quickening tempo of trade and finance greatly enlarged the number of white-collar clerkships, entrusted mostly to local sons and fresh arrivals from the American countryside who had contacts among the resident merchants. Alongside this new male office-worker group, the number and proportion of unskilled jobs—for dockworkers, draymen, porters, cartmen, day laborers of every kind—rose precipitously, while the growth of middle-class wealth widened the demand for female domestic servants, numerically the city's largest occupation at midcentury. These were the jobs for the city's blacks and the immigrant poor, especially the Irish: by the mid-1850s, more than half of the city's male Irish workers were day laborers or cartmen and about one-quarter of *all* the Irish females in the city were domestic servants.[8]

7. Rosenwaike, *Population of New York City*, 16, 33–54; Ernst, *Immigrant Life*, 20. The period of most intense overall growth coincided with the immigration of the late 1840s:

Year	Population of New York
1825	166,086
1830	197,112
1835	268,389
1840	312,710
1845	371,223
1850	515,547

For figures abroad, see B. R. Mitchell, *European Historical Statistics, 1750–1975* (New York, 1981), 86–89. In England, only Bradford, a singular demographic disaster, even approached New York's growth rate—and Bradford was only one-fifth New York's size.

8. Ernst, *Immigrant Life*, 206–17. On clerks, see Allan S. Horlick, *Country Boys and Merchant Princes: The Social Control of Young Men in New York* (Lewisburg, Pa., 1975). Overall, New York's occupation structure was similar to London's; compare the figures in Table 9 with those compiled for London's largest occupations by Henry Mayhew in 1850:

Occupation	Number
Domestic servants	168,701
Labourers	50,279
Boot and shoemakers	28,574
Tailors and breechesmakers	23,517
Dressmakers and milliners	20,780
Clerks (commercial)	20,417
Carpenters and joiners	18,321
Laundry keepers	16,220
Porters, messengers, and errand boys	13,103
Painters and plumbers	11,517

METROPOLITAN INDUSTRIALIZATION

Less readily understood was the expansion of local manufacturing production, an expansion that left manufacturing and craft workers as the largest sector of New York wage earners (Table 10). At a glance, commercial New York was an even more unlikely manufacturing city in the 1840s than it had been twenty years earlier. Rents in the central districts, already considered high in the 1820s, spiraled with the development of mercantile and transport facilities and with the squeeze for residential space, thus discouraging the building of factories and large central shops in all but a few trades. Manhattan's lack of any harnessable source of waterpower was even more glaring in the 1840s—the great age of American waterpower—than before. The inflow of easily transported manufactured goods from Britain, New England, New Jersey, and the Delaware Valley rendered superfluous the manufacture of numerous goods in New York. In all, New York, like London, might well have seemed, in Dorothy George's phrase, a city that would be passed over by the storm clouds of the industrial revolution.[9] But New York, also like London, had its ever expanding population—amounting to both the largest and most diverse consumer market and the largest concentration of surplus wage labor in the United States. Not only were workers needed to feed, house, and clothe these swarms, no matter how meanly; New York, with its immense labor pool, its credit facilities, its access to prefinished materials from Britain and New England, and its transportation lines, was a superb site for producing finished consumer goods, for local consumption or shipment elsewhere.

The interaction of these limits and incentives to manufacturing led to a uniquely metropolitan pattern of early industrial transformation, one as evident, mutatis mutandis, in mid-nineteenth-century London and Paris as in New York.[10] The chief distinguishing feature of early metropolitan

Morning Chronicle [London], February 4, 1850, in E. P. Thompson and Eileen Yeo, comps., *The Unknown Mayhew* (Harmondsworth, 1975), 274. Discrepancies appear primarily because some categories listed by Mayhew appeared under different headings in the New York census.

9. On rents, see *Niles' Weekly Register* [Baltimore], December 23, 1823; BAAD, December 5, 1831; J. B. D. De Bow, *Industrial Resources, Statistics, etc., of the United States* (New York, 1854); J. Clarence Davies, *The Value of Real Estate in the City of New York* (New York, 1860), 4–5. See also Albion, *Rise of New York Port*, 159–60; Allan R. Pred, *The Spatial Dynamics of U.S. Urban-Industrial Growth, 1800–1914: Interpretive and Theoretical Essays* (Cambridge, Mass., 1966), 155–59.

10. Cf. this account and Gareth Stedman Jones, *Outcast London: A Study in the Relationship of Social Classes in Victorian Society* (Oxford, 1971), 19–32; Peter Hall, *The Industries of London since 1861* (London, 1962); Sally Alexander, "Women's Work in Nineteenth-Century London: A Study of the Years 1820–1850," in *The Rights and Wrongs of Women*, ed. Juliet Mitchell and Ann Oakley (Harmondsworth, 1976), 59–111; Henriette Vanier, *La Mode et ses métiers: Frivolités et luttes des classes, 1830–1870* (Paris, 1960); Christopher H. Johnson, "Economic Change and Artisan

industrialization may be easily summarized: while manufacturing workers remained the largest group of New York wage earners, the established light handicraft industries—especially the consumer finishing trades—along with the building trades remained the most important sectors of the manufacturing economy. There were some important exceptions, those capital-intensive industries for which close proximity to specialized metropolitan markets was imperative, above all iron molding and casting. Other new, heavy urban industries—gas production, fine toolmaking—settled along the East River and at the edge of town; several older ones—brewing, distilling, sugar refining—all flourished and grew with the city's population. Yet while these industries fostered the rise of a significant factory sector in New York, far in advance of most American cities, and while they were important to the metropolitan economy, they employed no more than 10 percent of all New York manufacturing workers and only about 5 percent of all the gainfully employed in the 1850s.[11] As in the Jeffersonian period, the typical manufacturing worker in antebellum New York was not an iron molder or a brewery worker, but a tailor (or tailoress), a carpenter, a shoemaker, a baker—to name only the largest occupations.

Beyond the central importance of the crafts, the main lines of metropolitan industrialization before 1850 were more tangled. In general, manufacturing growth in New York, as elsewhere, entailed a steady increase in the size of individual enterprises, which soon dwarfed the infant manufactories of 1820; in 1850, nearly 600 enterprises hired more than twenty workers each; these firms, in turn, employed most of the manufacturing work force (Table 11). But these figures can be misleading if we equate the rise of large firms with the construction of large factories and the eradication of the city's small producers; in only one major metropolitan craft, printing, did the transitions of the 1830s and 1840s entail swift mechanization. Here, three additional features of early metropolitan industrialization complicated the pattern. First, the luxury and custom trade remained an important one in all branches of consumer production; New

Discontent: The Tailors' History, 1800–1845," in *Revolution and Reaction: 1848 and the Second French Republic*, ed. Roger Price (London, 1977), 87–114; Lees, "Metropolitan Types." There were also numerous broad similarities between early industrialization in New York and lesser commercial cities, as suggested (but not fully elaborated) in William H. Sewell, Jr., "Social Change and the Rise of Working-Class Politics in Nineteenth-Century Marseilles," *P&P*, no. 65 (1974): 75–109; and Gray, *Labour Aristocracy in Nineteenth-Cenutry Edinburgh*.

11. The 1855 census shows that 3.7 percent of the city's manufacturing work force worked in these heavy industries; see Ernst, *Immigrant Life*, 214–17. On iron, *see* Edwin P. Williams, *New York Annual Register for 1830* (New York, 1830), 159; *Niles' Register*, August 27, 1831; J. Leander Bishop, *History of Manufactures from 1608 to 1860* (Philadelphia, 1864), III, 122–36; Albion, *Rise of New York Port*, 148–51; Gold, "Manufacturing," 44–48. On sugar refining, see New York *Daily Tribune*, August 30, 1853; on the gas works, see Louis Stotz, *History of the Gas Industry* (n.d., n.p.), 20–50, 118.

York, after all, boasted the wealthiest elite market in the country, one that the Virginian George Fitzhugh (never one to praise the North lightly) would declare demanded "the most in skill and ability."[12] In· these branches of even the most rapidly industrializing trades, the artisanal conventions and small-shop production continued. Second, some entire trades grew enormously without significantly changing their production processes. These included those crafts that were tied exclusively to the local consumer market—above all the food preparation trades—as well as those maritime trades that still required highly skilled hands. Finally, and most important, most of the city's leading craft entrepreneurs, in line with the limits and incentives of the port, relied on an intensified division of labor and one or another form of out-of-shop contracting—innovations usually treated by historians as "transitional" or "proto-industrial" in character—to cut their costs and to multiply output. These arrangements varied from trade to trade, from urban outwork to garret-shop contracting, but the logic was always roughly the same: manufacturers, having subdivided their work into its minute details, relied on one of several kinds of underpaid worker—debased artisans, garret-shop hands, or outworkers—to perform as much of their labor as possible. In effect, they extended the innovations and the dilution of craft that had begun before 1825, but they did so on a far grander scale and with far more unsettling results. By 1850, this process of subdivision and putting-out had advanced to the point that most of the city's leading trades could barely be called crafts at all, even though some workers still clung to the appellations "mechanic" and "journeyman." In their place arose a bastard artisan system, one that would remain at the heart of New York manufacturing, even after the introduction of machines to some of the consumer finishing trades, through the age of Jacob Riis and well into the twentieth century.[13]

It was the ascendancy of this bastard system, along with the multiplicity of New York markets and the precocious mechanization of select sectors of the manufacturing economy, that was chiefly responsible for the proliferation of so many different kinds of work settings throughout Manhattan between 1825 and 1850 (Table 11). Of these, the factories re-

12. George Fitzhugh, "The Republic of New York," De Bow's Review 29 (1861): 181–87.

13. On "proto-industrialization," see Franklin F. Mendels, "Proto-Industrialization: The First Phase of the Industrialization Process," JEH, 32 (1972): 241–61; Eric J. Hobsbawm, "The Formation of the Industrial Working Class: Some Problems," 3e Conférence Internationale d'Histoire Economique, Congrès et Colloques, vol. 1 (The Hague, 1965), 176–77. On the interpenetrations of "proto-industrial" and "industrial" forms, see also Sidney Pollard, The Genesis of Modern Management: A Study of the Industrial Revolution in Great Britain (Cambridge, Mass., 1965), 30–47; Samuel, "Workshop of the World." On the New York manufacturing economy after 1870, see Moses Rischin, The Promised City: New York's Jews, 1870–1914 (Cambridge, Mass., 1961), 53–75.

mained of secondary importance; indeed, although a few New York trades mechanized very early, factory production was virtually nonexistent in New York in 1850 outside of the heavy industries, some small segments of the building trades, and in the book and periodical branches of the printing trades. In these places only did New York workers experience some approximation to the conditions of Lowell and Manchester, with their strictly enforced work rules, the constant surveillance of the patrolling foreman, and the unending din of the power machines. Even then, it was only an approximation: although the factories employed hundreds of hands, many, possibly a majority, were either highly skilled workers (for example, the most skilled compositors in the printing plants) or strictly manual laborers (for example, packers and delivery men); by no means did they constitute an undifferentiated mass of semiskilled factory operatives.[14]

Related to the factories but far better suited to New York's cramped conditions were the city's small mechanized workshops, which gathered between three and twenty workers each, to labor (if only part-time) on machinery ranging from the most primitive power saws to elaborate distilling equipment (Table 12). A few of the city's breweries and distilleries were in this category, as were some printing and engraving firms; the overall proportion of these enterprises, however, was small, and the proportion of wage earners who worked in them even smaller. Unfortunately, we know next to nothing about how work proceeded in these places—but it certainly would be mistaken to regard them, as a group, as either minifactories or the most exploitative workshops. Most employed fewer than fifteen workers each. Apart from the primitive strapping shops in the building trades, most tended to pay wages above the average for manufacturing workers. Above all, most were in the newer trades created by the industrial revolution—machine making, precision toolmaking, and the like—and were geared to specialized, flexible markets and not to mass production. Despite the presence of labor-saving machinery, a great deal of the work in these firms required the highest degrees of skill; indeed, wage earners in some of these trades remained among the most skilled workers in the country until well into the second half of the nineteenth century, even after production had moved into factories.[15]

14. The most detailed contemporary account of a New York factory describes the operations in the Harper Brothers printing office: Jacob Abbott, *The Harper Establishment* (New York, 1855). The importance of this segmented work force to any understanding of the uneven nature of industrial capitalist growth is explored in depth in Samuel, "Workshop of the World."

15. On the persistence of craft in one of the most important of these trades, machine production, see David Montgomery, *Workers' Control in America: Studies in the History of Work, Technology, and Labor Struggles* (New York, 1979), 9–31.

The manufactories and outwork manufactories were the headquarters of the bastard artisan system. The manufactory may be thought of as a machineless factory—defined here as a concentration of more than twenty workers, each of whom performed the old handicraft tasks in a strictly subdivided routine. As in the factories, manufactory work was closely supervised: the difference was that manufactory workers were literally debased artisans, men (for the most part) who completed only a portion of the labor that skilled journeymen used to do on their own. The outwork manufactories—the largest employers in the city—operated differently: only the most skilled jobs were completed on the premises (although again, as in the manufactories, in a subdivided regime); the bulk of the semiskilled assembly work was put out, either to contractors or directly to outworkers. The census records do not reveal the ratio of "in-shop" workers to outworkers in these enterprises, but a few existing reports on major clothing firms suggest that it was extremely low, perhaps one "inside" hand to every fifty outworkers. A conservative estimate suggests that while almost half of the city's craft workers were employed in outwork manufactories, only about 5.0 percent were "in-shop" workers; the rest—46.3 percent of all the city's craft workers—were outworkers.[16]

It was in the remaining work places—all small, all unmechanized—that most craft workers actually earned their livings. The small neighborhood shops—still the largest group of *shops* in New York in 1850—included the remaining custom firms in the most rapidly industrializing trades (fine shoemaking, independent custom tailoring) as well as those firms in trades relatively unaffected by bastardization and dilution of skill, like blacksmithing and butchering. Garret shops were slightly larger and were usually tied to the bastard system. Watched over by small masters and former journeymen, most garret workers either completed outwork for the manufacturers or prepared a single line of product to be sold off in bulk to wholesalers and local retailers. In either case, they worked in a divided regime according to piece rates set by the garret masters, who in turn adjusted their wages to suit the rates set by their patrons. Finally, there were the outworkers' homes—manufacturing sites unrecorded as such in the census—where entire families and groups of friends toiled at the assembly jobs handed to them by the manufacturers or contractors.[17]

This, then, was the New York manufacturing cityscape at midcentury, with its immense diversity of scale and its complex middle range of journeymen, contractors, small masters, and independent producers bridging

16. See *Hunt's Merchants' Magazine* 20 (1849): 347–48. Figures computed from the 1850 census.

17. The best contemporary descriptions of garret-shop conditions appear in George G. Foster, *New York Naked* (New York, 185?), 141–42; Edwin T. Freedley, *Leading Pursuits and Leading Men* (Philadelphia, 1856) 83–84; *Tribune*, November 15, 1845.

the gap between the largest manufacturer and the lowliest outwork hand. It was not, contrary to the most cataclysmic images of the early industrial revolution, a setting where all opportunity had been destroyed by invading merchant capitalists—where all artisans were plunged into the ranks of proletarianized wage labor. As Frederic Cople Jaher has pointed out, New York's commercial bourgeoisie had very little to do directly with the expansion of local manufacturing, apart from providing craft entrepreneurs with credit. Rather, with some important exceptions in the clothing trades, it was the city's leading master craftsmen who, after transforming their own operations or rising through the ranks of another's, came to dominate the manufacturing elite. Some did spectacularly well, meriting inclusion in lists of the city's wealthiest men; other masters made solid, if not outstanding, fortunes. They were not, to be sure, any more prominent in the merchant-dominated New York elite in 1850 than the old master craftsmen had been in the Jeffersonian period; a recent study by Edward Pessen indicates that the proportion of upper-class wealth held by manufacturers actually declined slightly between 1828 and 1845. Nevertheless, the craft entrepreneurs of Duncan Phyfe's generation and the one that followed remained an important presence in the city, both in the manufactories and workshops and in various "mechanics'" associations, including the General Society.[18] Similarly, small masters were still numerous, both in the fastest-changing trades and in those in which the artisan system persisted; as the census figures attest (Table 13), small masters, garret masters, and petty manufacturers still constituted the great majority of employers in 1850. As for the journeymen, not all were consigned to perpetual dependence, even in the most bastardized trades; the minuscule capital requirements necessary to set up as a contractor or a small master

18. Jaher, *Urban Establishment*, 199–200; Moses Y. Beach, *Wealth and Biography of the Wealthy Citizens of New York City*, 5th ed. (New York, 1845), passim, listings for Thomas Addison, Stephen Allen, George Arcularius, Robert Bache, Benjamin Brandreth, George Bruce, David Bryson, Richard F. Carman, Edwin B. Clayton, John Conger, Francis Cooper, Jacob Cram, Bersilla Deming, Samuel Demilt, Daniel Fanshaw, William W. Galatian, Jacob P. Giraud, Richard K. Haight, George W. Hatch, Edward R. Jones, Shepard Knapp, Benjamin Marshall, Michael Miller, Richard Mortimer, Anson G. Phelps, Duncan Phyfe, Jesse Scofield, Benjamin Stephens, Samuel St. John, Robert C. Stuart, John Targee, Samuel Thompson, Abraham Van Nest, James N. Wells, Abner Weyman; Edward Pessen, "The Wealthiest New Yorkers of the Jacksonian Era: A New List," *N-YHSQ* 54 (1970): 145–71; idem, *Riches, Class, and Power*, 47–49; Earle and Congdon, *Annals*, 358–415; New York Trade Agency Reports, 1851, N-YHS MSS; Dun and Company Reports, vol. 449, Baker Library, Harvard University; Elizabeth Ingerman, ed., "Personal Experiences of an Old New York Cabinetmaker," *Antiques* 84 (1963): 576–80. The point here is not to dispute Pessen's criticisms of the flaws in Beach's pamphlets and the directories (Edward Pessen, "The Occupations of the Antebellum Rich: A Misleading Clue to the Sources and Extent of Their Wealth," *Historical Methods Newsletter* 5 (1972): 49–52), or his contention that the mercantile and professional sectors retained command over elite wealth; it is only to note that some manufacturers made fortunes as well.

in the most debased crafts probably made it easier than ever, at least in principle, for journeymen to strike off on their own. Those who remained wage earners could, at least theoretically, vie for the more privileged posts in the custom shops and outwork manufactories.

Balanced against these abstract opportunities were the harsher realities of manufacturing work and the market for most craft workers and small masters. Access to capital, although widened greatly in the antebellum period, was not equal; nor was "upward mobility" a matter of succeeding in a free and impartial market. Bank committees closely scrutinized all requests for credit and discounted paper and naturally served those they knew to be good risks; Duncan Phyfe and his sons (still leaders of their trade in the 1840s) had a much easier time adding to their businesses than did unknowns entering the field with a few hundred dollars in assets.[19] Not surprisingly, the distribution of capital among the city's masters in 1850 was extremely uneven.[20] The deteriorating situation of the mass of craft workers, meanwhile, may be approached indirectly by examining some rudimentary statistics. First, there can be little question that average real wages fell in the city's major trades in the 1830s and 1840s. The entire logic of the bastard artisan system was based on the premise that employers could expand production by reducing their wage bills. While a small elite of workers was well paid, most men and virtually all women worked at piece rates that brought mediocre—for some, abysmal—incomes. The wage figures recorded in the census of 1850 suggest the overall effects of this downward pressure. In 1853, a report in the New York *Times* estimated that the minimal budget for a family of four (with the barest allowance for medical expenses) came to $600.00 per year. After adjustments for inflation, this would mean that a minimum family budget in 1850 was about 28 percent higher than the minimum for a family of *five* during the Jeffersonian period. According to the 1850 census, however, the average annual income for male workers in the trades was almost exactly $300.00, three-fifths of the minimum, and close to the rates paid *inferior* journeymen between 1800 and 1820 (Table 14). Even male workers in the best-paid of the major trades earned on the average only close to the estimated family minimum.[21]

Under the circumstances, male craft workers resorted to all sorts of

19. For details of the banking system and its partiality, see James S. Gibbons, *The Banks of New York* (New York, 1859), esp. 26–69.

20. Looking at the same trades sampled in 1816 in the 1850 census, we find the top tenth of all firms controlled 29.5 percent of total capital invested, while the bottom half controlled only 3.1 percent.

21. The figure for 1850 was derived by adjusting the 1853 figure (*Times*, November 8, 1853) according to the New York price figures in Arthur H. Cole, *Wholesale Commodity Prices in the United States* (Cambridge, Mass., 1938). Cf. Laurie, *Working People of Philadelphia*, 10–12.

adjustments to make ends meet, from cutting their purchases of food to scavenging; those female craft workers who had no man's income to help out—widows, young women with small children, the flood of country girls who came to New York in the 1830s and 1840s—faced an even greater crush to earn a bare subsistence.[22] The most common resolution was to rely on a spouse, children, other kin, or boarders for extra income. A simple random sample of 120 households in the lowly Fourth and Seventh wards in 1855, though tiny, hints at an emerging pattern. Of all the male "artisans"—employers and workers—located, 28.1 percent relied on some form of multiple-income arrangement, 22.5 percent supported a family on their own, and 49.4 percent were boarders. Half of the women craft workers without men in their households (45.2 percent of the women craft workers located) relied in part on the earnings of others. As much as the work itself and as much as the different standards of housing and income, the ubiquity of these arrangements (as well as those family-shop households not accounted for in the census), coupled with the rise of a "double-split" market in female labor (a large portion of it taken by women without men), set New York's workers apart from both the middle-class experience and the American Victorian image of the domestic sphere.[23]

Additional demographic evidence hints at how work in the leading trades had become a labor for the very poor. A clear sign of a severe depression in working conditions in 1850 was the presence of women; overall, women constituted about one-third of New York's manufacturing work force (Table 14) and their proportional numbers in the leading apparel trades, where the vast majority were outworkers, ranged from one-quarter to four-fifths.[24] The changing ethnic structure of the trades in the middle and late 1840s also offers some clues. A significant number of New York immigrants before 1850 were trained artisans; the Germans, in particular, included thousands of skilled men in the woodworking and food preparation trades. But so, too, as work was divided and put out, did

22. Stansell, "Women of the Laboring Poor," 57–75; New York Association for Improving the Condition of the Poor, First Annual Report, 1–8 and passim.

23. On the family economy and early industrialization, see Groneman, " 'Bloody Ould Sixth,' " 83–95; and Tilly and Scott, Women, Work, and Family. The sample represents 10 percent of all households in the Fourth Election District, Fourth Ward, and the Seventh Election District, Seventh Ward, 1855 census. Unfortunately, the 1850 census does not provide a breakdown on the ages of women workers. In the 1855 sample, however, 44.0 percent of all women workers were over the age of twenty-five—suggesting that the female labor force was not composed only of young women.

Carol Groneman (" 'Bloody Ould Sixth,' " 125–26) finds that in 1855 it was particularly common for Irish working-class wives to work for wages; she computed that, in all, 33.6 percent of all Irish "artisan" households in the Sixth Ward included a working wife. Almost all the women workers in the 1855 sample (93.2 percent) either lived in households headed by immigrants or were immigrant live-in domestics.

24. Computed from 1850 census.

a large share of underpaid work fall to the least-skilled, destitute immigrants (particularly the Irish) who would work for whatever price they could get: the Germans in cabinetmaking, the Irish in stone cutting and masonry, both groups in tailoring. That over three-quarters of the workers in the largest trades were immigrants (nearly half of them Irish) in 1855 —a year when about half the city's population had been born abroad—suggests further how New York manufacturing work had become underpaid labor (Table 15). That these immigrants (especially the Irish) tended to cluster in the largest and most fractured consumer finishing and building crafts makes the point even more clearly.[25]

But these figures are suggestive at best; even if they were more precise, they would not disclose how metropolitan industrialization transformed the social relations of production, transformations that affected everyone— large employers, small masters, and every variety of wage earner—in different ways. Any understanding of these changing social relations in turn requires a closer look at specific trades. No two New York crafts industrialized in exactly the same manner or at the same pace; some barely changed at all. It was this lack of uniformity in the social experience of New York's workers and employers that distinguished the metropolis from the most famous early industrial towns before 1850. It would prove a critical factor in shaping the contours of metropolitan class formation and class conflict in the 1830s and 1840s.

The Sweated Trades: Clothing, Shoes, and Furniture

In 1845, the New York *Daily Tribune* prepared a series of reports on the condition of labor in New York. What the *Tribune* reporters found shocked them, and they groped for explanations—especially to account for the outrageous underbidding and exploitation that riddled the city's largest trades. A few years later, after he had read the works of the greatest urban journalist of the age, a *Tribune* correspondent named George Foster had found the right term: it was "sweating," "the accursed system . . . so thoroughly exposed in the recent investigations of Mr. Mayhew in the 'Morning Chronicle,' " a system that had come to prevail "proportionally to as great an extent in this city as in London."[26] One or another variation of sweating emerged in almost all of New York's early industrial

25. Ernst, *Immigrant Life*, 214–18. Some 55.9 percent of all immigrant workers in 1855 worked either as domestic servants (and in related jobs), laborers, clothing workers, or shoeworkers. Some 73.0 percent of all Irish workers worked in these categories.

26. Foster, *New York Naked*, 141–42. On Foster, see George Rogers Taylor, "Gaslight Foster: A New York 'Journeyman Journalist' at Mid-Century," *NYH* 58 (1977): 297–312.

trades. It arose in its purest forms in the consumer finishing trades, and most notoriously in the production of clothing.

It took only ten years, from 1825 to 1835, for New York's clothing revolution to conquer the local market; by 1850, it had created and captured the lion's share of a national trade in ready-made clothes for men. The original instigators were the city's cloth wholesalers, auctioneers, and jobbers, whose command of the English import market and broadening avenues to New England invited further adaptation and expansion of the contracting schemes of the early slopshop entrepreneurs. Their success, and that of the master tailors turned manufacturers whom they supplied with cloth and credit, was neither an act of Providence nor an inevitable working-out of the growth of commerce. Of all of New York's middlemen and manufacturers, the clothiers were the most astute at perfecting aggressive merchandizing methods; more important, it was the clothiers who first mastered the art of extending liberal credit to local retailers and country dealers, to expand their own contacts and squeeze their competitors in other cities (and smaller New York dealers) out of the market. By 1835, they had turned the New York trade in ready-mades into one of the nation's largest local industries, with some firms employing between three and five hundred hands each. A large portion of their output was for the "cheap" trade—in precut apparel for southern customers (as well as the "Negro cottons" for southern slaves), dungarees and hickory shirts for western farmers and miners, and shoddy clothing for the urban poor. Beginning in the early 1830s, the clothiers also entered the respectable market, introducing superior lines, fiercely promoted by the jobbers and retailers, for clerks, shopkeepers, and wealthy patrons who lacked the time or money to patronize a custom tailor. There was some initial resistance to this noncustom work among the most cosmopolitan customers—but by the late 1840s the clothiers had changed people's minds. In 1849, a breathless report in *Hunt's* noted with admiration that the clothing of one ready-made firm was "adapted to all markets and for all classes of men, from the humblest laborer to the fashionable gentleman." With this democratization of product and the continued growth of the southern market, the New York clothing trade became an antebellum manufacturing giant. By 1850, the largest New York firms hired as many as five thousand tailors and seamstresses to turn out goods "with a degree of precision that would astonish the negligent observer."[27]

27. Fred Mitchell Jones, *Middlemen in the Domestic Trade of the United States, 1800–1860* (Urbana, 1937), 11, 17, and passim; Feldman, *Fit for Men*, 14–18, 25–34, 77–78, 93–94; Bertram Wyatt-Brown, *Lewis Tappan and the Evangelical War Against Slavery* (Cleveland, 1969), 226–47; Thomas Kettell, "Clothing Manufacture," in *Eighty Years' Progress in the United States*, [ed. C. L. Flint et al.] (Hartford, 1868), I, 309, 313–15; John C. Gobright, *The Union Sketch-Book* (New York, 1861), 40–41; *Hunt's*

The rise of the ready-mades metamorphosed New York tailoring at every level of production. Some of the old-fashioned master craftsmen did survive, largely in the fancy trade: New York business directories from the 1850s still boasted of Broadway's rows of custom fitters and gentlemen tailors. After about 1830, however, even the finest custom masters began to feel the competitive pinch. Some large custom firms like Brooks Brothers' entered the ready-made market for themselves and divided their shops into separate departments for custom work and the cheaper lines; as early as 1835, master tailors' advertisements stressed the availability of ready-mades as much as the skills of the proprietor and his journeymen. Some small custom masters who lacked the funds to finance a ready-made operation set aside defective work and tried to sell it off as "precut." Others went to work for the manufacturers, either as foremen or as semi-independent retailers, vending a specific firm's ready-mades and doing a bit of custom tailoring on their own. A few of these men went on to become large employers themselves; they, and the clothing merchants, oversaw not enlarged craft firms but entirely new kinds of enterprises.[28]

The focal point of the clothing outwork system was the New York version of the central shop—often an attractive structure when seen from the street, its shapely lines and graceful columns beckoning customers to inspect the stock (Plate 7). Once inside, a patron would see only the ample stores and the retinue of clerks; behind the scenes, the elite of the clothing work force, the in-shop cutters, prepared the predesigned patterns. The head cutters, the overseers of that elite, numbered about fifty in all in the city. With an average annual income of between $1,000 and $1,500 each, they were probably the best-paid craft workers in New York. Certainly they were the most privileged. Apart from their power to discipline workers, the head cutters (sometimes called "piece masters") were in charge of giving out all work to the journeymen, outworkers, and contractors. On the basis of their appraisal—or whims—a cutter or stitcher could earn a decent

Merchants' Magazine 20 (1849): 116, 347-48; 50 (1864): 233. New York's leading clothiers—C. T. Longstreet and S. H. Hanford among them—were merchant capitalists who entered the trade from the outside. They were not, however, alone. The Brooks brothers' success was one of several stories of custom tailors who adapted to the new regime; at least some (albeit, proportionally, a minuscule number) of the smaller men went on to become prominent manufacturers, such as Sylvanus B. Stillwell, a Long Island tailor who, thanks to a friendship struck with the New Orleans merchant H. B. Montross, built a major firm dealing to the southern trade. See Feldman, *Fit for Men*, 30-34, 41-49.

28. Measurement and Account Books, Unidentified master tailor, New York City, 1827-40, N-YHS MSS; Feldman, *Fit for Men*, 77-78, 82-83; Edwin Williams, *The New York Annual Register* (New York, 1836), 360; Kettell, "Clothing Manufacture," 309-15. On Brooks Brothers, see Brooks Brothers, Inc., *Brooks Brothers Centenary, 1818-1918* (New York, 1918), 11-25.

living or an excellent one. Impartiality in these matters was not among
the head cutter's virtues. "Generally," the *Tribune* reported, "he has his
favorites, perhaps a brother, or cousin, or a particular friend, who gets the
'cream of the shop' and is thus frequently able to make $30 or $40 per
week." With their incomes, with their close control over the daily operations and the lives of their subordinates, and with the confidence of their
manufacturer-employers, head cutters could reasonably expect one day to
open their own businesses.[29]

The cutters enjoyed relatively high wages (roughly $10 to $12 per week)
and regular employment, but none of the foremen's powers. Rapid, regular
work schedules prevailed in the cutting rooms. At the Devlin and Brothers'
firm, cutters were divided into bureaus for coats, pants, vests, and trim-
mings, while the entire production process, one reporter observed, "was
reduced to a system," in which every piece of work had its own number
and a ticket with the workman's name. Emphasis fell on speed and
accuracy in cutting predetermined designs; "Southern-trade cutting," a
term synonymous with rapid rather than artful work, was the most common task in New York's major clothing firms at least as early as the mid-
1830s. Any slip, momentary slowdown, or simple disagreement with the
foreman could deprive a cutter of the best work in the shop; if he could
not adjust to the pace, he was fired.[30]

From the cutting rooms (again, out of sight of the customers), the head
cutter or piece master distributed the cut cloth to the outworkers and contractors, and it was here that the worst depredations of sweating began. A
variety of outwork schemes existed. While most contractors were small
masters unable to maintain their own shops, or journeymen looking for

29. *Daily Tribune,* November 15, 1845; *Hunt's Merchants' Magazine* 20 (1849): 116.
See also Dun and Bradstreet Collection, vol. 449, Baker Library, Harvard University,
for numerous listings of successful clothing entrepreneurs. Some manufacturers hired
their sons or other close relatives as head cutters, both to protect their own interests
and to introduce the younger men to their businesses. In the 1840s, for example,
William Scofield worked as a cutter for his father, Jesse; in 1855, young Scofield had
assumed direction of the firm and was one of the wealthiest clothiers in the city. See
Beach, *Wealth,* 28; and idem, *Wealth and Biography of New York,* 10th ed. (New
York, 1855), 65.
The progress of James Shepherd illustrates the rise of a head cutter with no apparent
family connections to the trade. In the mid-1840s, Shepherd began work as the head
cutter at Jacob Vanderbilt's small clothing manufactory. By 1850, he was on his own,
the master of a custom and ready-made shop endowed with $2,000 in capital, the
employer to eight men and seven women—a "worthy and intelligent man," according
to credit-agency reports, whose business, though small, had a promising future. See
New York Trade Agency Reports, Shepherd, N-YHS MSS.
30. *Hunt's Merchants' Magazine* 20 (1849): 116, 346, 348; Feldman, *Fit for Men,*
79. For a sense of the degree of precision involved in cutting by the 1840s, see William
H. Stinemets, *A Complete and Permanent System of Cutting All Kinds of Garments
to Fit the Human Form* (New York, 1843).

the surest road to independence, some cutters and in-shop journeymen also managed to subcontract a portion of their work on the sly. Major firms dealt directly with outworkers. In all cases, the system invited brutal competition and a successive lowering of outwork piece rates. At every level of the contracting network, profits came from the difference between the rates the contractors and manufacturers received and the money they paid out for overhead and labor. Two factors turned these arrangements into a matrix of unremitting exploitation: first, the successive bidding by the contractors for manufacturers' orders (as well as the competition between manufacturers) depressed the contractors' income; second, the reliance of the entire trade on credit buying by retailers and country dealers prompted postponement of payment to all workers until finished work was done—and, hence, chronic shortages of cash. The result: employers steadily reduced the rates they paid their hands and often avoided paying them at all for as long as possible. To middle-class reformers, the great villain of the system was the contractor himself, the "sweater," the "remorseless sharper and shaver," who in league with the cruel landlord fed greedily on the labor of poor women and degraded journeymen (Plate 8). But the contractors and manufacturers had little choice in the matter, as they tried to underbid their competitors and survive on a wafer-thin margin of credit. "If they were all the purest of philanthropists," the *Tribune* admitted in 1845, "they could not raise the wages of their seamstresses to anything like a living price." Hounded by their creditors, hunted by the specter of late payment and bankruptcy, the contractors and garret masters lived an existence in which concern for one's workers was a liability and in which callousness (and, in some recorded cases, outright cruelty) became a way of life. Some were not above underhanded tricks to earn the extra dollar (the most widespread complaints concerned contractors who withheld wages on the pretense that an outworker's handiwork was not of the proper quality); all maintained their independence from the only source available to them, the underpaid labor of the outworkers and garret hands.[31]

The sufferings of the outwork and garret-shop hands—the vast majority of clothing-trade workers—taxed the imaginations of even the most sentimental American Victorians; if the reformers' accounts sometimes reduced a complex situation to a moral fable, they in no way falsified the clothing workers' conditions. All pretensions to craft vanished in the outwork system; with the availability of so much cheap wage labor, formal apprenticing and a regular price book had disappeared by 1845. At any given moment

31. *Tribune*, March 7, 1845; *New York Herald*, June 7, 1853; Jesse Eliphalet Pope, *The Clothing Industry in New York* (Columbia, Mo., 1905), 12; Foster, *New York Naked*, 142.

in the 1830s and 1840s, the underbidding in the contracting network could depress outwork and garret-shop piece rates so low that stitchers had to work up to sixteen hours a day to maintain the meanest of living standards: in 1850, some of the largest southern-trade clothing firms in the Second Ward paid their *male* workers, on the average, well below subsistence wages. Housing was difficult to come by and could amount to no more than a cellar dwelling or a two-room flat, shared with two or more families; single men crammed into outwork boardinghouses. During slack seasons or a bad turn in trade, the clothing workers struggled harder to make ends meet, with a combination of odd jobs, charity relief, and the starchiest kinds of cheap food. Poor journeymen tailors had little recourse but to sweat themselves and their families or, if they were single, to strike informal arrangements with girls and widows to work beside them, while they handled the negotiations with the head cutters or contractors: as a German immigrant later recalled, one New York adage from the 1850s ran, "A tailor is worth nothing without a wife and very often a child." The seamstresses and tailors' wives—consigned the most wearisome work (shirt sewing worst of all) and subjected to the bullying and occasional sexual abuse of the contractors—bore the most blatant exploitation; the men, working either as petty contractors or the patresfamilias of the family shops, enjoyed, by comparison, a measure of independence—but only that, as unionists noted in the 1850s.[32] By themselves, such conditions were difficult; they were aggravated by the tendency for outwork and garret-shop wages to diminish further as workers tried to increase their earnings by intensifying their labor and by taking on larger lots of work, thus causing short-term gluts in the labor market and still lower piece rates—what Mayhew elaborated as the principle that "overwork makes for underpayment." Even more, the rise of the ready-mades accentuated the seasonal fluctuations in labor demand. In April and October, when manufacturers prepared for the spring and fall sales seasons, regular work was relatively plentiful; for the rest of the year, as much as two-thirds of the clothing work force had to string together temporary work in an already overstocked labor market.[33]

Life for most New York shoeworkers was no better. Like clothing production, the boot-and-shoe trade changed dramatically with the expansion of the city's trade contacts and the wholesalers' pursuit of markets. By

32. *Hunt's Merchants' Magazine* 20 (1849): 346; *Genius of Temperance* [New York], February 29, 1832; Foster, *New York Naked*, 137; *Herald*, May 1, June 11, 1853; *Tribune*, August 20, 1853; U.S. Senate Committee on Education and Labor, *Testimony as to the Relations between Labor and Capital* (Washington, D.C., 1885), 413–14; Dolores E. M. Janiewski, "Sewing with A Double Thread: The Needlewomen of New York, 1825–1870" (M.A. thesis, University of Oregon, 1974); 1850 Census.

33. Thompson and Yeo, *Unknown Mayhew*, 384–88; *Tribune*, September 9, 1845.

1829, four major footwear jobbers had opened in Manhattan; by 1850, the number had increased tenfold. The most enterprising major concerns kept pace with the clothing dealers and extended their inland markets southward to Alabama and as far west as Texas. Unlike the clothiers, however, New York firms never took the national lead in the production of respectable ready-mades: most either relied on established firms in shoemaking capitals like Lynn or Haverhill or hired their own workers in outlying towns, where, the *Tribune* reported in 1845, "the workmen can live for almost half the sum it costs our city mechanics." What remained in New York, apart from a busy custom trade, was repair work, ladies' shoemaking, bootmaking and production of the cheapest lines of shoes, either for government military contractors or for wholesale exporters in the southern trade. The shoemakers were left either to what the English writer Joseph Sparkes Hall called "the cheapening system" or to an endless competition for custom orders.[34]

The transforming effects of credit, competition, and mercantile sponsorship were dramatized in one of the trade's success stories, the rise of John Burke. Burke, an Irishman, had learned the shoemakers' craft in Dublin, where he also dabbled in radical, anti-British politics. Disgusted with postfamine conditions and with Ireland's inability to break British rule, he determined to try his fortune in "the Great Republic," and in 1847 he arrived in New York. Having landed jobs in the leather-cutting rooms of some of the best custom shops, Burke quickly learned that the New York trade was very different from the Irish: to earn his competence, he would have to curry favor and credit from his employers' customers. The erstwhile radical craftsman became an entrepreneur. Within two years of his arrival, he proudly reported that "all the customers were my friends"; by 1852, thanks to a timely loan from Moses Beach, the editor and chronicler of the city's mercantile fortunes, Burke opened his own shop. Over the next ten years, Burke expanded his business (eventually buying out one of his former employers, an event he noted with blustery pride) and with Beach's backing eventually began to "gain first place in the shoe trade." He readily admitted that without the help of his "good friends," his life would have remained "a fight against mishaps, disappointments, and adversity." For the thousands of journeymen who lacked Burke's combination of skills, contacts, and charm, such a life of adversity was unavoidable: those who would gain their independence had little

34. Jones, *Middlemen*, 14; D. M. Marvin and Company, Ledger and Account Book, n.d. [ca. 1850], N-YHS MSS; Insolvency Assignment, Herschel and Camp Company, 1836, HDC; Dawley, *Class and Community*, 12–16; *Tribune*, September 5, 9, 1845, March 1, 1850, May 3, 1853; *Young America* [New York], October 18, 1845; *Champion of American Labor* [New York], April 3, 1847; Joseph Sparkes Hall, *The Book of the Feet* (New York, 1850), 82–84.

choice but to become contractors, to be stigmatized as "the greatest tyrants in the entire trade," in a competitive shoemakers' world where, as Hall remarked, "money *bulk* and not money *worth* becomes the only standard of business."[35]

The division of labor in boot- and shoemaking followed the same general pattern as in the clothing trade. Work in the custom shops and in the shops of the ladies' shoemakers and the bootmakers was divided into the very few skilled cutting chores (handled by men like Burke) and the simpler, more repetitive tasks of the crimpers, fitters, and bottomers. Most journeymen could expect to earn at best six dollars per week from the easier work; to supplement their incomes, they completed an array of ornamental "extras," the most time-consuming and exacting chores in the better branches of the trade. In the shops, apprenticeship, in decline even before 1825, was reported "pretty much done away with" by 1845.[36] Outside of the shops, the demands of garret work and outwork led the *Tribune* to reckon in 1845 that no class of mechanics averaged so great an amount of work for so little money as the journeymen shoemakers. Chronic unemployment and underemployment were even more severe in shoemaking than in tailoring, leaving the journeymen to labor at a breakneck pace whenever work came their way. Family-shop arrangements like the one that had shocked the Reverend Ely thirty years earlier became ever more common:

> We have been in some fifty cellars in different parts of the city [the *Tribune* reported], each inhabited by a Shoe-maker and his family. The floor is made of rough plank laid loosely down, and the ceiling is not quite so high as a tall man. The walls are dark and damp and a wide desolate fireplace yawns at the center to the right of the entrance. There is no outlet back, and of course no yard privilges of any kind. The miserable room is lighted only by a shallow sash, partly projecting above the surface of the ground, and by the little light that struggles down from the steep and rotting stairs. In this apartment often live the man and his work bench, his wife, and five or six children of all ages; and perhaps a palsied grandfather and grandmother and often both. . . . Here they work, here they cook, they eat, they sleep, they pray. . . .

Outwork binders, almost all of them women, were placed in backstairs chambers, where they worked from before sunrise until after sundown for piece rates that brought in as little as fifty cents a day. Small masters, in a losing battle against the wholesalers and the Lynn trade, made the

35. Diary and Recollections of John Burke, N-YHS MSS; *Tribune*, May 3, 1853; Hall, *Book of the Feet*, 83.
36. Horace Greeley, *Art and Industry* (New York, 1853), 110; [Flint], *Eighty Years' Progress*, I, 317, 323–24; *Tribune*, September 5, 1845, May 3, 1853.

cheapest grade of shoes and survived, the *Tribune* claimed in 1845, on "the chance job of gentlemen's or children's mending brought in by the rich people above ground in the neighborhood who are not celebrated for paying a poor cobbler high prices."[37]

Sweating assumed different forms and took slightly longer to develop in the furniture trades. The shift began in about 1830, when the larger master furniture makers, hoping to reduce their wage bills and circumvent the existing price books, solicited British and European artisans to emigrate to New York. Within five years, hundreds of cabinetmakers had settled in Manhattan, many of them Germans from declining craft towns, creating the oversupply of hands the masters wanted; one English cabinetmaker, upon his arrival in Manhattan in 1834, was advised to leave the overcrowded city as soon as he could, since steady furniture work was hard to find and since most available work was poorly paid. In their search for cheap labor, however, the masters also undercut their own position, as some of the Germans began entering the business for themselves and managed to undersell the established firms by hiring other Germans at low wages. Small German shops soon dotted the shores of the Hudson and East rivers, producing inexpensive goods for the wholesalers and paying piece rates well below those expected by native-born journeymen. In response, the established masters—including Duncan Phyfe himself—turned out cheaper lines (so-called butcher furniture) and cut some of their journeymen's wages accordingly, which only led the furniture jobbers to order more goods from the small garret shops. By the early 1840s, garret contracting operations had inundated the trades; agents prowled the city's wharves looking for immigrants to steer to the cheap shops. Furniture making, though immune to the usual forms of outwork, became a sweated contract trade.[38]

The majority of furniture workers divided into a small elite corps of custom workmen and the contract suppliers to the wholesalers and retailers. First-rate hands continued to turn and fashion elegant designs for the likes of Phyfe and Company and earned as much as fifteen dollars for a sixty-hour week, but by the mid-1840s such work was scarce, open to fewer than one in twenty furniture employees. Apprenticeship continued, although by one investigator's estimate in 1853, not one in fifty cabinetmakers was an apprentice; those who remained were taken on for periods of two to four years, a span the *Herald* claimed "those who have had an

37. *Daily Tribune*, September 5, 9, 1845, April 11, 1850; [Flint], *Eighty Years' Progress*, I, 324; *Man*, June 19, 1835.

38. *Tribune*, November 11, 1845; *Herald*, June 18, 1853; Christoph Vetter, *Zwei Jahre in New York* (Hof, 1849), 156; "A Working Man's Recollections of America," *Knight's Penny Magazine* [London], 1 (1846): 102; Ernst, *Immigrant Life*, 80–81, 101–2.

experience in the trade say is almost impossible to obtain a complete practical knowledge of it." The "second-class" or "botch" workers labored at restricted, repetitive tasks, either in the larger manufactories along the Hudson or in the colonies of cabinetmaking garret shops on the Lower East Side, places where, as the cabinetmaker Ernest Hagen remembered, the work was strictly divided and masters "generally made a speciality of one piece only." Their plight, as reported in the *Herald*, was quite similar to that of the tailors, as intense competition between contractors and small masters led to a system of underbidding "in which the contending parties seem to lose all sense of honor or justice." By 1850 the furniture journeymen complained that most furniture workers could not expect to earn as much as "the common standard prices paid to hod carriers and sewer-diggers, little better than starving prices."[39]

Tailoring, shoemaking, and furniture making were the most dramatic examples of consumer finishing trades beset by similar problems. In others— hat and bonnet making, umbrella making, and many more—one form or another of piecework, outwork, and sweating arose between 1825 and 1850; in still others, such as cigarmaking, the full force of the bastardization of craft would be felt within a generation.[40] In all of them, we confront, in the most extreme way, the divided legacy of early-nineteenth-century capitalist growth. There can be little question that the transformation of New York consumer finishing improved material life for millions of Americans, in the form of cheaper clothes, cheaper shoes, and cheaper furniture, in greater quantities (and of higher quality) than ever before. For those at the very bottom of the outwork network—especially, after 1845, the famine-ravaged Irish—even work in the sweatshops and outwork cellars and the driven life of a petty contractor were preferable to rural disaster and, for some, starvation; for the fortunate few like John Burke, it was still possible to expect to earn, by one means or another, an independent estate. But none of this alters what was the harder truth in the sweated trades—that the cost of productivity, of salvation from agrarian calamity, and of opportunity for some was the collapse of the crafts and their replacement with a network of competition, underbidding, and undisguised exploitation—all in a city where the mercantile elite and the more successful manufacturers accumulated some of the greatest fortunes in America. These changes were invisible to most customers and chroniclers, hidden from view in the back-room cutters' bureaus and in the out-workers' cellars. To upper- and middle-class New York, the onset of

39. *Tribune*, November 11, 1845; *Herald*, June 18, 1853; Ingerman, "Recollections," 577; 1850 census.

40. See *Tribune*, September 16, 17, November 7, 1845. On cigarmaking, see Dorothée Schneider's forthcoming dissertation (City University of New York) on German workers in New York after the Civil War.

metropolitan industrialization appeared mainly as a dazzling cavalcade of new commodities, "suited to every market." To the craft workers, it was the intensity of labor, the underpayment, and the subordination to the rule of another that was most apparent. Above all else, it was the very transparency of exploitation, the self-evident inequalities of power and material expectations at every level of production, that made the sweated consumer finishing trades the most degraded crafts in New York. It would also make these trades the most troubled of all during the city's labor upheavals after 1825.

Technology and the Division of Labor: Printing

Unlike the largest consumer finishing trades, printing experienced a technological revolution before 1850. As early as 1818, New York master printers, led by the brothers David and George Bruce, began experimenting with stereotyping processes to reduce the amount of composing work and increase the speed of their press runs. By 1833, New York's journeymen printers were complaining that the spread of stereotyping had rendered it steadily more difficult for compositors to support their families; a few years later, the complaints shifted, to denounce the introduction of steam-powered presses and the displacement of pressmen in the city's largest periodical and book-printing firms. By 1845, what had been a relatively small collection of local newspaper and printing offices a quarter of a century earlier had become the print capital of the United States, befitting its metropolitan status—but with the result, the *Tribune* reported, that most compositors' work was done by "mere typesetters and not printers or workmen in the strictest sense of the word," while nine-tenths of the city's pressmen had been thrown out of work. In all, the history of printing seems like one of the anomalies in New York, more like that of a classic "leading sector" of the industrial revolution than of a sweated trade. Problems arose, but ones very different in kind from those that confronted the tailors and shoemakers.[41]

Mechanization, however, was not the only, or even the primary, source of change in printing; indeed, to the journeymen (who naturally deplored the replacement of men with machines) the new technology was most effective in advancing the division of labor and the dilution of skill that were already underway in 1825 and that had led to a form of printshop sweating in the 1830s and 1840s. As before, the problem stemmed from

41. Bruce, "Autobiography," 1–11; Henry Lewis Bullen, "The Oldest Job Printing Office in New York," *Inland Printer* 50 (1913): 519–21; Ethelbert Stewert, "A Documentary History of the Early Organizations of Printers," *Bulletin of the Bureau of Labor* 61 (1905): 897; *Daily Tribune*, September 15, 1845. See also [Flint], *Eighty Years' Progress*, II, 286–97.

the overcompetition generated by the arrival of country printers in the city, men who, as the *Tribune* reported, were forced to underbid each other for merchants' orders. As the more unscrupulous master printers hired "half-way" boys or recent immigrants at low piece rates, established printers had to lower their own rates or be ruined. In 1836, one veteran master printer raised an alarm at the extended use of "half-way" apprenticing and at the "laxity of every sense of moral obligation produced by such a corrupting practice"; ultimately, the *Tribune* recounted in 1845, "the wages of the journeymen were by degrees reduced, until, instead of a uniform scale of prices, every man was compelled to work for what he could obtain." As mechanization in the periodical and book branches of production shut out most small masters from the most lucrative pursuits, conditions deteriorated in the unmechanized shops—those "Lilliputian garret offices, whose type, press, &c, would not bring more than fifty dollars at auction." By the 1840s, some employing printers were known to use boys almost to the exclusion of journeymen, and to practice all of the tricks of the clothing "sweaters," including the systematic withholding of wages, in order to maintain their profit margins.[42]

Thus the printers were caught in two distinct, but related, forms of early industrial innovation. The changing structures of the printing shops and of the printing work force reveal the uneven impact of these rearrangements. First, the division of labor in all branches of printing was as thoroughgoing as in any craft. As Horace Greeley remarked in a letter in 1836 (while he himself was still a journeyman), no printer could hope to succeed in New York unless he could "reduce the whole business to a system," dividing the master's duties between overseeing his shop and attending to the accounts, and leaving as much of the coordination of work as possible to his foreman and bosses; by 1850, journeymen printers, like the tailors, complained of the favoritism of the foremen's regime as one of the more annoying abuses of the trade. As this system proliferated in the mammoth steam-powered plants and the small garret shops, the printing work force broke down into three major groups. Roughly three-fifths of the city's printers worked in the largest periodical and book plants; these included both the best compositors and pressmen, who could earn as much as $16.00 a week in constant employment, and their helpers, who averaged about $6.00 per week. A second, much smaller group worked, usually on a part-time "sub" basis, in the press and composing

42. *Tribune*, September 11, 15, 1845; C. S. Van Winkle, *The Printer's Guide*, 3d ed. (New York, 1836), 22–27; Stewert, "Documentary History," 897–98. Journeymen printers complained of two kinds of ruses concerning wages: "bad pay," or failure to pay any wages; and "irregular pay," usually meaning payment once a fortnight, and then only in part and always in country bills instead of specie or city bills. See *Tribune*, May 22, 1850.

rooms of the most popular daily newspapers and normally received even better wages than the book printers—but were expected to work up to sixteen hours a day and had little or no security of tenure. The rest were employed in the smaller shops, a tiny fraction of them in the fine-engraving firms (where wages averaged as high as $20.00 per week) and the remainder in the competitive jungles of small-time job printing, where the best men's average wages ran to about $6.00 per week—figures the printers' union denounced in 1850 as "literally less than laborers' wages." Approximately two printers in five earned what the journeymen considered adequate wages; the rest did not.[43]

There were, of course, numerous reasons for printers to consider themselves privileged in comparison with other New York craft workers, despite the mechanization and despite the sweating. Overall, journeymen printers were among the best-paid wage earners in the city (Table 14). Those with steady situations, the *Tribune* noted, "live comfortably and in not a few instances in a certain style of gentility"; even the poorest-paid printers earned, on the average, more than the sweated tailors and shoemakers. A large sector of the printing workers had to be literate in English, a requirement that barred Germans and the poorest Irish from the composing rooms; in 1855, nearly half the printers were native born, and nearly one-third of the immigrants were from England, Scotland, or Wales. Neither technological improvement nor dilution of the labor force could entirely destroy the notion that the printers were craftsmen: "As a body," the *Tribune* claimed, "they pride themselves on personal appearance, and are not unfrequently select in their associations. . . ." Nevertheless, the gaps between the old standards and the new realities, already apparent in 1825, widened considerably between 1825 and 1850, both in the mechanized firms and in the jobbing offices. For some of the "genteel" printers, living well became a matter of keeping up appearances, leaving them, as the *Tribune* observed, "seldom overstocked with money." For others, it was the insecurity of employment, the constant "subbing" or running from office to office in search of temporary work, the flattery and deference expected by the foreman, that made a printer's life so difficult. Above all, for every printer it became steadily apparent that between the immense costs of opening a large printing works and the low wages and competition at the lower end of the trade, the chances of attaining an independence were dim. By the *Tribune*'s estimate, not more than one in twenty New York journeymen eventually opened his own shop, and those who did could at best hope to club together with friends to open a small, marginal business. The journeymen were well aware that this was so—indeed, they

43. Horace Greeley to B. F. Ransom, May 2, 1836, Greeley Papers, NYPL; *Tribune*, September 15, 1845, May 22, 1850. See also Abbott, *Harper Establishment*.

argued that even if wages were better, few workers would care to risk the anxiety and probable failure that attended the fledgling small master printer. Thurlow Weed's prediction had come true, to an even greater extent than he could have foreseen in 1816: to be a journeyman printer was to be a journeyman for life. Along with the ongoing substitution of juvenile "half-way" labor for skilled journeymen and the uncertainties that came with mechanization, this inevitability would lead the printers to join the shoemakers, tailors, cabinetmakers, and others, in common cause.[44]

Subcontracting and the Building Trades

As in printing, the skilled work in New York's building trades could not be given over to the poorest hands, but it could be divided and subcontracted along lines similar to those in the furniture trades. After the depression of 1819–22, the number of small-time New York builders and contractors mushroomed, a boon to local real-estate speculators interested in getting work done as quickly and as cheaply as possible, but a plague to the city's traditional "honest" builders and the city's journeymen. By thus extending the underbidding that had begun earlier in the century, building contractors threatened established tradesmen and, ultimately, the journeymen with a level of competition unknown in the Jeffersonian city.[45]

Amid the booms in New York public works and in residential construction during the 1830s and 1840s, the contractor-entrepreneurs changed the face of New York as well as the structure of the building trades. Self-styled carpenters, some of them former laborers and construction workers, snatched up building contracts throughout the city. Their work, labeled "Carpenters' Doric" and "Carpenters' Gothic" by the disdainful, replaced simple but sturdy edifices with monotonous ornate designs, sometimes of gimcrack standards. These builders executed as much as nine-tenths of the construction that erased the effects of the Great Fire of 1835; the most successful of them won enough favor and credit from municipal authorities, land speculators, and local banks to amass fortunes in contracting and real-estate deals—and managed in the process to cut off masters of smaller means from jobs in the newly developed parts of town.[46]

44. *Tribune*, September 11, 15, 1845; May 22, 1850; Ernst, *Immigrant Life*, 81–82.
45. *Courier and Enquirer* [New York], December 9, 1829; *Daily Sentinel* [New York], September 28, 1832. See also John R. Commons, "The New York Building Trades," *Quarterly Journal of Economics* 18 (1904): 409–36.
46. Union History Company, *History of Architecture and the Building Trades of Greater New York* (New York, 1899), I, 389–90; Bills and Receipts, Robert I. Brown Papers, N-YHS; Beach, *Wealth* (1845), 7; idem, *Wealth* (1855), 15, 28, 32. Reports on the consequences of gimcrack building began in the mid-1820s:

It is astonishing how carelessly buildings are erected in this city—six houses

Under the aegis of the contractors and the builders, the work on any one project was divided into dozens of smaller tasks, all open to bids from other entrepreneurs; each of the builders would then normally subcontract part of his work to others, who in turn hired the necessary help or subcontracted the job again. Consequently, the division of labor within single branches of the trades was intense; New York stonemasons, for example, unlike those in other cities, were quite distinct from stonecutters by the mid-1830s, while the stonecutters were divided into regular day workers and piece-rate hands. After the competitive bidding, the profit margins to those who actually oversaw the work were so narrow that sweating (along with occasional fraudulent bankruptcies) was guaranteed: by the mid-1840s, the construction trades were mazes of small speculative enterprises: well-paid honorable journeymen worked alongside sweated work crews on the building sites and received materials from a bevy of sweat-work strapping shops that supplied the subcontractors with ready-made items like window sashes and door frames. While they divided the work among well-paid men and pieceworkers, the builders and contractors remained ever alert to new ways to cut costs even further. The masonry contractors raised the most ire, when they turned to the state prisons to provide them with cheaper goods dressed and prepared by the inmates. Although the labor press tended to exaggerate the impact of convict labor, the use of prison-dressed materials in some very large projects, such as the building of New York University in 1835, seemed to confirm the employers' alleged indifference to their workers and to "the Trade." The adaptation, in the late 1840s, of various technical improvements to construction work—planing machines, steam-powered stone dressers—only exacerbated the situation, by allowing contractors to specialize even more in a single line of work and by permitting them to hire indifferent workmen to perform jobs that had once required great dexterity.[47]

Like the printers, the more skilled of the building tradesmen shared numerous advantages over the most degraded consumer trades. Despite the rise of sweating, the journeymen carpenters, the largest group of building workmen, were on the average among the best-paid craft workers in the city (Table 14). Immigrants, whose very presence traced the divi-

---

which were nearly finished in Reed-street, fell to the ground and broke three ribs of one of the workmen—this is the second time these houses have fallen . . . we understand that the thickness of the walls was only that of *one brick!*

New York Mirror 3 (1825): 71, quoted in Ford, *Slums and Housing*, I, 87.

47. *Daily Tribune*, March 6, 11, 12, September 19, 1850; *Herald*, July 6, 1850; Headley, *Great Riots*, 95–96; *Niles' Weekly Register*, March 27, 1819, July 17, 1824, June 11, 1834; *Journal of the American Institute* 3 (1838): 4, 9. See also [Flint], *Eighty Years' Progress*, I, 356–57; Sam Bass Warner, *The Urban Wilderness: A History of the American City* (New York, 1972), 66–67.

sion and sweating of labor, were far less common among the carpenters than among other craft workers. Through the 1830s and 1840s, even stonecutting, among the most heavily sweated branches of construction work, provided enough skilled labor on ornamental and fine work that John Frazee could still praise it as a noble craft, fit preparation for a career in the fine arts. For those with the stamina of an Alexander Masterson or a Richard Carman—the city's most renowned "self-made" builders—there were still fortunes to be won with the right combination of luck and ambition. Yet such comparison meant little to those in the sweated branches—above all piecework stonecutting, painting, and job carpentry—who saw their trades inundated with speculation and wage cutting; it meant even less to strapping-shop workers who spent as many long hours fashioning cheap sashes, shades, and frames.[48] Their concerns, along with those of the organized skilled carpenters over declining real wages in the inflationary 1830s, would bring the building trades to the forefront of union militancy.

The Persistence of Tradition: Shipbuilding and Food Preparation

Far from the outwork cellars, job printing offices, and building sites, some New York trades expanded without being divided and sweated. The city's leading maritime trades were among them, and no maritime trade required greater skill, commanded more respect, or held more tenaciously to established routines than did shipbuilding. "In every other art, the majesty of science holds out the sceptre of progress," John Griffiths told some fellow employers in 1854, "while in shipbuilding, traditional knowledge broods over the productions of philosophy . . . and sets bounds to the widening orbit of genius."[49] It was no complaint: to Griffiths, and to others connected to the port, these limits testified only to the high state of the art and to the skills of master shipwrights and their employees. Nowhere in America was the art practiced with greater pride than along the dry docks of the East Side. Between 1825 and 1850, the reputations of New York's master shipbuilders, combined with the tremendous increase in demand from local shippers, made Manhattan the most productive shipbuilding center in the country and, for a time, the busiest in the world.[50]

Despite the increased production and despite the larger scale of individual projects during the clipper-ship era, the key tasks involved in

48. Ernst, *Immigrant Life*, 73-75, 215; Frazee, "Autobiography"; *Tribune*, April 20, 1850; *Champion of American Labor*, April 24, 1847.

49. *Transactions of the American Institute* (1855), 95.

50. Albion, *Rise of the New York Port*, 287-311; Morrison, *History of New York Ship Yards*, 50-63.

designing and executing the body of a ship could not be placed in ordinary mechanics' hands or be directed by men new to the trade. Labor was organized according to a subcontract scheme, not unlike those in house construction, and a portion of the work was performed by semiskilled and unskilled helpers. However, because ship construction demanded the utmost skill and care (much as in a custom trade) and because the journeymen shipwrights themselves were vigilant about protecting their wages, these arrangements were not susceptible to sweating. The division of labor that did occur as a result of improvements in ship design involved the addition of entirely new trades—custom metalwork in particular—to the overall assembly process, not the splitting and degradation of existing skills. At the top, meanwhile, there was no room for entrepreneurs with a scant knowledge of the trade. Skilled master shipwrights, all of whom had served regular apprenticeships (usually in one of the adjoining yards) and who continued to supervise construction, ran all of the major firms. More than any other group of masters, the shipbuilders established their own craft dynasties, taking care to encourage proper, full-term apprenticeship and a paternal artisan order. Young boys reported holding the masters in awe; in William Webb's yards, apprentices were granted occasional peeks inside the masters' planning room, to be impressed by the ship models, drafting tools, and other paraphernalia of the craftsman-boss. From their experiences along the East River, trained apprentices took leading positions in shipbuilding firms around the country. For the hundreds of other shipwrights, carpenters, and joiners who obtained regular positions, work in New York, although taxing to the point of daily exhaustion, was rewarding (Table 14).[51]

While they expected first-rate work from their well-paid men, the masters indulged—indeed, openly encouraged—breaks from work as part of their customary paternal regime. "Saturnalias" were gotten up every time

51. "The Old Ship-Builders of New York," *Harper's New Monthly Magazine* 65 (1882): 221–32; *Herald*, December 31, 1852; Leonard H. Boole, *The Shipwright's Handbook and Draughtsman's Guide* (Milwaukee, 1858), 7–9. Boole, who eventually became a successful master in Wisconsin, noted with pride how after having worked for Webb as an apprentice for seven years—the last five without missing a day's work— he was taken on as a journeyman by Webb himself.

The accounts of Samuel Warshinge, a journeyman ship carpenter, are eloquent in describing the high wages in the trade. Warshinge worked at several yards between 1830 and 1852, at wages that varied from $1.75 to $2.50 per day; in the 1830s, he was able, in a single year, to place $100 in a bank account; he also dabbled in real estate. By 1839, when he won promotion to superintendent of the Fickett and Thomas yards, he was financially secure; with some irony, he reckoned, on the basis of his own accounts, that "a man that works in a common capacity can not save any of the Erning." See Samuel Warshinge, Account Book and Personal Notes, 1830–52, N-YHS MSS. Cf. Pollard, *Genesis of Modern Management*, 84–85; and see also Bishop, *History*, III, 136–44; *Tribune*, May 7, 1850; *Herald*, December 31, 1852.

a large vessel was launched, and the workmen's celebrations turned into impromptu public holidays along the East Side. One old carpenter recalled that the packet- and clipper-line owners "always insisted upon giving the workmen a 'blow-out' and usually paid the bills for the biscuits, cheese, and rum punch, and also for the champagne drunk by the guests. . . ." Each Fourth of July, the journeymen at the Webb yards built a special commemorative ship model, one of the last vestiges of the old festivals of "the Trade." If they no longer paid their workmen's wages in grog, as in the eighteenth century, New York shipbuilders entertained their employees with drink at different times of the day and permitted cake and candy vendors to patrol the docks to sell snacks during the long hours of building. At all times, each master took care to stress the personal touch, to preserve his image, in one journeyman's words, as "a genuine mechanic."[52]

The masters' paternalism did not completely insulate shipbuilding from some built-in structural crises and disputes between employers and employees. The very rapidity with which the master shipbuilders expanded their yards led to occasional shortages of employment, as every manner of shipworker (including many brought to the city by the masters) came to Manhattan in search of work. So long as the mercantile economy remained healthy and several building projects were engaged at once, there was more than enough work to go around; at peak periods, some shipbuilders even offered jobs to highly skilled carpenters from outside the trade. The slightest fluctuation or depression in trade, however, could cause employees to scatter, one retired ship carpenter recalled, "in as many directions, perhaps, as there are men, in search of some other three weeks' job." In some of the crafts ancillary to shipbuilding—rigging, sailmaking, and others—subcontractors complicated the traditional order by setting up small sweatshops near the shipyards. Generosity, meanwhile, could be turned to less than benevolent ends on the dry docks. "Often," an ex-journeyman recalled, "when the sun had set, one of the bosses invited his men to refesh themselves from a pail of brandy and water, and then suggested some timbers be raised, so that it was dark before the raisers reached home," unpaid for their extra labor.[53]

Masters and journeymen clashed over these problems, particularly over the hours of work; so, too, the periodic inflations of the 1830s and late 1840s prompted strikes for wages: journeymen ship carpenters, who had organized in the Jeffersonian period, did so again in the 1830s. What is re-

52. "Old Ship-Builders," 233–34; Adam Smith, The Wealth of Nations (1776; reprint, Harmondsworth, 1970), 172; George McNeill, The Labor Movement: The Problem of Today (Boston, 1887), 342.

53. McNeill, Labor Movement, 341; "Old Ship-Builders," 233.

markable about the disputes in the shipyards, however, is how different they were from those in the consumer finishing, printing, and house construction trades. On the most urgent question, the length of the work day, New York's ship workers mounted a determined campaign that demonstrated both their relatively elite status and the traditionalism of their trades. In 1831, fifty journeymen ship smiths and carpenters petitioned the Common Council, respectfully asking for "a correct standard for the different hours of commencing and letting off work," and offered to procure, at their own expense, a bell "of sufficient size to be heard and give notice at the various hours," so that they might have enough leisure time to enjoy their families and properly observe the Sabbath. The council and the masters agreed to discuss the issue; after two more years of negotiations between masters and men, the Mechanics' Bell, situated in the heart of the shipbuilding district, pealed at regular intervals to enforce a ten-hour day. It was, by any standard, a signal triumph for the journeymen, later to be hailed by the labor reformer George McNeill as the first major victory ever won by American workers in the cause of reducing work hours. It was also a victory won without the harsh rhetoric and public demonstrations common in other trades. Much as the artisans of colonial New York had appealed to local officials to redress their grievances, the shipbuilders turned to their own benevolent government to intervene for the common good. Their bill of particulars cited no evil intents on the part of their masters or any evidence that the employers were trying to cheapen the trade. Apart from everything else, the ship carpenters were among the few groups of wage earners well-paid enough to even contemplate winning their point by laying out money to cast and mount a bell.[54]

Other strongholds of the artisan system included the food preparation trades, above all butchering. Like other food tradesmen, the butchers had a long history of well-regulated production and close (if sometimes conflict-ridden) relations with the municipal government. Through the Jeffersonian period, they worked exclusively in one of the city's four major

54. Morrison, *New York Ship Yards*, 68, 84–91; Warshinge, Account Book; Petition of Isaac Hadders et al., CCFP, Street Commissioners, n.d. [1831], MARC; McNeill, *Labor Movement*, 345–47. On the shipbuilders' limited activity in strikes in the 1830s and in 1850, see below, Chapters 7 and 10. Other maritime trades also escaped many of the structural divisions of the era, if not as thoroughly as shipbuilding. Coopering is one example; although some barrel making was transformed and incorporated into larger manufactories—especially at the uptown distilleries—most of the trade remained artisanal in 1850. See Franklin E. Coyne, *The Development of the Coopering Industry in the United States* (Chicago, 1940), 11–23; Edward Hazen, *Panorama of Professions and the Trades* (Philadelphia, 1835), 56–57; Robert Taylor, "Diary and Autobiography," NYPL MSS; *Daily Tribune*, August 30, 1852; Ernst, *Immigrant Life*, 214–16; Herbert G. Gutman, "La Politique ouvrière de la grande entreprise américaine de l'age du clinquant': Le Cas de la Standard Oil Company," *Mouvement Social*, no. 102 (1978): 67–99.

markets at licensed stalls granted by the Common Council. Although procuring a license was not usually a difficult matter, prospective masters had to affirm that they had served proper apprenticeships. Once installed, the butcher stood a good chance of prospering in the regulated market. Normally, he would arrive at his stand early, accompanied by his apprentice and perhaps a journeyman, with just enough meat to sell for the day. By daybreak, the necessary cutting would be finished; by ten in the morning, most customers had completed their marketing and the butcher's major chores were done. His main competitive concerns were those forestallers, "shirkers," and other interlopers who might try to undersell him by setting up illegal private shops or by huckstering food in the streets. In such cases, the butcher, with his colleagues, demanded and usually received swift action from the clerk of the market and from the Market Committee of the Common Council.[55]

The system remained essentially the same through the 1840s. Still dependent on local drovers, meat suppliers, and creditors and still catering to a local trade in the licensed markets, the butchers had no need to change their ways; not until the mechanization of butchering in Cincinnati and Chicago in the 1860s and the perfection of refrigerated railroad transport in later decades did the New Yorkers have to contend with much competition from elsewhere. A few alterations hit the trade between 1825 and 1850: as the city's physical growth made a trip to market difficult for some patrons, the butchers agreed to make deliveries, which forced them to hire additional deliverymen and boys; improvements in refrigeration techniques in the mid-1830s allowed them to sell and store larger quantities of meat; the city loosened some of its restrictions on granting stalls and limitation of licenses, and by the 1840s some private shops operated along with the city markets. But these minor changes aside, butchering more than any other trade retained the work patterns, relations to municipal government and corporate spirit that were as reminiscent of the early modern guild crafts as of capitalist enterprises. The Market Committee continued to regulate meat sales, in cooperation with the Executive Committee of Butchers selected by the city's masters. Apprenticeship remained a critical step in any butcher's life and a prerequisite for setting up on his own. Sweating made little sense; while journeymen butcher boys in the city's markets earned only about ten dollars per month (in addition to board and lucrative perquisites), older journeymen earned as much as thirty dollars, plus board and perquisites. The continuing regulation of butchers' licenses by City Hall tied the structure of the labor force to politics, and with Tammany in control of the Market Committee through most of the

55. De Voe, *Market Book*, 210-11, 221-22, 228-29, 232, 345-47, 401-2, 425-26; Rock, *Artisans of the New Republic*, 209-11, 214-17.

1840s, German and Irish immigrants were assured a share of the trade; nevertheless, native-born men survived longer in the butchering trade than in most other crafts. The persisting corporate identity translated into the formation of the Butchers' Benevolent Association—with the sanguinary motto "We Destroy to Preserve"—that helped to enforce trade restrictions and organized social functions at least through the early 1840s.[56]

The butchers' daily routines also permitted them far more opportunities for public show, sport, and leisure than other craftsmen enjoyed. As much as the street hucksters and vendors whom they distrusted, the butchers occupied a hot spot in the city's street life, attending the swirl of the crowd, the spectacle of the market, all the while making their own pitch. Lined up with their bloody smocks, top hats, and bejeweled stickpins, renowned for their physical prowess, adept at the use of knives and cleavers, they looked—and smelled—like members of a masculine confraternity (Plate 9). The rickety confines of the city's markets were far less restrictive than the sweaters' garrets or the wholesalers' cutting rooms, and journeymen were known to slip off for a break at the nearby vendors of sweets, cakes, and liquors. Their work rhythms of intense labor followed by leisurely afternoons and evenings allowed the butchers considerable time for drinking and frolic: although the city's masters, many of them quite wealthy men, were widely regarded as "respectable, substantial, and sober," the apprentice and journeymen butcher boys had an unrivaled reputation for forming gangs and pulling roughneck pranks. Nothing in the expansion of the trade made these habits untoward; indeed, with the growth of the private shops in the 1840s and the infiltration of Irish provisioners and butchers into the trade, the associations in the public mind between butchers and drunken carousing grew even stronger. Within this order, conflicts between masters and journeymen were scarce; one labor journal reported in 1846 that the butchers only rarely acted together to advance their own interests.[57]

Baking, the other major New York food provisioning trade, was a singular case, in that the structure of the craft initially followed the pattern of butchering only to be overtaken by new forms of competition. Until 1821, the Common Council enforced a formal assize on bread and for decades afterward retained a standard measure for the weight of loaves. The restriction on overcompetition did not unduly bother the bakers, but the assize placed such strict limits on production that masters claimed they

56. De Voe, *Market Book*, 347, 402, 438–39, 506–7; *Tribune*, November 8, 1845; *Young America*, February 7, 1846. On the mechanization of butchering after 1860, see Sigfried Giedion, *Mechanization Takes Command: A Contribution to Anonymous History* (New York, 1948), 213–46.

57. Harlow, *Old Bowery Days*, 150–51; *Tribune*, November 8, 1845; *Young America*, February 7, 1846. See also Haswell, *Reminiscences*, 60, 89, 101.

could not bake enough bread to make a profit. A series of petition campaigns eventually convinced the council to loosen its grip; even with the abandonment of restrictions, however, baking remained in the hands of small neighborhood masters, whose greatest concern was to get enough flour when trade routes to western mills were shut by inclement weather. Like the shipbuilders, the master bakers changed work routines by extending the hours of labor rather than by dividing labor. Through the 1820s, the journeymen bakers complained most often about having to work long hours on Sunday; in the customary manner, they looked to relief not in strikes and boycotts but in petitions to the council that bemoaned Sabbath work as improper "in a moral and religious point of view, as well as an unnecessary labour on them."[58]

The situation worsened during the 1830s. Employing bakers, unmoved by their journeymen's complaints, did nothing to alter the hours of work in the bakeries: through the late 1840s, sixteen- to eighteen-hour days and Sunday work remained the norm. The lack of any technological innovation in baking probably redounded to the disadvantage of the journeymen; conditions remained as primitive and debilitating—and the manual work remained as arduous—as ever. Greatly compounding the situation was the masters' use of "half-ways" and fraudulent apprentices. In 1834, the journeymen bakers, organized for the first time in a trade union, cited this abuse above all and struck to force their employers to limit the number of apprentices to one per shop.[59] Despite the trappings of various bakers' benevolent societies and despite the absence of contracting, New York's baking operations generated abiding tensions. While it remained open to small entrepreneurs with limited capital (particularly German immigrants, who more or less took over the trade in the late 1840s),[60] and while it retained its small-shop character, baking became a hybrid of different forms of exploitation.

Craft Workers in the Industrializing Metropolis

By now, it should be obvious that no single model of early industrial change can account for all of the uneven innovations in the relations of production in New York between 1825 and 1850: if Dickens's Coketown, long regarded as the archetypal nineteenth-century industrial city, was, as Stephen Blackpool described it, a muddle, then New York was an even

58. Morris, *Government and Labor*, 161–66; Pomerantz, *New York*, 170; MCC, August 6, October 1, 9, November 12, December 10, 29, 1821; Rock, *Artisans of the New Republic*, 184–89, 196–97.

59. *Man* [New York], June 9, 10, 15, 1834; *Young America*, February 7, 1846; *Daily Tribune*, April 16, 1850.

60. Ernst, *Immigrant Life*, 87–88.

more confusing jumble. A summary of the main types of changes in different trades confirms this metropolitan diversity (Table 16). But some basic themes do run through the histories of all the crafts. In the very largest consumer trades, skilled tasks once performed by artisans were divided between a few well-paid journeymen and many more underpaid hands, including, in some cases, women and (increasingly) poor immigrants. Competition between entrepreneurs intensified as contractors and garret masters entered the field and as credit became the lifeblood of business. A primitive form of mass production for local consumption and the national market became the focus of work in the largest sectors of production; otherwise, except in a very few factory trades, the artisan system persisted at least until 1850.

Even in those trades most affected by metropolitan industrialization before 1850, innovations in production did not wash out all roads to self-advancement or completely destroy the dignity of skilled labor. Ambitious journeymen could still make a comfortable (if somewhat disreputable) living as contractors. In-shop work remained respected and relatively well paid. Luxury firms kept some of the higher standards of workmanship and paid higher piece rates than did the garret and outwork enterprises. Simultaneously, however, metropolitan industrialization, with its reorganization of the social relations of production and the thorough transformation of wage labor into a market commodity, also challenged fundamental assumptions about craft work and workshop relations that had been the heart of "the Trade." Independence, virtue, equality, cooperation, and a shared part in the work process had been the cardinal ideas of the artisan republic, as the trades eloquently expressed in their speeches and processions. But what was the independence of the small garret master, scrambling to meet the demands of the slopshops or the wholesalers? How could virtue be maintained in a sweatshop or outwork cellar, or in a universe dependent on capitalist favor and credit? How cooperative were the labors of in-shop workers who turned out pieces to fit the foremen's schedules? Where was equality to be found in the outwork manufactory? To what extent could the life of adversity and competition described by John Burke or the ceaseless insecurity of the "subbing" printers and the sweated shoemakers and tailors be described as an extension of the life of "the Trade"?

These questions did not arise in every craft; in those in which they did not, the older artisan solidarities remained strong in 1850 and afterward. But for most New York craft workers and their employers, the widening gaps between established principles and workshop conditions intensified debates over the artisan republican verities. Numerous developments intrinsic to metropolitan industrialization in New York—the ethnic and sexual segmentation of the work force, the persistence of the small masters, the social distance between privileged and debased workers—affected the course of these battles. But in spite of all that divided workers—and all that united some employers and workers across the emerging boundaries of class—the changes in the trades led to fresh disputes between entrepreneurs, radical spokesmen, and craft workers, disputes that gradually embodied clashing social visions. An ideological crisis—the crisis of artisan republicanism—accompanied the fracturing of artisan labor. In time, this crisis, accompanied by some ad hoc and eventually well-organized movements of workers from outside the crafts, brought distinctively American forms of class conflict to New York City.

III

Working Man's Advocates, 1825-1832

What is this you bring my America?
Is it uniform with my country?
Is it not something that has been better told or done before?
Have you not imported this, or the spirit of it, in some ship?
Is it a mere tale? a rhyme? a prettiness?
Has it never dangled at the heels of the poets, politicians, literats, of
  enemies' lands?
Does it not assume that what is notoriously gone is still here?
Does it answer universal needs? Will it improve manners?

Chants Democratic, I, 29

4

Entrepreneurs and Radicals

Gradually but decisively, the artisan republic disintegrated in the late 1820s. Rapid inflation punctuated by brief sharp depressions in 1825–26 and 1829 disrupted commerce and broke artisan businesses (Figure 1)— belying the brimming confidence that had arrived with the Erie Canal. Journeymen quieted their union activities after 1825, but a few strikes broke out, the most important of them led by laborers, semiskilled workers, and women. In politics, the unraveling of the "one-party" factionalism of the Era of Good Feelings and the rise of the Jacksonian Democrats anticipated the collapse of the old mechanics' interest. With these events, the ideological divisions within the trades became more complex, more profound, and more charged. New ideas and reformulations of old ones filtered through the shops. Two main lines of argument developed, one tending toward defenses of capitalist entrepreneurship, the other advancing one of several radical critiques of the emerging order. Advocates of each position proffered different explanations for the problems besetting the trades. All claimed to be championing the artisan republic.

Entrepreneurial Crusades:
Moral Reform and Political Economy

Many sources informed the more thoroughly entrepreneurial views of New York's leading master craftsmen, but none made more powerful ethical claims than did the new evangelicalism. After 1825, the city's well-to-do missionaries, led by the New School Presbyterian silk merchants Arthur and Lewis Tappan and by their associates in the New York Tract Society, made some headway in the field previously limited to the Methodists and the lower-class enthusiasts. Armed with the faith that all men could attain grace if they accepted Jesus and did His work, the Tappans and their friends fanned out into Manhattan's most impious realms—the prisons, the markets, the foulest of the slums—to distribute tracts, upbraid the ungodly, and collect wayward souls. Between 1825 and 1828, they concentrated on a Sabbatarian drive to pressure politicians into prohibiting all business on Sunday, from postal delivery to the sale of alcoholic spirits. As the campaign continued, the Sabbatarians decided to combat all forms of disorderly, intemperate behavior and to expand church membership with a great revival. Their efforts became a holy war in 1829 and 1830, with the founding of the New-York City Temperance Society, the establishment of the First Free Presbyterian Church on Thames Street, and the arrival of two of the nation's most successful revivalists—first Charles Finney's associate, the Reverend Joel Parker, and then Finney himself.[1]

In the trades, the evangelical reformers concentrated first on purging the shops of drink. Despite all previous efforts to encourage abstinence, alcohol remained very much a part of craft life in the late 1820s. Employers and jobbers still served copious amounts to friends and business associates; "I could scarcely visit New York on the most important business without getting Drunk," a shoe dealer from Newark remembered. Journeymen continued to indulge in drinking rituals and enforce what one called "certain bye-laws for the express purpose of obtaining liquor."[2] But with the advent of the united evangelical front and its attacks on intemperance, master craftsmen rethought the appropriateness of the old besotted customs as never before. Their testimonials to the city's evangelicals no doubt exaggerated the extent and popularity of reform, but by their earnest amazement they demonstrated a clear shift in attitude about unquestioned intoxication. In trades once notorious for having few sober men,

---

1. Rosenberg, *Religion and the Rise of the American City*, 70–97; Foster, *Errand of Mercy*, 187–88. On Sabbatarianism, see Bertram Wyatt-Brown, "Prelude to Abolitionism: Sabbatarianism and the Rise of the Second Party System," *JAH* 63 (1971): 316–41; Jentz, "Artisans, Evangelicals, and the City," 66–111; Johnson, *Shopkeepers' Millennium*, 83–88. Like Rochester's, New York's Sabbatarian and free-church movements began under the guidance of successful merchant capitalists and professionals and gradually encompassed others. The church movement was also particularly attractive to women. In its first two years of operation, the First Free Presbyterian Church admitted 326 members. Of these, 218 (66.9 percent) were females, of whom only one in seven (15.6 percent) were the wives and daughters of male congregants. Of the male members who can be identified, 22 (52.4 percent) were merchants, large retailers, or professionals; the rest included two printers, two tailors, and four other artisans; at least six of these artisans were prominent master craftsmen. See *Church Manual Number II for the Congregants of the Free Presbyterian Church* (New York, 1832).

2. George B. Dunn to Thaddeus Wakeman, September 5, 1842, American Institute Papers, N-YHS; Temperance Society, *First Annual Report*, 21.

one employer reported in 1829, "total abstinence is gaining ground" with "astonishing rapidity." The keeping of Blue Monday, while not completely eliminated, was "reduced to a limited extent," another observed, "where formerly it was generally the case." One master who had "for some years been in the habit of drinking some liquor and giving it to my apprentices" suddenly stopped doing so. Others prohibited drinking in the shop completely and kept watch lest their men take their drop elsewhere. Journeymen who wanted a drink now went out for it stealthily, and the more intractable faced sterner measures; as one master dryly observed on the decline of Blue Monday, "a certain discharge of employment has had a good effect." In a matter of months, the evangelical temperance cause attracted a following among some of the city's most eminent craft employers; early in 1829, when Lewis Tappan and others founded the city's first temperance society, some twenty masters immediately joined and nine leading craftsmen were named to the body's board of managers.[3]

The hatter Joseph Brewster, the most articulate of the artisan temperance men, typified the kind of skilled, pious, energetic entrepreneur most drawn to the cause. Born in Connecticut in 1787, Brewster served his apprenticeship in Norwalk and later worked as a journeyman in Northampton, Massachusetts. In about 1813, after he had sharpened his skills and saved a competence, he set up shop as a custom master in New York; over the next fifteen years, he built his fledgling enterprise into one of the largest businesses in the trade, earning enough to purchase a spacious mansion on Fourth Street. By all accounts, he was an exemplary master—an employer, one clergyman later recalled, "of a sanguine temperament [and] a sympathetic and generous disposition"—and his standing among his peers secured his election to the General Society and to the presidency of the Hatters' Benevolent Society. By the late 1820s, he was also a confirmed evangelical. Although he had not been raised in any religion, Brewster joined the Presbyterian Cedar Street Church shortly after his arrival in New York; about 1822, he had a conversion and publicly professed his faith; by the late 1820s, he was an active tract distributor.[4]

3. Temperance Society, *First Annual Report*, 19–23. The master artisans on the board of managers were J. P. Allaire (engine maker), Joseph Brewster (hatter), Lemuel Brewster (hatter), Benjamin De Milt (watchmaker), George Douglas (carpenter), Daniel Fanshaw (printer), William Mandeville (cabinetmaker), Charles Starr (bookbinder), Andrew Wheeler (butcher). Like the temperance societies elsewhere, the New York group remained largely a mercantile reform socieety; of the 113 subscribers whose occupations could be determined, only 17.5 percent (20) were artisans. The important point here is that several leading masters were attracted to it so early. See *The Free Enquirer* [New York], March 25, 1829.

4. Earle and Congdon, *Annals*, 69; Temperance Society, *First Annual Report*, 23–24; Colden, *Memoir*, 224; Asa Dodge Smith, *The Guileless Israelite: A Sermon on the Occasion of the Death of Joseph Brewster* (New York, 1852).

From his prestigious position in his trade, Brewster poured all of his energies not reserved for business into convincing artisans to stop drinking. The regularized routines now common in the shops, he explained, ruled out the use of beverages that disqualified the mind from "that systematic and methodical arrangement of business so indispensable to the good regulation of every establishment." Temperance was vital to the peace and good order of the firm, since "men, however well disposed, may, by the use of stimulus (though in small quantities) be excited to insubordination." Temperate employees would also work harder. Repeating the arguments of several masters that teetotaling journeymen were a great prize, Brewster meticulously laid out what was at issue: total abstinence would yield 25 percent more profits. Whatever the allures of alcohol, Brewster concluded, "facts speak loud."[5]

The new wave of artisan moralism peaked in May 1829, when a group of master mechanics led by Brewster and his associate, the master bookbinder Charles Starr, announced the opening of the Association for Moral Improvement of Young Mechanics. The employers, as Brewster and Starr explained, were distressed at the sinful and unindustrious habits still common among New York's journeymen and apprentices; their obligations— "to the city and to God"—demanded that they act as never before to encourage morality. At the association's meetinghouse in the heart of the Sixth Ward, interested mechanics would be able to improve their minds— and their work—by listening to free lectures on innovations in the mechanical arts. To improve their souls, they would be able to hear the gospel from the evangelical Reverend Henry Hunter and various temperance lecturers.[6]

It requires no great unmasking to discover the economic self-interest associated with these efforts; on this point, Brewster and company were quite open. It is equally important not to reduce artisan temperance reform to a mere rationale for acquisitiveness, as if the wily master craftsmen seized the arguments nearest to hand in order to advance their personal fortunes and secure a repressive social control. None of their points, even those on business and profits, were decisive ruptures with the benevolent entrepreneurialism that masters had begun to identify with the artisan republic before 1825. Surrounding the moralizers' more mundane arguments about increased returns and productivity there still glowed the halo of obligation, care, and patriotic duty: by helping younger artisans to be successful men—the Franklins and Fultons of tomorrow, as one put it—

5. Temperance Society, *First Annual Report*, 23-24.
6. *Man*, February 20, 1830, October 19, 1832. On Starr, see *Free Enquirer*, March 25, 1829; New-York Friendly Association of Master Bookbinders, "List of Prices" (1822), N-YHS Broadsides; Colden, *Memoir*, 231.

experienced craftsmen like Brewster hoped to rescue the young from the unvirtuous path of indulgence and dependence that rendered them, in one master's words, "mere slaves of creation."[7] The most committed evangelicals like Brewster certainly believed that by banning drink, they were helping to save souls, their own included. Other temperance men were less pious but still considered their motives to be as altruistic as they were self-interested. Closer to the spirit of their remarks was their fusion of the artisan republican emphasis on rights, virtue, independence, and the masters' obligations with the evangelical temperance argument—forming a powerful idealistic defense of the masters' position and clarifying a new individualist ethic of discipline, responsibility, and self-improvement. By finding their own moral bearings and getting their journeymen to work harder, the reformers helped all to gain their competence and, as Brewster contended, protected the security of republican institutions from a drunk, corruptible electorate. At the same time, they hoped to secure a more productive work force and a moral sanction for entrepreneurial competition. Each of these impulses reinforced the others in such a way that the masters could present themselves both as profit-seeking innovators and as benevolent craftsmen. That this struck them not as ironic but as self-evident eased their transition into the world of the industrializing metropolis: the artisan economy was changing but "the Trade" remained, supposedly directed by moral republican craftsmen and graced with a fundamental harmony of interests, governed by "the *energies* and decided *efforts and influence* of every good man who regards the welfare of his country."[8]

The General Society, now a stalwart friend of religion and morality, did its part in the Mechanics' School and Apprentices' Library—stirring some controversy along the way. The school enlarged rapidly, opening a department for girls in 1826 and admitting more than two hundred students by the end of the decade; to handle the numbers, the staff had to adopt the Lancastrian monitorial system, an apt introduction for students to the kinds of subdivision and coordination they would one day encounter in the shops. The controversy concerned the library and the complaints of some society members that its stock of poetry and plays—"suited to the taste of every description of readers"—was doing more to foul the minds of the apprentices than to purify and enlighten them. In 1828, the objectors proposed that all plays, romances, and novels be labeled "pernicious and immoral" and banned from the library shelves. The society's school committee responded with a thorough defense of the existing selection, and claimed that the controversial works were especially valuable "[a]s an incentive to the practice of reading, as a means of keeping from bad com-

7. Temperance Society, *First Annual Report*, 27–28.
8. Ibid., 30.

pany. . . ." Still, the committee mollified the critics by passing two new
rules, one that would permit any member to submit a list of works not to
be lent to his apprentices, and another that required all apprentices who
borrowed the lighter reading to take out some more "solid" material as
well.[9]

Apart from temperance and related moral issues, the master craftsmen
agitated the usual concerns of the mechanics' interest, especially those
connected with the entrepreneurial rights of craft employers. Building-
trade masters and contractors had long been perturbed by their lack of
adequate legal protection in the competitive construction market, in particular their liability for the costs of wages and materials on projects that
went bankrupt. In the early 1820s, as the effects of the panic of 1819
lifted, master masons, carpenters, and builders held public meetings
to demand a lien law from the state legislature. Faced with continued re-
buffs from Albany, they resumed their efforts in 1825 and 1828, with the
support of the leaders of the General Society. Their arguments hinged on
the idea that the lien would preserve sound credit and what more than
one builder called "equal rights": secure from failure, small speculative
builders would not be blocked from advancement; journeymen would be
spared some of the risks of dismissal and unemployment; consumers would
not be at the mercy of the richest building speculators.[10]

Another, more daring movement arose in opposition to the auctioning
system. Since 1815, British manufacturers and bankers had stepped up
their use of the New York auctions as conduits to the American market,
to save themselves time and expense and to sell off their surpluses as
quickly as possible. The practice infuriated the "regular" merchants shut
out from the licensed auction trade, as well as the master artisans alarmed
at the sudden influx of cheap imported merchandise. After petitioning
Congress on the matter for over a decade, the frustrated anti-auctioneers
took their cause to the voters in 1828, with a slate of independent pro-
Adams electors pledged to abolishing the auctions altogether. The group,
although dominated by such leading merchants as Lewis Tappan, was intent on winning the artisan vote; accordingly, it filled its journal, the *Anti-
Auctioneer*, with direct appeals to the mechanics, held a meeting of trades-

9. GSMT Minute Book, January 7, 1826, December 3, 1828; GSMT Minutes,
School Committee, June 5, 1826; December 31, 1827; Pascu, "Philanthropic Tradition," 409–14.

10. *Courier and Enquirer*, November 29, December 2, 1829; *Working Man's Advocate* [New York], December 12, 1829, January 9, 1830; Henry W. Farnam, *Chapters
in the History of Social Legislation in the United States to 1860* (Washington, 1938),
153–54; Jabez D. Hammond, *The History of Political Parties in the State of New York*
(Albany, 1842), II, 331. On similar agitation in Pennsylvania, see Louis Hartz, *Economic Policy and Democratic Thought: Pennsylvania, 1776–1860* (Cambridge, Mass.,
1948), 191–93, 221.

men chaired by the president of the General Society, and named one master, the builder Thomas C. Taylor, to its ticket.[11]

The anti-auctioneers fared badly at the polls, inundated by the popular vote for Andrew Jackson and his supporters: none of the three anti-auction candidates won, and only the one who ran jointly with the Adams slate gained a majority in any ward; the artisan auctioneer Taylor ran especially badly in the poor and middling central and eastern wards. The anti-auctioneers did manage, however, to extend the protectionist sentiments of 1788 to make them fit the new economic and political setting of 1828. Filling their speeches and articles with familiar republican rhetoric, anti-auction spokesmen like one "Plain, Practical Man" denounced the licensed merchants as "monopolizers" and "corrupt, selfish speculators" at war with "the genius of republican government." Like the lien-law advocates, they insisted that by aiding the entrepreneurial masters in their fight, journeymen and small tradesmen would help preserve their own jobs and future prosperity. "What is good for the head," one anti-auctioneer declared, "is good for the members." Undeterred by the debacle of 1828, they regrouped the following year, vowing to uproot auctions once and for all.[12]

The formation of the American Institute of the City of New York gave the masters' campaigns an additional political dimension and, in time, more coherence. The Institute was founded in 1827 as an offshoot of John Griscom's Mechanical and Scientific Institution; although headed by a diverse collection of manufacturers, merchants, and philanthropists (including several temperance leaders), it was guided by those craft entrepreneurs who were most friendly to the administration of John Quincy Adams. "Our aim," one Institute committee reported, "is to aid the diffusion of a more thorough and intimate knowledge of our natural resources— agricultural, commercial, and manufacturing." True to their word, the members began a string of projects for the collection of facts and the celebration of national genius, capped by an annual Institute fair. But un-

11. Horace Secrist, "The Anti-Auction Movement and the New York Workingmen's Party of 1829," *Transactions of the Wisconsin Academy of Science, Arts and Letters* 17 (1914): 149–66. The defense of the auctions as facilitators of trade appears in *The Beneficial Tendency of Auctioneering and the Danger of Restraining It: By a Friend to Trade* (New York, 1817); *Memorial of the Auctioneers of the City of New-York* (Washington, D.C., 1821). The campaign is well covered in *Evening Post*, October 14, 16, 17, 21, 31, 1828. See also Robert W. July, *The Essential New Yorker: Gulian Commelin Verplanck* (Durham, 1951), 139–40.

12. Secrist, "Anti-Auction," 155–58; Mushkat, *Tammany*, 108–9, 112–14; *Remarks upon the Auction System as Practiced in New-York: By a Plain Practical Man* (New York, 1828), 2; *Anti-Auctioneer* [New York], November 1, 1828, quoted in Secrist, "Anti-Auction," 154; *Morning Herald* [New York], May 8, 1829; *Working Man's Advocate*, December 12, 1829.

like the General Society, the Institute chose sides in the internecine struggle between different factions of self-proclaimed Republican politicians by adding spirited defenses of the Adamsite high-tariff American System to its agenda. "The NEW WORLD is old enough to take care of itself," one Institute broadside proclaimed; while trade and commerce were important to the commonwealth, manufacturing needed special support. In the spring of 1829, after New York's Adamsites had been crushed, the group emerged as the champion of all causes that stressed entrepreneurial reform. Demands for higher tariffs mingled with forceful attacks on the auctioneers, "a combination of monopolies . . . that must make the friends of equal rights tremble"; Institute committees added calls for wider credit for craft entrepreneurs, to be won by placing more master craftsmen in responsible banking positions, as had been done at the "signally useful" Mechanics' Bank.[13]

It was not that the Institute men—any more than the General Society, the lien-law reformers, or the anti-auctioneers—felt any ambivalence about capitalist expansion: they welcomed it, provided the masters had their share of sound bank credit. Even the most caustic American Institute reports on banking refrained from attacking financiers and banking in toto, and objected only to the cheapening of credit in the hands of reckless speculators. Rather, all these groups were interested in making America and the New World safe for craft capitalists, by ending "aristocratic" mercantile abuses and awakening "the spirit of American independence." More consistently than ever before, the masters emphasized the need to advance their own interests for the good of the entire trade—not simply to hold on to their opportunities but to enlarge them. Their fresh interpretation of artisan republicanism in turn fit well with the moral imprecations of the temperance men and the Association for Moral Improvement. In each case, the masters still claimed to be the patresfamilias of the trades who protected the mechanics' interest, including the journeymen, be

13. Allen, "Memoirs," 111–12; Charles Patrick Daly, *Origin and History of Institutions for the Promotion of the Useful Arts* (Albany, 1864), 28; John W. Chambers, *A Condensed History of the American Institute* (New York, 1892); *Report of the American Institute of the City of New-York on the Subject of Fairs* (New York, 1829), 5, 8, 10; *Report of a Special Committee of the American Institute on the Subject of Cash Duties, the Auction System, etc.* (New York, 1829), 2 and passim; *Memorial of the American Institute Praying for Certain Regulations in the Banking Capital of This State, March 14, 1829* (n.p., 1829), 9. For background, see Samuel Rezneck, "The Rise and Early Development of Industrial Consciousness in the United States, 1760–1830," *Journal of Economic and Business History*, supplement, 4 (1932): 784–811. Among the institute's early organizers were Adoniram Chandler, Clarkson Crolius, Henry Guyon, Robert Hoe, Peter Schenck, and Thaddeus Wakeman. Unfortunately, the earliest membership list in the American Institute Papers dates from 1840, but see *Officers of the American Institute in the City of New York from Its Origins in 1828 to and including 1892* (New York, 1892).

it against unrepublican speculators or the tyranny of drink. Each stressed the importance of individual initiative and industry, whether in overcoming alcohol or in securing credit and markets. Each insisted that by maximizing the masters' commercial opportunities, the public good—moral and economic—would be served. None suggested that any inequities in the workshops threatened the trades.[14]

The political implications of these views would be fully worked out only during the tumultuous summer and autumn of 1829. Long before then, however, New York's temperance men and craft entrepreneurs discovered that a small but growing number of artisans did not see things their way.

Impious Artisans and the Uses of Morality

On January 29, 1825, about forty self-professed freethinkers gathered in Harmony Hall to drink toasts and deliver eulogies in honor of Thomas Paine's birthday. Two years later, George Houston, an English immigrant printer, founded a new freethought newspaper, the *Correspondent*, featuring scientific and anticlerical essays "to bring man back to the path from which he has deviated." The Painites welcomed Houston by organizing the Free Press Association to defend him from the predictable attacks of the Sabbatarians and the regular New York press. Soon the freethinkers had started a weekly lecture series on theology and deism; by December 1827, when an additional lecture series was announced, an estimated three hundred persons regularly attended the freethinkers' programs. The following year, at least two new groups—the Society of Free Enquirers and the Debating Society—helped to sponsor the Temple of Arts, the Insitution of Practical Education (run by the Scot rationalist Robert Jennings), and a school, the Minerva Institution, administered by Houston's daughter. Abner Kneeland, the liberal minister of the Prince Street Universalist Church, was sufficiently swayed to lead a secession from his own congregation and to form the rationalist Second Universalist Society. Emissaries from the Manhattan societies delivered lectures and distributed freethought tracts in outlying towns. Copies of major freethought texts—Paine's *Theological Works*, Volney's *Ruins of Empire*—were available in cheap editions throughout the city. The Paine birthday celebrations, repeated annually since 1825, became elaborate affairs. Suddenly, two decades after Paine's death, New York was again a center of freethought agitation.[15]

14. *Report on Cash Duties*, 7; *Memorial*, 3; *Report on the Subject of Fairs*, 6; *Journal of the American Institute* 1 (1835): 3-5.

15. Albert Post, *Popular Freethought in America, 1825–1850* (New York, 1943); *Correspondent* [New York], January 20, March 3, 31, April 21, December 22, 1827,

The catalyst for the rationalist resurgence was a new element in artisan New York, an extraordinary collection of recent émigrés who had long been active in the clandestine enclaves of English deism. Houston, the most notorious of them, arrived in New York in the mid-1820s, shortly after he had served two years in Newgate for the offense of publishing a translation of Holbach's impious satire *L'Histoire de Jésus Christ*. Other British deists active in New York, included the shoemakers William Carver and Benjamin Offen and the printers Gilbert Vale and George Henry Evans; all shared Houston's interest in the eighteenth-century freethought classics and looked forward to promulgating their views in the less restrictive atmosphere of the New World. Their greatest hero was Paine, and their first efforts aimed at resurrecting Paine's reputation in his and their adopted country. The Sabbatarian controversy added new significance to the freethinkers' work: instead of simply promoting rationalism, they began to warn of a new ecclesiastical threat to republican liberties, one they deemed as dangerous as the one they had left behind. "Our country is saturated with . . . vile pernicious tracts," Jennings exclaimed, meant to "prepare the minds of our now politically free citizens" for passive submission to "lawless and ambitious puritans."[16]

Even more than the earlier deists, this new movement drew its primary support from small master and journeymen artisans—shoemakers, printers, stonecutters and assorted others. It offered its followers an updated version of older rationalist ideas on universal salvation and republican fears of ecclesiastical despotism, with the fillip that the new evangelicals loomed as the surest and most pressing threats to independence, reason, and virtue. Man, as Benjamin Offen explained, ceased to love freedom "only when he ceases to be rational or to exist." Revealed religion, by extinguishing rationality, robbed believers of the ability to form independent judgments or exercise their virtue, and thus served as a potent weapon of would-be tyrants. Once rulers understood the political uses of religious life, the freethinkers predicted, they could install a group of dependent clergymen, pamper them with luxury and privilege, and consolidate their

February 2, 29, March 22, April 5, May 24, June 6, 14, November 28, December 17, 1828; *Christian Advocate and Journal* [New York], December 7, 1827, cited in Post, *Popular Freethought*, 47; Abner Kneeland, *An Appeal to Universalists* (New York, 1829); idem, *Supplement to "The Proceedings of the Friends of Liberal Christianity in New York City"* (New York, 1829); Jentz, "Artisans, Evangelicals, and the City," 117-30.

16. *Correspondent*, July 7, 1827. On the freethinkers, see Post, *Popular Freethought*, 32-33, 45, 48-49; Hugins, *Jacksonian Democracy*, 95-96; D. M. Bennett, *The World's Sages, Thinkers and Reformers*, 2d ed. (New York, 1876), 695-99, 756-57; Lewis Masquerier, *Sociology: or, The Reconstruction of Society, Government, and Property* (New York, 1877), 123-24, 159-60; F. W. Evans, *Autobiography of a Shaker* (Mount Lebanon, N.Y., 1869), 10-11, 16, 26.

own position as the elect of God. Were such unrepublican clerics ever to take hold in the United States, as the evangelicals appeared to be doing, one freethinker declared, then "all that is estimable in the free institutions of our country will be endangered or lost."[17]

Ironically, the freethinkers repeated some of the themes found in the sermons of their worst enemies. In keeping with Paine's own writings, the Painites hailed commercial prosperity and technological improvement as worthy goals; one freethinking Fourth of July speaker praised the United States in 1827 for "rapidly increasing prosperity, by the scientific development of its vast internal resources." Like their pious entrepreneurial antagonists, the freethinkers also impressed upon their followers the importance of temperance, study, and reflection. Drinking worried them greatly, as a source of dependency, unreason, and disgrace; drunkenness, in Houston's view, was "a witch to the senses, a devil to the soul, a *thief* to the purse, the beggar's companion, a *wife's woe*, and *children's sorrow*." Rather like the American Institute, the freethinkers wanted to replace the customary habits of the workshop with their own reading groups and lecture series on the mechanical arts, natural science, and other forms of useful knowledge. Their exuberant autodidactism surfaced at their most lighthearted celebrations. They could find no higher praise for Paine on his birthday than that he "left us works that we may read/ And truth itself explore." For one leather-lunged freethinker, a toast to twenty-three freethinking heroes (including Wat Tyler and William Tell) was not complete unless it included Shakespeare, Pope, Burns, Shelley, Byron, "and all such philosophers, patriots, and poets."[18]

This superficial convergence on moral grounds, however, never dulled the warfare between infidel (a label the Painites gladly accepted) and evangelical—it was one thing, after all, to study the Bible, quite another to study Byron. The freethinkers had no interest in promoting respect for godly authority or obedience to a religious moral code: they sought rights— rights they claimed the Creator had bestowed to all, not to a select few,

17. *Correspondent*, February 3, 24, 1827, February 8, 9, 1829; *An Address to the Committee Appointed by a General Meeting of the Citizens of the City of New York, Held at Tammany Hall, January 31, 1829* (New York, 1829), 14–15. The social backgrounds of the deists are suggested by the occupations of those listed in the deist press as participants in the Paine birthday celebrations from 1827 to 1832: printers, three; shoemakers, two; stonecutters, two; draftsman, dry goods, grate setter, hatter, iron-chest maker, merchant, paperhanger, portrait painter, rule maker, tinsmith, teacher, and umbrella maker, one each. Only one, the shoemaker Elisha Tallmadge (a union leader in the 1830s) was identified clearly as a journeyman; of the rest, at least six were small masters. Most likely, the membership was dominated by a mixture of small masters and journeymen, along with a smaller number of petty retailers. See Jentz, "Artisans, Evangelicals, and the City," 117–30.

18. *Correspondent*, July 7, 1827; January 12, February 9, 1828. On freethought lecturing, see *Correspondent*, December 22, 1827.

rights the evangelicals were trying to destroy by legislating morality and enhancing their own power over others. As Offen explained, the religionists were set on a vicious, intolerant course, one that would destroy "the mutual aid and mutual respect that are necessary to our well-being." Sunday schools, missionary societies, and Sabbath regulations were all breaches of republican values and the constitutional separation of church and state, designed, "Veritas" charged, "to reduce the citizens of this country to abject slavery." Even though they encouraged sobriety, the freethinkers thought the temperance societies pernicious—examples, one of them asserted, of men "under the garb of sanctity, pushing themselves into the ranks of respectable citizens," to win a sober hearing and then steal the listeners' powers of reason. At bottom, the threat was as much political as theological, an attack by men of privilege on the people, those who should be enlightened and freed from crypto-aristocratic superstition. To counter the threat, the freethinkers posed their own cultural and educational institutions as a deistic, egalitarian alternative to the schools and libraries of the evangelicals. With these efforts, they would hasten their own rationalist kingdom, a world turned upside down where men would truly be able to think, reflect, and act for themselves, free of aristocratic and religious tyranny; where one would find, according to a freethinkers' toast, "soldiers at the plough, kings in the mines, lawyers at the spinning genney, and priests in heaven"; where Americans would enjoy "not the independence we now nominally have," the deist Edward Thompson proclaimed, "but the independence we may, and of right, ought to enjoy, by virtue of a declared and existing charter."[19]

Coming in the mid-1820s, this was not an especially penetrating analysis of American society and politics. While they berated priestly aristocrats in general terms, the freethinkers never tried to work out how, precisely, the New York evangelicals were linked to the republic's political institutions or to identify who the American aristocrats were. Since many of their leaders had only recently arrived from Britain, their broadsides on religion, monarchy, and moralism seemed oddly out of place in the post-Jeffersonian United States, as if the freethinkers were trying to transplant arguments pertinent enough in England without taking stock of American realities. Their political message was a reaction against evangelical excesses and remained trenchant only so long as religious proselytizers were active: any slackening of evangelical zeal would rob them of their only issue. Although some of the most thoughtful deists, including George Henry Evans, were aware of the writings of Thomas Spence and

19. *Correspondent*, February 9, June 14, 1828, April 25, 1829; Edward Thompson, *An Oration Delivered on the Anniversary of the Declaration of American Independence* (New York, 1829), 6.

the early English Ricardian socialists, they remained tentative in explaining how economic and social changes might also have contributed to what they saw as the loss of American liberty.[20]

What the freethinkers did kindle was an approach to knowledge that both set limits to evangelical reform and provided self-taught artisan democrats with an intellectual setting of their own, to judge the world's affairs in the light of Right Reason. By their very existence, the freethought groups challenged revealed religion and the moral reformers on their own ground. However narrow their vision, they saw an America where the rights of the many were in retreat, threatened by the evangelical ideas on grace and moral character increasingly popular among the city's craft employers. However derivative their arguments, they nurtured the political and cultural egalitarianism of the later eighteenth century—above all the notion that all men were capable, through reflection, mutual study, and debate, of challenging received wisdom and constituted authority and unlocking the mysteries of the universe. Along the way, they created numerous arenas for discussion and inquiry. In this freethinking radical milieu, ordinary artisans joined in a brace of popular forums and, guided by neither divine revelation nor clerics, preserved the secular republicanism of Paine and the traditions of anti-authoritarian political dissent, in the one land, a freethinking journal observed, where "heterodox truth [may] obtain an audience."[21] In time these inquiries were leavened by newer ideas, promoted by the associates and critics of Robert Owen, that challenged the very foundations of American capitalist development.

Property, Producers' Rights, and the Assault on Competition

The labor theory of value—the doctrine that all wealth is derived from labor—claimed a diverse array of supporters in antebellum America. The idea was at the core of Lockian theories of property; students of such different Enlightenment writers as Volney and Adam Smith held it axiomatic; so did public officials ranging from Andrew Jackson to Daniel Webster and John C. Calhoun. In New York, the theory percolated through Paine's radical republicanism, eighteenth-century attacks on luxurious speculators, and the freethinkers' denunciations of useless priests; the General Society emblematized the idea in its hammer-and-hand crest. If the notion was self-evident to working people, whose labor produced wealth every day, it had become, by the mid-1820s, a maxim of all versions of

20. On Evans and Spence, see Clifton K. Yearley, *Britons in American Labor: A History of the Influence of the United Kingdom Immigrants on American Labor* (Baltimore, 1957), 34–35.

21. *New Harmony and Nashoba Gazette*, October 29, 1828. For more on this periodical and its editors, see below, Chapter 5.

political economy. Such wide currency was possible because the concept of "labor" was very supple. A broad definition might include merchants, professionals, and bankers as productive citizens; a narrow one might exclude all but those who actually worked with their hands. Depending on one's point of view, the labor theory could be used either to defend "productive" capitalist entrepreneurship or to condemn it.[22]

The dissemination of the writings of the English radical Ricardians in the 1820s helped establish the theory as an attack on economic inequality, competition, and prevailing property relations. At the turn of the nineteenth century, several writers pointed out that England's wealth was being absorbed by "non-producing," parasitical landlords and the military; twenty years later, William Thompson, John Gray, Thomas Hodgskin, and other radical publicists turned these charges against the capitalist credit and wage system. Children of the Enlightenment, these pamphleteers expected that by exposing political and social inequality they would help bring about a social order based on the primacy of the producing classes; a few of the radicals, including Thompson, organized and supported community experiments to demonstrate a possible alternative.[23] Their influence in America intensified in the mid-1820s, with the arrival of Robert Owen (who helped popularize their work) and with the mounting publicity accorded the leading American religious communities, especially the Shakers. In New York, these developments quickened the activities of a small group of reformers who had already begun generating their own versions of the ideal producers' republic. The most celebrated of them was one Dr. Cornelius Blatchly.

Blatchly had not always seemed destined for a radical career. Born into a comfortable family in rural New Jersey, he made his mark first as a medical student at the College of Physicians and Surgeons, associated with that Episcopalian bulwark Columbia College. As he pondered his own religious views, however, the young doctor discovered a great deal that was radically wrong in his own city. Raised a Quaker, Blatchly was fast verging on the most unorthodox egalitarian professions of brotherhood, exceeding even the "radical" Quaker sects like the Hicksites; in 1829, he would declare himself a devout believer in the divinity of Christ but the follower of no man, woman, party, or church. In 1817, when he first collected his

22. Neufeld, "Realms of Thought," 8–13. See also Louis H. Arky, "The Mechanics' Union of Trade Associations and the Formation of the Philadelphia Workingmen's Movement," PMHB 76 (1952): 143–44; Laurie, Working People of Philadelphia, chap. 4.

23. On the Ricardians and preliminaries to Owenism, see Esther Lowenthal, The Ricardian Socialists (New York, 1924); Ronald M. Meek, Studies in the Labor Theory of Value (New York, 1969), 121–29; John F. C. Harrison, Quest for the New Moral World: Robert Owen and the Owenites in Britain and America (New York, 1969), 65–78; Patricia Hollis, The Pauper Press: A Study in Working-Class Radicalism of the 1830s (Oxford, 1970), 221–29.

thoughts in a brief tract entitled *Some Causes of Popular Poverty*, he turned this egalitarian pietism to the problem of the urban poor, in ways that stretched familiar republican themes beyond the boundaries of conventional wisdom. Insisting that those who worked with their hands were entitled to the full product of their labor, Blatchly located an American despotism, not in political or spiritual life alone, but in economic injustice and obnoxious conceptions of property. "Abundance of tyrants, vices, and oppressions," he argued bluntly, "are begotten by an abundant excess of riches in the hands of the few who are thereby often rendered proud, haughty, luxurious, profligate, lustful, and inhuman." Property—by which he meant property in land—had been bequeathed by God to man for "*general* use and benefit and not for *individual* aggrandizement"; therefore, he argued, only those who actually used or occupied property should hold it. The basic flaws of American society grew from violations of natural law that permitted nonlaboring rentiers, bankers, and other capitalists to accumulate land and exact usurious interest under the full protection of the law. To correct these abuses, he called for the abolition of inheritance and the redistribution of all the property of deceased citizens.[24]

Six years later, when a handful of professionals and master artisans formed the New York Society for Promoting Communities, Blatchly was appointed to write the group's constitution and a brief exposition of its central beliefs. Here, in *An Essay on Common Wealths*, Blatchly expanded his earlier argument even further, into a plan for the restoration of lost virtue through the organization of "pure and perfect communities." All men, he insisted, were entitled to four basic rights—health, the fruits of their labor, freedom from calumny, and liberty from injury. America, he claimed, repressed all four:

> For labour is cheated of its true reward by power, rank, interests, rents, *imposts*, and other *impositions*; health and life are ruined by many evils; liberty is destroyed by numerous injuries; and character is assailed continually, because envy, interest, and other evil passions and appetites are excited by the selfish nature of exclusive interests, power, *privileges*, and *grandeur*.

The legal sanctity of private property was itself an abomination that denied what Blatchly called society's religious obligation "to use and bestow her blessings and donations in the most wise, just, equal and social

24. *Working Man's Advocate*, November 14, 1829; Cornelius C. Blatchly, *Some Causes of Popular Poverty* in [Thomas Branagan] *The Pleasures of Contemplation* (Philadelphia, 1817), 199, 200–201, 206, and passim; Arthur Bestor, *Backwoods Utopias: The Sectarian Origins and the Owenite Phase of Communitarian Socialism in America, 1663–1829*, 2d ed. (Philadelphia, 1970), 97–100, 104; David Harris, *Socialist Origins in the United States: American Forerunners of Marx, 1817–1832* (Assen, The Netherlands, 1967), 10–19. Blatchly's religious views are mentioned in *Pleasures of Contemplation*, 176.

manner." In its place, he proposed new communities based on an ill-defined "inclusive system," where wealth would benefit all.[25]

There was an abundance of perfectionist millenarianism in all of this, not unlike that of the New York "mechanick" preachers, and harkening back to the sectarian radicals of seventeenth-century England. At every turn, Blatchly's argument cited and alluded to Scripture, starting with a quotation from Acts on his title page and continuing with repeated references to the Books of David, James, and Revelation. He discussed at some length the merits of religious communitarian sects, particularly the Shakers and the Rappites. His constitution for the Society for Promoting Communities stated outright that once the inclusive system became general, existing governments would be "supplanted by the government of Jehovah, and his annointed, the Prince of Peace." As in English and American millenarian tracts, a nostalgic, ahistorical air blanketed his radical observations, as Blatchly yearned for a golden age, a time before America's descent into indolence, luxury, and grandeur. Like the anti-aristocratic Ricardians, he said little directly about urban conditions, industrial innovation, or relations of production, but held closely to his preoccupation with rent and landlords. Even as Blatchly wrote in one of the fastest-growing cities in the world, his imagination was drawn to rural motifs, to "the wilds," to a Jerusalem of small landed producers.[26]

Yet Blatchly, like other sectarian radicals, should not be dismissed as an agrarian visionary or a pious crank and consigned to the oblivion of "utopian" socialism. If nothing else, his writings proved that an egalitarian Christianity could still inspire radical plans to counter the coercive measures increasingly characteristic of evangelical reform. No one more bitterly denounced the evangelicals, particularly those "false prophets" the Sabbatarians, than did Blatchly; no one was more insistent that "we should not meddle with religion politically, but let that be between God and every man's own conscience." Furthermore, Blatchly, although inspired by his religion, also made intelligent use of the secular literature on natural rights and the danger of inheritance and accumulation, in particular the Ricardians' discussion of usufruct and the American writings on the danger of privilege. While they led Blatchly to concentrate even more on the evils of rent and landed property, these nonreligious writings also led

25. Cornelius C. Blatchly, *An Essay on Common Wealths* (New York, 1822), 8–10, 25. Of the eighteen men listed in the essay along with Blatchly as members of the society, the occupations of fourteen have been identified from the 1822 city directory: five teachers and professors, three ministers, two attorneys, one physician, one merchant, one printer, one builder.

26. Blatchly, *Essay on Common Wealths*, 4, 6, 23–24, 29, 33, 36, 41. On related themes in nineteenth-century British millenarianism, see J. F. C. Harrison, *The Second Coming: Popular Millenarianism, 1780–1850* (New Brunswick, N.J., 1979), 3–10, 207–30.

him to a number of hardheaded efforts in the late 1820s and 1830s to defend New York's revived trade unions and to expose the plight of the outwork seamstresses.[27]

The crux of Blatchly's radicalism lay in his combination of Christian ethics, republican politics, and the labor theory of value. In concert with the beliefs of more orthodox Quakers, Blatchly's vision of brotherhood was rooted in an opposition to blasphemous human coercion. Chattel slavery was, of course, the paradigm of sinful domination, for Blatchly as for the Quaker abolitionists; Blatchly, however, extended that paradigm to cover all forms of economic inequality and competition, to declare that every society in which property was not "social and inclusive" was "under the domination of satan and antichrist." Simultaneously, he focused on economic inequality as a solvent of republican equality and community. His argument on accumulation referred above all to the enervating and corrupting influences of competition for wealth. Grasping, unvirtuous, "*selfish*" Americans, seduced by their own self-interest, were Blatchy's chief villains; selfishness, he wrote, was "the root of all national vices," destroying men's "equitable right to nature." Above all, Blatchly's Christian republican jeremiad blamed economic inequality not on political corruption alone but on private property and usury. So long as private property existed, all laws and privileges would favor the propertied; political reform was meaningless unless private benefits were turned into common wealth. And as the coup de grace, Blatchly singled out the United States as proof of his assertions, as a land perverted by private property, where "men's interests are now opposed to each other, in such a manner that only a little sympathy can exist."[28]

For all of its nostalgia, here was an argument to contradict the political economy of entrepreneurial benevolence. Blatchly remained a confident idealist, certain that social transformation would come with moral regeneration. His adoption of the labor theory of value brought no suggestion that the opposing interests of producer and nonproducer could not be reconciled with brotherly love. But his work also suggested that the radical Ricardians' critique, rather than the entrepreneurial brand of artisan republicanism, ran closer to the gospel as taught most eloquently in the Epistle of James:

> Behold, the hire of the laborers who have reaped down your fields, which is of you kept back by fraud, crieth: and the cries of them which have reaped are entered into the ears of the Lord of Sabaoth.

27. Cornelius C. Blatchly, *Sunday Tract* (New York, 1828), 2, 5; idem, *Essay on Common Wealths*, 7, 12–13, 21, 25; Hugins, *Jacksonian Democracy*, 98.

28. Blatchly, *Essay on Common Wealths*, 8–9, 24–25, and passim. A fine discussion of the broader patterns of Quaker religious and social thought appears in David Brion Davis, *The Problem of Slavery in the Age of Revolution, 1770–1823* (Ithaca, 1975), 241–54.

In short order, the essence of this message would help lead others to analyze the sources of social inequality.[29]

Robert Owen's arrival in New York two years after Blatchly published his *Essay* accelerated the pace of critical inquiry. Owen's reputation had preceded him, thanks in part to the controversies he had provoked in the *Edinburgh Review* and in part to the promotional efforts of the Philadelphian William Duane. Blatchly claimed to have run across *A New View of Society* only in 1822, just as he completed his pamphlet, but he quickly revised his text to note his affinities with the Englishman. By the time Owen came to New York, he was a communitarian hero, and he spent his first evening in the city as the honored guest of the Society for Promoting Communities. But Owen's fame was too great for him to be confined to the constricted radical circles of Blatchly and friends. Within weeks, he had visited prominent politicians, lawyers, and businessmen, all eager to learn more about the curious philanthropist. In Philadelphia, he stayed with Dr. James Rush, Benjamin's son, and addressed the Franklin Institute and the Atheneum; in Washington, he was received by John Quincy Adams, William H. Crawford, John C. Calhoun, and President Monroe. After his first trip to Indiana to inspect the site for his New Harmony community, he began a triumphant speaking tour that concluded back in Washington with two separate addresses in the House of Representatives. All the while, the New York press paid close attention to his progress and devoted space to his speeches. In the spring of 1825, a New York publisher released the first American edition of *A New View of Society*. A year later, Owen returned to New Harmony, in one historian's words, with "an intoxicating sense of a victory already won."[30]

To understand this whirlwind, it is imperative to recognize that Owen could mean different things to different people in the mid-1820s. Reactions to his treatises, certainly the most systematic radical writings to have arrived from early industrial Britain, were softened by Owen's reputation as a reforming industrialist—interested in improving society with a mixture of science and charity, in curing social ills with largesse, and in expanding production without creating classes. One can easily imagine a New York master, like his counterpart in the Franklin Institute, encountering Owen as another successful manufacturer with pertinent (if somewhat eccentric) ideas about reforming industry and labor while preserving social harmony: at least one founder of the American Institute, Peter Schenck, was greatly impressed by the man, despite some of his more outlandish views on property. Owen moved gracefully within the society of enlightened men of wealth, with backgrounds like his own; a crusty conservative like Chief

29. James 5:4. Blatchly quoted the passage in *Some Causes of Popular Poverty*, 204.
30. Bestor, *Backwoods Utopias*, 100–114, 133; Harrison, *New Moral World*, 106.

Justice Story could pronounce him "pleasant in his conversation" and of "considerable interest." If his charm won few actual subscribers to his project from the ranks of the well-to-do, Owen still won a respectful hearing, at least initially. In time, his religious views made him unacceptable, and by 1827 he found himself denounced by respectable newspapers and master craftsmen's societies across the country. Until then, his challenge was interpreted by some as more of an extension of the ideal of the harmony of interests than as an attack on capitalist entrepreneurs.[31]

Embedded in Owen's thoughts and in the writings of some of his followers were the elements of the more trenchant anticapitalism later associated with Owenism. Owen insisted, along with the Ricardians, that "manual labor, properly directed, is the source of all wealth." He denounced capitalists as parasites. He attacked private property and unearned profit. His steadfast rationalism and distrust of established religion as a source of oppression mingled well with similar currents of artisan anti-evangelicalism. Most important, Owen told his readers that it was by earthly economic arrangements, and not by divine sanction or their own moral shortcomings, that they had been cheated of their due. He retained the millenarian idealist perfectionism of a Blatchly but stripped it of its strictly Christian context, to offer a secular paradise open to believer and infidel alike.[32]

Owen's most immediate influence in New York was on the freethinkers. Briefly inspired by the possible marriage of deism to communitarianism, a group of them, led by the future editor of the *Correspondent* George Houston, purchased a farm in Haverstraw, in Rockland County, about thirty miles from the city, where they established in 1826 the Franklin Community, the third Owenist community in the United States. Hopes for the group ran high for the first few months, and Owen himself dispatched one of his associates from New Harmony to help the experiment along. Even before the land was formally bought, a number of families had settled in and begun farming. Once the community organized, however, the religious question quickly divided the members, as those attracted mainly by the lure of communal farming rebelled when Houston and his associate, the Painite Henry Fay, set up their Church of Reason.

31. Bestor, *Backwoods Utopias*, 105–7, 130–32. My appraisal of Owen owes a great deal to Harrison, *New Moral World*, and to Thompson, *Making of the English Working Class*, 779–806. I would also stress, however, that in the United States those who supported Owen for any appreciable period did so out of their attraction for his entire system, not just a few particulars. Thompson's portrayal—of English Owenists seizing on *parts* of Owenism and rejecting others—bears little resemblance to the history of Owenism in this country.

32. Robert Owen, *A New View of Society* (1817; reprint, London, 1927), 19–24 and passim.

Within five months, the community dissolved, virtually without a trace. When Houston returned to New York to start his paper, he did not even describe his brief community experience; indeed, scarcely a mention of co-operation would ever appear in the pages of the *Correspondent*. By the winter of 1828-29, Owenism seemed to have reached the limits of its influence.[33]

While Houston and his associates foundered, however, artisans in other corners of the city also read about Owen and his new moral world. One of them began work on a treatise that promised to incorporate elements of Owen's political economy but also to offer a very different kind of radical program. The book, entitled *Observations on the Sources and Effects of Unequal Wealth*, appeared in 1826, a few months after Owen departed for New Harmony. Its author, Langton Byllesby, was a thirty-seven-year-old printer who, as far as can be determined, worked as a journeyman proofreader for the Harper Brothers' firm. He had been born in Philadelphia, the son of English immigrants; orphaned as a child, he was raised by Thomas Ryerson, a Revolutionary veteran and member of the Pennsylvania legislature. Byllesby's early career had been successful enough: after learning the printer's trade, he experimented with various inventions, including a primitive flying machine, and earned his competence. By 1824 (after several changes of residence), he had settled down as the editor of a newspaper in Easton, Pennsylvania, and started a family. His fortunes dimmed, however, when his local political patron suffered a humiliating defeat in 1824, and in the following year Byllesby quit Easton, first for Philadelphia and then for New York, in search of journeymen's work. Once in Manhattan, he began writing out his reflections on the state of his trade—but transformed them into a stinging diatribe against capitalist development, one that would prove a primer for the most radical New York workingmen of the late 1820s.[34]

Byllesby began with an assertion of democratic republican faith, a claim that though men had long had "a generally correct idea" of a proper society, "it remained for the now sage and venerable Thomas Jefferson [in the Declaration of Independence] to give mankind a true description of their

33. Bestor, *Backwoods Utopias*, 203-4; John Humphrey Noyes, *A History of American Socialisms* (Philadelphia, 1870), 74-77; Post, *Popular Freethought*, 181.

34. On Byllesby's life and influence, see Joseph Dorfman's introduction to the 1961 edition of *Observations*, as well as Harris, *Socialist Origins*, 34-35; Charles Sotheran, *Horace Greeley and Other Pioneers of American Socialism* (New York, 1892), 98; Paul Conkin, *Prophets of Prosperity: America's First Political Economists* (Bloomington, Ind., 1980), 234-36. Byllesby reported that he discovered a copy of John Gray's *Lecture on Human Happiness* (1825) after his own book was in press; noting the "similarity in ideas," he included lengthy quotations from Gray at the last minute. See Langton Byllesby, *Observations on the Sources and Effects of Unequal Wealth* (New York, 1826), 105-13.

destiny." Byllesby's task was to elaborate how men could now secure their life, liberty, and happiness despite the obvious inequalities of American life. He assumed, like Blatchly and Owen, that wealth was "properly and only an excess of the Products of Labour," to be used for the subsistence and pleasure of all mankind; the problem was that in "civilized" societies, including the United States, "products of labour belong to almost any other than the producer, who generally obtains from the application of his power no more than a bare subsistence." Byllesby's first line of analysis paralleled Blatchly's, as he denounced private property in land and the denial of independence as violations of self-evident natural laws. But Byllesby went further, to describe as "the very essence of slavery," *all* systems whereby men are "compelled to labour, while the proceeds of that labour is [sic] taken and enjoyed by another." That a workingman was nominally free—that is, possessed of "the appearance of option whether to labour or not"—only cloaked his bondage; the ordinary hatter or shoemaker, though naturally endowed with the abilities and strength of other men, was trapped in a set of social relations that "takes from one man the products of two days' labour and gives him in compensation the product of only one day of another. . . ."[35]

Not satisfied with his discovery of these inequalities, Byllesby turned to history in order to understand better the etiology of oppression. In a gloomy synopsis, he traced how the defense against plunder, the creation of private property, and the invention of money gradually gave rise to a class of speculating merchant-capitalists and moneylenders; these men of commerce in time destroyed all economies based on the simple exchange of products; the subsequent introduction of new methods of production consolidated the new speculative order while it increased the wealth of the propertied and increased the suffering of the masses. Ultimately, society had arrived at a state in which labor-saving machinery enabled the propertied to increase production on a vast scale, displacing most workers and creating a pool of unemployed men. Assuming, as Byllesby did, that consumption would not rise to match the new levels of production (indeed, would only diminish, given the displacement of so many producers), the subjugation of the majority was complete: lower prices would not keep pace with lowered earnings, competition would lead to further labor saving and further unemployment, and those fortunate to find jobs would have their wages depressed by the existence of so many unemployed; all would suffer during periodic suspensions of operations to allow consumption to catch up with production. The competitive system, always a benefit to the few at the expense of the many, had saved its cruelest ironies for last: while an ever greater proportion of the population was reduced to penury,

35. Byllesby, *Observations*, 7, 10–11, 33, 42.

he wrote, "it had been reserved for the present times to see the paradox of an excessive production . . . overwhelm a large portion of the labouring classes with resourceless distress, and intense misery. . . ."[36]

Like his predecessors, Byllesby saw hope in establishing what he called "something approaching the nature of a community," but he was careful to distinguish himself from other communitarians. Earlier philanthropic critics—he mentioned Owen and William Thompson and might just as well have included Blatchly—had "intermingled their views with religious or moral sentiments" and had merely tried "to show how a more agreeable condition of mankind might exist, without enlarging on the intolerable nature of the prevailing one." Not only had these men had little self-interest in their social blueprints; they had confined themselves to "sublimated discussion of the malformation of the human character under prevailing institutions" and encouraged the sentimental notion that an appeal to the moral rich might abolish social injustice. "History," Byllesby countered, "does not furnish an instance wherein the depository of power voluntarily abrogated its prerogatives, or the oppressor relinquished his advantages in favour of the oppressed." Instead of new societies set off from the existing one, Byllesby proposed a new system of cooperative production. Artisans would invest a sum to pay for all materials and would themselves be paid in labor notes, in proportion to the amount of work they actually performed. Each member would be limited to one share in the cooperative and would have an equal voice in directing the enterprise. In time, the community, free of money, interest, and exploitation, would secure to each producer the full product of his labor, "from the incipience to the consumption."[37]

Even after a century and a half of sloganeering, these words lose none of their astonishing force: Byllesby the republican printer, in breaking with Owen and others, opened a line of social criticism in America quite similar to those which, in Europe, would lead to Proudhon, to the socialist writings of Marx and Lassalle and to various other strands of labor radicalism. Whereas Blatchly and his associates feared the Republic was threatened by selfishness and private property, Byllesby condemned systematic competition, manipulation of credit, and the social system of production as unrepublican denials of "true liberty and just Government." Although he concentrated on the impact of labor-saving machinery—not a surprising emphasis for a printer and an employee of the Harper brothers—he formulated his indictment in general terms, which could be applied equally to mechanized trades and to those in which skills were being divided and work put out:

36. Ibid., 124–54, 73–74, 87–100.
37. Ibid., 4–5.

[F]or every improvement in the arts tending to reduce the value of the labour necessary to produce them, must inevitably have the effect of increasing the value and power of wealth in the hands of those who may be fortuitously possessed of it, in an equal ratio with the decrease in price on those things which are the object of it.

Reliance on the social commonwealth or on Christian benevolence did not figure in Byllesby's account: only "those whose labour is the origin of the wealth they do not enjoy," he insisted, could eliminate the hierarchies between masters and men. In all, with Byllesby (even more than with Blatchly) we witness the acceleration of a fundamental shift in language and sentiment, away from a pure assertion of republican rights and the obligations of workshop "justice" typical of the early journeymen's associations and toward a recognition that a deeper matrix of exploitation and unequal exchange for labor was responsible for the plight of the mass—all presented as a message that linked republican equal rights to the rights of producers (small masters and journeymen) and to the exclusion of capitalists. Three years after Byllesby published his *Essay*, the power of that message would be revealed, in a revised and even more incendiary form, in the writings of an obscure machinist named Thomas Skidmore.[38]

Blatchly and Byllesby were scribblers. Neither wrote as the head of a significant artisan movement; Blatchly was not even a craftsman. The extent of their readership and influence through the late 1820s remains obscure. Nevertheless, within the context of the developing radical artisan milieu of freethinkers and artisan organizers, their critiques hinted at the kinds of discussions that were going on in the trades. As early as 1819, an English immigrant journeyman had been moved to write that even in glorious America, the masters' "only object is to accumulate money in the aggregation of which, they are perfectly regardless of the wants of the Journeymen whom they employ." Deist radicals like Houston had momentarily been attracted to Owenist communitarianism. In conjunction with the agitation of the freethinkers, the commentaries of the Owenists and the Ricardians circulated through the small network of freethought clubs and debating societies. By 1829, the spiritual egalitarianism of Blatchly and the more materialist contentions of Byllesby began to emerge in various places as one version or another of "political economy"; when Edward Thompson, the deist, addressed the Free Enquirers' Society in that year, he departed from the usual freethought arguments, to announce, "Ever since the science of political economy became familiar to my mind, it has struck me very forcibly that the very great inequalities among mankind in point of wealth, produced very serious evils. . . ."[39] Their immediate impact

38. Ibid., 8, 77.
39. *Evening Post*, July 13, 1819; Thompson, *Oration*, 10.

is unclear, but by the time Thompson delivered his remarks, different interpretations of this radical "science" were in the process of starting a political explosion.

The Outcasts Organize

While radical artisans listened to the freethinkers and read the American Ricardians, a group of tailoresses organized their own strike in 1825, the first in the country in which women alone participated. Little is known about the strike except that it concerned wages—but that it took place at all was the significant thing. By the mid-1820s, the expansion of outwork had brought an important shift in the sexual boundaries in the needle trades. Women, once confined to sewing female clothing in the regular female apprenticeship system, began to assume an ever growing share of slopwork and the easier chores in men's clothing work. For the journeymen tailors, the practice was more than an attack on their earnings—it offended their bedrock belief in the inherent superiority of skilled male labor. In 1819, when the panic and hard times forced the journeymen themselves to rely on slopwork, the men threatened to strike those employers who hired women. A spokesman summed up the men's views by mocking the female slopworkers as much as he berated the masters who hired them, taking due note of the "empiricism of women" and the "preposterous and truly ridiculous idea" that they could sew vests as well as men could: "Nothing can be offered in justification of women asking, or in employers giving work to women, other than the long continuance of an unwarrantable practice which is indeed . . . a slender excuse." In short, women craft workers were suspect, second-rate hands, potential "rats," who would undercut men's wages; any idea that they deserved sympathy or that they might be included as part of the men's union efforts was out of the question. Thus reviled and excluded, the women—even, as in 1825, tailoresses who had long been involved in regular shop production—were left to their own devices. The strike in 1825 was the first sign of their independent awakening. More would follow in the 1830s.[40]

The city's unskilled and semiskilled male workers also became more active in their own labor disputes in the 1820s. Collective action was nothing new to New York's laborers and dockhands; traditions of mobbing and resistance to authorities stretched back at least as far as the anti-impressment riots of the 1770s. Among the more recent Irish and British immigrants, industrial terror, collective bargaining by riot, and the sending of anonymous notes had for decades been standard tactics in times of agrarian and

40. *Evening Post*, July 13, 1819, April 12, 1825. Cf. Stansell, "Women of the Laboring Poor," 110–18.

labor unrest. Although they were bereft of any formal society or organization, New York's laborers turned to these tactics with increasing boldness to press wage demands on their employers. As early as 1816, day laborers in the building trades turned out for higher wages and marched from one construction site to the next to compel their colleagues to join them. In 1825, the riggers, stevedores, and wharf laborers (blacks and whites) allied in a strike for wages, formed a parade of one thousand men chanting, "Leave off work," and effectively shut down the port until the police arrived to disperse the crowd. Three years later, the stevedores and riggers struck shipowners who had cut their wage rates; before the strike was over, still another parade had swept along the waterfront, to battle with nonstriking workers.[41]

The weavers' strike of 1828 brought the most spectacular events. Handloom weaving, a degraded, former craft by 1825, was never as important a trade in New York as in other commercial ports, in part because of the competition from Philadelphia outwork firms and the early factories along the Schuylkill, and even more because of the ready availability of woven cloth from Britain. Although weaving would persist in Manhattan through the 1840s, it was largely restricted to the production of cheap rag carpets. For a short period, however, in the 1820s and 1830s, the flow of experienced British and Irish weavers into the city persuaded a few entrepreneurs to try to establish something of a local weaving industry. In June 1828, Alexander Knox, the city's leading textile employer, learned the perils of such endeavors when the journeymen struck for higher wages. One day, shortly after the turnout had begun, Knox found a note, addressed to "Boss Nox," that had been thrown through his office window:

> Sir
> I tak the chanc to let you no
> Either Quit the Busness
> Or else pay the price
> you ought to for if you
> dont you will be fixed
> We will neither
> lieve your house nor
> house stade you mind   The Black Cat

Knox unwisely ignored the message. A few days later, a crowd of from forty to fifty weavers "not in his employ" came to his home to demand that he raise his wages, "and threatened if not done to destroy every web that could be found." Knox was absent at the time, but his son ran to the police to report what had happened. Upon returning to the shop with a

41. *Columbian*, May 17, 1816; *Evening Post*, March 22, 1825, July 21, 1828; Gilje, "Mobocracy," 177–80; Weinbaum, *Mobs and Demagogues*, 83–84.

few watchmen, young Knox found that "the gang had been round" and had destroyed three webs and prevented the journeymen from working. Knox and the policemen eventually caught up with the strikers, only to be throttled by the crowd, one of whom hit Knox with a cut web. The workers then marched to the homes of Knox's weavers and destroyed the webs of those who had refused to quit work.[42]

At every level, the Knox affair (with its similarities to Irish rural violence, the weavers' uprisings in eighteenth-century Spitalfields, and other Old World crimes of anonymity) indicates that by the 1820s immigrant workers had successfully imported their own methods of bargaining to New York.[43] In the orthography of the "Boss Nox" note, one can detect the brogue of a writer who stood on the borders of literacy; like "Ned Ludd" or "Captain Swing," "The Black Cat" hid the identity of an easily victimized group of wage earners behind a threatening collective name. Along with the other violent strikes, the weavers' actions also showed what the city's less-skilled workers, native and immigrant, were up against. Lacking scarce skills and inherited trade institutions, caught in an increasingly overcrowded labor market, the city's dockers, weavers, and day laborers had to shore up their own ranks and limit the possibility of being singled out and fired. In every instance, their violence aimed either to coerce nonstriking men to join their turnouts or to frighten employers into negotiating. Given their predicament, their degree of organization was impressive; throughout, however, intimidation and covert threats were brutal, indispensable tools for the unskilled laborers and debased craftsmen.

These episodes introduced new elements to New York's re-emerging labor movement but at the same time raised problems for artisan radicals and organized journeymen. The strikes certainly proved that women, laborers, and weavers were capable of fighting for their economic interests. But how were the skilled men to react to the movements of people they had long deemed decidedly beneath them in status and ability—especially those who, like the tailoresses, seemed to threaten their own jobs? And how were organized journeymen and workshop radicals to respond to labor violence? How could they reconcile their own disciplined militancy— the traditions of the committee room—with attacks on persons as well as on property, attacks that seemed only to confirm the image of unskilled

42. Deposition of Alexander Knox, Jr., People v. Hamilton Radcliff and others, July 1, 1828, Court of General Sessions, MARC. On weaving in New York, see *Tribune*, September 20, 1845.

43. See E. P. Thompson, "The Crime of Anonymity," in Douglas Hay et al., *Albion's Fatal Tree: Crime and Society in Eighteenth-Century England* (New York, 1975), 255–344. See also George Rudé, *The Crowd in History* (New York, 1964), 66–78; Wayne G. Broehl, *The Molly Maguires* (Cambridge, Mass., 1968), 1–10; T. Desmond Williams, ed., *Secret Societies in Ireland* (Dublin, 1973), 13–36.

laborers as a heathenish lot? Through the early 1820s, as the logic of the laborers' violence began to unfold, the significance of these tensions over the constituency and tactics of organized labor were only faintly apparent. In later years, they would more emphatically distinguish between one form of protest and another.

Background to Crisis

Apart from the militant tailoresses, laborers, and weavers, two very different images of activism in the trades emerge from the events of the late 1820s: one of an improving master, a Joseph Brewster perhaps, proud of his craft but also a moralizer and entrepreneur, the other of a social critic, equally proud of his craft but more likely to turn to inspiration to a cheap edition of Volney, Paine, or Robert Owen. Gradually, as the disputes between these kinds of craftsmen became more evident, an ideological and social crisis took shape.

Still, as of 1829, it was difficult to discern irrevocable divisions within the trades. The movements of the period, for all their enthusiasm, were small: at best a slender fraction of the artisans supported the anti-auctioneering campaign and the efforts of the American Institute, while the freethinkers attracted no more than a few hundred devoted followers. The differences between these currents hardly conformed to strict class divisions: small masters could be found in entrepreneurial campaigns and radical efforts alike; the most radical tracts couched their arguments in terms of the rights of small producers, including both employers and employees. At times, the issues that divided the crafts were not altogether clear; the ideological tensions contained in the trade-union battles of the Jeffersonian period and the mid-1820s were not yet firmly associated with either entrepreneurial or radical views. Only when these developments became fully engaged in politics would the artisans, with their republican frame of mind, begin fully to comprehend the differences among them. Instead, the period before 1829 saw the circulation of radical ideas that had no immediate political impact. Events like the "Corrupt Bargain," the jostling for power by Andrew Jackson and his friends, and the machinations within Tammany Hall drew the most public attention. But circumstances changed dramatically as New York entered the age of Jackson. A combination of economic and political upheaval and the appearance of some exceptional radical leaders set in motion a chain of events that would make the crisis of artisan republicanism apparent to all.

5

The Rise and Fall
of the Working Men

1829 was an extraordinary year. It began with New York's economy locked in depression and with the city's politicians contemplating the coming to power of Andrew Jackson. By December, a radical popular movement—led by a committee composed primarily of journeymen mechanics—had emerged as a political force. For a season, the normal conventions of party politics were suspended and artisan voters pondered, not the usual rhetoric of the bone and sinew, but some of the most radical political proposals of the age of revolution. Ultimately, the movement was doomed, and its demise only reinforced the strength of the Tammany Democrats and the emerging Whig opposition. Even so, the brief history of the Working Men was a decisive episode, a moment of conflict that helped popularize and politicize radical ideas and that foreshadowed the class conflicts of the 1830s.[1]

Republicanism, Party Democracy, and Politics

The Working Men's movement did not originate in party politics or the old mechanics' interest, but its evolution owed a great deal to the Jack-

1. The standard studies of the Working Men include Frank T. Carlton, "The Workingmen's Party of New York City, 1829–1831," *PSQ* 22 (1907): 401–15; Commons, *History of Labour*, I, 231–84; Schlesinger, *Age of Jackson*, 133–43, 177–216; Seymour Savetsky, "The New York Working Men's Party" (M.A. thesis, Columbia University, 1948); Hugins, *Jacksonian Democracy*; Edward Pessen, "The Working Men's Party Revisited," *LH* 3 (1963): 203–26; idem, *Most Uncommon Jacksonians* 7–33, 58–79, 103–203 passim. As Pessen notes, the history of the Working Men is a much-told tale. It has, however, yet to be told accurately and adequately. Of the existing accounts, Pessen's runs closest to my own interpretation.

sonian political revolution. If we are to understand the "Workies," we must first recall what that revolution meant.

In New York, as elsewhere in the United States, a new system and ethos of party politics developed in the 1820s. After the Hartford Convention and the degeneration of the Federalist party, formal partisanship was widely distrusted. "We want no discord," the newly inaugurated president James Monroe declared in 1817, and politicians carried the message to the lowest echelons of public life. Local political battles, fought by unstable, shifting alliances, settled down to a form of "one-party" bickering, with all of the clarity and probity of politics in Hogarth's England. Amid this apparent regression, however, New York's feuding politicians came to divide sharply over the place of political parties in a popular democracy. Beginning in 1817, the Bucktail "outs," led by the young upstart lawyer Martin Van Buren, moved against the grain to attack the friends of Gov. DeWitt Clinton as a dangerous aristocratic faction that ruled through a network of family influences and connections. The Clintonians, ousted in 1820, countercharged that the more partisan methods favored by the Bucktails—with their veneration of the caucus and their attempts to enforce a party discipline—were antidemocratic threats to political harmony and consensus. Swept from office by a Clinton-led antiparty People's party in 1824 and later hounded by the rise of the antiparty anti-Masonic movement upstate, the Van Burenites looked for ways to repair their reputation and to reconcile party competition with popular government.[2]

The Bucktails' solution, anticipated earlier by the likes of Matthew Livingston Davis, forecast critical changes in the theory and practice of American politics in which, Michael Wallace has pointed out, "party discipline, from being essential to democracy, became the essence of democracy."[3] Contrary to the eighteenth-century consensus views of their opponents, the Bucktails insisted that conflict was imperative in any democratic society. Failure to accommodate these conflicts would result in either anarchy or oligarchy; the most suitable accommodation was a forthrightly competitive system of recognized parties, each responsible to a broad white male electorate and a party rank and file of ordinary voters, led by professional

2. The following section has been heavily influenced by Hammond, *History of Political Parties*, II, 1–291; Robert V. Remini, *Martin Van Buren and the Making of the Democratic Party* (New York, 1959); Benson, *Concept of Jacksonian Democracy*, 3–46; Richard Hofstadter, *The Idea of a Party System: The Rise of Legitimate Opposition in the United States, 1790–1840* (Berkeley, 1970), 212–71; Mushkat, *Tammany*, 75–101; and, above all, Michael Wallace, "Changing Concepts of Party in the United States: New York, 1815–1828," *AHR* 74 (1968): 453–91. The quotation, from Monroe's first inaugural address, appears in James D. Richardson, ed., *A Compilation of Messages and Papers of the President, 1789–1897* (Washington, D.C., 1896), III, 10.

3. Wallace, "Changing Concepts," 469.

politicians. In the orderly contest for office between these parties, the popular will and the public good would prevail; with the creation of truly
professional parties—their directors and members pledged to pursue the
party's welfare over personal ends, principles, or ideology—politics would
be purged both of aristocratic factions and of nefarious demagogues. "We
are party men, attached to party systems," the leading New York Bucktail
newspaper announced in 1822; "we think them necessary to the general
safety."[4]

Among other things, the Jacksonian triumph in New York in 1828
amounted to a stunning victory and vindication for the defenders of professional political parties. Van Buren, running for governor as a supporter
of Andrew Jackson, also masterminded the general's campaign, a beauti-
fully orchestrated assault on the antiparty Adams administration as an
elite faction perverted by aristocratic influence and corruption. The Jacksonians, in command of Tammany Hall, raised few issues apart from abstract references to states' rights and free trade, and stuck mostly to disciplined efforts to get out the vote with raucous political meetings and
liberal drafts of spirits. Although the National Republicans ran well statewide, losing narrowly, Adams's friends in the city—including members of
the American Institute, the anti-auctioneers, and the leading temperance
advocates—were swamped, unable to raise an issue to stem the Jackson–
Van Buren onslaught and incapable of matching the Jacksonians' organization (Table 17). A new form of party was now entrenched: the first
major political events under the Jacksonian regime—Governor Van Buren's
attempts to reward upstate pro-Jackson bankers with a new safety-fund
scheme, Jackson's endorsement of rotation in office and his sudden appointment of Van Buren as secretary of state—confirmed the view that
party service was now the measure of political virtue.[5]

What did the Jacksonian victory mean for the majority of New York's
masters, journeymen, and laborers in 1828? Certainly not a social revolution in politics, a coming to power of the city's common men via the
Jacksonian Democracy: the politicians in charge of Tammany, as well as
most of those elected in 1828, were either well-connected attorneys, merchants, financiers, leading master craftsmen, or allies of local banking interests, a situation that would change little over the next ten years. Nor
did the Jacksonians' campaign of 1828 promise any clear shift in policies
of particular interest to the small masters and journeymen, except perhaps
to those mercantile-trade producers who opposed high tariffs; although
they promoted a genuinely more democratic political culture, until 1830,
it would not be altogether clear where the New York Jacksonians stood

on any of the issues of the day.[6] The long struggle between Bucktail and Clintonian had yielded at least one important by-product, a liberalization of the white adult male suffrage that abolished tax-paying and property qualifications for voting after 1827—a matter of concern to the trades since the Revolution.[7] More directly, the decay of "one-party" politics and the Jacksonian victory upset the entire balance of politics. "The old party lines," as the *Journal of Commerce* would have cause to observe, were "newly obliterated." Those activists of the new "mechanics' interest" who had pursued principles in accord with the Adams administration's—above all the men of the American Institute and the anti-auction and lien-law movements—were temporarily broken, their candidates, their organization, their vision of politics repudiated. The very magnitude of the Jacksonian triumph in the city created a political vacancy into which some new movement—even, as it would turn out, a radical one—could enter to replace the crippled, ineffectual Adamsites. In the aftermath of 1828, meanwhile, those who had voted for the latest Man of the People found they had cast their lot with operational democrats, supremely interested (or so it seemed) in consolidating their party's power and strengthening its ties with loyal bankers and financiers. To some of these voters—especially to nominally Jacksonian journeymen and small masters with their own complaints—Tammany and the new men in Washington began to look no better than the corrupt aristocrats of the old administration.[8]

It was this political vacancy and this initial restiveness about the direction of Jacksonian rule that permitted the Working Men's movement to turn into a political insurgency from below; in this very limited sense, the rise and progress of the "Workies" was an outcome of disputes among established politicians.[9] The Working Men's roots, however, lay well outside the changing political establishment. As the vanquished Adamsites stumbled about for a political foothold, a curious collection of agitators—radicals who themselves disagreed about fundamental issues—began to gather support from journeymen and small master mechanics. Before long, they engaged the citizenry in debates on topics that no politician, Federalist or Republican, Clintonian or Bucktail, Adamsite or Jacksonian, had yet dared to mention.

6. Pessen, *Riches, Class and Power*, 284–87; Mushkat, *Tammany*, 119–27.

7. Benson, *Concept of Jacksonian Democracy*, 3–20; Chilton Williamson, *American Suffrage: From Property to Democracy, 1760–1860* (Princeton, 1960), 204–7.

8. *Journal of Commerce*, November 7, 1829.

9. Such is the main contention of Savetsky and Benson. Both are correct to point out the importance of shifting party structure in 1828–29; both fail to comprehend that the roots of the Working Men's movement lay outside of Tammany. They thus transform the history of a popular movement into a history of intraparty squabbling. See Savetsky, "Working Men," 14–23; Benson, *Concept of Jacksonian Democracy*, 33.

Dramatis Personae

On New Year's Day, 1829, Frances Wright, the Scots-born "Priestess of Beelzebub," disembarked in New York harbor. Wright's arrival and her announcement of the relocation of her newspaper, the *Free Enquirer*, from New Harmony to New York caused a sensation. Famous for her freethought, her admiration of Paine, and her advocacy of women's rights, she had already won a following among the city's freethinkers and anti-evangelicals and considerable notoriety from the conservative press. Her entire life had been a radical republican odyssey, from her childhood as the orphan of a prosperous Painite merchant, to her first visit to America in 1818, her liaisons with Bentham, Lafayette, and the French *carbonari*, her conversion to Owenism, and her establishment of the Nashoba community for ex-slaves in Tennessee in 1827. By the sheer power of her personality, as presented on lecture tours and in her writings, Wright had invigorated freethinkers in towns and cities across the North. Now dissatisfied with the isolation of the frontier and intent on reaching more urban workingmen, she set her sights on converting the nation's metropolis. Both the artisan freethinkers (long familiar with her work) and the radical circles of Cornelius Blatchly greeted her warmly, although with a hint of wariness at first; local journalists had a field day reporting her landing in New York and her immediate preparations for a new series of lectures. On January 3, more than fifteen hundred persons turned out to view the spectacle of her first public meeting. A few days later, a curious Philip Hone went to hear "this female Tom Paine" at the Masonic Hall. Her doctrines, Hone snorted, would "subvert our fundamental principles of morality if people were fools enough to believe them"; nevertheless, he admitted, "I found the room so full that I remained but a short time."[10]

Wright's performances—there is no other word for them—offered not so much an exposition of startling new ideas as a distillation of familiar ones into blistering diatribes against American inequality. Her political economy turned out to be a patchwork of Owenist mutualism and the labor

10. *New Harmony and Nashoba Gazette*, January 7, February 4, 11, 25, 1829; *New-York Spectator*, January 9, 13, 16, 1829; Nevins, *Diary of Philip Hone*, 9–10. A fresh, full-scale treatment of Wright is badly needed, but see William Randall Waterman, *Frances Wright* (New York, 1924); and Alice Perkins and Theresa Wolfson, *Fanny Wright, Free Enquirer: A Study of a Temperament* (New York, 1939). Of additional interest are Alice S. Rossi, "Woman of Action: Frances Wright (1795–1852)," in idem, *The Feminist Papers: From Adams to de Beauvoir* (New York, 1974), 86–99; and Margaret Lane, *Frances Wright and the Great Experiment* (Manchester, 1974). Wright and Owen first added the name Free Enquirer to their newspaper in 1828. For the sake of clarity, I shall refer to Wright and Owen's paper as the *Free Enquirer* only for the period after Wright and Owen moved it to New York. On the freethinkers' familiarity with Wright before 1829, see Perkins and Wolfson, *Frances Wright*, 249.

theory of value, stitched together by Benthamite references to the promotion of human happiness. Her deism was little different from Paine's or Owen's. The Jacobin feminism that brought her so much editorial abuse came directly from Wollstonecraft. Wright's genius lay in her ability to reformulate these different views as no previous freethinker had managed to do, and to proclaim them in polemics that struck to the core of Americans' political beliefs. She sounded her keynote in one of her most popular lectures on education:

> Is this a republic—a country whose affairs are governed by the public voice—when the public mind is unequally enlightened? Is this a republic, where the interest of the many keep in check those of the few— while the few hold possession of the courts of knowledge and the many stand as suitors at the door? Is this a republic where the rights of all are equally respected, the interests of all equally secured, . . . the services of all equally rendered?[11]

To this defiant rhetoric, Wright added an electrifying presence unmatched by any previous New York deist speaker, and possibly unmatched by any American speaker of the day. A sense of theater, of the strategic uses of histrionics, had been vital to the eighteenth-century British Jacobins, and Wright—the child of British Jacobinism—did her utmost to present her lectures as theatrical events. One hostile reporter recounted the scene at her first lecture:

> As the appointed hour sounded from St. Paul [i.e., St. Paul's Chapel] there was a general turning of heads. She came up the aisle, and attained the platform, accompanied by a bevy of female apostles and a single thick-set and well-constituted Scotchman [Robert Jennings]. He helped her in her little matters, received her cloak, and also her cap à la Cowper, which she took off as we men do, by grasping it with a single hand.[12]

Uncloaked, Wright appeared in the tunic costume adopted by the New Harmony Owenists in 1826, a suit of white muslin that announced her contempt for contemporary female fashion and her immersion in the cult of neoclassical reason (Plate 10). Thence she began to speak, with a voice and manner uniformly judged as exceptional. The curmudgeonly Mrs. Trollope, who had befriended Wright despite the younger woman's deistical views, was moved to record that "all my expectations fell far short of the splendor, the brilliance, the overwhelming eloquence of this extraordinary orator"; in time, even Hone grudgingly admitted her powers. Wright had her flaws as a thinker and organizer; the most severe were her occa-

11. Frances Wright, *Course of Popular Lectures* (London, 1834), 24–25.
12. *American* [New York], January 4, 1829.

sional self-centered glibness and her propensity to move on to new projects before completing those she had already begun. In early 1829, however, the excitement she generated overcame any doubts about her abilities.[13]

Almost immediately, Wright transformed the New York freethought movement by adding depth to its narrower interpretations of America's social ills and providing the deists with a positive program for reform. A firm adherent to the Ricardian labor theory of value, she revived the economic radicalism that had been dormant among the deists since the failure of the Franklin Community in 1826. Throughout the country that winter, she claimed in her lectures on the "causes of existing evils," she had seen honest mechanics out of work or toiling for atrocious wages; the source of the problem was that labor was being robbed not only of its political rights but of its just financial reward by an unprincipled aristocracy of useless, nonproducing parasites. "If the divisions of *sect* have estranged human hearts from each other," she insisted, "those of *class* have set them in direct opposition."[14]

Having demonstrated her social concerns, Wright turned to her pet topic, education. Many proposals had been tendered on how to correct existing social ills and ensure the perpetuation of equality; for Wright, the only reasonable first step was the implementation of a truly equal, national, and republican educational system—administered by the state and untainted by religion—to provide complete schooling for all American children. Private schools had for too long been a privilege of the rich; philanthropic religious and charity schools had for too long fouled the minds of impressionable youths with corrupting superstition, and curbed critical thought with Lancastrian precision. By replacing these instruments of oppression with free nonsectarian schools, Americans would establish the mental preconditions of social equality and "moral government."[15]

Wright's educational proposals were partly inspired and greatly fortified by the more detailed and dogmatic educational schemes of her comrade, the coeditor of the *Free Enquirer*, Robert Owen's son, Robert Dale Owen. An enthusiastic reformer whose concern for the poor was outdistanced only by his condescension toward them, Owen had long been intrigued by the possible social uses of education. As a young man reaping the benefits of

13. Frances Trollope, *Domestic Manners of the Americans* (London, 1832), 97–100; Nevins, *Diary of Philip Hone*, 15–16. See also *Commercial Advertiser*, January 4, 1829. Robert Dale Owen, writing years later, had his own reasons to be unkind, but his description of Wright's overly "sweeping," sometimes careless polemics reflects some of the distrust others felt in 1829. See Robert Dale Owen, "An Earnest Sowing of Wild Oats," *Atlantic Monthly* 34 (1874): 76.

14. *The Free Enquirer* [New York], April 15, 1829.

15. Wright, *Course of Popular Lectures*, 38–53; *Free Enquirer*, April 22, May 13, 27, 1829.

his father's financial success, he attended the Fellenberg school in Hofwyl, Switzerland, where education of the scions of benevolent wealth was extolled as the best means to lessen social inequity. These theories, along with his father's brand of perfectionism, shaped the younger Owen's social and political creed. At first, he was drawn to the possibilities of communitarian cooperation, and in 1825 he accompanied his father to New Harmony. The experiment only proved to Owen that inequality of education, and not, as some would have it, maldistribution of wealth, was the chief cause of poverty. In 1827, after he had met Wright at New Harmony, he joined the community at Nashoba and began writing for the forerunner of the *Free Enquirer*, the *New Harmony and Nashoba Gazette*. After his own removal to New York in June 1829, he filled his and Wright's weekly with discussions of the evils of private and sectarian education and with preliminary plans for a thoroughly secular state-supported system for all children.[16]

Owen's state-guardianship plan combined idealist social reform and environmental theories of education in a call for unprecedented state intervention in public schooling. All children would be removed from their homes at age two and placed in government-run academies until they were sixteen; all would wear the same clothing, eat the same food, and receive the same instruction, following Pestalozzian methods. Once safe from the degeneracy of slum life, the children would not be permitted to return home, even for a vacation; parents, with their possibly contaminating influences, would be allowed to visit at appropriate intervals but could not interrupt the school's regimen. From these egalitarian barracks of enlightenment—similar in design to the Fellenberg schools—would supposedly spring a "race . . . to perfect the free institutions of America."[17]

With Wright and Owen, especially Owen, it is tempting to see the rationalist autodidacticism and respect for order typical of earlier freethinkers and radicals overtaken by some of the more authoritarian impulses of post-Enlightenment Benthamite reform. Certainly Owen's descriptions of the poorer streets of urban America—places for "learning rudeness, impertinent language, vulgar manners, and vicious habits," he called them in 1830—betrayed a squeamishness toward those he would uplift; this frame of mind reappeared continually in Owen's quasi-Malthusian feminist tract of 1830, *Moral Physiology*, in which he defended birth control in part by blaming poverty in large measure on the thoughtless sexual indulgences of

16. Robert Leopold, *Robert Dale Owen: A Biography* (Cambridge, Mass., 1940), 3–102; Robert Dale Owen, *Threading My Way* (New York, 1874); *New Harmony and Nashoba Gazette*, October 29, November 5, 12, 19, 1828, January 7, 14, 1829; *Free Enquirer*, May 13, June 3, July 29, 1829.

17. *Free Enquirer*, March 4, May 6, 20, 27, November 7, 1829, May 1, 1830; Pascu, "Philanthropic Tradition," chap. 9.

the poor.[18] With even greater insistence than the *Correspondent* group showed, Wright and Owen promoted temperance, thrift, and industry, so much so that they publicized the New-York City Temperance Society and a new auxiliary Young Men's Society for the Promotion of Temperance before they had investigated the temperance movement's religious and political motives.[19] Their writings and lectures at times seemed out of step with previous work of the rest of the radical milieu: their stress on education, sexual equality and anticlericalism had little in common with either Blatchly's or Byllesby's pamphlets; their retreat from the elder Owen's very different paternal utopia led them to slight economic cooperation; their explicit plans to rely on the powers of the state broke with all earlier radical proposals, including the freethinkers'. By focusing primarily on uplifting education—an issue the city's entrepreneurs agreed was vital for the survival of the Republic—and by insinuating that they, the scientific Free Enquirers, were uniquely qualified to dictate proper republican ethics, Wright and Owen sometimes sounded as authoritarian and moralistic as the evangelicals they attacked.

Nevertheless, Wright and Owen were radicals, of a sort the twentieth century would call middle-class—eager to take unorthodox perfectionist ideas out of the parlors of genteel skepticism and into the darkest corners of the land, willing to brave the abuse (sometimes violent) that their activities provoked among the shocked defenders of conventional faith. In New York, they resided in a commodious mansion on the edge of town, but they easily found an intellectual home among the questioning rationalist mechanics. Their main arguments followed the familiar lines of artisan infidelity and Painite republicanism; their lectures and articles consisted largely of attacks on the clergy, divine revelation, and the "would-be Christian Party in politics." Simultaneously, Wright and Owen, by joining the mustier freethought rhetoric about aristocrats and priests to the Ricardian labor theory and by directing their barbs at specific moral reformers and pious editors, aroused the interest of journeymen and small masters outside the existing freethought milieu, including some who could not care less about piercing the mysteries of the universe. Simply by being so uncompromisingly blunt, by basking in their reputations as pariahs to respectable opinion, Wright and Owen won admirers: in time, self-proclaimed "Fanny Wright mechanics" began turning out pamphlets, crude by the deists' standards, with expressions of solidarity with the Free Enquirers

18. *Free Enquirer*, May 15, 1830; Robert Dale Owen, *Moral Physiology: or, A Brief and Plain Treatise on the Population Question* (New York, 1830); Sidney Ditzion, *Marriage, Morals, and Sex in America* (New York, 1978), 111–20; Linda Gordon, *Woman's Body, Woman's Right: A History of Birth Control in America* (New York, 1976), 82–83.

19. *Free Enquirer*, March 25, July 22, 1829.

and profane cartoons of Lewis Tappan and Ezra Stiles Ely (Plate 11). The old popular anticlericalism resurfaced, in lampoons and doggerel, to mock merchant-capitalists and the evangelical crusade:

> Arthur Tappan, Arthur Tappan,
> Suppose it should happen—
> Mind, I'm only *supposing* it should—
> That some folks in the Union
> Should take your communion
> Too often by far for their good.

At last, agitators had come along to tap these resources and expose, in terms far more pungent than those the *Correspondent* crowd used, what ordinary artisans considered to be the hypocrisy, arrogance, and unrepublican intents of entrepreneurial evangelical reform.[20]

Wright and Owen's greatest achievements, however, came less from what they said than from what they did to nourish a radical culture in the mechanics' wards. Beginning in April 1829, the Free Enquirers centered their efforts, puckishly enough, in the abandoned Ebenezer church on Broome Street near the Bowery, a ramshackle building that Wright dubbed her Hall of Science. "Raised and consecrated to sectarian faith," Wright declared during the elaborate rededication ceremonies,

> it stands devoted this day to universal knowledge—and we in crossing its threshold, have to throw aside the distinctions of class; the names and feelings of sect or party; to recognise in ourselves and each other the single character of human beings and fellow creatures, and thus to sit down, as children of one family, in patience to inquire—in humility to learn.[21]

Much as Wright's loose-fitting, Dianaesque garb announced her feminism, the very design of the hall advertised the freethinkers' devotion to rationality, its newly columned facade bidding all to a temple of reason (Plate 12). Here, in the heart of the city's small-artisan and journeyman neighborhoods, Wright established the office for her newspaper and tried to set up a nerve center for radical freethought activities. Sunday nights were reserved for the major weekly meeting; at other times the hall became an all-purpose lecture room for sympathetic speakers, a day school, a deist Sunday school for children and a reading room for adults; later, Wright and Owen's supporters added a free medical dispensary. A counterpart to Tammany Hall, located but a few blocks away, the Hall of Science was a

20. Perkins and Wolfson, *Frances Wright*, 240–41, 248–49; Owen, "Earnest Sowing," 73; *New Harmony and Nashoba Gazette*, January 11, 1829; *Free Enquirer*, March 18, 25, April 15, 1829; *Priestcraft Unmasked* 1 (1930): 116. See also, Lyon, *Recollections of an Old Cartman*, 123–24, for jocular distrust of proselytizing clergymen.

21. *New Harmony and Nashoba Gazette*, February 4, 1829; *Free Enquirer*, March 4, May 13, 1829; Perkins and Wolfson, *Frances Wright*, 236.

great improvement over earlier freethinkers' institutes, the first formal radical lyceum to serve the various physical, intellectual, and spiritual needs of its desired constituents. To complement its programs Wright and Owen's supporters, including George Henry Evans (who also printed the *Free Enquirer*), turned out fresh editions of radical deist classics, from Voltaire's *Dictionary* to Elihu Palmer's *Elements of Nature*, for sale at the hall and at Evans' shop.[22]

At least superficially, the experiment was a success, although there were distractions. Wright and Owen's views on sexual freedom—enough to make the normally serene Philip Hone rage that they would break down the moral and religious ties which bind mankind together—brought them some unwanted attention. On several occasions, police had to protect the Free Enquirers' lectures; at least once, shortly after her arrival, a man threw a smoke-barrel into the hall where Wright was speaking. Fascination with Wright—the first woman of importance to ascend a lecture platform in the United States—also must have swelled her audiences; surely many who attended came less to hear her speeches than to catch a glimpse. Still, the hall, which could accommodate twelve hundred persons, was regularly filled—largely, it seems, by mechanics—even when Wright was not on the program. The *Free Enquirer* sold well enough to cover its expenses; sales of the freethought books and pamphlets, priced at between five and twenty-five cents each, reached $3,000 per year. One subscriber was a Brooklyn house carpenter and Hicksite Quaker, Walter Whitman; his ten-year-old son Walt would later recall participating in the "frenzy" that attended Wright's lectures, and remember Fanny as "one of the sweetest of sweet memories: we all loved her, fell down before her; her very appearance seemed to enthrall us." Her ideas and Owen's would help stimulate the boy in later years to turn to poetry. So, in 1829, they would help direct ordinary small masters and journeymen to radicalism and to politics.[23]

If Wright and Owen won a following, however, they did not convert all of New York's disaffected artisans and craft workers, least of all the machinist Thomas Skidmore. Skidmore's rambling, caustic 1829 tract *The Rights of Man to Property!* contained none of the freethinkers' faith in the power of education to perfect the individual and society: Skidmore, building on Byllesby's work rather than on the freethinkers' or Owen's, looked to changes in existing property relations. "One thing must be obvi-

22. *New Harmony and Nashoba Gazette*, February 4, 1829, *Free Enquirer*, March 4, April 29, July 29, August 19, September 30, 1829, June 12, 1830; Leopold, *Robert Dale Owen*, 68–71; Perkins and Wolfson, *Frances Wright*, 234.

23. *Evening Post*, January 10, 1829; Nevins, *Diary of Philip Hone*, 10; Perkins and Wolfson, *Frances Wright*, 231–32, 235–36; Owen, "Earnest Sowing," 73–74; Horace Traubel, *Conversations with Walt Whitman in Camden* (New York, 1908–14), II, 204–6.

ous to the plainest understanding," he began, "that as long as property is unequal, or rather, as long as it is so enormously unequal . . . those who possess it *will* live on the labor of others." Mocking the plans of "political dreamers" like Robert Owen and his son, Skidmore asserted that the rights of labor and the poor would be won only if "we rip all up, and make a full and General Division" of property. Ultimately, the dispossessed, having seized their natural rights to property, would establish a secular commonwealth of independent producers, one that would destroy "both the oppressor and the oppressed; the victor and the victim, by preventing accumulation of power in one; and destitution, weakness, or poverty in another." In a stroke, the radical critique derived from the labor theory of value had turned into a call for social revolution.[24]

Thomas Skidmore's road to 1829 could not have been more different from Owen's or Wright's; indeed, his biography reads like that of the typical self-taught artisan scientist whom Owen and Wright tried hard to attract. Born into a struggling family in Newton, Connecticut, in 1790, Skidmore distinguished himself early as a brilliant schoolboy; as a thirteen-year-old, he helped support his family by teaching in the local district school. His childhood ended in 1808, when he demanded that he be permitted to keep half his wages for his own support rather than hand them over to his father (who, Skidmore's present-minded biographer of the 1830s claimed, tried to "monopolize" the boy's earnings). After leaving his family to live with an uncle (with whom he subsequently quarreled about politics), Skidmore left New England for good in 1809. He settled first in Princeton, New Jersey, but soon afterward began wandering down the eastern seaboard as far south as North Carolina, as an itinerant tutor. Still dissatisfied, he suddenly switched course in 1815 and traveled to Wilmington, Delaware, where he cultivated his interests in applied science and conducted experiments on various manufacturing processes: wiredrawing, papermaking, and the production of gunpowder. In all likelihood these too came to naught; in any case, in 1819 he moved to New York, where he set up shop as a machinist, married, and started on a new project to devise an improved form of the reflective telescope. Like many other tinkering artisans of the era, Skidmore might have seemed destined for the obscurity of his workshop, or, at best, for a mention in an ephemeral mechanics' journal—a man who, an acquaintance later recalled, did not lack "scientific attainments" but who "never held a distinguished place among men of science," one who worked "by practice and not in theory."[25]

24. Thomas Skidmore, *The Rights of Man to Property!* (New York, 1829), 3–4, 353, 369.
25. On Skidmore, see Amos Gilbert, "A Sketch of the Life of Thomas Skidmore," in

Skidmore's immersion in the theory and practice of politics, however, eventually changed his own life and the New York political scene. As a boy, he remembered, he had thrilled to the democratic pronouncements in William Duane's *Aurora*, where, almost certainly, he first encountered the writings of Thomas Paine and the English Jacobins. Through the late 1820s, he continued to read widely in political philosophy, fully digesting the works of Locke, Rousseau, Joel Barlow, and Jefferson. Paine made the deepest impression on him, as the patriot who "supported the rights of the people of all nations, with an energy, and an ability perhaps never excelled"; his closest associate in the late 1820s, the printer Alexander Ming, had been a prominent figure in Paine's freethinking circle at the turn of the century. But Skidmore also kept up to date with the latest pamphlets on political economy, particularly those of the Ricardians. The Philadelphian Daniel Raymond's treatise on the economic sources of unemployment caught his eye, as did, even more decisively, Byllesby's *Observations*. With considerably less enthusiasm, he read of Robert Owen's schemes and of the rise and fall of New Harmony. In 1828, he finally entered politics— as a delegate to the Adamsites' city nominating convention and as a member of the correspondence committee of the Friends of the American System. In retrospect, his passing link with the Adamsites may seem like something of an aberration. On certain discrete issues, however, the alliance made some sense. Skidmore abhorred the licensed auctions as barbaric monopolies; he favored prohibitive tariffs as a means to keep foreign capitalists from taking over the Republic's commerce and industry; he feared the party democracy and its portents for principled politics. Like Adams, he favored government aid for commercial improvements, "as necessary and useful public works, such as Roads, Bridges, Canals, &c. were concerned."[26] Yet, though Skidmore could join with the Adamsites temporarily, his own developing views on property, politics, and society were hardly in line with those of the national administration or the American Institute. Following the electoral fiasco, he returned to his study for yet another project, a compilation of the nation's ills and his remedies for them. The book would shock Adamsite and Jacksonian alike.

At a glance, *The Rights of Man to Property!*—the most thoroughgoing "agrarian" tract ever produced by an American—might appear to be but a recapitulation of earlier attempts to square doctrines of natural rights and

---

Free Enquirer, March 30, April 6, April 13, 1834; Edward Pessen, "Thomas Skidmore: Agrarian Reformer in the Early American Labor Movement," NYH 25 (1954): 280–94; Hugins, *Jacksonian Democracy*, 82–83; Harris, *Socialist Origins*, 91–139; Conkin, *Prophets of Prosperity*, 237–44.

26. *Free Enquirer*, April 13, 1834; *Rights of Man to Property*, 7, 12, 26–29, 66, 81, 89, 250–53, 385; Hugins, *Jacksonian Democracy*, 83. For Skidmore's views on tariffs, see *Rights of Man to Property*, 80, 271–82.

republican independence with the labor theory of value: Skidmore borrowed widely. His interpretation of labor and property relations, however, represented something of a theoretical breakthrough. Strictly speaking, he observed, labor did not, as many believed, have an intrinsic value but was only a human faculty that could increase the value of property. With this distinction in mind, Skidmore virtually stripped his theory of any Lockian connotations left untouched by previous radical writers. If even labor could not be equated with property, he asserted, nothing could justify the transformation of property into a private estate; at all times, property rightfully belonged to the entire community. Consequently, Skidmore reasoned, all laws that perpetuated *private* property, and its transmission through inheritance, violated the self-evident principle, "engraved on the heart of man," that each had an equal claim on the Creator's endowment. Most important, by Skidmore's definition, all *existing* property holdings were illegitimate. Rousseau, Byllesby, and others had shown that property was unequally distributed at the very time when governments were instituted; clearly, then, Skidmore reasoned, all accumulations, even those "earned" by individual labor, were based on a fundamental breach of natural rights. The many social and economic oppressions of which other writers complained, including the wage relation, stemmed directly from this initial maldistribution. Therefore, it was insufficient only to demand an end to inheritance or to devise means for the fairer distribution of the value of men's labor. Nothing less than the General Division could restore the laws of nature.[27]

Before Skidmore pressed these remarks to their logical conclusion, he scanned American political institutions and social life to show how thoroughly the sanctity of private property had corrupted men's minds. In contrast to his radical predecessors, he took special pains to point out the theoretical weaknesses of the most egalitarian of the founding fathers, Jefferson and Paine. Against their preoccupation with political rights, Skidmore held up the idea of a republic founded on private property as a sinister absurdity:

> Is the work of creation to be let out on hire? And are the great mass of mankind to be hirelings to those who undertake to set up a claim, as government is now constructed, that the world was made for them? Why not sell the winds of heaven, that man might not breathe without price? Why not sell the light of the sun, that a man should not see without making another rich?[28]

To refute latter-day political democrats, he went on to show how various American institutions, some of them overlooked by earlier radicals, only

27. *Rights of Man to Property*, 38–43, 79–81, 243, 359–66.
28. *Ibid.*, 59–67, 239.

reinforced the misrule of private property. Slavery—which Jefferson, then the Jacksonians condoned—was to Skidmore the quintessential American crime against nature, one that pitted propertyless whites against enslaved blacks and convinced at least some slaves that their bondage was preferable to a free but propertyless condition. Private banks, chartered monopolies and corporations (including those that entrepreneurs, for different reasons, complained about), private education, privately owned factories: all enhanced the power of corrupt men of wealth. The nation's political apparatus was marred by undemocratic features—Skidmore singled out the bicameral legislative chambers, appointed judgeships, and limitation of the suffrage to white males—all fostered by the fears of the propertied minority. Social and legal arrangements that repressed the civil and economic rights of Indians, Negroes, and women—Skidmore, like Wright, was both an abolitionist and an advocate of women's rights—marked the narrow limits of American "equality."[29] The very morality of the Republic was perverted by private property, a perversion typified by the opinion of one member of the New York Common Council, cited by Skidmore, "that he who would not work ought to starve." "Is it not quite as reasonable," Skidmore wondered,

> for a poor man to eat a good dinner, without having labored to earn it, as for a rich man to do it? Is there a difference in rights? Is there one sort of rights for one class of men, and another for another? May one do lawfully what another will do criminally; have we two codes of law among us? Have we a law for the Lilliputians, and another for the Brobdingnaggians?[30]

The answers, for Skidmore, were all too plain.

To each of these problems, Skidmore offered a thoroughly materialist, thoroughly democratic "agrarian" solution: the lawful seizure of government by the poor and the "friends of equal rights," and the expropriation and equal redistribution of all existing property. How would this seizure occur? Not with men "attached to the cause of a Clay or a Jackson," he went on to argue, but with a different use of established democratic forms. The dispossessed, presumably enlightened by Skidmore's tract, would combine into a great mass movement and elect enough representatives to the various state legislatures to call and control state constitutional conventions. Once assembled, the conventions would enfranchise all adults to consolidate the power of the poor. Then would begin the process of expropriation and redistribution. All forms of property—church buildings and lands, small as well as large fortunes, machinery and factories—would be subject to seizure; those forms of property incapable of division, in particular the manu-

29. *Ibid.*, 54–77, 158–60.
30. *Ibid.*, 242.

factories, would be retained by the community and operated in its name; so would the banks. After the redistribution, individuals—men and women, of all races—would be permitted to labor as they chose, in splendid cooperative independence, each with an equal stake of property. Of course, Skidmore concluded, persons of superior talent, diligence, and intelligence would inevitably produce more, to the greater benefit of themselves and the entire community, and would therefore accumulate some additional wealth, a form of private ownership he thought fully just, honorable, and egalitarian; Skidmore had no intention, as his opponents later charged, of turning America into a primitive communist state of total collective ownership. Provided, however, that inheritance was abolished and that all property, bestowed and accumulated, was confiscated when an individual died (to be redistributed equitably to persons who had just reached their majority) these natural differences would not congeal into exploitative privilege and permanent social inequalities. Gradually, social oppression and political force would disappear, "till there shall be no lenders, no borrowers; no landlords, no tenants; no masters, no journeymen; no Wealth, no Want"— and, he implied, the least possible government.[31]

It was a breathtaking analysis, as audacious in Skidmore's own time as Marx's description of the ultimate expropriation of the expropriators was in his. The text carried the questioning and ambitious temperament of the American artisan radical to new heights; Skidmore, the inquisitive tinkerer of broad self-education, brought to bear all of the resources he could muster, from Jonathan Swift to Langton Byllesby, in a relentless assault on institutions and hierarchies even his most radical predecessors did not challenge. He was hampered by the verbosity and occasional circumlocution of the autodidact; still, the argument burned with Skidmore's rage at personal disappointments and struggles.[32] Ever the "practical" man of science, he unfailingly pursued the broadest possible questions and pushed his inquiry and his proposals to their limit. As a political opponent was to observe, his combativeness and sometimes brusque self-assurance—"All else," he is reported to have replied to his critics, "is quackery"—signified, not ambition, but Skidmore's growing frustration with those unable or unwilling to follow his logic.[33]

The political thrust of Skidmore's work is understood most easily by contrasting it to the ideas of his chief radical rivals, the freethinking educational reformers. Simply put, Skidmore turned the Free Enquirers' analy-

31. [Thomas Skidmore], *Political Essays* (New York, n.d. [1831]), 22; idem, *Rights of Man to Property*, 137–44, 159–207, 385–86.

32. See, for example, Skidmore's bitter discussion in *Rights of Man to Property*, 227–28, of the meanness of parents who would dominate their young through property inheritance—an obvious reference to his own youth.

33. *Free Enquirer*, April 13, 1834.

sis on its head: maldistribution of wealth, he charged, was not an effect of mental superstition, but its cause. At best, the educational reformers were misguided; at worst, they were tricksters: while Skidmore planned for state-funded equal education after the General Division, he thought Owen's "sing-song essays" a hoax, that denied the poor were ready to exercise natural rights. At present, he charged, the only lesson the poor needed to learn was that they were entitled to what was theirs. Nowhere was the distinctive cast of Skidmore's program more obvious than when he clarified this point: the freethinkers wanted to bestow Right Reason upon the workingmen and lead them to equality; Skidmore sought a political movement in which the dispossessed fought for themselves.[34]

In all, Skidmore's reformulation of political economy reached the borders of a kind of plebeian, anticapitalist revolutionism not usually associated with Jacksonian America. He did not, of course, think in terms of bourgeois and proletarian; like the most radical sansculottes and English Jacobins of the 1790s and in keeping with Ricardian distinctions between producers and nonproducers, he expected that men of small fortunes and productive occupations would join with the propertyless against the parasites. In some respects, Byllesby's *Observations*, with their discussions of the inequalities of all systems of unequal exchange for labor and of the dynamics of capital accumulation, spoke more directly to conditions in New York's workshops. By comparison, Skidmore's agrarianism had an abstract, static, almost ahistorical quality. But Skidmore, with his persistent focus on the illegitimacy of private property, offered the startling prospect of a revolution in all social relations—including the new wage relations—at the direct expense of the wealthy. Gone was the exclusive focus of the old journeymen's unions on wages and self-protection. Gone, too, were the rural Christian communities of Blatchly, the philanthropic designs of Robert Owen and of the freethinkers, the alternative cooperatives of Byllesby. In their place, Skidmore offered direct and immediate political action to eliminate capitalist accumulation and to suppress the nonproducing rich.

Of what possible relevance or significance, though, were these revolutionary musings of a lowly machinist? Certainly Skidmore was not a typical artisan who espoused "representative" views—but then, agitators of his kind seldom are. If nothing else, the man and his writings proved that liberal Jacksonian America could produce, among the self-taught mechanics, an anticapitalist vision of extraordinary boldness. Even more, Skidmore's ideas, for all of their heresies, drew upon and promoted the most central artisan political and social ideals. It was the Revolution, and especially the work of Paine, that originally inspired his politics and gave him the title

34. *Rights of Man to Property*, 8, 72–76, 369.

of his book; to secure a truly egalitarian small producers' republic remained his ultimate goal; even his revolution would be conducted along carefully planned, thoroughly democratic lines. What Skidmore captured, in terms most accessible to New York's poor masters and craft workers, was the growing fear, expressed in all kinds of ways in the 1820s, that something was terribly wrong in America, something unforeseen by the Founding Fathers, something that was creating social privilege and inequality and destroying the Republic from within, something that had to be removed.[35] Skidmore's diagnosis and his cures were certainly not agreeable in every detail to any but a tiny minority of his would-be followers. But to small masters beleaguered by progress, and even more to journeymen who could foresee neither independence nor decent work, the essence of Skidmore's charges and solutions could at least appear more truthful, more persuasive than the rhetoric of the Jacksonians or the proposals of the Adamsites. The events of 1829 would make their potential appeal and political importance readily, dramatically apparent.

The Free Enquirers and Skidmore were to be the major radical influences (and rivals) in 1829, but there was also a third group of dispirited manufacturers, artisans, and petty merchants who would eventually vie for control of the Working Men's movement. These were the politically disappointed of late 1828 and early 1829—the anti-auctioneers, high-tariff advocates, temperance reformers, and American Institute members for whom the victory and consolidation of the Jacksonians had been a singular disaster. Among them was a commission merchant named Noah Cook. The few surviving sources about Cook suggest a picture of a petty entrepreneur, constantly on the move and eager to get rich quick, a Tocquevillian American if there ever was one. He served, at one point in the 1820s, as the New York agent of an Erie Canal boat line; other references have him vending cordwood, speculating on country real estate, and selling patent rights for a cast-iron gristmill and a filtering machine for purifying cider. In 1828, he was active in the Adams campaign and served as a delegate to the pro-administration state convention; he also became a prominent member of the American Institute. He stayed in New York City through the winter of 1828–29 and kept an active eye on political developments. Meanwhile, Henry Guyon, a master carpenter, was also looking for his political bearings. Guyon was one of the foremost employers in his trade, a member of the General Society of Mechanics and Tradesmen, a charter member of the American Institute, a subscriber to the New-York City Temperance Society, and an Adamsite in 1828. In 1828–29, he returned to his

35. For a brilliant discussion of this point, from a different point of view, see David Brion Davis, "Some Themes of Counter-Subversion: An Analysis of Anti-Masonic, Anti-Catholic, and Anti-Mormon Literature," MVHR 47 (1960): 205–24.

business and his duties at the General Society and the American Institute.[36]

Prior to 1830, neither Cook nor Guyon published any summary of his principles. Because of this, perhaps, they have been remembered mainly as opportunistic political connivers, interested more in advancing their own fortunes against the Jacksonians than in promoting any particular program.[37] Certainly both were deeply interested in politics and preferred the quieter role of the backroom fixer to the public position of the idealistic spokesman—but this alone did not make them unprincipled men. Guyon, in particular, had committed himself to causes that promoted a consistent entrepreneurial view of American economic growth. Having already worked for various groups and candidates, including Adams, whose views on political economy matched their own assumptions, Cook, Guyon, and others like them naturally turned to established networks of friends and allies rather than to pamphleteering and lecturing. Their major problem early in 1829 was that no issue appeared to be at hand to help them press a political response to the Jacksonians. With Adams gone, they had begun to switch their national allegiance to Henry Clay, but beyond that, little was in the offing to galvanize an anti-Jacksonian coalition. Anti-Masonry, that peculiar blend of egalitarian outrage and anti–Van Buren manipulation, helped gather the anti-Jacksonian forces in the raw canal towns and farming hamlets upstate, but made little headway in the metropolis. The anti-auctioneers geared up again, but promised to win little more than they had already achieved. As late as October 1829, anti-Jacksonians like the merchant William Lawrence hoped that they would be able to "avail themselves of some local issue" like Van Buren's banking schemes, but they remained pessimistic about the near future.[38] However, as Cook and Guyon would prove (in a most ungentlemanly way), anti-Jacksonian entrepreneurial causes could be advanced with the help of some very unlikely allies, amid some uncommon political circumstances.

The Radical Movement

The Working Men's movement began as a radical journeymen's protest. In early 1829, New York was in the grip of a serious recession, exacerbated by an unusually harsh winter and by squabbles between Manhattan bank-

36. On Cook, see Hugins, *Jacksonian Democracy*, 83–84; Henry M. Western, *An Address Delivered before the American Institute in the City of New York on the Fourth of July, 1828* (New York, 1828), 7. On Guyon, see Earle and Congdon, *Annals*, 404; Wiles, *Century of Industrial Progress*, 3; Temperance Society, *First Annual Report*, 22.

37. E.g., Pessen, *Most Uncommon Jacksonians*, 29, 70–71.

38. Benson, *Concept of Jacksonian Democracy*, 36; William Lawrence to Henry Clay, August 31, 1829, quoted in Mushkat, *Tammany*, 121. The best recent social analysis of anti-Masonry in New York State is in Johnson, *Shopkeepers' Millennium*, 62–71.

ers and Martin Van Buren over the governor's alleged partiality to upstate banking interests. Bankruptcy assignments, on the increase since 1825, hit the levels reached in the 1819 panic (Figure 1); thousands of mechanics were reduced to charity; some citizens held public prayer meetings. A violent, unsuccessful strike for wages by semiskilled journeymen stone polishers in mid-March heightened tensions in the trades.[39] In the spring, rumors spread that large employers, in unspecified trades, were about to lengthen the workday from ten to eleven hours, in order to recoup their recent losses. A group of journeymen considered calling a strike if the new hours were put into effect; instead, partially at the urging of Thomas Skidmore, they called a public meeting on April 23 to propose suitable action and, if possible, to pass a series of resolutions that might intimidate the employers. At what was later described as "a very numerous meeting of mechanics," the men voiced principles that an alarmed *Commercial Advertiser* claimed "would lead to the dissolution of society into its original elements." The resolutions bid all journeymen to refuse to work for more than ten hours, "well and faithfully employed," in order to preserve "the first law of society," the right to decent work and fair remuneration. More ominously, the journeymen backed their demands with the observation that "all men hold their property by the consent of the great mass of the community, and no other title." Suddenly, radical agrarianism was linked to a new form of trade unionism.[40]

The link was strengthened, five days later, when a crowd of mechanics—estimated at between five and six thousand—turned out for a public meeting in the Bowery, in the heart of the journeymen and small masters' neighborhoods. After declaring that "the Creator has made all equal," the meeting resolved that no man could give up his original right of the soil to become a mechanic or laborer "without receiving a guaranty [*sic*] that reasonable toil shall enable him to live as comfortably as others." The rights of the rich, "or, in other words, the employers," were no greater than those of the poor; any who demanded an excessively long workday were deemed aggressors against the rights of their fellow citizens. Forthwith, the meeting unanimously determined to strike any master who demanded more than ten hours of work per day, to publish the names of all

39. *Journal of Commerce*, January 11, 1829; *Morning Herald* [New York], February 26, March 4, 1829; Commons, *History of Labour*, I, 171–72; Henry Van der Lyn Diary, 23 February 1829, N-YHS MSS; *Democratic Press* [Philadelphia], March 24, 25, 1829; *Daily Sentinel* [New York], March 8, 1830.

40. *Radical* [Granville, N.J.], January 1842; *Commercial Advertiser*, April 25, 1829; *Morning Courier*, April 25, 1829. It is likely that the employers in question were carpenters and builders; existing evidence from before 1820 shows that the ten-hour day had been in force in the building trades for a generation. See Rock, *Artisans of the New Republic*, 250–52.

wage earners who worked longer hours, and to appoint a committee of fifty men, that would devise means of assisting journeymen on strike or those trying to organize one.[41]

There is no question that journeymen from the city's trades dominated these events: a journeyman locksmith and journeyman blacksmith presided on both occasions; George Henry Evans, at the time a protégé of Owen and Wright, recalled that on 28 April "very great care was taken to have no 'Boss' on the committee [i.e., the Committee of Fifty] who employed a large number of hands, and a large majority of the committee were journeymen." With their actions, they came as close as they ever had to forming an effective central association across trade lines, as Philadelphia's craft workers had done two years earlier.[42] Their demand to be "well and faithfully employed" and to suffer neither poor wages nor long hours made plain their anxiety about changing workshop relations; their attempt to explain the broader causes of poverty and unfair working conditions and their equation of "the rich" and "the employers" affirmed that their concerns went beyond the questions of hours and wages and had turned to emerging divisions of class. It remained only to be seen whether that analysis would hold and whether the Committee of Fifty could generate a sustained movement. The presence on the committee of Thomas Skidmore—then in the process of drafting *The Rights of Man to Property!*—gave a clue about the outcome.

Shortly after the meeting of April 28, the suspected masters renounced all plans to lengthen the workday; nevertheless, the Committee of Fifty continued to meet and to discuss what future actions the journeymen might take. By the summer, it had resolved to run a ticket of journeymen and poor small masters in the upcoming local legislative elections, and through the early autumn the members debated the merits of various proposed platforms. Having decided to enter electoral politics, the committee agreed to reach out beyond the journeymen and to demand a string of reforms of possible interest to small masters and wage earners outside the crafts—from the abolition of credit and banking to the suppression of the licensed auctioneers. On broader philosophical matters, the committee divided between the supporters of Skidmore and a more moderate minority that dissented from his views on property; all believed, however, that the

41. *Commercial Advertiser*, April 29, 1829; *Free Enquirer*, April 29, 1829; *Radical*, January 1842. The *Advertiser*, astonished at what was happening, could conclude only that the journeymen "could not have understood their own resolutions." It would soon prove a constant argument of those opposed to the Working Men and Skidmore. See *Commercial Advertiser*, April 25, 1829.

42. *Radical*, January 1842; Pessen, "Working Men's Party Revisited," 209; Laurie, *Working People of Philadelphia*, 52–54. The locksmith was James Quinn; the blacksmith, Oliver Hudson.

basic structure of American society and politics tended "to make the rich richer, and fewer in number, and the poor poorer and greater in number." For three months, the men hammered out the substance and wording of a political manifesto.[43]

Quite independently of the journeymen and the committee, Wright, Owen, and the freethinkers began their own organizing drive among the city's artisans. In March and April, Wright gave her lectures on working-men, the producing classes, and the "existing evils"; on April 26, while the journeymen prepared for their second meeting, she opened the Hall of Science. Over the summer, she became less directly involved in New York affairs, preferring, true to form, to undertake another hectic lecture tour, but Owen immediately took up the slack. After writing a string of articles on "the producing classes" and on his state-education plan, he established, in early September, the Association for the Protection of Industry and for the Promotion of National Education, to agitate for a state law for a system of equal republican education. Activists of a variety of faiths joined the cause; Cornelius Blatchly assumed a leading position in Owen's organization, as did Evans. While the association bid for support from all artisans for educational reform, Owen also directed editorials in the *Free Enquirer* at the discontented journeymen, supporting the ten-hour day and praising the efforts of the Committee of Fifty.[44]

Into the early autumn, radical ideas spread throughout the artisan wards, leavened by attacks on the party men in power. Mechanics complained that Tammany no longer belonged to "the true Jeffersonian school" and searched for a suitable replacement. Skidmore moved forward with his writing and committee work: in June he announced the forthcoming publication of *The Rights of Man to Property!*, and by October, on the eve of the delivery of the Committee of Fifty's report, he and his supporters had begun to hold agrarian public meetings in the Bowery. Repeat performances by Frances Wright, briefly returned from her tour, rocked the Bowery Theatre and the Hall of Science. Owen, when he was not denouncing superstition and professional parties in the *Free Enquirer*, organized his own lectures and meetings specifically for working-men.[45]

On October 19, the long-awaited public session of the Committee of Fifty met at Military Hall, in Wooster Street. Among the five thousand who attended was Robert Dale Owen, by his own account a stranger to

43. *Radical*, February 1842.
44. *Free Enquirer*, May 6, 27, August 19, 26, September 2, 9, 23, 30, 1829. Evans—no longer printer of the *Free Enquirer*—served as chairman pro tempore of the association's first meeting.
45. *Evening Journal* [New York], October 17, 1829; *Free Enquirer*, June 17, September 23, 30, 1829.

the proceedings. Owen was sympathetic to the growing movement, but concerned about the increasingly agrarian drift of the committee. Although he supported economic equality in principle, loose talk of equal property struck him as a dangerous distraction from the main task, educational re-form—a distraction likely to cost the mechanics public support. Spotted by the crowd and greeted as a friend, Owen agreed to act as secretary of the meeting, convinced that the journeymen would "require enlightened friends to aid them by prudent suggestion. . . ." Although powerless to control the substance of the resolutions or the vote, he remained hopeful that, in debate, his own brand of radical reform would dominate. Instead, his worst fears came to pass.[46]

The meeting heard and approved a document inspired and largely writ-ten by Thomas Skidmore, a recitation of specific demands headed by an agrarian preamble on property and politics. Arguments stretching back to the English Commonwealth radicals of the 1640s and filtered through Paine appeared early in an exposition of the origins of private property and the effects of the Norman Yoke:

> [W]herever government is organized upon such unjust and unequal principles as were established in England by William the Conquerer, and as have prevailed there ever since, the Almighty in vain for the poor has made the water to gush from its fountain, vegetation to flourish on the surface of the earth, and created the treasures of the quarry and mine. . . .

After demonstrating that neofeudal social relations characterized the capi-talist New World as well as the Old, the committee insisted that nothing could save the great mass of the community short of a civil revolution, one that would leave "no trace of that government which has denied to every human being AN EQUAL AMOUNT OF PROPERTY ON ARRIVING AT THE AGE OF MATURITY, and *previous* thereto, EQUAL FOOD, CLOTHING, AND INSTRUCTION AT THE PUBLIC EXPENSE." It was impractical, at that moment, to accom-plish this revolution all at once, but with the approaching election, it seemed sensible to the committee to seize the opportunity to prevent fur-ther calamities, by taking to the polls to elect "men who, from their own sufferings, know how to feel for ours, and who, from consanguinity of feel-ing, will be disposed to do all they can to afford a remedy." The commit-tee laid out its immediate demands: abolition of private commercial banks, first and foremost, and then of chartered public monopolies, li-censed auctions, and imprisonment for debt; passage of a lien law and a law taxing clerics and church property; and reform of various electoral pro-

46. *Working Man's Advocate*, October 31, 1829; *Free Enquirer*, October 31, Novem-ber 14, 1829, March 30, 1830; *Commercial Advertiser*, October 26, 1829.

cedures. Observing that "we have nothing to hope from the aristocratic orders of society," including the deceiving political parties, the report concluded by inviting those "who live by their own labor, AND NONE OTHER," to meet five days later to select candidates for the state senate and assembly.[47]

The new, plainly worded platform proclaimed as radical a body of political principles as the early industrial world had yet seen or would see for a generation. To be sure, the platform's immediate demands did not include a proletarian uprising or Skidmore's General Division. The hints of a compromise between Skidmore and the moderate minority on the committee can be detected: Skidmore obviously composed the preamble and the explanations of the demands, but most of the demands themselves, except for the first on banks, included nothing that far more moderate nonagrarians could not endorse, and a few points, notably those on the lien law and the auctioneers, that might appeal to artisan entrepreneurs as much as to truly radical Skidmorites. Wright and Owen no doubt had their share of support; although the report did not endorse Owen's plan, it at least mentioned equal education and demanded suppression of clerical tax exemptions. Nevertheless, in setting the context and aims of the insurgency's politics, Skidmore and his followers prevailed. In its first and only statement of purpose during the campaign, the new movement proclaimed as its central premise that the initial division of property and all subsequent property relations were barbarously unjust. Its manifesto focused mainly on credit and private banking, not to call for their reform but to urge their abolition. All of the main demands—including equal education—had figured in Skidmore's original program. While the movement supported discrete political changes, it forthrightly claimed to do so not to repair a flawed status quo but to hasten a revolution. This was the Working Men's challenge to the politics of party democracy that had triumphed in 1828. At the head of their ticket, they affixed the sign of the hammer and hand;

47. *Evening Journal*, October 20, 1829; *Working Man's Advocate*, October 31, 1829. On the Norman Yoke and its background, see Christopher Hill, "The Norman Yoke," in idem, *Puritanism and Revolution* (London, 1958), 50-122; Thompson, *Making of the English Working Class*, 86-89; Foner, *Tom Paine*, 76-77. H. W. Berrian, *A Brief Sketch of the Origins and Rise of the Workingmen's Party in the City of New York* (Washington, D.C., n.d. [1840]), 4-5, asserts that the platform was "said to have been prepared under [Skidmore's] direction, if it was not from his own pen." The unsubstantiated claim that the platform's mention of equal education was a demand put forward by an organized Owen *faction* seems to have begun with Helen Sumner, in Commons, *History of Labour*, I, 247. There is no evidence of such a faction within the movement prior to the November election; nor have I found any evidence for Pessen's claim (*Most Uncommon Jacksonians*, 68) that the meeting of October 19 and Owen's presence as the meeting's secretary launched Owen's "formal career" as a "leader" of the Working Men. Formally, Owen led nothing in 1829 save his own association—a minor point, but one, as we shall see, of some significance when assessing the Working Men's rise and fall.

the emblem was old, but it proclaimed a "mechanics' interest" with very new—and to some masters, dangerous—ideas.[48]

The meeting touched off a frenzy. The reconvened public session of the Committee of Fifty—a plenary assembly, now called the general meeting of the Working Men—took nominations from the floor and directed the committee to select twenty-two names for resubmission to the public. Three days later, the committee returned its list and, in a manner to defy Tammany usages, chose by lottery a ticket of eleven candidates for the state assembly; among the names drawn were those of Cornelius Blatchly, Skidmore's associate Alexander Ming, and Skidmore himself. The meeting then nominated Silas Wood, an Adamsite from Long Island, and Edward Webb—a deist, friend of Owen, and master carpenter—as candidates for the state senate.[49]

It was all very alarming to Owen, even though his agitation had helped encourage the unrest and even though three of his friends, Blatchly, Webb, and the whitesmith Robert Kerriston, were on the new Working Men's ticket. This was not his idea of a proper mechanics' movement; he would later claim that most of those at the meeting of October 19 probably did not understand the Committee of Fifty report, or they never would have supported it. Instead of simply returning to his own work, however, Owen lingered at the movement's edge. On October 30, the leaders of Owen's association met to discuss the campaign and tepidly endorsed peaceful measures to equalize property as "eminently useful to society"—a statement consistent with the Free Enquirer's general beliefs and a concession that agrarianism had its appeal. Nevertheless, the group insisted that the worst forms of inequality were those produced by unequal education; although monopolies, banks, auctions, and the rest were unrepublican, it seemed unwise to raise such "minor" issues until national education was instituted. "All other modes of reform," the association resolved, "are compared to this, partial, ineffectual, temporary, or trifling." The group then chastised the Working Men for nominating only small-master and journeymen candidates, and supported those nominees—and only those—who they believed were favorable to state guardianship.[50]

Only the brevity of the campaign insured that even this wispy support from the Free Enquirer leadership held. The Committee of Fifty had only seventy-five dollars left over from the strike fund collected in April, and its candidates had to rely on their own personal efforts and funds to get out the vote: Owen, with his own resources, swiftly tried to turn the insur-

48. *Evening Post*, November 3, 1829.

49. *Working Man's Advocate*, October 31, 1829. On Webb, see *Free Enquirer*, November 14, 1829; Hugins, *Jacksonian Democracy*, 95.

50. *Free Enquirer*, October 31, November 7, 1829.

gency to his own political ends. Having firmly dissociated himself from the Committee of Fifty's report, he assisted Evans in establishing the *Working Man's Advocate*, purportedly to serve as an organ of the Working Men. Through the association, Owen tried to exert his own influence in the name of the city's workingmen and mechanics. Edward Webb, following Owen's lead, renounced agrarianism, accused Skidmore of rigging the meeting of October 19, and concentrated mainly on promoting state guardianship and attacking Tammany corruption. Finally, near the end of the contest, Owen dickered with the Adamsites and Clay men (now regrouped as the Masonic Hall ticket) and tried at the last minute to force them to ally with him, in hopes of providing a radical alternative to both the Working Men and to the Democrats.[51]

The city's masters and the established press took different lines of counterattack. The General Society issued a terse disavowal of any connection with the Mechanics' ticket and pointed out that none of the "Workie" candidates was a society member. Adamsite and mercantile newspapers, such as the *Commercial Advertiser*, rang the tocsin of private property and conventional religion against the "anarchical character" of this new, "sans-culotte" "Fanny Wright ticket." A few singled out Cornelius Blatchly as a particularly baneful influence, a known friend of the Red Harlot and of Owen, a crackpot infidel who ran disguised as a Working Man but who was really a physician. The Democratic editors more perceptively noted that some former Adamsites had begun to infiltrate the ranks of the "Workies"; Silas Wood, in particular, struck them as a most unlikely workingman, since he had also been nominated for the senate on the Masonic Hall ticket and had played no role in the agitation until the last week in October. It seemed obvious to the Tammanyites that the Working Men's ticket was not a radical one at all, but "Clay at the bottom and tariff to the very destruction of the trade and commerce of this city. . . ."[52]

Despite the jockeying and the acrimony, ordinary artisans rallied to the Working Men. At least one trade benefit society, the painters', backed the ticket and aided the campaign. Meetings cheered assaults on speculators and their "hydra headed monster, PARTY." Shades of the Revolution

51. *Radical*, February, 1842; *Working Man's Advocate*, October 31, December 12, 1829. When Owen finally acknowledged the appearance of the *Advocate*, he noted only that it was "edited by a Mechanic, and devoted to the cause of the people"—even though he had known and worked closely with Evans for months and even though Evans was also distributing Free Enquirer tracts. Evans gradually dropped his guise between November and January 1829. See *Working Man's Advocate*, November 14, 28, December 5, 12, 1829; *Free Enquirer*, November 21, 1829. On Owen's early involvement with the *Advocate*, see also Frances Wright to William Maclure, January 3, 1830, quoted in Perkins and Wolfson, *Frances Wright*, 269–70.

52. *Evening Post*, November 2, 3, 1829; *Commercial Advertiser*, October 23, 1829; *Morning Courier*, October 28, 1829.

sometimes seemed to stalk the eastern and central wards. "Sydney" (one of several republican and radical pseudonyms taken by Working Men) called upon poorer citizens to rise to the crisis, to decide whether they would be freemen or forever dependent on aristocratic masters and "the drones of the State." More up-to-date appeals repeated the old republican language but fixed on "men who fatten on the fruits of your industry," and bid the artisans and craft workers to stage a different kind of political revolt than that of '76. Apprehension turned to exuberance as the three days of balloting began and early tallies showed the Working Men running well. Caught off guard, the *Journal of Commerce* moaned of the Republic's certain doom now that "every man that walks" could vote. The Jacksonian press exhorted the party faithful to go to the polls to stem the "Workie" turnout; the *Morning Courier* warned darkly that the new interest among the mechanics had been founded on "the most alarming principles to civil society."[53]

The final returns were a setback to the Jacksonians, a debacle for the remaining Adamsites, and an impressive debut for the Working Men, Skidmore, and the Committee of Fifty (Table 17). The overall turnout was lighter than that for the preceding year's presidential election, suggesting that, by comparison, this campaign left a portion of the electorate unmoved; the decline was lowest, however, in those poor wards that voted most heavily for the Working Men and in the wealthier wards that voted most heavily against them. Tammany was the chief beneficiary of the Working Men's challenge in the downtown wards, where it increased its percentage to the total vote over that in 1828 by from between seven and twenty-four points; some of the quondam Adams men who bothered to go to the polls no doubt turned to the Democrats as the strongest weapon against Skidmore and company. Elsewhere, the presence of the "Workies" cut deeply into both the Tammany and the Adamsite vote; in the strongest Working Men's wards, the poorer small-master and journeymen districts in the central and eastern parts of the city, the Tammany percentage dipped by about one-third, while the Adamsites' support, already minimal, virtually evaporated. In the Eighth and Tenth Wards Skidmore and the Working Men won small but convincing pluralities, and in the nearby Thirteenth Ward a large majority; in the city as a whole, the Working Men's assembly candidates polled nearly one-third of the adjusted total vote, two and one-half times that of the Adamsites. Although the Democrats won most of the assembly races, one Working Men's candidate, a journeyman carpenter named Ebenezer Ford, was elected to the assembly; Skidmore and Alexander Ming missed being elected by twenty-three and twenty-six votes respectively. Only Cornelius Blatchly—the man most clearly identified as a friend of Robert Dale Owen—failed to come close to winning, and even he captured more than four thousand votes. The state-senate races saw very different results. Silas Wood was elected, but his chief support came not from the Working Men's wards but from the same downtown districts that had voted most heavily for Adams; Webb the deist was defeated and ran behind the "Workie" assembly ticket. Overall, it was very encouraging for the leadership of the Working Men's movement; most of the candidates of their avowedly radical workingmen's ticket had won more than six thousand votes each.[54]

The election's larger significance was, as it continues to be, viewed in various ways. The Tammany and commercial newspapers predictably tried to slough off the result and charged that the Working Men's supporters had no idea for what or whom they had cast their ballots. Robert Dale Owen, who later suggested the same thing, knew better; his lament just after the election was that the announced program was all too clear and had cost the ticket even greater success. George Henry Evans somehow managed to interpret the vote as a victory for state guardianship, a most partial conclusion, given that the platform never endorsed Owen's specific proposal, given Owen's attacks on the movement just before the election, and given the turnout for Blatchly and Webb. Evans probably came closer to the truth more than a decade later, when he reversed himself, confessed that most of the Working Men's supporters favored an eventual redistribution of wealth, and reflected that the main cause for the Working Men's success "was that in their manifesto [i.e., the Committee of Fifty report] they boldly attacked every prominent system of oppression, of however long standing, under which they had suffered."[55]

Unfortunately, we cannot be certain how people voted in 1829 and why they voted that way; the multitude of candidates and the many opportunities for ticket splitting, as well as the dearth of background demographic data, cloud the results. But some conclusions can be drawn with reasonable confidence. First, the Working Men's campaign, more than that of any party of the era, benefited from some approximation of "class voting," and not from the usual party coalition. As in no other election in early-nineteenth-century New York, the results in 1829 drew a line between the city's richer and poorer wards—so much so that the best study of the ward-by-ward tallies concedes that the figures for 1829 were a true manifestation

54. *Working Man's Advocate*, November 7, 14, 1829; *Evening Journal*, November 9, 1829; *Evening Post*, November 10, 1829. On the ward-by-ward turnout for Wood, and its similarities to the preceding year's Adams vote, see Secrist, "Anti-Auction," 164–65.

55. *Morning Courier*, November 10, 1829; *Working Man's Advocate*, November 21, 1829; *Free Enquirer*, November 14, 1829, March 30, 1830; *Radical*, April, 1843.

of "lower-class" voting for the Working Men.[56] Second, if the Working Men were poor, they were not stupid or undiscriminating in their choices, as Tammany (and later Owen) implied. Had the Working Men's voters simply gone to the polls and blindly voted the "Workie" ticket, then Blatchly and Webb would have received many more votes than they did. Support for the Committee of Fifty—the movement's leaders—was strong, as the totals for Skidmore and Ming showed. Owen's friends in the movement also had their followers, who would vote for Blatchly and Webb even when others did not. Ebenezer Ford, the victorious candidate, was known only to be a journeyman carpenter—perhaps the strongest recommendation any "Workie" candidate could offer. In all, the returns corroborated what had seemed obvious since the spring—that the Working Men's movement was a radical movement of journeymen joined by small masters, probably as close to the beginnings of what Skidmore had in mind as his poor people's party as a movement or party could have been in New York City at the time.

The ideological ramifications of the election were just as important as the returns. If nothing else, the campaign and the related agitation compelled New York's small master artisans and craft workers to come to terms with the prospects of their political values in a city and nation of evident inequality. The Committee of Fifty report, the Free Enquirers' lectures, articles, and associations, the speeches and letters that invoked Paine, Jefferson, and the Revolution—all of these were radical, if divergent, expressions of fears that the Republic was endangered by its men of property and standing, above all its capitalist entrepreneurs. Whomever they supported, New Yorkers had to consider these arguments more directly than ever before. That so many were willing to break with their usual connections to vote for a forthrightly radical artisan ticket suggests that the ideological turmoil of the campaign was genuine enough. The two hundred odd votes cast for persons not on the ballot brought the point home with a satiric flourish. One man cast one of his assembly votes for George IV of England, another for Charles X of France, and another voted for Ferdinand VII of Spain; presumably, to them, a monarch was not much worse than (or, perhaps, preferable to) the assembly candidates. Others voted for a cosmopolitan range of radical heroes, from Praise God Barebones to Robert Emmet and Simón Bolívar. Seven men, meanwhile, voted for Frances Wright, seven for Fanny Wright, two for Miss Frances Wright, two for Miss Fanny Wright, and one each for Miss F. Wright and Frances Wright, Esq.[57] A new artisan political radicalism, in various forms, had begun to take hold.

56. Hugins, *Jacksonian Democracy*, 211–13. To say the least, the 1829 returns do not square with Hugins's overall interpretation of the Working Men's movement.
57. *Working Man's Advocate*, November 14, 1829.

The agitation continued in the immediate afterglow of victory. The Fifth Ward Mechanics and Other Working Men's Political Debating Society assembled in November to discuss labor, property, and education and to denounce the Democratic party; similar groups appeared in the Eighth and Eleventh wards. The Painters' Society pledged the Working Men's movement further support. The employers' New York Typographical Society, led by the American Institute master and evangelical temperance man Adoniram Chandler, denounced the Working Men and radical educational reformers as anti-Christian; several journeymen printers strongly protested and drafted a minority reply upbraiding the society for its impertinence. In December, another group of journeymen printers sympathetic to the Free Enquirers announced they would soon begin publication of a new daily devoted to the interests of the mechanics and workingmen. Skidmore and Ming produced a prospectus for still another newspaper to support the program of the Committee of Fifty.[58] Yet despite these abundant signs of life, the movement's future direction was far from assured. Indeed, more than anyone understood at first, its very existence was endangered, as much by the Owenite radicals as by the Democrats and Adamsites.

The Coup

During the election and the ensuing weeks, Robert Dale Owen remained blandly confident that his influence among the Working Men would increase. As the voters went to the polls, he allowed that the Committee of Fifty had called attention to crying abuses, and he cautiously remained on record as favoring an eventual equalization of property. Three weeks later, however, in a soothing editorial, Owen assured the city's conservative press that he and his colleagues "propose no equalization but that which equal national education shall gradually effect." Evans, meanwhile, claimed in the *Working Man's Advocate* that equal education was the Working Men's true interest, and asserted, without a hint of embarrassment, that he had never heard anyone support the "wild scheme" of equalizing property. Unable to deny the election results, the Free Enquirers tried to argue that the Working Men's movement, under Skidmore's leadership, had had nothing to do with its own success.[59] It was to be a prelude for more direct action by Owen and his friends.

The ticket's strong showing also attracted notice in new corners. The *Evening Journal*, normally a moderate defender of Clay and the American

58. Ibid., November 28, December 12, 1829; *Free Enquirer*, December 26, 1829, January 9, 1830.
59. *Free Enquirer*, November 7, 14, 28, 1829; *Working Man's Advocate*, November 21, 28, December 5, 12, 1829.

System, encouraged the Working Men in their quest to "gain a proper standing in the community," but cautioned them against passing violent resolutions or nominating any except men of "great ability and talent."[60] At the same time, men previously associated with either the Adamsites, the General Society, the American Institute, or all three began to gravitate to the "Workies." Noah Cook and Henry Guyon were among them; others included Adoniram Chandler, Clarkson Crolius, the prominent stoneware manufacturer and leading member of the American Institute, Abijiah Mathews, the anti-auctioneer furniture maker, and Joseph Hoxie, a General Society member and evangelical temperance leader. Some of these men probably had attended the Working Men's meetings as early as October, to help nominate Silas Wood for the senate. None had any sympathy with the freethinkers like Owen—whom Chandler singled out as a fraud, "hanging to the skirts of a deluded woman"—and they despised Skidmore.[61] Alarmed at the agrarians' power and eager for a better political base than the crippled Adamsite coalition, these men had decided to transform the movement into a party of their own. The first step, quite obviously, was to topple Thomas Skidmore. In this venture, they turned to those radicals who had sought them out before the election but whom they had rebuffed—the Owenites, who in their search to create a proper workingmen's movement would strike what alliances they could.

Political organization proved the deciding factor. Thus far, the movement had been a hybrid of centralized control and ostentatious defiance of Tammany-style procedures, but shortly after the election some members began to have second thoughts about such irregular arrangements. "Sydney" warned that the better-organized Jacksonians would do their best to set "Tammany traps," to steal the Working Men's issues and co-opt the membership. Thomas Skidmore worried more about the possible destruction of the movement from within. Like most successful popular leaders, he was driven to "keep jealousy and contention out of our works"; even more, he suspected that, if the movement was too improvised, a majority of "enemies" could enter and take command. To prevent fragmentation and manipulation, Skidmore urged the formal organization of a party along more regular lines, balancing ward committees with the general meeting and the Committee of Fifty.[62]

Evans, writing in the *Working Man's Advocate*, called Skidmore's plan

60. *Evening Journal*, October 22, 24, November 9, 1829.
61. *Working Man's Advocate*, December 12, 1829. The names of men who became active late in 1829 were drawn from Walter Hugins's manuscript list of Working Men activists, courtesy of Professor Hugins.
62. *Working Man's Advocate*, November 28, December 5, 1829; *Evening Journal*, November 25, 27, December 1, 4, 7, 10, 12, 1829. Skidmore wrote under the pseudonym "Marcus."

undemocratic and charged that the Committee of Fifty had been dilatory in proposing a new form of organization. With an ostensible desire to devise a plan acceptable to all, Evans demanded—and, to his delight, received—a call for a general meeting of the movement to discuss the matter. All along, Cook, Guyon, and Owen's friends were laying their own traps for Thomas Skidmore. An agreement was struck with the Committee of Fifty whereby any group within the meeting could form a committee to prepare a report for the plenary session; this done, Edward Webb joined with Noah Cook and several others in a conference committee and planned to take the floor of the general meeting as soon as it was called to order. Webb tested out an alliance with the entrepreneurial anti-auction movement, addressing one of its rallies in December with a stern warning about the "wild Agrarian scheme" as an impolitic and impractical menace. A few Owenites—possibly including Evans—prepared anti-Skidmore handbills intended for wide circulation; a self-styled "Real Working Man" bid mechanics to "defeat the desperate efforts of the Agrarian Minority" to "show this infatuated JUNTA, though [they] themselves are deluded, that the public mind is sane."[63]

Three thousand persons gathered at Military Hall on December 29. They attended, not a debate on strategy and tactics, not even a meeting of the Working Men's movement, but a coup de main. Owen's men and the friends of Cook and Guyon packed the hall and allowed Henry Guyon to take the chair; when Skidmore, the Committee of Fifty, and their supporters, unprepared and outnumbered, tried to take their positions, they were shouted down and then forcibly prevented from speaking. Suddenly, Noah Cook stepped forward to read what was supposed to be the conference committee report but was actually a new party manifesto. It was a document redolent with artisan republican rhetoric—of mechanics and workingmen fighting the monied aristocrats to reclaim the spirit of the Revolution—but its latent meanings were quite different from those of the Committee of Fifty report. Only the mildest of the demands from October—those on auctions, the lien, and imprisonment for debt—remained, stripped of all radical connotations and joined with a few even less offensive proposals and an ambiguous statement on universal education (a resolution Evans realized later had been "artfully framed" to confuse and placate the radical friends of state guardianship). Henceforth, Cook declared, the Working Men would not propose to interfere with men's sacred, individual rights to religion and private property—especially property, described in the report as "one of the greatest incentives to industry."

63. *Working Man's Advocate*, December 25, 1829, March 6, 1830; *Evening Journal*, December 12, 28, 30, 31, 1829; *Daily Sentinel*, February 26, 1830. It is not entirely clear whether, as Skidmore charged, Evans was directly involved in writing the handbills.

Banks would be respected as agents of prosperity but pressed to give more credit to manufacturers. The Working Men's movement, Cook concluded, would become a formal political party, but headed by a new general executive council in place of Skidmore's committee. The report stirred no debate and was approved; after it dissolved the Committee of Fifty, the meeting adjourned.[64]

The next day, the *Evening Journal* rejoiced that the "Workies" had "wiped away every stigma" of Agrarianism.[65] What in fact had happened was that the Owenite leaders and their new allies—men who thus far had either been on the fringe of the Working Men's movement or had opposed it—had created an entirely new organization in the Working Men's name. More precisely, as a close reading of the conference committee report, sensitive to every nuance, might have shown, the Cook-Guyon men had made a mockery of the October platform and used the Owenites to wrest the mantle of the Working Men for themselves. In less than an hour, the radical Working Men's movement had been displaced by the entrepreneurial Working Men's party.

A bitter struggle for legitimacy followed. The newcomers under the wing of Cook and Guyon wasted no time in consolidating control over their new party. In January 1830, they elected Guyon chairman of the new Executive Committee, and by March most of the party's posts were manned by mechanics unaffiliated with the Owenites—including some quite prominent master craftsmen. They did not succeed totally in removing radical influences. Clarkson Crolius lost a bid to be elected corresponding secretary to the Owenite painter Simon Clannon; the *Daily Sentinel*, the journeymen's newspaper established just after the election, had fallen under Owen's sway; Evans still ran the *Working Man's Advocate*. But the Cook-Guyon men were quick to dispel these disadvantages. Early in 1830, a group of Clayites bought out the *Evening Journal* and installed Noah Cook as associate editor. The Executive Committee passed a resolution barring all but committee members from attending its sessions; rumor had it that a doorkeeper would be hired to enforce order. Although they remained in the party, the bewildered Owenites began to understand that they, as much as the original Working Men, had been shut out. Like a confidence man who has just discovered he has been swindled, Evans blustered about the "anti-republican" moves to exclude "free citizens" from the party's councils. The Cookites, having learned the Jacksonian's organizing lessons well, restricted themselves to vague speeches on the

64. *Working Man's Advocate*, January 16, 1830; *Free Enquirer*, March 20, 1830; *Radical*, March, April 1843. The record of the meeting was also published separately, as *Proceedings of a Meeting of Mechanics and Other Working Men* (New York, 1830).
65. *Evening Journal*, December 30, 1829.

evils of Tammany and to petition campaigns in favor of the abolition of imprisonment for debt. More drastic divisions were in the making.[66]

Skidmore, although outmaneuvered, remained undeterred. In the days and weeks after the debacle at Military Hall, he and Ming dashed off letters to the *Free Enquirer* and the *Daily Sentinel*, to complain that Owen was misrepresenting their views, to explain what they meant by equal rights to property, and to charge that the Executive Committee was now headed by rich men who had no business calling themselves workingmen. At about the same time, Skidmore chaired a "well-attended" meeting for "those and only those who live by the labor of their hands" to discuss their future plans. In mid-February, a rump session of about forty Skidmorites voided the decision of December 29 and declared themselves the true Working Men's committee.[67] By April, when he brought out the first issue of his newspaper, the *Friend of Equal Rights*, Skidmore was engaged in a full-scale editorial war with the *Enquirer*, the *Advocate* and the *Sentinel*. Evans pronounced Skidmore's ideas on property preposterous and charged that "Mr. Skidmore's principal object is notoriety." Owen accused the "head strong and impudent schemer" Skidmore of "splitting and distracting the mechanic's party"; fortunately, Owen sneered, his influence was "confined chiefly to the idle and unemployed." Skidmore, for his part, indicted Evans for his role in the preparations for December 29 and attempted to distinguish his agrarian ideas and programs from the distortions of the Owenites' polemics.[68]

Skidmore's initial calm and confidence suggest that he was slow to understand the full significance of what had happened. Labeled as an unrepublican, violent fanatic who would make all possessions collective, robbed of the standard of the Working Men and incapable of taking over the now tightly managed Working Men's party, he found it impossible to regain his former position or to reassemble a following beyond a small band of devotees. Every newspaper in the city other than his own ill-funded sheet—including four "Workie" or "pro-Workie" newspapers—distorted his views and reported on the new committee as the Working

66. *Working Man's Advocate*, January 16, 23, 1830; *Evening Journal*, January 18, 1830; Owen, "Earnest Sowing," 78; Mechanics and Working Men, Executive Committee, Minutes, January 29, February 5, 1830, and passim, N-YHS MSS. Unfortunately, these minutes exist only for the period after December 29 and are spotty even then. They do show the extent to which the Cookites took over the party. Of those thirty-four committee members whose affiliations could be determined from Hugins's list (N = 50), twenty-two were Cookites and twelve were Owenites. Breaking them down by year shows that 52.4 percent of those active in 1830 were originally Cookites, compared with 83.3 percent in 1831.

67. *Free Enquirer*, January 9, 23, March 6, 20, May 1, 1830.

68. *Daily Sentinel*, February 26, 1830; *Working Man's Advocate*, March 6, April 17, 1830; *Free Enquirer*, March 20, 1830.

Men. The independent journeymen's movement that had first elevated him was now dispersed; he was almost completely isolated. "The Executive Committee is now universally recognized as the regularly nominated organ of the Mechanics of New York," Owen crowed. Skidmore's cause was not helped by the Jacksonians. Tammany, awakening to the need to find their own issues, read the results of the assembly elections well, and, as "Sydney" predicted, they set about making the milder of the "Workies'" issues their own. City bankers close to the Jacksonians opened their credit lines to small master mechanics. In Albany, Jacksonian assemblymen from Manhattan sponsored and helped pass a mechanics' lien law. Still denouncing the Working Men as a pack of Clayites—a charge that now began to stick—the Democratic press wooed those disaffected with the Working Men's party, propped themselves up as the true friends to the workingmen, and presented themselves as the only party strong enough to resist the Clayite-Working Men. Support for Skidmore, they implied, was now tantamount to support for the ex-Adamsites. It was all to prove too much for Skidmore to overcome.[69]

With these developments, the ideological splits among the artisans began to emerge, despite their common labels of "mechanics and working men." The backgrounds of the leaders of the respective groups suggested the social dimension of these divisions. They by no means conformed to strict boundaries of class: some journeymen, small masters, and masters could be found in all factions. Yet there were important differences. While grocers were common in all three groups, the Skidmorites tended to be small master artisans, journeymen, and laborers—brass founders, morocco dressers, and shoemakers seem to have been especially numerous (Table 18). The Cookites included far more men who listed themselves in the city directory as large-scale manufacturers and employers; its craftsmen included an unusually high percentage of master carpenters and builders, and at least some men of great wealth. The Owenites, meanwhile, included artisans—the vast majority of them journeymen—from widely scattered trades, and a large number of petty professionals and others from outside the trades, including editors, teachers, and attorneys. Residential patterns were less distinct, as all three groups drew from areas around the city; significantly, however, the Cookites included twice as many men from the "aristocratic" First Ward as the Skidmorites, while the Tenth Ward—the second-poorest per capita in the city, with 8.1 percent of the city's population—was home to 28.1 percent of the Skidmorite leadership, 5.9 percent of the Cookites, and 7.1 percent of the Owenites. Different connections with the city's two major

69. *Evening Post*, January 20, 25, 30, 1830; *Free Enquirer*, March 20, 1830; *Report of the Select Committee on the Petition of Sundry Builders* (New York, 1830). Owen listed the newspapers now friendly to the Working Men as the *Evening Journal*, the *Herald*, the *Working Man's Advocate*, and the *Daily Sentinel*.

craft groups were marked. Two of the Skidmorite artisans whose occupations can be traced were actually members of the General Society; these, however, included the entrepreneur, political adventurer, and baker Jonas Humbert, who was soon to renounce any association with Skidmore. Most of the rest do not appear to have been masters, let alone General Society men. Of the Cookite artisans meanwhile, nearly one in three was a General Society member, as was about one in every ten Owenite artisan. An accurate list of members of the American Institute in 1829 has not been located, but all of those men known to have been involved in both the Working Men's party and the Institute aligned with their fellow, Noah Cook. So did all those "workingmen" known as leading proponents of evangelical temperance reform.[70]

In all, three groups of broadly different backgrounds, and with three different visions of the artisan republic, had come to blows, shattering the Working Men's movement. It took time, however, for the fervor of 1829 to recede entirely. Discussions and debates continued among the rank and file. Journeymen excoriated monopolies and capitalists, men "who are not mechanics" who usurped the rights of small masters and wage earners. The Painters' Society declared its loyalty to state guardianship, while the Benevolent Society of Journeymen Bookbinders, meeting in May, took time to toast the Working Men of New York and Albany and "National Education, [t]he only true source of Liberty and Equality." Ward groups assembled and argued the merits of state education and property reform while the freethinkers continued to print their copies of Voltaire and Palmer. The Tammanyites were worried enough by the ongoing activity to drape themselves hastily in workingmen's garb in preparation for the fall election.[71]

The longer these popular initiatives continued, abetted by the *Sentinel*, the *Working Man's Advocate*, and the *Friend of Equal Rights*, the more they turned the labor theory of value and the language of the Republic against capitalists, dishonest employers, and corrupt officials. "Old Republican," in a letter to the *Advocate*, warned that the earnings of free-born Americans were being stolen by financiers and employers in order "to pamper a growing aristocracy." Others blamed invading capitalist employ-

---

70. On occupations, also see Hugins, *Jacksonian Democracy*, 124–25. In all, 7.0 percent of the Owenites and 19.0 percent of the Cookites appear as members of the General Society in Earle and Congden, *Annals*, 358–415. Those confirmed as members of the American Institute in 1829, according to membership lists from the 1840s in American Institute Papers, N-YHS, included Thomas Bussing, Adoniram Chandler, Clarkson Crolius, Jr., Henry G. Guyon, Joseph Hoxie, Thaddeus B. Wakeman, and Abijiah Mathews. The temperance men included Guyon, Chandler, and Hoxie. See Temperance Society, *First Annual Report*.

71. *Evening Journal*, February 18, 1830; *Free Enquirer*, May 29, July 24, 1830; *Working Man's Advocate*, May 13, 1830; Mushkat, *Tammany*, 124–26.

ers, still others the "standing army of Rag Money Makers" who, as Paine had warned a generation earlier, depreciated the currency to facilitate their own speculations and impoverish honest workingmen. Less radical disputants countered, in older republican form, that the economic system was less at fault than were selfish politicians who enacted laws contrary to the interests and rights of the people. It took several months of such debate before the fragmentation of the party was complete. The end was in sight when the Cookites, no longer in need of radical allies against the dangerous Skidmore, finally admitted what kind of workingmen they really were.[72]

The End

By the spring of 1830, ex-Adamsite supporters of Henry Clay were confident that with Cook and Guyon in command, the Working Men's party was theirs; one wrote directly to Clay to advise him that the party "will embrace most of the friends of the late administration . . . it promises well." The elimination of the Owenites became the Cookites' next priority. The breach opened in May, at a New York celebration of the recent formation of self-styled workingmen's parties at Troy and Albany. Noah Cook, by now an editor of the *Evening Journal*, used the occasion to offer some lessons about the dangers of fanaticism and to stress that while educational reform was laudable, the Working Men were primarily interested in "the protecting and fostering of our own industry." Two weeks later, at an Executive Committee session, a subcommittee chaired by Guyon delivered a stinging dissent from an Owenite report on education and branded state guardianship as "radically *wrong*" and merely "a specious attempt insidiously to palm off on the committee and the great body of the working classes the doctrine of *infidelity*." To the howls of the Owenites, the committee adopted the Guyon dissent. The heart of the Owenite program had been removed from the party.[73]

Over the next five months, the proceedings of the purported Working Men's party degenerated into fistfights and incessant plotting. When they were not smashing up each other's meetings or trading charges about fanatical infidelity and hypocritical piety, Owenites and Cookites planned to do each other in at the polls. By July, they had split, to run different candidates in a by-election for the Common Council; in September, the Cookites, in league with upstate Clayites, turned a statewide convention of Working Men into an anti-Jacksonian party conclave, finally capturing

72. *Working Man's Advocate*, July 3, 10, 1830.
73. Peter Porter to Henry Clay, May 25, 1830, quoted in Mushkat, *Tammany*, 124; *Working Man's Advocate*, May 20, 27, 1830; *Free Enquirer*, June 5, 1830; *Daily Sentinel*, June 16, 1830.

the Working Men's mantle for the Clay cause. Thomas Skidmore, meanwhile, struggled to regain what he had lost. Ostracized by Cookites and Owenites, commanding little more than his small newspaper and his most devoted followers, Skidmore had only the remotest chance of being heard amid the squabbles of the new Working Men; the press covered his activities and his attacks on Wright and Owen only to ridicule them as the ravings of a lunatic, savoring of "fanaticism of equality." Skidmore himself, meanwhile, embittered and on the defensive, diverted his energies from the elucidation of his program to ad hominem invectives against the Free Enquirers, as property-owning enemies of the people, guilty of "the willfull propagation of falsehoods . . . on subjects in which all mankind have an interest. . . ." Still a powerful polemicist, Skidmore had been reduced from the status of a popular leader to that of a man obsessed with those who had undone his plans, one whose diatribes only lent credence to charges that he was unstable. His Poor People's party did field a slate of candidates for the assembly in the fall election, but as much to expose Owen and Wright as to rekindle the movement of 1829.[74]

The election proved a reversal of the preceding year's returns. The Cookites, having finally declared their Clayite sympathies and having allied with the remaining Adamsites and the upstate anti-Masons, still claimed to be Working Men but built on the Adams constituency not on the "Workies." The Owenites, forced to go on alone, could rely only on the most determined radical voters; Skidmore's campaign mixed radical rhetoric with lampoons of his devilish, traitorous adversaries (Plate 13). Into the breach stepped the Jacksonian Democrats, happy to claim that they, the true party of the mechanics, had been correct all along and that the so-called Working Men were nothing but a collection of "ruffle-shirted lawyers" who favored Clay, corruption, and an aristocratic resurgence. Now that the old Adamsites were revived, the choice for most workingmen was plain; even Evans soon admitted that Tammany was preferable to the "piebald" Clayites. Tammany regained all of the "Workie" wards of 1829, while the Cookites finished a distant but not disgraceful second. The Owenite Working Men proved incapable of reassembling the original supporters of the Committee of Fifty and mustered only about 2,200 votes, about one-third of the total taken by the Working Men in 1829 and

74. *Free Enquirer*, June 19, July 3, 10, October 9, 1830; *Working Man's Advocate*, May 29, June 5, 1830; *Daily Sentinel*, June 26, July 3, 10, 27, 1830; Hugins, *Jacksonian Democracy*, 19–21. The details of the takeover of the state Working Men's convention—and thus of the party itself—by Clayites led by Thaddeus Wakeman of the American Institute are disclosed in Matthew L. Davis, Memoranda, 1830–1835, pp. 50–51, Rufus King Papers, N-YHS MSS; see also Hugins, *Jacksonian Democracy*, 21. For attacks on Skidmore, see *Free Enquirer*, September 4, October 2, 9, 16, 1830; for Skidmore's riposte, see *Free Enquirer*, October 2, 1830.

a mere 11 percent of the total in 1830. Skidmore's candidates received fewer than 200 scattered votes.[75]

Tammany's recovery did not end the ideological crisis; indeed, it was clearly exposed three weeks after the election when the trades gathered on Evacuation Day for the civic celebration of the revolution in France the preceding July. United in their respect for the French and for republican principles, the trades marched together (although with a singular lack of enthusiasm, according to one observer) and put on all the familiar craft shows. But after the public ceremonies ended amid shoving and catcalls, entrepreneurs and radical artisans went their separate ways, the first to toast Louis Philippe, Jacques Laffitte, and the new, liberalized French monarchy, the second to more spartan affairs that praised the Paris crowd, denounced the French "monied aristocracy," and bid New York's mechanics to redeem the country from monopolies, banks, "the poison of fashion and the canker-worm of party." The rituals of mutuality had become occasions for protest. Now, however, the radical forces lacked the tools, the momentum and the political room to carry their protests effectively into an election.[76]

The remnants of the Owenite faction lingered on for another year and a half. Late in 1830, Evans, having learned the perils of loose-knit organization, formed the Workingmen's Political Association, designed as a collection of private clubs divided along ward lines and closed to "pretended friends." The group courted all factions and parties in the city and actually got some of its men on the Clayite and Democratic tickets in the local elections in 1831, but its own slate fared dismally. In 1832, Evans accepted the inevitable and endorsed Jackson for president but tried to encourage a boomlet to nominate the anti-Sabbatarian congressman Richard M. Johnson for vice-president. The eventual selection of Martin Van Buren as Jackson's running mate was the final indignity; Jackson's bank-veto message, the shift of the last remaining Owenite radicals into the Jacksonian camp, and the smashing Democratic victory in the fall only ended the misery. The popular base of the old mechanics' interest had been recaptured, not by the Clayites, but by the Jacksonians. The Working Men's party—what was left of it—was dead.[77]

The end found the major figures in the events of 1829 scattered in their various pursuits. All save one went on to new careers; their personal fortunes were oddly emblematic of the fates of their movements. Frances

75. *Working Man's Advocate*, November 13, 20, December 4, 1830; Mushkat, *Tammany* 124-25; Hugins, *Jacksonian Democracy*, 22.

76. For details on the demonstration, see Wilentz, "Artisan Republican Festivals," 53-56.

77. *Daily Sentinel*, September 12, 13, 1832; Hugins, *Jacksonian Democracy*, 22-29.

Wright, who played no direct political role in either the Working Men's movement or the Cookite-Owenite party, had left New York in November 1829 for Haiti, where she tried to arrange for the transit of ex-slaves from Nashoba. She returned to New York briefly in the spring of 1830, just long enough to deliver a few speeches denouncing the Cookites and Skidmore, and then set sail for Paris. By 1831, she had attached her affections to the French educational reformer, Phiquepal D'Arusmont, whom, to the malicious amusement of her opponents, she eventually married. Although she would later return to New York, to considerable notice, to campaign for Martin Van Buren, and although her name remained one to be used by pious parents to frighten their children, Wright would never again recapture her former political influence. Robert Dale Owen, spurned by the Cookites and the New York electorate, had withdrawn from the party shortly after the 1830 election. In 1831, he sold the Hall of Science, ironically enough, to a new Methodist congregation. After marrying the daughter of a deist shoe manufacturer, he spent a year in Europe before he returned to New Harmony, where he would build a successful career as a Democratic reform politician on the ruins of his father's community. Cook and Guyon remained active in city politics and by 1832 were well along in their project of solidifying the coalition that would coalesce as the New York Whigs. Cook became a particularly prominent partisan, a "Pipelayer to the Whig Party," Evans later called him, "a man infamous for every species of political trick and fraud. . . ."[78]

Time was not left to Thomas Skidmore. In summer 1831, he published a response to Owen's birth-control proposals, *Moral Physiology Exposed and Refuted*, a short tract entitled *Political Essays*, and yet another attack on the "singular reform" of state education. He undertook one last radical effort, the New York Association for the Gratuitous Distribution of Discussions on Political Economy, before he withdrew to his shop to perfect a method for casting metallic shells for terrestrial globes. He died the following year at age forty-two, a victim of the cholera.[79]

Artisan Radicalism and the Paradoxes of Politics

"There are few persons who fully understand the principles and objects of the Working Men's Movement, while many totally misapprehend them," George Henry Evans wrote in 1842, "a necessary consequence of

78. Perkins and Wolfson, *Frances Wright*, 269–326; *Free Enquirer*, November 21, 1829; Leopold, *Robert Dale Owen*, 103–20; Hugins, *Jacksonian Democracy*, 83–84; *Radical*, February 1842.

79. *Working Man's Advocate*, June 23, 1830, August 11, 1832; *Free Enquirer*, December 17, 1831; Thomas Skidmore, *Moral Physiology Exposed and Refuted* (New York, 1831); [idem], *Political Essays*.

the flood of misrepresentation with which that Movement was assailed by a coalition of corrupt party presses."[80] Evans was being less than candid here; in 1829, he had contributed to the flood of misrepresentation as much as anyone. Still, his remarks are pertinent. The Working Men's movement was, has been, and continues to be described as any number of things: a proletarian party, an entrepreneurial interest group with some erratic radical leaders, a crusade for educational reform, a bunch of "nihilist" fanatics, an offshoot of Tammany Hall, an unstable coalition with three factions—as almost everything except as the popular movement that it was. It is the usual fate of such movements.[81]

To overcome these misapprehensions, we must discard the fiction, long assumed to be fact, that something called the Working Men's party came to life in the spring of 1829 and persisted, through various changes, for a few years afterward. That is, we must distinguish carefully between the Working Men's *movement* and the Working Men's *party*.

The Working Men's movement arose under the leadership of Thomas Skidmore and the Committee of Fifty in the wake of the enormous journeymen's protests in April 1829. It was this movement that linked artisan radicalism and journeymen's unionism, appointed the Committee of Fifty, approved the committee's program in October, nominated a Working Men's ticket, and polled one-third of the vote in the November assembly elections. This movement embraced the popular following of Wright and Dale Owen (although it had only tenuous connections with the Free Enquirer leadership); some entrepreneurs almost certainly began infiltrating its ranks as early as October 1829. Nevertheless, the movement was organized, planned, and led by militant journeymen, and then by a committee of wage earners and small masters, men whose ultimate object, Evans later admitted, "was a *Radical Revolution,* which should secure to each man the fruits of his own labor."[82] Generated from below, it was the one New York political movement in the late 1820s and 1830s that proved capable of gaining substantial support outside of the existing political parties.

The Working Men's party was born in December 1829, out of a marriage of convenience between the nonagrarian radicals and a group of craft entrepreneurs friendly to Henry Clay. The party seemed to be only an extension of the movement; in fact, it was an invention of the Owenites and Cookites, one that assumed the name of the Working Men in a political coup that stunned and isolated Skidmore and effectively killed

80. *Radical,* January 1842.

81. In addition to the authorities cited above, note 1, see Mushkat, *Tammany,* 122, on the Committee of Fifty report: "On a more nihilist tack, the Committee also substantially endorsed Skidmore's confiscatory notions and the Owen-Wright education scheme."

82. *Radical,* January 1842.

off what had been a radical political insurgency. It was this party that enunciated the entrepreneurial views sometimes described as "Workey-ism"; it was this party which, after its fragmentation in 1830, contributed to the rise of the Whigs on the one hand and the so-called Radical wing of the Jacksonian Democracy, led by Evans, on the other. The Working Men's movement, on the other hand, virtually ceased to exist after December 1829; attempts by its leaders to revive it as the Poor People's party failed amid the rise of the Clayite and Owenite Working Men and with the conciliatory gestures and "workingmen's" posturing of the Democrats. Faced with a resurgence of Adamsite-Clayite activity, most of the movement's constituency (as opposed to the party's) chose the relative security of Tammany; the political vacancy of 1829, filled first by the Working Men's movement, had been reclaimed by more conventional politicians; after 1832 the consolidation of a new brand of establishment politics, under the aegis of the Democrats and the emerging Whigs, would preclude the rise of anything like the Working Men's movement for twenty years.

It is a familiar-sounding story, one that is all the more significant when we consider when it took place: along with its counterpart in Philadelphia, the New York Working Men's movement, arising at the dawn of modern American party politics, was in effect the first modern American radical political movement—the first case study of a lower-class insurgency that emerged through the cracks in the party system, only to be beset by invasion, deflection, co-optation, and eventual ruin at the hands of outsiders and their radical pawns. We can hear the echoes of this drama in later years, most clearly in the Populist experience, but also in the history of scores of farmers' and labor parties in towns and cities across the country from the Civil War to our own time. Viewed from the standpoint of what they actually accomplished, the Working Men of 1829 set the standard for those future political movements, destined, in Richard Hofstadter's unflattering imagery, to sting the major parties into superficial reform before themselves dying, like certain species of insects, their historic mission fulfilled.[83] Viewed slightly differently, the Working Men were the first to confront the frustrating power of a professional American party politics just then emerging—the first to learn how, with the many misrepresentations and machinations of American party competition, a popular radical challenge could be turned into its opposite.

Less obvious are the important ambiguities and transformations that accompanied the Working Men's efforts. Despite their enormous differences, the movement and both factions of the party all resorted to the

83. Richard Hofstadter, *The Age of Reform: From Bryan to F.D.R.* (New York, 1955), 97.

same political language, that of the artisan republic. All spoke of being "mechanics," "producers," "working men," arrayed against an aristocracy of privilege and monied corruption; all lay claim to the heritage of the Revolution. Behind this language lay fundamentally different meanings and motives; the very language itself, however, and the ways in which Skidmore, Owen, and the Cookites each claimed to be fighting congealed privilege, helped to muffle these differences long enough that one group could infiltrate the Working Men's movement and, with the help of a second group, claim its name for its own uses. By the time the artisan radicals, agrarian and non-agrarian, had awakened to what was going on, it was too late. Even more important, by 1830 the Democrats, the foes of "aristocratic" politics, had also discovered the pertinence of the old language to their own cause, and they deployed it skillfully, to consolidate their own, decidedly nonradical democratic party. By 1832, when Andrew Jackson's veto message turned to the image of the republican small producer to rally popular support, the Democrats were even able to persuade nonagrarian artisan radicals that they were the true embodiment of the workingmen's interests.[84]

But even so, we should pause before judging the Working Men's movement an exercise in futility and ideological blurriness. In its way, the drama of 1829 made clearer than ever before that the ongoing social and ideological conflicts in the trades had begun to resolve into abiding conflicts of class. Of course, the Working Men's movement (let alone the party) was never composed entirely of embittered wage earners; journeymen and small masters could be found among the Cookites as well as among the Owenites and original Working Men. The Free Enquirers and Skidmore, no proletarian socialists, remained proponents of the broad Ricardian distinctions between producer and nonproducer, and not of that between wage earner and employer; so, in their way, did the Cookites. Through the election, the movement expressed and fed on different forms of *artisan* radicalism, distinct from the plebeian political democratic movements of the Revolution but very much a movement of the producers— "men who live by their own labor"—against capitalist parasites. But to assess the movement in essentialist terms obscures the most important fact—that 1829 brought an unprecedented social and political convulsion, led by an artisan committee that, whatever its disagreements, was united in a belief that rich entrepreneurs were destroying the Republic. Throughout, there were signs of new departures, of a joining of anticapitalist social radicalism with the incipient class consciousness of the earlier trade

---

84. The best reading of the veto message to date remains Meyers, *Jacksonian Persuasion*, 16–32.

unions. Skidmore's whole project, at least until December 1829, was to demonstrate to his journeymen allies how the sources of their complaints ran far deeper than they had thought; Owen—pushed, in part, by the journeymen's actions—tried to do the same, albeit with a different diagnosis. The journeymen's actions in April and the initiatives of the Committee of Fifty marked the first time that New York craft workers, organized across trade lines, looked beyond their immediate grievances to the deeper causes of social and political inequality—and then, joined by radical small masters, took their conclusions into politics. Without that journeymen's movement, the radical agrarians had no basis on which to launch a successful comeback after the coup; for as long as it lasted, the alliance proved far more powerful than anyone had imagined it would.

Above all, while the old language of the artisan republic survived, it was also in the process of being tested, reinterpreted, and fought over. If nothing else, the events of 1829 proved that, for thousands of journeymen and small masters, something was indeed radically wrong. The question was why: Why in a supposedly republican city were inequality and political "corruption" so evident, why did honest mechanics search for work and not get it, why, despite the rhetoric of "the Trade," did some masters seek to exploit their men by lengthening the workday? In trying to find an answer, ordinary men considered topics not normally taken up in ᴧ ' election campaign—the abolition of capitalist banking, radical education plans and neo-Jacobin freethought, the seizure and redistribution of property. The answers endorsed by the Working Men's movement remained tied to the ethos, to the values, of the artisan republic; they also invested those values with new, decidedly radical meanings. Despite the outcome of 1829–30, later movements would return to the same ideals and problems and continue to find radical answers.

Here lay the central paradox of the rise and fall of the Working Men. By entering politics, the artisan radicals, first the Skidmorites and then the Owenite leadership, left themselves open to distortion, infiltration, and defeat. Yet it was only by engaging in politics that the Skidmorites and the Free Enquirers widened their circle of followers to form, however briefly, a popular movement. For over five years, a spate of radical ideas had passed through the taverns and workshops with only limited apparent effect. Suddenly, in a political season, these ideas, and a culture of radical politics, celebrating reason, Tom Paine, equal property, and Praise God Barebones, took hold in the mechanics' wards—in popular debating societies, committees, and street-corner rallies—opposed to the politics of party and the political economy of capitalist entrepreneurship. At its height, the upsurge created a political challenge that managed to stage an electoral upset. Soon thereafter, to be sure, the movement was defeated and its constituents were dispersed. Yet it had also led to debates and commitments that would not be erased altogether from the public mind.

Such solace would, of course, have come as cold comfort to the artisan radicals in 1832. With Skidmore dead, the Hall of Science secured by the Methodists, and the Democratic Party seemingly impregnable, the radical milieu faded from view. The cholera epidemic, which killed Thomas Skidmore and hundreds of those he had hoped to organize, darkened the situation, as lists of the dead and dying replaced political news in the *Working Man's Advocate*.[85] Yet even then, craft workers, having learned some of the lessons of 1829, began plotting fresh activities. They would not finish until they had helped build, not a radical lyceum, not a poor man's party, but a journeymen's revolt.

85. *Working Man's Advocate*, August 11, 1832. On the medical history of the epidemic and its social and ideological consequences, see Rosenberg, *Cholera Years*, 13–64.

2. Duncan Phyfe (1768–1854), master cabinetmaker. The artist of this portrait is unknown, as is the date, though judging from Phyfe's looks it would seem to have been done about 1820. A triumph of self-presentation, the wealthy employer as skilled immigrant plebeian. *Photograph courtesy of Mr. Roger Halle.*

3. Duncan Phyfe's workshop and warehouse, Partition (now Fulton) Street, 1815, watercolor by J. R. Smith. Phyfe's house, located across the street, was just as imposing. *Courtesy, Metropolitan Museum of Art, Rogers Fund, 1922.*

4. The seal of the General Society of Mechanics and Tradesmen of the City of New York, designed in 1785.

5. "A Peep Into the Antifederal Club," dated New York City, 1793. Jefferson presides over this imaginary democratic gathering; in the audience, along with the drunken pirate and the shadowy Frenchman, is a man holding a pair of tailor's shears who looks suspiciously like Tom Paine. A typical conservative view of the Democratic-Republican opposition. *Courtesy, Free Library of Philadelphia.*

6. Trade emblems from the Erie Canal procession, 1825, printed in a contemporary description of the events. A kaleidoscope of artisan republican iconography. *Courtesy, Princeton University Library.*

7. Devlin's Tailoring Establishment, Broadway and Warren Street, 1854. Photograph by Victor Prevost. Devlin & Co. was one of the largest outwork clothing firms in the city in the 1840s and 1850s. In the foreground are the gates of City Hall Park. *Courtesy, New-York Historical Society.*

8. "Making Shirts for a Shilling; or, Misery and Magnificence." From *Godey's Lady's Book,* 1853. A vignette of greed, suffering, hypocrisy, and sentimentalism.

9. "The Butcher," watercolor by Niccolino Calyo, c. 1840. Calyo wandered about New York in the early 1840s, sketching and painting various street hawkers and peddlers. Mr. Brown, the butcher, was the most splendid and self-assured of them all, his cleaver at the ready, his ear cocked to his customers' queries, his top hat and white shirt unbesmirched. *Courtesy, New-York Historical Society.*

10. Frances Wright, c. 1826. The Red Harlot of Infidelity, resplendent in her Owenist feminist costume. The most electrifying radical speaker and polemicist of her day.

11. An anti-evangelical cartoon by a self-styled Fanny Wright Mechanic, [1831]. From a ribald pamphlet, *The Magdalen Report Burlesqued*, issued in response to a Finneyite exposé of ungodly prostitution in the metropolis. *Courtesy, New-York Historical Society.*

12. The Hall of Science, Broome Street, 1830.

13. A Skidmorite cartoon, 1830. An "aristo," backed by the Tammany, Cookite, and Owenite newspapers, does the devil's work, while the brawny true workingman votes with Liberty, the American version of the sans-culottes' allegorical Marianne. An unintentional testimonial to just how isolated the Skidmorites were after December 1829, opposed by superior forces, on the defensive. *Courtesy, Kilroe Collection, Columbia University.*

A Voice from the People!

Great Meeting in the Park!!

14. An appeal to the GTU faithful, 1836. By hammer and hand, the union would stand. Nearly thirty thousand supporters responded, in a rally to protest the conviction of the union tailors' leaders for conspiracy. From *The Union*, 1836. *Courtesy, New York Public Library.*

15. Announcement of a meeting to support the seamstresses, 1836. Obviously, the seamstresses were well-organized. Notice, though, that sympathetic middle-class men dominated the list of speakers; notice, as well, that the women sang of their plight with an adapted revivalist hymn. Evidence of how religion—far more influential among working women than workingmen before 1837—could be turned to support the wage-earners' cause, a precursor of the plebeian Protestant movements of the mid- and late 1840s. Evidence, also, of the problematic public position of women workers and of early middle-class concern for the peculiar plight of exploited females. *Courtesy, New-York Historical Society.*

ORDER OF EXERCISES,

FOR THE

Public Meeting in behalf of the Talloresses and Seamstresses' Benevolent Society,

WEDNESDAY EVENING, DEC. 28th, 1836.

1. Address of the Committee to the Public,
   By GEORGE FOLSOM, Esq.
2. Music, by the Choir of Volunteers from different churches, under the direction of
   Mr. GEORGE ANDREWS.
3. Resolution and Address,
   By WILLIS HALL, Esq.
4. Resolution and Address,
   By H. M. WESTERN, Esq.
5. Original Ode, - - - - - By the CHOIR,
   Written for the Occasion.
6. Resolution and Address,
   By DAVID M. REESE, M. D.
7. Resolution and Address,
   By WM. B. MACLAY, Esq.
8. Collection, Subscription, and
   Music by the CHOIR.
9. Concluding Address,
   By DAVID GRAHAM, Jun. Esq.
10. Motion of Adjournment.

DAUGHTER OF ZION.

1. Daughter of Zion, awake from thy sadness,
   Wake! for thy foes shall oppress thee no more;
   Bright o'er the hills, dawns the day star of gladness,
   Rise! for the night of thy sorrow is o'er.

2. Strong were thy foes; but the arm that subdued them,
   And scattered their legions was mightier far;
   They fled like the chaff from the scourge that pursued them,
   Vain were their steeds, and their chariots of war.

3. Daughter of Zion the power that hath saved thee
   Extolled with the harp and the timbrel should be;
   Shout! for the foe is destroyed that enslaved thee,
   The oppressor is vanquished, and Zion is free.

16. "The Soaplocks," watercolor by Niccolino Calyo, *c.* 1840. A montage featuring the pleasures of the Bowery republic, with the B'hoys in the middle of everything. Though already somewhat stylized as the sporty worker, Calyo's B'hoys are still closer to the down-and-out reality than later, softened images of the hearty, jolly fireman-Bowery-ite. *Courtesy, New-York Historical Society.*

17. The annual fair of the American Institute, Castle Garden, 1846. *Courtesy, New-York Historical Society.*

18. James Harper (1795–1869), printer, publisher, nativist, Mayor of the City of New York, 1844–45. Harper aged well; though this portrait was executed toward the end of his life, it evokes the uncharismatic sobriety of the American Republican leader of the 1840s.

19. Mike Walsh in action, 1843. From the frontispiece of a collection of Walsh's early speeches. The artist only slightly exaggerated Walsh's horny, calloused hands; it is unclear whether the look in Walsh's eyes owed more to enthusiasm or to drink. In any case, a telling bit of political portraiture, to promote the image of the first radical Bowery B'hoy Democrat. *Courtesy, New-York Historical Society.*

20. The National Reform Association's blueprints for homestead republican townships, 1844. The plans were reproduced and explained in the land reform press, particularly in the NRA's newspaper *Young America*.

21. The masthead of *The Champion of American Labor*, voice of the American Laboring Confederacy, 1847. Dimly visible, in the lower right corner, is the hammer-and-hand, which appeared atop the editorial column on page two. *Courtesy, New-York Historical Society.*

IV

The Journeymen's Revolt,
1833-1836

I will confront these shows of the day and night!
I will know if I am to be less than they!
I will see if I am not as majestic as they!
I will see if I am not as subtle and real as they!
I will see if I am to be less generous than they!

Chants Democratic, I, 45

6

"A Phalanx of Honest Worth": The General Trades' Union of the City of New York

Class consciousness joined New York craft workers across trade lines in the 1830s. While the radical remnants of the Working Men's party disintegrated in 1831, the journeymen printers formed the Typographical Association, separate from the polite mutual-aid society run by their masters. Two years later, following a bitter strike for higher wages by the carpenters, representatives from nine trades organized the General Trades' Union of the City of New York. Over the next four years, the GTU led a series of offensives that saw New York wage earners organize over fifty unions and nearly forty strikes (Table 19). Without raising a barricade (although with occasional violence), the journeymen in the most rapidly dividing crafts sundered remaining solidarities between craft employers and employees. In time they honed their own critique of capitalist wage labor and built a new brotherhood of craft workers—one they hoped would prove, in a sympathizer's words, "a phalanx of honest worth and independence that the aristocrat and the speculator does not dare attack."

1. A. F. Cunningham, "An Oration Delivered before the Trades' Union of the District of Columbia, at the City Hall in Washington," in *National Trades' Union* [New York], August 30, 1834. On activity in 1831, see *Working Man's Advocate*, May 21, 28, 1831; McNeill, *Labor Movement*, 336; Stevens, *Typographical Union*, 105–13. Standard secondary sources on the G.T.U. include Commons, *History of Labour*, I, 232–33, 459–52; Schlesinger, *Age of Jackson*, 192–98; Philip S. Foner, *History of the Labor Movement in the United States* (New York, 1947–   ), I, 140–66; Hugins, *Jacksonian Democracy*, 51–80; Pessen, *Most Uncommon Jacksonians*, 3–8, 34–51, 80–99, 103–203 passim. The phalanx image was a common one, well before the advent of American Fourierism; note, for example, the New York journeyman house carpenters' description of the trades' unions as "one great phalanx against the common enemy of workingmen, which is *overgrown capital* supported by AVARICE, and carried on by

The origins and implications of the journeymen's revolt were similar in many respects to those of comparable movements across the Atlantic in the 1830s. Economic problems, caused by the dislocations of metropolitan industrialization in this country and by the rapid inflation of 1835-36, help explain the upsurge, but only in part. Far from being single-minded, "wage-conscious," "bread-and-butter" craft unionists—the most favored of all craft workers looking to preserve their privileges and high wages—the New Yorkers included skilled and semiskilled hands, interpreted their economic distress broadly and connected their workshop grievances with the health of the Republic. Their deliberations did not, to be sure, sustain a unified, sharply calibrated proletarian force, armed with a thorough critique of the capitalist system as a whole. Cultural and political differences abounded, within organized trades and between those trades that organized and those that did not; important divisions separated male craft workers from unskilled laborers and women workers (although these divisions narrowed in the course of the revolt). Rather, thousands of workers in the unions declared their mutual interests as wage earners against capitalist employers and entrepreneurs, fought for those common interests, elaborated their own version of political economy and property rights, and, for a moment, considered allying with common laborers in a general strike. In doing so, they emerged from the maelstrom of Jacksonian reform movements to launch an early industrial attack on both capitalist inequities and workshop exploitation, one that captured concerns similar to those driving the British and French craft workers' movements of the 1830s, but that framed these concerns within an American idiom.[2]

Union Men

Perhaps the most impressive features of the craft workers' movement were its size and the rapidity with which it grew. In 1833, only nine trades organized the General Trades' Union; a year later, when twenty more trades had organized, 11,500 men had joined the New York unions and those in Brooklyn—somewhere between 20 and 30 percent of Manhattan's entire white male workforce, skilled and unskilled combined. By 1836, when twenty more unions had organized (most of them in the GTU), the *Evening Post* argued that "it is a low calculation when we estimate that two-thirds of the working men in the city" had joined trade unions. By com-

SPECULATION ON HUMAN WOE, perpetually wringing from the honest and industrious that portion of comfort and happiness which the God of Nature destined him to enjoy." See *National Trades' Union*, December 12, 1834.

   2. On movements abroad, see G. D. H. Cole, *Attempts at General Union, 1830-1834* (London, 1953); Prothero, *Artisans and Politics*; Moss, *French Labor Movement*; Sewell, *Work and Revolution in France.*

parison, it is unlikely that the proportion of American workers in trade unions reached much more than 15 percent of the total before 1900. Although their numbers were but a fraction of the 100,000 who manned New York unions in the 1870s, it is safe to say that the percentage of New York craft workers who enrolled in the unions in the 1830s was among the highest at any time in the nineteenth century.[3]

As these figures suggest, the unions made impressive efforts to include second-rate and sweated hands as well as the most skilled craftsmen. The broadening of the union base was neither immediate nor total. Early in the revolt, a moderate spokesman claimed that "clumsy" hands were usually barred from the unions. Some societies, such as the carpenters', initially excluded those who could not affirm they had served regular apprenticeships; women craft workers were never admitted to the men's unions or the GTU.[4] By 1835, though, it was clear that the movement was no narrow association of the "aristocracy" of the trades. At least one society, the bakers', claimed to have enlisted every journeyman in the city trade. Unions in some of the most rapidly dividing crafts—the tailors', stonecutters', shoemakers', cabinetmakers', and saddlers'—embraced pieceworkers and sweated journeymen, heard their complaints, and fought on their behalf; still others, like the handloom weavers, were composed largely of semiskilled operatives.[5] And if the majority of unionists were better off than the city's day laborers, they did not live in anything approaching secure comfort. The vast majority of the GTU delegates and the rank-and-file unionists whose names can be traced in city directories were propertyless; as the directories tended to exclude poorer citizens, it is plausible that less than 10 percent of the unionists owned more than their tools (perhaps), their clothing, and other personal effects. The delegates tended to dwell

3. *Working Man's Advocate*, June 21, 1834; *Evening Post*, June 13, 1836. The membership figures on the 1830s are, admittedly, very rough. I am more inclined than Maurice F. Neufeld is to assume that the 1834 report was reasonably accurate, and to project that the number in 1836 in New York alone exceeded 10,000. Neufeld is quite correct, though, to suspect that historians have exaggerated the extent of union membership *nationwide* in the 1830s. See Maurice F. Neufeld, "The Size of the Jacksonian Labor Movement: A Cautionary Account," *LH* 23 (1982): 599–607. On national and New York union membership in the heyday of the labor movement of the 1860s and 1870s, see Montgomery, *Beyond Equality*, 140–41, 189. Given Montgomery's conclusion that there were 3,546,300 industrial wage earners in the United States in 1870, his estimates of union membership indicate that between 8.4 and 16.8 percent of the industrial labor force was unionized. From these figures, Montgomery argues that "[i]t is probably safe to say that a larger proportion of the industrial labor force enrolled in trade unions during the years immediately preceding the depression of 1873 than in any other period of the nineteenth century" (140).
4. *National Trades' Union*, August 9, 1834; Constitution and Bye-Laws, New York Union Society of Journeymen House Carpenters, NYPL MSS.
5. *Working Man's Advocate*, June 11, 14, 1834; *Man*, May 31, 1834, February 5, 1835; *National Trades' Union*, February 7, April 4, May 9, 16, 23, 1835.

in the poorer (although not usually the very poorest) and most densely populated sections of the city, particularly in the Eighth, Tenth, and Thirteenth wards; while many unionists moved every year (some to leave the city altogether), most shuttled to rented homes within a few blocks of their previous residence. Few were destined to establish a permanent competence in New York: of all the delegates identified, only 15.2 percent were masters or retailers in New York in 1850.[6]

The unions' ethnic diversity confirmed their openness despite the early signs of ethnic segmentation of the city's leading trades in the 1830s. Although native journeymen dominated the GTU hierarchy, they freely allowed that the immigrants were necessary to the cause and that they had, in some cases, been instrumental in getting the journeymen to organize. The house carpenters opened their union to naturalized immigrants, at least some of whom must have been sweated hands; the union's membership list shows that by 1836 a large and growing number of Germans and some Irish were admitted (evidence, perhaps, that the organized men had come to admit untrained immigrants). Federated unions like the cabinetmakers' appealed directly to the immigrants to join and support them and made it a point to condemn employers who attempted to deceive and sweat the many "strangers and foreigners in our trade." One anonymous cabinetmaker described how his shop was struck in 1836; although the Americans in his multi-ethnic shop were the noisiest of the strikers, they tried hard to organize the immigrants. Of the twenty journeymen tailors tried for conspiracy in 1836, four were unnaturalized immi-

6. In all, the names of 183 union delegates were gathered from the proceedings recorded in John R. Finch, *Rise and Progress of the General Trades' Unions of the City of New-York and Its Vicinity* (New York, 1833); and Commons, *Documentary History*, V, 208–303. Only two delegates, Levi Slamm of the locksmiths and John Keane of the stonecutters, were not listed in the city directories of 1833–36 as craft workers; both were listed as grocers. Three delegates were noted in the tax lists of 1834 and 1835 as assessed property owners: Seth T. Clark of the leather dressers ($3,000 real property), Thomas W. Lewis of the sailmakers ($1,550 real property), Joseph Parsons of the leather dressers ($2,000 real property). William N. Black ("Union of Journeymen House Carpenters," 31) finds that, of the 259 rank-and-file house carpenters in the union whose addresses can be identified, 25.3 percent owned some form of assessed wealth. This figure is not altogether surprising, given the relatively high wages of carpenters; a similar check of rank-and-file members of the stonecutters union (*Man*, June 7, 1834) in the tax list of 1834 turned up no property owners. Black also shows (52–56) that most union carpenters moved regularly in the 1830s, although they tended, as far as possible, to remain within a few neighborhoods, mainly in the Eighth and Ninth wards. Regarding social mobility: unfortunately, there is no comprehensive reliable list of master and small-master craftsmen for the 1830s and 1840s; by checking against the 1850 directories and census, I overlook those men who (a) became masters but who died or left the city before 1850, (b) left the city to become masters, or (c) had names too common to identify exactly. Even so, the scarcity of delegates in the 1850 schedules at least suggests that the great majority of union men did not become independent producers in New York.

grants. Vehemently antinativist, union leaders did their utmost to discourage ethnic disputes. At the least, the declaration of one journeyman in 1834 prevailed—"We know no distinction nor will have any other title than that of "American citizen.' " In some unions, such as the tailors', even that distinction was overlooked.[7]

Far more important than skill or ethnicity in determining who formed or joined unions was the uneven pattern of metropolitan industrialization: quite clearly, unionism flourished where the bastardization of craft and the emergence of new forms of wage labor were most pronounced. Although trades from every sector of the economy organized at some point, and although the GTU helped organize several crafts that had never unionized before, the consumer finishing, building, and, to a lesser extent, printing trades composed the bulk of the movement (Table 19A). Butchers were conspicuously absent. The skilled maritime trades were scarce: although the ship joiners and coopers sent delegates during the GTU's early months, they dropped out soon afterward, before the GTU began coordinating strikes; the coopers organized again in 1836 but never went so far as to call a turnout. Of the unions that remained in the GTU from its founding, seven came from the consumer finishing, printing, or building trades, leaving only the bakers (suddenly faced with dilution of skill and "half-way" apprenticing) and the sailmakers as exceptions. The consumer finishing trades, conducted the most strikes, including the most acrimonious of all, the tailors' turnouts of 1833 and 1836 (Table 19B). The shipwrights and ship carpenters organized to strike for higher wages at the height of the inflation but had no role, direct or indirect, in the GTU; there is some question whether the shipwrights actually struck.[8] In contrast, the majority of the strikes sanctioned and led by GTU involved consumer finishing trades.

The unionists' connections with earlier union and political movements were more complex. It comes as no surprise that several union leaders had also been active in earlier trade associations and radical groups. At least one GTU delegate, the tailor Mansfield Shelley, had been indicted for conspiracy for his attempts to organize his trade in the mid-1820s.[9] A tiny core of union leaders—including six GTU delegates, 3.3 percent of the total—had been preeminent either in the Working Men's movement, the Owenite wing of the party, or both; such leading personalities of 1829 as

7. Membership List, New York Union Society of Journeymen Carpenters, 1835–36; *National Trades' Union*, March 14, April 4, 11, 18, 1835; "Workingman's Recollections," 108; *Man*, April 5, June 24, 1834, April 4, 1835; *Union*, June 7, 10, July 2, 1836.

8. *National Trades' Union*, March 4, 1836.

9. People v. William Smith and others, August 12, 1824, Court of General Sessions Records, MARC.

Ebenezer Ford and Joseph Parsons (both candidates for the state assembly) represented their trades in the GTU convention.[10] The affinities between deism and labor radicalism also lasted. At least three GTU delegates and one officer of the printers' union were among the most outspoken freethinkers in the city and participated in the continuing annual celebrations of Thomas Paine's birthday. The carpenters' strike manifesto of 1833 included among its grievances an attack on clerical tax exemptions, considered by the journeymen as tools "to deprive the creators of wealth of the fruits of their labors." Later that year, the printer John Finch, in an address to the newly formed GTU, invoked "the God of Nature" as the bestower of all blessings. Outside of the union, the GTU found some of its few supporters among such freethinking radical master craftsmen as George Henry Evans and Edward Webb; Evans, despite his strong misgivings about the strikes, edited and published an unofficial union newspaper.[11]

Two men typified how earlier radical movements met in the journeymen's revolt. John Windt, the printer, joined the freethinkers while he was a journeyman in his mid-twenties. In 1829 and 1830, he printed, edited, and proofread several of Frances Wright's essays and worked closely with Evans; it was Windt, along with a few of his colleagues, who roundly attacked the Typographical Society's homiletic salvos against Robert Dale Owen and the state-guardianship plan. Through the 1830s, Windt was a prime mover in the Paine birthday celebrations and a supporter of Benjamin Offen's new deist organization, the Society of Moral Philanthropists. He also helped organize the printers in 1831 and served in the union, first as president and then as treasurer. Windt was more fortunate than most journeymen: in 1833, he was one of a tiny proportion who owned some assessed property, and in 1834, after being fired and blacklisted because of his pro-Jackson political activities, he established his own small printing shop and a components works. By 1835, he had won enough

10. The names on Hugins's list were checked against the names of union delegates: the identified Skidmorite and Owenite unionists were John Commerford (chair makers), Ebenezer Ford (carpenters), Willoughby Lynde (printers), Joseph Parsons (leather dressers), James Quinn (locksmiths), and Henry Walton (cordwainers).

11. *Working Man's Advocate*, June 8, 1833; Finch, *Rise and Progress*, 12. *Man*, May 13, 1835; Jentz, "Artisans, Evangelicals, and the City." GTU Painites included David Kilmer (ladies' cordwainers), J. D. Pearson (cabinetmakers), and John Witts (umbrella makers); John Windt was the printer-deist. Evans took ample account of the Painites' ongoing activities, and occasionally included articles on Paine in his "union" newspaper, *The Man*. See *Man*, January 10, 31, 1834, April 24, 1835. People outside the GTU certainly associated it with infidelity, at least during the early stages of revolt; one "Long Island Farmer" fiercely denounced the unions as attempts "to foist atheistical works and infidel doctrines upon the public." See *National Trades' Union*, June 27, 1834. On Evans, and his ambivalence about strikes, see *Man*, June 5, 1835; on Webb, see *Man*, May 13, 1835.

prestige to be consulted as a leading member of a newly formed Mechanics' Institute, and elected secretary of the Democratic General Executive Committee. He remained, through it all, a stalwart rationalist and a union sympathizer, "a friend to the rights of the laboring man," one associate recalled, ever appreciative of "the hardships of the wages and hours system."[12]

John Commerford was the most energetic and respected of the GTU leaders and was destined to be a leading figure on the New York radical scene for decades to come. He began his career in the late 1820s as a journeyman cabinetmaker in Brooklyn; in 1830, he joined an Owenite Working Men's group and campaigned for its nominees in the fall election. After moving to Manhattan the following year, he joined the agitation against the Bank of the United States and state prison labor. In 1834, the newly established Journeymen Chairmakers' Society elected him its president and delegate to the GTU convention. Described by a contemporary as an extraordinary speaker, Commerford immersed himself in union business, served on over three dozen GTU committees, and represented the New York labor movement at meetings and rallies from Newark to Boston. In 1835, he was elected to replace Ely Moore as president of the GTU, and he remained at the post until the group collapsed. His speeches and his articles in the GTU newspaper *The Union* (which he also found time to edit) revealed the most searching mind in the union movement. In sympathy with the anti-evangelicals, he mocked pious reformers, those "jugglers" who tried to distract wage earners from the material sources of their plight. Eventually, he picked up the labor theory of value to expose a range of problems, from workshop exploitation to the evils of unfair distribution of the public lands.[13]

If, however, radicals like Windt and Commerford became an important influence, theirs were not the only voices in the GTU. As the unions reached out to a wide array of journeymen and craft workers to press for their common welfare, they inevitably included men who had little or no sympathy for deism, educational reform, or agrarianism. Several turned up in the GTU leadership, at least temporarily. Two of the carpenters' delegates, Isaac Odell and Robert Townsend, Jr., had been among the foremost journeymen Cookites in 1830; Townsend had also supported the Sab-

---

12. Hugins, *Jacksonian Democracy*, 74–75; Stevens, *Typographical Union*, 106; *Mechanics' Magazine* 7 (1836): 267; Tax Assessments 1833, MARC; Masquerier, *Sociology*, 106–7.

13. *Working Man's Advocate*, October 23, 1830, September 19, 1835; *Man*, April 15, May 9, August 29, September 2, 17, 1834, February 26, June 15, July 6, 1835; Commons, *Documentary History*, V, 223–24, 233, 236, 239–53, 256–57, 262–65, 271–75, 278–82, 292–98; *National Trades' Union*, July 5, August 9, 1834; Hugins, *Jacksonian Democracy*, 72–74.

batarian and temperance campaigns of the late 1820s. Both of them, along with the GTU delegates David Scott of the tailors and Robert Anderson of the printers, became avowed and active Whigs in 1834. Ely Moore, the first president of the GTU, came from a different but equally nonradical background. Born in New Jersey in 1798, Moore had been an apprentice printer, but in the early 1820s he improved his situation considerably by moving to New York and marrying the daughter of Gilbert Coutant, a wealthy grocer and Tammany fixer. After turning some lucrative land deals, Moore entered politics in 1830 as Coutant's protégé and won an appointment as assistant county registrar. Two years later, he struck out on his own, joined the brief movement in support of Richard M. Johnson for vice-president, and made a quick impression with his anti-Sabbatarian speeches. The deist journeymen of the Typographical Association heard of his diatribes and had him address them; Moore, no radical, regaled the printers but also wasted no time in rejoining Tammany in the fall election, an enthusiastic supporter of Jackson, Van Buren, and the war on the U.S. Bank. Thanks to his reputation as a maverick, his prominence as an anti-Sabbatarian Democrat, his artisan background—and the strong backing of the printers—Moore was in 1833 elected the GTU's first president. As he somewhat ruefully admitted at his inauguration, he took office with no previous experience in helping to direct an organization of any kind, let alone a trade union. Under his leadership, he promised, the GTU would strive to keep to a moderate course.[14]

As for the majority of GTU delegates and the rank and file, active participation in the unions of the 1830s probably marked their first sustained involvement in anything resembling a dissenting New York movement. Many of the immigrants could have arrived in the city only in the 1830s; other unionists either had no experience in earlier journeymen's societies or the Working Men's movement, played a quiet, unrecorded role, or worked in previously unorganized trades. With such a broad following, the unionists were well aware that they held diverging views. Most probably voted for Jackson and the Democrats, but certainly not all; to be safe, the GTU, mindful of the Working Men's experience and distrustful of party politics, explicitly renounced all formal political endorsements and alliances. Only a small minority of unionists could have been practicing freethinkers in the 1830s, most were probably unchurched, and no doubt some were swept up by the evangelical crusades of the 1830s (although

14. *National Trades' Union*, July 5, August 9, September 20, 1834, March 28, June 27, 1835; Hugins, *Jacksonian Democracy*, 69–71; "A Sketch of the Speech of Col. Ely Moore," in [William Emmons], *Authentic Biography of Col. Richard M. Johnson of Kentucky* (Boston, 1834), 86–92; Commons, *Documentary History*, V, 220, 225. On Moore, see also Walter E. Hugins, "Ely Moore: The Case History of a Jacksonian Labor Leader," *PSQ* 65 (1950): 105–25.

their numbers appear to have been very small). Without an exhaustive search of New York's scattered and fragmentary church records, it is impossible to be precise about the union rank and file's religious affiliations; what is certain is that the GTU and the individual unions considered the membership diverse enough to prohibit any discussion of religious questions.[15]

Thus, despite the radical presence, the ideological character of the union movement was far from settled, at least at the outset. Even if the radicals were to predominate, meanwhile, it was not altogether clear where they would lead the rank and file. The most familiar artisan radical programs of 1829 had only limited relevance for union organizers. Although their critiques of the sources of American inequality were apposite enough, the writings and speeches of Skidmore, Owen, and Wright contained little to guide a movement of employees taking coercive economic measures against their masters: even Skidmore, who had his strongest contacts with the journeymen of the Committee of Fifty, had counseled that political action, and not strikes, were the order of the day. The ill-fated progress of the Working Men's movement and the Owenite wing of the party pointed out more about pitfalls to be avoided—party politics, factionalism, co-optation—than about strategies to be emulated. In 1833, as the journeymen formed their unions, they faced every imaginable decision not only on strategy and tactics but on broader questions concerning the social philosophy of their movement. A sense of their direction emerged quickly when they set about designing their own institutions.

Union Democracy

During the second quarter of the nineteenth century, we are told, Americans were bedeviled by institutions and by fears that old models of social order had grown obsolete and broken down. In the new spheres of middle-class reform, these fears bred a fresh resolve to build social mechanisms that would foster moral regeneration, individual liberty, and social harmony. From these schemes, so well delineated by David Rothman, supposedly sprang the most powerful impulses of Jacksonian social reform, to promote social stability "at a moment when traditional ideas and practices appeared outmoded, constricted, and ineffective."[16]

15. Stevens, *Typographical Union*, 151; Commons, *Documentary History*, V, 293; *Union*, April 21, 1836. See also Michael Floy, *The Diary of Michael Floy, Jr., Bowery Village, 1833–1837*, ed. R. A. E. Brooks (New Haven, 1941), 93. Floy, a devout Methodist, was also a firm Jacksonian and was impressed by a Fourth of July oration by Ely Moore. On the failure of evangelical revivalism in New York, see below, Chapter 7.

16. David J. Rothman, *The Discovery of the Asylum: Social Order and Disorder in the New Republic* (Boston, 1971), xviii and passim.

By focusing exclusively on one variety of American reform, such accounts illuminate the background to later reform efforts but also obscure the history of the 1830s. It is not that middle-class visions of stabilizing uplift were unimportant. Alone, however, they were but one of several American responses to the institutional crises of the early industrial age. The professional party system of Martin Van Buren was another approach; Owenist and, later, Fourierist communitarian schemes another; the dedicated anti-institutionalism of a Garrison, a Thoreau, a Whitman still another. So, too, the New York unionists of the 1830s had their own ideas about institutions. With them, they built an organization that stressed discipline and harmony but that by its very design described a social and political philosophy quite different from those of the asylum builders and middle-class evangelicals.

It was one of the many ironies of the 1830s that conservatives attacked the unions as "undemocratic"—for the unionists, from the start, were practically obsessed with democracy, and with how to establish and maintain their movement as an open one without falling into the traps of the Working Men. The individual craft unions, like their predecessors of the Jeffersonian years, paid particularly close attention to decorum and democratic procedures. The membership elected union officers and delegates regularly (GTU delegates annually) by majority vote, although with provisions that officers who failed their duties could be removed from office. Firm ground rules governed discussions and debate, forbade slurs, and punished dilatory participation. Discipline and accountability in and out of the union were stressed; the carpenters' union, for one, included a clause in its constitution depriving a member of all sickness payments if he was found wasting his benefits in taverns or bordellos.[17]

The more ambitious and elaborate structure of the GTU also tried to insure a regular and scrupulously egalitarian system of checks and balances (Fig. 2). At the union's foundations were the individual craft associations, each of which selected three delegates to the main GTU body, the convention. The individual unions had full responsibility for watching over conditions in their respective trades; the GTU was charged mainly with sanctioning and coordinating strikes, corresponding with other city central unions, and holding debates on matters of universal interest to the journeymen. The GTU delegates met monthly with their colleagues from other trades and elected the GTU officers and a finance committee, all of whom were responsible to the convention. Most GTU business took place

17. E.g., Stevens, *Typographical Union*, 111-13; Constitution and Bye-Laws, New York Union Society of Journeymen House Carpenters. For typical attacks on "antidemocratic" unions, see *Journal of Commerce*, June 1, 1833; *Evening Star* [New York], December 3, 1833; *Niles' Register*, May 9, 1835.

in the convention and was handled by ad hoc committees selected by the entire body. Trade-society delegates reported back to the individual unions, who then debated GTU actions, requested delegates to air specific grievances before the convention, and arranged for the support of approved strikes through the networks of taverns and hotels that served as the local journeymen's meeting places. To fund the organization, each trade paid monthly dues, supplemented by a monthly per capita payment by each journeyman directly to the GTU treasury.[18]

By 1834, the GTU, lacking any precedent, had created a body that, at least in principle, was at once regular in its procedures, capable of acting with dispatch, and responsive to the opinions of the rank and file. The constant flow of information between the unions, the delegates, and the convention gave each journeyman a chance to assess events quickly and have some effect on making GTU policy. Delegates who did not match their membership's wishes could be—and were—removed from office. The ad hoc committee system, for all its apparent casualness, hindered the emergence of small oligarchies within the convention. The limited powers of the president and the vice-president made it difficult for any one man or small group to take the union over against the will of the membership. Before the panic of 1837, the experiment proved quite successful. Over the years, a few exceptionally active members assumed more posts than did others, but union responsibilities were generally dispersed among numerous delegates from a wide range of trades. Union men criticized the leadership in debate without appearing to damage seriously the group's stability. A number of heated disputes did arise, mainly about the jurisdictions of different unions from related trades; a protracted debate pitted delegates from the larger trades, who insisted they were entitled to more representatives, against those from the smaller trades, who naturally wanted to keep the original GTU plan of equal representation. At one point, Ely Moore lamented that a spirit of jealousy had overtaken the convention, "sullied its reputation and threatened its destruction." But such fears proved exaggerated; even the most troublesome questions were settled by the ad hoc committees, in accordance, as one subcommittee report put it, with the principle that "in all governments and communities, every person is obliged to yield a little to the other."[19]

Dry as such matters of organization are, the GTU's solutions suggest something about its members' intents and abilities. Clearly the unionists

---

18. This discussion is based on the GTU constitution, on scattered materials in Commons, *Documentary History*, V, 214–322, and on *Man*, June 22, 29, 1835. In 1835, the constitution was amended, so that the Finance Committee would be composed of one delegate from each trade, elected by the trade.

19. *Man*, November 24, 1834; Commons, *Documentary History*, V, 284.

had learned something from the dismal episode of 1829-30, an object lesson in the dangers of loose organization: the GTU's structure avoided the haphazardness of the Working Men's movement without raising insurmountable objections about centralization and expense or degenerating into a union movement in name only. Without sacrificing unity, the GTU turned an ethic of union discipline and personal dignity into a day-to-day practice of ordinary workingmen going about their own business and solving their own problems. It proved, amid all of America's institutional experiments of the time, a modus operandi far more democratic than that of virtually any other reform group or any political party. The contrast with Tammany Hall is most striking, but the GTU was also considerably more open than the moral reform societies, with their permanent committees and sanctified directors; apart, perhaps, from the sectarian communitarian societies, the GTU was probably the most democratic major institution founded in the United States in the 1830s. Here, more in the tradition of Paine than in the emerging traditions of middle-class reform and the political parties, was the truly democratic element in the Jacksonian city.[20]

Institutional democracy and discipline, however, were but the first steps toward unity and success. In planning their course, the union men still had to sort out their grievances and choose their weapons. Their activity would take them from self-protection to militancy.

Strikes and Politics

"[S]trikes," a moderate New York unionist claimed in 1834, "are scarcely considered, by the projectors of Trades' Unions, as essential to their purpose."[21] Such pronouncements were common in New York in 1833 and 1834, as some journeymen, a mite defensively, stressed that they had confederated primarily for benevolent and social ends. Whatever their original intentions, however, the unionists quickly saw the folly of such circumspection and learned to defend their rights to associate and fight their employers on the picket line. Why, then, did they strike?

Whether historians place the blame on President Jackson for his destruction of the Bank of the United States, or on more impersonal international flows of capital, the economic exigencies endured by wage earners in the mid-1830s look the same—a brutal inflation of commodity prices that quickly diminished real wages. The strikes and union drives in New York

20. On the structure of the moral reform societies, see Rosenberg, *Religion and the Rise of the American City*, 80–96; Wyatt-Brown, *Lewis Tappan*, 113–15.

21. *National Trades' Union*, September 27, 1834. See also ibid., July 5, August 23, 1834.

were clearly linked to the inflationary spiral. Most of the strikes raised demands either for higher wages or for an end to reductions. Strike messages consistently referred to rising prices; in a typical statement from 1835, "Justice" computed that it cost a journeyman cordwainer nearly $650 to support a family at a minimal level, while at the prevailing wage rates, the average regular journeyman, making shoes six days a week, fifty-two weeks a year, could expect to earn just over $400. Not surprisingly, the timing of the organization of the GTU and the tempo of strike activity fit with changing price levels (Fig. 3); the general effects of the inflation explain why so many trades, including a few only marginally disrupted by metropolitan industrialization, sent delegates to the GTU or organized on their own.[22]

The inflation was not, however, the journeymen's sole or even main concern. The unions were just as interested in obliterating the new lines of power in the trades—to succeed, where earlier journeymen's unions had failed, in winning some permanent control over the workshop regime and in resisting metropolitan industrialization and the subordination of wage labor. The successful hatters' strike of 1834–35, for one, began not as a wage dispute but as an attempt to resist repression of the union and blacklisting of society men by the master hatters, to end what the unionists called the masters' "practice of prescribing to the journeymen what they may and what they may not do. . . ."[23] Even when the journeymen ostensibly struck for wages, they were less intent on winning more money than on ending the exploitation of contracting and sweating by getting their employers to agree to a regular tariff to be followed throughout the trade. Use of a regular bill or book of prices had, of course, been general in New York's workshops long before the GTU; by the 1830s, however, the established lists in several trades had either been abandoned or had failed to account for the new kinds of subdivided work the masters expected their men to perform. Without having to adhere to a standard rate, masters could pay their men virtually what they chose for unenumerated tasks; more often, they used the lack of an effective measure to justify putting work out and underpaying less skilled hands. Simultaneously, the piece rate for enumerated jobs was subject to continual disputes between employers and individual journeymen—disputes that the masters usually won. By striking for an equalized rate, one group of unionists proclaimed,

22. Ibid., June 6, 1835. See also ibid., April 4, 1835, February 20, April 16, 1836; New York Transcript, April 3, 1835; Man, July 1, 1835; Niles' Register, November 12, 1836; Horace Greeley, Recollections of a Busy Life (New York, 1868), 87. On the sources of the Jacksonian inflation, the conventional wisdom on Jackson's responsibility and the primacy of the Bank War is stoutly challenged by Peter Temin, The Jacksonian Economy (New York, 1969).

23. On the hatters' strike, see Man, December 18, 1834, January 1, 6, 1835; National Trades' Union, December 20, 27, 1834; January 3, 10, 24, 1835.

the journeymen would benefit the trade as a whole by setting an "efficient standard," by ending "the necessity of giving work out of the shop," and by halting "the formation of a system which will ultimately (if not promptly met) lead us to the annihilation of our rights and cause us finally to become mere vassals of the wealthy employer."[24]

Two particularly well documented episodes in 1835 point out how the character of the wage relation was as central an issue as the level of wages. In March, the journeymen cabinetmakers met to air their complaints and to express special concern that the price book used by their masters was more than a quarter of a century old. Not only had the old book failed to keep up with cost of living; its use also encouraged employers to resort to "lumping"—contracting—and then sweating immigrant garret hands. Two weeks later, the journeymen presented their own book and declared that the "Employers wish to abolish the system of working by a *scale of prices.*" After affirming their special concern for the sweated German workers, the journeymen called a general strike of the trade, one that eventually won a standard rate for all. The stonecutters' strikes of the same year raised almost identical problems. After a brief turnout, employers granted their more skilled men (paid by the day) a wage increase but denied one to the less skilled pieceworkers. A second strike of the entire trade commenced in May, when day workers stayed off the job for the sake of their brother workmen "who are *not fully* paid" and in order to stave off the "unprincipled, uncontrolled competition" they claimed was overtaking the trade. After a stormy, month-long impasse, the labor press happily reported that the stonecutters had won their general rate for all hands.[25]

On other fronts, the unionists attacked a range of problems that had intensified with the acceleration of metropolitan industrialization. As early as 1831, the printers denounced a long list of practices, including contracting and the use of "half-ways." In 1834, the bakers, in the first strike originated under GTU auspices, demanded an end to Sunday work, the enforcement of a five-year apprenticeship period, and the limitation of apprentices to one per shop. As the strikes continued, union men also began contemplating some drastic reforms of the workshop. "Regulus" suggested that an eight-hour working day was both an appropriate and practical way to ensure that "the demon of individual gain" would cease feeding off "the working man's labor, his health, his social usefulness, and

24. *National Trades' Union,* April 4, 1835. See also *Man,* April 3, June 29, 1835.

25. On the cabinetmakers, see *National Trades' Union,* March 14, April 4, 11, 18, 1835; *Man,* April 3, 4, 1835. On the stonecutters, see *National Trades' Union,* April 25, May 9, 16, 23, 30, June 6, 13, 1835; *Man,* May 9, 20, 21, 24, 26, 1835; Commons, *Documentary History,* V, 236–37.

his happiness"—thus anticipating by more than a generation the arguments of the Eight-Hour Leagues, the Knights of Labor, and the American Federation of Labor. The formation of the journeymen's shops, a useful strike tactic earlier in the century, took on new significance, as journeymen claimed they could remove capitalist masters once and for all by redesigning the work, as the tailors put it, "according to true principles of Political Economy." Some GTU leaders, John Commerford the most important among them, included calls for land reform among the unionists' demands; others spoke of supplanting all existing forms of production with a cooperative system.[26]

On a tactical level, the disciplined strikes were something of a reform, an attempt to replace the wave of sporadic threats and violence of the late 1820s with more orderly responses to the employers. The unionists did not always succeed. The most famous case of labor violence in the 1830s, the stonecutters' riot of 1834, saw journeymen angered by wage differentials and the use of prison labor attack strikebreakers and buildings erected by offending masters. During the cabinetmakers' strike of 1835, a group of journeymen allegedly mutilated some imported furniture on display for sale, to insure that no product would be sold while they were striking for their price book. That same year, a band of pianoforte builders tarred and feathered another worker, whom they accused of being a "Black" (that is, a "blackleg"), one who regularly worked at wages below union scale. In and out of the trades, particularly in the dockworkers', coal heavers', and tailors' strikes of 1836, violence and the threat of violence recurred, an upsurge of physical force that appeared to some to presage a turn to a more brutal style of unionism—a charge repeated often by the conservative press. Yet such incidents were remarkable for their infrequency, given the extent of labor unrest, and the unions always denounced them in the strongest possible terms; in one instance, the GTU disclaimed any connection with a group of journeymen horseshoers who, while on strike, had not acted "with that propriety becoming good citizens." On more than one occasion, especially during the most riotous disturbances in 1836, the violence turned out to be the work of police provocateurs. As a movement,

26. National Trades' Union August 9, September 27, October 25, 1834, June 20, 1835, March 12, 1836; Man, March 29, May 28, 31, June 12, December 12, 1834, June 29, 1835; Working Man's Advocate, September 19, 1835; Union, May 23, 1836. On cooperatives, trade-union shops, and houses of call, see Man, June 19, 1834, January 15, 1835; National Trades' Union, February 20, 1836. On the significance of the eight-hour day, see Montgomery, Beyond Equality, 230–60; Irwin Yellowitz, "Eight Hours and the Bricklayers' Strike of 1868 in New York City," in idem, ed., Essays in the History of New York City: A Memorial to Sidney Pomerantz (Port Washington, N.Y., 1978), 78–100. Although the eight-hour demand never became a GTU proposal, that it was proposed by anyone suggests that the class identities that Montgomery sees emerging in the 1860s and 1870s had their roots in the 1830s.

the union men stood for dignified opposition, undertaken with what they called "manly conduct."[27]

While they attacked broad structural problems and refined their organization, the unionists also looked beyond purely local grievances. The GTU leadership recognized that their problems were national in scope, exacerbated by those improvements in transportation that made the shipment of cheap goods (and, when appropriate, of strikebreakers) far easier than before. Several efforts followed to assemble trade unionists from around the country to discuss their common plight. At the simplest level, the GTU corresponded with individual unions and city centrals elsewhere to notify them of the prevailing prices in New York and to make sure that no union man would come to Manhattan while a strike of his trade was in progress. More ambitious were the attempts to form national union councils. Most auspicious was the National Trades' Union, founded at the request of the New York GTU in 1834. Without approaching the powers of a genuine national union assembly, the NTU served for two years as a valuable clearinghouse for reports on the state of labor and suggestions on how to control conditions of work, whether in the New England mills or the garret workshops of Philadelphia. GTU men, particularly Commerford and Moore, dominated the NTU's proceedings and helped to draft numerous position papers on topics ranging from women's work to cooperative labor. The New York societies of journeymen cordwainers, handloom weavers, and printers added to the national ferment by helping to form national craft bodies, in order to aid colleagues in other cities in funding strikes, publicizing union complaints, and forming their own unions.[28]

In this atmosphere, the unionists' various benevolent projects, more than attempts to encourage mutual aid, proclaimed a unity of all organized journeymen as wage earners, regardless of craft—creating, in effect, a trade-union culture. For the first time, newspapers appeared that presented the views of the journeymen alone; two of them, the *National Trades' Union*, edited by Moore, and Commerford's *Union*, were started in order to help mobilize protests. The Typographical Association tried to offer the unionists an array of activities and diversions, including a library and a reading room. By 1835, the idea of building a central union hall, or a "Labor Temple," aroused considerable interest. Ely Moore proposed an alternative journeymen mechanics' institute for lectures on self-improvement and scientific subjects. In 1834, a group of journeymen in the mili-

27. *National Trades' Union*, May 2, 30, June 13, November 14, 28, 1835; *Man*, May 4, 1835; *Working Man's Advocate*, May 9, 1835.

28. *National Trades' Union*, August 1, 15, 22, 1835, February 5, March 26, 1836; *Man*, February 20, 1834, May 7, 27, June 19, 1834. On the importation of strikebreakers, see *National Trades' Union*, August 1, 1835. On the NTU, see also Commons, *History of Labour*, I, 424–53.

tia suggested forming "The Trades' Union Guards" to march on civic occasions; while their efforts seem to have failed, the GTU unions did parade, en masse, on various holidays and in union celebrations. A panoply of union songs, banners, and insignias appeared, especially on the Fourth of July, new emblems of the journeymen's cause.[29]

Politics proved more troublesome. In the aftermath of the Bank War, the revolution in party politics begun by the Van Burenite Bucktails completed its course, and by 1834 the New York Whig party was virtually in place. Now that electoral politics were firmly in the grip of party professionals and their well-to-do political allies, there was little opportunity for a radical movement of wage earners to enter politics on its own. A schism in Tammany ranks in 1835, led by the Radical antibanking Democracy of the ex-Owenite Evans, did create a new Equal Rights (or Loco Foco) party, an effort that won the backing of some influential unionists, including Commerford. But while the Loco Focos updated the Owenite "Workies" radicalism, their position vis-à-vis the labor movement remained problematic. Their politics, echoing Paine, aimed primarily to purify government and eliminate aristocratic corrupt influences, particularly the new Tammany pols and their banker friends; their program, as formulated by such publicists and allies as William Leggett, was vitriolic in its denunciation of monopolies, banking, and paper money, but contained no hint of Skidmorite agrarianism, Owenite rationalism, or (at least until the labor crisis of 1836) trade unionism. The Loco Focos' laissez-faire appeals—to restore "the landmarks and principles of true Democracy"—were as appropriate for petty entrepreneurs in search of wider business opportunities and nominal Jacksonians on the outs with Tammany as for exploited workers in search of a deflationary currency and an end to banks. The party's leadership and following, far from being that of a popular movement, was a cross-class coalition much like the Democrats' or Whigs', led by professionals, petty and middling mechants, and disgruntled renegades from the Democratic General Executive Committee. A few radicals like Commerford could see the line of convergence between the Loco Focos' cause and the journeymen's, but this was not enough to risk a formal union alliance with a small Democratic splinter group.[30]

29. Stevens, *Typographical Union*, 153; Commons, *Documentary History*, V, 247; *National Trades' Union*, September 6, 1834, January 17, May 2, 1835. On GTU parades, see also Wilentz, "Artisan Republican Festivals," 57–60; on songs, see Philip S. Foner, *American Labor Songs of the Nineteenth Century* (Urbana, 1975), 18–19.

30. On the Loco Focos, see Hugins, *Jacksonian Democracy*, 36–48, 148–202 passim (but beware Hugins's merging of the Loco Focos and the earlier Working Men's movement as a *single* movement); Hofstadter, "William Leggett"; Carl N. Degler, "The Locofocos: Urban 'Agrarians,'" *JEH* 16 (1956): 322–33; Mushkat, *Tammany*, 167–68; Stephen Hasbrouck to Alexander F. Vaché, October 14, 1836, Mrs. Gouverneur

Under these circumstances, the unionists faced a dilemma. Clearly, they had abundant reasons to avoid getting caught up in party affairs or allying with regular politicians—to the *Union*, those "wire pullers who move the juggling machines of 'the party.'" Yet while they felt compelled to preserve their political independence, the unions could ill afford to renounce politics entirely. Issues like those raised in the Bank War were of direct concern to union men, regardless of the motives of some of the politicians who agitated them; although not "intended to interfere in *party* politics," the *National Trades' Union* observed, the unions recognized that "many of the evils under which the workingmen are suffering are of a political origin and can only be reached in that way." Rather than stand in fixed opposition to political action, the journeymen looked for ways to influence public questions without becoming dupes.[31]

With surprising success, the unionists walked a tightrope between compromising commitment and outright abstention. On matters of broad significance, like the rechartering of the Bank, the GTU made its preferences clear in every way short of formal endorsement or political merger. Reactions to the mayoral election of 1834—a virtual referendum on the Bank—exemplified union policy. Although the GTU maintained its official silence, the union leadership helped to organize a monster rally of "Democratic Mechanics and Working Men" to cap the anti-Bank Tammanyite Cornelius Lawrence's campaign; eleven of the seventy-one signers of the meeting's anti-Bank memorial were union delegates, as were seven of the twenty men chosen as ward captains to oversee the balloting; by the rally's end, there was little doubt about the sentiments of the most prominent union men and of hundreds of rank-and-file journeymen.[32] The pattern reappeared the next autumn when the Democrats selected Ely Moore (who never cut his personal ties to the party) to run for Congress as "labor's" nominee: even with its president on the hustings, the union remained neutral, but individual unions and unionists, led by the printers, worked hard and in the end successfully to elect him. On issues of more direct concern to the trades, meanwhile, the unions took firmly political,

Morris Phelps Collection: Equal Rights Party, N-YHS MSS. On Commerford and the Loco Focos, see Fitzwilliam Byrdsall, *History of the Loco-Foco or Equal Rights Party* (New York, 1842), 17, 36, 51, 54, 75–79, 93. For a useful discussion of the "hard-money" New York Democracy, see Sharp, *Jacksonians versus the Banks*, 297–305.

31. *Union*, June 8, 1836; *National Trades' Union*, September 20, 1834. See also *National Trades' Union*, March 28, 1835; *Union*, April 21, May 20, June 22, 1836. There were, to be sure, always some men in the union who thought the journeymen should take a political turn. See *Man*, March 28, 1835. On what became of that sentiment, see below, Chapter 7.

32. *Man*, February 8, April 3, 4, 5, 26, May 7, 12, 15, 17, 1834. At least one individual union, the cordwainers', did see fit to support the Democratic candidate and to issue a broad statement backing President Jackson.

if nonpartisan, stands. Their gravest concern was over state prison labor, an offense to all journeymen and something of an economic threat to men in the building trades. Beginning in March 1834, the stonecutters' and marble polishers' unions revived earlier protests to the legislature about the system; several local union men, including John Commerford, helped arrange for a convention in Utica the following summer to arouse public opinion. Over the next two years, the unions repeated their complaints, sometimes in concert with politicians but always independently of party, always in the name of journeymen's rights.[33]

With all its political caution, this was hardly narrow-gauge, "bread-and-butter" unionism, an abandonment of broad political and social goals in favor of the pursuit of higher wages and better conditions. Although the unions did not organize a party of labor (a perfectly understandable refusal after the debacle of 1829-30) and although they did not elaborate radical appeals or platforms as Skidmore and the Free Enquirers had done, they certainly understood that they confronted systematic changes in the social relations of the workshops—changes with direct political connections. From the start, as the *National Trades' Union* announced, the movement aimed to address "the whole extent of evils under which the producing classes are suffering";[34] as the later strikes and protests proved, this meant opposing the central thrust of metropolitan industrialization. Instead of risking co-optation and defeat, however, the unionists created their own independent institutions and, like other antebellum radicals and reformers, marshaled their collective power to challenge the course of American progress.

Yet while the union men were social reformers, their approach to reform also encompassed different, at times conflicting, ideological perspectives. As they came to grips with these differences, the journeymen turned to far headier topics than wage differentials and the inflation. Once they did, they began to fashion a new language—and a new consciousness—of social conflict.

Class Consciousness and the Republic of Labor

"The time has arrived when the people of the United States must decide whether they will be a Republic in fact, or only a Republic in name. . . ."[35]

33. *Man*, June 7, 23, August 27, September 26, October 30, November 3, 1834; *Working Man's Advocate*, May 8, June 7, October 18, November 15, 1834; Hugins, *Jacksonian Democracy*, 158-62. Employers also continued their own protests against prison labor; see *Working Man's Advocate*, March 5, 19, 1831; *Man*, May 24, 31, July 1, 1834; *Proceedings of the State Convention of Mechanics Held at Utica* (New York, 1834).

34. *National Trades' Union*, July 5, 1834. Cf. Hugins, *Jacksonian Democracy*, 79.

35. *Man*, February 18, 1834. See also Finch, *Rise and Progress*, 11-12.

In a phrase, George Henry Evans' union newspaper *The Man* disclosed the abiding power of republican ideals among the journeymen and indicated that they interpreted their situation as part of a crisis in fundamental American values. Over the next three years, different groups of craft workers delivered similar messages and turned the familiar terms of artisan republican discourse against their employers. For some, the journeymen's cause was not unlike that of the earlier mechanics' interest: as good republicans, these moderates insisted, the journeymen sought their equal rights as middling producers against unvirtuous men of wealth and power. Others, however, were less certain the old artisan republican verities alone could fully explain their predicament or defend their actions. "Democratic Republicanism," one observed in 1834, "good, excellent, and blessed though it may be, does not necessarily imply the *perfection* of human society—much wrong is still experienced within its sacred pale—much internal improvement is yet wanting; and many of its parts require to be adjusted to one another."[36] Without abandoning their republicanism, these men turned to ideas similar to those which had inspired Blatchly, Skidmore, and the educational reformers—above all, the radical interpretation of the labor theory of value—but transformed them into a distinctly American trade unionism. As much as the strikes and protests, it was the ideological transition, from moderation to an early form of class consciousness, that dominated the union's rise and progress.

The moderate position, articulated best by Ely Moore, may be called classical republican trade unionism. Decidedly conciliatory in tone, the classical argument was quick to divorce the unions from all previous radical departures, particularly from the agrarian Skidmorites'; at most, Moore contended, the unionists were "truly conservative" mechanics, who wanted to restore the trades to the balanced harmony that had supposedly reigned in Jefferson's day. Far from desiring "a perfect equality of rights," Moore declared, the moderates saw their problem in eighteenth-century terms, as a political battle of "the intermediate classes" against a few men of great wealth and power, against a new aristocracy "prostituted to lust, avarice and ambition" that threatened the Republic with the specter of luxury and that had construed "the essence of politics as corruption, corruption, corruption!" Although cognizant of economic inequality, Moore and his associates remained vague about the economic sources of the journeymen's plight and paid, at most, only passing attention to the radical implications of the labor theory of value. Indeed, Moore's ideas on political economy often differed little from those popular in entrepreneurial circles: in 1833, he took the position that self-love—"this prevailing

36. *Man*, June 12, 1834.

disposition of the human heart"—was essential to social welfare, and held that "[t]he *selfish* generate the *social* feelings." By such lights, the unions were not bodies of exploited wage earners—those Moore called "the breadless and impotent"—but movements of respectable small producers looking out for their "self-interest and self-preservation," out to recapture, as the Typographical Association put it, "the virtue and happiness of the governed."[37]

Despite all of its anachronisms, the classical critique made some new points. Men like Moore did, after all, deploy the old rhetoric to defend a completely new kind of movement; simply by being active in the union, they helped provide a context in which sharper conflicts could develop. Moore's overblown exhortations to the city's journeymen to "cherish *'the Union'*; 'tis the only palladium that can protect you—'tis the only *Sacred Mount* to which you or your posterity can flee for refuge," may have sounded trite, even in Daniel Webster's America: they still marked Moore, at least for a time, as something of a rebel, outside the normal boundaries of respectable political opinion.[38] But Moore and others who clung to the classical lexicon were not ones to introduce fresh ideas or build upon the radicalism of the 1820s.

Moderate influence had considerable power through 1834 but waned dramatically as the strikes and protests proceeded. The moderates' downfall was hastened by the political disgrace of Ely Moore. Shortly before his election to Congress, Moore was appointed to a Democrat-controlled state commission to investigate state prison labor, an issue the Democrats (who had approved state-prison-labor plans) wanted to remove from the political agenda. The commission did not release its findings until after Moore was elected; when finally published, the report's vindication of prison labor caused an uproar among the organized journeymen. Moore, some delegates charged, had "deserted the cause" by signing the report; others demanded that he resign the GTU presidency for his adherence to his party's line against the journeymen's interests. Although he received a polite farewell before packing off for Washington, he would never again command the full allegiance of the journeymen's movement.[39] With Moore's departure and with John Commerford's elevation to the GTU presidency, the unionists'

---

37. Ely Moore, *Address Delivered before the General Trades' Union* (New York, 1833), 7–8 et passim; *National Trades' Union*, August 9, 1834; *Union*, May 20, 1836. Moore did refer to the war between labor and capital in his famous reply to Waddy Thompson in the House of Representatives in 1836—long after he had ceased to be an active force in the GTU.

38. *National Trades' Union*, August 9, 1834.

39. *Man*, February 9, 19, 26, March 2, 7, 1835; *National Trades' Union*, March 28, 1835; Commons, *Documentary History*, V, 235. Moore did get some support—from the paper he edited, *National Trades' Union*, February 28, 1835.

ongoing struggles with their employers (and, in time, the courts) led them in a more radical direction.

The impetus for this more class-conscious trade unionism came, somewhat ironically, from the Bank War. As planned by Jackson and his aides, the president's refusal to recharter the Bank of the United States and the release of his veto message aimed to remove what they had come to consider a bastion of illegitimate elite power and to win Democratic votes, not to stir radical controversy outside the party. Among New York's journeymen, it had been the Bank issue, along with anti-Sabbatarianism, that had first elevated the Democrat Ely Moore to prominence. While the Jacksonians got their support, however, they also helped redirect popular attention to economic inequalities and quickened radical inquiry. The shift was particularly evident in the editorial columns of the *Working Man's Advocate*. As early as 1831, George Henry Evans had turned his back on educational reform, to wonder whether Skidmore had not been correct after all and to declare that the source of the workingmen's difficulties lay not in the scheming of the church–and–state aristocracy but in the credit and banking system. Through the mid-1830s, Evans and the hard-money Jacksonians publicized how a "privileged class" robbed the producers; New York's journeymen adapted their arguments to suit their own problems, much as earlier radicals and workingmen had adapted the writings of Robert Owen. At first, they, like Evans, focused primarily on how credit helped financiers, capitalist entrepreneurs, and contractors at the expense of honest artisans. A "Journeyman Printer" of melodramatic imagination outlined the situation in a vignette that compared the fortunes of three characters "familiar to all," the merchant jobber Simon Squeezem, the speculative boss builder Ichabod Log, and their victim, the honest, upright carpenter Peter Plane: whereas Squeezem and Log made fortunes from speculative credit, Plane was shut out of a system designed to help "great wealthy employers to compete and crush little ones"—and prevent honest journeymen from becoming employers. "Justice," in an address to the striking carpenters in 1833, listed the credit system as the journeymen's worst foe, a "usurpation of republican pride." Fuller radical critiques, such as the one offered by "Journeyman Mechanic," attacked paper money on radical Ricardian grounds, as a device used by capitalists to manipulate the value of labor and rob workingmen. Proposed solutions, echoing Byllesby's, ranged from the establishment of labor cooperatives to the substitution of labor notes for currency.[40]

Such anticapitalist arguments updated the standard classical republican

40. *Working Man's Advocate*, January 28, July 8, September 3, October 8, 29, December 24, 31, 1831, February 18, 1832, April 6, June 8, 29, November 30, 1833, April 15, 16, 1834; *Man*, May 10, 22, 1834. On the Bank message, in addition to Meyers, *Jacksonian Persuasion*, see Lynn L. Marshall, "The Authorship of Jackson's Bank Veto Message," *MVHR* 50 (1963): 466–67.

and Ricardian formulations about the primacy of the virtuous producing classes but did not in themselves define the conflict as one over the relations of workshop production. They remained an important feature of the unionists' arguments through the end of the revolt, as union spokesmen attached a defense of their rights to organize to assaults on perfidious aristocratic politicians and the manipulators of "fictitious capital"—those Commerford called the promoters of "the paper or Hamiltonian scheme," who had imported the English banking system and "imbued it with the governmental engine."[41] But there was more: steadily, as the union men and the rank and file probed the questions raised by the Bank War and their own strikes, analyses of the peculiar problems of wage earners appeared with increasing regularity in union broadsides, speeches, and public appeals. In an address to the GTU in 1833, John Finch charged that the battle loomed not simply between producers and nonproducers but between masters and men: as if by decree, Finch announced, it seemed that "the *employer* was rapidly running the road to wealth [while] the *employed* was too often the victim of poverty and oppression, bound to the vassalage of inadequate reward for his labor." Ely Moore mentioned the point later that year; others went on to elaborate it as the revolt continued. The ladies' shoemaker Oramel Bingham noted that wages did not rise in periods of high prices and labor shortage—proof, he claimed, that the concerted interests of the masters, and not an impartial law of supply and demand, governed journeymen's earnings. "We are led to believe," the journeymen cordwainers concurred, "that [the employers] are dependent upon the profits they acquire from the labor of our hands"; all this really meant, however, was that the "fat task masters" established their independence—and sometimes great personal fortunes—by keeping wages as low as possible and feeding on the profits of their employees' labor. Under the existing arrangements, the GTU insisted, unjust laws and customs made the employer and the journeyman "two very different persons with regard to the measurement of privileges." To John Commerford, the enemy was plainly "capital"—a class of men *including* exploiting masters who with "deep and matured design" so controlled society that they could reward themselves by virtually "filching from labor." "While there are employers and journeymen," Commerford declared in 1836, "it is necessary, from the avarice that so generally pervades employers, that organized bodies of journeymen should exist, to neutralize the schemes and effects of upstart mushrooms."[42]

41. *Union*, April 30, 1836. See also *Union*, April 21, July 1, 1836, and passim.
42. Finch, *Rise and Progress*, 10; *Man*, June 16, 1835; *National Trades' Union*, June 19, July 1, 1835; *Transcript*, April 2, 15, 1836; *Working Man's Advocate*, September 19, 1835; *Union*, June 2, 1836; Moore, *Address*, 10.

Having made these connections, the unionists returned to the labor theory of value and critiques of prevailing property relations to set forth an axiom that had been raised only faintly before: they, the journeymen, and *only* the journeymen, had the right to judge the value of their labor. "It has been said, and truly said," Finch told the journeymen "that labour is wealth"; unfortunately, it was less than clear who had the legitimate power to fix their labor's worth. Obviously, to Finch, the masters did not, since they had shown that they believed it was in their interest to depress wages "and grow rich upon the depression." Only the journeymen—"you who are interested in supporting yourselves and your families by a fair consideration of your services"—could establish a fair wage. By 1835, this argument had swept throughout the union movement, coupled with the idea that the wage earner's labor was not a market commodity but his own personal estate. "We hold that our labor is our property," the sailmakers declared, "and we have the inherent right to dispose of it in such parcels as any other species of property." "We, the working-men," the journeymen house carpenters argued, "consider that we are by far the most competent judges of the value of our labor." To the journeymen cordwainers, any attempts by employers "to say how much . . . journeymen shall receive for their labor" amounted to "a usurpation of authority." "[A]ll we ask," Oramel Bingham implored, "is to set the price of labor," since "we know its value best."[43]

Here lay the essentials of a new, more coherent trade-union theory, one foreshadowed in the Jeffersonian period and influenced by the debates of the 1820s but representing a more cohesive, class-conscious rupture with entrepreneurial assumptions about capitalist wage labor. Superficially, it marked a retreat from earlier radical positions; although they attacked capitalist accumulation and the new wage relations, the unionists, unlike Blatchly, Byllesby, and (especially) Skidmore and the Working Men, never questioned private property per se. Nor did they adopt Skidmore's distinction between labor and property. But by claiming their labor as their *own* property, by linking that definition to what they perceived as the new inequalities in the workshops, and by then asserting their exclusive rights, as wage earners, to regulate their wages, the organized journeymen turned the most fundamental of entrepreneurial ideas—the very notion of labor as a commodity—on its head and threw it back at their employers. If property was indeed sacred, they reasoned, then their masters were guilty of theft, for their exploitation and plunder of their employees' labor. Under existing property relations, an inalterable antagonism between mas-

43. Finch, *Rise and Progress*, 16–17, 23; *National Trades' Union*, October 24, 1835, March 5, 1836; *Man*, June 16, 1835. See also *Man*, May 27, 1835; *Union*, March 14, 1835, April 25, 27, June 16, 1836.

ters and journeymen was inevitable; everything favorable to the property rights of employers could be expected to be oppressive to the property rights of workers. Faith in a natural, self-adjusting market in labor and products was absurd in a world of selfish competition, a world of capitalist robbery, a world where arrogant masters could be expected "to *coerce* the independent spirited men who [take] upon themselves the unquestionable right of affixing a value to their own labor."[44]

In every important respect, this fusion of anticapitalist "producerism" and the analysis of workshop exploitation—and the defense of an inter-trade union—was as profound a critique of early industrial capitalism as any that appeared among the craft workers' movements of Britain and France in the 1830s; indeed, the New Yorkers' reformulation of natural property rights into an attack on the effects of capitalist wage relations had close parallels with the most articulate expressions of working-class consciousness abroad.[45] By 1835, these ideas had supplanted what remained of classical trade unionism in the GTU; a year later, a GTU report delivered after the indictment of twenty-five journeymen for conspiracy revealed the depths of the New Yorkers consciousness of class and its links to their own conception of natural rights and political economy. As a summary of what had become of the journeymen's movement in less than three years, it is a document that bears quotation at length.[46] The report began with what was now the standard argument on labor, property, and exploitation, that unless the "operatives of this country" could exercise "the right of graduating the prices of their own constitutional

44. *National Trades' Union*, March 5, 1836.
45. See especially Sewell, *Work and Revolution*, 201–18; Iorwerth Prothero, "William Benbow and the Concept of the 'General Strike,'" *P&P*, no. 63 (1974): 132–71; and (although the emphasis is different), Stedman Jones, "Language of Chartism." Of course, the French and the English, still subjects to crown and nobility, sometimes pushed their *political* conclusions to include calls for revolution. The Americans, as we shall see, hoped to alter class relations by redeeming their republic. The structure of their analysis, however—the adaptation of older radical political ideas to a critique of wage relations—bore a strong resemblance to arguments presented abroad. Indeed, given the extent to which English and French labor radicals still divided society (as Prothero argues concerning William Benbow) "in terms of political, not economic rôles" (144), the GTU's ideas might be considered more exacting on the question of wage labor. The New Yorkers were quite aware of the writings and activities of English and European radicals, trade unions, and Robert Owen's Grand National Consolidated Trade Union; rather than try to emulate these movements, however, the New Yorkers were content to point out their similarities, noting that "like causes produce like effects." See *Working Man's Advocate*, March 15, June 14, August 30, November 29, 1834; *Man*, May 24, June 24, 1834, and, for a full review, Peter G. Roberts, "The Response of American Labor to English Industrial Experience, 1828–1848" (M.A. thesis, Columbia University, 1971).
46. "Report of the Committee . . . of the Trades' Union of the City of New York" reprinted in *Transcript*, April 2, 1836.

and natural property," they would be left with only "the mock ostentation of liberty." Any wage earner not given sufficient return for his labor had reason to distrust not only his employers but his government, so long as laws and the political system favored masters over men. Such certainly seemed to be the case in New York, especially following the indictment of the tailors; even in the Republic, Shakespeare's lines held true:

> Plate sin with gold and
> The strong lance of justice hurtless breaks;
> Clothe it in rags, and
> A pigmy's straw doth pierce it.

Under such conditions, no country, "whether controlled by a monarchy or a republic," could enjoy internal tranquility. The masters' plea that they only followed the laws of supply and demand was a fraudulent ruse, an impudent denial of the "best motives" of the Revolution and the Constitution:

> [T]here is a class of persons who takes upon themselves the affixing of a price of our labor, and this they have always attempted, utterly regardless of the state of trade; these men have always endeavored to make the laborer work for low wages, without any reference to the prosperity of the country.

The conflict was everywhere, in the clash of workshop property rights, in the laws, in the very ethics of the offending masters—no longer selfish individuals or corrupt politicians but "a class."

What, then, became of the journeymen's artisan republicanism? In the Old World monarchies, the class consciousness of the 1830s was always bound up with the most radical republican ideas; in France, especially, and above all in Paris, craft workers' militancy mingled with antimonarchical politics, in what Alain Faure has described as the *république des ouvriers* of 1833–34.[47] If, as the GTU report claimed, capitalist inequities were as glaring in the American Republic as in the Old World, had the unionists shed their artisan republicanism? Not at all. Much as the radical craft workers in France turned established corporate idioms and the political language of French republicanism to their own uses, the most militant New York unionists drew upon their own ideals of "the Trade" and upon the egalitarian ideas of the Revolution, in a manner that shaped and, in their own eyes, fortified their consciousness of class. In their view, resistance to capital, defense of the Republic, and preservation of their rights to associate and to set the price of their labor were one and the same

47. Faure, "Mouvements populaires et mouvement ouvrier à Paris (1830–1834)," *Mouvement Social*, no. 88 (1974): 51–92.

cause; above all, the notion of independence, central to both republican politics and the order of the artisan system, propelled their critique of proletarianization. Rather than scoff at the legitimacy of the artisan republic, they celebrated it—but in new ways, altogether different from those of the old artisan celebrations and of the proclamations of the Jacksonian regulars, the emerging Whig opposition and those anti-union entrepreneurs who also laid claim to the republican legacy.

John Commerford's writings and speeches detailed the terms of this new transformation of meaning. For all his criticisms of capital and exploitative masters, Commerford, like countless artisan spokesmen before him, fixed on the fragility of republican institutions; like his predecessors, he referred to the ancients to show how avarice and luxury bred corruption and decline. The measure of capitalist tyranny, in his view, was precisely that it obliterated republican independence, equality, and commonwealth, not simply by creating a corrupt hierarchy of wealth and privilege (as some claimed) but by attempting to make one class of citizens "the willing tools of other men." Once secure, capital perverted every blessing that Americans had the right to enjoy in common. Labor-saving machinery, among "the most valuable acquisitions rendered by Philosophy to the Arts," had become "a mere tributary of capital," concentrated in the hands of a few for their own benefit. America's storehouse of public lands, snatched up by "a knot of speculators," remained outside the grasp of would-be independent workers, thus bottling up what Commerford recognized as "surplus labor" in the eastern cities, where it depressed the wages of all. While capitalist employers claimed that all men of honest industry could become rich, thousands toiled incessantly without ever obtaining riches in proportion to their industry. Politics, supposedly the testing ground of the popular will, had become a showplace of personal ambition, manned by the "agents of brokers and shavers." How, Commerford asked, could a worker cherish and maintain "the independent character of an American citizen" amid such degradation? Obviously, he could not, unless he joined with his fellow workers as a counterpoise to capital, to effect "a reform and revolution"—labor's "day of retribution"—to establish "a true system of political economy" in which those who earn all of the wealth of a nation should no longer secure the least.[48]

More graphic testimony to the unionists' outlook appeared in the GTU's various public festivities and emblems. Like the early national artisans, the unionists took their public presentations seriously. In one of its first actions, the GTU convention voted to hold a procession to announce

---

48. *Working Man's Advocate*, September 19, 1835; *Union*, April 21, May 17, 25, June 22, August 19, 1836. On Commerford's support of cooperative ideas, see the report he helped write for the NTU, in Commons, *Documentary History*, VI, 298–99.

and celebrate the founding of the union. For at least the next two years, the GTU repeated these marches as anniversary festivals, complete with speeches from the union president. Individual trade unions held their own, separate Fourth of July functions. As previous gatherings had celebrated the mechanics' interest, the unionists took to the streets to proclaim their new identity as a class apart, ready to march behind such new standards as the GTU's banner of Archimedes lifting a mountain with a lever. "Can you," Ely Moore asked at the first celebration, gesticulating to the union's freshly painted emblem, "as mechanics and artists, look upon that *banner* without being reminded of your united strength?"[49]

While declaring their new identity, however, the journeymen also re-dedicated themselves to republican—and specifically artisan republican—ideals. The GTU convention chose November 25, "the anniversary of our entire liberation from *foreign* thralldom," as the original date for its inaugural procession in 1833. Journeymen's Independence Day celebrations turned rapidly from attacks on capital and unfair laws to celebrations of the principles of American government—"emphatically a government of the people," the stonecutters heard, with all its flaws "the finest on earth." Despite their distance from their masters, they managed, however grudgingly, to march in a joint civic parade to mourn Lafayette in 1834—so long as it was to honor the memory of a departed French hero and a secular saint of the Revolution, and so long as they marched separately from their employers and every other civic association. The class identity evoked by the GTU's new banners did not replace the customary craft regalia. The Union Society of House Carpenters' banner featured the carpenters' trade emblem (supported by two workmen using their tools), a temple ("finely executed") and the slogans "The Art Conservative of All Arts" and "We Shelter the Houseless." The journeymen ladies' cordwainers also featured the arms of their trade, along with two female figures, one holding a slipper, the other a ladies' gaiter boot. Journeymen from other trades mounted pageants. A grand union parade in 1836, in support of striking tailors, was headed by the old Adam-and-Eve banner, "indicating thereby," a reporter observed, "that tailoring was the first trade started after the fall of man." The anniversary marches ended with the singing of a national air. To rally the journeymen after the tailors' conspiracy trial in 1836, the *Union* turned to the old image of the hammer and hand (Plate 14). There was no mistaking the message of this "band of brothers," as one journalist described a GTU parade; the union, borrowing from a speech by Ely Moore, had spelled it out as early as 1834:

49. *Working Man's Advocate*, November 30, December 6, 21, 1833, September 19, 1835; *Evening Star* [New York], December 3, 7, 1833; *National Trades' Union*, September 20, 27, 1834; *Man*, June 25, 26, 1834.

We the JOURNEYMEN ARTISANS and MECHANICS of the City of New York, and its vicinity, therefore, believing as we do, that in proportion as the line of *distinction* between the employer and employed is widened, the condition of the latter inevitably verges toward a state of vassalage while that of the former as certainly approximates towards supremacy; and that whatever system is calculated to make the many dependent upon, or subject to, the few, not only tends to the subversion of the natural rights of man, but is hostile to the best interests of the community as well as to the spirit and genius of our government. . . .

The masters, having adopted capitalist, and therefore undemocratic, antirepublican, ways, were not even entitled to march with their men in the trappings of "the Trade."[50]

In one sense, these artisan republican themes might be taken as symbols of respectable dissent; by appropriating the Republic and "the Trade," the journeymen were able to justify their protests as being in keeping with established political and social traditions. Such legitimation was certainly important to men like Moore. But the links between artisan republicanism and the unionists' developing consciousness of class were also far more profound. The artisan republic, more than an emblem of legitimacy, had long incorporated a moral vision of social obligation and political liberties. The chief consequence of metropolitan industrialization, as the journeymen experienced it, was to desecrate this vision and replace it with a sinister new system, detrimental to the community at large. In reaction, the unionists reasserted the old values, not as a nostalgic reverie or as a bid for public approval, but as something approaching an alternative system, one that would offer a cooperative path to republican progress and that would be different from the one designed by their capitalist employers—a system that would, at the very least, give the journeymen the control over their labor and eliminate capitalist domination and the "demon of individual gain." In completing this transformation the unionists did more than assert their devotion to the artisan republican legacy: they decided that the protection and extension of that legacy could be insured only by wage earners. Whereas the workshop had once been the repository of republican values, it was now the union of journeymen, "embodying hundreds of honest and industrious mechanics of virtue, worth and talent, in one great brotherly association," Finch declared, "having in view their own mutual protection and support. . . ."[51] The Revolution had become the journey-

---

50. Finch, *Rise and Progress*, 9; Robert Walker, *Oration Delivered at Clinton Hall to the Journeymen Stone Cutters' Association* (New York, 1833), 14; *Man*, June 26, 1834; *National Trades' Union*, August 9, September 27, 1834; *Herald*, April 11, 1836; *Union*, July 2, 3, 1836; *Transcript*, August 29, 1835.

51. Finch, *Rise and Progress*, 13.

men's cause. The republican mutuality of "the Trade" had become the republican mutuality of the union.

The Boundaries of Class

While the journeymen's revision of artisan republicanism helped them to define themselves as a class, in opposition to their employers, it also pointed out problems regarding the unionists' links with other segments of the community that might logically have joined them. Women and day laborers, for example, had long been kept at arm's length by journeymen as dependent persons, despite their sporadic movements; women craft workers, in particular, had appeared to the journeymen primarily as a threat. How, in the class-conscious atmosphere of the 1830s and with the expansion of women's work and semiskilled work in the trades, were these groups to be treated by the unions? And how were the unionists to treat the many "honorable" small masters—including radicals—who continued to respect their employees' rights and pay them fair wages? If anything, these men were as endangered by metropolitan industrialization as were the journeymen—yet the unionists' declaration of separate interests appeared to preclude any alliance with them. As they wrestled with these questions, the unionists reached the boundaries of their own consciousness of class and rethought some of their traditional social solidarities.

Women workers, by their own organized efforts, most persistently raised questions about their place in the labor movement. Some—probably most—journeymen still assumed in the early 1830s that women had no clear sense of their rights, let alone any capacities to fight for them. As late as 1836, one unionist asserted that "the natural weakness of the sex—their modesty and bashfulness—their ignorance of the forms and conduct of public meetings, and of the measures necessary to enable them to resist the oppression under which they labor—will ever prevent their obtaining by their own unassisted efforts any melioration or improvement of their condition." Yet contrary to such bland assumptions, New York's women craft workers had proven themselves capable of actions that were anything but modest, bashful, and incompetent. The tailoresses, who had struck for wages in 1825, organized again in 1831 and 1836; in 1835, female bookbinders and the newly established Ladies' Shoe Binders' Society followed suit, as did female umbrella makers the following year. These groups were, at best, evanescent; nevertheless, for as long as they lasted, they showed the women's abilities to organize in the name of their own republican rights, despite the employers' hostility and the indifference of male journeymen. The most startling demonstrations came during the tailoresses' uprising of 1831, in which sixteen hundred female outworkers organized their own

Tailoresses' Society and mounted a bitter, three-month strike against wage reductions. Along the way, a core of articulate, able leaders arose from the tailoresses' ranks to refine a distinctively female working-class consciousness. "It needs no small share of courage for us who have been used to impositions and oppressions from our youth to the present day, to come before the public in defense of our own rights," Sarah Monroe told her sisters at one strike meeting. "But, my friends, if it is unfashionable for the men to bear the oppression in silence, why should it not also become unfashionable with the women? or do they deem us more able to endure hardships than they themselves?"[52]

The male unionists—even those who had thrilled listening to Fanny Wright—never regarded these efforts as being on a par with their own. The practical consequence of these attitudes was female exclusion from both the GTU and the individual craft unions. To justify their policy, some unionists proclaimed a plebeian cult of domesticity—a cult quite unlike its emerging middle class counterpart, one based not on a feminized evangelicalism, but on older notions of the primacy of male authority and duty. Some spoke of being sickened by the spectacle of wives and daughters—and, even worse, single girls—leaving their preordained positions as homemakers. A woman's very "physical organization, natural responsibilities, and . . . moral sensibility" an NTU report opined, "prove conclusively that her labors should be only of a domestic nature." Once out of the household, women were subject to the whims of greedy and, sometimes literally, rapacious overseers and masters, who would treat them like slaves (a term the men used repeatedly). By depicting the women wage earners as victims, "pearls of princely value" depraved by the demands of poverty, the unionists elevated themselves as women's natural protectors, whose manly efforts would raise their own wages high enough to support their own wives, daughters, and sisters and drive the offending masters from the trades. Such condescension offered little hope that the journeymen's sense of equality and mutual respect would extend beyond their own sex.[53]

But condescension was not contempt. Even with their patriarchal prejudices, the unionists of the 1830s came to regard the plight of women craft workers very differently than the journeymen tailors of the Jeffersonian period had. As early as 1831, during the tailoresses' strike, "A Mechanic" repeatedly urged the women on, suggesting that they open their own shop

52. *National Trades' Union*, July 11, 1835; *Daily Sentinel* [New York], March 5, 1831. On women's unions and organizing in the 1830s, see *National Trades' Union*, August 30, 1834, June 6, 20, July 4, 11, 1835; *Man*, May 27, June 19, 1835; *Evening Post*, July 10, 1835. See also Stansell, "Women of the Laboring Poor," 118–28.

53. *Working Man's Advocate*, September 20, 1834; Commons, *Documentary History*, VI, 282, 285. On middle-class domesticity, see Nancy F. Cott, *The Bonds of Womanhood: "Woman's Sphere" in New England, 1780–1835* (New Haven, 1977).

and receive work based on their own price list. By mid–decade, unionists in other trades were prepared to take more formal actions. When the women shoe binders organized in 1835, one union member offered a detailed exposé of the atrocious conditions in which the women labored and concluded that "it is high time, in this republic, that such slavery is done away with." The all-male shoe binders' union agreed and passed a strong resolution of support. In the same spirit, a special meeting of the New York Association of Journeymen Bookbinders noted a few days later that "the females connected with this business are at present endeavoring to better their conditions by making a small advance in their list of prices"; quickly, the society approved a public address expressing its deep interest in the women's struggle and vowing to use "all honorable means" to help them. Other journeymen pledged similar support for women on strike; the National Trades' Union went so far as to suggest that all trades affected by female labor add women's auxiliaries to their unions.[54]

In the context of the 1830s, these gestures of support were as significant as the journeymen's stubborn patriarchy. The union men clung to an ideal of the decent life that required, as one NTU committee wrote, a "wife or relative at home, to perform the duties of the household." They still expected that by winning higher wages for themselves, they would enable the heads of households to support themselves and their families—the surest way to end the exploitation of female labor. Yet these were times, as the union men told the city constantly, when a decent life was impossible, when more of their own wives and daughters faced the likelihood that they would work for wages. As Barbara Taylor has observed about London tailors in the 1830s, it was a moment of greater flexibility in the men's attitudes: if their anger at masters and their rhetorical solidarity with the women's unions stopped well short of a spirit of sexual equality, their attitudes marked a blurring of once stark sexual preconceptions, at least for a time.[55] Given the earlier history of the journeymen's unions, given the world in which the journeymen worked, it was no small change.

A similar shift was noticeable in the journeymen's relations with unskilled men. Like the women craft workers, New York's day laborers continued to organize, but on an ad hoc basis, through the mid-1830s. In 1834, local sailors struck for an advance in pay. The riggers and stevedores followed in early 1836, emulating earlier strikers by marching along the

54. *Working Man's Advocate*, July 3, 1831; *Man*, May 28, June 15, 19, 23, 1835; Commons, *Documentary History* VI, 288–89.

55. Commons, *Documentary History*, VI, 283, 287–89; Barbara Taylor, "'The Men Are as Bad as Their Masters . . .': Socialism, Feminism, and Sexual Antagonism in the London Tailoring Trade in the Early 1830s," *Feminist Studies* 5 (1979): 7–40.

city's wharves, pulling more than eight hundred men off their jobs, and effectively shutting the port. As the dockworkers struck, more than two hundred building laborers, mostly Irishmen, also demanded higher wages and forced work to stop on local building projects. The city's coal heavers began their own walkout in 1836. Far from being docile, indolent men, the laborers showed all the signs of effective organization despite their lack of a union. Their efforts also displayed some familiarity with the culture and the political economy of the unions. At the very least, the stevedores and riggers knew enough to publish a lengthy exposition of their grievances, in which they declared their right to fix their own wages; as they paraded along the waterfront, they carried their own "trade" banner.[56]

Unlike their counterparts in Philadelphia, the New York journeymen never seized upon these developments to admit unskilled men to their general union (although they did include the outwork weavers); nor did they ever walk off their jobs in solidarity with the unskilled, as Philadelphia journeymen did to support striking coal heavers on the Schuylkill in 1835. This social distance between skilled and unskilled was recognized by the laborers themselves: when the building laborers struck in 1836, for instance, they did not even ask the skilled masons and bricklayers who worked beside them to join their walkout. It was thus all the more remarkable when, during the climactic New York labor crisis of 1836, the unionists began to speak of the problems faced by day laborers and reconsidered their relationship to the unskilled. In February, a meeting of mechanics and laborers, led by delegates from the GTU, tried to establish a common front, outside of the GTU itself, to lead a united effort by all male wage-earners, raising fears of a general strike. While the project came to nothing, the idea that skilled and unskilled men shared common problems and interests persisted. By the late spring, John Commerford, writing in the *Union*, referred to the stevedore's strike and bid the mechanics to come to the aid of those strikers who had been arrested at the behest of a few "swollen exchangers of other men's labor"; "like the mechanic," Commerford commented, "the stevedore has as good and just a right to ask what he pleases for his labor as the merchant has for his commodities." Through the summer, craft workers and laborers met in joint protest demonstrations. One by one, the social and ideological barriers that had long separated the skilled from the unskilled began to fall.[57]

Very different kinds of problems beset the journeymen's relationships with the city's small masters. The issue was raised as soon as the GTU or-

---

56. *Man*, July 25, 1834; *National Trades' Union*, September 27, 1834, February 27, 1836. See also below, Chapter 7.

57. Laurie, *Working People of Philadelphia*, chap. 5. *Herald*, February 24, 25, 1836; *Union*, June 2, 23, 1836.

ganized, when John Finch noted that "[m]any employers (and be it said to their lasting honour) have shown a noble and generous disposition to do their journeymen mechanics justice." Others echoed Finch's insistence that the worth of these small masters was priceless and claimed that the unions were not out to harm them. It was more difficult, however, to say where, precisely, the unions were to stand vis-à-vis these men. Were they, like the Boston equivalent of the GTU, to admit small masters, as friends to "the Trade" and therefore to the unions? One Boston journeyman urged the readers of the *Man* to do so, "since the bos [*sic*] is often brought to journeywork by hard luck, and the journeyman may expect in his turn to become an employer. . . ." All men who "obtain their living by honest labor," the Bostonian contended, "have a common interest in sustaining each other against the rich men, the professional men," those "whose interest is promoted by working us hard and working us cheap." The more moderate New York unionists—joined, predictably enough, by radical small masters like George Henry Evans—counseled a similar course.[58]

The journeymen's own artisan republicanism, as well as their experiences on strike, further clouded the situation. So long as the unionists hoped to retrieve what Finch called the proper "mutual dependence" between employer and employee, it was not altogether clear why they should break with those masters who respected that mutuality. Some dinner celebrations of individual craft unions, most of all those of the more moderate groups like the Typographical Association, spent as much time toasting those gallant employers who treated them well as they did berating those who hired "rats." Strike appeals included fulsome praise for masters who came to terms quickly. At times, it appeared that the journeymen's genuine appreciation of sympathetic employers would overwhelm their critique of exploitation and replace it with the more familiar moral distinctions, between good men and bad; even as the GTU geared up for the climactic strike movement of 1836, its leaders (including Commerford) were able to endorse a statement that denounced the wage earners' "abject state of vassalage," but also noted that the unions' original object "was not to trample upon the rights of employers" or "create a feeling of enmity against the non-producers."[59]

Ultimately, however, the journeymen declined to admit even friendly radical small masters. It was not that the journeymen ceased to seek or value the masters' support; rather, they pointed out, wage earners could

---

58. Finch, *Rise and Progress*, 13, 23; *Man*, May 30, June 4, 16, September 22, 1834, May 13, June 5, 1835; *Working Man's Advocate*, April 12, 1834; *Union*, April 21, 1836. See also *National Trades' Union*, September 6, 1834.

59. Finch, *Rise and Progress*, 12–13; *Working Man's Advocate*, June 29, 1833; *Man*, June 16, 1834; *National Trades' Union*, February 27, 1836.

not be sure that seemingly honest masters would always remain so; many who called themselves honorable, the cordwainers' remarked, only later turned out to be "part-time friends." More to the point, a joint organization of masters and journeymen would prove impossible to hold together, especially during strikes. As the *Man* admitted in 1835, the journeymen "possess themselves of a great power over employers . . . from having only one side of a dispute"; allowing masters to join would lead the unions to pull in different directions "when it is in their interest to pull together."[60] While they hoped, one day, to achieve a lasting cooperative mutuality, the unionists' new consciousness of class held firm, even if their hearts and minds remained somewhat divided. The small masters could contribute to the cause by treating their men fairly and setting an example to others. They could do no more.

In all, by the mid-1830s, it was possible to see the journeymen's movement—open in new ways to solidarity with women and laborers, adamant in its refusal to admit any masters—turning into still another kind of working-class movement extending beyond the trades. Indeed, it was even possible to see, in the unionists' editorials, demonstrations, and speeches, a still wider consciousness of the New York journeymen's place, as part of a larger American working class, restricted neither to New York nor to the crafts. Quite apart from their involvement in the NTU, the New Yorkers took an active interest in conditions and strikes throughout the country; the GTU, along with individual unions, came to support not only their fellow New York journeymen but also the female factory workers of Lowell, the operatives (including the children) of Paterson, organized wage earners in every conceivable trade and occupation. The unionists' rhetoric grew more expansive as well, to match their widened concerns. John Commerford fastened onto this sense of a larger unity of interest and tried to find the words to describe all the nation's wage earners as one, first as mechanics and workingmen, then as operatives, finally as the "family of labor," the "working classes."[61] So brief was the life of the union movement of the 1830s, so new were its institutions, that this broader working-class consciousness never translated into a general association of New York's wage earners, let alone a national confederation of all workers. But that consciousness flickered in 1836, a mere three years after the journeymen had first set about organizing their own general union. It would burn long enough that the unionists, during the great wave of strikes in 1836, nearly found themselves at the head of an unprecedented kind of insurgency.

60. *Man*, April 1, 15, June 24, 1835.
61. *Man*, May 24, 1835; *National Trades' Union*, August 1, 8, 1835; *Working Man's Advocate*, September 19, 1835; *Union*, April 21, 1836.

Radicalism and the Union

The rise and progress of the GTU, and its equivalents in other cities, was a central, transforming event in the history of American class relations. Although hardly "revolutionary" in the usual political sense (or in the sense in which Thomas Skidmore and his Working Men friends used the term), the New York journeymen's movement, like its allies elsewhere, established a new frame of reference for wage earners' protests, as a contest over clashing conceptions of labor and property. It also raised points that would remain important to labor movements over the rest of the century. Discussions of the effects of credit and the overexchange of commodities in the labor press of the 1830s prefigured the positions of the Greenback-Laborites of the 1870s and 1880s. The promise of land reform and producers' cooperatives, presented in the speeches of Commerford and others, would constantly reappear in radical political platforms and some trade-union programs. In the numerous GTU attacks on exploitation at the work place, we find the elements of a working-class (as opposed to "artisan" or "producerist") political economy of a kind that would be developed and elaborated by such later theorists as Ira Steward. It is no exaggeration to consider the emergence of the GTU and its counterparts elsewhere to be the birth of nineteenth-century American working-class radicalism, in almost all of its forms other than Marxism.[62]

The power, the possibilities, and the limitations of these radical notions and the GTU's consciousness of class became fully clear during the events of 1836. To understand these matters, however, requires looking well beyond the trade unions and the GTU. Many other kinds of unions appealed to New York's craft workers and their employers in the 1830s, each of them with professed republican intents. Some complicated the trade unionists' efforts, others clashed directly with GTU. Each affected the others. Each by turn shaped the progress and the meaning of the journeymen's revolt.

62. See Montgomery, *Beyond Equality*, 135–96, 230–60, 425–47. Maurice F. Neufeld presents some parallel observations, but with a very different emphasis, in "The Persistence of Ideas in the American Labor Movement: The Heritage of the 1830s," *Industrial and Labor Relations Review* 35 (1982): 207–20; cf. Neufeld's argument and David Montgomery, "Labor and the Republic in Industrial America, 1860–1920," *Mouvement Social*, no. 111 (1980): 201–15.

7

Oppositions:
To the Crisis of 1836

The sober constitutionalism of the GTU carried an important strain of radical artisan culture into the 1830s: like the earlier journeymen's associations and freethinkers' societies, the unions promoted a code of radical rectitude that would have taken their men out of the taverns, cockpits, and brothels and into committee rooms and lecture halls to combat their common enemies. Union procedures and rules captured this attitude only in part. For some unionists, moderate and radical, the cause required a complete transformation of character centered on temperance. Among the reasons Ely Moore cited in favor of a trade-union institute was that "it would induce [the journeymen] to forsake their accustomed places of resort (where temptations too often beset them). . . ." Of all the causes of poverty and ignorance other than low wages, John Commerford wrote, "there is none more preeminently conspicuous than that of alcohol." Others claimed that "all talk of the hard heartedness of the employers [and] their mean maneuvers" would prove abortive "while we remain indifferent to the destroying effects of spiritous liquors."[1]

Against this thoroughgoing reformism, most journeymen (including the union rank and file) retained some loyalty to their usual haunts and pleasures. Even dedicated unionists saw nothing wrong with organizing their efforts in taverns and hotel bars, their customary meeting places. Nor did they necessarily object to drinking at work. As one immigrant cabinetmaker recalled, his shop mates, union supporters all, automatically assumed that the right to drink went along with the right to control their own labor.

1. *Man*, November 24, 25, 1834; *Union*, May 23, June 1, 1836. See also *National Trades' Union*, August 9, 1834; *Man*, February 22, 1834.

Frequently, he noted, after a stretch of especially hard toil, the men would begin "a simultaneous cessation from work":

> No one could tell why, though no surprise was manifested that, in one case, we placed ourselves near an open window, or in the other that we drew round the stove. Then, as it were by tacit agreement, every hand held out its contribution of "loose change"; the apprentice was sent on his errand and speedily returned laden with wine, brandy, biscuits, and cheese. The appropriation of these refreshments was sure to call forth songs from those who felt musical; after which came a proposition for a further supply, which provoked a more noisy vocalization, while the conversation which had been animated became excited.

Journeymen in unorganized trades showed even less of an affinity for abstemiousness.[2]

Moving out of the workshops and into the journeymen's leisure spots and neighborhoods, one found the radicalism of the unions crowded by a more generalized dislike of outsiders and formal official authority, especially of the police. This was a world of street gangs, masculine bravado, and noisome entertainments—where Melville's mariners, renegades, and castaways mingled with the workingmen, where the young Whitman could loiter to watch the butcher boy–dandy exchange his killing clothes for his "duds" and launch into his repartee, his shuffle and breakdown. It was also a world where mobbing still served as an instrument against injustices, public and private. At times, this more boisterous culture intersected with that of the unions: in one of the more curious riots of the 1830s, several hundred artisans and apprentices, furious at the arrest of a young woman accused of robbing a shoe store, smashed into the store in question and raised the cry "State Prison Monopoly!"[3] But at the extremes, this culture—what some historians have construed as working-class "traditionalism"[4]—proved a hedge against the unifying and sophisticated class consciousness of the unions. So long as most journeymen, including the union faithful, kept at least one foot in the republic of the streets and taverns, there would always be important tensions between the most committed union organizers and those they hoped to lead.

While the unions tried, with only limited success, to change the journeymen's habits, they also confronted the increasingly coherent entrepreneur-

2. "Workingman's Recollections," 107.

3. Herman Melville, *Moby-Dick*, ed. Harrison Hayford and Hershel Parker (New York, 1967), 104; Walt Whitman, *Leaves of Grass: The First (1855) Edition*, ed. Malcolm Cowley (New York, 1959), 34; *Commercial Advertiser*, July 1, 1834; Weinbaum, *Mobs and Demagogues*, 53, n. 55.

4. Alan Dawley and Paul Faler, "Working-Class Culture and Politics in the Industrial Revolution: Sources of Loyalism and Rebellion," *JSH* 9 (1976): 466–80; Laurie, *Working People of Philadelphia*, chap. 3.

ial republicanism of the city's major craft employers. By the mid-1830s, the masters' defense of their own interests and of the values they associated with the Republic were far more consistent and more sanctimonious than ever before. To at least some of New York's journeymen, this conception of republican rights and obligations was so compelling that they shunned both the taverns and the unions; for many more, the masters' professions of republicanism only sharpened their own resistance. At all events, by 1836 the unionists found themselves at war with articulate and well-organized movements of masters, supported by the municipality and the courts. This war, tempered by political and cultural developments outside the unions, ultimately defined the meaning of class conflict in Jacksonian New York.

The Republic of the Bowery

To find New York's lower-class world of rough amusement, a traveler had only to visit the Bowery. Bisecting the northeastern section of the city, with its heavy concentration of workers' and small masters' dwellings, the Bowery in the 1830s was swiftly becoming New York's plebeian boulevard, the workingmen's counterpart to fashionable Broadway. "To a philosopher," George Foster later wrote, "a walk through the Bowery would furnish abundant food for thought and contemplation."[5] Those otherwise inclined would also have found enough to keep them occupied. Here journeymen and apprentices from nearby butcheries, furniture shops, and shipyards mixed with other craft workers, small employers, and day laborers, in what one chronicler described as a constant parade of "kaleidoscopic contrasts." Here were the groggeries, oyster houses, dance halls, gambling dens, and bordellos that catered to workingmen and adventuresome tourists from around the world. Here too, especially on a Saturday night, after weekly wages were paid, could be heard "the clink of glasses in the taverns and porter houses punctuating arguments over 'free trade' [. . .] 'foreigners,' and 'native Americans' (with now and then a fight)."[6]

The Bowery's most renowned attractions were its scores of sideshows and theatricals, especially those staged at the Bowery Theatre. The Bowery, built in 1826 and originally intended for a well-to-do audience, was becoming by the mid-1830s a new kind of popular arena, New York's showcase for melodrama and traveling players like the minstrel T. D. "Jim Crow" Rice—a theater designed specifically for shopkeepers, small masters, and wage earners. The Bowery management, directed by the enterprising

---

5. George G. Foster, *New York in Slices, by an Experienced Carver* (New York, 1850), 121.
6. Haswell, *Reminiscences*, 356–58; Harlow, *Old Bowery Days*, 174–75.

Englishman Thomas Hamblin, departed from customary practices and fixed a uniform rate for tickets in the boxes and the pits, at prices low enough that even mechanics, their pockets replenished at the end of the week, could afford admission. The third tier was reserved for prostitutes, bringing workingmen patrons an amenity long available at respectable theaters. The proscenium proved no barrier to active participation: accounts of Bowery productions—in which, as Whitman put it, the audience was "as much a part of the show as any"—evoke the frenzy of an Elizabethan theater. On Saturday nights, Whitman recalled, the Bowery was "pack'd from ceiling to pit with its audience mainly of alert, well-dress'd full blooded young and middle aged men, the best average of American-born mechanics. . . ." This was "no dainty glove business," he explained, "but electric force and muscle"—or, as another writer put it, a "shrieking, cat-calling, true Bowery crowd." It was not all noise and backslapping: the mechanics' performances were tied to a sense of provincial loyalty and neighborhood identity that bordered on defiance. Bowery audiences reserved their greatest praise for local talent, especially the Manhattan-born Shakespearian actor Edwin Forrest. A visitor to the theater who was unknown to the regulars could expect to be removed forcibly and passed to the rear, his seat yielded to one of the Bowery's own. Fortified by drink, armed with an arsenal of peanut shells and rotten vegetables, the Boweryites felt perfectly at home and interrupted the action on stage at will, to applaud the performers or comment on the unfolding drama.[7]

As mass entertainments, the Bowery productions—on and off stage—became charged, almost ritualistic affairs, expressing some of the deepest solidarities and resentments of their lower-class audiences. Theater rioting was one important extension of the audience's prerogatives to act out; although common as early as the eighteenth century, the practice reached new heights in the late 1820s and 1830s, usually to chastise obdurate, snobbish English actors. The Bowery itself became the target of a theater crowd in 1831, when the management made the mistake of engaging Joshua Anderson, known to the Bowery's denizens as a supercilious champion of the superiority of English letters; after two separate riots, in which the audience chased Anderson from the stage with volleys of spoiled fruit and pennies, the management had to drape the theater in patriotic bunting. The most popular of the new productions, the set-piece minstrel shows,

7. Theodore Shank, Jr., "The Bowery Theatre, 1826–1836" (Ph.D. diss., Stanford University, 1956), details the transformation of the Bowery into a popular theater; see also David Grimstead, *Melodrama Unveiled: American Theater and Culture, 1800–1850* (Chicago, 1968), 52–57; Walt Whitman, *Complete Prose Works* (New York, 1902), III, 184–95; George C. D. Odell, *Annals of the New York Stage* (New York, 1928), III, 254–56, 678–79, IV, 69; Joseph N. Carland, *Records of the New York Stage* (New York, 1867), 55–56; Haswell, *Reminiscences*, 360–63.

caught the public fancy and expressed the tensions within the Bowery culture in very different ways. Invented by city-born entertainers for lower-class urban audiences, the shows took racism for granted; at the simplest levels, the scenes of benign plantation life and of "jump Jim Crow" offered an opportunity for white mechanics to berate and laugh at blacks. But as the form developed, the real object of scorn in these shows was less Jim Crow than the arriviste, would-be aristo—either the white interlocutor or the dandified black, both parodies of unmerited self-satisfied condescension. In the blackface burlesque, the minstrels turned from racist humor to mocking the arrogance, imitativeness, and dim-wittedness of the upper classes in "permissible" ways, as in a kind of carnival; as refined through the 1830s and early 1840s, the figures became stock characters, either the foolish white "straight" or a would-be gentleman colored in cork like Zip Coon or like Zeke (who would go on to win his greatest recognition in Anna Cora Mowatt's hit comedy, *The Fashion*):

> Dere's a coat to take de eyes of all Broadway! Ah Missy, it am de fixin's dat make de natural *born* gemman. A liberry for ever!

As Alexander Saxton points out, it was this carnival that set the minstrel audiences roaring; by keeping the shows' structure loose enough to permit ad-libbing, revisions, and audience participation, the minstrels also kept up-to-date, inserting, where appropriate, allusions to public figures and controversies that set the democratic mass against the elite purveyors of high culture and salvation.[8]

This communal identity also pervaded the premier workingmen's social clubs of the 1830s, the volunteer fire companies. The fire laddie was becoming a new social type in Jacksonian New York. In the early years of the century, the city's volunteer force was staffed by a mixture of prominent merchants—"the city's very best classes," according to one historian of the department—along with independent shopkeepers and master craftsmen. Company meetings were polite and decorous, with the feel of a proper dining club; when they actually fought fires, the bluestocking companies relied on other citizens to join them in the bucket brigade. By the 1830s, the city's physical growth rendered this older system obsolete, and as the force expanded its membership became decidedly more lower class.

8. *Gazette and General Advertiser* [New York], October 14, 17, 18, 1831; *Sun* [New York], July 8, 11, 1834; *Morning Courier*, July 10, 1834; Grimstead, *Melodrama Unveiled*, 65–75; Weinbaum, *Mobs and Demagogues*, 37–38; Anna Cora Mowatt, *The Fashion* (New York, 1845), quoted in Robert C. Toll, *Blacking Up: The Minstrel Show in Nineteenth-Century America* (New York, 1974), 29; Alexander Saxton, "Blackface Minstrelsy and Jacksonian Ideology," *AQ* 27 (1975): 3–28. On popular violence at the theater, see also Peter G. Buckley, "'A Privileged Place': New York Theater Riots, 1817–1849" (Paper delivered to the Organization of American Historians, Philadelphia, April 1982), 4–6, 11–12.

Some of the city's wealthiest merchants and craft employers, including the iron founder James Allaire and the shipbuilders Henry Eckford and William Webb, retained their connections with the firehouses, but they were steadily outnumbered: as Richard Calhoun has shown, the volunteers of the 1820s and 1830s were "increasingly less propertied—and therefore increasingly in violation of the eighteenth-century standard of property owner as property defender." Entire companies of journeymen, with names like "Black Joke," "Live Oak," and "Mechanics'," were composed almost entirely of journeymen shipbuilders, who protected their highly vulnerable places of work as well as their homes. Apart from the shipyard workers, carpenters, men peculiarly suited to saving burning buildings, were the most conspicuous fire-fighting tradesmen.[9]

In addition to protecting the citizenry, the companies offered the men a break from work and a chance to take part in more exciting pursuits. Peter Warner, a veteran fire fighter, recalled that mechanics "would throw down their tools, leaving them exposed where they fell," and sacrifice as much as a full day's wages in order to fight a fire. Each company was also a fraternal order, with its own mottoes, insignias, and freshly minted traditions. Station houses eventually became arenas for pugilism, dogfighting, and other blood sports. On more formal occasions, a company might hold one of the famous firemen's chowder balls or stage a parade. On the Fourth of July and on Washington's Birthday, the entire force marched by company, trimmed out with all of the firehouse paraphernalia the laddies could carry. Rivalries between the different companies—discreetly labeled "emulation"—reinforced the firemen's sense of loyalty and camaraderie and won the affection of the surrounding neighborhood; according to Zophar Mills, a turpentine maker and one of the most renowned of the firemen, it was this "pride and ambition" of each company to be the first

9. Augustine F. Costello, *Our Firemen: A History of the New York Fire Department* (New York, 1887), 145, 609–10, 619–21, 623–24; Minutes, Oceanus Fire Company No. 11, 1780–1819, N-YHS MSS, November 9, 1784, November 8, 1787, November 2, 1789, and passim; Richard B. Calhoun, "From Community to Metropolis: Fire Protection in New York City, 1790–1875" (Ph.D. diss., Columbia University, 1973), 147–48. Calhoun contends that the force was largely "working class" from the early nineteenth century through 1860; he draws that conclusion by describing all masters and craft workers as "working class." Given (as Calhoun discusses) that men who could not prove they were independent were formally excluded from the force before 1820, and given Calhoun's figures on property ownership among firemen, it is clear that the balance of the membership shifted from masters to journeymen between 1820 and 1850. As for the later occupational breakdowns, Calhoun presents figures drawn from samples of the fire-department register in 1820, 1830, 1840, 1850, and 1860. In 1830, 40.4 percent of the masters and craft workers identified ($N = 109$) were either in the shipbuilding or house construction trades; ten years later (with $N = 90$), 28.9 percent of the masters and craft workers were from these trades. Calhoun, "Community to Metropolis," 354–55.

to arrive at a fire and the first to quench the flames that drove the men on. Every company had its own venerable hero, such as the butcher Moses Humphreys of the Lady Washington Engine, a man respected for his fists as well as his ability to fight fires. The most active irregular partisans were young boys, called "runners" or "volunteers," who frequented the houses, ran odd jobs, and accompanied their heroes to the fires to help them extinguish the flames. Older folks sang the individual laddies' praises in songs and poems. Occasional scuffles marred the proceedings, as "emulation" turned into ruder battles to win the rights to a fire; on one occasion, in 1835, a scuffle between a company on duty and some Irish gas workers led to a nasty brawl. Through it all, a new form of popular culture and lore took shape, one distinct from "the Trade" and the unions, one with its own fiercely masculine rituals and with its own cherished neighborhood emblems—the fire hose, the company crest, the fire chief's trumpet.[10]

Not surprisingly, the political parties, always on the lookout for ways to increase their votes, tried to tap these resources of popular organization. The politicization of the companies began in part as an elite reaction to the companies' lower-class roughhousing, when city fathers suggested, to no avail, that the department be reorganized into a more sedate, disciplined professional force. The firemen, for their part, were largely successful in securing their control over the companies—by the mid-1830s, they had won the right to elect their own chief and assistant engineers—but controversies still pitted them against the Common Council. In the most famous dispute, in 1835, the municipal board of fire and water commissioners (dominated by Democrats) voted to remove James Gulick (a Whig) as head of the department, prompting Gulick and his men, upon hearing the news, to leave the scene of a terrible blaze at one of the public markets. The more astute of the city's politicians tried to capitalize on the bickering by defending the companies and their leaders, hoping to convert the firemen's popularity into votes. Firemen-heroes like Gulick (chosen by the Whigs shortly after his resignation) adorned the lower end of electoral tickets as an extra inducement to voters. By the middle of the decade, fire-department politicking led genteel public figures to despair for the city's safety; Philip Hone thought the firemen "so courted for political

10. Warner, quoted in Costello, *Our Firemen*, 452; Mills, quoted in George Sheldon, *The Story of the Volunteer Fire Department of the City of New York* (New York, 1882), 20. On fire department life and rowdiness, see Costello, *Our Firemen*, 145–60 and passim; Abram C. Dayton, *Last Days of Knickerbocker Life in New York* (New York, 1877), 214–16; Lowell Limpus, *History of the New York Fire Department* (New York, 1940), 161–65; Stephen F. Ginsberg, "The History of Fire Protection in New York City, 1800–1842" (Ph.D. diss., New York University, 1968), 294–314; Calhoun, "Community to Metropolis," 316–42. For charges and countercharges about firemen's violence, see *Evening Post*, January 6, 1835, August 31, 1835.

objects that they appear to consider themselves above the law." It would not be long before service as a fireman would be an apprenticeship for a career in the party clubhouse.[11]

The legendary fire-company battles shaded into the even less respectable continuing gang rivalries of the era. In the 1830s, the gangs, once considered "normal," seemed to have gotten out of hand, to the extent that anxious journalists and officials bewailed the onset of an American "reign of terror." They exaggerated; nevertheless, the gangs of the 1830s at least appeared better organized and more prone to use physical violence than ever before. The most famous of them, the butchers' Chichester Gang, seems to have been the first to stick together over a period of years, with a semblance of regular organization of adult leaders and younger troops. With their own sense of personal pride and their own crude uniforms and weapons, the gangs turned the fire companies' pride and mastery of turf into rougher—and, to city officials, even more threatening—sport.[12]

For the most part, the gangs were concerned with private vendettas and the protection of street honor. The press could only see their outbursts as arising from "a mere spirit of insubordination and love of mischief," but the gang members' appearances in court bespoke more serious intents—vindicating a slight, avenging a betrayal, attacking an unscrupulous madam. In time, the gangs also found their own public duties. Some served as informal neighborhood constabularies: members stood about on street corners with a studied, watchful glower, making sure, as one New Yorker recalled, that anyone who was "exotic or unfamiliar" would not cause trouble or linger too long. In the Bowery gambling halls and licensed groceries, the gangs also made political connections with local party saloonkeepers. In a tight race, the "boys" might be summoned to serve as "sluggers," to vote as often as they could; when the results of a particular election district were in doubt, the publicans sent the gangs down to take sterner measures, stealing ballot boxes or destroying polling booths.[13]

To say the least, a Saturday night on the Bowery or a race with the fire companies or gangs had little in common with a meeting of the GTU. In

11. Philip Hone Diary, May 6, 1836, quoted in Stephen F. Ginsberg, "Above the Law: Volunteer Firemen in New York City, 1836–1837," NYH 50 (1969): 165–66; Calhoun, "Community to Metropolis," 197–215.

12. Weinbaum, Mobs and Demagogues, 55–75, 151, 155; Commercial Advertiser, October 26, December 28, 1836, January 6, 1837.

13. Commercial Advertiser, October 1, 1834; Mushkat, Tammany, 358; Weinbaum, Mobs and Demagogues, 5–10, 151. More anecdotal accounts of the gangs include Harlow, Old Bowery Days, 167–88, 196–97, and Herbert Asbury, The Gangs of New York: An Informal Social History (New York, 1927), 5–96. For a sampling of court cases stemming from gang brawls, see People v. Morris Ragan, March 17, 1836, People v. Francis Hanratty et al., April 8, 1836, People v. John Chichester, April 8, 1836, People v. Peter Meredith, June 10, 1836, People v. James McCorwin, June 10, 1836, People v. James Doyle, July 15, 1837, Court of General Sessions, MARC.

the rough-and-tumble world of the streets, bellicose, at times brutal notions of rights and duties arose alongside the instrumental radicalism of the unions—notions of insular independence, distrust of outsiders, and freedom from interference that could be directed as easily against a foreign actor or a rival company as against employers and capitalists. It would appear to deserve being called a "traditional" view of the world, since it celebrated old customs (above all those which involved prodigious physical prowess) and distinguished primarily between plebeian white "insiders" and everyone else. But it was also a very new culture, one that emerged only as the social distance between New York's rich and poor widened—one that matured in such new institutions as the lower-class fire companies and became a cause for concern to city officials only as elite perceptions of the lower orders began to darken into fears of the "dangerous classes."[14] As it developed, this culture acquired a new ideological significance as well, a sort of republicanism of the streets that connected the workingmen's pride, resentments, and simple pleasures to the language of republican politics. The fire companies were among the first to suggest the connections, in their Fourth of July parades and in their patriotic firehouse icons. The Jacksonians went further, by turning popular distaste of cultural proscription into a political creed of opposition to Whiggish moral reform, in their bids to add the votes of the Bowery to their disparate coalition. In all of these institutions and appeals, we can detect the egalitarian robustness that Whitman knew intimately, a truculent anti-authoritarianism that a New England reformer could describe only—and archly—as "Boweriness."[15] But the republic of the Bowery had its uglier features as well.

Popular anti-abolitionism, and in particular the anti-abolitionist mobs, exposed the depths of the journeymen's and small masters' cultural fears outside of more sharply defined class conflicts. Antislavery sentiment was, of course, far from negligible in the New York trades; by the mid-1830s, artisans and craft workers, including union radicals like John Commerford, were the largest group of signatories of New York abolitionist petitions to Congress.[16] Most craft workers and white laborers, however,

14. Weinbaum, *Mobs and Demagogues*, passim, argues persuasively that the press, especially the Whig press, lost no opportunity in exaggerating the level and extent of popular violence in the 1830s.

15. Thomas Wentworth Higginson, *Cheerful Yesterdays* (Boston, 1898), 230, quoted in Larzer Ziff, *Literary Democracy: The Declaration of Cultural Independence in the United States* (Harmondsworth, 1982), 246. Higginson was describing Whitman as he remembered the poet in the 1850s.

16. *Union*, May 23, 28, June 7, 22, 1836; John B. Jentz, "The Anti–Slavery Constituency in Jacksonian New York City," *Civil War History* 27 (1981): 101–22. Radicals and Painites were not, however, the only—or even the most important—abolitionist constitutency in the trades. Consistent support also came from evangelical master artisans like Joseph Brewster, Joseph Hoxie, and Charles Starr—all of whom signed at least one abolitionist petition. See Jentz, "Artisans, Evangelicals, and the City," 162–233.

retained a deep distrust of the small, unskilled black community as a class of supposedly abject dependents. Several factors exacerbated the situation. Sensitivity to racial issues increased as New York became the national center of organized abolitionism. Tammany Hall, in accordance with national party policy, portrayed abolitionist efforts as an attempt to destroy the Constitution and states' rights; whether slavery was an evil or not, the Democrats declared in 1835, was a local question to be resolved by "the States in which it is tolerated," not by the actions of mostly Whig abolitionist outsiders. Outright racism, a fact of lower-class life even in good times, intensified as white craft workers and laborers poured into New York to find blacks well entrenched in some key sectors of the unskilled work force, especially along the waterfront. That the leadership of the abolitionist societies was composed primarily of wealthy evangelical reformers like Lewis and Arthur Tappan only reinforced popular resentment.[17]

Almost inevitably, racial tensions mounted along with the inflation of the mid-1830s, to the point where lurid rumors circulated in the poorer wards, hinting that local blacks, with the help of their abolitionist friends. planned to take over white neighborhoods and "mullatoize" them. Periodically, interracial and anti-abolitionist violence broke out: the worst incident, in early July 1834, saw crowds storm abolitionist meeting halls, sack Arthur Tappan's store and Lewis Tappan's house, and pillage black homes and churches over an eight-day period. The labor press swiftly denounced the rampage as a disgrace; George Henry Evans charged that the riots had been led by southerners and "the dregs of society." But as the rioting subsided and the arrestees were led away, it became clear that the crowd had consisted largely of small master artisans, tradesmen, and journeymen—including at least one union member, arrested on the scene.[18]

A closer look at the 1834 riot, the most destructive disturbance of all in what later generations would call New York's "year of the riots," shows just how multifarious the crowd's concerns were—how revived traditions of political mobbing blended with racism, dislike for entrepreneurial reformers, and repugnance for foreign "aristocrats," in a belligerent form of popular republicanism. In general, the participants followed the rules of classic "preindustrial" urban mobs by choosing their targets with care, at-

17. *Man*, August 1, 1834; Mushkat, *Tammany*, 163; Linda K. Kerber, "Abolitionists and Amalgamators: The New York City Race Riots of 1834," *N-YHSQ* 48 (1967): 34.

18. Kerber, "Abolitionists and Amalgamators," 28–39; *Man*, July 12, 1834; Leonard L. Richards, *"Gentlemen of Property and Standing": Anti-Abolition Mobs in Jacksonian America* (New York, 1970), 115–22, 152, 174–75. According to Richards, 45 percent of those arrested were artisans, "tradesmen," or their sons. Among those arrested was one William Gilbert; the same name appears on the membership list in 1834 for the Union Society of Journeymen Carpenters, NYPL MSS.

tacking property but not persons, and by taking advantage of every symbolic opportunity. At the height of the riot on the evening of July 9, the crowds shifted between three carefully selected sites in a steady progression of popular wrath. The violence began at Lewis Tappan's house, where more than one hundred men smashed through windows and doors, piled art work and fine furniture in the streets, and burned as much as they could. One rioter discovered a portrait of Washington, and at the insistence of his friends—"For God's sake, don't burn Washington," one bellowed—he preserved it. The crowds left the scene in triumph, bearing the painting as its standard. At about the same time, a crowd estimated at between two and three thousand gathered at the Chatham Street Chapel—Charles Finney's church—where an abolitionist meeting was scheduled to assemble. The abolitionists, forewarned, never arrived, but the crowd broke into the chapel anyway, where it vowed to disrupt any future abolitionist meetings. The Tappan rioters and a segment of the Chatham Street crowd then converged on the Bowery Theatre, where yet another disturbance was under way, to protest the hiring of an Englishman, George Farren. Farren, it seems had little respect for his American audience, and when a story circulated that he had punched a local butcher, insulted the American flag, "cursed the Yankees, and called them jackasses, and said he would gull them whenever he could," republican tempers flared. Four thousand persons mobbed the Bowery, while between five hundred and a thousand others broke into the theater and drove the actors from the stage. They were quelled only when the manager, Hamblin, rushed in from the wings to apologize, waving an American flag in each hand and summoning an American singer to perform Zip Coon.[19]

A lot was at stake for the rioters; taken together, their actions proclaimed a political culture of the streets, distinct from that of the unions. A trace of anticapitalist sentiment was evident: Lewis Tappan, after all, was a former editor of the New York *Journal of Commerce*, the city's most vociferous journalistic foe of trade unionism—a man who mingled with the Simon Squeezems and who presumed to preach evangelical morality to the Peter Planes. But this crowd fought Lewis Tappan on a very different front, and with very different weapons, from those chosen by the GTU. In the streets, there was no sign of permanent organization or political pressure: direct, purposeful violence, by the people "out-of-doors," remained the people's weapon. A multitude of associations spurred the rioters on: racism went hand in hand with hatred of antirepublican British snobs; an attack on Tappan and the evangelical Chatham Street Chapel was closely linked with expressions of patriotism, plebeian pride, and

19. Richards, "*Gentlemen of Property and Standing*," 118; *Courier and Enquirer*, July 9, 10, 1834; *Sun*, July 8, 9, 10, 11, 12, 1834; *Evening Star*, July 10, 1834; *Man*, July 11, 1834; Headley, *Great Riots*, 84–87; Harlow, *Old Bowery Days*, 291.

white supremacy on the stage of the recaptured Bowery Theatre. In their own way, the crowds, like the firemen, were protecting their neighborhoods—and, like the gang members, their turf—from those they deemed external threats, while they vindicated the American workingman's honor from the insults and abuse of English aristocrats and meddlesome, evangelical entrepreneurial reformers.[20]

Related themes appeared, in a very different way, in the nativist turbulence of the 1830s. Nativism was not nearly as virulent in Jacksonian New York as racism and anti-abolitionism, nor was it as widespread and pronounced among workers as it would be in the 1840s. Although rural, mostly Irish Catholics became a larger component of the immigrant population after 1830 and although untrained hands were increasingly numerous at the bottom of the most debased crafts, most of the immigrants remained consigned to manual laboring jobs. Because so many immigrants in the trades were still trained artisans, the nativist equation of immigrant invasion with the degradation of the crafts was more difficult to make than it would be later. In the workshops, the rudiments of a rough hierarchy of privileged native workers (including foremen) and immigrant hands emerged, but only gradually; journeymen might play upon national stereotypes, but their jesting could affirm that native artisans and newcomers, Protestant and Catholic, still managed to find room for mutual respect. The anonymous English cabinetmaker who remembered his shop mates' drinking rituals also related scenes he took to be characteristic of the city's ethnically mixed shops:

> On my first entrance, the foreman, an American, called out to the representative of the emerald isle, "Look here, Paddy; here's another John Bull come over to be civilized." John Bull, however, can afford to be laughed at. After we became acquainted we went on very pleasantly together; the superior skill of the Germans and Frenchmen was of the highest service to me, who had much to learn, never having worked outside of a provincial town in England.

This sense of harmony (at least on the job) carried over to the union; the more violent nativism usually associated with the Jacksonian period would arise with full force only after the panic of 1837.[21]

Nevertheless, ethnic tensions were far more intense in the mid-1830s than earlier. In 1837, one immigrant newspaper suggested that at least some native workers had grown wary of the Irish newcomers, leaving the immigrants in a difficult position: "If they go to work at the old price the journeymen at once cry out, 'those d——d Irishmen are always ratting'

---

20. See Richards, "Gentlemen of Property and Standing," 65-71. See also Davis, "Themes of Counter-Subversion." Many of the conspiracy themes Davis discusses were at work in the riot.

21. "Workingman's Recollections," 102.

and if they 'strike' the employers at once exclaim 'those d——d Irishmen are always uprorious [sic].' So that between them all, poor Pat is treated like a football in a ring—every body gives him a kick." Outside the shops, ethnic riots erupted from time to time, primarily between gangs of Protestants (natives and immigrants) and Irish Catholics. In March 1835, a crowd of Irishmen broke up a meeting of the middle-class nativist New York Protestant Association; three months later, crowds of up to five hundred Irish and natives battled for three days in and around the Five Points.[22] More important, amid the confused party politics of the mid-1830s, nativism became a potential political force, fusing elite Protestant distaste for party politics and freshly arrived papists, Whig political ambitions, and craft workers' republican fears of ecclesiastical despotism and economic dependence.

The political nativist movement began in May 1835, in the wake of the Irish attack on the NYPA. A faction of the Whigs, in search of a popular issue and well aware that Tammany had a lock on the Irish and German Catholic vote, tried to offset their disadvantage by campaigning on a frankly xenophobic platform that called for stiffening the naturalization laws and putting new restrictions on immigrant office holding. Joined by nativist Jacksonians, including the artist-inventor Samuel F. B. Morse, the group dubbed itself the Native American Democratic Association; with dispatch it organized ward committees, established its own newspaper, the *Spirit of '76*, and won the endorsement of several city editors. Declaring that the effect of foreign influence and intrigue, unless checked, would "prove the overthrow of this Republic," the association took to the hustings, the nation's first explicitly nativist political party.[23]

The nativist association can hardly be described as an artisan or craft movement, let alone a working-class movement; its leaders—like those of the major parties—did their utmost to yoke together merchants, professionals, petty retailers, master craftsmen, and wage earners, "all classes of citizens," in Morse's words, against the alleged monarchical papist threat. The association did, however, pin its electoral hopes on a mobilization of native small masters and journeymen—a reassembly of the mechanics' interest in politics, but now under the guidance of nativist politicians. The *Spirit of '76*, edited by the idealistic morocco case maker and ex-Jacksonian Uriah C.

22. *European* [New York], April 8, 1837, quoted in Ernst, *Immigrant Life*, 101–2; *Commercial Advertiser*, March 18, June 22, 23, 24, 1835; Leo Hershkowitz, "The Native American Democratic Association in New York City, 1835–1836," *N-YHSQ* 46 (1962): 49–50; Louis Dow Scisco, *Political Nativism in New York State* (New York, 1901), 22–23. On ethnic rioting, see also Weinbaum, *Mobs and Demagogues*, 66.

23. Scisco, *Political Nativism*, 24–25; Leo Hershkowitz, "New York City, 1834–1840: A Study in Local Politics" (Ph.D. diss., New York University, 1960), 113–21; *Spirit of '76* [New York], June 20, 23, 24, 25, 30, July 1, 2, 3, 7, 1835. The quotation appears in the issue of July 11, 1835.

Watson, wrapped the movement in the most venerated symbols of the Republic and the trades, and linked the nativist cause to that of the producing classes. The main lines of the argument raised long-recessive republican fears: the immigrants, above all the Catholics, supposedly threatened republican institutions, their political souls having been captured by despotic powers intent on enslaving the entire world. Once in America, these trammeled unskilled men fell under the sway of the new politicians, whose "base and selfish spirit of party" had led them to denigrate republican principles and to clear the path for immigrant domination. Politics shaded easily into economics, as the artisan nativists, led by *Spirit of '76*, insisted that all of the mechanics' troubles sprang from immigrant (and especially papist) perfidy. State prison labor, they argued, was a sinister, nineteenth-century version of the Popish plot, hatched with the aid of Democratic politicians in order to enrich immigrant contractors at the expense of true Americans. Likewise, the nativists blamed immigration for the bastardization of craft. "The land is becoming overrun with swarms of foreign artisans," the *Spirit of '76* declared, "who are more destructive to native American industry than the locusts and lice were to the Egyptian fields." The nation's wealthy nonproducers, far from perturbed by this threat, made fortunes off the new arrivals: "They employ the European-spawned mendicant at the half price you cannot afford; they build the warehouses and the marble palaces, from the starved labor of the tools of Jesuit priests; they roll along the streets on the carriages trimmed with the trappings of despotic countries." Such rhetoric did not, to be sure, represent the views of all the city's nativists, least of all the ex-Whig leaders who showed no willingness to turn the movement into an all-out assault on the nonproducers. But the nativists' approach to the trades—as ever, "the bone and sinew of the body politic"—did appeal to at least some journeymen, including one "Native American" who tried to persuade the readers of the *Union* that nativism and the fight for journeymen's rights were inextricably linked. Even John Commerford, a stalwart antinativist, had to admit that such an argument had considerable logic "in its particulars."[24]

24. Samuel F. B. Morse, *Foreign Conspiracy against the Citizens of the United States* (1835; reprint, New York, 1844), xii; *Spirit of '76*, April 23, May 5, 21, 28, June 10, 12, 13, August 21, 26, September 14, 1835; *Union*, May 15, 1836. A search in the 1836 city directory and tax list for the occupations of the nativist ward leaders and delegates (their names drawn from the *Spirit of '76*), revealed the following breakdown (in percentages):

Merchants and professionals	26.9
Shopkeepers, retailers, and petty professionals	26.9
Master craftsmen and manufacturers	15.7
Small masters	7.4
Journeymen	17.6
Laborers and unskilled	5.5
TOTAL (N = 108)	100.0

The movement fell apart, the victim of its internal divisions, before it could test its strategy fully. Nativist Whigs, determined to use the association as a counter to the Jacksonians, grew impatient with the egalitarian, sometimes radical-sounding pronouncements of the *Spirit of '76*, while Watson, unwilling to launch a foursquare attack on the Jacksonians and Loco Focos, tempered his nativism. In September, 1835, the Whig nativists founded their own newspaper, and within a month, the *Spirit of '76* turned its back on the Whigs by giving early support to the Van Buren-Johnson ticket in the next year's presidential election. In the November races for Congress and state assembly, the erstwhile cross-party nativist coalition had become a virtual stand-in for the Whig party, and collected more than 40 percent of the vote; by the spring of 1836, however, local Whigs, wary that they were being fully displaced by the NADA, had regrouped and decided to mount a more determined campaign on their own in the April mayoral election. The NADA's problems were compounded when, after a long, fruitless search for a mayoral nominee, it decided to run Morse—a self-described man of "democratic principles of the *Jeffersonian school*, as they stand opposed to aristocracy in all its shapes, to ruinous monopolies, to a union of church and state." But for its nativist twist, this was Loco Focoism pure and simple, hardly a set of doctrines to please Whig nativist voters. Despite last-minute attempts to deny his Democratic leanings, Morse won less than 6 percent of the mayoral vote; thereafter, nativist ideologues (reorganized as the Democratic American Association) contributed to local Whig victories but had virtually no independent power.[25] Theirs, however, would not be the last movement of its kind.

It would be convenient to see each of these manifestations, from the insular street republicanism of the Bowery Theatre to the first stirrings of an organized craft nativism, as wholly distinct and separate from the union movement. To a degree, they were. The GTU leadership and its press opposed anti-abolitionism as strongly as they counseled against dissipation. Nativism, according to the *Union*, was at bottom a cruel attempt by politicians and capitalists to "glut their vindictiveness against the common people, by arraying the native-born laborer against his fellow being."[26] The fire companies and gangs made their primary alliances with the political parties, contrary to the very spirit of the unions. The most salient cultural-political movements of the 1830s would seem, from the scrappy evidence that survives, to have drawn their vital support from trades relatively unaffected by metropolitan industrialization. The fire companies, for example, included disproportionately large numbers of shipbuilders but relatively few tailors and shoemakers. Journeymen and apprentice butchers

---

25. *Spirit of '76*, August 26, September 2, October 7, 1835; Scisco, *Political Nativism*, 26; Hershkowitz, "New York City," 167.
26. *Union*, May 30, 1836. See also *Union*, June 1, 1836; *Man*, July 1, 1835.

were the most notorious gang members. The nativists' secondary leadership included a fair number of printers and building tradesmen, but only a minority were men in those sweated trades where the immigrant presence was strong; none of their ward-association officers had any recorded connection with the GTU.[27] At the extremes, the typical citizen of the Bowery republic experienced the 1830s quite differently from the shoemakers, tailors, cabinetmakers, and others in the unions; in this sense, the republic of the streets encompassed those sectors of the emerging working class least open to radical union appeals. But it is important not to draw this distinction too severely. Union men who drank on the job and met in taverns most certainly knew the delights of the Bowery. If the GTU men were unlikely to be gang members, at least some of them were firemen; John Commerford himself was close enough to the world of the companies to alert readers of the *Union* to parades and festivities in which local firemen would "play the *soger*."[28] The union member picked up during the anti-abolitionist rioting had almost certainly been assisted by others who eluded the police. Nativism made sense to at least some native journeymen in the most debased crafts.

Rather than construct two opposing mutually exclusive ideal types—pleasure-seeking, benighted "traditionalists," abstemious enlightened "rebels"—it is more useful to consider the republicanism of the Bowery and the republicanism of the unions as different but at times overlapping expressions of the journeymen's fears and aspirations—one focused on the economic and political sources of inequality and exploitation, the other stressing cultural autonomy and manly independence. One of the unionists' great achievements was to develop their discussions of class conflict, solidify their union institutions, and reach out beyond the most radical journeymen, gathering thousands of workers in the most exploited trades to the cause. But they never managed the impossible, to mold all of their followers into sober, tolerant, eternally dedicated trade unionists. As the journeymen's revolt reached its greatest crisis in 1836, so the union men's

27. The identified nativist masters and small masters included three carpenters, two butchers, two jewelers, two printers, two tailors, and one of each of the following trades: baker, builder, coach painter, cooper, electrician, harness maker, hatter, pump maker, saddler, sash maker, ship joiner, shoemaker, stonecutter, and trunkmaker. The journeymen came from both highly skilled and from some of the worst sweated trades; they included four carpenters, two printers, two shoemakers, two tailors, and one of each of the following: chair maker, engraver, jeweler, morocco-case maker, painter, rigger, ship carpenter, ship joiner, and smith. Obviously, the numbers here are too small to allow any firm generalization; they do suggest, however, that to the extent that the nativists recruited among the trades, they drew largely on masters in trades with proportionately few immigrants and on two sorts of journeymen—those in "traditional" trades with few immigrants, and a smaller proportion from the most debased crafts.

28. *Union*, June 1, 1836.

ability to narrow the cultural divide and hold the movement together would face its sternest test.

The Masters: Toward an Ideology of Free Labor

The ideology and activities of New York's leading craft employers in the 1830s had a familiar air, reminiscent of the old mechanics' interest and of subsequent efforts to reform the journeymen. But with the tumults that accompanied the rise of the GTU, the masters' views on wage labor and the harmony of interests in the trades also sharpened their entrepreneurial republicanism in contrast to the unionists' class consciousness. With the impact (albeit limited) of evangelicalism and the temperance movement, these differences acquired an added cultural dimension. Although they did not yet use the phrase, New York's craft employers and their allies began to proclaim what later historians would call an ideology of free labor.[29]

Indicative of the masters' work were the programs of the General Society of Mechanics and Tradesmen. Now in its fifth decade, the society had become one of the city's most respected civic institutions. Having weathered the depression of 1829, the group expanded its educational efforts to include several lecture series on science, philosophy, economics, and the fine arts, and resolved to impart, by its examples and its teachings, the supreme importance of frugality and industriousness—the lesson, as one latter-day Franklin put it, that an ounce of prevention is worth a pound of cure. To this end, the society offered instruction on the history of medieval Spain, warnings on the danger of running with the fire companies, and sermons by the veteran Presbyterian missionary Gardiner Spring on the importance of keeping regular habits.[30]

While the society's useful information tended to be predictable exercises in moral temperance, the American Institute made more daring and more telling forays into political economy. Having failed to prevent the defeat of the American System at the polls, the Institute disseminated a flood of papers on business, finance, and manufacturing. It was in the Institute's journal that the young Henry Carey, the future economist-in-residence of the Republican party, published his collection of "Maxims of Political Economy," ranging from Hamilton's arguments for public finance to Say's observation that "a productive establishment, on a large scale, is sure to animate the industry of a whole neighborhood." More original studies included statistical inquiries on wage rates among early industrial

29. See Eric Foner, *Free Soil, Free Labor, Free Men: The Ideology of the Republican Party before the Civil War* (New York, 1970), 11–39.

30. Earle and Congdon, *Annals*, 81–100; GSMT Minute Book, January 5, 1833, May 7, 1834, January 22, 1837.

wage earners in England, France, and the United States (with the usual pro-American results) and reports on the latest advances in all fields of manufacturing. The Institute also continued its fairs, making them more elaborate each year. By 1835, the exposition was a major tourist attraction, cited in city guidebooks and attended by tens of thousands of visitors. Five years later, Cyrus Mason, flushed with pride at the rows of new machines and blue-ribbon products, declared the affair "the appropriate festival for the working men of this country."[31]

A third venue of activity was the Mechanics' Institute. Founded in 1831 by a group of prominent craft employers (including some members of the General Society, some former Working Men, and some Jacksonians), and joined by a small number of professionals, the Mechanics' Institute steered clear of political commitments and pledged itself primarily to educational work: without education in science, ethics, and economics, a spokesman declared, the "laboring classes of the community . . . will be doomed to an intellectual and political slavery by the better educated classes." By 1836, it had attracted over five hundred members and launched its own annual fair, extensive lecture series, a journal, and a mechanics' institution with rooms in the basement of City Hall. Rejecting the Whiggery of the American Institute, the Mechanics' Institute became particularly favored by liberal Democratic entrepreneurs and employers, led by George Bruce and David Bruce, Jr.; the body defined its purposes and constituency so broadly that in 1833 it selected the bookbinder and GTU officer James McBeath as one of the chairmen of its board of managers; by the mid-1830s, the deist small masters Edward Webb and John Windt were also active members. Throughout, however, the group was something of an American equivalent of the London Mechanics' Institute of the 1830s, dominated by manufacturers and masters, careful to avoid any hint of radicalism or any deviation from the ethic of self-improvement and study. There was no explicit battle, as there had been in London, over the Institute's views on the political economy of labor. From the start, on this question, entrepreneurial assumptions prevailed.[32]

31. *Journal of the American Institute* 1 (1836): 526-31; 2 (1837): 554, 579-86; 3 (1838): 113-17; T. B. Wakeman, *An Introductory Lecture Delivered for the American Institute of the City of New-York* (New York, 1835); Thomas McElrath, "Sketch of the Rise and Progress of the American Institute," *Transactions of the American Institute* (1860): 86-87; *New York As It Is, in 1835* (New York, 1835), 84; Cyrus P. Mason, *The Oration on the Thirteenth Anniversary of the American Institute at the Broadway Tabernacle* (New York, 1840), 5

32. Gulian C. Verplanck, *A Lecture . . . before the Mechanics' Institute of the City of New York* (New York, 1833), 6 and passim; Mechanics' Institute of the City of New York, *First Report of the Board of Managers* (New York, 1831), 3-7; *Mechanics' Magazine* [New York], 1 (1833): 285; 3 (1834): 180-82; 6 (1835): 250-64. On McBeath, see Mechanics' Institute, *Second Report*; Commons, *Documentary His-*

Both the General Society's lectures and the more ambitious work of the institutes revealed that the values of "the Trade" were as alive among New York's employers as among the union men, though in very different ways. Their repetitions of the old rhetoric of craft pride—"Of all the pursuits of life," declared a Mechanics' Institute member in 1833, "none more surely offers comfort and respect than that of a mechanic"—were neither coincidental nor antiquarian. In the 1830s, as before, the masters insisted that all who engaged in artisan and manufacturing work, employers and wage earners, deserved honorable reputations and shared common interests. These interests, moreover, remained inseparable from the nation's republican ideals, the main bulwark against the kinds of inequalities that had arisen in industrializing Britain. Contrary to those who attacked industrial improvement, the employers claimed that the spirit of the Republic nourished harmonious growth: "the effects of a republican form of government," as one writer for the American Institute's *Journal* put it, gave the United States "a spirit of commercial enterprise and manufacturing . . . unequalled in any other country," a spirit which united all. Any compari-

---

tory, V, 214ff. Of the 59 institute officers and directors elected in 1836 (*Mechanics' Magazine* 7 (1836): 267), all but 5 could be identified; all were either master craftsmen, small masters, or professionals. Their occupations broke down as follows:

1. *Professionals*		(5)
chemist	(3)	
other	(2)	
2. *Masters and small masters*		(49)
machinist	(5)	
plumber	(3)	
stonecutter	(3)	
builder	(2)	
carpenter	(2)	
cord manufacturer	(2)	
hatter	(2)	
pencil case maker	(2)	
printer	(2)	
shoe manufacturer	(2)	
others	(24)	
TOTAL	54	

Nine of the 54 (16.7 percent) had been active in the Working Men's party, 7 as Owenites, 2 as Cookites. A former union carpenter, Robert M. Lang was among the officers; see Minutes, New York Union Society of Journeymen Carpenters, April 8, 1833. Among the notable manufacturers on the list, apart from Bruce, were Richard M. Hoe (machinist) and Henry O. Kearsing (piano maker). On Bruce, see Hugins, *Jacksonian Democracy*, 99. On the London Mechanics' Institute, see Thompson, *Making of the English Working Class*, 743–45. The New York *Mechanics' Magazine* regularly featured articles first published by its London counterpart, as well as excerpts from the work of English promoters of manufacturing, including Charles Babbage and Andrew Ure. See, e.g., *Mechanics' Magazine* 1 (1833): 178; 6 (1835): 220–22; 9 (1837): 2–11, 100–108.

son with unrepublican Europe bore out the difference: the self-evident disparity in the standards of living of workingmen in the New and Old worlds, one article quoted by the Mechanics' Institute journal claimed, should shame into silence all those who charged that America's employers were oppressors. Like the master craftsmen in earlier artisan republican speeches, the employers envisioned an inevitable American economic expansion without tears.[33]

A mounting paradox did emanate from this sanguine entrepreneurialism, for while the employers looked forward to innovation, they continued to describe themselves and others in increasingly old-fashioned terms. The American mechanic so frequently mentioned in their remarks usually entered as the practical tinkerer, the small producer with an irresistible instinct for innovation and self-improvement. The enduring image of the mechanic as yeoman, blessed, as the American Institute spokesman Caleb Cushing observed, with "the prosperity and glory of a Republic," admitted of no acquaintance with permanent wage earners or sweated outworkers. Industrialization, seen as an accretion of piecemeal improvements by independent men, augured no social dislocations, no disruption of the fraternal links between masters and men. The transformation of the wage relation went unnoticed. Economic change signified only the growth of national wealth, in ways that would preserve—indeed, enhance—what Cushing called the necessary "domestic and social ties, the attachment of individual to individual."[34]

To buttress these happy conclusions, the entrepreneurs, starting in the wake of the Working Men's challenge, built a modified Smithian political economy to contradict the gloomier assessments of artisan radicals and, in time, the city's unionists. They began with a polemic against all "agriculturalists" and "agrarians," from the eighteenth-century French physiocrats to the American Old Republicans. The *économistes'* notion that cultivators of the soil were more productive than all others was most offensive: all labor, the masters argued, adds value to the materials to which it is applied. Farm labor, if anything, was less valuable than mechanical labor, Tristam Burges told the American Institute in 1830, since agricultural abundance came as much from the fertility of the soil as from the cultivator's work. The doctrine of rural moral supremacy, which portrayed the farmer as the most useful of all citizens, was to the masters a mischievous deception, one that maligned all mechanics and threatened to keep the United States permanently dependent on Britain for manufactured neces-

33. *Journal of the American Institute* 1 (1836): 529; *Mechanics' Magazine* 1 (1833): 166; 7 (1836): 64.
34. Caleb Cushing, *An Address Delivered before the American Institute* (New York, 1836), 10–11.

sities. The "true doctrine" of Adam Smith owed nothing to such so-called political economy.[35]

If the physiocrats were, in the employers' eyes, deluded, then radical theorists, especially the more radical Ricardians, were dangerous. The prices of all commodities including labor, the masters insisted, were not governed by an "engrossing or monopolizing spirit" on the part of landlords or employers but by the limits of supply and demand; in Malthusian terms, as population rose and as increasingly infertile land was ploughed, costs and prices increased. To blame these effects on the possessors of wealth was simply to recast the physiocratic prejudices and redraw the artificial and pernicious line between productive and unproductive men—thereby, Burges observed, exciting "hostile feelings among men, all equally engaged in one great community and brotherhood of labor for mutual benefit." Man-made inequalities, other spokesmen insisted, arose not from the privileges of the few, and certainly could not be ended by those starry-eyed idealists who assumed that "the love of individual property can be got rid of by a very short process of reasoning." The only true oppressors were those "warriors" who, like the agrarian radicals and trade unionists, would plunder their neighbors' wealth. In the peaceful operations of the market and the search for individual profit, there was no such robbery. Inequality was best mitigated by allowing that search to continue in order to increase material abundance for all.[36]

Within this framework, outlined in numerous addresses, speeches, and articles, the United States was a republican capitalist utopia, "a country of busy men," John Kennedy of Baltimore told the American Institute, where "whatever gives facility and aid to labour benefits every class of the community." "It is not the wealthy that rule in our legislative councils, in societies, in politics, in town meetings, and the everyday concerns of life," a member of the Mechanics' Institute declared; "it is not the aristocratic part of our community that have sway over the rest; but it is the educated, the active, the intelligent. . . ." Republican government specifically prohibited all instruments that would turn any one man's ambition into unassailable privilege; in this nation, where "all men are workingmen," all received the fruits of their labor. Never before, Burges and others claimed, had a nation existed where the harmony between the individual and the commonwealth had so swiftly produced such staggering material and spiritual improvements as in the United States. The surest way to continue

35. Tristam Burges, *Address of the Hon. Tristam Burges Delivered at the Third Annual Fair of the American Institute of the City of New York* (New York, 1830), 16–17. See also Edward Everett, *Address Delivered before the American Institute* (New York, 1831), 5–7; *Journal of the American Institute* 1 (1836): 236, 283–88.

36. Burges, *Address*, 17–28.

this progress was to promote increased output, to lower production costs, and to secure the largest possible domestic market for American producers.[37]

Developments outside of the society and the institutes—and outside the trades—reinforced these liberal assumptions. In politics, the Jacksonian party revolution did not bring unanimity among the masters, but it did create political coalitions with different approaches to liberal ends. The Whigs staked out the high-tariff, pro-Bank, pro-internal-improvement positions favored by the American Institute. Other prominent merchants, masters, and manufacturers—including General Society stalwarts like the now elderly Stephen Allen and a host of more recent arrivals—stayed with the Democracy, even though some prominent men of business had their misgivings about the hard money Jacksonians' more fiery anti-Bank appeals to the producing classes. A very few joined the Loco Foco revolt in 1835. After 1832, election battles at times seemed to assume the character of a fundamental social breach, between the defenders of capitalism and its enemies; the presence of some radical GTU men, first in the Jacksonian coalition and later in the Equal Rights party so enhanced this appearance that for generations afterward, historians mistook New York City electoral politics as a direct translation of class conflicts. In fact, no party was solely or primarily a party of "capital" or "labor," in leadership, following, or ideology; none, even the truly radical anti-bank Equal Rights Democrats, opposed capitalist labor relations as the unions did; the major parties proffered wholly liberal programs for entrepreneurial improvement and innovation. Regular politicians certainly appealed for the votes of class-conscious workers, with broad republican rhetoric that at times blurred their liberal outlooks. Otherwise, they offered New York's entrepreneurs and craft employers, not a single identity, but various possibilities, open to different interests and groups (high tariff versus low tariff; "positive" government versus "negative" government) in which the leaders took for granted the desirability of one form or another of continued entrepreneurial growth.[38]

37. John J. Kennedy, *An Address Delivered before the American Institute of the Chatham-Street Chapel* (New York, 1833), 27; *Mechanics' Magazine* 1 (1833): 285; Burges, *Address*, 18–27. See also Cushing, *Address*, 17–20.

38. A thorough social history of party politics in Jacksonian New York—including an account of the party affiliations of manufacturers and master craftsmen—has yet to be written. It has been amply demonstrated, however, that both Whigs and Democrats were led by men from the city's upper classes. Lee Benson suggested as much using Moses Beach's pamphlets; Edward Pessen, highly critical of Beach, utilized his own list of wealthy men but came to broadly similar conclusions about who ran city politics. In the most exacting and persuasive study to date, Brian J. Danforth examined the political affiliations of New York's merchants from 1828 to 1844 and found that they split fairly evenly between Whigs and Democrats, before and after the Bank War. Although further study is needed on the political economy of New York party conflict,

Meanwhile, in religion and in church-related reform movements, some masters found a moral analogue and spiritual reinforcement for their views on labor and the market. In the least successful of their efforts, the attempt to raise a great revival in New York, middle-class evangelicals tried as never before to move beyond reform to a thorough conversion of the city's workers. In six years, the free-church movement begun in 1829 pushed into the East Side mechanics' wards and convinced Charles Finney himself to settle in New York. The Episcopalians, who thus far had restricted themselves to opening Sunday schools and distributing tracts, started their own free churches. Methodists and Baptists, still the largest denominations in the central and eastern wards, tried to keep pace. As in other cities, master craftsmen helped to spearhead church efforts.[39]

Among the most active Finneyites was the ubiquitous temperate hatter Joseph Brewster. In 1834, Brewster, ever the idealist, moved his family from their Fourth Street mansion to a shabby Bowery dwelling on Rivington Street, where he immediately joined the Brainerd Presbyterian congregation, a free church founded a year earlier to tend to the "glaring spiritual wants" of the Eleventh Ward. Brewster's co-congregants included the future Whig polemicist Calvin Colton and the evangelical abolitionist and bookseller Jonathan Leavitt, but the hatter was second to none in his zeal. It was Brewster who, one Sunday shortly after his resettlement, led a raiding party on a nearby saloon—fittingly enough, "The Fort Washington"—and demanded that the owner stop selling alcohol on the Sabbath. In his shop, Brewster took to slipping evangelical tracts inside his newly sold hats. By 1836, when Brainerd Presbyterian published a manual and list of members, Brewster sat as a church elder and president of the board of trustees, administering all of the congregation's secular affairs.[40]

Among the Episcopalians, it was John McVickar, a man well-known to the city's masters, who led the free-church movement. A professor of moral philosophy at Columbia, McVickar had won his reputation as a political economist with his *Outline of Political Economy* (1825), an eloquent and reasoned defense of the harmony of capitalist expansion and a direct riposte to the Owenists and writers like Cornelius Blatchly.

---

there is every reason to believe that New York's manufacturers also divided their support. See Benson, *Concept of Jacksonian Democracy*, 84–85; Pessen, *Riches, Class, and Power*, 45–74; Danforth, "Influence of Socioeconomic Factors," passim. Again, the key point to bear in mind here is not that class was unrelated to political structure and political development; rather, it is that all successful parties were elite-led, cross-class coalitions. See also Wilentz, "On Class and Politics."

39. Rosenberg, *Religion and the Rise of the American City*, 70–159.

40. Smith, *Guileless Israelite*, 11–25; *Manual for the Communicants of the Brainerd Presbyterian Church Worshipping in Rivington Street, City of New York*, No. 1 (New York, 1836), 3–8.

Eight years later, having espied depravity and spiritual poverty in the Stanton Street area (only a few blocks from Brainerd Presbyterian), Mc-Vickar started a weekly prayer service and quickly won the backing of church elders to turn the effort into the city's second free Episcopalian church, the Church of the Epiphany. Along with the Baptist and Methodist churches already in place, the free churches helped make the area just east of the Bowery into a would-be seedbed of spiritual redemption.[41]

Although the theologies of the new free churches were not identical, their aspirations and messages converged. The New School Presbyterians, inspired by Finney, used a panoply of measures to excoriate the sinful corruption of worldly indulgence and the profligacy of idleness. "The agency," Finney and his followers roared, "is the sinner himself"; the revival sprang from the sinner's "obeying the truth," by "*his* acting right"; to act right, the converted sinner had to be disciplined, temperate, and a Christian steward to his fellow men. Conversion brought freedom in Lord Jesus; it also demanded elimination of unseemly habits and constant self-inquiry. The more active Brainerd congregants tested their devotions at a weekly lecture and a weekly prayer meeting, in addition to Sunday services. Every day, they were expected to take a moral inventory with a long list of "questions for self-examination":

> Are you of a *lowly mind*? Do you esteem others better than yourself? Are you condescending? Can you bear reproof?
>
> . . . .
>
> Are you prudent, diligent, and strictly honest in all your *secular business*?
>
> . . . .

—and so on, eventually touching, relentlessly and methodically, all the foibles and excesses that the flesh is heir to. By these lights, worldly success was no sign of degeneration, provided the successful did not turn to base pursuits or luxury; indeed, if men were responsible to society and God, such success, honestly earned, was a sign of grace. But more important than success was the ethic of individual exertion in the Lord's name, to come to Jesus and to overcome temptation, to attend to secular business and to hasten the coming of the Kingdom by mastering a dignified self-control and spreading the gospel.[42]

41. John McVickar, *Outline of Political Economy* (1825; reprint, New York, 1966); Church of the Epiphany, Index to the Minutes, MSS, 21–77; Charles Howland Russell, *The Church of Epiphany, 1833–1958* (New York, 1956); Rosenberg, *Religion and the Rise of the American City*, 139–41. On McVickar's political economy, see also Conkin, *Prophets of Prosperity*, 111–15.

42. Charles Grandison Finney, *Lectures on the Revival of Religion* (1835), ed. William G. McLoughlin (Cambridge, Mass., 1960), 9–13; *Manual . . . Brainerd Presbyterian Church*, 37–40.

The Episcopalians, though intent on changing people's habits, did not go to such millennial, nearly Arminian extremes. Nor did they turn to spiritual terror: "This transformation of character we propose to effect by the simple agency of plain instruction and cheering counsel," the Episcopalian New York Mission Council noted in 1832. Where they agreed with the Finneyite evangelicals, apart from their desire to reach poorer New Yorkers, was in their ideal of an "efficient morality," of "a spirit of independence and self-estimation, which"—once spread among the lowly—"will produce habits of thoughtfulness and reliance on their own resources." Even more explicitly than the Finneyites, they attached this morality to a secular, entrepreneurial political economy:

> In the older countries of Europe, there is a CLASS OF POOR: families born to poverty, living in poverty, dying in poverty. With us there are none such. In our bounteous land individuals alone are poor; but they form no poor class, because with them poverty is but a transient evil . . . save paupers and vagabonds . . . all else form one common class of citizens; some more, others less advanced in the career of honorable independence: *but none without having in their hands, under God's providence, the means of attaining it*; and all, with individual expectations, going on, by industry and economy, to acquire it.

All this might have appeared in the journal of the American Institute or the Mechanics' Institute, or been spoken at an anniversary meeting of the General Society. Coming from John McVickar or from the preacher at the Church of the Epiphany, Lot Jones, it promised spiritual salvation as well as social harmony and abundance.[43]

Had the New York missionaries succeeded, as they did in the Burned Over District upstate, they would have reached master and journeyman alike, teaching the first his responsibilities to himself, his family, and his community, and compelling the second to abandon sinful dissipation and the wrongheaded earthly hatreds of the unions. But while New York was the headquarters for national organizations of the evangelical front, the city itself was to be no Rochester, no "shopkeeper's millennium," despite Finney's ministrations and the support of some of the wealthiest entrepreneurs in the city. The elite's high-church Episcopalian traditions (diluted but not destroyed by the ongoing influx of New England merchants to New York) limited the "Presbygational" influence of the most extreme Finneyites: William Leete Stone of the *Commercial Advertiser*, the journalistic mouthpiece of mainstream mercantile opinion, pronounced the most dedicated "new-measure men" deluded, professors of the worst

---

43. *Churchman* [New York], November 17, 1832; New York Protestant Episcopal Church Mission Society, *Sixth Annual Report* (New York, 1837), 15–16, quoted in Rosenberg, *Religion and the Rise of the American City*, 155–56 (italics mine).

"ultraism of the day, in matters of philanthropy and religion." The free-church Episcopalians fared rather better but did not reach the mass of New York workers. Although the Methodists expanded their activities, they barely held on to their proportional share of the city's population; all of the Baptist churches founded in the Bowery in the 1830s disbanded before the decade was out. New York, with its immigrants, its Bowery, its traditions of popular anticlericalism, and its sheer size, lacked almost all the prerequisites for a successful revival; when that revival was attempted, it brought few journeymen to Jesus. Its major effect was not to close the growing breach of class but to provide some craft entrepreneurs and small masters with an enhanced sense of moral purpose and righteousness.[44]

The records of Joseph Brewster's Brainerd Presbyterian—among the most determined of the missions to the workers—allow a close evaluation of the New York revivals' limited successes, and even greater failures. Like evangelical churches across the North, Brainerd was overwhelmingly female; indeed, the proportion of women and girls in the congregation (78.5 percent) was even higher than in the congregations of the Burned Over District. Of the women, nearly half—48.1 percent of the total adult membership—were unmarried and without any direct kin in the church: women who were either live-in domestic servants or who lived alone, with a sibling, or with a family too lowly to be listed in the city directories. A large number appear, from the records, to have come from nearby rural areas; most were probably drawn from the regiments of young women that poured into New York in the late 1820s and 1830s to take up work as seamstresses and domestic servants. Of the married women, meanwhile, only 4.8 percent were married to artisans or craft workers. The male membership, small as it was, included a variety of occupations; apart from a sprinkling of wealthier men like Colton, most were small shopkeepers and petty entrepreneurs. Only 31.0 percent were men from the crafts, and of these, 55.6 percent were, like Brewster, master craftsmen. All told, of the entire adult membership, only 9.5 percent had any recorded connection with a craft household, and of these, most were either master craftsmen or married to master craftsmen.

The limits of the revival are even clearer if the Brainerd's converts are distinguished from those who transferred in from other churches. The vast majority (63.0 percent) of Brainerd congregants in 1836 had been converted *before* they joined the new church. Of the new converts, 87.0 percent were women, 30.0 percent were single women, and 21.3 percent were widows or daughters of widows. Only 14.9 percent of all the new converts came from artisan or craft workers' households, all but one headed by master craftsmen; in three years, between 1833 and 1836, the church converted only one man from the trades, a journeyman painter named Frederick Byrd. Brewster and his friends had found their "depraved" working people—but they tended to be single women and not male craft workers or the wives of craft workers.[45]

The multiplying reform associations sponsored by the united evangelical front, above all the temperance societies, had a far greater influence than the free churches—but, like the churches, they appealed to craft employers more than to journeymen. In 1832, the New-York City Temperance Society, under the pious guidance of the merchant evangelical Robert Hartley, imitated the tract societies and reorganized into ward groups, in order to reach more effectively the families of small masters and journeymen. Joined by such artisan temperance veterans as Brewster and Joseph Hoxie, the society became increasingly absorbed with the crusade in the workshops; individual masters and the General Society received a barrage of letters and circulars from temperance leaders. In January 1835, Hartley, with an eye on "the excitement which has existed in the community for some months past," singled out the journeymen as the society's most important target and suggested that craft temperance societies might be more useful than ward committees. Yet another union was in the making, one that would explicitly oppose the trade unions' efforts.[46]

Artisan temperance groups had already proliferated. The New-York Apprentices' Temperance Society, founded in 1830 by thirty-three boys, claimed over seven hundred members in 1834. Gold- and silversmiths, stonecutters, and house carpenters formed their own groups between 1833 and 1835. The General Society and the Mechanics' Institute applauded the upsurge and invited representatives of the apprentices' society to address their members. The American Institute did the same and made special note of the metal tradesmen's temperance work. In 1836, the City

45. *Manual . . . Brainerd Presbyterian Church*, 9–14. The surviving records of McVickar's church are far too fragmentary to be useful. Of the ten men identified as members, however, six were small master craftsmen. See Parish Register, Church of the Epiphany, 1833–36, MSS. On the growing "respectability" and wealth of the Episcopal free congregations in the 1840s, see Rosenberg, *Religion and the Rise of the American City*, 140–44. On women and revivals in the Burned Over District, see Ryan, *Cradle of the Middle Class*.

46. Minutes of the Proceedings of the Executive Committee of the New-York City Temperance Society, June 8, 1832, December 3, 1833, January 8, 1835; Black Temperanceana Collection, NYPL Annex; Emil Christopher Vigilante, "The Temperance Reform in New York State, 1829–1851," (Ph.D. diss., New York University, 1964), 144–63.

Temperance Society boasted that, by gaining the influence of "the leading mechanics," the reformation had made "an amazing change both in sentiment and practice," exceeding even the rosy predictions of 1829.[47]

To judge from its pamphlets and reports, it might seem that the temperance movement swept through the trades; in fact, the evangelicals, as ever, looked to the masters, those "whose profits will greatly depend upon the care and skill of sober workmen," as their chief allies. Even the young apprentices, a valuable asset to the cause, centered their proselytizing on the masters, not on fellow apprentices. From their pecuniary interests alone, the apprentices' society reasoned in 1832, "master Mechanics will receive more benefit from the success of this society than almost any class of citizens"; so the enlightened employers, as the natural leaders of their trades, would do the movement the most good, exemplifying and enforcing abstemiousness in what the City Temperance Society discreetly called their "stations of influence over a very numerous class of [their] fellow citizens." Journeymen, on the contrary, required more convincing and could not be counted on for lasting support. Employees, the City Temperance Society admitted in 1835, "can only be reached with great difficulty"; when they confronted the journeymen, temperance advocates only "awakened feelings of opposition and, in some cases, a spirit of determined resistance." Wage earners could, in time, see the light and become genuine temperance men; nevertheless, artisan temperance remained a reform to be imposed from above.[48]

As in the late 1820s, the temperate masters were quite frank about the need to resort to coercion in order to turn their men into independent, morally responsible individuals. "J.W.," responding to a temperance circular, recalled how he took the pledge in 1830 and then posted strict temperance rules banning workmen from bringing liquor into the shop. Others had few scruples about even stricter enforcement. "T.M." wrote that he never kept on any hands who got drunk and that when trade slowed he always fired the least steady and least sober men first. For "M.C.," no precaution against drunken workingmen was too mild; just as mischievous beasts were caged, he wrote, "if men will be drunken unless bound to be sober, bind them, I say. . . ."[49]

While they returned to these old themes, the temperate masters also

47. New-York Apprentices' Temperance Society, *Second Annual Report* (New York, 1832), 3–5; New-York City Temperance Society, *Fourth Annual Report* (New York, 1833), 8; idem, *Eighth Annual Report* (New York, 1837), 13–17, 43–48; Circular Letter to New York Gold and Silver Smiths' Temperance Society, June 1836, American Institute Papers, N-YHS MSS; GSMT Minute Book, December 12, 1832.

48. Apprentices' Temperance Society, *Second Annual Report*, 7–8; City Temperance Society, *Eighth Annual Report*, 13–14.

49. City Temperance Society, *Eighth Annual Report*, 54–56.

tied them ever closer to the political economy of entrepreneurial republican improvement and workshop harmony. It was in "the interest of the employer as well as the employed" that the cause succeed, one master wrote, since it brought the promise of independence to the first and greater profits to the second. The traffic in spirits, one temperance essayist noted, violated "the first principles of political economy by decreasing the productive labor of the country." An American Institute member summed up the point neatly in 1833 with the observation that "industrial growth is most intimately concerned with temperance and good morals, and good morals cannot be expected where intemperance prevails." Beyond profits, temperance was a bulwark of the Republic, a reform for patriots as well as philanthropists, one advocate claimed, that would secure "the virtue and intelligence of the people" and prevent political demagogues from floating into office.[50]

Temperance also emerged as an anti-union weapon in the 1830s. By focusing on the drinking question, the masters found an alternative explanation for the journeymen's economic problems. In America, one temperance pamphleteer contended, none could "ascribe social evils to a bloody tyrant [or] an excess of population"; nor were explanations "to be fished out of the maze of political economy" or found "in the systems and complexities of commerce." The problem lay with the drunken journeymen. Unions and benevolent societies hid this reality behind foolish nostrums, panaceas, and social hatreds; even worse, by meeting in taverns and porterhouses, they had become, as one employer described them, "prolific sources of intemperance." The journeymen's best hope—their only hope— was to leave such groups and join with their masters in the mutual aid and self-discipline of the temperance societies. Once they did, they would receive the same steady work and better wages enjoyed by other sober employees.[51]

No doubt the temperance movement converted a fraction of the journeyman population—although temperate masters remained eternally suspicious that those who claimed to have sworn off liquor were only shamming to save their jobs. More important, temperance met the spiritual and secular needs of hundreds of employers and small masters in a time of acute social crisis. It was no more a movement of cynics than its predecessors of the 1820s had been. The blunt sincerity of masters like the one who admitted that he was "long a disbeliever in temperance societies," and would "only go so far as I think them temperate," is as arresting as it

50. Ibid., 47; New York State Temperance Society, *Fourth Annual Report* (Albany, 1833), 13–24.

51. Alvah Stewart, *Prize Address . . . for the New York City Temperance Society* (n.p., 1834), 7–8; City Temperance Society, *Eighth Annual Report*, 50–58.

is indicative of how widespread the appeal of temperance had become; so, too, must the reformers' faith that, with the triumph of temperance, "earth will soon bloom like Eden" be judged sincere.[52] At a time when their moral stewardship of the trades, already eroded, was being challenged by the unions, master craftsmen found in temperance both an explanation for conditions in the crafts and an envigorated social purpose, to set things right for everyone. Once more, the employers were good republican masters, whose efforts to perfect the abilities of all artisans to accumulate their competence (and, not coincidentally, to increase their own profits) would expand national prosperity and increase the store of virtue.

This tone of moral authority—along with the entrepreneurial, individualist political economy now associated with it—also permeated the masters' most direct engagements in the class conflicts of the 1830s, led by the dozen or so employers' trade associations formed to combat the unions. Central to the masters' argument was their view, first stated outright a quarter of a century earlier at the cordwainers' trial, that the organized journeymen violated all standards of republican comportment. In a typical statement, the Society of Master Tailors called the unions "subversive of the rights of individuals, detrimental to the public good . . . restrictive of our freedom of action, . . . and oppressive towards industrious journeymen who are not members." To these reprises, the masters added that the unions had been gotten up by drunken demagogues, infidels, and second-rate hands.[53] The best antidote to their unrepublican viciousness (and to the deluded union sympathizers) was to instruct the journeymen on the fundamentals of republican capitalism. And it was here that the masters clarified just what was at stake in the journeymen's revolt.

The masters' counterlessons, rehearsed throughout the strikes of 1835 and the crisis of 1836, refuted the unionists' interpretation of property rights and the labor theory of value with the maxims of a Mechanics' Institute lecture. "[L]abour, *like every other commodity*, will seek its own level, and its true value, in an open and unfettered market," the Society of Master Curriers asserted. Low wages did not come from avarice or exploitation; by heeding demand—"the true regulator of prices"—masters paid only what the market warranted. No master dared to underpay his men, lest he find himself priced out of the labor market. Any artificial disruption of this balance by the unions only compelled employers and retailers to raise their prices and force an already overburdened public— including the journeymen themselves—to pay more for necessities. In time

---

52. City Temperance, Society, *Eighth Annual Report*, 56.
53. *Transcript*, February 19, 1836. The charge that the trade unionists were unindustrious men or drunkards was a common one. See, for example, Diary of Philip Hone, June 6, 1836, N-YHS MSS; *Herald*, February 29, June 14, 1836.

New York's craftsmen would suffer competitive disadvantages compared with producers in other American cities and overseas. Bankruptcy and unemployment would follow. While their union leaders promised them higher wages, the journeymen, by attacking employers, were only cutting their own throats.[54]

The truly republican journeymen, the masters agreed, would learn these simple truths, honor the fundamental harmony of interests between employers and employees, respect the market's absolute and impartial dictates, and support efforts to improve themselves and their masters' fortunes. Temporary hardships could be endured and conquered by spurning intemperate, spendthrift ways and ignoring pleas of the "idlers and loungers" of the trade unions. The workers would not be abandoned: to aid them in their quest for success, the masters would offer an array of wholesome lectures, books, and exhibitions, to improve the mind, steady the soul, and enlarge personal savings. By remaining loyal to their employers, the journeymen would achieve the manly independence that was every American's birthright.[55]

There is a familiar, at times almost eerily contemporary, ring to these pronouncements: by 1836, New York's masters, in defining their political economy of labor, their politics, and their reformism, and in turning these ideas against the unions, had perfected the essentials of a republican defense of capitalist growth and wage labor. The supposed harmony of interests between employer and employed, the reciprocity and essential fairness of the wage, the promise of social mobility and an independent competence for all industrious men, a model of private charity and benevolence, a nearly religious devotion to the market as an economic arbiter—all of these still current articles of American economic faith, foreshadowed in the Jeffersonian period, added up to a self-evident case against the unions, despite the changes in New York's crafts. Above all, the masters explained their vision in terms of the proliferation of the small independent American producer, the American mechanic for whom industrial change would mean only greater abundance and opportunity. In appealing to this image, the masters were no more "backward-looking" than the unionists; while they retained the republican ideal and while they clung to the rhetoric of the small producer, they also transformed the old terms to accentuate the possessive individualist elements of artisan republican thought. Even when they announced their personal concern for their journeymen, they did so to defend—in ways only hinted at in the 1820s—the abstract shared interests of employers and employees in the market and the justice of the

54. *Courier and Enquirer*, March 9, 26, 1836 (italics mine). See also *Journal of Commerce*, June 10, 1835.
55. *Courier and Enquirer*, March 9, April 11, 1836.

new relations of production, in that Republic where opulence, in John Kennedy's metaphor, was "a gilded pyramid" built on a pedestal of ice, "its foundations . . . perpetually melting in the sun."[56] This was not nostalgic. It was a one-sided view of metropolitan industrialization that saw an unbroken continuity between the old workshops and the new order, that celebrated social wealth and virtuous independence but admitted to no exploitation, no inequalities of opportunity. It was a social vision that, in its fully elaborated form of the 1830s, truly merited the term "bourgeois."

This vision was the basis of the masters' own consciousness of class; by the mid-1830s, it had acquired the force of natural—and, to masters like Joseph Brewster, divine—law. So it jibed with ideas that had come to pervade almost every feature of Northern political and social life—including the law itself. The transformation of American law proceeded on several fronts in the Jacksonian era; as always, it was the question of conspiracy, and the legality of journeymen's associations, that most directly concerned the trades. In 1829, the state legislature reinforced what had long been the employers' position by revising the champerty law to cover all confederations injurious "to trade or commerce." Six years later, in a conspiracy trial involving several union journeymen from Geneva, New York, the state supreme court ruled that the new statute explicitly forbade strikes. In itself, the ruling brought a significant shift, by placing the power of statute law behind a verdict that to this point had been derived from debatable common-law precedent. The decision, written by Chief Justice Edward Savage, revealed even more plainly that the court assumed, like the masters, that trade-union coercion represented "an injury done to the community, by diminishing the quantity of productive labour, and of internal trade."[57]

In 1836, armed with the Geneva ruling, certain in their own minds of the legitimacy of their cause, New York's employers started a counteroffensive to crush the journeymen's revolt. It would lead New York City, in one journalist's words, to the brink of a kind of "local revolution."[58]

The Crisis of 1836

If 1834 was New York's year of the riots, 1836 was the year of the strikes: ten major turnouts hit the skilled trades, and convulsive strikes took place on the waterfront and building sites (Table 19B). In response, employers,

56. Kennedy, *Address*, 27.

57. On the Geneva case, see Stephen Mayer, "People v. Fisher: The Shoemakers' Strike of 1833," *N-YHSQ* 62 (1978): 7–21; Commons, *History of Labour*, I, 406–8. On the law in general, see Morton J. Horwitz, *The Transformation of American Law* (Cambridge, Mass., 1977).

58. *Herald*, February 25, 1836.

backed by city officials, the courts, and military force, mounted an unprecedented counterattack—which only led workers to consider even more active forms of resistance. Talk of insurrectionary violence and revolution never got beyond some panicky jottings by the city's men of property and some inflammatory letters and handbills—but that there was such talk at all, in a democratic republican city, was the extraordinary thing. After thirty years of union organizing, radical politics, and recurrent strike waves, a new order of labor crisis gripped New York City.

It began in late January, when two master stonecutters brought members of the Journeymen's Stonecutters' Society to court in order to recover damages arising from a strike the preceding autumn. Little went well for the journeymen's defense at first; halfway through the trial, the judge announced to the jury that as far as he was concerned, the masters' case was proven. Under cross-examination, however, the chief prosecution witness revealed that both he and the masters who had brought the case were all former union members who had been dismissed for strikebreaking and for working with prison contractors. The jury—persuaded by the defense's argument that the masters were prejudiced, but unwilling to vote an acquittal—lowered the award from the $1,000.00 the plaintiffs demanded to $32.50. It was only a skirmish compared with the confrontations to come.[59]

Undaunted by the decision in the stonecutters' case, various groups of masters, led by the tailors, formed their own employers' associations and accelerated the pace of legal action. Similar associations had appeared sporadically in other trades in 1834 and 1835; the tailors, however, took the step of nullifying the price book they had negotiated with their men the preceding spring and announced that henceforth they would employ no union members. The journeymen tailors, stunned by this "strike of the masters," responded by turning out and asked the GTU and other trade unions for support. Three members of the Society of Master Tailors in turn swore out affidavits against five union strikers, accusing them of riotous and disorderly conduct. Support for the employers ran strong in the press. Over the next few weeks, announcements that several other masters' societies had been organized promoted speculation that the tailors' strife would soon engulf the entire city.[60]

All along, the individual trade unions and the GTU had been preparing for the expected strikes at the start of the spring business season. Thus far, their attempts to standardize wages had been largely successful; the inflation of the winter of 1835–36, along with the likelihood that masters would follow the tailors and cut their wages, made a renewed union offen-

59. Ibid., January 20, February 3, 1836; *Sun* [New York], January 21, 1836.
60. *Transcript*, January 30, February 12, 1836; *Herald*, February 18, 1836; *Journal of Commerce*, February 16, 1836; *National Trades' Union*, February 13, 1836.

sive all but inevitable. News of the stonecutters' trial and the tailors' strike hastened their activity and elicited denunciations of the employers' "assumed and insolent meddling with that which properly belongs to us." By mid-February, journeymen clothing cutters, house carpenters, and hatters had met to formulate their demands. "These are truly striking times," the anti-union New York *Herald* noted sourly.[61]

On February 22, attention shifted dramatically to the waterfront, where the stevedores and riggers struck for higher wages and paraded from ship to ship to gather support. The next day, as the protests continued, two policemen tried to disperse a group of two hundred strikers. Harsh words, then a scuffle followed: one policeman landed in the hospital with a fractured skull. At almost precisely the same time, a few blocks away, laborers working to rebuild the downtown district that had a few months earlier been destroyed by fire walked off their jobs and formed a parade of between five and eight hundred men. The high constable, alerted to the disturbance on the waterfront, ran head-on into the building laborers and, thinking fast, assured them that they had the right to strike but not to interfere with other workmen. The laborers—satisfied that the municipality was on their side—cheered the good officer and went back to work. The police, however, remained on the scene and rounded up nine workers in connection with the fracas at the dockside.[62]

Meanwhile, Mayor Cornelius Lawrence—the anti-Bank Democrat first elected two years earlier with informal union support—prepared to take sterner measures. Concerned about the size of the protests, fearful that the city's commercial economy might be drained by a strike in the port, alarmed by the attack on the police, Lawrence called up the twenty-seventh Regiment of the National Guard and ordered it to report to City Hall the following morning. The mayor had no desire to shed working-men's blood; although he ordered the guardsmen to be armed, he did not send them to the waterfront but instead had them parade in City Hall Park. It was enough to convince the riggers and stevedores to return to work, their demands unmet. It also marked the first time in New York history that the municipality called upon the military to help break a strike.[63]

61. *Sun*, January 20, 1836; *Transcript*, February 1, 13, 15, 17, 18, 19, 1836; *National Trades' Union*, January 16, February 13, 20, 1836; *Herald*, February 24, 1836.

62. *Transcript*, February 23, 24, 25, 1836; *National Trades' Union*, February 27, 1836; *American*, February 24, 1836; *Commercial Advertiser*, February 24, 1836; *Herald*, February 24, 1836; People v. Edward Hallahan et al., March 12, 1836, Court of General Sessions, MARC. See also Weinbaum, *Mobs and Demagogues*, 77–78.

63. *American*, February 24, 25, 1836; *Commercial Advertiser*, February 24, 25, 1836. Mayor Lawrence also issued a standing order to the regiment to intervene if any further strife broke out. See Emmons Clark, *History of the Seventh Regiment of New York, 1806–1889* (New York, 1890), I, 243. The regiment had also been called up in 1834 in a somewhat different situation, to suppress the stonecutters' riot.

Although the military show accomplished its aim, it also redoubled the militancy of skilled and unskilled workers from around the city. Within twenty-four hours of the call-up, a protest meeting of journeymen and laborers, led by several GTU delegates, sought to widen the union cause. The meeting resolved to hold an emergency session of representatives from all the city's trades and laboring occupations, in order to agree on their respective wage lists. Once these proposals were approved by a general meeting, the workers would present their demands in unison; if rebuffed, all the city's wage earners would discuss taking further measures. A general strike seemed imminent; the new group, though, did not last more than a few weeks beyond its initial meeting. Whatever its fate, it was another first, the first attempt by skilled men in New York to join with day laborers in a single organization and to threaten a general strike. The arrival of the military appears to have united the city's workers as never before—as wage earners, all "worthy of their hire."[64] While no general strike was attempted, the boundaries between craft workers and laborers remained blurry in the weeks that followed.

By the end of February, the strikes and protests appeared to the *Herald* to have become "a general movement over the city." A dozen journeymen's unions and several groups of laborers either were on strike, had won strikes, or were organizing one; even the shipwrights, their real wages eroded by the inflation, announced their intention to turn out. The tailors' strike, meanwhile, had turned into a protracted, violent affray. Unruly scenes unfolded at the city's clothing shops, where strikers, strikebreakers, and officers held running battles. A policeman provoked one incident by dressing in plain clothes and pretending to return some finished articles to a colluding master; several union lookouts spotted him and took chase, until the officer stopped short and arrested two of them for criminal harassment. Another journeyman, Edward Ney, was arrested on a masters' complaint; Ney defended himself and left the nonplussed court a free man, roundly denouncing the police, the city government, and his employers. By early March, the tailors' union raised the stakes by establishing its own cooperative shops, to provide the journeymen with some income and to demonstrate that they could create an alternative to the sweated wage system. James Gordon Bennett of the *Herald*, who knew the masters' minds as he knew his own, had some prudent advice: "read your Bibles—say your prayers—and raise at once the wages of journeymen moderately."[65]

64. *Herald*, February 27, March 4, 1836.
65. *National Trades' Union*, February 20, 27, March 5, 12, 26, 1836; *Transcript*, March 1, 2, 12, 16, 25, 1836; *Herald*, March 3, 4, 5, 7, 8, 1836. On the coal heavers' strike, see People v. Patrick Donahan et al., and People v. John Sullivan et al., March 15, 1836, Court of General Sessions, MARC. On the shipwrights' strike, see *Sun*,

Over the frenzy hung the threat of the Geneva conspiracy case decision. Several unions tried to warn the city's masters of the dire consequences of a conspiracy trial; the national cordwainers' union contended that if Savage's decision was allowed to stand and become general, "the feudal system may as well be established at once." The master tailors pressed ahead anyway, and in late March a grand jury handed down the expected conspiracy indictment against twenty journeymen tailors. The unions' immediate response was an impressive march of several thousand workers up Broadway, headed by the striking tailors and complete with musical bands, trade banners, and signs announcing the journeymen's intention to regulate their own wages. Individual unions hurled abuse at banks, party politicians, and chartered corporations, as well as that combination of men "who have evinced an unrepublican taste in dubbing themselves *master tailors*. . . ." Their remarks were not lost on the press. "Are we not on the eve of another revolution as we witnessed among the mechanics in 1829?" the *Herald* wondered. "Every thing looks that way."[66]

The lines of opposition sharpened over the next two months. In some trades, the resumption of the spring trade season compelled masters to settle with their men; in others, fresh strike activity began, in some cases for the second time that year, to advance wages even further. Emboldened by the conspiracy indictments, the masters in several more trades formed their own employers' associations; at one point, the master cordwainers suggested that delegates from all the city's trades meet at a general employers' convention to counteract the GTU. The journeymen replied to their "patriotic" bosses with pungent satires on the "ebullition of purse-proud fools who seek to put down the only *justifiable* combination that exists," joined with an attack on those who would build their so-called independence from "the PROFITS *on the labor of the men in* [their] *employ*." The tailors, still on strike, remained at the head of the journeymen's movement; in mid–April, the tailoresses, apparently undaunted by the possible legal repercussions, announced that they would turn out as well. In May, the awaited trial of the journeymen began.[67]

The trial, and the activity that surrounded it, both recapitulated the social and ideological divisions in the trades and signaled the possible commencement of a new kind of uprising. The legal arguments followed

---

March 1, 3, 1836. Their demand was for $2.50 per day; by comparison, the house carpenters' demand was for fourteen shillings (i.e., $1.75) per day. See *Sun*, March 4, 1836.

66. *Herald*, March 8, 11, 12, 14, 17, 28, April 1, 1836; *Transcript*, March 18, 19, 25, April 1, 2, 1836; *National Trades' Union*, March 12, 19, 26, 1836.

67. *Herald*, April 2, 6, 11, 14, May 14, 1836; *Transcript*, April 15, 1836; *National Trades' Union*, April 9, 16, 1836.

the pattern in the Geneva case, as did Judge Ogden Edwards's charge to the jury, described by a court reporter as "decidedly against *Trades' Unions*, stigmatising them as illegal combinations." When the jury returned its verdict of guilty, all appeared lost to the unionists: not only had their arguments been repudiated, but their right to unionize had also been denied by a supposedly impartial republican American court. Their reaction was decisive. *The Union* tried to remain calm but could conclude only that Judge Edwards had succeeded in "an unhallowed attempt to convert the working men of this country to slaves"; John Commerford suspected that even in England, "aye, in England, at this very time, a judge could not be found" who could have acted as Edwards had. Others drew more dramatic and more militant conclusions. "The long agony is over! American mechanics no longer have any rights in the community!" one wrote:

> If an American judge will tell an American jury that the barriers which the poor have thrown up to protect the growing avarice of the rich are unlawful, then are the mechanics justified the same as our own fore Father's [*sic*] were in the days of the revolution, in ARMING FOR SELF DEFENSE!![68]

Still others, presumably well-schooled in the art of the anonymous note, plastered the city with an ominous handbill headed by a coffin:

> The Rich against the Poor! Judge Edwards, the tool of the Aristocracy, against the People! Mechanics and workingmen! a deadly blow has been struck at your Liberty! The prize for which your fathers fought has been robbed from you! The Freemen of the North are now on a level with the slaves of the South! with no other privileges than laboring that drones may fatten on your life-blood! Twenty of your brethren have been found guilty for presuming to resist a reduction in their wages! and Judge Edwards has charged an American jury, and agreeably to that charge, they have established the precedent, that workingmen have no right to regulate the price of labor! or, in other words, the Rich are the only judges of the wants of the Poor Man! On Monday, June 6, 1836, these Freemen are to receive their sentence, to gratify the hellish appetites of the Aristocracy! On Monday, the Liberty of the Workingmen will be interred! Judge Edwards is to chant the Requiem! Go! Go! Go! every Freeman, every Workingman, and hear the hollow and the melancholy sound of the earth on the Coffin of Equality! Let the Court-room, the City-hall—yea, the whole Park, be filled with Mourners! But, remember, offer no violence to Judge Edwards! Bend meekly, and receive the chains wherewith you are bound! Keep the peace! Above all things keep the peace![69]

68. *Union*, June 1, 1836.
69. Commons, *Documentary History*, V, 317–18. On the handbill, see also *Herald*, June 7, 1836; *Union*, June 8, 1836.

The mood was just as ugly among the masters and their allies. While the masters' societies expressed satisfaction that their liberties had been vindicated and that the unions were dead, merchants and employers excoriated the union men as criminals and miscreants. Philip Hone, who earlier had exulted in his diary that the law had at last begun to strike against the unions, now wrote a succinct celebration of the conviction of these "Knights of the Thimble," these "vile foreigners," these mere tailors who had once mistakenly been dubbed "the ninth part of man," but who in fact played their "full part in mischief."[70] The *Herald*, abandoning its role as prudent counselor to the masters, took the opportunity to discuss what the recent events had shown about the nature of trade unionism. No pithier summary of the masters' attitudes toward labor—or of the morality of entrepreneurial republicanism—was delivered in the 1830s:

> The mechanic who attends quietly to his business—is industrious and attentive—belongs to no club—never visits the porter-house—is always at his work or with his family—such a man gradually rises in society and becomes an honor to himself, his friends, and to human nature. On the contrary, look at the Trades Unionist—the pot-house agitator—the stirrer-up of sedition—the clamorer for higher wages—After a short time, he ends his career in the Penetentiary or State Prison.[71]

Beneath this jubilation was the uncomfortable truth that the mischievous clamorers for higher wages now headed what was becoming a general movement of the New York working class and its supporters.

That movement quickly gained momentum. A large crowd turned out at City Hall to hear Edwards proclaim that "in this favoured land of law and liberty, the road to advancement is open to all, and the journeymen may by their skill and industry, and moral worth, soon become flourishing master mechanics." As soon as he announced his sentence, union men set up a relief fund, to be collected in local taverns and shops, to pay the men's fines.[72] One week later, an evening rally of mechanics and workingmen met at City Hall to protest the entire affair. It was, by all accounts, one of the most remarkable public events of the Jacksonian period. Nearly thirty thousand persons attended, to that point the largest protest gathering in American history, a crowd that represented about one-fifth of the entire adult population of New York City. They heard speakers—"chiefly radicals," the press reported—denounce Edwards, bankers, merchants, employers, and the two major parties for being "at variance with the spirit and genius of Republican government." After a flurry of angry resolutions,

70. Diary of Philip Hone, June 6, 14, 1836, N-YHS MSS. For Hone's reflections on earlier events, see Diary, February 23, March 26, 1836.

71. *Herald*, June 14, 1836.

72. *Union*, June 4, 7, 8, 1836.

the assembled listened to plans to call a convention to meet in Utica in September, in order to consider the possibility of starting "a separate and distinct party, around which the laboring classes and their friends can rally with confidence." After a final cheer, the crowd headed home, its path illuminated by the flickering effigies of Justice Savage and Judge Edwards hung from the main gates of City Hall Park. At last, the newspapers reported, the radical mob of labor had risen—a mob of tens of thousands, a mob with politics on its mind. The *Herald's* earlier prediction—that New Yorkers should beware "the melting of the snow," since warm weather would bring "one of the most remarkable agitations . . . which ever took place in New York"—now seemed prescient.[73]

Over the next three months, the journeymen's fury abated, in part because of a signal success, in part because of political difficulties. The success came only days after the City Hall rally, at a conspiracy trial of journeymen cordwainers in upstate Hudson. All of the facts and arguments in the case were similar to those in the New York tailors' trial; if anything, the Hudson men, who freely admitted that they had tried to enforce a closed shop, had been even more audacious than the New York tailors. Few expected any change in the recent pattern of decisions, especially after the presiding judge delivered his charge to the jury; it came as a stunning surprise when the jury returned an acquittal. The *Union* was exultant, as were the union men in general; although, "A Mechanic" wrote, Edwards's decision might yet be sustained, the journeymen could still look to Hudson with hope, as a rallying point for all "unprejudiced freemen."[74]

Building a political party of labor proved more vexing. The decision of the mass meeting was a bold new step for the journeymen's movement, out of keeping with what had been strict union policy from the beginning. The GTU stood firm and took no formal role in the preparations; in the usual pattern, however, individual union men, including Commerford, participated on their own, joined by activists from the Loco Foco party, and gave the new initiative the informal imprimatur of the union movement. As the committee charged with preparing for the September convention met, however, it soon became clear that the Loco Focos dominated the group—including two recent members who had considerable experience in political manipulation, the former Cookite journeymen Isaac Odell and Robert Townsend, Jr. By the time the "new party" convened, its meeting had been turned into the nominating convention of the state-

73. Ibid., June 14, 15, 1836; *Evening Post,* June 14, 1836; *Journal of Commerce,* June 18, 1836; *Herald,* March 4, June 11, 1836. The size of the crowd was estimated as 27,000 by the Boston *Reformer;* see *Union,* June 20, 1836.

74. *Union,* July 2, 1836.

wide Equal Rights party; there, Whig sympathizers in the ranks of the Loco Focos (including Odell and Townsend) helped nominate several joint Whig–Loco Foco candidates, Townsend among them. The union journeymen remained without their party of labor.[75]

The Hudson decision and the political fiasco cooled the situation, but the calm did not mean that the class-conscious militancy of the unions was broken or that the crisis had been resolved. Through the autumn and early winter of 1836–37, the GTU added new members and new unions. Strikes—usually uncommon after the spring—were called by the carpenters (again), the riggers, and the female umbrella makers; the seamstresses, with some unique middle-class support, held a meeting (Plate 15). In the weeks after the Hudson trial, the unionists continued to recite the message of the New York tailors' verdict, namely, that one class of citizens was trying to rob another of their rights and their independence. As "A Mechanic" put it in early July, it all made a mockery of the ideals of July 4, 1776:

> A day is fast approaching, which must call forcibly to mind the state of liberty in republican America. To tailors, the conspiracy class, it must be a sad day; disguise the matter as we may, they were treated no better than tyrants treat their subjects, and for them to shout in commemoration of their freedom would be hollow mirth indeed.

As similar sentiments were coming from city central unions across the Northeast, there was every indication that the crisis of 1836 would lead to renewed and even wider conflict in 1837.[76]

The Legacy of Union

What finally ended the crisis and wrecked the union movement was neither official repression nor political co-optation but dearth and economic collapse. In the summer of 1836, swarms of Hessian flies had devastated the wheat crop in western New York, Pennsylvania, and the border states, stripping northeastern cities of major sources of supply; in the early months of 1837, flour prices on the New York market soared (Fig. 4). To make matters worse, the speculative mania of the mid-1830s reached its peak and began to bottom out in late 1836. By May 1837, when the crisis hit the New York banks and specie payment was suspended, the American economy was teetering; by June, it had fallen apart. More than one-third of New York's workers reportedly lost their jobs in the immediate wake of the panic; where the ensuing contraction did not displace

---

75. Byrdsall, *History*, 61–93; *Proceedings of the Convention of Mechanics, Farmers, and Working-Men of the State of New-York* (n.p., n.d. [1836]).

76. *Union*, July 2, 1836. On developments in other cities in 1836, see Commons, *History of Labour*, I, 397–401.

union men, master craftsmen singled them out, happy to take the opportunity to rid themselves of troublemakers without risking reprisals. A few militants attempted to regroup—the carpenters and painters struck for wages, and a committee of printers called upon their fellow journeymen to resist layoffs and firings—but to no avail.[77] As the flour shortage and then the depression hit, journeymen turned to other more immediate concerns, above all to insuring that their families had enough to eat. Under the circumstances, unions were both a costly indulgence and a futile one; more direct action, to punish those who appeared prepared to profit from economic hardship, seemed in order. The change in mood was clear as early as February, when a crowd of hundreds of artisans and laborers broke away from a Loco Foco meeting protesting the high price of food and rents to carry their complaints to the flour merchants. Several speakers at the meeting, witnesses recalled, had urged that some such protest be mounted; an onlooker later testified that one speaker had told his listeners to go to the flour stores the next day and offer a just price of eight dollars per barrel, "and if they don't take it, let us offer them our Heart's blood." But the crowd could not wait. In scenes reminiscent of an eighteenth-century *guerre des farines*, the protesters, joined by irate women, marched to the warehouses of three prominent merchants, broke into the storerooms, seized the flour, and fended off the police (and, in time, the mayor) with wads of dough. The techniques and class consciousness of the unions were laid aside, replaced by the direct action and moral economy of a food riot, the street tactics of the Bowery. By summer, the union movement was dead. It was to prove a portent of the difficulties faced by New York's labor radicals for nearly a decade.[78]

A dual legacy remained. Measured by their grandest hopes, the union men had failed—failed to win control over their labor, to reorder the relations of production and power in the workshops, to change their followers' habits, to achieve labor's day of redemption. But they had also succeeded, despite the obstacles, in uniting craft workers as a class, in winning (for a time) concessions from their employers, in instilling a sense of purpose and competence that allowed ordinary journeymen to battle intimidation, in the courts and in the shops. Briefly, they had even tried to bring together the entire family of labor. And, like their counterparts in Britain

---

77. Commons, *History of Labour*, I, 484; *Evening Post*, June 29, 1837.

78. On the riot, see *Evening Post*, February 14, 1837; *Courier and Enquirer*, February 14, 1837; *Sun*, February 14, 1837; *Journal of Commerce*, February 14, 1837; Byrdsall, *History*, 103. For eyewitness accounts, see the depositions in People v. John Windt et al., and People v. William Louge et al., February 17, 1837, Court of General Sessions, MARC. In March, the Loco Focos held another protest meeting; the mayor called out the militia to insure order and disperse the crowd. See Byrdsall, *History*, 109, 113.

and France, they had transformed a political language into a new under-standing of class divisions and wage earners' rights. The bifurcation of artisan republicanism was complete, leaving two very different sets of ideas about independence, virtue, commonwealth, and equality, two different orders of citizenship, two different conceptions of labor and property. Even in the hard times of the late 1830s and 1840s, when the class con-sciousness of the unions was driven to the margins of public life, this split would not be healed completely. Although class antagonisms softened, the conflicts and the memory of 1836 persisted—to reappear, in new forms, within a generation.

V

Hard Times and Politics,
1837-1849

Around me I hear that éclat of the world—politics, produce,
The announcements of recognized things—science,
The approved growth of cities, and the spread of inventions.

Chants Democratic, XXI, 1

8

Panic and Prejudice

Panic turned into despair for New York's workers in the late 1830s and early 1840s. The mass unemployment that followed the financial collapse was bad enough, prompting one newspaper to wonder how this "awful fact" had come to pass in the free and equal United States.[1] The situation worsened over the next five years. Wage rates for those craft workers and laborers lucky enough to find work fell by about one-third between 1836 and 1842; in the worst years, real wages also fell (Figs. 3 and 5). Unemployment deepened. In 1843 New Yorkers finally glimpsed the start of a recovery of business and higher wages—but within two years of the depression's end the city was swamped with refugees from the Irish famine and from agrarian and political crises in Germany. With this sudden expansion of the supply of cheap labor, New York's manufacturers and master craftsmen, already buoyed by the return of commercial prosperity, further expanded and extended the subdivision and contracting of work. By the late 1840s, New York's position as the nation's leading manufacturing site was secure, and the split labor market and the fragmentation of the artisan system were complete.

Under the circumstances, radical and trade-union activities were difficult to sustain, at least until the recovery was more thoroughly under way. Although journeymen's benevolent associations and a few unions in the leading consumer crafts continued to meet, a visitor from Albany remarked in 1842 that New York's craft workers and small masters evinced

---

1. *New Era* [New York], May 25, 1837. The best concise account of the social impact of the panic and the depression in New York appears in Samuel P. Rezneck, "The Social History of an American Depression, 1837–1843," AHR 40 (1935): 663–76.

little more than "apathy and indifference" toward the cause of the mechanics.[2] Inflation had bred union militancy, but hard times and their aftermath demanded defensive strategies for dignified survival. As the depression dragged on, workers clung to their situations and tried to salvage some decency and pride; now faced with the certainty of dependence on wage-labor, they looked for ways to become what had once been thought a contradiction in terms—self-respecting wage earners for life. Collective action did not end, but its goals changed, as workers either tried to alter themselves and help each other through the disaster or took to the republic of the streets.

The most obvious signs of despair were to be found along the Bowery, where chiliastic sects sprang up along with new congregations of distinctly lower-class Methodists and Baptists, in what soon became the greatest plebeian Protestant revival in the city's history. Millerites roamed the sidewalk, distracted from their normal pursuits, predicting the approaching destruction of the world. Meanwhile, at least one of the Irish Bowery gangs, the True Blue Americans, dressed in plug hats and long coats, and gave streetcorner harangues about the fiery downfall of the British Empire. On other fronts, the fire-company competitions and "emulations" turned increasingly nasty, becoming less distinct from the ever more fierce gang battles; in the most celebrated encounter between Mose Humphreys's Lady Washington company and Hen Chanfrau's in 1839, more than one thousand men and boys battled with sticks and brickbats for over an hour to support their favorites.[3]

A different but related development was the appearance of the "soap locks," better known as the Bowery B'hoys (Plate 16). Contrary to later myth, the B'hoys were not the members of a single body or ethnic group, but represented an updated version of still another metropolitan type, the youthful working-class dandy. John W. Ripley recalled the B'hoys when he reminisced about his days as an engraver in the 1840s:

> I was at that time what was known as a "Bowery Boy," a distinct "gang" from either the "know-nothing" or "Native American" parties. The gang had no regular organization, but were a crowd of young men of different nationalities, mostly American born, who were always ready for excitement, generally of an innocent nature.

Almost invariably a journeyman or an apprentice, the B'hoy came into his own in the gloom of the postpanic years and had become a journalistic

2. *New York State Mechanic* [Albany], December 19, 1842.

3. Greenleaf, *History of the Churches*, 124–330; Harlow, *Old Bowery Days*, 208, 227–28, 286; Costello, *Our Firemen*, 100–101; Weinbaum, *Mobs and Demagogues*, 152–35.

stock figure by the late 1840s. By day he either worked in the shops or looked for work, but in the evening, as Charles Haswell recalled, he "appeared in *propria persona*, a very different character":

> His dress, a high beaver hat, with the nap divided and brushed in opposite directions, with the hair on the back of his head clipped close, while in front the temple locks were curled and greased . . . a smooth face, a gaudy silk neck-cloth, black frock coat, full pantaloons, turned up at the bottom over heavy boots designed for use in slaughterhouses and at fires. . . .

A habitué of the fire companies and the theaters, a sentinel of the new army of unemployed, the B'hoy became a kind of popular hero, proud of his sporting ways, willing to defend them against all comers with a punkish gaze. He appeared to be, as a sympathetic George Foster described him, a young man out of step with the calculations of the marketplace or the union meeting, a rebel without prospects other than those of the street corner or dance hall, a worker who "thinks little of his future destiny, and seems unconscious of any powers other than those brought into play by a race for a fire plug or a scamper on the avenue."[4]

From the anxieties and straitened hopes that goaded the sects and the B'hoys also came the impulses for the most significant popular movements of the early and mid-1840s, for lower-class temperance and for nativist reform. From them, as well, came the redoubled efforts of the city's employers and master craftsmen to strengthen and celebrate the free-labor republic. With the unions temporarily crushed, New York's craft entrepreneurs consolidated their views of the 1830s. Although shaken for a time by the panic, their faith in the market and in a classless America was fully restored with the return of prosperity. Their engagements and pronouncements, although bland in comparison with the popular movements, set the decade's ideological keynote, that adversity and hard times arose not from social antagonisms but from individual incapacities to adapt to the demands of a competitive economic order. To those who could discern only the surface of things, the masters' commanding logic and the journeymen's panic made it seem that class conflict and class consciousness had been eradicated once and for all in the industrializing metropolis, amid a resurgence of pious moralism, sobriety, and ethnic pride.

4. John W. Ripley, "Account of Astor Place Riot of 1849, written by John W. Ripley, a Participant (1897)," Seventh Regiment Archives, N-YHS, p. 1; Haswell, *Reminiscences*, 270–71; Foster, *New York in Slices*, 43–47; Harlow, *Old Bowery Days*, 192–97. See also William Bobo, *Glimpses of New York, by a South Carolinian* (Charleston, S.C., 1852), 162–67. I am grateful to Peter Buckley for bringing Ripley's memoir to my attention.

Free Labor and the Republic of Capital

Late in 1837, as the effects of the panic settled on New York's workshops, the young minister Alonzo Potter—soon to become a bishop of the Protestant Episcopal church—polished off the revisions of a long article on trade unions for the *New-York Review*. It was, in its way, a brilliant piece, a sophisticated exposition of what had become the masters' republican position on labor and the evils of the unions; Potter would soon incorporate it almost verbatim in an even more ambitious and influential work, his *Political Economy*, published in 1841. Taking quick stock of Anglo-American political theory, from Edmund Burke to the Founding Fathers, Potter found in radical trade unionism the symptoms of an Old World disease imported to the Republic by the victims of oppression—men who no sooner arrived on these shores than they set up as Apostles of Liberty agitating not for civil equality but for an equality of condition. By pitting one class against another, these unionists and their supporters committed horrendous violations of equal rights, against employers, against the agricultural classes (who paid more for manufactured goods because of the unions' wage demands), and against those workers who did not join their plots. More to the point, the unions arrested the American spirit of improvement by trying to persuade workers that they were fixed in some permanent condition of inferiority—to Potter an obvious absurdity. Distilling arguments that had been in the air for decades and making apposite use of Henry Carey's writings, Potter announced the true American principle that "the highest welfare of the laboring classes depends, after all, upon themselves, and without virtuous principles and habits, no increase of compensation can either enrich or elevate them."[5]

Coming when they did, after the panic, Potter's remarks had lost some of their timeliness. As a codification of republican free-labor principles mingled with religious beliefs—delivered not by an employers' association but by a reflective clergyman—they also beckoned to the future, to the fullest expressions of an American bourgeois ideal. It took a few years for New York's masters and manufacturers to rally their confidence, to carry themselves through the depression and refine these views even further. Conventions of manufacturers and businessmen, hastily assembled by the American Institute, had to affirm that only faster industrial development would bring national economic recovery. The institutes and the General Society had to renew their calls for individual self-improvement and the expansion of workers' education, in their schools, lectures, and fairs (Plate 17). Throughout, even as scores of firms lay shattered by the depression, New York's craft entrepreneurs kept their basic faith in the United States

5. Alonzo Potter, "Trades' Unions," *New-York Review* 2 (1838): 5–48.

as a classless, capitalist dream fulfilled, where politics and the market enhanced what one spokesman called "the moral dignity of labor."[6] By the mid-1840s, those entrepreneurs who survived had turned the gist of Potter's remarks into a social creed, couched in the language of republican capitalism.

Four propositions came to frame the masters' thinking, and it fell to a southern Whig sympathizer of industrial growth to make explicit the axioms that others took for granted. Addressing the American Institute in 1844, Alexander H. H. Stuart struck the optimists' note in yet another comparison between the United States and Great Britain:

> Here we see no class of our population subsisting on wages of sixpence or a shilling a day! Here we have no necessity for factory bills, or a system of legislative police to guard the operative against the exactions of his employers. Here a competency is within the reach of every man who is disposed to exercise ordinary industry and frugality; and the labouring population is prosperous and happy.[7]

Proposition One, on the classlessness of American society, repeated the longstanding republican defense of virtue, independence, and equality, and linked it to the masters' liberal views on labor and the market; as other spokesmen put it, Americans had learned to outlaw all corrupt institutions that would cause the wealth of the few and the abject poverty of the many. Where republican institutions could not insure economic opportunity, America's natural abundance and storehouse of land would, since, as Cyrus Mason pointed out, the ready availability of cheap lands would allow the laboring classes to escape the clutches of any improbable would-be manufacturing aristocracy. Proposition Two, that all Americans of industrious habits could better themselves, followed as a corollary; manufacturers never tired of noting that America was a land of "self-made men, the architects of their own fortunes," men who, thanks to republican equality, had been compelled to earn their competence by hard labor. Proposition Three, that American wage earners were prosperous, seemed self-evident from any comparison between New York and Old World cities.[8]

It was Proposition Four, on the mutuality of interests, that provided the employers' favorite theme. As in decades past, they deemed employer and wage earner—yet again, "the bone and sinew"—as part of a wider network

---

6. GSMT Minute Book, January 31, 1840, February 3, 1841, February 2, September 28, 1842, February 1, 1843, February 5, 1845, February 3, 1847; *Mechanics' Institute Lectures for 1844 and '45* (New York, 1845); James J. Mapes, *Inaugural Address Delivered before the Mechanics' Institute of the City of New-York* (New York, 1845), 3–4 and passim.

7. Stuart, *Anniversary Address before the American Institute* (New York, 1844), 10.

8. In addition to Stuart's *Address*, see Mason, *Oration*, 32–33; H. G. O. Colby, *Anniversary Address before the American Institute* (New York, 1842), 11.

of the Republic and "the Trade," what Harman Westervelt, the president of the American Institute, defined as "a community of friendly feeling," joined by "a desire for the mutual benefit of the establishment." As latter-day masters, the employers retained their watchful prerogatives, unceasing, the General Society reported, in their attempts to help apprentices and journeymen become "accomplished mechanics, useful citizens, and good and happy men"—ever mindful, in Westervelt's words, that "instruction is their aim, and their country and not Mammon is the only shrine at which they worship." Simultaneously, the masters spoke with greater assurance and sophistication of an *economic* harmony of interests in the shops. H. G. O. Colby imagined a binding and natural Lockian consensus among employers and men, in which all were devoted to "the same object—the same portion of wealth," and in which all sought to protect private property. Since their desires did not conflict, there was no reason for hostility between the rich and the laboring classes, "but the strongest reason, on the contrary, for mutual friendship and the most cordial unions." Stuart went even further, to explain the social compact in detail, with a social vocabulary of dazzling abstractions new to the city's craft entrepreneurs:

> The two great subjects of all governments are persons and property, and the two great elements of every society are *Labour* and *Capital*. These subjects are intimately connected. Capital is the product of Industry—Labour is the agency by which Capital is acquired. Capital gives employment to Labour and Labour repays Capital by its profits. They are natural allies and mutually beneficial . . . and he who wars against the one necessarily wars against the other.

Capital, that term of opprobrium for the GTU, had become in the masters' explanations a benevolent instrument for the commonweal, the republican comrade of labor.[9]

By vaunting capital as labor's partner, the employers proclaimed their republican anti-unionism ever more strenuously, secure that the union movement itself was in disarray. Colby conceded that at times "a feeling of prejudice does exist between the wealthy and the labouring classes, even in this country," but he blamed this sourness of spirit on demagogues who "declaim in bar-rooms and grog shops, with surpassing eloquence, upon equal rights, when the only species of equality they desire is that the loafer shall share the wages of the labourer." If such jealous passions were

9. H. C. Westervelt, *An Address Delivered before the American Institute* (New York, 1846), p. 10; Colby, *Address*, 12–14. Stuart, *Address*, 10. See also Daniel D. Barnard, *Anniversary Address Delivered before the American Institute* (New York, 1843), 6–10; Luther Bradish, *Opening Address of the Seventeenth Annual Fair of the American Institute* (New York, 1844), 3, 7–8. On "the bone and sinew," see Mahlon Dickerson, *Address Delivered at the Opening of the Nineteenth Annual Fair of the American Institute* (New York, 1846), 7.

ever allowed free reign, Westervelt charged, then "riot and disorder will take the place of truth and right, while our republic will recede into the original barbarism which devours a beastly subsistence."[10]

The masters' more pronounced religious tone extended earlier evangelical ideas and reflected the religious responses to the depression among the city's better classes. The assault against workingmen infidels, dating back to the 1820s, still preoccupied some employers in the late 1830s; as late as 1840, Cyrus Mason felt it necessary to demonstrate that industry and morality were intimately connected with pure religion and to claim that science, far from disproving infidelity, had exploded all grounds for skepticism.[11] The years during and after the depression, meanwhile, brought a significant rise in middle-class Protestant church membership, in more conventional Episcopalian and Presbyterian congregations as well as in the evangelical churches. There, the congregants heard of the panic as God's judgment; they also learned of the resumption of commerce as God's blessing, His renewed bestowal of providence on the young industrializing Republic. By the mid-1840s, the major organizations of the city's employers, never circumspect about religious matters, were making a stolid pandenominational Protestantism into an article of entrepreneurial faith, the spiritual expression of republican capitalist harmony. The august Presbyterian clergyman Stephen Tyng made the argument most eloquently in 1848, when he reminded the American Institute that nowhere but on Christian soil were men secure in the peaceful possession of their labor. Like republicanism, Christ's message of spiritual humility and equality made "the cunning artificer the perfect equal to the eloquent orator"; by devising their Declaration of Independence and Bill of Rights as Christian documents—"to grow and flourish upon the word of God"—the Founding Fathers had assured their progeny economic security and political freedom. For Tyng and his audience, the Protestant Lord, the one true master craftsman, became, like the employers themselves, an agent of capitalist growth. Where profane radicals would build a blasphemous republic of man, the improving entrepreneurs would build a republic of God.[12]

The sum of the masters' political economy and their moralism was less than the combined whole, and the two merged only gradually; one effect of the precipitous decline of union radicalism was to permit the masters to do so without much fear of contradiction. Yet even as the entrepreneurial rhetoric of the 1840s fell into place, best summarized in the Reverend Tyng's celebration of "free labor upon a free land," the employers' image

10. Colby, *Address*, 14; Westervelt, *Address*, 11.
11. Mason, *Oration*, 27–28.
12. Greenleaf, *History of the Churches*, 110–11, 220–22; Stephen Tyng, *An Address Delivered to the American Institute* (New York, 1848), 8–10.

of America still reflected old concerns, in ways that at once transformed old usages and stressed continuity with the past. Their more up-to-date political economy allowed them to extend the labor theory of value to cover all Americans in the marketplace, entrepreneurs and wage earners, as producers; although they sometimes recalled the idea of the employer as small producer, their vocabulary of capital was broad enough to enable them on occasion to say, as Mahlon Dickerson did, that even capitalists "who avoid productive labor" were still useful citizens, "absolutely necessary to the well being of the republic. . . ." Meanwhile, their discussions of America, although far removed from the speeches of the master craftsmen of Jefferson's day, still remained consistent (at least in their own eyes) with older artisan republican themes. Cyrus Mason spelled out the connections in 1840:

> The accumulation of wealth is to be made by the people, and remain in their hands. It will not be collected by hundreds of slaves for the luxury and pride of one master; nor by hundreds of serfs for one lord; nor by thousands of subjects to be lavished on the pomps and vices of royalty; but the commonwealth will be advanced. The industrious and virtuous of the people at large will be better housed, better clothed, better fed, and better learned. The log cabin will give way to the tasteful and commodious dwelling. The deep forest will become a fruitful field. The desert will blossom as the rose.

It was an ideal that less fortunate journeymen and small masters, meeting on their own, would try to claim for themselves, in very different ways.[13]

The Jovial Hurrah: Washingtonian Temperance

Of all the developments of the depression years, the mass movement for temperance reform best expressed the workingmen's shock at the prolonged depression and the collapse of the unions. Within a year of the panic, a brace of new temperance groups formed the Temperance Beneficial Association to encourage journeymen and day laborers untouched by the earlier evangelical crusade to give up alcoholic beverages. More of a craft mutual-aid society than an adjunct of the evangelical front, the TBA scolded established temperance societies for their failure to attend to the economic needs of the city's wage earners, and set about improvising soup kitchens. Instead of delivering godly injunctions and enforcing coercive rules, the new societies extended a hand to the unchurched and the down-and-out. Street corners as well as churches and public halls became their pulpits; speeches and testimonials came from reformed alcoholics and hard-bitten mechanics as well as from preachers and reformers. In a year,

13. Tyng, *Address*, 10; Dickerson, *Address*, 8. Mason, *Oration*, 32.

the TBA made more progress among the craft workers than the evangelicals had managed in nearly a decade. It was to prove the start of a passionate lower-class temperance reformation.[14]

In 1840, four Baltimore craftsmen, drinkers all, attended a temperance
lecture meeting intending to mock the speakers, but returned to their tavern convinced temperance men, and persuaded two of their friends to
swear off liquor. Reports of the men's conversion and their establishment
of the Washington Temperance Benevolent Society quickly reached New
York, and in March 1841 Robert Hartley, at the request of the New-York
City Temperance Society, invited the Baltimorans to send five of their
number to Manhattan. In a frenzied lecture series, the reformed men addressed thousands of New Yorkers to explain their transformation and to
call for the establishment of temperance groups modeled on their own;
soon thereafter, fifty-four journeymen and small master craftsmen started
the New York Washington Temperance Society. Within six months, the
group claimed to have won more than twenty thousand male members
and thousands more women, gathered in more than fifty chapters. Even
with the inevitable exaggerations about their numbers, temperance reformers could claim with justice that theirs was now the largest popular movement in the city's history, one that made New York, as one temperance
newspaper rejoiced, the "banner city" of Washingtonianism.[15]

The Washingtonians immediately made it clear that their crusade would
be very different from that of the evangelicals of the 1830s. Quickly, the
new movement brought together the kinds of men who had differed
sharply over temperance only a few years earlier. Several prominent merchants, professionals, and masters took leading positions in the Washingtonian chapters, but so did an equal number of shopkeepers, workers, and
small masters from a wide range of trades. The busiest Washingtonian lecturers included the journeyman hatter John H. W. Hawkins and the visit-
ing erstwhile bookbinder John Gough. Masters and journeymen in at least
five trades—bakers, butchers, hatters, printers, and shipwrights—organized
their own Washingtonian chapters; so did a citywide group of apprentices.

14. *Constitution and Laws of the Temperance Beneficial Association* (New York,
1838); Ian R. Tyrrell, *Sobering Up: From Temperance to Prohibition in Antebellum
America, 1800-1860* (Westport, Conn., 1979), 168–69.

15. Vigilante, "Temperance Reform," 167–73; Minutes, New-York City Temperance
Society, March 15, 1841; *New York Washingtonian*, May 21, 1842; *New York Organ
of the Washington Temperance Benevolent Society* [New York], June 11, 1842. An
excellent concise survey of Washingtonianism appears in Tyrrell, *Sobering Up*, 159–224,
but see also Milton A. Maxwell, "The Washingtonian Movement," *Quarterly Journal
of Studies on Alcohol* 11 (1950): 410–51. In 1842, the New York Washingtonians
claimed more than twenty thousand members, according to figures in *Organ*, May 2,
1842; Tyrrell (*Sobering Up*, 205) claims that by 1843 the New York Washingtonians
boasted over sixty thousand members.

Although originally invited by the Prebygational evangelicals, the Washingtonians established their chapter meetings among the lower-class sects and congregations of Methodists and Baptists that had grown since the panic.[16]

Following the TBA's example, the Washingtonians took their cause directly to the craft workers as well as to such workingmen's haunts as the fire companies. A down-to-earth egalitarianism lacking in the City Temperance Society pervaded their literature: "Exclusiveness was never intended to constitute any part or have anything to do with Washingtonianism," one temperance journal remarked; "all who disapprove of the use as a beverage of alcoholic drinks" could join without risking any violation of conscience. Their parables drawn from life—the highly publicized, pathetic chronicle of Edward Allen, a besotted and choleric ship carpenter saved by the pledge, was typical—at once aimed to persuade craft workers and avoided the evangelicalism and political economy of earlier tracts. "[W]e write plain things for plain people," the Washingtonian *New York Organ* observed. Whatever Hartley's intentions in bringing the Washingtonians to Manhattan, and whatever the desires of its middle-class supporters, the organization became a movement from below, of and for the journeymen and laborers who had shown little love for the missionaries of evangelical reform.[17]

The Washingtonians' message and goal were simple: alcohol made hard times worse and had to be avoided completely. The group's chosen means were considerably more complex. Washingtonian temperance men, survivors of daily imbibing and repeated binges, understood far better than the abstemious evangelicals that drinking was a central part of the lower-class way of life, part of the texture of good natured sociability that defined the male workingmen's world—a habit that could not, and should not, be handled with pious coercion. As the evangelical temperance leader John Marsh observed, the Washingtonians had no patience with those who be-

16. *Organ*, September 10, 1842, and passim. The names of Washingtonian chapter officers were gathered from the *Organ* and the *New York Washingtonian* for 1842–43. Of those identified, in the city directories and tax lists, the occupational breakdown (in percentages) was as follows:

Merchants and professionals	44.4
Shopkeepers, retailers, and petty professionals	2.2
Master craftsmen and manufacturers	6.7
Small masters	4.5
Journeymen	28.9
Laborers and unskilled	13.3
TOTAL (N = 45)	100.0

Cf. Tyrrell, *Sobering Up*, 166. On the crafts, see *Organ*, May 2, June 25, 1842, January 21, 1843. Gough never formally joined, but he often addressed the Washingtonians.

17. *Organ*, August 13, 20, 27, 1842.

lieved that committed drinkers could be reasoned or compelled into reform; alcohol had to be fought with different weapons, to enable "masses of men [to] throw off the monster evil, either with a spirit of indignation or a jovial hurrah." Instead of prayers, they offered to help the men get back on their feet, by feeding and clothing them and getting them work; they also invented alternative forms of leisure that would permit mechanics weaned on strong drink to unburden themselves of their troubles, share in the rough camaraderie and frivolity of the tavern, and preserve their dignity and some kind of independence, all without a drop of spirits or beer.[18]

Their main forum was the weekly experience meeting, where reformed men and new recruits would tell of their past dissipation and of the personal satisfactions of sobering up. The polarities of their before-and-after stories were stark, following the melodramatic conventions of the day, contrasting the shadow of inebriation with the sunshine of sobriety. What they lacked in subtlety they more than made up for in a graphic power, blasphemous in comparison with the evangelicals' tracts and speeches. There was a knowing quality to their testimonials, a preoccupation with the details of *just* how bad life on the bottle could be, spoken to fellow regenerates who could spot fraudulent rationalization in an instant, each of whom had their own stories to tell. Heads nodded in recognition and tongues prepared their own lurid recollections as each speaker reached the climax:

> He stated [one critic recalled of a Washingtonian testifier] that for years he had loafed around the markets and wharves without any regular means of subsistence, sleeping in the markets and on the sidewalks, almost without clothes, or friends, and that all he sought for was rum; and that his appetite was so craving that he would stoop to the meanest calling to obtain a little rum.[19]

Here was barroom boasting stood on its head, a recitation of past exploits transformed into a confession, setting the boundaries of a new fellowship of those who not only were sober but knew another life and had rid themselves of it.

Once purged of the past and pledged to temperance, the Washingtonians enjoyed the substitutive culture of lower-class teetotalism. As far as possible, the societies tried to re-create tavern life with songs, poems, and activities almost obsessive in their exuberance. The standard Bowery shows were relocated to temperate theaters; Charley White, one of the best-

18. *Journal of the American Temperance Union* 6 (1842): 138; Maxwell, "Washingtonian Movement," 429–436; Tyrrell, *Sobering Up*, 163–64, 176–79.
19. Benjamin Estes, *Essay on the Necessity of Correcting the Errors Which Have Crept into the Washington Temperance Movement* (New York, 1846), 6, quoted in Tyrrell, *Sobering Up*, 163–64.

known Jim Crow troupers in the 1840s, began his career with the Kentucky Negro Minstrels by playing in New York's Teetotaler's Hall.[20] At the temperance meetings, former regulars of the Bowery grogshops sang of the joys of sobriety; entire companies of firemen joined the chorus:

> Come forth ye rummer come,
> Come to the Clinton Hall,
> The pledge of Freedom sign—
> Come banish alcohol,
> Rum, brandy, beer, and wine[21]

During the rest of the week, converts could pass as much time as they cared to with their pals, at temperance picnics, temperance bazaars, temperance concerts, temperance reading rooms, and temperance fishing trips. The opening of the Croton Aqueduct in 1842 was the perfect opportunity to put this culture on display, to troop the temperance colors and repeat the old "Trade" pageants in praise of the restorative qualities of pure water. More than a reform movement, the Washingtonians built a replica of the Bowery republic, minus drink.[22]

The religious overtones of this explosion of goodwill are too obvious to be overlooked. The testimony of the experience meeting, the charisma of the itinerant Washingtonian lectures, the stewardship of the societies with their motto "Every man brings his man," bespoke at least some Methodist influence. The very act of turning sober had all of the dimensions of a conversion experience, as recalled by one member who attended the first series of Washingtonian meetings:

> As they stepped confidently, but unassumingly, within the precincts of the altar, the conviction settled down into my very soul that they had enlisted for life in the temperance war. . . . When I reached home I asked myself what can I do to help the glorious reformation. What can I do to save others from the mental suffering I have endured?[23]

The inclusion of women, organized into auxiliary Martha Washingtonian Societies, intensified the aura of propriety. Even more than the middle-class evangelical temperance groups, the Washingtonians encouraged women in craft workers' and laborers' households to help their men sober up. Women were largely responsible for coordinating the Washingtonians'

20. Tyrrell, *Sobering Up*, 195.

21. Sheldon, *Volunteer Fire Department*, 145. See also *New York Washingtonian*, May 21, 1842; *Organ*, June 25, 1842. The president of the Firemen's Temperance Auxiliary was James Gulick.

22. *New York Washingtonian*, May 2, 1842; *New York Crystal Fount*, March 1, 1843; *Organ*, June 18, 25, October 8, 15, 1842; Tyrrell, *Sobering Up*, 176–79.

23. *Organ*, June 11, September 10, 1842.

charity work; often, they outnumbered the men at the experience meetings. It was the first time that females had their own formal sphere within a temperance cause, and the first successful attempt to base temperance reform among the lower classes with an appeal to the preservation of harmonious families. The plebeian cult of domesticity had found its own movement.[24]

It is important, however, not to confuse forms with intentions: while Washingtonianism cannot be understood as an attempt by workingmen to "internalize" middle-class evangelical norms, neither should it be interpreted as a mere extension of the plebeian panic revival. There were, to be sure, a good number of pious masters well-placed in the New York Washingtonians' ranks, men like the Methodist publisher James Harper (Plate 18) who, though independent of the Finneyites, still considered temperance a religious reform. The Washingtonian press reflected their views, summarized in the *New York Organ's* insistence that sobriety was meaningless unless it also instilled "the glorious traits of our religion"; the pan-Protestant moralism characteristic of the entrepreneurs always found a place in the new movement's public ceremonies. But many others were also taken up with the cause, their views ranging from indifference to hostility toward organized worship and the godly free-labor republic. To the consternation of the more religious members and to the outrage of the older temperance groups, a few Washingtonians were said to have claimed that their work had nothing to do with religion or abstract morality and that they used the Bible only to confute its arguments against temperance. More commonly, Washingtonian lecturers simply denied any sectarian motives, recited their openness to all persuasions—including men of no faith—and stressed that their only concern was to provide a human agency to help defenseless men escape utter degradation.[25]

From the start, the more secularist—even rowdy—sentiments prevailed. As one Washingtonian song related, the men were interested in improving life in the here and now, not in preparing some future millennium:

> The world's not all a fleeting show
> For man's illusion given;
> He that hath sooth'd the drunkard's woe,
> And led him to reform, doth know,
> There's something here of heaven.[26]

24. *Crystal Fount*, November 16, December 14, 1842; Lorenzo Dow Judson, *Martha Washingtonianism: or, A History of the Ladies' Temperance Benevolent Societies* (New York, 1843); Tyrrell, *Sobering Up*, 179–83.

25. *Organ*, December 21, 1842; Tyrrell, *Sobering Up*, 195–206; John B. Gough, *Autobiography and Personal Recollections* (Springfield, Mass., 1870), 192–94.

26. *Washingtonian Pocket Companion*, ed. A. B. Grosh (Utica, N.Y., 1842), quoted in Maxwell, "Washingtonian Movement," 438.

A gruff humanist perfectionism, an emphasis on overcoming man-made problems with manly exercises of will, was evident in the Washingtonians' pledge, a plain promise to work "as gentlemen" for the mutual benefit of the membership and to remain sober—without any mention of Jesus, His love, or attaining grace, and without the slightest hint at what temperance would do for profits. A parody catechism prepared the loyal for the inevitable questions of the curious:

> Q. Were there no other requirements specified in the pledge?
> A. None.
> Q. Nothing respecting a moral life?
> A. Nothing directly.[27]

Without renouncing religion, but by refusing to teach any lessons except total abstinence, the Washingtonians achieved what the earlier movements could not: a temperance drive joined by some religious entrepreneurs, by more radical, godless proponents of self-improvement, and by thousands of journeymen, laborers and their families, who were simply trying to find their bearings in a city with little work and with descending wages.

Predictably, Washingtonianism, for all its good will, soon proved anathema to the city's older temperance advocates; their differences exposed abiding social and ideological tensions within the cold-water army. Within a year of Hartley's invitation to the Baltimore reformers, the American Temperance Union, now the umbrella group of evangelical temperance reform, began criticizing the Washingtonians' "vulgar tone" and took umbrage at the "spicy narratives of drunken orgies" featured at the experience meetings. Far from having converted the wayward, the ATU charged, the new reformers only created additional (albeit temperate) strongholds of noisome sin; even worse, the Washingtonians permitted licentious men to remain members even if they had strayed from the pledge. In the mid-1840s, the dispute widened into an all-out war over the importance of religion and the efficacy of moral suasion. The New-York City Temperance Society had long insisted that the reformers had a duty "to acknowledge their dependence on God," and as the evangelicals reaffirmed their faith they scorned the Washingtonians. The Washingtonians in turn renounced the neo-Sabbatarian attempts by the ATU and its allies to push their crusade into politics with demands that local and state governments enforce a virtual prohibition of the liquor traffic—to the Washingtonians an unnecessary entanglement in party politics and a denial of the openhearted sympathy to all (including liquor sellers and manufacturers) on which they based their entire strategy. These differences in approach, compounded by the older groups' alarm that the growth of Washingtonianism had

27. *Organ*, January 14, 1843.

robbed them of potential members and financial support, barred any possibility of merging the movement from below and the movement from above.[28]

While these battles sapped the Washingtonians' strength, the structural weaknesses of the loose-knit, hastily organized Washingtonian societies had even more telling effects in 1843. Despite their earnestness, the most dedicated members found it difficult to keep track of everyone who had taken the pledge, and virtually impossible to bring backsliders into the fold again. As early as January 1843, the New York *Crystal Fount* admitted that many who had signed had since returned to their former course. It is not difficult to understand why so many left: lack of abiding resolve, weariness with the relentless exuberance of the experience meeting and the sing-alongs, and the slow return of prosperity in 1843 all helped drive men from the ranks. Some choice scandals, including the discovery of John Gough, the most eloquent of the lower-class lecturers, lying in a drunken sleep in a downtown bordello, did not help the group's credibility. The rifts over religion within the movement, as well as between the movement and the older groups, proved to be the coup de grace. "Washingtonianism is dead," went an evangelical cry in 1845—killed, supposedly, by infidelity. The second claim was debatable, but the first was not: by June 1845, the New York Washingtonian movement, its numbers dwindling, had fallen under the control of a new group, the Sons of Temperance, who insisted on respectable comportment, dress, and language at meetings and pledged the society's support of prohibition. Although still tied to the trades—the Oliver brothers, the Sons of Temperance leaders, were ex-journeymen and former Washingtonians—Washingtonianism, had been changed from a haven of boisterous self-respect into a society of more circumspect respectability.[29]

Nonetheless, with all its meteoric qualities, Washingtonianism had an abiding influence. Lower-class temperance was not extinguished in the mid-1840s; at least two groups, the Rechabites and (even more) the Order of the Good Samaritans, picked up the cause and resisted any alliance with or endorsement of the evangelical prohibition campaigns. The Good Samaritans, in particular, stressed the needs of drunkards and sought them out in their lower-class haunts; in the early 1850s, the Samaritans claimed to have enrolled more former alcoholics than any other of the city's active

28. Vigilante, "Temperance Reform," 184–86; Minutes, New-York City Temperance Society, March 10, 1836; *Christian Article* [New York], February 4, 1843; *Crystal Fount*, October 5, 1842.

29. *Crystal Fount*, January 25, 1843; Gough, *Autobiography*, 194–96; *Police Gazette* [New York], December 13, 20, 27, 1845; Tyrrell, *Sobering Up*, 204. Tyrrell points out (206–7) that some Washingtonians also blamed the political parties—and the customary "treating" of the campaigns of 1842 and 1844—for drawing men from the cause.

temperance societies had. Outside of temperance circles, meanwhile, the creed of lower-class mutuality and self-help, linked to sobriety, proliferated in the city's surviving artisan benefit societies and in the few remaining unions; the Mechanics' Mutual Protection Association (which we shall encounter again) enrolled thousands of workers across New York State in the mid-1840s, preaching the Washingtonian creed of alcohol avoidance and cooperation.[30]

Apart from its institutional legacy, Washingtonianism also represented an important interlude for its adherents. As they departed from the well-beaten temperance path, the Washingtonian societies offered their members more than hope and a hot meal: they brought the idea that ordinary men and women could collectively benefit each other—or at least escape further degradation—without the assistance of God or their social betters, through patience, toleration, and joy. The mordant hymns of the evangelicals gave way to the strains of the temperance glee club; personal self-control was joined to a robust celebration of life. Given their circumstances, it was no less noble or heroic an effort to retrieve independent "self government" than the unions' had been. Yet, the Washingtonian experience was also an ambiguous one, its ambiguities stemming from the harder times of the early 1840s and the turn to temperance as a balm. For all of the Washingtonians' enthusiasm, independence, and self-organization, their hopeful vision of mutuality and collective aid without social conflict showed how thoroughly the depression had changed the context of workers' lives, quieting the class antagonisms of 1835 and 1836 without fully abolishing class and cultural tensions. Occasionally, there were hints that the splits within the movement had led to some awareness of the clash of social assumptions that lay beneath the surface; at one point, the temperance press reported that some New Yorkers were complaining of attempts by "the silk stocking gentry" to take over the movement by pitting "the rich against the poor." But there was nothing in Washingtonianism—as a movement, as a solution to people's problems—that encouraged members to think about those differences, to handle them in ways that might explain why the rich would have a different approach to temperance reform than the poor. In the long run, Washingtonianism and its image of sober manly self-respect would have a profound impact on all varieties of journeymen's movements, including some with decidedly radical views. More immediately, in the early 1840s, it reinforced the idea that the source of workers' worst distress lay outside the maze of political economy, that hard times were bad, "but they might be worse and despondency makes them so," that with courage, perseverance, and a little cooperation, all would go well.[31]

30. Tyrrell, *Sobering Up*, 206–18. On the Mechanics' Mutual, see below, Chapter 9.
31. *New York Washingtonian*, May 21, 1842.

American Republicanism:
Nativism, Mutuality, and Liberty

Just as temperance became a mass movement, political nativism returned to New York with a vengeance, stirred initially by the continuing controversies over public education and by attempts by the political parties to expand their popular base. In 1839 and 1840, Gov. William H. Seward shocked New York's pious Protestants and emboldened Catholic leaders with calls for equal educational funding for all the state's children, including those in Catholic-run schools. Seward's suggestion, a masterstroke of Whig opportunism, was also perfectly in keeping with his brand of political Whiggery, which would have joined all Americans in a pluralist harmony of interests. Church leaders like Nathan Bangs and Gardiner Spring, and the Protestant-controlled Public School Society—less reconciled to the Catholic presence—saw the governor's position as a direct threat to their command over public education. When the vicar of New York's Catholic church militant, Bishop John Hughes, took up Seward's remarks and applied to the Common Council for a portion of the funds allotted from the state, the Protestants fought back hard. The issue became thoroughly politicized in 1841, when Hughes named a separate Carroll Hall ticket of Democrats pledged to secure funds for the parochial schools from the state legislature. The Democrats, after regaining control of the legislature that year, did not give Hughes his money, but did replace the PSS with a board of education, to be elected annually by the voters.[32]

Coming five years *before* the arrival of the famine wave, these disputes arose only in part from the growing numbers of Catholic immigrants in New York. The main questions, even more than in the 1830s, centered on native distress at the political parties, municipal misdeeds, and public immorality. Democrats had long made appeals to the Irish as an important part of their campaigning; with the immigrant vote secure, the nativists charged, Tammany had enriched itself with shady public contracts, at the taxpayers' expense. Seward's statements and the increasingly professional, nonideological appeals of the Whigs seemed to antipapists like utter capitulation to the dupes of Rome. They quickly led to another outbreak of independent nativist politics.

The agitation began in the summer of 1843, when a group of Protestant

32. On the school dispute, see Kaestle, *Evolution of an Urban School System*, 151–58; Diane Ravitch, *The Great School Wars: New York City, 1805–1973* (New York, 1974), 33–82; Ira M. Leonard, "New York City Politics, 1841–44: Nativism and Reform" (Ph.D., New York University, 1965), 98–194; Mushkat, *Tammany*, 192–207. Stephen Allen, by now a venerable city father, was a powerful trustee of the Public School Society; for his denials that the society was sectarian and for his embittered recollections of this affair, see his "Memoirs," 192–97.

butchers and market men, enraged by Tammany's alleged favoritism in distributing market licenses to Irish Catholics, called for the organization of a new party, independent of both the priest-ridden Democrats and the ineffectual Whigs. Nativist idealists and politicians, no longer an effective party, seized upon the butchers' complaints, added their own about flagrant financial mismanagement and patronage abuses by the Democrats, and organized once more. Their fledgling American Republican party, far from trimming on the immigration issue, made its key demand the requirement that all foreigners have lived in the United States for twenty-one years before being allowed to vote, in order to sever the connection between politics and religion. It also urged repeal of the 1842 school law. With this simple platform, the American Republicans polled a surprising 8,600 votes—22.9 percent of the total—in the fall elections for local offices. By December, the party's General Executive Committee was planning for the charter elections the following spring. Promising "thorough reform in our city government" to end the "great extravagance and wasteful expenditure of the people's money," the new group appeared able to accomplish the earlier nativists' dream of uniting disparate anti-immigrant, anti-Catholic, and "antiparty" opinion.[33]

Like its predecessor, the NADA, the American Republican party was led by a cross-class coalition: although started in part by the butchers, it attracted some of the city's foremost professionals, editors, and men of affairs, from Samuel F. B. Morse to the attorney and erstwhile Painite freethinker Henry Fay. Also like the NADA, but with far more success, the American Republicans established a base with elements of the old mechanics' interest—masters, small masters, and journeymen united under the leadership of the larger employers. More specifically, American Republicanism appealed most strongly to masters and journeymen in those trades in which the effects of metropolitan industrialization were slight, the numbers of immigrants were proportionally few, or both. Butchers, carpenters, and printers were among the more conspicuous in the party's secondary leadership; none or proportionally few came from the largest sweated outwork trades, most notably tailoring and shoemaking, where immigrants (and, in the 1830s, interethnic trade unionism) were most prevalent. Within these limits, the party included men of widely different backgrounds, from prominent members of the General Society of Mechanics and Tradesmen like the publisher James Harper to the brush maker and former GTU delegate Joseph Hufty. In all cases, the decline of unionism and the apparent willingness of the parties to yield to Irish Catholic pressure revived republican antipapist fears and redirected attention to the

33. Ira M. Leonard, "The Rise and Fall of the American Republican Party in New York City, 1843–1845," N-YHSQ 50 (1966): 162–64.

state of local political institutions. As a popular political movement, American Republicanism amounted to a rally of "the Trades" in those crafts in which some semblance of economic mutuality or ethnic homogeneity among masters and journeymen could still be discerned, a movement driven less by workshop grievances than by revulsion at the supposedly corrupting moral and political consequences of Catholic immigration.[34]

Ideologically, American Republicanism stuck to all of the older artisan and republican ideals and language. "[T]he true science of politics," the General Executive Committee declared in 1844, was based on one great question, "viz., the best POLICY of maintaining and perpetuating our glorious republican form of government. . . ." It was not strange, the American Republican argued, that pauperism, crime, and immorality had increased wherever the Catholic immigrants settled—Catholics, after all, were reared to believe that the priest could release them from their sins. Nor was it a coincidence that so many Irish Catholics gained their foothold in the city thanks to political patronage from "faithless sentinels and corrupt politicians." By their mutual depredations, the immigrants and the politicians—under whose hand "political virtue is rapidly becoming extinct"—were accountable for all the ills of city life.[35]

The connections between nativism and the world of "the Trade" were made at several points in the nativist press, but they were best emblematized in the career of the American Republicans' most respected spokesman, James Harper. Harper was an outstanding member of that genera-

---

34. Names of the presidents and officers of the American Republican party ward associations were drawn from the American Republican Party Papers, N-YHS. The occupations of those who could be identified in the city directories and tax lists broke down as follows:

Merchants and professionals	30.7
Shopkeepers, retailers, and petty professionals	21.3
Master craftsmen and manufacturers	28.0
Small masters	0.0
Journeymen	16.0
Laborers and unskilled	4.0
TOTAL $(N = 75)$	100.0

Those in the trades included five carpenters, three butchers, jewelers, cabinetmakers, and brush makers, two printers and one of each of the following: carriage maker, combmaker, cooper, electrician, hatter, mason, ornamental painter, painter, refractory slater, ship carpenter, shoemaker, typefounder, upholsterer, and varnisher. David Montgomery points out an almost identical pattern of artisan participation in the Philadelphia American Republican movement, in "The Shuttle and the Cross," 430.

35. Address to the People of the State of New York by the General Executive Committee of the American Republican Party of the City of New York (New York, 1844), 5; American Republican, August 2, 1844, quoted in Benson, Concept of Jacksonian Democracy, 116–17. See also Address of the General Executive Committee of the American Republican Party (New York, 1843), 3–6.

tion of master craftsmen who turned a successful rise through the crafts into an extraordinary success in capitalist enterprise; nevertheless, he always insisted (and by all accounts genuinely believed) that he owed his rise "to character and not to capital." Born on Long Island, the son of a dour, temperate Methodist carpenter and his ex-Dutch Reform wife, Harper had arrived in New York in 1810 at age fifteen, hoping to learn the printers' craft. Thurlow Weed, an early shop mate, remembered him as a young man of punctilious attention to his duties and of seemingly limitless stamina, an ambitious journeyman who would press others (including the less determined Weed) to join him in doing extra work. By the 1840s, Harper's character, as well as the business acumen of his brother and partner, John, had paid off handsomely, making the House of Harper the largest and fastest-growing publishing enterprise in the United States. In literary circles, the firm was best known for its inexpensive, sometimes pirated editions of English and American fiction, reproduced by the tens of thousands on the Harpers' battery of steam-powered Hoe presses. Their mainstay, though, was their line of religious books, ranging from the Episcopalian prayer book and texts for the Methodist Sunday schools to a stylish illuminated Bible, a multivolume edition of the complete works of Hannah More, and the Reverend Potter's contribution on political economy.[36]

While he printed what he preached, Harper became one of the city's most respected craft employers, and in 1831 he was admitted to the General Society. Eventually, his concern for sober habits and political purity took more public and political forms. In 1841, he helped to organize the second of the New York Washingtonian auxiliaries and served as its president; four years later, after the Washingtonians' demise, he became an officer in the local chapter of one of the smaller temperance societies, the Brotherhood of Temperance. A liberal benefactor of the Whig party, he joined the American Republicans as soon as they organized, and became one of the city's most visible nativists. With his pious artisan background, his impeccable reputation, and his connections, Harper was an obvious choice to be the party's mayoral nominee in 1844.[37]

It is hard not to regard Harper as something of a parody of the dull, upright craft entrepreneur, as if a Cruikshank or a "Phiz" in one of his cheap editions had sprung to life. He certainly looked the part, his long-nosed, awkward gaze stirring little of the romance of the popular leader (Plate 18). In his personal affairs, he was occupied mainly with reflecting on the state of his business and with playing practical jokes on his friends;

36. Eugene Exman, *The Brothers Harper* (New York, [1965]), 3–145; Weed, *Autobiography*, 61–62.

37. Earle and Congdon, *Annals*, 398; *New York Washingtonian*, May 2, 1842; Rules and Regulations, Brotherhood of Temperance (n.d.), Harper Papers, N-YHS.

his motto—"Observe carefully three rules and happiness will attend you: Trust in God, pay your bills, and keep your bowels open"—said as much about the character of his intellect as about his spiritual and worldly priorities. He read little of what he published other than the Bible. Yet Harper also exuded the spirit of the skilled benevolent artisan craftsman that had once guided the trades—a throwback, despite his wealth, to the moralistic small masters of the first two decades of the century. He held conspicuous displays of affluence in contempt and always claimed that, for all his success, he was only "a humble maker of books." While his brother attended to the receipts, he would walk among the pressmen and compositors, to instruct and exchange banter as well as to oversee the operation. He was the kind of master who would applaud a job well done, reminisce with his workers about his experiences in the trade, and slip an extra ten dollars to an employee in financial trouble.[38]

Harper perceived American political institutions in ways as reminiscent of a New York master artisan of the age of Jefferson as of a nativist Whig of the 1840s. He valued the obligations of virtuous citizenship above all, with views he himself deemed identical to those of John Quincy Adams. The very essence of American political duty, he wrote an associate in 1845, was that "every citizen in return for the protection, the rights, and privileges which he enjoys, is bound to give his services to his fellow citizens in whatever form or mode the latter may prescribe." To this bedrock republicanism, he added "some aspirations of professional pride," a hope that his own political success would "do some honor . . . to the mechanical calling generally, and especially to that which I had been engaged since boyhood. . . ." As much as his fear of Catholics, Harper's conception of an American free of political corruption, partisan conflict, and social complexity led him to the nativist cause; it could only have come from a successful master whose life bridged the last days of the artisan republic and the seeming chaos of the industrializing city, a fatherly employer who still called himself "a mechanic." His political slogans, like his personal mottoes, were deceptively simple; behind the watchwords "The Bible—liberty—My country or death" lay a steadfast refusal to admit that the social transformations of a quarter of a century—transformations that Harper had helped to initiate and complete—had altered the small producers' republic. Poverty, crime, immorality, and pauperism could never spring from any sickness of the American soul; the disease must have been imported by Catholics, the "base mercenary hirelings and Priests" of European monarchies, aided by unvirtuous, selfish politicians.[39]

38. Exman, *Brothers Harper*, 4, 45, 94, 122.

39. James Harper to ?, January 9, 1845; "Remarks to the Citizens of New York," Draft, n.d. [1845]; "To the Electors of the City and County of New York," n.d. [1844], Harper Papers, N-YHS.

With some timely aid from the Whigs, this appeal led to a stunning upset in the 1844 spring election. American Republican organizers perfected a network of ward associations, solicited funds from sympathetic merchants, and named a solid nonpartisan ticket headed by Harper and composed largely of master craftsmen. The Whigs, as Greeley's partner Thomas McElrath explained in a private apology, could not support any local organization as a matter of national party policy, despite the sympathy of many Whigs for the nativist cause; they agreed, however, to lend tacit support and to put up "a *show* of [a] fight," in exchange for American Republican support in the fall presidential election. Most of the Whig dailies backed Harper. The Democrats, vulnerable to nativist attacks on municipal corruption and favoritism, tried to reverse themselves with promises of reform, coupled with counterattacks on the nativists' bigotry and charges that the American Republican party was a Whig front. Their campaign was hopeless. In all, the nativists carried twelve of seventeen wards in the Common Council races; even more convincingly, Harper carried more than two-thirds of the city's election districts and won nearly one-half of the vote for mayor, crushing his Democratic rival and the Whigs' token nominee. Not surprisingly, a majority of the Harper vote— some 60 percent, according to contemporary estimates—came from nominal Whigs; far more significant was the nativists' ability to cut into Democratic support and win, very roughly, about one in five normally Democratic voters. Especially alarming to Tammany must have been the returns from those central and eastern wards, with their heavy concentrations of mechanics and Democrats, where Harper won with percentages higher than his percentages in the city as a whole (Table 20). Despite their Whiggish, pious connections, the nativists had won over at least a segment of the Bowery.[40]

An outpouring of popular nativism followed Harper's inauguration. Fears of papist insurrection, heightened by news of bloody nativist-immigrant riots in Philadelphia, reached epidemic proportions in early summer. Thurlow Weed reported to Harper that a Mr. Bromer, a builder in the Thirteenth Ward, had learned that men had been seen late at night carrying large boxes—of sufficient length and width to contain guns—into the basement of St. Mary's Catholic Church. The American Republican Executive Committee heard similar tales and warned the new mayor to station armed men at the almshouse, to prepare for a Catholic attempt to

40. Thomas McElrath to James Harper, n.d. [1844], Harper Papers, N-YHS; Scisco, *Political Nativism*, 44–46; Leonard, "Rise and Fall," 167–70; *Tribune*, April 12, 1844; Mushkat, *Tammany*, 214–15. Overall, the Democratic vote declined from 56.3 percent in 1843 to 40.8 percent in 1844, while the Whig vote declined from 43.7 percent to 10.5 percent.

free the inmates and run amok. When the papist plot failed to material-
ize, more mundane moral concerns, quite apart from the Catholic menace,
came to the fore. Letters from small masters and shopkeepers streamed into
City Hall to complain of raucousness in grogshops, of street-corner gatherings of youths and young adults, and of boys who pitched pennies while
using bold and profane language. One H. H. Dennison wrote to ask
whether something could be done to halt the Sunday performances of the
Messrs. J. Ahrens and Company, a traveling troupe that featured "a distinguished professor with black moustaches" and a singing "'lady in
black' (with her arms bare and her bosom nearly so)" who accompanied
herself on the harp. For these good citizens, nativist reform meant above
all the promotion of order, the use of political muscle to rid the city of
what one called "the largest group [sic] of Human Depravity on the continent of America."[41]

With all of their seeming paranoia and pettiness, such complaints
flowed from the heart of nativist idealism—the hope for a larger reformation of American politics and culture, a return to republican first principles to recover the harmony, virtue, and purity supposedly undone by the
pols and the Papists. Daniel Coolidge, an aging small master, epitomized
nativist opinion in his periodic, crudely penned messages of support and
advice. "May the Lord Bless you," he greeted Harper, "and enable you to
see Republicanism in that Beautiful and Heavenly form that our Worthy
Fore-Fathers were essating [sic] to see it in Early Times." Lest Harper
should be unclear about his meaning, Coolidge repeated that he referred
to the republicanism "Of Heavenly Birth—not that republicanism seen by
Tom Paine—Bucktails of old Tammany-Hall notoriety, prostituting men
to work all uselessness with grandness." Coolidge's father, it seemed, had
been a hero of the Revolution, and he had loved New York; his son, while
admitting that "truly New York is a great city," found it swarming with
gamblers, grifters, and paupers, all at war with the strivings of the Revolution. Harper, he wrote, had to take quick action to curb immigrant political power and remove the immoral from the streets, before the "Old-
Country Democrats" and others who had "abandoned heaven to go there
own Hook" plotted a return to power. Only then would Americans be
assured that their country and city would be governed not "by Brick Bats
or Bullets but by Love, Joy—Peace."[42]

41. Thurlow Weed to James Harper, n.d. [1844]; A. H. Stoughtenberg to James
Harper, July 18, 1844; Thomas Ritter to James Harper, May 25, 1844; George Coles
to James Harper, June 4, 1844; W. H. Byrnes to James Harper, June 13, 1844; H. H.
Dennison to James Harper, January 25, 1845; Daniel Coolidge to James Harper, March
23, 1845, all Harper Papers, N-YHS.
42. Daniel Coolidge to James Harper, March 23, April 15, May 5, May 16, 1844,
Harper Papers, N-YHS.

Harper did his best to implement his proposals, with symbolic gestures and substantive repressive reforms. On several occasions he ventured to enforce strictly the tavern laws prohibiting Sunday sales. His most famous proclamation, delivered in June 1844, banned the erection of booths and sheds for selling alcohol on the Fourth of July (still the custom in New York), a fitting blend of patriotism and propriety. Far more significant was the nativist attempt to reinforce New York's haphazard, eighteenth-century police system with a disciplined, salaried force. For over a decade, demands for police reform had intensified; in May 1844, the state legislature, responding to local Democratic initiatives, passed a law authorizing the complete reorganization of the city's police force. The new, nativist Common Council, incapable of following the Democratic plan and unwilling to break with precedent entirely, decided to supplement the existing constabulary with a uniformed police of 200 men. The nativist scheme was deeply flawed: the new professionals were too small a group to patrol the city effectively; the council's requirement that they be American citizens provoked immediate hostility among party politicians and ordinary immigrants. Within months, the nativist police system was scrapped. Police reform, however, was not: in 1845, goaded by the nativists' failure, a newly-elected Democratic Common Council abolished the old constabulary and enacted the original plan, for a department of 800 professional policemen.[43]

Harper's crusade failed to bring the sudden reformation expected by his supporters. Lacking any real power as mayor under the terms of the city's charter, Harper had to rely on a coordination of reform efforts with the Common Council; in this regard, he proved amateurishly inept. In July, "A Real Native" complained bitterly that on a Sunday walk through the city, he had found "the porter houses, taverns, cigar and candy shops the same as heretofore." Political exigencies kept Harper's reforms—and the American Republican party—from proceeding any further. In the elections of autumn 1844, the party supported the Whigs' candidates for national office, as promised, and formed a fusion ticket for local candidates; although they could not prevent the Democrats from winning the presidential electors, they did help elect two congressmen, two state senators, and two assemblymen, in what they considered a ringing endorsement of nativist principles. Even so, the nativists' total vote declined; thereafter, the party's coalition with the Whigs collapsed. Harper, with his intransigence about back-room political dealings, alienated local Whig professionals; upstate Whigs, led by Seward and Thurlow Weed, denounced the nativists as a threat to the Whig party itself. Over considerable protest, the Whigs decided to mount a serious challenge for the

43. Proclamation, n.d. [July, 1844], Harper Papers; Leonard, "Rise and Fall," 179–80.

mayoralty in 1845. American Republican loyalists, including the *Journal of Commerce*, stuck with Harper, who with characteristic humbleness accepted the nomination. The election all but destroyed the nativists' hopes, as the Democrats, running the respected merchant William Havemeyer for mayor on a reform ticket, reclaimed City Hall and won thirty of the thirty-four seats on the Common Council. Harper polled 36.1 percent of the vote, far ahead of the Whig, but a distant second to Havemeyer (Table 20). Apart from a successful candidate for ward constable, the American Republicans were swept clean from municipal government.[44]

The American Republicans' hasty decline—another example of the difficulties faced by a political movement outside of the major parties—ended political nativism in New York for several years. It hardly marked, however, the passing of nativist sentiment. In the streets, some of the roughest battles between nativist and immigrant gangs occurred in the late 1840s. More respectable activities engaged the several nativist secret societies and semisecret societies that blossomed just as Harper's regime collapsed. The largest, the Order of United Americans, founded its first chapter in 1845, joining merchants, masters, and journeymen with "the combined objects of patriotism and fraternal benevolence." Within two years, the OUA grew to include ten New York chapters; in 1847, it was joined by two more distinctly working-class nativist bodies, the American Laboring Confederacy and the Order of United American Mechanics. A failure at the polls, nativism persisted as a brotherly bond in the clubby atmosphere of the gang and the mutual-benefit society.[45]

As nativism survived, so it continued to influence at least some of New York's wage earners. Alone of all the political and extraparty movements of the first half of the nineteenth century, the nativists came close to practicing a true politics of nostalgia. While they offered no criticism of the ethics of liberal economic expansion—indeed, encouraged industriousness and sobriety—their cultural approach to political disorder revealed a genuine longing for a supposed golden age, before poverty, before immigration, before social conflict. Whereas the regular parties accommodated themselves to changing social realities and whereas the unions had looked to overcome new oppressions, the nativists clung to ideals of a way of life and a political order that had passed—and they did their best

---

44. *Tribune*, December 24, 1844, quoted in Spann, *New Metropolis*, 38–39; Scisco, *Political Nativism*, 54–61; Leonard, "Rise and Fall," 179–92; Mushkat, *Tammany*, 224; *Tribune*, April 18, 1845.

45. Spann, *New Metropolis*, 335–39; Scisco, *Political Nativism*, 69–70; Robert Ernst, "Economic Nativism in New York City during the 1840's," *NYH* 29 (1948): 170–86. On the OUA, see also [William W. Campbell], *Address and Poem Delivered at the Dedication of the Hall of the Alpha Chapter of the O.U.A.* (New York, 1845); Alfred B. Ely, *Oration: American Liberty* (New York, 1850).

to bring them back, by repressive means if necessary. Such cultural conservatism was not lost on some workers—especially not on those in trades in which the necessity or logic of interethnic solidarity was less than self-evident. The main rhetorical themes remained those of republican independence and mutuality—the republicanism of peace, joy, and love. In nativism, however, a significant minority of New York's workers had come to judge men's republican commitments, not by how they made their money or how they treated their employees or fellow workers, but by how they spoke, how they prayed, and by what version of the Bible they read.

Reformation

In some respects, Washingtonianism and American Republicanism were very different kinds of movements. The first attempted to reform the workingman, regardless of his religious faith (or lack of it) in a collective effort; the second, suffused with Protestant republican zeal, tried to reform the city by excluding Catholic immigrants from office. The Washingtonians rejected political action; the American Republicans were fixated on politics. The lower-class temperance movement united (for a time) masters and journeymen, craft entrepreneurs and former radicals, deists and former Bowery "traditionalists," but it never made a sturdy alliance across religious and class lines; the political nativists more convincingly joined entrepreneurs, some former unionists, and Boweryites, at least in 1844. The Washingtonians offered a new, secular, lower-class vehicle for self-preservation; the American Republicans combined old republican fears of cultural disinheritance and degradation with a morality of pious repression.

Despite these differences, however, the rise of lower-class temperance and the resurgence of political nativism were related. Several American Republican leaders, including James Harper, were also active Washingtonians. Nativist rhetoric and reforms invariably linked disorderliness and papist tyranny with alcohol. It is safe to assume that reformed Washingtonian Boweryites cast their ballots for Harper in 1844. Above all, both movements defined a new mood in the trades, an apparent quieting of the class turbulence of the 1830s and a more conservative approach to social and personal problems. They were not, as twentieth-century social scientists have suggested, the products of some ill-defined "irrational" "status anxiety"; nor were they the result of an evangelical counterassault on secular radicalism. Rather, they arose from workers' fully "rational" fears of dependence, from the search for an adjustment to what looked like permanent hard times.[46]

46. See Joseph R. Gusfield, *Symbolic Crusade: Status Politics and the American*

Yet if temperance and nativism marked a softening of class divisions, they did not eradicate class antagonisms or labor radicalism. The tensions between temperance evangelicals and reformed workingmen that helped undo Washingtonianism indicated abiding class tensions; later developments would show how similar tensions could divide different kinds of New York nativists. Outside of the temperance and nativist movements, meanwhile, veteran radicals, some trade unionists, and newcomers preserved radical ideals, in new organizations and (in some cases) with new kinds of cures for exploitation and inequality. Through the late 1840s, most of these men either worked in obscurity or occupied the lower echelons of political power. By the decade's end, some of them were ready to help lead a new wave of labor unrest.

Temperance Movement (Urbana, 1963); Seymour M. Lipset and Earl Raab, *The Politics of Unreason: Rightwing Extremism in America, 1790–1970* (New York, 1970); Anthony F. C. Wallace, *Rockdale: The Growth of an American Village in the Early Industrial Revolution* (New York, 1978).

9

Subterranean Radicals

Labor radicalism slipped into a political netherworld in the late 1830s and early 1840s. Labor's spokesmen, a motley collection of street-corner socialists, Fourierists, trade unionists, land reformers, and so-called shirtless Democrats, won only a few isolated victories. Even their most promising projects were doomed, in the long run, to neglect, deflection, or co-optation. Simply by staying together, however, the diverse groups of subterranean radicals kindled some of the ideas of the 1830s and added a few new ones of their own. While they toyed with what historians have generally dismissed as utopian panaceas, and while some appeared to retreat from the confrontations of the 1830s, they also repeated the argument that the roots of privilege, corruption, and "wage slavery" were located in prevailing property relations. After 1845, their efforts to remind New Yorkers that theirs was still a city of economic inequality and exploitation, combined with the struggles of the city's new Irish and German workers, began to move the labor question back to the center of popular awareness.

Mike Walsh and the Shirtless Democracy

New York party politics came of age in the aftermath of the panic. Office holding and party leadership remained in the hands of the city's merchants, financiers, lawyers and like professions; the maturation of the Whigs as a successful professional party, however, altered the structure and context of political activity, forcing politicians to develop new means to secure and incorporate a mass following. The Democrats—shocked by Whig victories nationally and locally in the panic years, and increasingly vulnerable to internal divisions over banking, slavery, and municipal re-form—adjusted their institutions and their rhetoric to consolidate their position as the party of both the Bowery and the immigrant. Without abandoning economic issues like the tariff, Tammany campaigns blended lower-class racism and anti-abolitionism, class and ethnic resentments, and nationalist jingo to establish the Democracy as the antinativist, red-blooded party of the patriotic workingmen, the eternal foe of the aris-tocratic, Tory, "Federal Whig Coon Party." To reinforce party loyalty, Tammany distributed a considerable share of middling and lower party offices to recent immigrants and humble wage earners. Always, the party paid special attention to craft workers. Former GTU men like Ely Moore and the locksmith Levi Slamm were absorbed into the party hierarchy. Separate Democratic craft committees organized in each of the major trades. Firemen and gang leaders (including the notorious Isaiah Rynders of the Empire Club) became party fixtures. By 1844, the New York Democracy, although far from invincible, had built the institutional base for a modern urban party machine.[1]

Among those who entered the party from below was an unorthodox group of largely working-class partisans, the "shirtless" Democrats, who instead of riding the high road to party spoils tried to wrest a measure of power from the party's leadership. After 1843, their egalitarian (and eventually anticapitalist) diatribes and their roughneck Bowery tactics made them a genuine force in party affairs. Their leader was a flamboyant Irish immigrant, a sometime engraver and newspaper editor, the chairman of the Spartan Association, Michael Walsh.

Walsh was born in Youghal, county Cork, in 1810, the son of a cabinet-maker and veteran of the United Irishman uprising of 1798. While the boy was still a toddler, his family emigrated to America, where his father set up a furniture store and mahogany yard; Michael, a Protestant who arrived before the famine wave, always considered himself a "true Ameri-can." After serving an apprenticeship with an engraver, young Walsh

---

1. Pessen, *Riches, Class, and Power*, 284–85; Sharp, *Jacksonians versus the Banks*, 297–304; Mushkat, *Tammany*, 185–241; Anthony Boleslaw Gronowicz, "Revising the Concept of Jacksonian Democracy: A Comparison of New York City Democrats in 1844 and 1884" (Ph.D. diss., University of Pennsylvania, 1981), 43–81; Hugins, *Jacksonian Democracy*, 66–67. On Moore's descent into ideological bathos, see Ely Moore, *Oration Delivered before the Mechanics and Workingmen of the City of New-York on the Fourth of July, 1843* (New York, 1843), a mélange of classical republican rhetoric, Christian piety, and lightly veiled encouragements to vote Democratic. On Rynders, see Matthew P. Breen, *Thirty Years of New York Politics Up-To-Date* (New York, 1899), 307–14; *Evening Post*, January 25, 1845; *Working Man's Advocate*, October 19, 1844. On the New York Democrats' party image, purported political philosophy, and cultural appeal, see above all the fine analysis in Benson, *Concept of Jacksonian Democracy*, 227–37.

traveled across the South in the 1830s, only to surface in New York as a newspaper reporter in 1839. He remained a journalist, first as a correspondent for the Democratic New York *Aurora* (edited for a time by another footloose artisan, Walt Whitman) and then as editor of his own newspapers, the *Knickerbocker* and, later, the *Subterranean*. By 1843, he was in the thick of that ebullient movement of youthful, ambitious, and fiercely democratic writers who aimed to create a new literature in the name of Young America.[2]

Walsh also aspired to his own niche in the Democratic party. In 1840, he founded the Spartan Association, a rough amalgam of an Irish secret society, a political gang, and a workingman's club, complete with its own banner, rituals, and unrepentant plebeian style. A year later, Walsh, enraged at Tammany's refusal to give the Spartans an independent voice within the party, ran for Congress on Bishop Hughes's Carroll Hall ticket, and drew enough votes away from the Tammany nominee to elect the Whig. Their point made, Walsh and his Spartans quickly returned to the Democrats—only to resume the attack on Tammany, the Van Burenites, and the Van Burenite "radical" Slamm (who edited the party's "workingmen's" paper, the *Plebeian*), for their cliquish management of the party and their cozy relations with local banking interests. Basking in his reputation as a consort of the B'hoys—a reputation cemented by his friendship with the pugilist hero and pol Tom Hyer—Walsh directed his supporters to stampede Tammany meetings with cries of "Go it, Mike"; escorted to the podium, he then broke into cocky tirades against office-seeking beggars, Democratic power brokers, and others "who fawn upon us and call us the bone and sinew of the country . . . and who would use us until there was nothing but bone and sinews left of us." Profane, sarcastic, and belligerent, Walsh hardly invented the use of crowds as party political tools, but he certainly helped perfect the craft, and turned it to new, insurgent political ends. The strategy worked, at least in winning Walsh a following. In 1842, the Spartans temporarily took over the Tammany nominating convention, named its own candidates (including Walsh), and vowed never to support the regulars. Although the Tammany chiefs eventually nominated and elected their own men, Walsh's muscular challenges and his angry denunciations—all recorded copiously in the *Subterranean*—kept him in the public eye. In 1846, Tammany

2. The best accounts of Walsh are Robert Ernst, "The One and Only Mike Walsh," *N-YHSQ* 26 (1952): 43–65; and Frank C. Rogers, "Mike Walsh: A Voice of Protest" (M.A. thesis, Columbia University, 1952). See also Schlesinger, *Age of Jackson*, 408–9, 412, 416, 428, 490–91, 508. On the cultural background of Young America, Perry Miller, *The Raven and the Whale* (New York, 1956), remains unsurpassed, but see also Peter G. Buckley's forthcoming dissertation on culture and politics in Jacksonian New York, State University of New York at Stony Brook.

finally relented and nominated Walsh as a regular candidate for the state assembly.[3]

In his restless search for a political voice and a public persona, Walsh came to embody a new and curious figure in New York politics, the radical Bowery B'hoy politician. He by no means lacked the competitive guile and personal ambition of the hungry journalist or party professional; writing to his son in 1854, he counseled the boy above all to learn to think and act quicker than others, to "keep ahead" in the "fast age" in which they lived—remarks that may be taken as Walsh's political watchwords. For all his abuse of Tammany, Walsh was a shrewd hand at party politics and journalistic infighting, capable of turning apparent disgrace—including a conviction for libel—into personal political advantage. Yet despite his bullying and his vainglorious, at times antic self-promotion, Walsh was neither a common ward heeler nor a cynical rabblerouser. Few doubted his sincerity: men as different as John Tyler, James Gordon Bennett of the *Herald*, George Henry Evans, and the deist radical Gilbert Vale all hailed his integrity (although not always his judgment).[4] He never attempted to use his Spartans to establish a mock populist regime of the kind the twentieth century would know. His use of force was perfectly in keeping with the roughhouse standards of the 1840s; if anything, it was exceeded by that of the regular party gangs like Rynders's Empire Club. Rather, Walsh, like Tammany but with a different rhetoric—and without elite directors—assembled disparate groups of lower-class New Yorkers in a new radical coalition, dedicated both to advancing his own political fortunes and to social reform. His basic support came from the men of the Bowery, "muscular Christians," one contemptuous contemporary called them, "of the class of Rowdy young New Yorkers who run with the Forty and Kill for Keyzer," men for whom Walsh's workingman's garb, stagy mannerisms, and contempt for aristocratic snobs must have seemed a political extension of the performances at the Bowery Theatre (Plate 19). Despite his criticisms of the "insolence of foreigners" and the "clannishness and pro-Tammanyism of some of the new arrivals," Walsh defended the immigrants against the "paltry and bigoted principles" of the nativists; his unyielding Anglophobia and support for Irish political freedom did not harm his standing with the city's largest group of downcast newcomers. Simultaneously, Walsh developed good relations with some of the most

3. *Subterranean* [New York], May 24, June 14, 21, 26, 28, August 30, October 18, 1845, February 28, May 16, 1846; Michael Walsh, *Sketches of the Speeches and Writings of Michael Walsh* (New York, 1843), 9–16, 21–32; Breen, *Thirty Years*, 302–7; *Working Man's Advocate*, March 30, 1844; Rogers, "Mike Walsh," 35–40.

4. Michael Walsh to ? [son], January 7, 1854; John Tyler to Michael Walsh, February 16, 1843, Walsh Papers, N-YHS; *Working Man's Advocate*, October 12, 1843; *Herald*, November 2, 1843; *Beacon* [New York], July 8, 1843.

radical ex-unionists, including John Commerford. Above all, Walsh looked to the city's journeymen, day laborers, and marginal small masters who harbored few hopes for a secure independence, "honest, hard-working young men who are dependent solely on the labour of their own hands for a subsistence," men like the Spartans, who Walsh claimed were "Radical in everything." Breaking with party norms and radical precedents, Walsh molded these men into a political movement—inside the party but outside of Tammany Hall—that celebrated Bowery bravado (with all its racism and insularity) and promised radical political action.[5]

Walsh's radicalism developed quickly between 1842 and 1846. In his earliest pronouncements, he claimed that his movement was a logical extension of the Loco Focos and of William Leggett's war on "feudal corporations": the original rules of the Spartan Association mentioned political reforms like the abolition of corporation charters as the group's major goals. Ever restless, Walsh then gravitated to reform movements throughout the Northeast. The Dorr Rebellion in Rhode Island caught his fancy as a plebeian uprising, and in 1842 he and about twenty Spartans joined an abortive raiding party to help Thomas Dorr capture the Providence arsenal; as late as 1845, well after the Dorrites had been repressed, Walsh threatened to lead five hundred Bowery B'hoys northward to flatten the Rhode Island state house and pillage Providence. A sudden interest in land reform and cooperation prompted Walsh to make a pilgrimage to Brook Farm in 1844, where he struck a temporary alliance with L. W. Ryckman, the Fourierist shoemaker. On the same trip, Walsh paused to address the striking mill girls at Lowell. Back home, he publicized these campaigns and for a time joined George Henry Evans's land-reform association, while he turned his sarcasm against those he described as New York's equivalents of New England's lords of the loom. He took special delight in taunting John Jacob Astor, a man who had saved—"from what the world calls his industry"—as much as thousands of laborers could collectively earn in twenty years. On a broader front, Walsh took aim at the leading entrepreneurial reformers and temperance groups, "a fanatical hypocritical set of imbecile humbugs," unconstitutional in their actions and unrepublican in their intents. "They regard God as a cruel and capricious tyrant," he bellowed. "How is it possible for such servile slaves to be republicans at heart?"[6]

5. Thomas L. Nichols, *Forty Years of American Life* (London, 1864), II, 157; *Subterranean*, December 23, 1843, March 23, 1844, March 7, 14, April 14, May 2, September 26, 1846; *Working Man's Advocate*, October 19, 1844. Commerford was nominated to the state assembly on the Spartans' insurgent "ticket" in 1843; *Subterranean*, October 28, 1843. The Forty referred to a fire company, "Keyzer" to a prominent butcher.

6. Walsh, *Sketches*, 13–16; *Subterranean*, September 21, 1844, June 14, July 26,

What set Walsh apart from the mainstream of the New York Democracy was his increasingly vitriolic anticapitalism. Walsh readily accepted the working-class critique of workshop labor relations, and he lashed out against "the slavery of wages"; in the mid-1840s, he published numerous exposés, some original, some borrowed from the *Tribune*, of the sordid condition of most workers in the city's major trades. Yet for Walsh, trade unionism was only part of what, ultimately, he saw as a political struggle, to retrieve genuine democracy from all forms of capitalist greed and power. In 1843, he paused from his polemics long enough to announce his credo and to distinguish it from that of mere political democrats:

> I care not what man it is that subscribes to the democratic creed; if he's a spit-licking, cringing, crawling journeyman, an overbearing employer, a tyrannical landlord, a haughty overbearing acquaintance—such man is no democrat. No man can be a good political democrat without he's a good social democrat.

To achieve the social democracy, Walsh later proclaimed, the working classes—all who lived by their own labor—had to look to themselves and refuse to follow the usual party politicians, utopian "bran-bred philosophers" and middle-class men who worshiped moral reform "on the glutted altars of Mammon." Once in the field, the new Democracy would naturally oppose the most pernicious Whig programs, especially the protective tariff—to Walsh, a measure that protected "not industry but capitalists." But so, too, would the movement strike at the deeper sources of evil in which regular politicians of both parties acquiesced, above all the contracting network, "that infamous system by which bloated purse-proud knaves can drive around in their gigs abusing the poor forlorn laborers." To charges that such a program made him a leveller, Walsh replied that he gloried in the name.[7]

Walsh's diatribes amounted to yet another reworking of artisan republican ideals, reminiscent in both tone and principles of some of Skidmore's formulations. The true aim of republican government, the *Subterranean* argued in 1845,

> should ever be the peace and happiness of its whole people. No people can ever be virtuous or happy while a large portion of them are in absolute want of the commonest comforts and even necessities of life. The peace, power, virtue, and glory of a country consists in the com-

---

August 30, September 6, October 4, 1845, January 19, 1846; *Working Man's Advocate*, October 12, 19, 26, 1844. On Walsh's growing interest in land reform, see *Subterranean*, February 24, March 23, 1844. On the Walsh-Evans alliance, see also Helene S. Zahler, *Eastern Workingmen and National Land Policy, 1829–1862* (New York, 1941), 37.

7. Walsh, *Sketches*, 12; *Subterranean*, March 22, 29, May 3, June 14, July 25, September 5, 1845, April 25, 1845, May 16, September 20, 1846.

fort, industry, and happiness of the whole people—not the aggrandizement of an idle few.

To this, Walsh added the anticapitalist connotations of the labor theory of value. "What is capital," he asked,

> but that all-grasping power which has been wrung, by fraud, avarice, and malice from the labor of this and all ages past?—It is the great—the icy-hearted despot of civilization, whose swords, spears, and battle-axes are shin-plasters, silver dollars, and doubloons. . . .

The Declaration of Independence, Walsh contended, guaranteed every person who was willing to labor the right to do so; man, he continued in Skidmoresque language, "must have an equal right to the share of the means which nature provided." To deny these rights would be to "deny the wisdom, the justice, and even common humanity of the God who created us."[8]

Capital, then, was unnatural, ungodly, and unrepublican—yet all about him, Walsh saw the effects of capital's ascendancy. With a frequency and bite unmatched even in Skidmore's writings, Walsh repeated the idea that wage slavery and the tyranny of capital had reduced republican producers to dependent menials. In a typical column of 1845, the *Subterranean* exploded:

> Demagogues tell you that you are freemen. They lie—you are slaves, and none are better aware of the fact than the heathenish dogs who call you freemen. No man devoid of all other means of support but that which his labor affords him can be a freeman, under the present state of society. He must be a humble slave of capital, created by the labor of the poor men who have toiled, suffered, and died before him.

The third sentence, here, was the critical one: the deadly blow feared by the unionists of 1836 had at last devastated the trades. "Nothing but revolution or legislation," Walsh concluded, "can effect the indispensable change." It was enough to win him nearly twenty thousand votes in 1846.[9]

Already, of course, Walsh had chosen the politics of legislation within the Democratic party, and although the outcome unfolded only in the 1850s, it is useful to examine it here. Once in the assembly, Walsh became an active legislator, cultivating his image as a hard-drinking brawler and workingman dandy—with his disheveled clothes, diamond ring, and silver-tipped cane—while he introduced legislation to end butchers' and builders'

---

8. *Subterranean*, November 8, 1845.

9. Ibid., September 13, 1845. See also ibid., April 25, 1846. In all, Walsh won 19,841 votes: *Daily Tribune*, November 9, 1846.

monopolies, abolish contracting on public building projects, and regulate conditions for apprenticeship. By the mid-1840s, however, Democratic politics had begun to turn more on the slavery question than on working-men's reform. Walsh, the Boweryite, had always regarded political inter-ference with slavery as a violation of democratic rights by Yankee entre-preneurs and as a diversion from the war on capital; his position hardened in 1843 when he joined with labor reformers as different as Orestes Brown-son and John Commerford to support the low-tariff Calhounites, whom the radicals considered friends of the workingmen.[10] Once the New York Democracy shattered into Barnburners and Hunkers—and even more after the Van Burenite Free Soil revolt—Walsh tied his political future ever more tightly to a defense of southern political interests. Rewarded with a nomination to Congress in 1852, Walsh arrived in Washington as much as a northern champion of southern rights as labor's voice in the House of Representatives. He made his grandest effort during the momentous de-bate on the Kansas-Nebraska Bill in 1854, when he trotted out to de-nounce the emerging Republican opposition as servants to the barons of wage slavery. The only difference between the free-labor and the slave sys-tems, he declared, was that in the South the Negro had a master without asking for one, while in the North the wage earner had "to beg for the privilege" of becoming a slave. George Fitzhugh could not have put it any better; although Walsh expressed contempt for his southern colleagues' mock chivalry and although he tried to raise other issues, he counted as only an addition to the prosouthern chorus. The scourge of unprincipled office seekers had become a political pawn.[11]

Ensnared in party intrigue and the slavery debate, incapable of taking any other position on the southern and slavery questions, Walsh's radical political departure was doomed. His personal limitations quickened the demise of his movement: Walshism, in the end, was nothing without Mike Walsh. Although he eschewed the role of party dictator—such a use of prolabor rhetoric would await the arrival of the Fernando Wood

10. Rogers, "Mike Walsh," 75–85. I have profited from reading an unpublished paper, written at Yale, by Michael A. Bernstein, now of Princeton University, "In the Interest of the Working Class: John C. Calhoun and the Radical Democracy." See also J. F. Jameson, ed., *Correspondence of John C. Calhoun* (Washington, D.C., 1900), II, 861–62, 874–78, 940–42, 965–67; Arthur Schlesinger, Jr., *Orestes A. Brownson: A Pilgrim's Progress* (Boston, 1939), 157–62; Charles G. Sellers, *James K. Polk, Conti-nentalist, 1843–1846* (Princeton, 1966), 25–26. On Commerford's admiration for Calhoun, see *Subterranean*, March 7, 14, 1846.

11. Ernst, "Mike Walsh," 58–62; *Congressional Globe*, 33d Cong., 1st sess., 1854, 27, pt. 2, pp. 1097, 1232, 1691, 1956–57. Walsh won 60 percent of the vote in 1852 and represented the Fourth ("Bowery") Congressional District (Wards 4, 6, 10, 14). See *Herald*, November 3, 1852. On Walsh's reactions to Washington, see Rogers, "Mike Walsh," 115–16.

regime, in the late 1850s—Walsh did manage, with some success, briefly to usurp the role of the one great political representative of the city's wage earners and struggling small producers. As egotistical as he was combative—the Spartans at one point referred to him as "our Napoleon"—he began to charge that other reformers had stolen his ideas; with his prodigious drinking and spoken slang—"like any tramp who had graduated from the gutter," an offended politico later wrote of his speechmaking—Walsh came to consider himself the only man two-fisted enough to lead the city's lower classes. His followers agreed, only to be led into the constraints of regular party politics. Had another equally dedicated radical—John Commerford, perhaps—been able to assemble and command Walsh's forces, the Subterranean Democracy might have led to a more durable, independent organization. As it happened, Walsh's success in the party and the personal traits that broadened his appeal also helped destroy him and his movement. For all practical purposes, the end was in sight in 1848, and by 1850 Walsh was more of a follower than a molder of dissent. The rest was pitiful anticlimax. By 1854, he had lost touch with his constituency, which was more concerned with a resurgence of labor activity than with slavery and the debates in Washington; "Where is Mike Walsh?" went the cry of one machinist on strike, "Mike Walsh is in Congress!" Defeated for re-election, Walsh traveled to Europe to help arrange a series of business deals for some local shippers. Along the way, his alcoholism overcame him, and he returned to New York riding steerage on a clipper, desperately ill, a political corpse. On March 16, 1859, he was spotted with some friends in several Broadway saloons, drinking into the following dawn. The next afternoon, Saint Patrick's Day, some strollers discovered his battered remains on the steps of an Eighth Avenue shop, stripped of his trademark watch and ring, a curiosity later gawked at by thousands alerted to the scene.[12]

Destined for the ignominy of a penny dreadful, Walsh nevertheless made his share of contributions to the preservation of labor radicalism in hard times. Alone of all the prominent local political figures of the early and mid-1840s, he spoke in an unvarnished language of class conflict, thrusting the labor theory of value into his listeners' faces, attaching the cause of the "wage slaves" to that of the social democracy. If his radicalism did not extend to the question of slavery and race and if he ultimately led his followers into a disastrous political alliance, he also brought an anticapitalist variant of artisan republicanism out of the workshops and meeting halls and into the streets, to challenge the moral reformism and nativism of the 1840s and to bridge the gap between labor radicalism and Bowery

12. Rogers, "Mike Walsh," 43; Breen, *Thirty Years*, 302–3; *Subterranean*, July 25, 1846; *Tribune*, April 11, 1853; Schlesinger, *Age of Jackson*, 491.

republicanism that the unionists of the 1830s had never fully overcome. The achievement fell far short of Walsh's original promises. The message would help vitalize a new labor movement, even as Walsh himself began to drown in party politics and liquor.

Land Reform

Outside the Democratic party, other labor reformers (some of whom temporarily supported Walsh) contended that the wage slave would be freed only if he could obtain a patch of land. The argument had long been a familiar one to artisan radicals versed in radical republican and Ricardian socialist writings. Thomas Spence, the English Jacobin artisan, had most eloquently turned his political egalitarianism into an "agrarian" attack on landlords in the 1790s; Paine in his *Agrarian Justice* (1796) had raised similar issues, although he drew back from Spence's radical assaults on private property; among Spence's and Paine's American admirers, Byllesby and Skidmore had argued that land should be titled for use alone. The argument had reappeared at various points in the 1830s. George Henry Evans began assaulting the land monopoly in the *Man* in 1834. John Commerford declared that apart from union strikes, distribution of cheap public lands was "the great outlet of relief in view." Now that the union was gone, land reform appeared to some ex-unionists and union sympathizers as the only remedy left.[18]

National politics and the depression made the land issue even more prominent after 1837. In Washington, the disposal of public lands had been hotly contested for two decades as an issue ancillary to battles over the tariff and the currency. Democratic support for western cheap-land programs helped pass a series of pre-emption bills between 1838 and 1841, but important questions about the price of lands, the distribution of profits from land sales, and the state control of lands remained open. In the early 1840s, different factions within the national parties and shifting sectional alliances focused on land as never before, turning positions on different versions of redemption and graduation into political litmus tests. And as land dominated the congressional agenda, the depression brought the issue closer to home for eastern craft workers. With unemployment high, unions in abeyance, and immigration swelling, removal to the West (long a temporary solution for New York journeymen in hard times) now seemed a possible way out; rather than tramp, some craftsmen now reluc-

13. *Man*, March 26, May 22, 1834; *Working Man's Advocate*, September 19, 1835. On Spence, see Thompson, *Making of the English Working Class*, pp. 161–63; on Spence's influence on the land reformers, see *Radical*, April, 1841.

tantly considered becoming western pioneers, once they had the necessary funds—and once Congress made cheap lands readily available.[14]

By the mid-1840s, land reform had captured the imagination of almost every labor radical still active in New York. Among them were some former activists from the GTU and the Loco Foco Democracy, along with the Painite deists (who doggedly continued to meet every January 29 to honor their hero). George Henry Evans was the prime mover. Evans had removed to Rahway, New Jersey, some thirty miles from Manhattan, in 1835; a year later, citing exhaustion and poor health, he suspended publication of the *Working Man's Advocate*. By 1841, when he returned to publishing with a new monthly, *The Radical*, his interest had shifted entirely to land reform. "If man has any right on the earth," he wrote in an early editorial,

> he has the right to land enough to raise a habitation on. If he has a right to live he has a right to land enough for his subsistence. Deprive anyone of these rights and you place him at the mercy of those who possess him.

Evans's "agrarianism" arose not from a simple nostalgia for rural life (although he had, to be sure, retreated to the countryside) but from his interpretation of how the free-labor regime had subverted republican rights. For Evans, no less than for Walsh, the laboring population of the North was in a state of "white slavery," in which "a large portion of they who perform the most useful labor are allowed to consume a less proportion of the fruits of their labor than the colored slaves of the south." While he affirmed (unlike Walsh) that he supported abolition, Evans also maintained that "reform should begin at our own firesides":

> The white laborers [he wrote] are beginning to understand that *liberty* means something more than the privilege of exchanging taskmasters, and that it is not a *law of nature* that labor should be rewarded in an inverse ratio to its usefulness; and philanthropists, if they would have an influence, must no longer confine their sympathies to *color*.

To retrieve these lost rights and the full reward of labor, Evans concluded, the white laborer had to be "emancipated . . . *by restoring his natural right to the soil*"; with access to the land, he insisted, "the laborer would

---

14. The standard work on land reform and eastern workers remains Zahler, *Eastern Workingmen*. I have also found useful Roy M. Robbins, "Horace Greeley, Land Reform and Unemployment, 1837–1862," *Agricultural History* 7 (1933): 18–41, and (with caution) John R. Commons, "Horace Greeley and the Working-Class Origins of the Republican Party," *PSQ* 24 (1909): 468–88. On the politics of land reform, George M. Stephenson, *The Political History of the Public Lands from 1840 to 1862* (Boston, 1917), though old, is still useful.

not be *dependent* on the employer, and would consequently rise to his proper rank in society . . ."[15]

Evans's old associates agreed. John Windt and the freethinker Gilbert Vale contributed speeches in praise of cheap land; by 1843, the Thomas Paine's birthday celebrations included toasts to "An end to the land monopoly," and "Our Public Lands; the workingman's remedy." John Commerford, now a struggling small master chairmaker, invoked the union legacy in support of Evans's proposals. A three-point program—for free public lands to actual settlers, for limitation of the quantity of land held by any individual, and for exemptions of homesteaders from debt—became their rallying point.[16]

Land reform also attracted a collection of associationists and communitarians, ranging from the New York Fourierists to artisan cooperative builders. Interest in communitarianism had all but disappeared in New York in the 1830s; when it revived, the followers of Charles Fourier, notably Albert Brisbane, made the greatest stir. Brisbane, the studious son of a wealthy landowner, had traveled to Europe in the early 1830s to study with Hegel and Heine, but returned a thorough convert to the Frenchman's theory of the passions and communal life. In 1840, he published his notebooks crammed with Fourier's pronouncements, under the title *The Social Destiny of Man*. With diagrams and taxonomies, he sketched a geometry of the injustice and wastefulness of competitive production and called for American versions of the phalanxes designed by his master. Capital would not be abolished in Brisbane's utopia; rather, men's and women's work would be so matched to their fixed passions, and production made so much more efficient and bountiful, that the portion of wealth absorbed by the capitalist would not be missed by the workers. Civilization, with its antisocial spirit, its "apathy and intellectual death," would end; association—the adjustment of inner passions to social relations, the fulfillment of man's social destiny—would replace it.[17]

Almost immediately, Brisbane captured his most influential disciple, Horace Greeley. By the early 1840s, Greeley was the most important Whig editor in the country; unlike his more conventional colleagues, how-

15. *Radical*, January, 1841, March, 1841, June 1841; Zahler, *Eastern Workingmen*, 34–36.

16. *Radical*, February, 1843; Zahler, *Eastern Workingmen*, 52–53.

17. On American Fourierism, Arthur Bestor, "American Phalanxes" (Ph.D. diss., Yale University, 1938), is still unsurpassed. On Fourier, see Frank Manuel, *Prophets of Paris* (New York, 1962), 195–243. A useful biography of Brisbane is Maurice Buchs, "Le Fourierisme aux Etats-Unis: Contribution à l'étude du socialisme américain" (Thesis, Faculté du Droit, University of Paris, 1948); more analytical is Michael Fellman, *The Unbounded Frame: Freedom and Community in Nineteenth Century American Utopianism* (Westport, Conn., 1973), 3–19. See also (but with caution) Redelia Brisbane, *Albert Brisbane: A Mental Biography* (Boston, 1893).

ever, Greeley, who had tasted poverty as a journeyman printer in New York in the 1830s, perceived the wage earners' plight as a social disorder and not as a series of individual failures. "To talk of Freedom of Labor," he would write,

> when the fact is that a man who has a family to support and a house hired for the year is told, "if you will work thirteen hours per day, or as many as we might think fit, you can stay, if not you can have your working papers, and well you know that no one else hereabout will hire you"—is this not the most egregious flummery?

Greeley's concern led him to devote more space than any other main-stream New York editor did to reports on the foul conditions in the trades and to suggestions on how they might be improved. His profound distaste for any cause that promoted class conflict and strikes—what he would later call "industrial warfare"—tempered his views on trade unionism: Greeley's mercurial career may be read largely as a search for a democratic solution to exploitation that would preserve the supposed harmony be-tween employer and employee and the benefits of capitalist growth. Owen-ism might have suited him well, but in 1841 he read a similar message in Brisbane's compilation. For over a year, from 1842 to 1843, Greeley gave Brisbane a free hand in a column in the *Tribune*, to broadcast American-ized versions of European communitarian ideas to a mass American readership.[18]

Thanks largely to Greeley and Brisbane, Fourierism bound together an odd alliance of New England intellectuals, philanthropic reformers, evan-gelized provincials, and New York radicals. While the Fourierist lumi-naries of Brook Farm charmed, amused, and infuriated the sophisticated reading public and opened their arms to workingmen, other experiments, funded by absentee philanthropists, relied almost entirely on the labors of humbler urban craftsmen. Between 1843 and 1845, some twenty-six Fourier-ist communities were founded, almost half of them in the burned-over areas of western New York and Ohio. The metropolis also felt the move-ment's reverberations. At the North American Phalanx in New Jersey, less than thirty miles from Manhattan, sixty shopkeepers and tradesmen from Albany began the most successful Fourierist community; the Sylvania As-sociation, a short-lived affair in western Pennsylvania, consisted largely of New York City mechanics.[19]

18. *Daily Tribune*, April 10, 1846; Greeley, *Recollections*, 146–50. On Greeley, see Daniel Walker Howe, *The Political Culture of the American Whigs* (Chicago, 1979), 184–97. On Greeley's early contacts with Brisbane, see *New Yorker*, December 26, 1840, January 2, 16, 1841.

19. Bestor, "American Phalanxes," 74–75, 225–38. Dolores Hayden, *Seven American Utopias: The Architecture of Communitarian Socialism, 1790–1975* (Cambridge, Mass., 1976), 149–59, 183–85; Anne C. Rose, *Transcendentalism as a Social Movement*,

Revamped for Americans, the body of Fourierist doctrine never won as many thoroughgoing adherents as its promoters hoped it would. The architectonics of balanced passions, as idiosyncratic as their creator, never figured as prominently in the American phalansterians' remarks as did more straightforward cooperative concerns. The Sylvania Association, for example, although it conformed to Fourier's plans, claimed only that it had been started by "intelligent and energetic working-men, who, despairing of obtaining the aid of men who have capital, have determined upon building an Association for their own labor." Cooperative production and the abolition of unproductive profit and accumulation were their major aims, to be won by their own toil: differences over religion, educational theory, and stock-holding arrangements remained, causing the swift decline of most of the Fourierist experiments. Where Fourierism succeeded, it revived interest in cooperation and the communitarian alternative, to restore independence, virtue, and mutual obligation—which in turn led directly to wider support for land reform. When, in 1843, Evans and his band asked for the phalansterians' support, several, including Greeley, Brisbane, Lewis Ryckman, and the former Owenist Lewis Masquerier, joined them. When some Fourierists, notably the restless Greeley, finally abandoned phalansterian associationism, they became all-out advocates of cheap western lands.[20]

A third column of support came from those associationists and self-professed socialists who drew their ideas not from Fourier but from English labor reformers and the Chartists. In Britain, Owenist communitarianism had firmly attached itself to working-class radicalism, passing from the labor exchanges and the Grand National Consolidated Trades' Union of the 1830s to various utopian commonwealths of cooperative nonwage labor in the 1840s. Their cause was strengthened by the American-born John Bray, whose *Labour's Wrongs and Labour's Remedy* appeared in cheap editions on both sides of the Atlantic in the early 1840s, to restate the argument against unequal exchange of labor and the land monopoly. An array of land and producers' cooperatives sprang up across the North of England; although the most successful of them, the Rochedale Pioneer Society, eventually reconciled itself to capitalist enterprise, it retained the collectivist spirit through the 1840s. Simultaneously, the more political Chartists devised a land program quite similar to Evans's and put it into practice in the Land Cooperative Society of 1845. Feargus O'Connor, well

1830–1860 (New Haven, 1981), 140–61. Rose presents an especially valuable discussion of the links between Brook Farm, Fourierism, and the New England labor movement.

20. *Daily Tribune*, October 28, 1842, January 17, 1843; *State Mechanic*, March 4, 18, 25, 1843; Zahler, *Eastern Workingmen*, 53–54. On the Sylvania Association, see also *Phalanx* [New York], October 5, 1843.

acquainted with agrarian issues in his native Ireland, based most of his economic theory on the land question, arguing that restoration of land was "the only means of promoting industry, independence . . . and the great principle of self-reliance." Bronterre O'Brien and other Chartist leaders filled their speeches and the *Northern Star* with similar points; land reform remained on the lips of the Chartist exiles Thomas Devyr and Peter Bussey, who organized Chartist and socialist meetings in Manhattan in 1840 and 1841. The socialism of the democratic cooperative system— defined, in contrast to the competitive system, as a combination of common property, equal rights, and mutual labor—soon found its advocates in the deist press friendly to land reform. One conservative, Moses Beach, could see the entire land-reform movement only as "neither more nor less than English Chartists transported to this country."[21]

The different tendencies favoring land reform joined in 1844 under Evans's aegis in the National Reform Association. The first meeting of the association was held at John Windt's home and included Evans, Windt, Masquerier, the Irish Chartist Devyr, and James A. Pyne, a baker and former activist in the Loco Foco Democracy. John Commerford joined shortly thereafter. Mike Walsh served as coeditor of the association's newspaper, *Young America*, before breaking with Evans after a year of personal wrangling. By September 1845, land-reform groups had spread to several other states, and were being trumpeted in the *Tribune* as the most important labor movement of the day. The NRA's program, mingling the republican theme of independence and renewed attacks on banking and credit with the republican emphasis on political action, had found a slogan: "Vote Yourself a Farm." More fancifully, the group invented neo-Jeffersonian plans for the future development of republican townships—harmonious, virtuous parallelograms of equal, 160-acre plots traversed by roads to the outside world, the building blocks of an America of independent labor (Plate 20). In November, a collection of New York activists, including Walsh, Commerford, and Masquerier, took the program to the voters in campaigns for state and local offices.[22]

From the start, the National Reformers appealed directly to the city's

21. Sidney Pollard, "Nineteenth-Century Cooperation: From Community Building to Shopkeeping," in *Essays in Labour History*, ed. Asa Briggs and John Saville (London, 1967), 74–112; Joy MacAskill, "The Chartist Land Plan," in *Chartist Studies*, ed. Asa Briggs (London, 1959), 306–9; Alice Mary Hadfield, *The Chartist Land Company* (Newton Abbot, 1970), 11–44; Harris, *Socialist Origins*, 140–42; Ray C. Boston, *British Chartists in America, 1839–1900* (Manchester, 1971), 21–44; Zahler, *Eastern Workingmen*, 77–79; *Beacon*, May 14, December 5, 1840; *Diamond* [New York], May 1840; Thomas Devyr, *The Odd Book of the Nineteenth Century* (New York, 1882), II, 25, 139.

22. *Tribune*, July 31, 1845; *Young America*, October 11, 1845; *Herald*, November 5, 1845.

small masters and journeymen, always making sure to note their own arti-san backgrounds. Commerford continually remarked how the agitation re-minded him of 1835 and 1836 and dwelled on the importance of land re-form to workingmen, in addresses to such groups as the journeymen stonecutters' association and the nativist American Laboring Confedera-tion. Evans went out of his way to speak to any of the surviving trade societies that would listen, to remind his audience of the GTU's position on land reform in the 1830s. *Young America*, one of several NRA news-papers, seized the mantle of Thomas Skidmore, the Working Men, and the GTU—land reformers all, according to one editorial. Outdoor public meetings and banners proclaimed that American labor was "fast verging on the servile dependence" common in the Old World. As the NRA's mem-bership grew, it became a movement of disaffected artisans. Small groups of journeymen blacksmiths, cordwainers, and tailors formed their own benevolent societies affiliated with the NRA; the Spartans joined in, as long as their hero did; journeymen and, even more, small masters domi-nated the leadership. In a bid for even wider support, the NRA estab-lished a preliminary industrial congress in 1845 to prepare for political action and to formalize its links with the New England Workingmen's Association. Evans, even more than in the 1830s, cautioned against re-liance on trade unionism and strikes—as at best partial solutions, at worst disastrous debacles—but his revived *Working Man's Advocate* publicized and encouraged union activities in and out of New York. By 1847, under the name of the Industrial Congress, the land reformers had backed such demands as the ten-hour day for factory workers.[23]

It was a heady effort, but an inauspicious one. For too many urban wage earners, resettlement to the West seemed in the end impractical, even with government aid. "We could not travel to the West without money," an English traveler heard from eastern workers, "and we can-not save money." Even if land, tools, and seed could be bought, exile to what one journeyman called "the horrors of wilderness life" seemed a relegation to purgatory. The remaining city trade unions and benefit so-cieties—wary, no doubt, of Evans's position on strikes—listened politely to the land reformers before declining to join them officially. The nativists of the American Laboring Confederation invited Commerford and Evans

23. *Working Man's Advocate*, March 30, April 6, 20, June 8, 26, May 25, June 29, July 13, September 21, October 12, 1844, March 15, 1845; *Young America*, July 5, September 20, 1845; *Champion of American Labor*, April 3, 1847; Zahler, *Eastern Workingmen*, 57–67. Of those active land reformers identified in the NRA press and city directories (N=62), the vast majority (71.4 percent) were from the trades; of these, 80.0 percent were small masters or journeymen. On the NRA Industrial Congress, see also Norman J. Ware, *The Industrial Worker, 1840–1860: The Reaction of American Industrial Society to the Advance of the Industrial Revolution* (Boston, 1924), 222–26.

to speak, but quickly dismissed their proposals as diversionary and unrealistic. The twin causes of cheap land and labor reform found a more popular spokesman in Mike Walsh, but following his break with Evans in 1845, Walsh lambasted the NRA as a collection of "would-be philanthropists," who by their "milque-toast cowardice" to confront capitalists had proven themselves out of touch with the wage slaves. In its first bid for office, the group's leading candidates could not even muster one hundred votes; after a few months of further agitation, they increased their total, but to a mere five hundred votes.[24]

The land reformers' significance was far greater than their numbers indicated; the difficulty is in sorting out what that significance was. Given common historical standards, the NRA might appear to have been the city's first truly petit bourgeois radical movement, the final resolution of eighteenth-century Painite republicanism into a lower-middle-class enthusiasm divorced from the concerns of wage-earners. Although many of its leaders had been outspoken supporters or leaders of the GTU, the NRA turned away from "industrial warfare" to an effort to join honorable masters and journeymen against the common antirepublican foe, the land monopoly. Although they accepted the label "agrarian" and spoke respectfully of Thomas Skidmore, Evans and his associates never came close to espousing Skidmore's General Division. Coming *after* the journeymen's revolt and the early struggle over capitalist wage relations, the land reformers' antimonopolism purposefully obscured the lines of class drawn by the GTU, to inspire democratic small master craftsmen infuriated by capitalist privilege but wary of a renewed wage earners' insurgency. To succeeding generations of Gompersites and Marxists, such ideas would be the very soul of petit bourgeois radicalism.

Yet such a classification (with the polemical air of opprobrium that it still evokes) distorts the historical context of the 1840s and misses the NRA's genuinely radical approach to labor; it also slights the land reformers' importance in maintaining at least the semblance of a labor radical milieu. Many years later, after the repression of the slaveholders' rebellion and after the labor movement's failed courtship of the Radical Republicans, the middle-class assumptions behind some of the land reformers' views would become more obvious. Greeley's ideological pilgrimage, from land reform in the 1840s to self-help and Liberal Republicanism in the 1860s and 1870s, is the classic example of this gradual revelation. But in the 1840s, such distinctions were still only beginning to be worked out. Be-

24. Commons, *Documentary History*, VII, 54–55; Zahler, *Eastern Workingmen*, 57–59; *Working Man's Advocate*, February 22, March 8, 15, 22, 1845; *Champion of American Labor*, April 3, 1847; *Subterranean*, July 14, 25, 1845; *Herald*, November 5, 1845. For the vote, see *Young America*, April 12, 1845; November 8, 1845.

fore 1850, the land reformers' stress on labor's plight and, in particular, on the economic relationships that undermined independence explicitly linked their cause to the concerns of exploited wage earners as well as to those of petty producers. Their opposition to strikes was based, at least partly, on their contention that trade unionism would accomplish little unless some larger social transformation was achieved; their opposition never dampened their sympathy for wage earners' activities. Their anti-capitalism took complaints about conditions in the trades beyond the exigencies of the moment, to sketch out (far more concretely and in greater detail than the earlier unionists had done) an alternative American republic and the political means to achieve it. More important, the land reformers' conceptions of labor and property relations did not contradict those formulated by the trade unionists in the 1830s; although its solutions were different, the NRA, like the GTU, aimed to end the transformation of labor into a commodity, to restore to labor the character of a personal estate—or, in Evans's somewhat different terminology, to restore capital to its "true relation" as "the representative of voluntary labor," always found "in possession of those who have produced it."[25]

The land reformers' ability, meanwhile, to hold together a coherent, articulate, independent radical organization (however small) was remarkable enough in itself in the mid-1840s. By 1846, the land-reform movement had become a haven for all sorts of New York labor radicals. More than any other movement of its time, it also kept open communication between Americans and Old World radicals, publishing excerpts from the Chartist and English socialist press and welcoming émigrés as soon as they arrived in the city. It created, in the National Industrial Congress, a forum for wage earners' grievances on matters that had nothing directly to do with land reform. To be sure, for most of the 1840s, the land reformers (like many later generations of socialists) remained, as Walsh charged, out of step with the mainstream of working-class opinion. Their influence would prove far greater in 1850.

Plebeian Protestants:
The American Laboring Confederacy
and the Mechanics' Mutual

Until the coincidental demise of both Washingtonianism and the Harper regime, in 1845, the assertion of Protestant norms and cultural superiority dulled class antagonisms. Thereafter, however, the spread of temperance

25. *Working Man's Advocate*, August 31, 1844. It is perhaps worth noting that Marx and Engels considered the NRA, along with the Chartists, as a "working-class party," although obviously not a communist one. See Marx and Engels, "Manifesto of the Communist Party," 354.

and nativism among New York's wage earners helped feed the most curious of all the popular movements of the 1840s, the largely working-class nativist and Protestant benefit societies. Although far less militant than the class-conscious unions, these Protestant groups described the limits of cross-class solidarity in moral and nativist reform: their emergence helped to reshape cultural politics to account for economic antagonisms. Ironically, they helped clear the way for a possible reconciliation of journeymen and radicals across ethnic and religious lines.

The arrival of the Order of United American Mechanics in New York brought first evidence of the changing contours of workingmen's nativism. Founded in Philadelphia in 1845, the OUAM was as forthright in its moralism as in its nativism. Members, sworn to a pledge of "Honesty, Industry and Sobriety," were expected to forsake blasphemy, brothels, and drink, on pain of expulsion. Primarily a benevolent society, the group encouraged sympathizers to patronize American-born mechanics and sponsored lectures and roundtable discussions on how to secure individual economic independence. Yet while they endorsed the industrious ethos, the United American Mechanics also distinguished themselves from more elite nativist groups: theirs was to be a nativism of and for the small master and journeyman artisan. They barred nonproducers—merchants, professionals, financiers—as well as immigrants from their meetings. OUAM lectures included discussions on the labor theory of value and on the evils of financiers and other capitalists. Without questioning its nativism, the Order claimed one of the keystones of artisan radicalism as its own.[26]

The implications of the marriage of nativism to the labor theory of value became clear only between 1845 and 1847, when the arrival of the famine migration from Ireland and the great German emigration sparked a new form of lower-class economic nativism. In March 1847, a notice signed "Many Mechanics" greeted the city's workingmen with an invitation to meet and adopt measures for self-preservation through immigration restriction. By all appearances, the call had the full approval of the city's established nativist organizations—the hall designated for the meeting was owned and lent for the occasion by the American Republicans' Native American Association—but within weeks, the new movement established its own identity. The organizing meeting was directed by a diverse group of small masters and journeymen—including the ex-Washingtonian painter J. D. Young—primarily from the sweated consumer finishing crafts and the building trades, a constituency very different from that of the Ameri-

26. Scisco, Political Nativism, 65–67; Champion of American Labor [New York], May 29, June 5, 1847; Laurie, Working People of Philadelphia, chap. 8. Three chapters of the OUAM were operating in New York in 1847. See Champion of American Labor, August 14, 1847.

can Republicans. Their grievances centered almost exclusively on economic problems—how immigration contributed to the contracting system, the depression of journeymen's and women's wages, and the elimination of honest independent craftsmen. Although the immigrants, particularly the Irish, deserved some sympathy, Young told the meeting, the presence of so many poor newcomers had knocked wages down to disgraceful levels. Other speakers cited dismal piece rates for trades in which the immigrants were most numerous. Six days later, a meeting of two thousand "Working Men and Women" turned the movement into a formal organization, the American Laboring Confederacy; after electing a central committee of two delegates from each of the trades, the body initiated a petition campaign calling for a direct head tax on every foreign arrival and penalties for importers and contractors who hired illegal immigrant labor.[27]

At first, the Confederacy emphasized its dedication to the harmonious interests of "the Trade," its abhorrence of radicalism, and its belief that there was "no class of men in this country whose interests would suffer in consequence of the cessation of immigration." At the original gathering in March, Young tried hard to eliminate any suspicions that "this meeting will lead to radicalism." The Confederacy's newspaper, the *Champion of American Labor*, singled out the National Reform Association for attack, conflating land reform with revolutionary "agrarianism." One "Old Mechanic," in a letter to the *Champion*, argued that immigration should be stopped so that employers could hire American workers, "conservative in their views on religion, political economy, etc."; with these "active and intelligent" men on the job, "then will all the radicalisms of the present take flight from this once happy land." Temperance poems and celebrations of the Protestant Sabbath appeared beneath the *Champion*'s masthead; the paper's iconography returned to all the old themes—the small shop artisan, the Revolutionary patriot, and the hammer and hand (Plate 21). "We say to the capitalists," the editor William S. Tindale declared, "look to your interests as *we* look to your interests: we are your friends, be you friends to yourself. Preserve our friendship . . . by unitedly endeavoring to shut out the *cause* of all our differences, the *only* cause, ALIEN CHEAP LABOR."[28]

By the summer, however, the call for unity grew strained, as the Confederacy began to assess why its arguments had failed to win support in high places. Such a change in attitude had been likely almost from the start; these new nativists, after all, took their lead not from prominent Whigs or craftsmen in trades that had escaped bastardization but from

27. *Champion of American Labor*, April 3, 1847. See also Ernst, "Economic Nativism," 177–79.
28. *Champion of American Labor*, April 3, 17, May 8, 1847.

building tradesmen, shoemakers, and tailors, whose complaints about the blight of immigration were in part the result of metropolitan industrialization. As reports reached the *Champion* about how insensitive capitalists and employers turned the immigrant invasion to their own advantage, anger replaced the appeal to artisan honor and mutuality. "The exclusiveness of capitalists is proverbial," wrote one nativist correspondent, "and most justly are they charged with that which is natural to them as the change their natures undergo from the accumulation of wealth." "Old Mechanic," eager to return the trades to conservative hands, also realized that American wage earners and small masters would not long abide the contracting system; unless it was abolished, he remarked, "I shall not attempt to say how long property will be safe." Sympathetic reports of strikes and the New England movement for the ten-hour day began to appear in the *Champion*. The great material promise of America—the promise of "Roast Beef and two dollars a day"—had not been realized, several nativists pointed out, and the problem had led to a direct clash of interests among native Americans. Thus, the Confederacy's petition resolved:

> WHEREAS, Tariffs have been put forth by the political parties affording no *direct* competition to farmers, mechanics, laborers, seastresses, factory girls, sewing women, and American land laborers and operatives, but reserving all protection for the rich capitalists, to mammoth manufacturers, extensive railroad speculators and contractors in the public works . . . all these latter having it in their power to *compel Americans* to work for 50 cents per day, by reason of their having the cheap pauper labor of Europe ready at hand, to work for that price if Americans refuse—

> Therefore,

> Resolved, that AMERICAN LABOR ought to be protected against foreign competition—directly and not by reflection, because the shadow is infinitely thin in comparison with the substance—

If this was a far cry from the class consciousness of the 1830s, it also was very different from the nativism of James Harper and the American Republican party and far more insistent on economic questions than the NADA of 1835. Immigration restriction, once an instrument of political reformation and cultural homogenization, had become a means to check capitalist greed and underpayment.[29]

Similar themes appeared in the Christian workingmen's republicanism of the Mechanics' Mutual Protection Association. The Mutual was started in Buffalo in 1841 by a former dyer, the Scots immigrant Robert MacFarlane, to help displaced and underpaid small masters and journey-

29. *Champion of American Labor*, April 17, 24, May 1, July 3, 1847. The petition appears in *Champion of American Labor*, July 24, 1847.

men pool their available resources, set up labor exchanges, and dispense sickness benefits. The idea quickly caught on in Ohio, Pennsylvania, Wisconsin, and Michigan, where every major town and city soon boasted a Mechanics' Mutual chapter. In 1846, MacFarlane brought his organization to New York, where, he observed, more than anywhere in America, the mechanics had suffered evil from unjust competition and worked for wages by which no American could live "as the citizen of the Republic should." Within months, six Mechanics' Mutual chapters had been started in Manhattan, along with several others in Auburn, Rochester, and other upstate towns.[30]

Even more than the nativists, the Mechanics' Mutual fused previously antagonistic cultural and political themes. The familiar artisan republican imagery reappeared in MacFarlane's speeches and in the group's literature, attached to a glorification of sobriety and social harmony that far exceeded the GTU's and that most evangelicals and entrepreneurs would have heartily commended. To "go-a-head," the *Mechanics' Mirror* admonished wage earners, they had to practice perseverance, temperance, enterprise, and assiduity, to turn themselves into the kind of thrifty, industrious workers who could safely be recommended to employers. To understand the origins and meaning of the republican commonwealth meant first accepting God and following the golden standard of Christian love. Collective education and self-respect, and not social conflict, was MacFarlane's aim:

> We do not war against wealth; we would not tear down the proud pinnacles which have been erected above us. We are not the levellers of the French Revolution, that would drag down the rich to the miserable condition of too many of ourselves, but with the means at our command and the tools in our hands, we would raise the battlements as high as their lofty towers.

The Mutual explicitly opposed the unions and strikes and insisted that "we believe in the rights of labor and the rights of capital and we wish the protection of both"; disputes were best handled with "mutual good will" and Christian understanding. With education and benevolence, the group would reinforce this charitable spirit and cultivate what MacFarlane summarized as "simplicity of habits: a mechanic simple in tastes, intelligent in conversation, industrious in his habits, moral in his deportment, in all a fit representative of a republic."[31]

To these quiet counsels, with their implied resignation to the free-labor

30. Robert MacFarlane, *Address Delivered . . . before the Mechanics of New-York, in the Broadway Tabernacle, June 10, 1847* (New York, 1847), 9, 16; *Mechanics' Mirror* 1 (1846): 296. On MacFarlane, see Yearley, *Britons in American Labor*, 34–36.
31. *Mechanics' Mirror* 1 (1846): 77–79; MacFarlane, *Address*, 4, 11–12.

regime, the Mutual added some more disturbing ideas. No degree of good-will could blind MacFarlane and his followers to the misery of the mass of mechanics; their suffering was to be explained not with the Bible alone but with the science of political economy and its account of the effects of capitalist expansion. "It is a mistaken idea, seldom reflected on . . . ," wrote one correspondent in the *Mirror*, "that the circulation of capital by the creation of Labor is the means of good in which ever way it is circu-lated. . . ." Here, the group drew a strict line against nonproducers: only "practical mechanics," small masters and journeymen, were eligible to join. In addition to aiding the unemployed, MacFarlane promised campaigns to reduce the hours of labor, to improve the conditions of apprenticeship, and to abolish the "half-way" system. "[L]ike Gideon of old . . . ," Mac-Farlane proclaimed, mixing the sacred with the verbose, "we shall lean down with the swoop of the falcon, and the victorious shout of A FAIR REMUNERATION FOR AMERICAN MECHANICAL LABOR AND A TEN HOUR SYSTEM FOR AMERICAN FACTORY OPERATIVES!" To one of MacFarlane's supporters, the counterattack was critical if Americans were to retain that society of "small but universal ownership," which was "the true foundation of a stable and firm Republic": "if we love, and would protect the liberties of our country," he concluded, "we must watch the insidious approaches of combined capital with a more jealous eye than the advance of an invad-ing enemy."[32]

These two lines of argument, far from contradictory, established the Mechanics' Mutual as a Protestant republican equivalent of the Christian workingmen's circles of Europe in the 1840s. The Mutual members wor-shiped Jesus and His sacred cause, but He was Christ the workingman, "the Reformer of Judah who laboured himself as a carpenter, and chose from among the working class the sharers of his toils, the beholders of his benevolent acts." They believed in independence and virtue, but not in the kind of individualism that would countenance low wages for honest toil or praise the mere pursuit of wealth. "Man is a social being," one member wrote, "and we are mutually dependent upon each other; the very weakest has something of which the most powerful may be deficient"; con-sequently,

> there is no *true* independence but in the reciprocation of good acts and good will towards one another among all classes, and the cultiva-tion of this principle for general happiness is more obvious in a repub-lican country like ours, than in any other. . . .

The only cure for capitalist disorder was a moral crusade, to uplift the op-pressed, "to give that dignity to labor which it deserves," and to Chris-tianize the oppressors. "The balm is in Gilead," the Mechanics' Mutual

32. *Mechanics' Mirror* 1 (1846): 119–22, 141–42, 153–54, 197–98; MacFarlane, *Address*, 5, 10.

instructed the faithful; "each class of society must be enlightened in their particular duties to their God and fellow men."[38]

To describe the new nativists and the Mechanics' Mutual as radical might seem wrongheaded if not perverse. Ethnic bigotry is never pretty, and it certainly has never been in the mainstream of radical thought; Christian love, in the era of Little Eva, often looks more like an artifact of feminized sentimentalism than an article of faith for embittered workingmen. In different ways—by continuing to fracture wage earners along ethnic and religious lines, by upholding the ideal harmony of interests between honorable employers and employees, by exhorting small masters and journeymen to sober industry—these movements would appear to have had more in common with the Washingtonians and the American Republicans than with the subterranean radicals. Set against the depression years, however, the emerging radicalism of the later Protestant plebeian groups is more obvious. Unlike the earlier temperance and nativist movements, both excluded capitalist nonproducers. Both came to attack sweating and competition. Both connected their cultural concerns with the economic and social inequalities of the industrializing metropolis, to turn nativism and Christian piety into a cause for displaced small masters and underpaid journeymen. Although their conception of the labor theory of value explicitly rejected the trade union radicalism of the 1830s, their revision of the cultural issues of the early 1840s augured an important, though subtle, break: If, they asked, respectable workingmen, industrious and temperate, were doomed to unending toil and struggle, who or what was to blame? The very question, along with the responses that began to appear in the nativist and workingmen's press, beckoned to a new form of labor radicalism, based on a social Christianity that would restore the independence of the wage earner and small producer by uprooting the ungodly capitalist.

Trade Societies, Immigrants, and Labor Radicalism

Finally, an assortment of craft societies, benefit clubs, and social groups, organized by natives and immigrants, either survived or sprang to action in the middle and late 1840s. Of these, the remaining journeymen's unions

33. *Constitution and By-Laws of Mechanics' Mutual Protection Number 41 of the City of New York* (New York), 1848, 4; MacFarlane, *Address*, 8; *Mechanics' Mirror* 1 (1846): 7, 162, 253–55. On Roman Catholic working-class radicalism in Europe, see Edgar Leon Newman, "Sounds in the Desert: The Socialist Worker Poets of the Bourgeois Monarchy, 1830–1848," *Proceedings of the Third Annual Meeting of the Western Society for French History* 3 (1975): 269–99. Similar Christian themes remained a mainstay of American labor movements into the twentieth century. See Gutman, *Work, Culture, and Society,* 79–118; Nick Salvatore, *Eugene V. Debs, Citizen and Socialist* (Urbana, 1982), 62–65.

are the most impenetrable, in part because of the unionists' wariness about drawing attention to themselves in the years after the panic. Organized printers literally went into hiding to form the secret Order of Faust. Basically a fraternal body with its own complicated rituals, insignias, and mutual-aid plans, the Order also pledged to put pressure on employers who mistreated their journeymen or who hired "half-ways"—but beyond that, little for certain is known about the group. Journeymen shoemakers, bookbinders, upholsterers, stonecutters, and tailors also kept their benefit societies, without the printers' secrecy and (at least through the early years of the decade) without declared trade-union objectives. As a workers' movement, they represented the faintest echo of the GTU; before 1844, they might have gone unnoticed but for their respectful appearance in a parade to mourn the death of President William Henry Harrison.[34]

Hard as times were, however, the trade unionists preserved some links with the militant days of 1835 and 1836. In 1840, workers at the office of the *Gazette*, the *Courier*, and Harper & Brothers (possibly organized by the Order of Faust) struck to protest wage cuts. Four years later, when the depression lifted, a resurgence of trade unionism ensued; employers, mindful perhaps of the Hudson verdict, negotiated. The printers thwarted the publisher John Trow's attempt to cut his piece rates. A burst of strikes hit the city's bookbinding, upholstering, shoemaking, and tailoring shops; at the peak of what turned out to be a successful five-week strike, the tailors mounted a torchlight procession two thousand strong, led by two musical bands and men carrying the republican banners of old. The hatters and tailors held conventions to organize national confederations and to consider new price lists. The carpenters began to plan for a strike for higher wages in 1845; the shoemakers struck in 1846; the cigar makers formed their own benevolent society.[35]

The movements of women workers, although short-lived, were even more extraordinary. In 1845, women from six trades, led by the straw sewers, organized a citywide federation, the Ladies' Industrial Association, modeled very roughly on the GTU. Some seven hundred women—lowly slopworkers as well as tailoresses and seamstresses—assembled for the group's first meeting, to hear their chairwoman, Elizabeth Gray, explain their aims in familiar artisan republican terms as those of "daughters of the Patriots of '76." "Too long have we been bound down by tyrant employers," Gray declared, "but the time has now come for us to stand up for our rights, and to let our employers see that we can do more than they think we can." Emphatically independent, the women neither sought nor trusted the direction

34. On the Order of Faust, see *Transcript*, April 19, 1836; Stevens, *Typographical Union*, 141–42; on the remaining trades, see *Evening Post*, April 10, 1841.

35. Stevens, *Typographical Union*, 567–68; *Working Man's Advocate*, April 25, June 29, July 13, August 3, 17, 24, 1844; *Tribune*, April 20, August 28, September 11, 1845; *Young America*, April 26, August 30, 1845; Ware, *Industrial Worker*, 229.

of men; when one male offered to help the new association draft an address, "the women instantly rebuked his impertinence by saying that they were competent to manage their own affairs." The brief openness of the 1830s ended, while persistent sexual divisions in the trades took their toll; women, with their special problems, had to fight their own battles in order to win a secure position in the labor force and to guard against peculiar forms of oppression. The more comprehensive feminism of Fanny Wright and the tailoresses of 1831 did not appear in the association's rhetoric; if anything, Gray (reflecting, perhaps, evangelical as well as republican influences) played upon the imagery of domestic womanly virtue, to assure the public that the group did not intend to extort higher wages but wanted only to enable women workers to be "more cheerful at their work and still more earnest and willing to serve their employers." Economic survival in the double-split labor market framed their concerns; as a step toward winning a larger, more appropriate sphere for women in the labor force, some Association members urged employers to replace male clerks and office workers with women, to harmonize women's gentler nature with their occupations. Although the attempt failed when the Association lost a strike for higher wages, it demonstrated a new and ambiguous development among the city's workers: the emergence of an ever more sophisticated and militant female sector of the working class that defined its interests as distinct from those of male workers.[36]

Otherwise, craft organizations were dominated by the old benefit societies and a few new associations. The most radical of them, the New York Protective Union, formulated a class-conscious critique of wage relations but claimed that neither strikes nor political reform would secure workers' rights. Their alternative project, begun in 1847, virtually duplicated Langton Byllesby's proposals of 1826—a series of cooperative shops, in which all workers earned the value of their labor, without employers or wages. The PU fully expected that as these shops proliferated capitalism would collapse and the group's ultimate object—"equality of condition"—would be secured. More typical of the 1840s was the Pioneer Temple Number One, begun in 1844. The Temple, ostensibly a protective union for house carpenters, admitted employers as well as employees and undertook to assist unemployed members, promote knowledge of the craft and related sciences, and advance brotherly feeling. Guiding the group, at all times, was the familiar maxim that "the interests of the employer and the employed are one and the same." Little dissent emanated from such quarters before 1850.[37]

Of all the city's workers, however, it was the immigrants—after mid-

36. *Evening Post*, March 7, 1845; *Working Man's Advocate*, March 8, 1845.

37. On the Protective Union, see *Tribune*, August 13, 1850; on the Pioneer Temple, see *Tribune*, April 13, 17, 1850.

decade, an emerging majority of the labor force, in and out of the trades—
who contributed most to the sustenance of a local labor movement, as they
settled into their own ethnic working-class communities. By the late 1840s,
the Irish constituted the largest immigrant group in the city, and, by all
accounts, the most miserable. Predominantly rural in origin and possessing
few of the skills necessary to enter any but the sweated sectors of the
trades, the famine Irish clustered at the very bottom of the occupational
scale. Their settlement in New York did a great deal to discourage any turn
to political dissent or labor militancy. For the penniless, the possibility of
work, any kind of work, outweighed the hardship of low wages; already
well-schooled in suffering, the Irish, if only to survive, would endure far
worse conditions than most native-born craft workers were prepared to accept—precisely the grievance of the plebeian nativists. For the refugees of
the blighted handkerchief potato patch, the closest approximations to
familiar cultural settings—the taverns, public markets, and street corners—
were the most inviting gathering places. For Catholics in a Protestant city
swept by various forms of nativism, the embrace of a Tammany ward
heeler, of an aggressive church—one increasingly hostile to social and
political reform—or of a vigilant Irish gang could be most welcome. It was
enough to lead a more refined Irish political radical émigré like Thomas
D'Arcy McGee to despair for the poorest of Irish New York as a "perverted peasantry."[38]

But Irish life in Manhattan was not all novenas and barroom punch-
ups; nor were the Irish, as one historian has recently described them, "en-
feebled and bewildered," an "uprooted population." Most either arrived in
family groups or quickly established ties once they settled; although desperately poor in some cases, the Irish banded together in family, town,
and kin networks to bring in enough money to support themselves. Although nominally Catholic, the majority of the immigrants knew little or
nothing of church dogma and practices and could not be expected to follow the church's lead on all social issues; despite determined efforts by the
parish clergy, religious indifference remained far more prevalent in the
Irish neighborhoods than piety; as late as 1865, one Irish priest would
lament that "half of our Irish population here is Catholic merely because
Catholicity was the religion of the land of their birth." Until his death, in
1847, Daniel O'Connell had as much of a purchase on Irish-American enthusiasm as any parish priest: although it failed to lead masses of immigrants into broader currents of social reform, the Repeal agitation in New

38. John T. Smith, *The Catholic Church in New York* (New York, 1905), I, 143.
The most comprehensive recent treatment of the Irish in mid-century New York is Jay
P. Dolan, *The Immigrant Church: New York's Irish and German Catholics, 1815–1865*
(Baltimore, 1975); but see also Ernst, *Immigrant Life*, passim.

York contributed mightily to what one historian has called "the first major Irish nationalist movement of consequence in America."[39]

On labor questions, meanwhile, neither the city's Irish press nor the rank and file showed any of the deference and pessimism usually ascribed to the famine refugees. The shoemakers' union, still active through the late 1840s, was kept alive almost entirely by Irish outworkers. In 1843, Irish building laborers helped organized the first mutual-aid society for the city's unskilled, the Laborers' Union Benevolent Association; by the decade's end, the LUBA had called for higher wages and the elimination of sweating, and had enlisted more than six thousand members, making it the largest labor "society" in any American city. The most celebrated strike in the New York area involved, not native journeymen artisans, but Irish laborers who struck their jobs on the Brooklyn waterfront in 1846. Alongside the usual promises to promote the common welfare, the laborers asserted in sweeping republican prose their own "immutable rights to self-government," to protect their own "freedom and equality."[40]

The German societies, meanwhile, belonged to a category of their own, both in the coherence of their organization and in their receptivity to radical political ideas. As early as 1845, German bakers, cabinetmakers, upholsterers, turners, tailors, and shoemakers had arrived in New York in large numbers; by the 1850s, Germans composed a disproportionately large segment of the work force in the city's woodworking, clothing, and baking trades. Thousands settled in the *Kleindeutschland* that began to overtake sections of the old Bowery district in the late 1840s; others could be found throughout the East Side, from East Broadway to the impoverished, uptown shanties along "Dutch Hill." In these enclaves, the Germans tried, much of the time in testy harmony with their neighbors, to re-create the social life of the Fatherland. The German artisan clubs were among the most prominent of the numerous New York *Liedertafeln* and *Vereine*; in these circles, members of a particular trade would gather to sing, listen to lectures, perform amateur theatricals, drink lager, plan German-language festivals, and otherwise enjoy each other's company.[41]

39. Spann, *New Metropolis*, 27; Groneman, " 'Bloody Ould Sixth,' " passim; Dolan, *Immigrant Church*, 56–57; Gilbert Osofsky, "Abolitionists, Irish Immigrants, and the Dilemmas of Romantic Nationalism," *AHR* 80 (1975): 901.

40. *Tribune*, September 16, 1843, September 9, 1845, May 2, 1846, May 8, June 5, 10, July 3, 1850. A copy of the LUBA constitution and bylaws is kept at the N-YHS. The group's first officers were Daniel B. Taylor (later a Tammany politician), James B. O'Donnell, and David S. Roach. For typical comments on labor in the local Irish press, see *Irish-American* [New York], May 19, August 10, 1850.

41. Ernst, *Immigrant Life*, 41–43, 130–32; Dolan, *Immigrant Church*, 37, 80–81. Dolan notes that the Germans tended to live together in large clusters more than the Irish did. All, of course, was not harmonious between Irish and Germans; in 1846, New York German scabs were successfully brought in to break the Irish dock laborers' strike

The *Vereine* sponsored mainly leisurely attempts at self-improvement, but talk of the trades, politics, and religion inevitably entered their conversations. The best-known of them all, the *Turnvereine*, or gymnastic clubs, had strong reputations as hotbeds of German liberal and republican politics. Ideas on cooperative production floated through the clubs and neighboring beer halls, as did the militant rationalism that had flourished in the disintegrating German urban trades: one impious German saloon-keeper was renowned for haranguing Sunday crowds of workingmen from his barroom "pulpit" on the tyranny and superstition of organized religion. Eventually these sentiments crossed the language barrier and drew some German craft workers into the radical underground.[42]

Attempts to direct the Germans into American political activity began with Hermann Kriege. Kriege, a Westphalian journalist and member of the outlawed Communist *Bund der Gerechten* (and a bitter opponent of Marx and Engels), arrived in New York in 1845. He soon fell into the circle of that eager cosmopolitan host George Henry Evans; with the support of the National Reform Association (and with the disdain of the conservative mercantile German Society), Kriege launched an agrarian *Deutsche Jung-Amerika Gemeinde* and started a newspaper, the *Volks-tribun*. For months, the exile, still a self-professed communist, combined arguments for land reform with blistering salvos against monopolists, clerics, and the rich in general. "The *Volkstribun*," he wrote in the first issue,

> must be our journal, for us, the poor, the tortured, the oppressed. The rich oppressors are not going to find it a personal savior. As for the priests, lawyers, office seekers, it has nothing to say to them, they have no reason to look at it. As for you, you who torment yourself one day to the next and are bound to all suffering . . . to earn your miserable piece of bread; you who have been nothing and will be all, you and you alone have been the people whom I wish to serve, whom I wish to defend from wicked designs.

Jung-Amerika and its offspring, the NRA-affiliated *Sozialreformassoziation*, had some impact, drawing several hundred Germans to its meetings and inspiring the formation of chapters in over half a dozen other cities. But despite Albert Brisbane's observation that "the Germans rose in all their force," the movement fizzled within a year. Kriege proved unequal to the task he had set for himself; by 1846, he had pledged to support the Democratic party once the party supported some version of the land-reform program. This Tammany readily did, drawing Kriege into the party; before

---

in Brooklyn. See *Tribune*, May 2, 1846. On "Little Germany," see also Stanley Nadel, "Kleindeutschland: New York City's Germans, 1845–1880" (Ph.D. diss., Columbia University, 1981).

42. Carl Wittke, *The Utopian Communist: A Biography of Wilhelm Weitling, Nineteenth-Century Reformer* (Baton Rouge, 1950), 140–41. See also Ernst, *Immigrant Life*, 130–31.

long, the erstwhile communist had turned his pen to agitating for a more drastic form of land reform, the annexation of Mexico.[43]

German artisan radicalism revived briefly in 1847 with the arrival in New York of Kriege's mentor, the journeyman tailor turned radical exile, Wilhelm Weitling. Weitling already had a small reputation. For a decade, since his initial flight to Paris in 1837 and his first contact with the *Bund der Gerechten*, he had been publicizing his own critique of capitalist property relations; by the time he settled in Manhattan, he had refined the basics of his proposed "kingdom of love and science," yet another variation on anticapitalist and cooperative themes long familiar to New York's radical artisans. The great enemy for Weitling was not the employer but the capitalist and financier; the money system, rather than the system of production, was the matrix of oppression, for wage earners and small employers alike. The solution (also echoing parts of Byllesby's proposals) lay in centralizing the basis of exchange, by founding a new banking system in which workers would receive labor notes for the amount of actual labor they performed. Cooperative production, overseen by journeymen's trade associations, would follow; the new bank, meanwhile, would serve as a socialist provider, using the profits from its labor note exchange to fund education, old-age pensions, and hospitals for all its members. It was, in Carl Wittke's words, a scheme of social harmony that captured "the rage and fire of the craftsman, the artisan . . . who was beginning to disintegrate under the impact of large-scale industry." Although derided by his fellow *Bund* members Marx and Engels as a hopeless, befuddled petit bourgeois, "the king of the tailors," Weitling found some sympathy among those New Yorkers who read his tracts. Brisbane and the Fourierists immediately took him in and encouraged him to keep writing. Still immersed in conspiracy, Weitling formed a new secret society, the *Befreiungsbund*, a sort of German-American *Bund der Gerechten*. His efforts were cut short only when news arrived early in 1848 of the uprisings in Paris, Vienna, and Schleswig-Holstein; in haste, Weitling assembled a delegation of New York German radicals (including Kriege) to return home and join the revolution for which they had long yearned.[44]

Weitling's following was no doubt minuscule at this point, even among

43. *Der Volkstribun* [New York], January 5, 1846, quoted in Herman Schlüter, "Die Anfänge der deutschen Arbeiterbewegung in New York und ihre Presse," in *New Yorker Volkszeitung*, February 21, 1903; Ernst, *Immigrant Life*, 113; Karl Obermann, "Germano-Américains et la presse ouvrière, 1845–1854," in *La Presse ouvrière, 1819–1850*, ed. Jacques Godechot (La Roche-sur-Yon, 1966), 70–72; on the German background, see Peter Wende, *Radikalismus im vormärz: Untersuchungen zur politischen Theorie der frühen deutschen Demokratie* (Frankfurt, 1975), and David McLellan, *Karl Marx: His Life and Thought* (New York, 1973), 137–38.

44. Wittke, *Utopian Communist*, 6–109, is a fine introduction to Weitling's thought, and discusses his departure; see also Ernst, *Immigrant Life*, 114; Obermann, "Germano-Américains," 73.

the Germans. Prominent German merchants and masters spurned him as a radical lunatic; humbler members of the *Handwerkervereine* suspected that his clandestine plotting was the work of a greenhorn, out of touch with republican political realities.[45] He did succeed, though, in making some limited contact with American radicals. His hazy plans for banks of exchange and labor cooperation in the United States at least began to connect the older American sentiment for cooperation with the German artisan cooperatives of the same period. Almost imperceptibly, native radicals and Germans began to understand that although they spoke different languages, they articulated similar hopes and fears. In short order, meanwhile, the *Vereine* would begin to reorganize as protective unions in alliance with English-speaking craft workers. Weitling, the wandering radical, would prove vital in promoting this upsurge when, in 1849, he returned to New York, a defeated man.

Radicalism and Self-Respect

The 1840s have long been interpreted as years of reaction and humanitarian utopianism, when (especially in the seaboard cities) the labor radicalism of the preceding decade disintegrated into nativism, Protestant piety, a search for social respectability, and a few woolly-headed projects of obtrusive intellectuals. On the most superficial level, such was the case in New York. The city's masters consolidated their political economy of free labor and merged it ever more thoroughly with a Christian morality of discipline, industriousness, and charity. Thousands of journeymen buried their differences with masters and capitalists to join in attacks on Romanism and rum. The one party politician who dared to castigate capitalist accumulators, Michael Walsh, led his forces into a self-destructive liaison with the southern wing of the Democratic party. Those professed radicals who remained—the ruins of the deist-GTU circles—turned to land reform as their main issue and found themselves cut off from most of those whom they hoped to lead. Other associations of workers, apart from the unions, emphasized the rhetoric of moderation, social harmony, and self-control.

Beneath the surface the situation was in fact far more complex. Although the class consciousness of the GTU faded, entrepreneurial reformers did not bring about class harmony. Journeymen and small masters who joined temperance societies and nativist groups still harbored suspicions about the city's capitalists and employers. If Walsh was on the road to political disaster, he did manage to elaborate a radical anticapitalist republicanism at odds with the usual Tammany rhetoric. The land reform-

45. Ernst, *Immigrant Life*, 115.

ers, at the very least, kept alive a network of labor radicals first built in the 1830s and extended it to reach newly arrived German socialists. The Mechanics' Mutual and workingmen's nativist groups combined the quest for self-government with a determination to resist contracting and underpayment. Unionists, including immigrant day laborers, perceived their circumstances in familiar terms, as those of free-born republicans protecting their property and their self-ownership. New York labor radicalism, although muted, hardly succumbed to what one writer has described as the great "evangelical counterattack," the assault of "Christian industrialism" of the postpanic years.[46]

A subtle but important series of divisions did arise, one that is too easily misconstrued as a split between "labor" and "intellectual" reform. In the 1840s, with the depression, the decline of mass trade unionism and the resurgence of political nativism and temperance, the concerns of rank-and-file New York workers and those of their former leaders and allies were not clearly identical. The unions' and the plebeian Protestants' indifference to land reform (and to John Commerford) was one example of this fragmentation, as was Walsh's eventual denunciation of the NRA and all "bran-bread philosophers": increasingly, labor radicalism, apart from Walsh's movement, seemed the province of a few marginal visionaries who had lost contact with the more mundane concerns of the city's beleaguered workers. But these splits were neither as straightforward nor as hard and fast as they might appear in hindsight. Far from being narrow, "intellectual" groups, the land reformers and cooperativists established some links with working-class groups and publicized and sympathized with trade union activities. The larger, more popular labor associations of the period, meanwhile, sought some fundamental reformation of prevailing class relations. Walshites, plebeian nativists and teetotalers, Mechanics' Mutual members, and immigrant unionists—all followed a vision of a new cooperative artisan republic, free of the effects of capitalist accumulation and permanent dependency; all held that America had not sunk so deep into the morass of Old World ways that some kind of radical moral, economic, and cultural change was outside their grasp. What did occur in the 1840s was both a change in emphasis and a loss of apparent unity—a return, in most instances, to the broader terms of social conflict, of "producer" versus "nonproducer" rather than of workers versus employers, compounded by a deflection of purpose and new ethnic stratification and tensions, that drove labor radicals and wage earners in several different directions. Through the mid-1840s, this disruption and deflection made it appear that class consciousness had been extinguished, that social reform had been irrevocably severed from labor's cause, and that ethnic prejudice

46. Wallace, Rockdale, 296–397 passim.

had destroyed working-class solidarity. In 1850, however, these divisions proved illusory. The great antebellum uprising of radical republican labor had not been averted in the panic of 1837 and its aftermath. It was yet to come.[47]

Two portents of that uprising closed the decade. News of the Paris revolution in February 1848 reached New York in early March, and before long, a diverse committee began making plans for an elaborate demonstration of support for the latest republican breakthrough. Unlike that of 1830, this one was turning into a genuinely republican French revolution—but also unlike that of 1830, it saw the continuing arrival of strange, exciting dispatches immediately after the new regime was installed, reports of national workshops, of calls for the abolition of contracting, of the bloody crescendo in June. No civic celebrations greeted these later events, only shock, bewilderment, and curiosity at the rise of a workers' movement that took to the barricades against self-proclaimed republicans, for something it called the social republic. Continuing events in Europe, and especially Germany—the debates of the Frankfurt Assembly and the convening of the radical Frankfurt Congress, the socialist and workers' activities in Cologne and in Berlin (Weitling's headquarters), the suppression of the resistance—captured even more attention in *Kleindeutschland*.[48]

A year later, workingmen's blood was spilled in New York, although in a very different kind of cause. For months, Edwin Forrest, the American Shakespearian and hero of the Bowery Theatre, had been feuding with the renowned English tragedian William Macready. When Macready announced that he would close a tour of the United States with a performance of *Macbeth* at the elite Astor Place Opera House, the stage was set for an old-fashioned New York theater riot. Macready appeared, as planned, at the Astor Place, only to be chased from the stage by a shower of hisses, rotten eggs, and street muck, hurled by pro-Forrest Boweryites who had managed to slip into the theater. But Macready's friends would not be denied so rapidly. In a public petition, some of the city's leading writers and men of fashion deplored the violence and urged Macready to defy the mob; in response, placards appeared throughout the city asking patriotic workingmen to resist the attempted imposition of British rule in New York and to disrupt any future appearance by the Englishman. Three nights after the first debacle, Macready was persuaded to try again, but only with the protection of two hundred policemen and three hundred

47. On "intellectual" versus "labor" movements, see Ware, *Industrial Worker*, 163–239.

48. *Tribune*, March 29, 1848. Among the New Yorkers who traveled to Germany and witnessed or participated in the revolution—apart from Weitling, Kriege, and the other former exiles—was Albert Brisbane. For his impressions, see Brisbane, *A Mental Biography*, 273.

militia stationed outside the theater—the first mobilization of the military to quell the New York "mob" since the dockworkers' strike of 1836. Somehow, Macready completed his performance, but only after the police had repulsed several attempts by the throngs outside to crash their way in. Shouts that Macready had finished inflamed the crowd to attack the police; some taunted the troops—"You durst not shoot, you durst not shoot," repeated one—confident that the old theater-riot conventions would be followed, without personal violence. Suddenly, the soldiers lowered their sights and opened a rapid volley, killing twenty-two persons. The next day, a mass protest meeting in front of City Hall heard several inflammatory speeches (delivered by Mike Walsh and John Commerford, among others) about the murderous New York aristocracy. Philip Hone drew very different conclusions. "The fact has been established," he wrote in his diary, "that law and order can be maintained under a Republican form of government."[49]

Compared with the revolutions of 1848 or with the GTU activities of the 1830s, the Astor Place Riot was a cruel comedy, an atavistic explosion void of organized politics, radicalism, or anything approaching an articulate consciousness of class. Yet for the people of New York, its significance was far more profound. Though obscured by the farce of an actors' quarrel, the social antagonisms that led some New Yorkers to call on lethal military force, and others to stone the theater and the troops, were real enough—it was to be war, here expressed in violent cultural terms, between rich and poor, between the Anglophile aristocrats and the lawless mob, between Astor Place and the Bowery. A nebulous form of class conflict, to be sure—but one that challenged the faith of the 1840s that social harmony and peace were freely grasped, that America had escaped the internecine strife and gore of the Old World.

Over the next two years, in scenes far more reminiscent of insurgent Paris, that faith would be assaulted again, in one of the most unsettling labor crises in America before the Civil War.

49. *Account of the Terrific and Fatal Riot* (New York, 1849); *Tribune*, May 11, 12, 1849; Nevins, *Diary of Philip Hone*, 877.

VI

Class Conflict in the American Metropolis, 1850

What is your money-making now? What can it do now?
What is your respectability now?
Where are your theology, tuition, society, traditions, statute-books now?
Where are your jibes of being now?
Where are your cavils about the Soul now?

Chants Democratic, II, 13

10

The Labor Crisis of 1850

The crisis began at a time when New York's economic and political fortunes seemed sounder than ever. Local prices had recovered briefly in 1844 and 1845, only to dip again from 1846 until early 1847; by 1850, the recovery had resumed and the metropolitan economy was in full swing. City government was in the gentlemanly hands of the Whigs, their way to office opened by fresh splits within the Democracy; in the mayor's office sat the stalwart lawyer and businessman Caleb Woodhull, a man of the new mercantile elite, a humanitarian who proposed building parks and improving sanitary conditions in the slums to uplift the poor, but who showed no reluctance about calling on the military to suppress lower-class unrest. The benevolent middle-class God was in His heaven; on earth, New York's city fathers, businessmen, and manufacturers were busily doing His work, "heralding our modern civilization," one clergyman proclaimed, "to conquests and results not possible before."[1]

Like the breakneck expansion of the mid-1830s, the city's renewed prosperity had its perils for local wage earners. Although business was brisk, their incomes did not keep pace with rising retail prices and rents. Their jobs were no more secure with the ongoing division of labor and consequent sweating. Their confidence in city government was not reinforced by Mayor Woodhull's handling of the Astor Place affray. As a committee of journeymen printers was to observe in May, the midcentury boom made it seem to some an unlikely time for workers to organize; the problem was that even then, "with the prospects of the journeymen

1. *Independent* [New York], May 2, 1850, quoted in Spann, *New Metropolis*, 16. On Woodhull, see [Joseph Scoville]; *The Old Merchants of New York City* (New York, 1863–66), I, 142–43; Spann, *New Metropolis*, 101, 129, 163.

brighter than they usually are," strikes and radical experiments appeared to be the only effective remedies for lagging wages and permanent dependency.[2] As these fears and resentments spread, they brought New York's workers back into the committee rooms, and then into the streets.

A sense of both déjà-vu and novelty pervaded the workers' movements from the start. The class-conscious trade unionism of the GTU reawakened—but was joined by the agitation of the immigrants, the land reform organizations, the Protestant benefit societies, and the cooperative socialists. Once these groups met, they posted familiar demands and some very new ones; in their fight, they encountered the old nemeses of internal dissension and party politics, but in new ways; they again faced repression, but in the form of a new and deadly official violence. Ultimately, the uprising failed, wracked by internal dissent, leaving behind a reinvigorated but still unfulfilled republican labor radicalism and numerous blueprints for industrial reform. But although they ended in pathos, these events also marked the culmination of the artisan republican crisis, beginning the new decade with a sudden reassertion that the republican metropolis was riven by class.[3]

Movements and Men

Althougl. a variety of groups with wide-ranging interests took part, the uprising of 1850 must be recognized as an expression of working-class unrest—it was, as Norman Ware discerned, "a legitimate industrial movement."[4] The instigators and mainstays of the insurgency, the union delegates and representatives in the New York Industrial Congress, were all propertyless men, most of whom lived in the city's poorer wards (Table 21A). They represented a rough ethnic cross-section of the New York work force; more than half of those located were immigrants, mostly Germans, British, and Irish (Table 21B). The pattern of union organization bore the mark of uneven metropolitan industrialization, just as the GTU had; once again, those trades most disrupted by structural change were the most active, while those relatively unaffected remained relatively quiet (Table 22). Small masters and middle-class labor advocates like Greeley assumed important roles, but they retained their influence only as long as they were able to enlist and maintain working-class support.

The diversity of the revived labor movement bespoke the ideological

2. *Tribune*, May 22, 1850.

3. No adequate history of the events of 1850 has yet been written. Most accounts have discussed the various lines of development but have treated them as separate histories, without fully interpreting the multiplicity of forces at work and how they affected each other. See Commons, *History of Labour*, I, 552–607; Ware, *Industrial Worker*, 229–39; Carl Neumann Degler, "Labor in the Economy and Politics of New York City, 1850–1860" (Ph.D. diss., Columbia University, 1952), 11–95, 258–341.

4. Ware, *Industrial Worker*, 235.

diversity of the workers themselves. Two distinct types of trade organizations emerged, with very different agendas. The craft benefit societies, including several previously incorporated by the state legislature, were the quieter of the two, open to masters and journeymen and devoted to mutual aid rather than to organizing strikes. The cordwainers' benefit society—one of the few surviving societies from the Jeffersonian period—pointedly stressed that its activities pertained only to sickness and burial benefits; its charter obligated the group's secretary to file an annual affidavit with the county clerk, affirming that the body had neither directly nor indirectly undertaken any project beyond "extending the right hand of fellowship to each other when in distress, sickness, or hour of death."[5] A few of the benefit societies (including the cordwainers') eventually reorganized in 1850, to assume some of the features of the protective trade unions; others—the tailors', the masons', and the jewelers' benefit societies—helped their members organize independent protectives or cooperatives or both. For the most part, however, the benefit societies were important primarily as fraternal groups and gatherers of information—information that other societies cited in support of their demands.[6]

The protective unions were more militant. Although statistics are scarce, it appears that only a minority of the workers in the organized trades actually joined their respective protective unions; however, by consulting with nonunion workers in open meetings, the protectives were able to lead several impressive strikes.[7] Their grievances were reminiscent of those of the 1830s—enforcement of fair, standard wage rates in all the city's shops, regulation of apprenticeship, strict adherence to the ten-hour day, and commencement of an eight-hour day were typical demands. Like the earlier unions, they stressed the importance of interethnic harmony, in some cases to the point of conducting their meetings and rallies with continual dual translation into English and German.[8] Even more emphatically than the GTU, the most articulate protectives insisted on their right (indeed, their duty) to strike, and voiced opposition to the prevailing struc-

5. *Tribune,* June 6, 1850.

6. *Ibid.,* April 23, 1850. For a concise contemporary discussion of the differences between protectives and beneficials, see the account of the coach makers' meeting in the *Herald,* May 1, 1850.

7. Union membership appears to have varied considerably from trade to trade, and possibly by ethnicity. The cordwainers' union, for example, claimed only 300 members, the upholsterers' only 140, the cabinetmakers' 800 (of 2,000), and the ladies' cordwainers' only 150; the German joiners', however, claimed about 1,000. Unfortunately, no record of these unions has been found other than what appears in the newspapers, making it impossible to know more about size and membership. See *Tribune,* April 20, 23, 26, May 7, 23, 25, 1850. The important point to bear in mind is that many workers not formally in the unions would follow the unions' lead in strikes, cooperatives, and related activities.

8. See, for example, the meetings described in the *Tribune,* April 20, May 25, 31, June 3, 19, 22, July 1, 25, 1850; see also Commons, *History of Labour,* I, 589–90.

366 CLASS CONFLICT IN THE AMERICAN METROPOLIS, 1850

ture of contract capitalist wage labor in New York—what some now called the "wages system." Honorable small producers—those the bricklayers called "legitimate employers"—caused them no trouble; the problem lay with those who had taken over the workshop economy and transformed the wage relation, those "butchers and tinkers who never learned the trade," who would "drive [men] like slaves that they might enrich themselves from the blood and sweat of those whose necessity knows no law. . . ." The preamble to the constitution of the window-shade painters' protective cooperative set out the broader points at issue:

> We . . . have formed ourselves into an Association . . . for the purpose of protecting ourselves from the trickish system of speculators—that make use of us like machines limiting the Painters' industry to suit the demand, or pushing it to meet the supply; or using or abusing us as the employers please—starving us into low wages, or pushing us, in their necessity, to the utmost toils that a Painter's nature can sustain. They have endeavoured always to keep us wholly in their power, driving us to work or throwing us into idleness, as suits their market—while they always obtain and retain the profits of our labor. We, the undersigned, deem it our duty to oppose such a system.[9]

Or, as a committee of printers more bluntly phrased it, only with the abolition of the "wages system" would labor "be forever rescued from the control of the capitalist."[10]

Some of the protectives in turn helped oversee a spate of local producers' cooperatives, the most systematic attempts to find a practical alternative to capitalist production. Some of these projects—including the Working Shoemakers' Union, organized by L. W. Ryckman—were inspired by the associationists and communitarians of the 1840s, others by the German co-ops and by Weitling; by combining regulated joint-stock ownership with payment of a "fair" price schedule, they all represented the old dream of Langton Byllesby and the failed projects of the GTU come to life again. They were not, any more than the other reform associations, solely the preserve of "intellectuals" or Germans. Native unionists like Peter Demarest and George Moulton helped establish and run the shoemakers' cooperative. Other co-ops—the carpenters', the window-shade painters', the scale makers', and the tailors', as well as the Protective Union—were administered largely or in part by native-born and British workers. The *Irish-American*, self-appointed voice of Irish labor during the uprising, argued that cooperative plans and "the principles of association" were "the surest means to better the conditions of labor."[11] Although al-

9. *Tribune*, April 4, 12, 16, June 3, 13, 1850.
10. *Ibid.*, July 8, 1850.
11. *Ibid.*, March 1, 19, 1850; *Herald*, April 18, July 27, 1850; *Irish-American*, June 15, 1850. Both Demarest and Moulton were born in the United States, according to

ways controversial—some workers interpreted them as a socialist menace, others as a distraction from the strikes—the cooperatives exposed both the depth of working-class alienation from existing relations of production and a faith, reinforced in the 1840s, that small producers and wage earners could unite to build a new system free of the "intermediate capitalists, alias bosses."[12] Their efforts were aided by those of several consumers' cooperatives, based loosely on similar organizations begun in Britain and New England in the 1840s.[13]

Cooperation also dominated the work of two holdovers from the 1840s, the Mechanics' Mutual and the Pioneer Temple. The Mutual stood by its program of practical industrial reform and Christian morality, but as the strikes continued, the New York chapters relied less on the rhetoric of self-respect than on direct assaults on competition and support for cooperation. In June, George Clark, a Mutual spokesman, announced plans for a protective grocery store, to aid the strikers and to generate funds for additional producers' cooperatives. The Pioneer Temple remained distinct from the carpenters' protective and still stressed the overriding harmony of interests between employer and employee, but it also established the House Carpenters' Eight Hour Protective Home Association to collect funds for a building-and-loan cooperative and to agitate for a further reduction of working hours to eight per day. Although decidedly less influential than even the mutuals, the Pioneers' work signaled a shift from the simpler mutual-aid schemes of the benefit societies to a wider program, emphasizing social reform as well as personal propriety.[14]

Far more curious were the chapters of a new group called the Brotherhood of the Union. The Brotherhood had been founded in Philadelphia in 1847 by that most peculiar of labor reformers, the Christian socialist pulp novelist George Lippard; by 1850, it claimed 25,000 members across the nation and about 260 members in New York. Heavily influenced by Lippard's admiration for the Founding Fathers and Jesus Christ, the Brotherhood was at once an agency of moral uplift and an anticapitalist lodge. The group restricted itself neither to wage earners nor to men of a single trade; nor did it attempt to supplant the protective unions. Organized into local circles—the Ouvrier, Nazarine, and Supreme circles in New York—Brotherhood members (with titles like the Chief Washington and the Herald of the Union) mixed Masonic and artisan ritual with the code of self-improvement; their major concerns were mutual aid and land

---

the 1850 census manuscript population schedule. On the co-ops as "intellectual" and German-inspired reforms, see Commons, *History of Labour*, I, 568.

12. *Tribune*, April 17, 1850.

13. *Ibid.*, July 1, 15, 16, 30, August 10, 1850. On the New England movement, see Edwin C. Rozwenc, *Cooperatives Come to America: The History of the Protective Store Movement, 1845–1867* (Mt. Vernon, Iowa, 1941), 3–95.

14. *Tribune*, April 13, 17, May 11, June 1, 4, July 3, 12, 16, October 10, 1850.

reform. No one was admitted who did not believe in God and prove that he was of a temperate moral character; Brotherhood rules demanded a decorous solemnity and encouraged members to establish libraries and other wholesome institutions. Yet behind these arcane rites and pious professions stirred more radical impulses. America, several members proclaimed, was supposed to be the "Palestine of redeemed labor," where exploitation was outlawed; instead, it had been taken over by "usurers of capital who degrade labor," men "subversive of morality, religion, and virtue." In all of its important elements, the Brotherhood was a precursor to the "secret" working-class reform societies of the late 1860s and 1870s, including the early Knights of Labor. In 1850, it attracted both union leaders and sympathetic radical reformers—including John Commerford.[15]

Another variety of Christian radicalism appeared in the form of a small sect, the Church of Humanity, led by the journeyman printer K. Arthur Bailey. Bailey was among the most active labor leaders in 1850, the president of his benefit union as well as a member of the Brotherhood of the Union. His church, located in the Eleventh Ward, stressed all of the now familiar moral reforms but also worked in appeals to the labor theory of value and attacks on monopoly. Bailey's sermons evoked the vision of Cornelius Blatchly; his style was that of a midcentury mechanic preacher, self-educated and unafraid. While ridiculed by anti-union newspapers as a marginal fanatic, he spoke mainly about such down-to-earth concerns as the growing power of the railroad magnates and other large capitalists—to Bailey, unholy men out to increase their wealth at the direct expense of America's workers, blasphemous destroyers of God's plan, that all of creation be the common property of His children.[16]

Several other organizations either advised the trade unionists or helped them coordinate their activities. *Kleindeutschland* became a center of these activities, above all those of the Central Committee of the Trades, headed by Wilhelm Weitling. After the failure of the Frankfurt Congress and the 1848 revolutions, Weitling returned to New York; momentarily beyond the polemical reach of his antagonists, Marx and Engels, he established a newspaper and gathered support for his cooperatives and banks of exchange. As soon as the strikes began in 1850, he redoubled his efforts, speaking first to the cabinetmakers and confectioners and then to any of the predominantly German trades that would listen to him. By April, he had founded the Central Committee, composed of delegates from the German unions and sections of unions; three months later, the

15. *Ibid.*, July 3, 16, 31, August 6, 15, 1850; Roger Butterfield, "George Lippard and His Secret Brotherhood," *PMHB* 79 (1955): 285–301. Butterfield argues that Uriah Stephens, later a founder of the Knights of Labor, was well acquainted with the Brotherhood, and may have imitated it when he set the rules and rituals for the Knights. On similar organizations in the 1860s, see Montgomery, *Beyond Equality*, 136–37.

16. *Tribune*, March 21, August 13, 1850; Ware, *Industrial Worker*, 166.

committee claimed to represent some 4,500 members of seventeen protective unions. Over most of the year, the committee divided its time between debating Weitling's reform projects and lending financial and organizational aid to journeymen contemplating strikes. The tailors' strike in July and August kept the committeemen at their busiest; by the time it was over, they had helped the journeymen tailors establish a cooperative shop. Weitling, meanwhile, was everywhere, cajoling native-born unionists to expand their co-ops, outlining his schemes for workers' banks and payment in labor notes. Other German labor groups, like Charles Schiff's small but outspoken socialist cooperative, the Economic Exchange Association, supported him.[17]

The land reformers, although less intimately involved with the unions, also continued their agitation. The National Reform Association was nothing if not tenacious. Throughout the year, it sponsored demonstrations and banquets, culminating in a mass meeting in late August addressed by Isaac Walker, the leading land reformer in Congress. As the strikes came to dominate the crisis, the NRA also made some unprecedented alliances with the trade unions. Not all of the land reformers were pleased by this spectacle: the ex-Chartist Thomas Devyr, for one, nettled several activists with his claims that the strikes were irrelevant where they were not harmful, and that land reform alone should be the workingmen's cause. But most land reformers were flexible enough to join with the union men and the German socialists. Their attention to wage earners' grievances and labor reform, reaffirmed when their National Industrial Congress reconvened in Chicago in May, added to the strike ferment in New York. Even the normally acerbic Weitling—a man whose unswerving adherence to his own ideas easily rivaled Devyr's—came to applaud the land reformers' work.[18]

Associated with land reform but hardly limited to it was the omnipresent Horace Greeley. Of all the major New York newspaper editors, Greeley stood alone as a sympathizer of the labor movement, and he covered it at length, winning the resounding approval of the protective and benefit unions. Greeley also restated his hatred of strikes and began a personal campaign to get the unions off the picket lines and into cooperative workshops. In April, he addressed the Working Shoemakers' Union with a measured plea for prudence and deliberation; two months later, he urged the bricklayers' and plasterers' protective to follow the lead of the shoemakers' cooperative and renounce all strike plans. By August, he had won enough influence to be chosen secretary of the tailors' cooperative; at no

17. *Ibid.*, April 23, 24, 30, May 16, June 6, 8, July 3, 26, August 21, 1850; Wittke, *Utopian Communist*, 144–97; Obermann, "Germano-Américains," 74–75; Ernst, *Immigrant Life*, 115–16. On Schiff and his association (with its forty-four members), see *Tribune*, August 15, 1850.

18. *Tribune*, March 19, 20, 23, May 3, 23, 30, August 28, 30, 1850.

point, though, did he endorse class warfare. Greeley's radicalism rested as ever on his insistence that the workers' plight was a social problem, not a collection of individual ones; his solution now, as in the 1840s, was to harmonize the interests of capital and labor.[19]

Unskilled laborers also held their own meetings and aired their complaints. By 1850, the Laborer's Union Benevolent Association was by far the largest organization of wage earners in the city. As an incorporated benefit society, the LUBA was ostensibly limited to mutual-aid work, but in the militant atmosphere of 1850, the group took the offensive. Monthly LUBA meetings became forums at which building laborers discussed the effects of arbitrary hiring practices, wage cutting, and sweating. In one of its several public rallies, the group supported the craft unions on strike and listened to its founder, the hod carrier turned politician Daniel Taylor, and Mike Walsh (who still had some fire in him) denounce speculators and building contractors. Finally, in May, the group supported a rank-and-file demand for a raise in wages and called its men out. Other previously unorganized laborers, the quarreymen and public porters, followed the LUBA's example, formed their own protectives, and threatened to strike if the "competition system" was not abolished.[20]

Working women proved a different case, in part because of the machinations of reformers, in part because of a resurgence of plebeian paternalism in the unions. In July, an obscure activist named A. W. Goff announced the formation of the American Industrial Union, a cooperative shop designed (or so Goff claimed) to help the city's seamstresses become their own employers. The union lasted at least through August, when Goff spoke at a Methodist church to ask for funds. The effort, however, struck most unionists and their allies as a fraud; Greeley, long a defender of the seamstresses and no enemy to cooperation, advised his readers to stay away from the AIU until its financial affairs were in safer hands than the dubious Mr. Goff's. Otherwise, the unions, with one exception, largely ignored the women; only the shoemakers, recognizing the splits in the labor market, admitted women and girls to membership, provided they were wives or daughters of workingmen in the trade. The Industrial Congress of 1850 took some note of the plight of the seamstresses and shirt sewers and invited a few of their number to address the delegates, but on the matter of representation, the congress would go no further than to

19. *Ibid.*, March 6, 12, 25, April 11, 26, June 1, August 23, September 17, November 29, 1850. Greeley was so busy spreading his ideas that his chief rival, Bennett of the *Herald*, declared that the entire strike movement was but a prelude to a campaign to elect Greeley mayor of New York. See *Herald*, April 23, 26, July 13, 1850.

20. *Tribune*, April 18, May 8, 10, June 11, 14, 20, 1850; *Herald*, May 12, June 16, 1850. There is some question about whether the public porters ever struck; Bennett charged that the report that they had done so was a fraud perpetrated by Greeley. See *Herald*, May 1, 1850.

permit two male representatives to be selected to oversee the women's problems. Only in 1851, when the seamstresses established their own cooperative, did the Congress take steps to support them actively—but by then the Congress itself was in difficult straits. Otherwise, the women were left with only the unionists' paternal insistence that women's work was degrading and ought to be abolished. On this point, the movement of 1850 backed away from the possibilities opened in the 1830s.[21]

This mélange of organizations and reform proposals revealed a great deal about the inherited ideas of New York's workers—and about all that had changed since the 1830s. Old themes reappeared: the labor theory of value; celebrations of mutuality and cooperative production; attacks on plundering, aristocratic nonproducers, capitalists, and employers; the antirepublican implications of the "wages system"; defense (and some criticism) of strikes. At the same time, new views emerged. The overtones of deism and irreligion, still present in the GTU, were almost gone among native-born workers, replaced by a Christian message of piety, morality, and resistance to oppression. Land reform, a logical outgrowth of older republican ideals of independence and virtue, tried to take working-class action back into political channels; along with the benefit societies, cooperatives, and Christian groups, the land reformers united small producers and workers under a single rubric—the industrials. In most cases, these groups opposed strikes; they also proposed, in far more concrete terms than the GTU's (and in less audacious terms than Skidmore's), a radical reform of property relations. Immigrants, although always important in the union rank and file, now built their own labor organizations with their own ideas about reform. The Germans, in particular, demonstrated how newly arrived immigrants had become a critical force; so did the numerous Irishmen like the tailor Joseph Donnelly who rose to the leadership of individual craft unions and helped organize the unskilled. Although women were largely excluded, the participation of the organized laborers in their own benefit and protective societies marked a degree of unity and formal activity outside the crafts unattained fifteen years earlier: "Our interests are identical, one and the same," a union carpenter told the LUBA, "and we must act in concert to elevate our moral and social situation."[22] Several streams of working-class opinion flowed in 1850; steadily, these streams drew together.

They met in the New York Industrial Congress. Although its exact origins are unclear, the congress was well established by the summer of 1850 as the chief standard-bearer of the labor movement. At no point did it turn into a revival of the GTU: its purposes were broader, to unite delegates from all the city's labor reform groups into a single body and to enun-

21. *Tribune*, July 1, 18, August 6, 1850.
22. *Irish-American*, May 19, 1850.

ciate a coherent common program. Greeley captured its intentions perfectly when he noted that several proposals had been tendered on how to do justice to labor: "For our part, we believe in exclusive devotion to [none] but in contending for each of all as occasion may occur." The congress proclaimed the terms of consensus in its constitution: confronted with "the hostility of relations which now exist between capital and labor," the delegates pledged to "secure the laborer the full product of his toil and to promote union, harmony, and brotherly feeling among all workmen of whatever occupation." By the end of the year, more than ninety unions and labor organizations had endorsed these broad precepts.[23]

The rise of the Industrial Congress (with all its diversity) proclaimed the reappearance of the New York working class as a presence in the city's social and political life; its progress and eventual failure marked the limits of working-class unity and power. Quite apart, however, from both the Congress and its constituent organizations, one more group played a key role in the events of 1850 and their aftermath—the Democratic party. Badly fractured over the slavery question and local political matters—and about to fracture again—the Democrats were in momentary need of some unifying force to consolidate their base and regain control of city government. The last thing the party wanted was an unpredictable, independent movement of labor, one that might well turn to political agitation on its own. For most of the year, Democratic spokesmen were content to stand aloof from the union struggles, apart from a few forays by sympathetic working-class politicos like Mike Walsh. By December, some were prepared to take the labor movement into the party's electoral coalition. Their efforts, as much as anything, shaped the final outcome of the protests.

To City Hall

The battles of 1850 began with the militant craft journeymen. As early as 1848, the tailors had established a new protective union, followed soon thereafter by the gilders and the printers, but the crisis began to take shape only in March 1850, when the cordwainers and carpenters announced that they had formed labor cooperatives and the carpenters went on strike. Both groups cited contracting and wage cutting; the carpenters went on to capture the city's attention by staging a series of grand parades and rallies (with suitable regalia) and by winning some encouraging words from Weitling's *Republik der Arbeiter*. The sight of one master builder after another agreeing to terms persuaded other journeymen that they should organize, and by the end of February at least five more protectives had posted demands for higher wages and changes in work rules. The shoe-

23. *Tribune*, July 30, 1850, January 2, 1851. Full reports on the congress's early sessions appear in the *Tribune*, May 24, 25, 30, June 4, 5, 12, 13, 14, 20, 25, 26, 1850.

makers, meanwhile, mapped out their cooperative and suggested that others might want to adopt similar plans. Immediately, city editors and the party press took alarm: the *Herald*, once again at the forefront of anti-union opinion, likened the new organizations to those undertaken by Skidmore, Wright, and Owen in 1829, and warned New York's workers to gird themselves against the "vast importations of foreign socialists" who would attempt to destroy the old political parties and construct "a new and remarkable one, under the banner of socialism."[24]

In April, protectives and cooperatives appeared in almost all of the consumer trades, particularly in those with large numbers of Germans: ten German unions or trade "sections" organized between April 18 and April 29. Weitling's influence was decisive. At least one German section, the tailors', announced it was forming a cooperative only hours after listening to a speech by Weitling; another, the confectioners' proclaimed that it was "following the *Republik der Arbeiter*" to support cooperation, labor exchanges, and workers' banks. The *Tribune* took stock on April 23 and noted that "no class goes to work harder than our German artizans. . . ." On the same day, the newspaper disclosed the formation of the Central Committee of the Trades.[25]

Weitling and the Germans were not alone. In early April, the mostly British and native window-shade painters formed their own protective and cooperative associations. On April 21, the printers held a mass meeting to announce that they had formed a committee to investigate the state of the trade and to report back to the membership. Veteran radicals also began to take a more active interest in labor's revival. Albert Brisbane attended a meeting of the house carpenters to encourage their efforts and to promote association. Thomas Devyr penned a long letter to the *Tribune*, urging the journeymen to support land reform more directly. Greeley, while not going over the dispatches from his roving reporters, could be spotted all over town, speaking to cooperatives, recording the unionists' speeches, and keeping in touch with each of the new labor groups as it formed.[26]

Within the union meetings, craft workers engaged in remarkable debates over their common problems and the proper relationship between trade unionism and other movements for social reform. Radical workers rose to explain their positions and to argue that what they proposed was in line with most journeymen's aspirations for self-independence. At a carpenters' union meeting, a native American unionist, incensed at the out-

24. *Tribune*, March 1, 6, 7, 9, 14, 19, 20, 24, 25, 28, 1850; *Republik der Arbeiter* [New York], March 1850.
25. *Tribune*, April 4, 5, 6, 8, 9, 11, 12, 13, 15, 16, 17, 18, 19, 20, 22, 23, 24, 25, 26, 27, 29, 30, 1850; *Herald*, April 3, 12, 14, 18, 19, 21, 24, 26, 29, 1850.
26. *Tribune*, April 22, 26, 1850.

cries of James Gordon Bennett of the *Herald* and other "capitalists," explained his views. "I am one of the men that they call socialists," he began:

> Now suppose instead of working journeywork for a "boss," twelve of you take a place of your own and work for yourselves—is that socialism? The "boss" lives out of town, and keeps a splendid house, gets up at nine o'clock in the morning and drives into town, but you can never have a chance of buying a lot, and your thirteen shillings [$1.62] a day are spent before the end of the week. . . . Mr. Bennett says, "To array capital against labor would be to destroy, to a great extent, both." That's all very true; but it is already arrayed against labor, and therefore they refuse to give you fourteen shillings a day. It appears to be the capitalists' intention to reduce the laborer.

Another socialist followed the same logic: "We believe that by our own energies, we might make our labor benefit us more than it does at the present time." Other workers were more skeptical and insisted that although they too sought independence, it would be bad policy for the carpenters "to engraft themselves onto Fourierism or any other ism." One pointed out, "We are all carpenters here; but we are not all socialists." At least one labor group, the ship sawyers' benefit society, flatly repudiated socialist and cooperative ideas.[27] The debates would continue over the next six months.

As the spring brought New Yorkers out of doors, the power and diversity of the mounting agitation became evident to all. In late May, several protectives held mass meetings to announce their grievances, to vote on a course of action (almost invariably for a strike), and otherwise to display their unity. The union democracy, virtually absent from view since 1837, reappeared in the streets, most often in front of City Hall. Two of the largest unions, the printers' and carpenters', used their rallies to present lengthy reports on conditions in their trades; both concluded with ringing denunciations of wage cutting, contracting, and competition. The printers renounced all intentions to strike, but called for a thorough reorganization of the shops into printers' chapels, preparatory to an eventual conversion of all production to a cooperative system, in order to end the "perpetual antagonism between labor and capital." By the first week of June, at least ten protective unions had either gone on strike or begun making plans to do so; the laborers of the LUBA and the quarrymen's and public porters' protectives also raised their demands. Outside of the strike movement, the cooperative projects made further headway. A few trades, with Greeley's support, urged the creation of a formal labor exchange, along the lines of the French *bourses de travail*, to reduce competition in the labor market, curtail unemployment, and coordinate the activities of the various craft

27. *Herald*, April 19, 29, 1850.

societies. The Mechanics' Mutual announced that it had decided to start its consumers' cooperative. Anti-union spokesmen struck back, calling themselves the "honest and sincere friends of the working classes" and repeating the familiar rhetoric on the harmony of interests and the limitless opportunity of the American republic.[28]

About this time, the Industrial Congress was born. Despite its similarity in name to the land reformers' National Congress, the group began entirely independent of the NRA; the impetus for its organization seems to have been strongest among the cabinetmakers' and turners' protectives. As the delegates gathered for their first meeting, on June 5, the power of the trade unionists was obvious. The vast majority of delegates came from the protectives in the consumer trades. K. Arthur Bailey, the journeyman printer, was quickly elected president. Of the thirteen other officers whose affiliations have been identified, ten were from the protectives.[29] Nevertheless, the Congress was a mixed assemblage from the start. Land reformers (including George Henry Evans), Christian labor radicals, and co-operativists all took seats as delegates; President Bailey embodied the numerous ideological tendencies at play. In this, their first formal gathering, the various groups showed more than passing suspicion for each other. Greeley applauded the Congress but expressed concern at the numbers of trade unionists in its ranks; the body's initial sessions were given over to squabbles about organizational matters. The confusion prompted the *Herald* to liken the group to a bunch of "little boys attempting to represent a play of the great Shakespeare."[30]

Divisions within the Congress, however, were quickly overshadowed by the ongoing unrest within the trades and by unions' clashes with intransigent employers. On June 8, the largest trade of all, the tailors', staged its first mass meeting of both "English" (that is, English-speaking) and German sections; the cabinetmakers' and button and fringe makers' protectives rallied on the same day. Disagreement had cropped up between the natives and Germans in the cabinetmakers' and cigarmakers' unions, centered on their wage demands and the desirability of cooperative shops; rank and filers and Weitling's Central Committee soothed the tensions and hammered out shaky compromises.[31] The unrest had reached a critical stage, approaching the most intense of the strike waves of the 1830s. Attention turned for a moment to the Industrial Congress, for a sign about where the rebels were headed. As it turned out, they were bound for City Hall.

28. *Tribune*, May 1–June 2, 1850, passim; *Herald*, May 1, 3, 4, 6, 9, 12, 15, 22, 26, 27, June 2, 1850. For the printers' remarks, see *Tribune* May 22, 1850. For anti-union views, see *Herald*, May 5, 1850.

29. *Tribune*, June 6, 1850.

30. *Ibid.*, May 24, 30, June 5, 1850; *Herald*, June 7, 1850.

31. *Tribune*, June 9, 1850.

The idea of using City Hall as a meeting place and labor exchange had first been proposed in mid-May, by a native tailor interested in merging his "English" brethren with the German tailors and the Central Committee. At the time, the proposal was passed over as a "curious novelty," but in the headiness of late spring it quickly won support. On June 11, the Industrial Congress, in one of its first official acts, petitioned the Common Council to set aside space, citing the council's duty to make at least a small recognition of labor's cause. A response was not forthcoming: while the appropriate committee of the council stalled, the Congress, meeting at the baker's cooperative shop, debated various reform proposals and complained about the city's delays. Finally, on July 1, word reached the Congress that the Board of Alderman had reversed the committee's negative report. We can only guess at the board's motives; presumably, the labor movement, and whatever friends it might have had among those close to the board, had persuaded the aldermen that the cession of a single room would be a prudent, even politic gesture. In any case, after July 1, the congress moved its deliberations to the supreme court chambers in the New City Hall, an annex building next to the original hall.[32]

The move, seemingly quite insignificant when compared with the strikes and cooperatives, carried powerful associations. Only two years after the fledgling French republic had created the Luxembourg Commission and German radicals had formed their own congresses to forward recommendations about the social organization of labor, New York's Industrial Congress had persuaded its own local authorities to allow it to sit at the very center of municipal government. Like the French and German bodies, the congress had no mandate to enforce reforms; most important, it was not empowered to negotiate or ratify wage agreements. None could deny, however, that an unprecedented degree of political legitimacy had befallen the militants. Without even discussing a formal alliance with the political parties, they had entered the New City Hall by themselves. New hopes beckoned: if the council permitted the Congress to use the hall, might it not also lend its authority to enact some of the Congress's proposals? Would not the mere sight of journeymen mechanics and laborers parading through the corridors of justice help persuade politicians and the public of the justice of their cause and the depth of their commitment? Might not the Republic at last save itself—and might not the Americans, with their ingrained republicanism, succeed where the French and the Germans had failed?[33]

32. *Tribune*, May 15, June 12, 25, July 2, 1850. In 1834, the GTU had tried to persuade the council to give up some space for the first convention of the NTU. The council refused, enraging the unionists. It is likely (although the incident was not brought up) that some men in the Congress—and the Council—recalled these events and pursued a more conciliatory course. See Commons, *Documentary History*, V, 269–75.

33. *Ibid.*, July 2, 3, 5, 1850.

Immediately, the delegates' deliberations picked up momentum. On the same day they received word from the Common Council, the men approved the Congress's constitution. Several committees went to work, to draft position papers on contract labor and the eight-hour day. On July 3, the Congress passed a resolution demanding that the city set aside a portion of municipal property to be turned into a public bath, a workingmen's reading room, and a labor exchange. Weitling and others appeared before the delegates to press for support for the cooperatives.[34] Outside of the Congress, meanwhile, the strike movement also entered a new phase, as the tailors organized at full strength. The bloodiest and most divisive of all the strikes of 1850—indeed, in antebellum urban American history— was about to begin.

The Tailors' Strike

Although the carpenters were initially at the head of the uprising (as they had been in 1833), the tailors were expected to join them. Apart from being the largest trade in the city, the tailors suffered from what the unionists and their sympathizers acknowledged were the worst working conditions in New York. "As a class," ran one article typical of 1850, "they are the worst oppressed of God's creatures." Not surprisingly, the *Tribune* took special notice of a mass meeting of German and "English" tailors on July 10 and rejoiced that they had "aroused from their lethargy and awakened to a sense of duty at last." The meeting proposed a scale of prices, and by the fifteenth some nine hundred tailors had turned out; the following week brought another meeting and a further expansion of the strike. On both occasions, organizers and rank-and-file tailors stressed the need for unity across ethnic lines as well as between the custom and ready-made branches, lest the employers should try to play one group against the other. By the twenty-fifth, the ranks were secure, as the Germans announced that they would adopt the pay scale of their "English" brethren and the custom workers declared that they would refuse to handle any article destined for the southern trade.[35]

In the midst of their mobilization, the tailors soon discovered that they faced a threat unknown to the GTU, the professional police force organized in the wake of James Harper's failed nativist reforms. First blood was drawn on the afternoon of the twenty-second, during a march of some three hundred tailors to present their bill of prices to Longstreet and Company, a southern trade firm notorious for its low wages and opposition to trade unionism. At least nineteen other such marches to tailoring establishments had taken place during the preceding week without incident;

34. *Ibid.*, July 5, 12, 1850.
35. *Ibid.*, July 10, 26, 29, 1850.

even the *Herald* had grudgingly approved of the strikers' conduct. Upon reaching Longstreet's, however, the tailors were met by a member of the firm, one J. H. Bates, who ordered them to step aside. When the strikers refused, Bates bid some of his men to shut the doors, provoking a rock fight between those within the shop and those outside. Within minutes, a detachment of police—alerted to the scene by two officers posted to watch over Longstreet's—was wading into the crowd, nightsticks flying. At least one spectator was arrested for protesting the policemen's rough handling of the prisoners; others were beaten when they tried to rescue those who had been arrested.[36]

Over the next fortnight, the tailors' strike and outrage at the police action overwhelmed other matters. The strikers, undeterred by the violence, declared a general strike of the trade and set up shop committees to coordinate their actions. Joseph Donnelly, representing the tailors, pleaded with the Industrial Congress for additional support; although the tailors—most of them German—had turned unruly at Longstreet's, Donnelly argued, it was largely because they could not understand what Bates was saying; certainly they were "more sinned against than sinning." Donnelly won his resolution of support, both for the strikers and for eventual aid to help the tailors to set up a cooperative. A series of protective public meetings, meanwhile, drew familiar lessons from the tailors' experience. It was imperative, one speaker proclaimed, for all workers to support the tailors but also to

> prevent the growth of an unwholesome aristocracy, whose only aim is to acquire wealth by robbery of the toiling masses; to place themselves in a position to successfully combat capital; to bring labor up to its proper elevation and take that position which God intended man should fill—truly independent of his fellows, and above the position of a mere "wage slave."

On July 27, untold thousands of sympathizers "densely crowded" City Hall Park for a mass rally. Three separate speakers' stands were erected to keep the crowd within earshot; those who listened heard every variety of labor radicalism and trade unionism proclaimed, now unified in support of the tailors. "English" spokesmen like John Commerford and Albert Brisbane reinvoked republicanism and the labor theory of value; for Commerford, the event brought back memories of 1835 and 1836, as once again, he remarked, the wage earners fought capital as their forefathers had fought the British. Others agreed, but also compared their efforts to those of the workingmen of Paris and argued that only cooperatives would restore the

---

36. For clashing accounts of the riot, see *ibid.*, July 24, 1850; and *Herald*, July 22, 1850. Seven men were arrested: Robert Barr, Daniel Gedney, James Mayher, Henry Brown, Conrad Sneider, Charles Frank, and a Mr. Britykar.

republican trades to a state of mutuality and independence. All the while, anti-union opinion hardened: "The Devil To Pay Among the Tailors," the *Herald* declared, noting that the violence that attended the tailors' march was a "striking illustration of socialism" and what it would bring.[37]

As the trade unions flocked to the tailors' aid, the Industrial Congress tried to consolidate its own unity—thereby exposing the first serious signs of division. Although they managed to agree on several points—support for the tailors, a report calling for the abolition of contracting on public building projects, the eight-hour day—the delegates did not see eye to eye about what the Congress should do next. A few of the protective unions, especially the bricklayers', were especially wary of the influence of the land reformers and benefit societies. Both groups, they argued, included at least some employers and therefore could not be counted on to support the strikes; even more, previous movements had failed precisely because unfriendly persons, under the guise of support for labor's rights, had infiltrated them; only the GTU, restricted to wage earners, had managed to survive for a time. The benefit unions, led by Charles Crux of the upholsterers', responded that no one in the congress would dream of denouncing or thwarting the protectives' efforts, even though some delegates were opposed to strikes. All agreed that the tailors' cause was just, all supported them against Longstreet and the police. A GTU was fine in principle: the object of the Congress was simply a different one, to ally all opponents of capital in a broad front to coordinate disparate efforts at labor reform. The protectives, although displeased, backed off for the moment. The basis for future disputes had been laid.[38]

Back outside of City Hall, the unionists continued to clash with police and began to consider forming their own group to supplement the congress. The escalation of the violence shocked even the most militant journeymen. "We did not expect to find in this free country a Russian police," the Central Committee declared, "nor do we believe that the people will sustain these officials in their evident abuse of power." Newspaper reports claimed that journeymen tailors had begun provoking policemen assigned to protect strikebreakers; several tailors were arrested for an assault on a Catholic church that had reputedly been distributing work to scabs. The police in turn stepped up their efforts, regularly harassing the strikers and going under cover to protect the city's shops.[39] On August 3, the Central Committee held another mass meeting of Germans and "English" to condemn the police actions. John Commerford reportedly referred to the police force as "seven hundred thieves," who had colluded with the city's

---

37. *Tribune*, July 26, 29, 1850; *Herald*, July 23, 26, 27, 31, August 1, 1850.
38. *Tribune*, July 3, 4, August 12, 1850.
39. *Ibid.*, July 26, 1850; *Herald*, July 31, 1850.

employers. Speakers addressing a contingent of Irish-born tailors berated the police and issued fresh proposals. William Barr, a tailors' delegate to the Industrial Congress, urged that once the tailors had won their strike, they should join with others in a united movement for an eight-hour day; another Irishman, proving that the long tradition of artisan rationalism was not completely dead, observed that "even in this liberal country, the middle class stands above the workingmen, and every one of them is a little tyrant in himself, as Voltaire said." The Germans matched the Irish tailors' rhetoric and called upon all of the protective unions to form a provisional committee roughly similar in structure to the GTU; further-more, they suggested that this committee begin planning for a general strike of all the trades.[40] Once more, the crisis was assuming unfamiliar proportions. Deadly violence was not long in coming.

On the next day, August 4, as the Irish, English, Scotch, and American tailors met formally to align with the Germans, a row broke out at the home of one Frederick Wartz, a journeyman who reportedly had been performing work at home at below union scale. Reports conflict on what happened. The police, Wartz, and several eyewitnesses charged that a mob of some one hundred German tailors had ransacked Wartz's shanty be-fore being repelled by the police. The *Tribune* and several tailors countered that the story was a complete fabrication and that Wartz's home, although the site of a protest, had been attacked by a company of fire laddies called to the scene by the police. In any event, a detachment of twenty police-men patrolled the immediate vicinity of Wartz's through the late after-noon.[41]

At roughly 5 P.M., another party of about three hundred tailors, again mostly Germans, set out to confront Wartz and then to proceed north, to follow up a rumor that two subcontractors were quietly giving out south-ern work below scale. At the corner of Thirty-eighth Street and Ninth Avenue, the marchers found their way blocked by the police. Without warning, the officers attacked, clubbing tailors to the ground amid a shower of stones and brickbats; "part of the time," the *Herald* reported, "it appeared to be a more formidable riot than at the Astor House." Once again the more disciplined police prevailed, and the tailors scattered into the dusk. All told, at least two tailors were killed, dozens were severely wounded, and forty were arrested; a few policemen reported injuries rang-ing from knife wounds to bruises.[42] For the first time, urban American workers had been slain by the forces of order in a trade dispute.

40. *Tribune*, August 5, 1850; *Herald*, August 4, 5, 1850.
41. *Herald*, August 6, 7, 8, 9, 1850, presents details of the events at Wartz's home, including the affidavits filed with the police court by Wartz, his wife, and three other eyewitnesses. *Tribune*, August 5, 6, 1850, presents the tailors' side of the story, and their contention that the firemen were responsible for the damage.
42. *Herald*, August 6, 7, 1850; *Tribune*, August 5, 6, 1850. It is possible that many

Predictable indignant speeches and editorials followed. The anti-union press had a field day with the "tailors' riot": how ineffective, the *Herald* sermonized, were the efforts of "overzealous and highly excited laborers" who would wrest power by violence rather than through the ballot box. Labor spokesmen, although jarred by the affair, stood by the tailors and demanded a full investigation. The tailors held additional mass meetings on the ninth and the twelfth. K. Arthur Bailey declared that "it is the imperative duty of the industrial classes throughout the city to aid and support the operative tailors." Trade unions and benefit groups from as far away as Boston expressed their solidarity with the New Yorkers; the Industrial Congress pledged to provide defense funds for the arrested men. If anything, the incident only emboldened the tailors' movement and hastened the implementation of new departures. By August 21, some 3,000 German and "English" tailors had established a cooperative association. By month's end, the union, now with the crucial backing of the cutters and foremen in the southern as well as the custom branches, had brought almost every employer to terms. The German sections elected delegates to get the proposed central labor union underway.[43]

The unity that followed the riot softened the controversies within the Industrial Congress and the unions; through early autumn, there was no reason to believe that the unity would cease or that the labor movement would stall. By September, the journeymen's Cooperative Union Tailoring Establishment was advertising its wares in the *Tribune*. The German socialists held a picnic celebration. Greeley printed a flurry of articles describing the Parisian cooperative workshops and urging New Yorkers to emulate them. The congress returned to its reform agenda and repeated its call for an eight-hour day; both the carpenters' protective and a committee of workers from the Eleventh Ward added their support for the measure.[44] Yet in spite of the tailors' victory, a pall gradually settled over the militants. Not every union had won its demands; indeed, as Greeley observed in November, irregular wages and price differentials remained as common as ever in most trades. Some of the more successful unions, such as the carpenters', discovered that employers could easily break earlier agreements and force the unionists to begin all over again. The bloodshed of August, though it gave the labor movement a rallying point, also con-

more than two tailors died. The *Herald* reported on August 6 that "a considerable number of wounded escaped and were taken away from them, i.e., the police—some of them perhaps mortally." The list of arrestees appears in *Herald*, August 7, 1850; the great majority were German. Only eight were eventually brought to trial and convicted; one was fined $50; six were fined $5; one was released "on good advice." On the trial, see *Tribune*, December 12, 16, 1850.

43. *Tribune*, August 10, 12, 13, 14, 15, 19, 20, 21, 24, 28, 1850; *Herald*, August 7, 8, 13, 14, 1850.

44. *Tribune*, September 5, 10, 18, 1850.

fused and intimidated some who were not fully prepared for such repression in a republican metropolis and who wanted to preserve the labor movement's reputation for discipline. A meeting of Irish tailors supported the Germans but also registered "deep regret" and apologies concerning the riot. Other unions stressed as never before that they respected law and order and would not countenance violence from their members. The Industrial Congress, some of whose members had feared strikes all along, quietly backed off from its promise to aid the arrested tailors.[45]

The autumn also brought the elections and with them a turn away from labor disputes and toward politics. All year, the House and Senate had been debating the Fugitive Slave Bill and related matters, raising the distinct possibility of national disunion. With the passage of the compromise, local attention focused on the battle between abolitionists and conservatives over the rights of one James Hamlet, a runaway slave, who had been arrested in New York.[46] The labor movement for the most part could not have cared less. Racial animosities and distrust of Whiggish moralizers remained strong among the membership, particularly among the laborers; even those who opposed slavery construed the emergence of sectional issues in politics as a distraction from their own cause. One group of workingmen in the Eighth Ward argued that it was important "to abolish Wages Slavery before we meddle with Chattel Slavery." The radicals of the Industrial Congress could do no better than to pass a resolution stating that they "utterly detest[ed] the entire system of American slavery, black and white," and would work to end both. More typical was the attitude of the Brotherhood of the Union, that only when workingmen had freed themselves of monopoly would they "consider the propriety of unfettering those who are better off than to be let loose under the present Competitive System of labor. . . ."[47]

In searching for ways to redirect political debate, the Congress and the unions faced an old dilemma: How could labor engage in politics without making dangerous entangling alliances? The entry to City Hall had opened up one possibility—although the recent actions of the police raised obvious questions about the municipality's commitment to labor. To strengthen its position, the Congress adopted what would become a familiar union strategy, devising a questionnaire to be delivered to all local candidates and allocating their support on the basis of the candidate's replies. The questions reflected the mixed character of the Congress, although land

45. *Herald*, August 9, 1850; *Tribune*, September 11, 1850.
46. On the Hamlet case, see Stanley W. Campbell, *The Slave Catchers: Enforcement of the Fugitive Slave Law* (Chapel Hill, 1970), 115; Sean Wilentz, "Crime, Poverty, and the Streets of New York City: The Diary of William H. Bell, 1850–51," *History Workshop* 7 (1979): 132–33.
47. *Tribune*, August 15, 22, October 8, 1850.

reform did receive more attention than any other concern. The results were equally mixed. In several races, no candidate agreed to support the labor movement, and the Congress had to endorse its own; although the Congress eventually took credit for helping to elect nine assemblymen from the major parties, none of its independent nominees came close to a majority. Retrieving a sense of victory, the Congress went on to describe political action as the surest means whereby "the producing classes" could end their various "oppressions and grievances"; nevertheless, the election, and the quieting of strike activity, set the labor movement adrift.[48] Although the effects of that drift were not immediately apparent, it was already becoming clear to a few in the trade unions that the labor movement was moving toward just the kind of political alliances and divisions they had feared.

Party Politics, Dissolution, and the Aftermath

The Industrial Congress began the new year optimistically, certain that the labor movement was stronger than ever. In a reiteration of their shared principles, the delegates endorsed a ringing appeal to republican rights, to wit:

> That all men are created equal—that they are endowed by their Creator with certain inalienable rights, among which are the right to Life, Liberty, and the fruits of their Labor, and to the use of such a portion of the earth and other elements as are necessary for their subsistence and comfort, to Education and paternal protection from society.[49]

The well-organized land reformers began to dominate the body more than ever, their hands set free by the abeyance of strike activity. Numerous petitions bid the House and Senate to pass some sort of homestead bill; outspoken land-reform politicians, including Walker, won the Industrial Congress's commendation. Still, land reform did not force other items off the agenda entirely. Throughout the winter, the group condemned subcontracting and proposed its abolition in all state building projects. The co-ops held the Congress's support. In April, it approved a proposal reversing its previous stance on women workers and offering to aid a new shirtmakers' cooperative with a subsidy "no less liberal . . . than was the grant to the file makers' association of Paris." New approaches to financial and currency reform, including Edward Kellogg's *Labor and Other Capital*, were discussed and publicized by Industrial Congress committees.[50]

In late May, however, the Congress had to consider a truly novel pro-

48. *Ibid.*, December 2, 1850.
49. *Ibid.*, January 2, 1851.
50. *Ibid.*, January 6, 17, February 11, 14, March 22, April 9, 1851.

posal, when Bailey announced that the delegates had been invited to attend a mass meeting at Tammany Hall "of all those in favor of land and other industrial reform, to be made elements in the presidential election of 1852." A hot debate ensued, notable more for personal invective than for discussion of the merits of political action; in the end the majority voted to accept the invitation. They gathered at Tammany Hall on June 3 to find the place filled with trade unionists, committed political friends like Walsh, and more conventional Tammany professionals. As one representative of Tammany and another from the congress chaired the meeting, the men listened to familiar denunciations of the land monopoly, but with a new twist—an appeal for all "friends of the workingmen" to use the leverage of the Democratic party to win their reforms. The argument seemed to be in line with the Congress's opinion on politics; in principle, they would support only those men who favored their own programs, and stay formally independent of party affairs. A series of resolutions urging the Democrats to support freedom of public land and to nominate Isaac Walker for president passed without a vote in dissent.[51]

The Congress was doomed. By joining the Democrats, it had finally put political action for land reform before all other questions; gradually, the delegates from the protective unions and a few of the beneficials found themselves shut out when they tried to raise other matters. The splits that had appeared the preceding July widened, as trade unionists caught up in the land reform drive joined with nonunionists against the protectives and the LUBA. By early 1852, any semblance of solidarity had disappeared. Patrick Dillon of the LUBA explained that at least since late 1850, the Congress had been taken over by "irresponsible men," less interested in industrial reform and supporting the strikes than in pursuing their own will-o'-the-wisp; with a few exceptions, the trade-union organizations had ceased to participate. After that, the decay could not be arrested. Reorganized into ward associations, rather than by trade, the Industrial Congress became a political reform auxiliary, its activities limited to little more than staging demonstrations in favor of Walker and land reform. When the Walker insurgency failed and Franklin Pierce was elected president, the Industrial Congress dissolved. Only sixteen men were reported present for its final meetings.[52]

The trade unions and cooperatives, now fighting on their own, found it much more difficult to sustain themselves in 1851 and 1852. Another brief downturn in prices, in 1851, dashed the wage advances of 1850 and dampened any further union activities. The cooperatives survived rather longer; Greeley was hopeful enough in 1851 to print copies of an "associative

51. *Ibid.*, May 30, June 2, 1851; *Herald*, June 12, 1851.
52. *Tribune*, July 5, 1851, November 8, 1852.

manual" by the English radical Charles Sully, complete with suggested bylaws. In most cases, however, lack of ready capital and adequate legal protection proved too forbidding to keep the shops alive; by the autumn of 1851, only four of the German producers' cooperatives were still in existence. Although a few strikes followed in 1852, the journeymen returned in large numbers to the quieter benefit societies, including a new one, the Mechanics' Union Association.[53]

Once prices did improve, in 1853, the protectives geared up for strikes, but by then the labor movement's character had changed dramatically. A new central labor congress, the Amalgamated Trades' Convention, assembled delegates from a range of trades; excluded, however, were all land reformers and socialists not also active in a trade union. The new convention frowned, at least initially, on political action and on anything else that would divert it from winning its strikes; without reconciling themselves to the "wages system," the trade unionists turned to the most direct shop-floor issues, above all work rules; even if they won higher wages, *Hunt's Merchants' Magazine* gasped, these unionists would "go on to enact laws for the government of their respective departments to all of which the employer must assent before he can be allowed to proceed to his business."[54]

Fresh political activities also began, especially among the Germans, but these, too, initiated very different approaches to the labor question. While the NRA foundered and while Weitling, frustrated by his latest failure, made plans to move west, a different breed of socialist appeared in *Kleindeutschland*. In January 1852, a recent immigrant, Joseph Weydemeyer, established a paper, *Die Revolution*; by spring, he had published the first edition of *The Eighteenth Brumaire of Louis Bonaparte*, by his friend and political associate Karl Marx. It took time for Weydemeyer to establish himself, but by the winter of 1852-53, his articles and his group, the *Proletarierbund*, had attracted the attention of a few hundred German mechanics. Much of their talk stuck to familiar topics—how industry served capital alone and how the capitalist robbed the wage slave—but their political vision, and their vision of America, was entirely different from those of earlier movements. The Republic, they claimed, was a fraud; the only difference between the Old World and the New, as Weydemeyer put it, was that "there the bourgeois is monarchist and over here republican." Strikes alone, though necessary, would not liberate the proletarians; neither would reliance on utopian schemes or naïve principles of virtue,

53. *Tribune*, February 13, March 18, 20, 27, 1851; *Republik der Arbeiter*, September 1851; Degler, "Labor," 50–51.
54. *Hunt's Merchants' Magazine* 28 (1853): 594; *Tribune*, September 1, 14, 21, 28, 1853.

independence, and commonwealth. The first step, rather, was for the wage slaves to understand that they were nothing more than that; they then had to form a genuine workers' party, one that aimed to seize control of the state and transform it utterly, stripping the bourgeoisie of all claims to power. American workers, in short, had to learn the lesson of the *Eighteenth Brumaire*. Weydemeyer's arguments, which sounded odd to the ears of American republicans, never got much beyond *Kleindeutschland*; Weydemeyer himself, analyzing the growing sectional controversies of the late 1850s and the coming of civil war much as his German friends did, went on to enlist in the army of the bourgeois republic, and make his mark as a Union artillery officer. He ended his days in St. Louis in 1866 as a notable in local radical and Republican party circles. Back in New York, his writings, along with the continuing efforts of his mentors Marx and Engels, still had their champions among the Germans. They would eventually win more—including a young cigarmaker, Sam Gompers—to make Marxism the leading form of socialism in New York.[55]

Conclusion: "The Most Radical City in America"

What had happened? In the most abstract sense, the crisis of 1850 had turned into a familiar chronicle of defeat, of internal splits hastened by political manipulation and deflection—a flash of anger quickly dissipated. For all of their early hopes, the rebels of 1850 had accomplished, if anything, less than their predecessors of 1829 and the mid-1830s. The land reformers, German radicals, and cooperativists, capable of lending coherence, organization, and radical imagination to the trade-union uprising, never came to terms with the aspirations and exigencies of the unions—and without the unions, they faded back into insignificance. The union movement, though it provided the numbers and the power behind the uprising, could not sustain itself as an independent force in the face of the intimidating superiority of the police and employers and the vicissitudes of the business cycle. For a few months, the separate lines of labor agitation of the 1840s were joined; in the end, it was the Democrats, reaching out for political support, who picked up the labor movement's shattered remains, leaving the causes of labor reform and wage earners' rights as fragmented as ever.

In spite of the collapse, though, 1850 was also important to those who took part, both as an experience of conflict and as a signal of things to come. A comparison, here, to the failed rebellion of the German and (even

55. Weydemeyer, quoted in Hermann Schlüter, *Die Anfänge der deutschen Arbeiterbewegung in Amerika* (Stuttgart, 1907), 141. On Weydemeyer, Karl Obermann, *Joseph Weydemeyer: The Pioneer of American Socialism* (New York, 1947), remains the standard work, but see also David Herreshoff, *American Disciples of Marx from the Age of Jackson to the Progressive Era* (Detroit, 1967), 59–68.

more) the Paris workers in the spring of 1848 is not completely amiss. The events in New York were, of course, of an entirely different order of magnitude from those in Europe: New York saw no revolutionary crisis, no June Days, no insurrection by workers or anyone else. To the extent that the New York labor movement took a political turn, it was to the ballot box and not to the barricade. Quite apart from the evocation of the Luxembourg Commission and the Frankfurt Congress, however, New York knew something of the reconsolidation and transformation of class consciousness and labor radicalism that one historian of France has discussed as the central event of 1848.[56] The temporary union of organized journeymen with laborers, assorted radicals, and immigrants had produced a plethora of programs and demands, as well as a new model of institutional centralization for the labor movement. In the trade unions, new immigrants joined with native journeymen in an impressive show of multiethnic working-class unity—a repudiation of nativism after the tribulations of the middle and late 1840s. For the first time, organized workers made demands directly on the municipality to provide important reforms—not simply to abolish abusive practices but to supply workers with public baths, labor exchanges, and reading rooms; several of these demands, and several of the labor movement's cooperative projects, would remain at the heart of labor agitation through the Gilded Age and afterward. And, more important than all this, was the very scale and sharpness of conflict that galvanized the city for nearly six months. Despite all that divided them, the unions and reform associations had found their common enemy once more, a class of employers and all their supporters, ranged against them with a new kind of official force, a "Russian" police. Of the major newspapers, only Greeley's *Tribune* treated the labor movement's activities with any degree of respect or sympathy; no significant political support was forthcoming from either party until after the strikes had died down; otherwise, the Industrial Congress and its constituents were left on their own, inside the very halls of power, but incapable of breaking the phalanx of opposition. Some workers held to the possibility of a new regime of "honorable" cooperation or even (with Greeley) reconciliation; others recoiled in horror; nevertheless, the lesson was plain to all, rehearsed in the strikes, written out in the blood spilled at Longstreet's and at Frederick Wartz's shanty: this was a conflict of class.

In back of this renewed clash was more than half a century of political dissent, painful re-evaluation, and conflict. In an important sense, its origins stretched back at least as far as the primal political events of 1774–76, when resistance to Britain had turned into republican revolution. Tem-

---

56. Sewell, *Work and Revolution in France*, 243–76. See also Rémi Gossez, *Les Ouvriers de Paris*, vol. 1, *L'Organisation*, 1848–1851 (La Roche-sur-Yon, 1967), 221–389.

pered by war and elitist resurgence, the artisan republic had established
its political presence in the 1790s and the first decades of the nineteenth century, only to run into the challenges and divisions of a new
workshop order, imposed in the name of individual liberty and republican
bounty. So the new conflict had begun, ebbing and flowing in the city's
most rapidly changing trades from the mid-1820s to 1850, washing away
the old craft connections and creating new solidarities, the burdens of
necessity forcing men and women, in the span of a single lifetime, to some
of the most creative popular engagements in this nation's history. The nub
of the matter in 1850—as James Gordon Bennett hinted—was the same as
in the 1820s: Did metropolitan industrialization and the transformation
of wage labor into a commodity enhance the independence and mutuality
of the Republic itself? Middle-class employers, having already laid powerful claims to the legacy of the commonwealth, had no doubts; in 1850,
they were willing to sanction the use of force to support their claims in
the name of social order. In response, New York's organized workers and
labor radicals once again turned inward, to reflect on what America was
supposed to be; their replies varied, but, as before, they carried a message
of negation, resistance, and reform.

The obstacles that confronted the labor movement were as formidable
at midcentury as they had been in the days of the Working Men. The
fissures between those workers and radicals who looked primarily to social
and political reforms (and, in some cases, class reconciliation) and those
who would also take (or, in some instances, only take) to the picket line
still ran through the ranks and widened under the stress of confrontation.
No consensus had been reached on what the matrix of exploitation actually
was, on whether the greatest enemy was the monopolistic aristocratic financier or land jobber, the corrupt party politician, the exploitative employer,
or all of these men. The perils of politics—the power of the Democrats to
absorb discontent, the hopes of some labor reformers that a regular party
or political reform might be a vehicle for creating a new social order—remained. Unity across the lines of craft and ethnicity had been achieved
(the second with effort) as had formal unity between skilled and unskilled men; there was no guarantee the achievements would endure. The
problem of where that veritable city within a city of laboring women belonged had not been sorted out. Nor had the issues of race and slavery—
issues of relatively little moment to earlier labor movements but ones that,
once engaged, played upon cultural fears and class antagonisms in ways
that bound most workers' loyalties ever tighter to the Democracy. Behind
1850 was the legacy of class formation. Decades more of struggle, over what
the working-class presence meant and over what its project should be, lay
ahead.

And yet that presence was unmistakable in New York in 1850, as it would continue to be in later years. So was the special place of the metropolis as a center of working-class action and labor radicalism in the industrializing Republic. Many other cities had seen strikes and radical committees rise and fall over the preceding twenty years. None had witnessed anything like the unrest that unfolded in Manhattan in 1850. Although the classic scenes of industrial capitalist growth were to be found elsewhere, New York remained the focal point of the American economy, a manufacturing center that generated staggering wealth and sharp inequalities, a haven for radical émigrés, an immigrant metropolis. For millions of Americans, New York was becoming an alien, menacing, almost un-American place; as in Britain and on the Continent, however, it was here, in the metropolis, that the ideas and movements that would inspire radicals (and their opponents) for generations took shape. Mike Walsh had sensed New York's peculiar importance as early as 1843, telling his followers that nothing like the shirtless democracy could have originated in any other part of the country: ". . . New York is to the Union what Paris is to France—what ancient Rome was to its vast Empire—what the heart is to the body."[57] Nearly a decade later, another artisan "rough," like Walsh a man steeped in the artisan republican tradition, put it slightly differently. Walt Whitman, more than others, was at home in the workshops, the taverns, the meeting halls, the theaters where New York's workingmen met and debated; although no exponent of trade unions or class conflict, he knew something of their origins and sympathized with the hard-pressed small masters, craft workers, and laborers. In a few years he would begin to poetize the soul of the artisan republic in his democratic chants; in 1852, his mind was more directly on politics, and on how New York's workers might be converted to antislavery—as it turned out, a fruitless enterprise. He based what hopes he had, however, on something he thought unique to New York, its working people, its radicals. "I have been at Washington and know none of the great men," he advised the anti-slavery politician John P. Hale,

> But I know the people. I know well (for I am practically in New York) the real heart of this mighty city—the tens of thousands of young men, the mechanics, the writers, &c., &c. In all of them burns, almost with a fierceness, the divine fire which more or less, during all ages, has only waited a chance to leap forth and confound the calculations of tyrants, hunkers, and all their tribe. At this moment, New York is the most radical city in America.[58]

57. Walsh, *Sketches of the Speeches*, 42.
58. Edward Haviland Miller, ed., *The Correspondence of Walt Whitman* (New York, 1961–69), I, 46.

22. Hudson Street, 1865. *Courtesy, New-York Historical Society.*

Epilogue
Hudson Street, 1865

Where the city stands with the brawniest breed of orators and bards,
. . . .
Where thrift is in its place, and prudence is in its place,
Where behavior is the finest of the fine arts,
Where the men and women think lightly of the laws,
Where the slave ceases and the master of slaves ceases,
Where the populace rise at once against the never-ending audacity of
    elected persons,
. . . .
Where outside authority enters always after the precedence of inside
    authority,
Where the citizen is always the head and ideal—and President, Mayor,
    Governor, and what not, are agents for pay,
Where children are taught from the jump that they are to be laws
    to themselves, and to depend on themselves,
Where equanimity is illustrated in affairs,
. . . .
There the greatest city stands.

Chants Democratic, II, 10

In August 1865, the photographer Marcus Ormsbee stood at the corner of
Hudson and Chambers streets and took a formal portrait of several groups
of craft workers in their different shops (Plate 22). Perhaps unconsciously,
Ormsbee left a vivid record of the changes in the New York trades—and
the continuities—since Peter Stollenwerck's day. At the center of the photograph, at Outcault's carpentry shop, stands the conventional artisan trio
of master, journeyman, and apprentice, still at the heart of the city's workshop world—yet class differences mark these craftsmen's every feature. Only
the apprentice smiles; the future alone will tell whether he will wind up
like the tophatted employer to the right or the middle-aged journeyman

to the left. Nearby, Croker, the job printer—his business tied to the mercantile trade—has adapted more decisively to the metropolitan industrial logic of his craft; four of his employees are young men, and one is a young woman. Over at No. 5, Leonard Ring has built a large house-painting business in his seventeen years in the trade, but Ring himself is nowhere to be found; his men rest as a clump with the break in work, possibly thinking about how they might prefer to join the men in the nearby sample room. Brooding above everyone, a new brick manufactory seals off its employees from the street and from public view. Small shop and large enterprise converge; New York remains a blend of old and new. Only the immigrant presence goes unrecorded.

For the moment—as in Stollenwerck's city of 1815—the workmen in Ormsbee's photograph bask in peace; with the slaveholders' rebellion crushed and the armies returned, there are freshly cut planks to be stacked, cards to be printed, houses to be painted. But peace in the workshops had proven illusory before, and would again. New York in 1865 lives with the class differences and tensions that had taken shape over the first half of the century. New Yorkers still confront their uncertainties and conflicts over the fate of the Republic in an industrializing world.

The trajectory of New York's social and economic development was much the same in the Civil War era as it had been before 1850. Having consolidated its position as the nation's commercial metropolis, New York remained America's premier manufacturing center, fed by a continual flow of poor immigrants through the mid-1850s. Metropolitan industrialization entered a new phase, with the adaptation of machinery (most important, the sewing machine) to some spheres of production and with the rapid decline of some trades, shipbuilding and furniture making among them.[1] Still, New York production continued to be based largely in the craft industries; the diversity of scale and markets characteristic of the 1830s and 1840s remained; one or another variation of contracting and bastardized craft work prevailed in most of the leading trades, including those that had turned to machines.[2]

1. On the introduction of the sewing machine, see Degler, "Labor," 33–37; and the lively account in Ruth Brandon, *Capitalist Romance: Singer and the Sewing Machine* (Philadelphia, 1977), 67–140. On the decline of New York shipbuilding, see Morrison, *History of New York Ship Yards*, 153–65, and Pred, *Spatial Dynamics*, 197–202. On cabinetmaking, and the flood of Grand Rapids furniture onto the New York market in the 1870s, see Ingerman, "Recollections," 442–43; and Giedeon, *Mechanization*, 392–408.

2. In 1860, more than one in four New York manufacturing workers were involved in clothing production; in all, 74.5 percent worked in the craft industries. For a breakdown, see U.S. Bureau of the Census, *Eighth Census of the United States: Manufac-*

As the scale of local enterprise—and poverty—grew more bewildering, the mission of middle-class New York became more coherent. Reform efforts, spearheaded by the Tract Society's successor, the New York Association for Improving the Condition of the Poor, mixed Christian stewardship with a new, more "scientific" approach to philanthropy; rather than simply convert the laboring poor, the new uplifters would try to erase the environment of slum life and degradation, and cure social disorder by offering the lowly decent housing, domestic regularity, all the basic amenities the reformers assumed were necessary for a wholesome, thrifty, proper life.[3] Along with the blessings of reform went the material bounty of further industrial and commercial expansion, the unquestioned social improvements of republican entrepreneurship. Manufacturers and politicians repeated what had become familiar doctrines of American capitalist political economy. "With our growth in wealth and power," Charles King told the General Society of Mechanics and Tradesmen, in a review of half a century's progress, "I see no abatement in those qualities, moral and physical, to which so much of our success is owing. . . . The sun shines not upon, has never shone upon, a land where human happiness is so widely disseminated, where human government is so little abused, so free from oppression, so invisible, so intangible, and yet so strong." The opening of the New York Crystal Palace in 1853 turned the rhetoric closer to reality, with an industrial exposition to dwarf all previous efforts by the American and Mechanics' institutes, an extravaganza of American mechanical ingenuity and republican pride. Four years after the Crystal Palace opening, the *Times* reminded the city's "intelligent workingmen" of the genius of America, a land where workers were supposed to scorn "degradation and dependence": "It is the possession of this proud independence that makes America the workingman's paradise. . . . Fortune, to be sure, showers her favors unequally. Some succeed and some fail—but no one thinks of blaming his neighbor for his bad luck."[4]

The city's workers and labor radicals were less sanguine about the efficacy of entrepreneurial moral reform and the preservation of the social harmony of interests. As before, their counteractivities took several, at

---

tures (Washington, D.C., 1865). On the adaptation of contracting to the factory, and of the machine to the outwork system, see Stansell, "Women of the Laboring Poor," 94–110. On the New York manufacturing economy in general in the Civil War and post–Civil War era, see Spann, *New Metropolis*, 403–10; David C. Hammack, *Power and Society in Greater New York* (New York, 1982), chap. 2.

3. Rosenberg, *Religion and the Rise of the American City*, 245–76; Christine Stansell, "Women, Children, and the Uses of the Streets: Class and Gender Conflicts in New York City, 1850–1860," *Feminist Studies* 8 (1982): 309–36.

4. Charles King, *Progress of the City of New-York* (New York, 1852), 79; New York *Times*, November 10, 1857.

times seemingly contradictory forms. Land reform and other would-be workingmen's political movements fared worst after a brief show of strength in the mid-1850s; at decade's end their members and leaders either rejoined the Democracy or drifted—with Greeley and, eventually, Commerford—into the sparse ranks of the New York Republican party; those who survived into the 1870s found themselves lured to the dreamlike world of sentimental labor reform. Gang and mob violence (laced with Irish-nativist antagonisms and tied more closely than ever to the shifting factional alliances within Tammany) continued unabated, in protests against transgressions of customary norms by meddlesome police and public officials. 1857 brought the greatest upheaval, in the wake of the reorganization of the city police force by the state legislature and the passage of a New York version of the Maine temperance law; for two weeks, Irish and Germans mounted pitched battles against the new state-controlled Metropolitans, to protest their presence and attempt to ward off any enforcement of the new liquor regulations.[5]

So, in very different ways, the trade unions and a series of organized labor movements asserted their presumed right to self-government. The Amalgamated Trades Convention collapsed shortly after it commenced, split by fresh disputes over the place of political reform on its agenda—but individual trade unions led a wave of strikes in 1853–54, halted only by the abrupt downturn in trade and prices and by the consequent unemployment of late 1854 and early 1855. As earlier, trade unionism retreated with the business cycle, but labor activism did not. Through the winter of 1855, New York's first movement of the unemployed continually took to the streets, supported by a loose coalition of labor radicals and land reformers, to debate and (successfully) to demand jobs and financial assistance from the Common Council, in the name of republican commonwealth. Even grander demonstrations followed the panic of 1857, prompting new fears of class warfare and revised lectures from the Democratic and Republican press about how the workingmen's ideas ran counter to true Americanism. Industrial movements were not, of course, confined to New York; labor discontent in New England, the scene of accelerating industrialization and mechanization in the 1850s, would in a few years culminate in the nation's largest turnout before the Civil War, the shoemakers' strike of 1860. But the metropolis remained the barometer of discontent to those who watched such developments closely. To the British consul in New York, the sudden destitution of 1857–58 and the city's reactions to the crisis had a familiar air; now, he reported to his superiors,

5. Degler, "Labor in the Economy and Politics," 157–75; Montgomery, *Beyond Equality*, 387–424; Paul O. Weinbaum, "Temperance, Politics, and the New York City Riots of 1857," *N-YHSQ* 59 (1975): 246–70.

even in America, "bands of men paraded in a menacing manner through the streets of the city demanding work or bread."[6]

The gradual lifting of the depression and the coming of sectional conflict redirected public attention and popular action to other matters, but it did not end the tensions of class or the ongoing struggles in the workshops: the history of New York provides little evidence to support the contention that the fight for the Union cooled working-class resistance or that "an entire generation was sidetracked in the 1860s because of the Civil War."[7] Loyalty was one thing, and New York workers proved theirs by enlisting heavily in the army and by ignoring the political appeals of the Copperhead Peace Democrats of Mozart Hall and supporting the Union Democrats of Tammany. But loyalty never stretched to the point of subservience or willing surrender to the perceived inequalities of the free-labor republic. The explosion of mob violence and street republicanism against the draft in July 1863 disturbed the city's labor leaders as much as it did the bluestockings of the Fifteenth Ward; it still manifested (with all its racism) the hatreds and collisions of class—in David Montgomery's words, the "grotesque reflections of Paris's Bloody June Days."[8] So did the more disciplined actions of the city's trade unions, which took to the offensive during the wartime inflation. Over ninety trade-wide strikes were recorded in New York during the war, forty-two of them in the year 1864 alone. Many more actually took place without any formal union guidance. James Dawson Burn, an English emigrant hatter, recalled that often as many as four shop calls were made in the course of a single day in the different departments of the shops in which he worked; New York, to him, was the scene of "constant struggle between men and their employers about prices." The Workingmen's Union, consisting of delegates from about half of the city's unions and representing about 15,000 men, organized in 1864 and took the lead in coordinating political action; in its first year, the union called several huge rallies to protest a new bill before the state senate that would have stripped the unions of all coercive powers. By the winter of 1865, the union's campaign had inspired the German trade unions to form their own *Arbeiterbund*. Returning from the front, the demobilized New York infantry found an experienced labor movement well entrenched in the city's shops and along the waterfront.[9]

6. Degler, "Labor in the Economy and Politics," 157–97 (quotation appears on 196).
7. Dawley, *Class and Community*, 238.
8. Montgomery, *Beyond Equality*, 103–7. On the riots, see also Adrian Cook, *Armies in the Streets: The New York City Draft Riots of 1863* (Lexington, Ky., 1972).
9. Montgomery, *Beyond Equality*, 97–100; [James Dawson Burn], *Three Years among the Working Classes in the United States* (London, 1865), 186–87; Lawrence Costello, "The New York City Labor Movement, 1861–1872" (Ph.D. diss., Columbia University, 1967), 558–64, 577.

That movement received no single strategy for change or labor activism. All of the questions that attended the rise of the working class were asked and would be asked again, as often as not in German or with an Irish brogue—on the sources of inequality, on the merits of political action and political parties, on women, race, small employers, and the boundaries of class. What the working people of 1865 did inherit was a legacy of battle, one that honored independence, equality, and commonwealth but that would have been incomprehensible to the generation of the American Revolution, one that had intensified since the uprising of 1850. The Union army dead were buried; the workers of Whitman's radical city resumed their struggles, to insure that the Union would be, as they saw it, a republic in fact and not just a republic in name.

Appendix

A Note on Tables and Figures

The available historical statistics on labor in the United States before 1850 are poor. Many of the tables and figures offered here were assembled from disparate and fragmentary sources. Deriving the results involved numerous problems of judgment.

The New York City Jury Book for 1816 (microfilm, N-YHS) was the basis for Tables 2, 3, 4, 5, 7, and 8. This compilation includes the names, occupations, and household sizes of every head of household in the city, as well as information about wealth and, for the artisans, about master-journeyman status. Unfortunately, not all of the returns have survived, and those which have are inexact regarding wealth and inconsistent in their notations regarding masters and journeymen. Given these obstacles, I elected to analyze the returns from three contiguous wards for which the returns were available—the third, fifth, and eighth—thereby covering a section of the city along the west side from the elite downtown wards to the outskirts of concentrated settlement. I also selected six trades that covered the range of different kinds of trades in Jeffersonian New York. With these limits, the total figures for all trades reported in the relevant tables do not necessarily represent the situation in the city's trades as a whole; I made no attempt to construct a sample that would reflect the proportions of different trades in the craft economy. Rather, the tables are intended to show variations in residential and wealth patterns in different trades.

In order to be more precise about wealth and stratification, I checked all of the names gathered in the Jury Book sample against the city's Tax Assessment Lists for 1815 and 1816 (MARC). If an individual was assessed in either year, the amounts were recorded; when an individual appeared in both lists, the *higher* figures were included in the computations. I made no attempt to trace any individual's wealth other than that recorded at his home or place of business; nor did the assessment lists account for an individual's holdings of corporate wealth, if any. Consequently, the figure computed for concentration of wealth among the masters is probably quite conservative, while the figures on property-holding journeymen probably overstate slightly the extent to which wage earners owned assessable wealth in any given year.

Of the wards sampled, only the returns for the Eighth Ward stated categorically whether an artisan was a master or a journeyman. Otherwise, I considered any artisan listed as eligible for jury duty or as a fireman or artilleryman as a master; those listed as single men or simply as "exempt," I considered journeymen. It was impossible to tell from the Jury Book whether aliens, blacks, or men over sixty were masters or journeymen, although most probably were journeymen. For my statistical impressions of small masters, I looked at only those masters with $1,000 or less in assessed property. This figure is arbitrary, but it yielded a sample large enough to offer some conclusions; there was no detectable difference in the results for those small masters who owned some property and those who did not.

The 1850 manufacturing census (NYSL) is the earliest comprehensive account of the size, wages, and work force of New York's shops, manufactories, and factories. In order to distinguish between different kinds of workplaces, I rearranged the manuscript schedules according to the following scheme: firms with 0–5 employees were designated as neighborhood shops; those with 6–20 employees, as garret shops; those with 21 or more employees (and, in the case of the consumer finishing trades, those with 21–49 employees) without steam machinery, as manufactories; those with 21 or more employees with steam machinery, as factories; and those outwork consumer finishing trade firms with 50 or more employees, as outwork manufactories. Of course, these categories are arbitrary; however, they generally coincide with both contemporary and recent descriptions of the size of different sorts of urban workplaces at midcentury. I excluded a few firms in which the return was illegible and those which were obviously not craft or manufacturing firms.

I decided to use the figures gathered in the 1855 New Yorfk State population census for Tables 9, 10, and 15 for two reasons: first, the 1850 population census schedules do not list the occupations of women and children wage earners in male-headed households; and second, Robert Ernst's careful collection of the 1855 data made use of the later figures far more convenient. Some problems remain. The 1855 schedules do not distinguish between employers, self-employed craftsmen, and workers in a given trade; hence, these figures are not an exact accounting of the proportion of employees in any given sector or trade. They are, however, a close approximation, although given the ratio of employees to firms in 1850 they probably tend to slight the relative size of the consumer-finishing-trade sector. More important, the proportion of immigrants, in any given trade and in the city's economy as a whole, was certainly higher in 1855 than in 1850.

Establishing occupational categories, and distinguishing masters from journeymen and small masters from leading entrepreneurs in the 1830s and 1840s involved a series of steps. Any individual who appeared in the city directory with more than one address was automatically considered a master; so was anyone who appeared in the tax list with more than $150 assessed property. The rest were considered journeymen. Masters with $1,000 or less in assessed wealth, I considered small masters. The results, again, are necessarily somewhat arbitrary; it is likely that some of those listed as journeymen were in fact small masters and that some listed as small masters were in fact far wealthier. However, by applying these standards uniformly in analyzing the various movements of the era, I expect that the arguments in the text about the comparative social appeal of each movement are valid. In discussing the movements I have, of course, often had to draw judgments on the basis of available information about their primary and secondary leadership—an imperfect process. By keeping the basis for comparison consistent, however, I believe that a reasonable basis for comparison and interpretation is established. Whenever possible, I have also based my interpretations on what evidence exists about the social character of the membership.

As for the occupational groups outside the trades, I included as merchants and professionals all men listed in the city directory simply as "merchants," bankers, brokers, commission merchants, attorneys, physicians, and government officials. All others with non-manual occupations, I listed as petty professionals. I reluctantly decided to include clerks and office workers in this category; in no case did they number more than two in any given movement. Laborers and unskilled consist of all those with manual occupations who were not in the craft or manufacturing sector, including cartmen.

A final caveat: the purpose of this Appendix is to show the basis upon which I drew my conclusions. Given the inescapable guesswork involved, given the innumerable possibilities for human error, these figures should be considered as less reliable than the estimates generally employed in the text.

Table 1. New Yorkers with $5,000 or more personal wealth, 1815, by occupation group

Occupation	%	% of total found in directory
Merchants	33.3	55.6
Professionals	6.3	10.5
Retailers and grocers	7.5	12.5
Artisans and manufacturers	8.3	13.9
Widows and estates	4.2	7.0
More than one listing in city directory	14.1	—
No occupation listed in city directory	12.7	—
Not listed in city directory	13.3	—
Other	0.3	0.5
TOTAL	100.0	100.0

(N = 996)

Average holding for total: $17,807.
Average holding for artisans and manufacturers: $12,060.
Percentage of total wealth over $5,000 owned by artisans and manufacturers: 5.6.

SOURCES: R. S. Guernsey, *New York and Vicinity during the War of 1812* (New York, 1895), II, 483–94; *Longworth's American Almanac . . . for 1815* (New York, 1815).

Table 2. Percentage of artisans with taxable property, selected trades, Wards 3, 5, 8, New York City, 1816, by trade

Trade	Real	Personal	Any property
Cabinetmakers (74)	14.7	27.0	27.0
Coopers (43)	18.6	39.5	39.5
Metal trades* (35)	31.4	45.7	45.7
Shoemakers (275)	14.5	41.1	42.2
Stonecutters and masons (240)	14.6	28.3	33.8
TOTAL (N = 667)	15.1	33.6	37.5

* Includes brass founders, coppersmiths, goldsmiths, nail makers, silversmiths, and tin workers.

SOURCES: Jury Book, New York City, 1816; Tax Assessment Lists, New York City, 1815, 1816.

Table 3. Percentage of masters and journeymen with taxable property, selected trades, Wards 3, 5, 8, New York City, 1816, by trade and status

Trade	Masters			Journeymen		
	Real	Personal	Any property	Real	Personal	Any property
Cabinetmakers	40.7	66.6	66.6	—	4.3	4.3
Coopers	70.0	90.0	90.0	3.0	24.2	24.2
Metal trades	55.0	65.0	65.0	—	20.0	20.0
Shoemakers	64.7	82.4	86.3	3.1	31.7	32.1
Stonecutters and masons	48.0	62.0	66.0	5.8	19.5	25.3
TOTAL	54.4	70.2	74.0	3.5	24.0	26.1

SOURCES: See Table 2.

Table 4. Residence by Ward, masters and journeymen, selected trades, Wards 3, 5, 8, New York City, 1816, by trade

Trade	% in Ward 3		% in Ward 5		% in Ward 8	
	Masters	Journeymen	Masters	Journeymen	Masters	Journeymen
Cabinetmakers	59.3	8.9	37.0	80.4	3.7	10.7
Coopers	60.0	15.2	30.0	39.4	10.0	45.5
Metal trades	65.0	6.7	35.0	53.8	—	39.5
Shoemakers	39.2	5.0	43.1	60.0	17.7	35.0
Stonecutters and masons	4.0	6.8	66.0	62.1	30.0	32.0
TOTAL	36.1	6.2	49.3	61.8	12.5	32.0

SOURCE: Jury Book, New York City, 1816.

Table 5. Percentage of propertied masters and journeymen in different wealth groups, selected trades, Wards 3, 5, 8, New York City, 1816, by trade and status

Trade	Total amount of assessed wealth				
	$0–499	$500–1,999	$2,000–3,999	$4,000–5,999	$6,000+
Masters					
Cabinetmakers	62.9	—	11.1	7.4	18.5
Coopers	40.0	20.0	10.0	20.0	10.0
Metal trades	45.0	—	—	35.0	20.0
Shoemakers	35.3	23.5	17.6	13.7	9.8
Stonecutters and masons	72.0	18.0	4.0	2.0	2.0
Journeymen					
Cabinetmakers	100.0	—	—	—	—
Coopers	95.7	0.3	—	—	—
Metal trades	100.0	—	—	—	—
Shoemakers	97.8	1.8	0.4	—	—
Stonecutters and masons	94.8	4.2	0.5	—	0.5

SOURCES: See Table 2.

Table 6. Artisans and manufacturers with $5,000 or more personal wealth, New York City, 1815, by occupation group

Occupation	% of Artisan total
Heavy manufacturing (15)	18.1
Leather (8)	
Other (7)	
Shipbuilding and maritime (10)	12.1
Tailors and merchant tailors (9)	10.9
Building trades (8)	9.6
Butchers and bakers (8)	9.6
Other clothing (6)	7.2
Heavy metal (5)	6.0
Shoemaking (5)	6.0
Printing and publishing (5)	6.0
Precious metal (4)	4.8
Furniture (3)	3.6
Other (5)	6.0
TOTAL ($N = 83$)	99.9

SOURCE: See Table 1.

Table 7. Percentage of masters and journeymen in different age groups, selected trades, Wards 3, 5, 8, New York City, 1816, by trade

Trade	Age			
	<20–29	30–39	40–49	50+
Masters				
Cabinetmakers	33.3	45.8	16.7	4.2
Coopers	20.0	20.0	50.0	10.0
Metal trades	35.3	17.6	17.6	29.4
Shoemakers	13.7	43.1	29.4	13.8
Stonecutters and masons	29.2	45.8	20.8	4.2
TOTAL	24.7	40.0	24.6	10.6
Journeymen				
Cabinetmakers	66.0	17.0	12.8	4.3
Coopers	27.3	39.4	24.3	9.0
Metal trades	50.0	21.4	21.4	7.2
Shoemakers	52.6	27.2	14.6	5.6
Stonecutters and masons	39.9	36.7	14.4	9.0
TOTAL	47.8	30.4	14.9	6.8

SOURCE: See Table 4.

NOTE: Excludes individuals whose ages are unclear.

Table 8. Percentage of masters and journeymen with taxable wealth, selected trades, Wards 3, 5, 8, New York City, 1816, by trade and age

Trade	Age			
	<20–29	30–39	40–49	50+
Masters				
Cabinetmakers	37.5	63.6	100.0	100.0
Coopers	50.0	100.0	100.0	100.0
Metal trades	33.3	66.6	100.0	80.0
Shoemakers	71.5	77.2	100.0	100.0
Stonecutters and masons	35.7	77.2	70.0	100.0
TOTAL	43.2	75.0	93.1	93.8
Journeymen				
ALL SELECTED TRADES	16.6	28.8	36.0	29.4

SOURCE: See Table 2.

NOTE: Excludes individuals whose ages are unclear.

Table 9. Twenty principal occupations in New York City, 1855

Occupation	Number	% of total
Domestic servants	31,749	15.2
Laborers	20,238	9.7
Clerks	13,929	6.7
Tailors	12,609	6.0
Dressmakers and seamstresses	9,819	4.7
Food dealers	8,300	4.0
Carpenters	7,531	3.6
Shoemakers	6,745	3.2
Merchants	6,299	3.0
Bakers and confectioners	3,692	1.8
Masons, bricklayers, and plasterers	3,634	1.7
Cabinetmakers and upholsterers	3,517	1.7
Painters, varnishers, and glaziers	3,485	1.7
Retail shopkeepers	2,646	1.3
Blacksmiths	2,642	1.3
Laundresses	2,563	1.2
Printers	2,077	1.0
Tobacconists	1,996	1.0
Peddlers and traders	1,915	0.9
Drivers, coachmen, and hackmen	1,741	0.8
TOTAL	147,127	70.4 (of 208,891)

SOURCE: Robert Ernst, *Immigrant Life in New York City, 1825–1863* (New York, 1949), 214–17.
NOTE: Figures include employers *and* employees in each occupation.

Table 10. Distribution of work force in major sectors, New York City, 1855

Sector	Number
Crafts and manufacturing[1]	91,947
Domestic servants, laundresses, and cooks	35,067
Laborers, porters, cartmen[2]	32,260
Clerks and government employees[3]	15,750
Professional workers[4]	6,912
TOTAL	181,936

SOURCE: See Table 9.
[1] Including building trades.
[2] Including drovers, stevedores, boatmen, expressmen, drivers, coachmen, and hackmen.
[3] Including policemen.
[4] Includes actors, architects, artists, authors, clergy, lawyers, musicians, physicians, and teachers.

Table 11. Percentage of work force in different workplaces, New York City, 1850, by trade

Trade	Neighborhood shop	Garret shop	Manufactory	Factory	Outwork manufactory
Clothing and tailors	0.5	3.5	4.2	—	91.9
Hats, caps, millinery	1.7	10.6	9.2	—	78.5
Shoes and boots	14.3	20.0	22.4	—	43.3
Iron	0.8	5.6	—	93.6	—
Printing	4.4	23.4	8.9	63.3	—
Shipbuilding	4.2	7.1	84.1	4.5	—
Cabinetmaking and chair making	14.4	33.4	50.4	1.8	—
Stonecutters	—	34.0	37.9	28.1	—
Carpenters and builders	9.3	65.7	21.7	3.3	—
Sash makers	28.2	71.8	—	—	—
Bakers	48.9	42.0	9.1	—	—
ALL TRADES (N = 84,940)	5.0	15.5	11.3	19.6	48.6

SOURCE: Manufacturing Schedules, MS, 1850 Census, New York County.

Table 12. Small mechanized workshops, New York City, 1850, by trade

Trade	Number of shops	Number of workers	Average male wage per month
Brewing	5	46	$30.95
Distilling	6	45	31.28
Machine and tool making	25	263	33.06
Printing and engraving	23	217	31.68
Others	130	1466	30.37
TOTAL	189	2037	30.59

SOURCE: See Table 11.
NOTE: Male workers = 94.3% of total.

Table 13. Percentage of shops of different sizes, selected trades, New York City, 1850, by trade

	% of Total shops in trade				
Trade	Neighborhood shop	Garret shop	Manufactory	Factory	Outwork manufactory
Clothing and tailors	18.3	37.9	19.2	—	24.6
Hats, caps, millinery	27.3	43.9	9.2	—	19.6
Shoes and boots	60.9	24.4	9.0	—	5.7
Iron	20.0	33.3	—	46.7	—
Printing	29.5	51.7	5.5	13.2	—
Shipbuilding	45.0	31.7	21.7	1.6	—
Cabinetmaking and chairmaking	43.8	45.9	8.8	1.5	—
Stonecutters	—	60.9	26.1	13.0	—
Carpenters and builders	30.4	62.3	5.8	1.5	—
Sash makers	55.0	45.0	—	—	—
Bakers	79.0	19.1	1.9	—	—
ALL TRADES (N = 3202)	43.8	38.0	7.6	5.5	5.1

SOURCE: See Table 11.

Table 14. Monthly wages and sexual composition of the work force, selected trades, New York City, 1850, by trade

Trade	Average male wage	Average female wage	% Male	% Female
Clothing and tailors	$11.53	$ 6.99	48.5	51.5
Hats, caps, millinery	27.51	17.14	43.5	56.5
Shoes and boots	24.32	10.43	75.2	24.8
Iron	28.65	15.00	99.8	0.2
Printing	36.28	14.48	71.3	28.7
Shipbuilding	48.27	—	100.0	—
Cabinetmaking and chair making	25.22	12.41	98.6	1.4
Stonecutters	31.12	—	100.0	—
Carpenters and builders	35.97	—	100.0	—
Sash makers	27.47	—	100.0	—
Bakers	23.79	11.16	87.6	12.2
ALL TRADES	24.76	7.79	63.4	36.6

SOURCE: See Table 11.
NOTE: Estimated family wage in 1850 = $42.84 per month ($514.00 per year).

Table 15. Percentage of immigrants in selected trades, New York City, 1855

Trade	Irish	German	British	Other Immigrant	Immigrant	Black
Glassworkers (143)	58.7	14.0	11.9	13.9	98.6	–
Gunsmiths (126)	34.1	40.5	19.8	3.2	97.6	–
Shoemakers (6,745)	31.4	55.2	5.3	4.3	96.2	*
Stonecutters and polishers (1,914)	65.4	10.9	17.6	2.4	96.2	–
Tailors (12,609)	33.1	53.2	5.5	4.3	96.0	–
Roofers and slaters (78)	35.9	15.4	38.5	1.3	91.0	*
Bakers (3,692)	23.3	53.8	8.2	4.7	90.0	*
Locksmiths (394)	15.2	55.8	10.7	4.0	85.7	–
Cabinetmakers and upholsterers (3,517)	11.6	61.2	4.7	5.5	82.9	*
Turners, carvers, and gilders (1,126)	14.5	52.0	8.6	7.2	82.2	*
Blacksmiths (2,642)	50.7	20.0	8.8	2.2	81.7	*
Riggers (482)	29.5	15.8	24.6	11.6	81.5	–
Masons, bricklayers, and plasterers (3,634)	60.6	9.2	8.3	*	79.0	*
Umbrella makers (270)	58.1	9.3	9.2	2.2	78.9	–
Painters, varnishers, and glaziers (3,485)	30.7	26.0	15.3	8.5	77.9	*
Coopers (1,018)	40.6	26.4	4.1	2.8	74.0	*
Brass workers (442)	38.0	11.7	19.0	4.1	72.9	–
Coppersmiths (207)	36.2	26.2	6.8	*	70.5	–
Tinsmiths (897)	29.3	25.6	11.4	2.7	69.0	*
Dressmakers and seamstresses (9,819)	46.4	9.5	7.2	4.1	67.4	1.1
Precision-instrument makers (607)	9.6	29.7	14.2	13.7	67.0	*
Musical-instrument makers (836)	7.3	38.8	10.9	9.2	66.1	–
Carpenters (7,531)	29.6	22.1	9.6	3.3	64.6	*
Plumbers (1,053)	40.8	4.4	16.2	1.5	62.9	–
Hatters (1,422)	20.3	29.7	5.7	7.0	62.7	*
Gem and precious-metal workers (1,705)	10.4	28.3	10.2	14.2	60.8	*
Ship carpenters (1,146)	32.5	5.8	13.9	7.2	59.4	–
Coach and wagon makers (757)	31.4	8.1	7.3	2.2	59.0	–
Printers (2,077)	25.0	11.4	14.3	5.0	55.7	*
Smiths (various) (595)	20.6	15.0	11.9	5.5	53.0	*
Iron molders (593)	27.3	7.8	15.1	2.9	52.4	*
Bookbinders and folders (1,315)	10.9	9.5	2.3	–	51.1	–
Sailmakers (281)	24.9	3.6	10.0	4.3	42.7	–
Boat builders (99)	22.2	3.0	4.0	5.1	34.3	*
Caulkers (378)	22.2	1.6	3.2	4.5	31.5	–

SOURCE: See Table 9.

* Less than 1% of total.

Table 16. Summary of effects of metropolitan industrialization in various New York crafts, ca. 1820–1850

Trade	1	2	3	4	5	6
Consumer finishing						
Clothing production	X	X	X	X	X	–
Shoemaking	X	X	X	X	X	–
Furniture making	–	X	X	–	X	O
Other consumer						
Printing	–	O	X	O	O	X
Building trades	–	X	O	–	O	O
Maritime						
Shipbuilding	–	X	–	–	O	O
Food preparation						
Butchering	–	–	–	–	O	–
Baking	–	–	X	O	X	–

1: Put out
2: Contracting
3: Apprenticeship disrupted
4: Employment of women
5: Employment of immigrants
6: Some factories and/or mechanization

X: Strong tendency
O: Mild tendency

Table 17. Voting returns, New York City, 1828–1830, by ward

Ward	(President) %T	(President) %N	1829 (Assembly)* %T	1829 (Assembly)* %N	1829 (Assembly)* %W	1830 (Assembly) %T	1830 (Assembly) %C	1830 (Assembly) %O	1830 (Assembly) %S	Per capita wealth 1830
1	49.3	50.7	73.0	17.0	10.0	51.4	42.4	4.4	1.8	$4,104
2	43.8	56.2	51.0	35.0	11.0	47.0	46.4	6.4	0.3	1,685
3	49.2	50.8	66.0	15.0	16.0	48.3	43.1	8.4	0.2	1,721
4	56.9	43.1	66.0	16.0	16.0	51.7	39.2	8.9	0.3	741
5	56.7	43.2	59.0	17.0	24.0	48.8	31.9	18.8	0.5	701
6	67.1	32.9	64.0	10.0	25.0	53.5	36.5	9.6	0.4	628
7	69.1	30.9	58.0	13.0	28.0	64.0	26.1	9.0	0.9	532
8	64.2	35.8	42.0	11.0	46.0	45.2	38.9	15.3	0.6	401
9	65.8	34.2	50.0	9.0	36.0	53.7	33.7	12.4	0.2	638
10	66.5	33.5	46.0	6.0	48.0	58.0	28.0	12.8	1.2	287
11	69.4	30.6	48.0	3.0	49.0	58.8	27.0	14.0	0.2	403
12	67.4	32.6	74.0	4.0	21.0	65.5	27.5	7.0	—	687
13	65.0	35.0	40.0	5.0	55.0	51.0	42.7	5.3	1.0	214
14	64.3	35.7	55.0	7.0	35.0	60.5	28.2	10.6	0.6	451
TOTAL	61.6	38.4	55.0	12.0	31.0	53.7	34.9	10.7	0.6	820

T Tammany
N National Republican
W Working Men

C Cookites
O Owenites
S Skidmorites

SOURCES: *Evening Post*, November 10, 1828, November 10, 1829, November 13, 1830; Walter Hugins, *Jacksonian Democracy and the Working Class* (Stanford, 1960), 209.
* Adjusted total.

Table 18. Social composition of Working Men's leadership, 1829–1830

Occupation	Faction		
	Cookite	Owenite	Skidmorite
Merchants and professionals	7.5	5.4	3.0
Shopkeepers, retailers, and petty professionals	28.3	25.6	15.2
Master craftsmen and manufacturers	34.0	17.0	18.2
Small masters	9.4	7.2	18.2
Journeymen	17.0	40.3	39.4
Laborers and unskilled	3.8	4.5	6.0
TOTAL	100.0	100.0	100.0
	(N = 53)	(223)	(33)

SOURCES: Hugins List, *Longworth's American Almanac . . . for 1829* (New York, 1829); Tax Assessment Lists, 1829, 1830.

Table 19. Trade unions and strikes in New York City, 1833–1836

A. Trade Unions	
1833	**1835**
Bakers*	Bakers*
Blacksmiths and machinists	Bookbinders*
Block and Pump Makers	Bookbinders (female)
Bookbinders*	Brush makers*
Brushmakers	Cabinetmakers*
Cabinetmakers*	Carpenters*
Chairmakers	Chairmakers*
Carpenters*	Cordwainers (ladies')*
Carvers and gilders*	Cordwainers (men's)*
Coopers*	Curriers*
Cordwainers (ladies')*	Glass cutters*
Cordwainers (men's)*	Hat finishers*
Gilders and looking glass frame makers	Hatters*
Hat finishers*	Hatters (silk)*
Hatters*	Horseshoers*
Hatters (silk)	Leather dressers*
House painters	Locksmiths*
Jewelers	Piano makers
Masons	Printers*
Morocco dressers	Sailmakers*
Printers*	Saddlers*
Rope makers	Shoe binders (female)
Sailmakers*	Steam-boiler makers
Stonecutters*	Stonecutters*
Ship joiners*	Tailors*
Tailors*	Tin workers*
Tin plate and sheet-iron workers*	Weavers
Typefounders*	Weavers (hand loom)
Willow basket makers	
	1836
1834	Bakers*
Bakers*	Bookbinders*
Bookbinders*	Brush makers*
Brushmakers*	Cabinetmakers*
Cabinetmakers*	Carpenters*
Carpenters*	Chairmakers*
Chairmakers*	Cordwainers (ladies')*
Cordwainers (ladies')*	Cordwainers (men's)*
Cordwainers (men's)*	Coach makers
Hat finishers*	Glass cutters*
Hatters*	Hat finishers*
Printers*	Hatters*
Sailmakers*	Hatters (silk)*
Stonecutters*	Leather dressers*
Tailors*	Locksmiths*
Tin workers*	Masons
Weavers (Brussels carpet)	Millwrights and engineers

sources: John R. Finch, *Rise and Progress of the General Trades' Unions in the City of New-York and Its Vicinity* (New York, 1833); John R. Commons et al., *History of Labour in the United States* (New York, 1916) I, 472–75; John R. Commons et al., *Documentary History of American Industrial Society* (Cleveland, 1910), V, 208–322.
* Confirmed as represented in the General Trades' Union.

Table 19 (*Continued*)

Morocco beamsmen*
Printers*
Riggers
Sailmakers*
Tailors*
Tailoresses

Tin workers*
Umbrella makers*
Upholsterers and paperhangers
Varnishers and polishers*
Weavers (handloom)*

B. Strikes in New York, 1833–1836

1833	Cordwainers (men's)*
Carpenters	Glass cutters*
Tailors*	Sailmakers*

1834	1836
Bakers*	Tailors*
Cordwainers*	Shipwrights=
Sailors	Stevedores and riggers
Carpet weavers	Building laborers
Locksmiths	Coal heavers
Hatters*	Sheet-iron workers
	Machinists
1835	Tailoresses=
Cabinetmakers*	Handloom weavers=
Cordwainers*	Coach makers
Arsenal mechanics	Varnishers and polishers*
Stonecutters*	Masons=
Ship carpenters	Cordwainers*
Saddlers*	Shoe binders (female)
Piano makers	Leather dressers*
Horseshoers*	Carpenters*
Bookbinders (female)	Riggers=
Leather dressers*	Umbrella makers (female)

SOURCES: John R. Commons et al., *History of Labour in the United States* (New York, 1916), I; *National Trades' Union*, May 2, November 14, 28, 1835; February 20, 26, April 9, 16, 1836; *Herald*, February 23, 24, 25, 1836.

* Strike coordinated by the GTU
= Unclear whether or not strike took place.

Table 20. Voting returns, New York City, 1840, 1842, 1844-45, by ward

Ward	1840 President		1842 Congress		1844 Mayor			1845 Mayor		
	% D	% W	% D	% W	% D	% W	%N	% D	% W	%N
1	32.8	67.2	41.7	58.3	42.5	13.0	44.5	52.8	23.5	23.7
2	32.4	63.6	39.6	60.4	32.7	16.2	51.1	39.3	21.6	39.1
3	31.6	68.4	36.6	63.4	25.8	17.2	56.9	33.7	27.4	38.9
4	50.8	49.2	57.6	42.4	58.1	4.8	36.4	65.0	10.2	24.8
5	44.6	55.4	47.8	52.2	36.4	14.6	49.0	44.8	17.8	37.4
6	60.3	39.7	56.0	44.0	63.8	7.5	28.9	69.0	12.0	19.0
7	50.3	49.7	49.1	50.9	35.5	11.6	52.8	49.3	12.9	37.8
8	52.9	47.1	50.8	49.2	36.7	12.0	51.3	47.6	16.1	36.3
9	56.7	43.3	56.8	43.2	37.4	10.0	61.2	45.0	15.4	39.6
10	54.7	45.3	52.7	47.3	37.3	11.7	51.0	49.9	11.3	38.8
11	70.0	30.0	65.3	34.7	43.0	6.1	50.9	54.7	7.4	37.9
12	64.2	35.8	51.5	48.5	51.4	3.5	45.0	56.6	6.3	37.1
13	59.3	40.7	57.3	42.7	40.4	8.6	51.3	50.6	9.9	39.5
14	55.0	45.0	57.4	42.6	53.3	8.9	37.8	58.1	50.6	29.1
15	32.1	67.9	32.1	67.9	24.0	14.9	61.1	30.5	21.4	48.1
16	57.6	42.4	45.0	55.0	48.1	11.4	40.4	51.6	12.8	35.6
17	53.2	46.8	53.2	46.8	38.1	7.7	51.2	48.4	10.8	40.8
TOTAL	51.1	48.9	49.1	50.9	40.8	10.5	48.7	49.6	14.3	36.1

D Democrat
W Whig
N American Republican

SOURCES: *Evening Post*, November 10, 1840, November 12, 1842, April 12, 1844, April 14, 1845.

Table 21. Birthplace and residence of trade-union delegates, 1850

		A. Birthplace			
NYC	U.S. Not NYC	Germany	Ireland	Britain	Elsewhere
25.8	13.6	6.1	37.8	12.1	4.6
(N = 66)					

B. Residence in New York

Ward	% of delegates	% of city population in ward
1	—	3.8
2	—	1.3
3	—	2.0
4	12.8	4.5
5	7.7	4.4
6	2.6	4.8
7	6.4	6.3
8	11.6	6.7
9	6.4	7.9
10	7.7	4.5
11	2.6	8.5
12	2.6	2.0
13	9.0	5.5
14	12.8	4.9
15	3.8	4.4
16	3.8	10.3
17	6.4	8.5
18	2.6	6.1
19	1.2	3.6
TOTAL	100.0	100.0
(N = 78)		

SOURCES: *Daily Tribune,* 1850; U.S. Census Office, Seventh Census, Population Schedule, MSS, New York County; *Doggett's Directory of the City of New York,* 1850.

Table 22. Labor organizations in New York, 1850, with dates of founding

Old craft benefit societies
Cordwainers (1805)
Smiths (1832)
Saddlers (1836)
Bookbinders (1839)
Masons (1843)

New craft benefit societies,
founded 1850
Carpenters
Iron molders
Jewelers
Lithographers
Plumbers
Riggers
Ship sawyers
Shipwrights and caulkers

Cooperatives, founded 1850
Bakers
Blacksmiths
Cigar makers (German)
Coopers
Confectioners (German)
Dyers
Hat finishers
Scale makers
Shoemakers Workers' Union
Silversmiths
Tailors (German) (through July)
Tailors (after July)
Tobacco pipe makers
Turners (German)
Window-shade painters
Shirt Sewers' Cooperative (1851)
Mechanics' Mutual (consumer)
Protective Union (producer and
    consumer)

Protective societies,
founded 1850
Bakers
Block and pump makers
Bricklayers and plasterers
Brush makers
Button and fringe makers
Cabinetmakers
Carpenters

Carpenters (Bloomingdale)
Carvers
Coach makers and painters
Coachmen
Confectioners
Coopers
Cordwainers (ladies')
Cordwainers (men's)
Hat finishers
House painters and smiths
Iron- and metalworkers (German)
Iron molders
Joiners (German)
Manufacturing jewelers
Marble polishers
Operative masons (bricklayers)
Painters
Porters
Printers
Printers (chronopress)
Quarrymen
Sailmakers
Sash and blind makers
Ship sawyers
Silversmiths
Smith and wheelwrights (German)
Steam-boiler makers
Stonecutters
Turners
Tin and sheet-iron workers
Upholsterers
Varnishers
White-work weavers
Window-shade painters

Other societies
Brotherhood of the Union (1847)
Central Committee of the Trades (1850)
Church of Humanity (1846)
Economic Exchange Association (1850)
Laborers' Union Benevolent Association
    (1843)
Ladies' Industrial Association (1850)
Mechanics' Mutual (1841)
National Reform Association (1844)
Pioneer Temple Number One (1843)
Protective Union (1847)
United Workingmen's League (?)

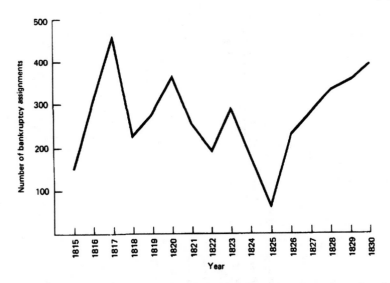

Figure 1. Number of bankruptcy assignments, New York City, 1815–1830, by year. Source: Index, Bankruptcy Assignments, Historical Documents Collection, Queens College, City University of New York.

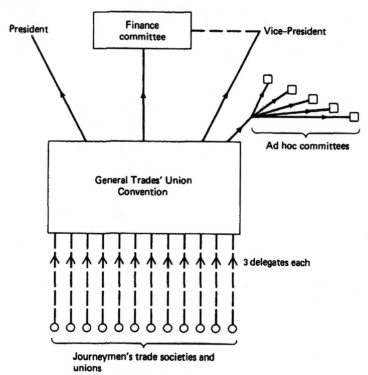

Figure 2. Structure of the General Trades' Union, 1833–1834. Source: John R. Commons et al., *Documentary History of American Industrial Society* (Cleveland, 1910), V.

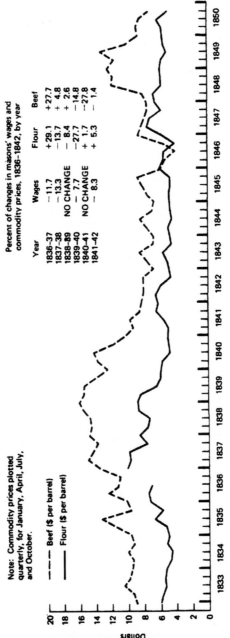

Figure 3. Wholesale commodity prices, New York City, 1833–1850. Source: Arthur Harrison Cole, *Wholesale Commodity Prices in the United States, 1700–1861, Statistical Supplement* (Cambridge, Mass., 1938).

417

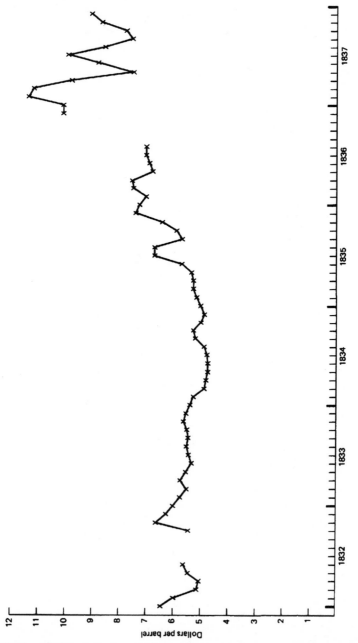

Figure 4. Price of one barrel of superfine flour, New York City, 1832–1837, by month. Source: Arthur Harrison Cole, *Wholesale Commodity Prices in the United States, 1700–1861, Statistical Supplement* (Cambridge, Mass., 1938).

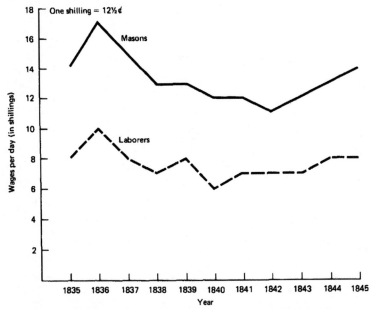

Figure 5. Wages per day in shillings, for masons and building laborers in the month of May, New York City, 1835–1845, by year. Source: *Mechanic's Mirror* 1 (1846): 146.

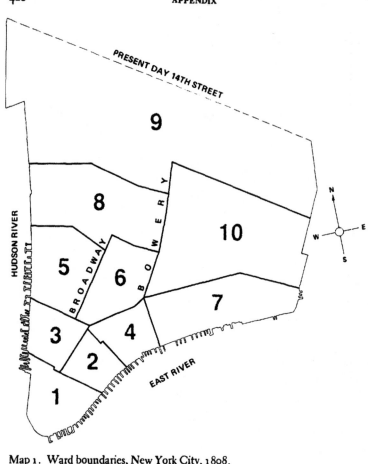

Map 1. Ward boundaries, New York City, 1808.

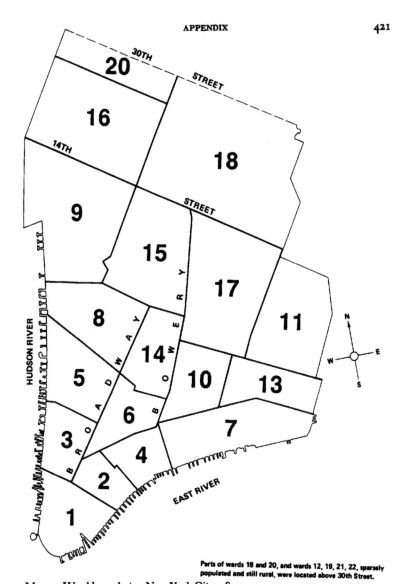

Parts of wards 18 and 20, and wards 12, 19, 21, 22, sparsely populated and still rural, were located above 30th Street.

Map 2. Ward boundaries, New York City, 1850.

Bibliographical Essay

This bibliographical essay does not include all of the sources used in the preparation of this book, or even all of those cited in the notes. Such a list would be excessively long and largely redundant. I have tried, as far as possible, to discuss the relevant literature, particularly secondary sources, in the notes. In order to help students of early-nineteenth-century America and of the early labor movement, I have listed those manuscript collections which I found to be of even marginal interest, including a few which did not find their way into the notes. Otherwise, I have included only those sources which I relied upon most heavily for information, as well as those which most influenced my interpretations.

Manuscript Collections

Collections of personal papers are not especially rich in material about the early history of the New York working class; the few that are are have already been heavily mined. Nevertheless, I found the following collections useful:

Stephen Allen Papers, N-YHS
Elisha Blossom Papers, N-YHS
Robert I. Brown Papers, N-YHS
John Burke Papers, N-YHS
Matthew Livingston Davis Papers, N-YHS
Horace Greeley Papers, NYPL
Greeley-Colfax Papers, NYPL
James Harper Papers, N-YHS
Philip Hone Diary, N-YHS

Rufus King Papers, N-YHS
Thomas Lawrence Papers, NYPL
Gideon Lee Papers, N-YHS
Samuel F. B. Morse Papers, Library of Congress
John Petheram Papers, N-YHS
Mrs. Gouverneur Morris Phelps Collection, N-YHS
Michael Walsh Papers, N-YHS
Samuel Warshinge Papers, N-YHS

A few scattered account books were also helpful, in particular the account book of Solomon Townsend, 1795–97, N-YHS; the ledger book of an unidentified builder, 1815–19, NYPL; and the D. M. Marvin and Company ledger and account book, N-YHS. The Dun and Bradstreet Collection, Baker Library, Harvard University, contains copious notes on the credit worth of hundreds of New York enterprises at the end of the period under discussion; these should be supplemented with the jottings in the New York Trade Agency Reports, 1851, N-YHS.

Institutional archives and collections were of far more value. The minute books, miscellaneous reports, and ephemera of the General Society of Mechanics and Tradesmen, kept at the society's headquarters, 20 West 44th Street, New York, N.Y., are of utmost importance in sketching the society's history. The American Institute Papers, N-YHS, make up a large, intimidating collection, much of which concerns the Institute's fairs and related activities; the collection also contains some important correspondence and pamphlet material. The surviving papers of the General Executive Committee of the Working Men's party, N-YHS (unused by previous historians) are fragmentary, but offer some clues about the group's activities and preoccupations under the leadership of Noah Cook and Henry Guyon. The minute book of the New-York City Temperance Society, NYPL, is a critical source on the evangelitical temperance movement from 1829 through the early 1840s. The American Republican Party Papers, N-YHS, are extremely helpful when used in conjunction with the Harper Papers.

Three sets of contemporary trade society papers have survived: the minute book of the New York Society of Journeymen Shipwrights and Caulkers, 1816–19, NYPL; the New York Typographical Society Papers, Eisenhower Library, Johns Hopkins University (although much of the valuable information here can be readily consulted in George A. Stevens, *Typographical Union No. 6: Study of a Modern Trade Union and Its Predecessors* [Albany, 1913]); and the constitution, bylaws, and membership list of the New York Union Society of Journeymen Carpenters, 1833–36, NYPL.

Government Reports and Official Documents, Unpublished and Published

For the period before 1825, there are several important bodies of official material in manuscript. The Jury Lists for 1816 and 1819 are available on microfilm at N-YHS. The City Clerk's Filed Papers are of use on day-to-day life in New York; they are kept at the Municipal Archives and Record Center, 52 Chambers Street, New York, N.Y. Probate inventories and the city's insolvency assignments are located at the Historical Documents Collection, Queens College, CUNY, ably administered by Professor Leo Hershkowitz.

The manuscript returns for the 1850 census are in the New York State Library, Albany, and are available on microfilm. The schedules for the 1855 New York State census for New York County are in the County Clerk's Office, Surrogate Court Building, 31 Chambers Street, New York, N.Y.

Of exceptional use for the entire period after 1800 are the indictment papers for the Court of General Sessions, kept at the Municipal Archives. These archives also have the complete collection of tax assessors' lists for the period studied here.

Published government sources were helpful, though not as much as I had hoped they would be. *The Minutes of the Common Council of the City of New York*, 1785–1831, 16 volumes, contain a great deal of miscellaneous information about citizens' complaints and civic response. The published documents of the Board of Aldermen and the Board of Assistant Aldermen are similarly informative, and contain some useful reports on poverty in the 1830s and 1840s. Of practically semi-official status are the city directories, especially *Longworth's American Almanac, New–York Register, and City Directory*, published annually. A complete collection, dating from 1786, is kept at N-YHS.

Newspapers and Periodicals

Contemporary newspapers and periodicals were by far the most valuable primary source for this study. Because my subject ranged over a long period of time and because the number of newspapers published in New York is immense, I was forced to be selective. The following were of the most use: 1788–1825: *American Citizen, American Mechanics' Magazine, Columbian, Courier and Enquirer, Evening Post, Independent Mechanic, Mechanics' Gazette, New-York Journal, New York Packet, Niles' Weekly Register* [Baltimore]; 1825–37: *Commercial Advertiser, Courier and Enquirer, Daily Sentinel, Evening Journal, Evening Post, Free Enquirer, Herald, Man, Mechanics' Magazine, National Trades' Union, New Harmony and Nashoba Gazette, Spirit of '76, Sun, Transcript, The Union, Working Man's Advocate;* 1837–50: *Beacon, Champion of American Labor, Daily Plebeian, Diamond, Herald, Hunt's Merchants' Magazine, Irish-American, Mechanics' Mirror* [Albany]; *New York Crystal Fount, New York Organ, New York State Mechanic* [Albany], *New York Washingtonian, People's Right, Phalanx, Radical, Republik der Arbeiter, Subterranean, Tribune, Volkstribun, Working Man's Advocate* [2d ser.], *Young America.*

Contemporary Speeches, Convention Proceedings, Books, and Pamphlets

A number of important speeches and proceedings are collected in what is still the best starting point for serious research on American labor movements before 1880, John R. Commons et al., eds., *Documentary History of American Industrial Society*, 10 vols. (Cleveland, 1910–11). Included are the records of some of the main proceedings of the Working Men, the GTU, and the Industrial Congress. The collections of broadsides and pamphlets located in the Library of Congress, NYPL, and N-YHS are extensive and informative. Speeches that I found particularly valuable include the early national Fourth of July orations (N-YHS), John Finch, *Rise and Progress of the General Trades' Union of the City of New-York* (New York, 1833), and Edward Thompson, *An Oration Delivered on the Anniversary of the Declaration of Independence* (New York, 1829), a revealing statement about the intermingling of freethought and political economy in the late 1820s. A vast and rewarding selection of speeches, pamphlets, and reports on every aspect of temperance reform is included in the Black Temperenceana Collection, NYPL. Walsh's early efforts are collected in *Sketches of the Speeches and Writings of Michael Walsh* (New York, 1843).

Contemporary books of which I made considerable use include two works by Cornelius C. Blatchly, *Some Causes of Popular Poverty* (Philadelphia, 1817) and *An Essay on Common Wealths* (New York, 1822); Langton

Byllesby, *Observations on the Sources and Effects of Unequal Wealth* (New York, 1826), and Thomas Skidmore, *The Rights of Man to Property!* (New York, 1829). On New York in the 1840s, and early 1850s, the writings of George G. Foster present thoughtful and lively descriptions of workshop conditions and popular amusements; see especially *New York in Slices, by an Experienced Carver* (New York, 1850) and *New York Naked* (New York, 185?). Jabez D. Hammond's venerable *The History of Political Parties in the State of New York*, 2 vols. (Albany, 1842) is still worth reading; so is Fitzwilliam Byrdsall, *History of the Loco-Foco or Equal Rights Party* (New York, 1842).

Autobiographies, Memoirs, and Reminiscences

Although fraught with personal idiosyncrasies, these works provide important material on social conditions and contemporary political movements. Of considerable value are the unpublished reminiscences of Stephen Allen, David Bruce, John Burke, John Frazee, and John Petheram, all at N-YHS. See also the unpublished memoir of Robert Taylor, a cooper who went on to become a leading nativist-Whig politician in the 1840s, NYPL. Harriet A. Weed, ed., *Autobiography of Thurlow Weed* (Boston, 1883), throws light on artisan life before 1825 and on subsequent developments in the New York Whig party. Robert Dale Owen, "An Earnest Sowing of Wild Oats," *Atlantic Monthly* 34 (1874), is a genre piece, of an aging reformer looking back on his wild youth, but it contains some useful facts about Owen's activities in 1829. Horace Greeley, *Recollections of a Busy Life* (New York, 1868), was written while Greeley was nuturing his presidential ambitions and slights his socialist interests in the 1840s, but still contains some pertinent information. Of more help on politics and reform in the 1840s are Thomas A. Devyr's peculiar but fascinating *The Odd Book of the Nineteenth Century* (New York, 1882) and Lewis Masquerier's *Sociology; or, The Reconstruction of Society, Government, and Property* (New York, 1877). By far the most helpful recollections about social life in nineteenth-century New York, moving outside the world of the elite, are in Charles H. Haswell, *Reminiscences of an Octogenarian of the City of New York* (New York, 1897). Elizabeth Ingerman, ed., "Personal Experiences of an Old New York Cabinetmaker," *Antiques* 84 (1963): 576–80, is an arresting memoir by Ernest Hagen, a cabinetmaker who worked in New York in the 1840s and 1850s. Even better is the anonymous "A Workingman's Recollections of America," *Knight's Penny Magazine* [London], 1 (1846), written by a cabinetmaker who worked in New York in the mid-1830s.

Biographies

Not surprisingly, given the available sources and the preoccupations of earlier historians, there are few modern biographies of New York artisans and workers. An exception is Ellen Vincent McClelland, *Duncan Phyfe and the English Regency* (New York, 1929). A few figures, in and out of the trades, who were active in politics and labor reform movements have received some attention. Robert Leopold, *Robert Dale Owen: A Biography* (Cambridge, Mass., 1940), is an impressive piece of work, filled with valuable source material and shrewd judgments about Owen's work in New York. Less satisfactory are William Randall Waterman, *Frances Wright* (New York, 1924), and Alice Perkins and Theresa Wolfson, *Frances Wright, Free Enquirer: A Study of a Temperament* (New York, 1939), although the latter volume does reproduce liberal excerpts from Wright's correspondence. Edward Pessen, "Thomas Skidmore: Agrarian Reformer in the Early American Labor Movement," *NYH* 25 (1954): 280–94, and Walter E. Hugins, "Ely Moore: The Case History of a Jacksonian Labor Leader," *PSQ* 65 (1950): 105–25, are the best studies of these two very different leaders; George Henry Evans's early life is covered in his brother's autobiography, Frederick W. Evans, *Autobiography of a Shaker* (Mount Lebanon, N.Y., 1869). There exists no full-scale biography of John Commerford. Eugene Exman, *The Brothers Harper* (New York, 1965), includes an exacting portrait of the nativist leader. On Walsh, see Robert Ernst, "The One and Only Mike Walsh," *N-YHSQ* 26 (1952): 43–65. Glyndon G. Van Deusen, *Horace Greeley: Nineteenth-Century Crusader* (Philadelphia, 1953), sticks largely to Greeley's activities as a Whig, and is less helpful on land reform and Fourierism. Weitling is well served in Carl Wittke, *The Utopian Communist: A Biography of Wilhelm Weitling, Nineteenth-Century Reformer* (Baton Rouge, 1950).

Books, Articles, Etc.

Although no longer in academic vogue, the first volume of John R. Commons et al., *History of Labour in the United States* (New York, 1916), like the *Documentary History*, is a basic resource for all students of early labor history, in New York and the rest of the country. So is the first volume of Philip S. Foner, *History of the Labor Movement in the United States* (New York, 1947), although, as in the case of Commons, there are grounds for disagreement with some of Foner's interpretations. On the history of New York City, I. N. P. Stokes, *The Iconography of Manhattan Island, 1498–1909*, 6 vols. (New York, 1915–28), remains the starting point for all scholarly research. Edward Pessen, *Riches, Class, and Power before the Civil War* (Lexington, Mass., 1973), is extremely valuable on social stratification in New York from 1828 to 1845. Edward K. Spann's sprawling *The New Metropolis: New York City, 1840–1857* (New York, 1981) confirmed my own impressions about poverty and social divisions in the 1840s, with a wealth of detail.

On the eighteenth-century social and political background, before the Revolution, I learned most from Richard B. Morris, *Government and Labor in Early America* (New York, 1946); and Gary B. Nash, *The Urban Crucible: Social Change, Political Consciousness, and the Origins of the American Revolution* (Cambridge, Mass., 1979). Patricia U. Bonomi, *A Factious People: Politics and Society in Colonial New York* (New York, 1971), is very informative on political mobilization before 1776; on the Revolution and the 1790s, Alfred F. Young, *The Democratic Republicans of New York: The Origins, 1763–1797* (Chapel Hill, 1967), is indispensable. In addition, see the conflicting interpretations offered in Edward Countryman, *A People in Revolution: The American Revolution and Political Society in New York, 1760–1790* (Baltimore, 1981), and Pauline Maier, *The Old Revolutionaries: Political Lives in the Age of Samuel Adams* (New York, 1980). On the ambiguities of American artisan political ideology in the age of the democratic revolution, Eric Foner, *Tom Paine and Revolutionary America* (New York, 1976), is superb. My conception of the age as a whole has been deeply influenced by David

Brion Davis, *The Problem of Slavery in the Age of Revolution, 1770–1823* (Ithaca, 1975).

Much of what I have to say on the Jeffersonian period complements and extends points raised in Howard B. Rock, *Artisans of the New Republic: The Tradesmen of New York City in the Age of Jefferson* (New York, 1979). Still valuable for its coverage and interpretive clarity is David Montgomery, "The Working Classes of the Pre-Industrial American City, 1780–1830," LH 9 (1968): 3–22. On ideology and society before 1825, I have profited from Linda K. Kerber, *Federalists in Dissent: Imagery and Ideology in Jeffersonian America* (Ithaca, 1970), and Richard J. Twomey, "Jacobins and Jeffersonians: Anglo-American Radicalism in the United States" (Ph.D. diss., Northern Illinois University, 1974). Like other American historians, I have been greatly stimulated by the continuing debates stirred by the work of J. G. A. Pocock on the character of eighteenth- and early-nineteenth-century American republicanism, above all by Pocock's synthesis in *The Machiavellian Moment: Florentine Political Thought and the Atlantic Republican Tradition* (Princeton, 1975).

On the economic history of New York City, Robert G. Albion, *The Rise of New York Port, 1815–1860* (New York, 1939), has yet to be replaced. Allan Pred's work on early metropolitan manufacturing is most useful, especially his "Manufacturing in the Mercantile City, 1800–1840," *Annals of the Society of American Geographers* 56 (1966): 307–25; see also David T. Gilchrist, ed., *The Growth of the Seaboard Cities, 1790–1825* (Charlottesville, 1967). Bruce G. Laurie, *Working People of Philadelphia, 1800–1850* (Philadelphia, 1980), suggests useful comparisons to similar developments in New York, with respect both to early industrialization and to all of the other themes developed here. August Baer Gold, "A History of Manufacturing in New York City, 1825–1840" (M.A. thesis, Columbia University, 1932), is full of information, but develops little in the way of an analytic framework. More generally, my understanding of the state of the American economy after 1825 has been drawn from George Rogers Taylor, *The Transportation Revolution, 1815–1860* (New York, 1951), Stuart Bruchey, *The Roots of American Economic Growth, 1607–1861* (New York, 1965), and Peter Temin, *The Jacksonian Economy* (New York, 1969).

The historiography of Jacksonian politics and the labor movement in the 1830s and 1840s is, of course, immense. Edward Pessen, *Jacksonian America: Society, Personality, and Politics* (Homewood, Ill., 1969), and Ronald P. Formisano, "Toward a Reorientation of Jacksonian Politics: A Review of the Literature, 1959–1975," *JAH* 63 (1976): 42–65, are instructive guides to the major debates through mid-1970s; I have attempted to update the lines of controversy, at least tentatively, in "On Class and Politics in Jacksonian America," in *The Promise of American History: Progress and Prospects*, ed. Stanley I. Kutler and Stanley N. Katz (Baltimore, 1982), 45–63. Although many of its specific formulations have been challenged and, in some cases, refuted, Arthur M. Schlesinger, Jr., *The Age of Jackson* (Boston, 1945), still stands as the most comprehensive (and the most provocative) historical survey of the 1830s and 1840s. I also found much value in rereading another book usually thought of as woefully outdated, Frederick Jackson Turner's *The United States, 1830–1850* (New York, 1935). Three other works that discuss Jacksonian politics in very different terms strongly affected my thinking: Richard

Hofstadter, *The American Political Tradition* (New York, 1948), Marvin Meyers, *The Jacksonian Persuasion: Politics and Belief* (Stanford, 1957), and William A. Williams, *The Contours of American History* (Cleveland, 1961). Party politics in New York are copiously covered in the existing literature. For an overview, see D. S. Alexander, *A Political History of the State of New York*, 3 vols. (New York, 1906). On the period before the panic of 1837, see Lee Benson, *The Concept of Jacksonian Democracy: New York as a Test Case* (Princeton, 1961), Brian J. Danforth, "The Influence of Socioeconomic Factors upon Political Behavior: A Quantitative Look at New York City Merchants, 1828–1844" (Ph.D. diss., New York University, 1974), and (for clarification of the endless intricacies of the New York Democracy) Jerome Mushkat, *Tammany: The Evolution of a Political Machine, 1789–1865* (Syracuse, 1971). On the years after 1837, in addition to these works, see Herbert Donovan, *The Barnburners* (New York, 1925), and James Roger Sharp, *The Jacksonians versus the Banks: Politics in the States after the Panic of 1837* (New York, 1970). The Whigs, in New York as elsewhere, have received less attention than the Democrats, but see, in addition to Benson's *Concept of Jacksonian Democracy*, Daniel Walker Howe, *The Political Culture of the American Whigs* (Chicago, 1979). Of central importance to my understanding of politics is Michael Wallace, "Changing Concepts of Party in the United States: New York, 1815–1828," *AHR*, 74 (1968): 453–91, as well as Pessen, *Riches, Class, and Power*.

On the Working Men and the New York labor movement in the 1830s, two works are vital: Walter E. Hugins, *Jacksonian Democracy and the Working Class: A Study of the New York Workingmen's Movement, 1829–1837* (Stanford, 1960), and Edward Pessen, *Most Uncommon Jacksonians: Radical Leaders of the Early Labor Movement* (Albany, 1967). On the radical political economists, Joseph Dorfman, *Economic Mind in American Civilization, 1606–1865*, 2 vols. (New York, 1946), slights their radicalism, while David Harris, *Socialist Origins in the United States: American Forerunners of Marx, 1817–1832* (Assen, The Netherlands, 1967), is most interested in matching their work against Marx's. Nonetheless, both are stimulating and informative. Paul Conkin has more recently contributed intelligent, concise surveys of Byllesby and Skidmore, in *Prophets of Prosperity: America's First Political Economists* (Bloomington, Ind., 1980). The 1840s are less than adequately treated in the literature, but some important leads can be found in Norman J. Ware, *The Industrial Worker, 1840–1860* (Boston, 1924). On the crisis of 1850, the works of Commons and Stevens, already cited, provide some basic information, but see also Carl Neumann Degler, "Labor in the Economy and Politics of New York City, 1850–1860" (Ph.D. diss., Columbia University, 1952).

Evangelical religion and the reform movements of the 1830s and 1840s are analyzed in Carroll Smith Rosenberg, *Religion and the Rise of the American City: The New York Mission Movement, 1812–1870* (Ithaca, 1970); see also Richard Carwardine, *Transatlantic Revivalism: Popular Evangelicalism in Britain and America, 1790–1865* (Westport, Conn., 1978). My thoughts on these matters have been strongly influenced by Paul E. Johnson's *A Shopkeeper's Millennium: Society and Revivals in Rochester, New York, 1815–1837* (New York, 1978). On temperance after 1837, I found a great deal of useful material in Ian R. Tyrrell, *Sobering Up: From Temperance to Prohibition in Antebellum America, 1800–1860* (Westport, Conn., 1979).

Louis Dow Scisco, *Political Nativism in New York State* (New York, 1901), is still the place to start on organized nativism. More detailed examinations of specific movements appear in a series of important articles: Leo Hershkowitz, "The Native American Democratic Association in New York City, 1835–1836," *N-YHSQ* 46 (1962): 41–59, Ira P. Leonard, "The Rise and Fall of the American Republican Party in New York City, 1843–1846," *N-YHSQ* 50 (1966): 151–92, and Robert Ernst, "Economic Nativism in New York City during the 1840's," *NYH* 29 (1948): 170–86. A thorough history of ethnic and racial conflict in Jacksonian New York has yet to be written, but some important materials and perceptive observations appear in Paul O. Weinbaum, *Mobs and Demagogues: The New York Response to Collective Violence in the Early Nineteenth Century* (Ann Arbor, 1979). Leonard L. Richards's "*Gentlemen of Property and Standing*": *Anti-Abolition Mobs in Jacksonian America* (New York, 1970) is valuable, especially since it sets the New York pattern of (lower-class) anti-abolitionist violence apart from those Richards detected in smaller towns and cities. On related themes of race and lower-class outlooks, see Alexander Saxton, "Blackface Ministrely and Jacksonian Ideology," *AQ* 27 (1975): 3–28. On fire companies, see Richard B. Calhoun, "From Community to Metropolis: Fire Protection in New York City, 1790–1875 (Ph.D. diss., Columbia University, 1973).

The land-reform movement has attracted one significant monograph, Helene S. Zahler, *Eastern Workingmen and National Land Policy, 1829–1862* (New York, 1941). Henry Nash Smith, *Virgin Land: The American West as Symbol and Myth* (Cambridge, Mass., 1950), and Arthur Bestor, "Patent-Office Models of the Good Society: Some Relationships between Social Reform and Westward Expansion," *AHR* 58 (1953): 505–26, illuminate the social and political significance of the West in Jacksonian and antebellum northern thought. Bestor has also made critical contributions to our understanding of communitarianism. His "American Phalanxes" (Ph.D. diss., Yale University, 1938) is still the most comprehensive study of American Fourierism; his study of Owenism, *Backwoods Utopias: The Sectarian Origins and Owenite Phase of Communitarian Socialism in America, 1663–1829*, 2d ed. (Philadelphia, 1970), contains much useful material on New York. My conception of Owenism's meaning has also been strongly influenced by John F. C. Harrison, *Quest for the New Moral World: Robert Owen and the Owenites in Britain and America* (New York, 1969). On the British influence in the 1840s, see Ray C. Boston, *British Chartists in America, 1839–1900* (Manchester, 1971).

Immigrant workers are treated in extraordinary depth in Robert Ernst's *Immigrant Life in New York City, 1825–1863* (New York, 1949). To supplement Ernst, it is now important to consult Jay P. Dolan, *The Immigrant Church: New York's German and Irish Catholics, 1815–1865* (Baltimore, 1975), and Carol Groneman [Pernicone], "The 'Bloody Ould Sixth': A Social Analysis of a New York City Working-Class Community in the Mid-Nineteenth Century" (Ph.D. diss., University of Rochester, 1973). On German workers and the labor movement, the essential source is Hermann Schlüter, *Die Anfänge der deutschen Arbeiterbewegung in Amerika* (Stuttgart, 1907), but see also Karl Obermann, "Germano-Américains et la presse ouvrière, 1845–1854," in *La Presse ouvrière, 1819–1850*, ed., Jacques Godechot (La Roche-sur-Yon, 1966).

Although this study ends in 1850, my analysis has been strongly influenced by works on labor, politics, and ideology in the Civil War period and beyond.

Many of the ideals I have described as aspects of capitalist entrepreneurial republicanism—and, indeed, many of the proponents of those ideals—reappeared in defense of American "free labor" in the 1850s and 1860s, as Eric Foner discusses in *Free Soil, Free Labor, Free Men: The Ideology of the Republican Party before the Civil War* (New York, 1970). The extent to which similar ideals took hold in the northern Democratic party—particularly among its more conservative elements in cities like New York—remains to be determined. On the labor front, the changes and continuities in the working-class outlooks and radical strategies that I have discussed are treated in detail in David Montgomery, *Beyond Equality: Labor and the Radical Republicans, 1862–1872* (New York, 1967). As Montgomery demonstates, New York workers remained at the forefront of labor agitation into the Gilded Age. The long-term fate of working-class republicanism has also been the subject of a great deal of recent interest. In addition to Montgomery's "Labor and the Republic in Industrial America, 1860–1920," *Mouvement Social*, no. 111 (1980): 201–15, see Leon Fink, *Workingmen's Democracy: The Knights of Labor and American Politics* (Urbana, 1983), and Nick Salvatore, *Eugene V. Debs: Citizen and Socialist* (Urbana, 1982).

Finally, although I have tried to preserve the proper historical context, my thoughts inevitably have been shaped by works on English and Continental social and labor history. From the start, the writings of Maurice Agulhon, Christopher Hill, and E. P. Thompson helped me to consider the problems of class, ideology, and politics in their broadest terms. Since then, a number of works have initiated important debates over the character of class consciousness in early industrial cities; the debates have in turn raised a number of questions and lines of inquiry pertinent to my own concerns. Among these are Alain Faure, "Mouvements populaires et mouvement ouvrier à Paris (1830–1834)," *Mouvement Social*, no. 88 (1974): 51–92, Gareth Stedman Jones, "The Language of Chartism," in *The Chartist Experience: Studies in Working-class Radicalism and Culture, 1830–1860*, ed. James Epstein and Dorothy Thompson (London, 1982), 3–58, Iorwerth Prothero, *Artisans and Politics in Early Nineteenth-Century London: John Gast and His Times* (Folkestone, 1979), and William H. Sewell, Jr., *Work and Revolution in France: The Language of Labor from the Old Regime to 1848* (New York, 1980).

Index

INDEX

439

habits, 55; associations, 55–59; strike, 56–59; scab, 57; political unity with masters, 76–77; associations, participation in parades, 88; and masters, opposing interests, 96, 100; in 1829 workday disputes, 191–92; republican mutuality, rise of, 237–48; wages, unionists' stand on, 241–42; social habits, 255–56; volunteer firemen, 260; and temperance movement, 283–84; crisis of 1836, 286–94. *See also specific trade*
Journeymen Chairmakers' Society, 225
Journeymen's Cordwainers' Society, 97
Journeymen's Stonecutters' Society, 287

Keane, John, 222n
Kearsing, Henry O., 273n
Kellogg, Edward, 383
Kennedy, John, 275, 286
Kerriston, Robert, 196
Keteltas, William, 66–67
Keyser, 329, 330n
Kilmer, David, 224n
King, Charles, 393
King, Thomas, 84
Kleindeutschland, 353, 354n, 358, 368
Kneeland, Abner, 153
Knickerbocker, 328
Knights of Labor, 368, 368n
Knox, Alexander, 169–70
Kriege, Hermann, 354–55, 358n

labor: workers' conception of, 17; Byllesby's view of, 165–67; Skidmore on, 185; value, unionists' stand on, 242; as property, unionists' stand on, 242–43; employers' views on, 274, 284, 292
labor crisis of 1850, 363–69; participants, 364; significance, 386
labor exchange, 374
labor-saving machinery: Byllesby on, 165–67; Commerford's critique of, 245
labor theory of value, 157–58; Wright on, 178
laborers, 399; unskilled, 10, 10n, 110; manual, 26–27; unskilled, wages, 50n–51n; day, 110; strikes, 168–69, 250–51; day, strike, 1836, 288; unskilled, unions' relations with, 250–51; skilled and unskilled, attempt to join forces, 1836, 289; unskilled, organization, by 1850, 370

Laborers' Union Benevolent Association (LUBA), 353, 370, 384
Ladies Industrial Association, 350–51
Lambert, John, 27
Land Cooperative Society (Britain), 339
land reform, 335–43, 356–57, 369, 383, 384, 394; unionist call for, 233; Walsh's interest in, 30, 331n
Lang, Robert M., 273n
Lasch, Christopher, 16
Lawrence, Cornelius, 236, 288
Lawrence, William, 190
leather tanning, 30, 37
Leavitt, Jonathan, 277
Lee, Gideon, 37, 41n
Leggett, William, 235
Lewis, Thomas W., 222n
Liberty Boys, 65
lien law: agitation for, 150; proponents, 194; passed, 206
Lippard, George, 367
Livingston, Edward, 73
Loco Foco party, 235, 269, 276, 293–95
London, 6, 111; occupation structure, 1850, 110n
London Mechanics' Institute, 272
Lorrilard, Jacob, 74
Lynde, Willoughby, 224n

machine making, 114, 114n
MacFarlane, Robert, 346–48
Macpherson, C.B., 102
Macready, William, 358–59
Madison, James, 61
Man, The, 224n, 238, 252, 253
manufacturers, political affiliations, 277n
manufactories, 112, 115, 398; early, 30–31, 31n; outwork, 115, 398
Marsh, John, 308–9
Marx, Karl, 4, 343n, 354, 355; *The Eighteenth Brumaire of Louis Bonaparte*, 385–86
Mason, Cyrus, 272, 303, 305, 306
Masquerier, Lewis, 339, 340
master craftsmen, 27, 35, 398; Marx on, 4–5; earnings, 29; removal from production, 33; wealth and property, 35–36; condemnation of journeymen's demands, 100; rise to wealth, 116; and reform movement, 257, 277; and ideology of free labor, 271–74; political affiliations, 276; in temperance movement, 282–84; class consciousness, 286; position on unions, 301,